STORMY WEATHER

Also by JAMES GAVIN

INTIMATE NIGHTS: *The Golden Age of New York Cabaret*
DEEP IN A DREAM: *The Long Night of Chet Baker*

The Life of
LENA HORNE

James Gavin

ATRIA BOOKS

NEW YORK   LONDON   TORONTO   SYDNEY

ATRIA BOOKS

A Division of Simon & Schuster, Inc.
1230 Avenue of the Americas
New York, NY 10020

First Atria Books hardcover edition June 2009

ATRIA BOOKS and colophon are trademarks of Simon & Schuster, Inc.

For information about special discounts for bulk purchases,
please contact Simon & Schuster Special Sales at
1-866-506-1949 or business@simonandschuster.com.

The Simon & Schuster Speakers Bureau can bring authors to your live event.
For more information or to book an event, contact the Simon & Schuster Speakers
Bureau at 1-866-248-3049 or visit our website at www.simonspeakers.com.

Designed by C. Linda Dingler

Manufactured in the United States of America

10 9 8 7 6 5 4 3 2 1

Library of Congress Cataloging-in-Publication Data
Gavin, James.
   Stormy weather : the life of Lena Horne / James Gavin. — 1st Atria Books
hardcover ed.
      p. cm.
Includes bibliographic references and index.
   1. Horne, Lena. 2. Singers—United States—Biography. 3. African American
women singers—Biography. I. Title.
ML420.H65G38 2009
782.42164092—dc22
[B]
2009008170
ISBN: 978-0-7432-7143-1

For Gene Davis (1939–2007)
who believed in me and this book

you are beautiful
and you are alone

NICO
(from the song "Afraid")

STORMY WEATHER

INTRODUCTION

ON A GRAY, rainy Manhattan day in April 1994, I walked to the Wyndham, a midtown hotel, to do an interview for the *New York Times*. My heart was pounding, for I was about to meet Lena Horne, an intimidating show-business and cultural icon. Her first new album in years was due out shortly. It was a bold move for a singer who would soon turn seventy-seven, and who was so identified with her beauty and her feral stage presence that most of her records had sold poorly. "You've got to see her," went the explanation.

But she'd found a reason to brave the studio once more. *We'll Be Together Again* was a tribute to the friend she missed most: composer-arranger Billy Strayhorn, Duke Ellington's right-hand man and Horne's soul mate until 1967, when he died of cancer. Horne herself had drifted in and out of view since 1985, when she closed a forty-two-city tour of *Lena Horne: The Lady and Her Music,* her one-woman evening of revisionist autobiography. The show had run fourteen months on Broadway in 1981–1982 and earned her a Tony, two Grammys, and an avalanche of raves.

The publicity extolled her as a black woman who had battled racism and crushing loss with ultimate dignity, while conquering almost every corner of white-dominated show business—Hollywood, Las Vegas, Broadway. In an age when black film actresses were confined either to low-budget "race movies" or to playing maids or whores, Horne was the screen's first Negro goddess and bowed to no one. Regal and classy, she helped redefine white America's image of the black female.

But for a long time, much of her own race had seen her as something else: a Hollywood-groomed aristocrat, out of touch with their hardships. When she sang her theme, "Stormy Weather," in a haughty voice of satin, it was hard to accept her as anything more than a cunning supper-club seductress. What did anyone who looked like that have to be unhappy about?

In *The Lady and Her Music,* she told them. Horne talked about the pain that racism had caused her—particularly in Hollywood, where roles she'd wanted desperately were held out of reach. In interviews she spoke of the strain of carrying a mantle for her race; of personal battles subverted to the cause; of losing four key men in her life, starting with Strayhorn, in four years. Finally, in her sixties, this long-suffering freedom fighter had triumphed over every demon. The closing number of *The Lady and Her Music* found her shouting out, "You've got ta believe in yo-*self*!" like a southern evangelist. At every show, her audience—the first substantially black one of her career—leapt to its feet, bursting with the glory of human potential.

But as Horne told more than one reporter in that dreamlike late flowering, it was all "too little, too late"; the wounds and the rage went too deep. Not much had changed since 1942, when the "Negro Cinderella," as she was once called, filled out a questionnaire for the PR department of her new employer, M-G-M. Asked for her philosophy of life, the twenty-four-year-old replied: "Never hope too hard—never pans out."

That attitude carried through to 1994, as the Blue Note label prepared to release her new CD. "I'm sorry this poor record company's gonna have trouble!" she said wistfully.

Yet here she was, submitting to an interview that might prove helpful. On that April day, Horne met me in the lobby of the Wyndham. By her side was a black man in his seventies, Sherman Sneed, her now-feeble longtime manager. Horne lived across town, but had stayed at the hotel before, and still used it sometimes for interviews. She wore a baggy white suit with a white cap and big dark glasses. Even so, she was unmistakable—the skin near-flawless, the exquisite bone structure, the smile as blindingly white as ever.

I felt the famous Horne jolt, and my mouth fell open; involuntarily I stepped back. At that moment I understood, like never before, the power of the beautiful, who live on pedestals. They inspire awe and envy; we covet or resent them. Whatever the case, they're not like the rest of us, and we don't let them forget it. Horne had seen reactions such as mine since childhood—certainly since 1933, when she entered the Cotton Club as an unknown chorine. She "couldn't sing" and was a "*bad* dancer," as she put it, yet wound up with the solo spot the other girls wanted, followed by a part in a Broadway play. Eight years later, M-G-M chose her as the Negro beautiful enough—in a Caucasian fashion—for white Americans to accept.

The experience, for Horne, had not ended happily, and it showed. By the 1950s, her sweet presence in her early films was gone, replaced by a calculating, fire-spitting nightclub vixen. "Beautiful" had become a permanent prefix to her name—a constant reminder of what had pushed her to the top, even as colleagues and critics proclaimed her artistry. "Her command of the stage, and her ability to mesmerize an audience, were awesome," said the singer Abbey Lincoln. But no amount of hard-earned vocal finesse could outshine her looks, which "weren't anything I really earned," said Horne. To her, "beautiful" took on a dismissive subtext: "She looks good but she can't do nothin'."

Peggy Moffitt, a top model of the 1960s and '70s, recalled sitting among Horne's adoring audience at the Cocoanut Grove in Hollywood, circa 1962. "I thought she hated us all," said Moffitt. But she marveled at how ingeniously Horne disguised that loathing: "She used it as though it were sexy." By then, the singer was also turning her wrath upon Lennie Hayton, her white husband and musical director. "Lena is a very nasty woman, honey," said a fellow Hollywood beauty and Vegas headliner.

Having heard such impressions, I panicked when Sherman Sneed left me alone with Horne after a brief hello. She and I took the elevator to her suite—a seemingly endless ride. But the woman who some had been described as "scary" wasn't that at all; she seemed warm, funny, and more than a little sad. The pressure of living as a symbol had taken its toll; weariness showed in her movements and her voice. Once we'd sat down in her room, she spoke with a candor that startled me—a seventy-six-year-old unburdening herself to a thirty-year-old. "Why am I here?" Horne wondered aloud, and she wasn't talking about the interview. "My kid left, my father left, my husband left, Billy left—why am *I* still here?"

Word was that she hadn't wanted to make this album at all; that its executive producer, Shirley Cowell, an heiress and longtime benefactor of Horne's, had talked her into doing it. In the Horne myth, such stories were old news. For years she'd claimed she'd never wanted her career; she'd succumbed to it only to support her family or empower black Americans. The reluctant Lena, socially responsible yet victimized by the injustice of the times, made good copy. Over the years, she'd crafted her bio to fulfill every expectation the public had of her. Icons aren't allowed to be human beings.

Now, Horne seemed too tired to maintain the old façade. Her memories were edged in regret and only fleeting pride. "I was never able to *enjoy* this damned thing," she said of her career. "It was always a hassle. A fight."

Horne described herself as "evil and angry and jealous and possessive," and her life had grown quite solitary. She lived alone in a spacious East Side apartment; apart from her select public appearances, she saw few people besides her daughter, Gail Lumet Buckley; her son-in-law, Kevin; and her grandchildren. She spent most of her private time reading books, watching old movies on TV, and ruing her past. It included a stage mother who was so jealous she had once stooped to blackmailing her daughter; and the downfall of her beloved son, Teddy, who died at thirty of drug-induced kidney failure—a fate for which Horne felt guilty.

We spoke for over two hours, during which she ruminated for minutes at a time. "I never speak to people," she said with a smile, "so when I'm with someone like you I talk too much." Eventually she turned hoarse, and I decided I'd better quit while I was ahead. Down we went to the lobby, where Sherman Sneed waited for us. Horne kissed me good-bye. I walked home, my feet barely touching the ground.

Her renaissance lasted on and off until 2000—further albums (one of which won a Grammy), two sold-out Carnegie Hall concerts, a TV special taped at New York's Supper Club, gala benefits in her honor. Then she vanished from public view.

There's no telling how much longer it might have taken for black women to get even a fraction of their due onscreen had it not been for

Horne. The black dancer and choreographer Louis Johnson felt profoundly indebted to her. "Lena is the mother of us all," he said. Playwright Arthur Laurents, long one of her closest friends, watched her play "a lot of roles offstage," far more than she ever got to enact as a performer. "In a way she's not black," he said. "In a way she's universal."

But who was the real Lena Horne? Even in her seventies she seemed confused. As for all she'd achieved, none of it seemed to bring much comfort. Before we left her suite at the Wyndham, Horne took one last troubled stare into her past and asked out loud, "What was it all worth?"

CHAPTER 1

LORRAINE GERARD, the wife of a bebop pianist named Vinnie Gerard, was nearing eighty in 2005, but time had not dimmed a particular memory from her Depression-era childhood. She grew up in Canarsie, a bayside neighborhood in Brooklyn, New York. Her family took her for weekend fun to the shore, where buskers entertained for coins on a well-known pier.

In 1933, Lorraine got her first glimpse of a lovely, waiflike teenager whose name, she heard, was Lena Horne. "Every Saturday and Sunday she used to sing and dance on the beach for pennies," Lorraine recalled. "She appeared to be extremely poor. I thought she had the ugliest legs, and I wasn't the only one that thought that. Scrawny, you know? Her dresses were skimpy-looking; you could tell that she was in need." Lorraine's family never spoke to the girl, but she earned their sympathy, and they tossed some change her way.

Her household needed all the help it could get. Lena's mother was a jobless and sickly actress; her Cuban stepfather was unemployed, too. They could barely pay the rent on their small Brooklyn apartment and lived on groceries from relief organizations. For Lena—who'd been born into the well-heeled respectability of the black middle class—life now held considerable shame.

A decade later she had good reason to obscure her past. M-G-M had signed her to a long-term contract, the likes of which no one of color in Hollywood had ever known. In the black community, all eyes were on her. As a sex symbol of uncommon refinement, Horne would have to revolutionize the Negro persona in Hollywood. Among the reams of press she received was a profile in *PM*, a Manhattan leftist newspaper. For an article called "The Real Story of Lena Horne," she told reporter Robert Rice about her distinguished family, which included school-teachers, activists, and a Harlem Renaissance poet. Apropos of nothing, Horne mentioned that an interviewer had asked her if she'd ever "danced for pennies on the street" as a youngster.

"I told him no," she said.

KEEPING up appearances would always be crucial to Horne, as it was for so many black people throughout her lifetime. They had to take great pains to counter the stereotypes that the white community associated with them. A veneer as painstakingly wrought as Horne's wasn't easily dropped; it was the armor she needed to survive, and it hid lots of se-crets. Only in 1963, when the civil rights movement had forced much of America to take an honest look at what it meant to be black, did Horne start delving behind her own mask. She did so for an autobiographical article in *Show* magazine, "I Just Want to Be Myself."

"I came from what was called one of the First Families of Brooklyn," Horne explained. They shunned discussing the slave ancestry that had spawned them all—"yet it was the rape of slave women by their masters which accounted for our white blood, which, in turn, made us Negro 'society.'" Home was an immaculate four-story brownstone in Brooklyn's Bedford-Stuyvesant section. An iron fence with sharp black spikes pro-tected 189 Chauncey Street on three sides. That barrier told passersby to keep their distance; and for Lena's grandmother Cora, the lady of the house, it shut out the neighborhood's seamier elements—the poor Irish in tenements across the street, the Swedes who ran a garage a few doors down.

Cora and her husband, Edwin, had lived on Chauncey Street since 1896. That year they joined a northward migration of approximately forty thousand blacks who fled the growing horrors of southern life. Post–Civil War Reconstruction had collapsed, toppled by white supremacists. Negroes had lost most of the rights they'd gained, and segregation was flaring. Hundreds of lynchings had occurred—each a symbolic warning of what might happen to Negroes who stepped out of line, or even to those who didn't. In contrast, the northern cities—New York, Chicago, Detroit—seemed like oases of safety and opportunity.

A small percentage of the newly settled black families were considered special. This was the "black bourgeoisie," a prosperous middle class of teachers, doctors, businessmen, and others of education and grooming. They or their elders had descended from "favored slaves"—privileged blacks who, by virtue of their brains or their sexual allure to their masters, had worked in the house, not in the field. During the decadelong heyday of Reconstruction, they'd used their cachet to start businesses and gain social standing. Now, in the North, they were helping pave the way for a new Negro image—one that challenged every cliché of black women as household help, black men as shiftless loafers. The Negro aristocracy tended to shun anyone who embodied a past they wanted to bury. "Uppity" became a popular word to describe ambitious blacks.

Respectability was their gospel, and they upheld it at all costs. Actress Jane White, whose father, Walter White, became the executive secretary of the National Association for the Advancement of Colored People (NAACP) in 1931, recalled the code of behavior dictated by the black bourgeoisie. "You didn't laugh too loud," she said. "You didn't go out in messy clothes, you were always polished and ironed; you learned how to speak well, and with a modulated voice. It was a tight cage you were in."

The Whites lived at 409 Edgecombe Avenue, the most prestigious address in Harlem. At fourteen stories, it towered above the rest of Sugar Hill, a gold-ring neighborhood for the Negro elite. Residents through the years included NAACP cofounder and preeminent activist W.E.B. Du Bois; Jimmie Lunceford, one of Harlem's star bandleaders; and Thurgood Marshall, the lawyer who worked for the NAACP before becoming the Supreme Court's first black justice. In the 1940s, Marshall often dropped by the White apartment for poker nights. "There would be hootin' and hollerin' and drinkin'," said Jane, "and they would let their hair down, and Thurgood talked one way amongst them. When he argued in court he talked another way. One may laugh, but it's rather sad." In public, she said, "you couldn't be what you were."

Many in the black bourgeoisie wound up emulating the values and even the looks of middle-class whites. From the 1920s through the 1960s, magazines for black readers advertised lye-based skin-lightening creams and hair-straightening treatments. "'Lighter is brighter'—that was an actual expression then," said Gene Davis, who produced dozens of black cultural documentaries before his death in 2007. "The social structure in the black community until recently was based on how light you were. And the lighter you were, the more acceptable you were." The notion that "black is beautiful" did not appear until the civil rights movement, when African roots were flaunted, not hidden, and the Negro slave ancestry celebrated for its strength.

In his 1957 book *Black Bourgeoisie*, sociologist E. Franklin Frazier defined that group in terms that could have applied to Lena Horne. In Frazier's view, it lacked "cultural roots in either the Negro world with which it refuses to identify or the white world which refuses to accept it." By struggling so hard for the respect of both, he wrote, members of the black bourgeoisie suffered from a constant identity crisis.

But a more enlightened age could never have come without bridges, and the black bourgeoisie was uniquely equipped to fight for change. Its members had education, social access, and manners a white society might come to heed. If they had to deny their history in order to find a foothold in the white man's world, they didn't hesitate.

So it was at the Horne residence, the hub of a family with a sprawling history explored by Gail Lumet Buckley in her book *The Hornes: An American Family*. Before Lena's birth in 1917, six people lived in the house. Reigning over them was Cora Calhoun Horne, her dictatorial grandmother. Fifty-two when Lena arrived, Cora was a community activist of warrior determination. She looked the part, with her austerely pulled-back salt-and-pepper hair, steel-rimmed glasses, and near inability to smile.

Cora battled for so many Negro civic groups that her gentler husband seemed to wilt by comparison. Back in Chattanooga, Tennessee, where he was born, Edwin had published and edited *Justice*, a prominent black newspaper; later he worked as a schoolteacher and politician. In Brooklyn he became secretary-general of the United Colored Democracy of Greater New York.

Astonishingly, Edwin wasn't even a Negro, but the son of a white Englishman and a Native American mother. During Reconstruction, Native Americans had suffered worse discrimination than blacks. For his children's sake, he'd decided to "pass" as Negro. Apparently that went undiscussed among the Hornes—no surprise, given their disdain for whites.

Edwin and Cora had four sons. Edwin Frank Horne, Jr., the handsomest of the boys, lived on the top floor with Edna, his wife. Errol had served as a sergeant in an all-black army troop until influenza killed him. Burke and Frank were teenagers when Lena was born.

The Hornes seemed like a model family. Outsiders didn't know that Edwin and Cora slept in separate rooms and barely spoke. One of the rumored causes was a past affair between Edwin and a white editor of *Vogue*. But in a Catholic household like theirs, divorce was as verboten as philandering; best to avoid discussing either. "As a family," said Lena, "we were very reticent, hiding feelings."

Certain parts of their lineage went unmentioned, too—especially by Cora, whose café au lait skin, thin lips, and delicate nose betrayed generations of intermingling with whites. Her maiden name, Calhoun, came from her father's and grandmother's slave master in Georgia, Dr. Andrew Bonaparte Calhoun. His uncle, Senator John C. Calhoun, had championed slavery as God's will—another unvoiced source of shame among the Hornes.

But Cora had revered Moses, her mulatto father. After decades as a house slave, he'd become a top Atlanta business owner and had married a white woman. Cora and her sister, Lena, had more white blood than black; this along with their father's means brought them great privilege. As young women they lived like debutantes, earning university degrees at a time when few women of any race did. In 1887, when she was twenty-two, Cora took her own white husband, Edwin Horn (he added the *e* later). Lena married Frank Smith, a mixed-blood, light-skinned doctor.

Once settled in Brooklyn, Edwin and Cora focused on raising their sons. But according to Gail Lumet Buckley, child rearing bored Cora. Once the boys were old enough to fend for themselves, she began working for a dizzying array of community causes. They included the Urban League, the National Association of Colored Women (NACW), and the NAACP, formed in 1909 in response to the growing scourge of anti-Negro brutality. Cora lectured hookie-playing black youths on how they were jeopardizing their futures and shaming their race. She led demonstrations to demand voting rights for black women. She aided unwed Negro mothers, and fought to get scholarships for worthy young blacks—one of whom, Paul Robeson, entered Rutgers University in Newark, New Jersey, due partly to Cora's efforts.

Her bedrock strength left little room for warmth. Lena Horne recalled her as a "violent, militant little lady" who never caressed her or uttered a loving word. To Cora, sentimentality meant weakness. Having come from a line of women who cooked the white man's meals and washed his clothes, she wouldn't stoop to anything that evoked servitude. She left such tasks to her husband. The ironies were many: A white man (albeit one in hiding) did housework for his (partly) Negro wife, who wore the pants in the family—and who detested whites.

Edwin had already fallen a rung in society. He'd lost his job as a teacher to a less experienced white man; now he worked as an inspector for the fire department. He sought comfort in life's finer things. At home in his parlor, he relished his sweet-smelling Havana cigars while listening to Caruso on the Victrola. He applauded the great tenor at the Metropolitan Opera. Edwin's looks held their own distinction; Lena would recall his gray mustache and hair and his "beautiful, sad blue eyes." Even as a child, she understood her grandfather's loneliness.

Edwin, Jr.—better known as Teddy—spat in the face of the family high-mindedness. Teddy had proudly skipped college, knowing his charm and pretty-boy looks would get him further. He smirked behind the back of any "sucker"—usually white—whom he could coax into doing his bidding. By the time he'd grown, the illegal gambling business had found a master hustler in Teddy Horne.

In 1916, he wed a girl from an even cushier Brooklyn background. Edna Scottron was the fair-skinned, green-eyed daughter of a Native American mother and a successful Portuguese Negro inventor. Like Teddy, Edna lived for her whims. She dreamed of stardom in the theater; meanwhile she'd landed a lady-killer for a husband.

She and Teddy moved into the top floor of the Horne brownstone, where Edna became pregnant quickly. She hoped for a son. Instead, on June 30, 1917, she bore a brown-eyed, freckled, copper-skinned girl. Edna and Teddy named her Lena Mary Calhoun Horne. Lena would report later that her father wasn't at the hospital when she was born; he'd gone to play cards, ostensibly to earn money to pay the hospital bill. As she saw it, her father was "pursuing his own interests"; to Lena, this constituted rejection at birth. Not surprisingly, she remained an only child.

If Teddy and Edna were embarrassments to the family, grandmother Cora took steps to ensure that Lena set forth on the right track. In October 1919, the NAACP newsletter, the *Branch Bulletin*, welcomed one of the organization's "youngest members." Lena was just two and barely walking when Cora signed her up. "She paid the office a visit last month and seemed delighted with everything she saw," explained the *Branch Bulletin.*

Above that caption was a photo of a joyless toddler wearing a white lacy dress and a frown; the rose placed in her hands did nothing to brighten the scene. Her face mirrored the mood at home. By that time, Teddy wanted out of family life and had devised a ruse for escape. He was sick, he said, perhaps with tuberculosis, and had to head west for health reasons. Edna knew he was lying, but she was powerless to keep him. Later she told Lena that her father "was too young, too handsome, and too spoiled by the ladies to be ready for marriage."

Teddy had an action-packed new job in store. He became a numbers runner—"a pimp and a hustler," as Horne further explained. Illegal gambling was a popular profession among Negro men of his day. Whatever their education, only menial jobs—or none at all—tended to await them. Many Negro men thumbed their noses at the system and took to the streets. "You worked with criminal attitudes," said Lena. "It took a lot of guts. You chose that rather than have *the man* make a slave of you."

But no danger befell Teddy Horne, who gave off an invincible air. Photos of him from the twenties show a slick, grinning operator with pomaded hair, three-piece suits, and Stetson hats. By then he had a new woman on his arm, Irene, whom he'd married as soon as he was free. From Seattle, where they lived, he sent his daughter gifts and an allowance. She opened each package with glee, but then came a stab of longing: Why had her father deserted her?

Edna had her own concerns—namely, her dreams of acting. She moved to Harlem, where the action was, and left Lena behind. Now both parents had abandoned the child. Before going to sleep each night, Lena said her prayers, then kissed the bedside photos of her mother and father.

Cora would have none of her granddaughter's tears. As soon as Lena was old enough to understand, she told the child that she must never be like her mother, with all her silly ambitions. Relentlessly she drilled Lena on how to be a proper Horne: "Think for yourself. Don't make excuses. Don't lie. Never say 'ain't.' Learn how to read. Learn how to listen. Hold your head straight, look people in the eye, talk to them distinctly." Most important: "You will never let anyone see you cry."

Lena obediently followed her to meetings. As Cora's women friends held grave discussions, Lena got a lesson in manners: It was her job to serve the ladies tea and cake, then to sit silently in the corner. "She never made a child of me," said Lena. "I was always an adult." Once home, Cora would drill her as to what she'd learned.

In *The Hornes*, Gail Lumet Buckley described Cora as "a very neurotic woman," obsessed with what others thought of her and her family. Carmen de Lavallade, an influential black modern dancer whose career burgeoned in the fifties, knew the stifling effects of such an upbringing. "At that time if you came from certain families, you had to grow up to be a lady!" she said. "I grew up that way. It doesn't give you allowance for anything—for temper, for sorrow. You can't be yourself."

Cora's militancy involved deep prejudice. Horne would later tell reporter Sidney Fields that she'd "been raised to dislike white people intensely." Cora forbade her to play with white children, but wouldn't explain why. When she got older, she heard that white men wanted only one thing from black women, and it wasn't marriage. Cora looked with equal disgust at lower-class Negroes. Gail Lumet Buckley gave a dismaying example in *The Hornes*. When Lena's fair-skinned cousin Edwina fell for a dark-hued, unpedigreed black man, the family broke it up, all but forcing her to marry someone else. Even the lusty sounds of gospel and blues made Cora cringe; in her home, anything that signified a loss of control was shunned. Instead, she listened to Bach and Gregorian chants, cutting off the musical part of Lena's black heritage.

Cora sneered at Edna's ambitions, but they weren't so outlandish as she thought. By now enough black beacons had burst onto the show-business scene to keep Edna hopeful. Comic Bert Williams had conquered vaudeville, Broadway, and the recording field to become the nation's first Negro star. Audiences knew him as a downtrodden clown whose laughing-through-tears quality touched the heart. Florence Mills was black America's sweetheart, a lovely young waif who sang in a lilting, birdlike voice. Mills had shot to prominence in an off-Broadway smash, *Shuffle Along,* and seemed on the verge of great things. Actress Rose McClendon had moved from South Carolina to New York and won a scholarship to the hallowed American Academy of Dramatic Arts; eventually she became known as "the Negro first lady of the dramatic stage."

McClendon reached that zenith via Harlem's Lafayette Theatre, nirvana for an aspiring black actor. Billed as "America's Leading Colored Theatre," the two-thousand-seat hall hosted the Lafayette Players, a legitimate Negro stock company. Founded in 1915, the ensemble was a big step forward from minstrel shows, vaudeville, and many silent films, where blacks were usually portrayed as thick-lipped, nappy-haired buffoons. Instead, the Players performed everything from Shakespeare to all-black versions of Broadway hits, such as *Dr. Jekyll and Mr. Hyde.*

In 1921, Edna walked into the Lafayette during an open audition and recited a monologue from *Antony and Cleopatra.* Her flair for melodrama served her well, and she walked out of the theater as a Lafayette Player. Edna had never known such joy. Soon she was emoting her way through ingénue roles in plays like *Madame X.*

Now a working (if meagerly paid) actress, she sometimes reclaimed her four-year-old from Cora and showed her off at the theater. Lena retained a happy memory from that time. Edna had a part in *Way Down East,* a popular Victorian tragedy that had just made it to the silent screen. The stage set contained a fireplace, and before curtain time one night, Edna sat Lena behind it and allowed her to watch the show through a little hole. Even at four, the stage thrilled her.

The Lafayette Players had a branch in Philadelphia, and Edna went there in 1921 to perform in *Madame X.* Although Cora was dead set against it, Edna took Lena. There, the child made her "acting" debut. One scene depicted a little girl lying in her sickbed. Lena played the part impeccably. In her 1950 memoir, she recalled wandering around backstage, in and out of dressing rooms, awestruck by the theater and fantasizing about stardom. The most dazzling sight of all was her mother, whose beauty and talent overwhelmed her. "I was certain that she must be the most wonderful actress in the world," said Horne. Cora's warnings about Edna fell aside; Lena dreamed of doing exactly as her mother had done.

For a while, Edna's career seemed to thrive. "I can understand why she believed she was on the threshold of a brilliant future," observed Lena.

The girl was home in Brooklyn in the autumn of 1922 when Edna trekked for the Lyceum Theatre in Stamford, Connecticut. She'd been cast in the ninety-three-member, all-black company of a musical revue, *Dumb Luck*. Its name bespoke the producer's wishful thinking. He'd taken that huge company to Connecticut with hardly any budget, praying the reviews would attract investors who would pay for a move to Broadway. *Dumb Luck* lasted two nights. "The show was lousy, so they closed it," said blues singer Alberta Hunter, one of its stars. The cast was left stranded. Headliner Ethel Waters had been in that bind before, and wangled a sale of the costumes in order to pay for everyone's ride home. The incident would become all too familiar to Edna as her short career wore on.

By now Lena was enrolled in the brand-new Ethical Culture School in Brooklyn. No one had to force her to do her reading; at home she spent hours in her bedroom, the covers pulled up to her chin as she turned the pages of storybooks. She'd taught herself to read before kindergarten; now she devoured children's tales—especially ones about orphans, with whom she empathized.

Apparently her grandmother had called a strict halt to any further visits between the child and her wayward mother. In 1923, Edna had to resort to subterfuge to see her daughter. One day she showed up at a neighbor's house on Chauncey Street and asked the woman to fetch Lena. The two had a tearful reunion, but Edna warned her not to tell her grandmother. Soon thereafter, a relative spirited Lena away to Edna's apartment in Harlem. The little girl found her mother sick in bed, and spouting a dire warning—her father was plotting to kidnap her, and they had better leave town fast.

Edna was lying, of course; Teddy Horne had moved to Seattle with his new wife and had no desire to abscond with the child he'd run away from. But Edna was feeling vengeful—not only toward the husband who'd deserted her but toward Cora for daring to withhold Lena from her.

Her days with the Lafayette Theatre were through. Soon Edna stood on a train platform, holding a suitcase in one hand and leading her daughter by the other. They boarded a segregated train for Miami. There, Edna hoped, she could act in tent shows—Negro vaudeville that played the outskirts of southern towns for a few days at a time. The actors faced "hellish" odds, as Bill Reed wrote in his book *Hot from Harlem*. Police gladly arrested them if they were out on the street at night—the very time they worked. "Unscrupulous management and inadequate food and lodging were a commonplace of black show-business life. . . . That these performers managed to shoulder the burden of racism . . . and still get the job of entertainment done was a miracle."

Horne later reflected on the hard knocks they were willing to endure in order to practice their craft. She herself paid a harsh price for her mother's ambitions. For the next six years, Edna would drag her from town to town as she searched, mostly in vain, for acting work; she would leave her child in foster care, then vanish, sometimes for months. More than once, she would reappear in the middle of the night and snatch Lena away, claiming her father was about to kidnap her.

But Lena could never have foreseen all that as she rode the train to Miami with Edna, whose illness left her moaning all the way. There in the sweltering South, the two carted their bags to their temporary new home, a little frame boardinghouse. It stood behind a railroad track in a Negro slum. Lena recalled it as a "tumble-down shack with a sagging porch, broken stairs, and no plumbing." The kitchen had a dirt floor; cinders blew in the window when a train passed. Each room sheltered anywhere from two people to a family, all of whom shared "a foul outhouse." Young as Lena was, this descent into rural poverty must have seemed an unexplainable fall from grace.

Edna's professional fortunes in Miami proved slim. She took on odd jobs—salesclerk, maid—to support her and her daughter. For the first time, Lena learned what lay behind much of the antiwhite talk in Brooklyn. From almost any white she felt a cold draft or downright hostility. Her feet hurt because her new shoes didn't fit; Negroes weren't allowed to try on merchandise, for if they didn't buy the item, no white person would, either. At home, fellow boarders at the house spoke hatefully of "crackers"—a popular southern term for bigots.

Some kindness awaited Lena at the one-room schoolhouse where Edna sent her. *The Hornes* contains a touching photo of the child flanked by two classmates. She grins proudly as she hugs both girls close; one of them beams at her adoringly. But Lena was also learning that sometimes no one was meaner to Negroes than other Negroes. Perhaps because of her reading skills, the six-year-old had been placed a grade ahead. Her resentful schoolmates called her "dumb." Worse still, they taunted her for her northern accent and light skin, which to them meant she was "high yaller"—in a drawled pronunciation of "high yellow," which denoted the child of a mixed-race union. Up North, her lighter skin gave her advantages. Lighter-skinned Negroes there were perceived to be "better"; here that look signaled the blood of the reviled white man.

The jeers crushed her. But Edna was too preoccupied to offer much comfort. In their travels, she did find a few tent-show jobs. But much of the time, recalled Lena, Edna wound up "stranded, and starved, and once she was caught in a company where one member was lynched." Lena saw her mother turn frustrated and sad. She took it out on her little girl; minor infractions, such as leaving her sweater at school, brought beatings.

In her self-centeredness, Edna also unthinkingly exposed her daughter to outside dangers. Their next stop was Jacksonville, Florida's largest city. She left Lena with a theatrical couple and disappeared again. Back one day for a visit, she made plans with the couple to see a nearby tent show. With Lena in the car, they drove off into the night, laughing and telling stories. Suddenly they saw a black man up ahead, waving his arms. He warned them frantically, *"The crackers are out killing tonight!"* The gay mood turned to terror; they swerved around and sped home.

Soon Edna and daughter fled Jacksonville and took aimlessly to the road. Lena recalled boarding in a house where the police broke in during the night and used their guns to beat a black man mercilessly. Everyone else in the room looked on in terror. Afterward, Lena sobbingly asked her mother to explain. "They're mean down here," was all Edna said.

When money ran so low that she couldn't afford Lena's care, Edna scraped together what cash she could to buy her a train ticket to Brooklyn. Traveling alone with a tag on her lapel, the little girl returned to what she later called her "only sense of roots." But invariably Edna plucked her away again. It seemed odd that Cora—who battled for the rights of young people she didn't even know—would not have taken steps to keep Lena home. And did the moneyed and connected Teddy Horne know or care about his daughter's plight? Teddy, of course, had deserted the family, and surrendered his fatherly control. Time and again Lena toted her bag down the staircase of the Chauncey Street brownstone, heeding a familiar command: "Come on, Lena, we're *going!*"

The child next found herself in southern Ohio, where Edna placed her with a doctor and his family. They treated her affectionately, and she had her own room in a comfortable house. But she knew it wouldn't last, and she began having terrible nightmares. In 1974, she told reporter Nancy Collins that every time she developed a loving relationship with her caregivers, her mother snatched her away. She became "*afraid* of people . . . of letting myself be close to them," lest she get her feelings hurt. From then on, she lived with lowered expectations. "I made my peace that no one really did love me," she said, "regardless of my color."

In 1927, Edna got word of possible work in Macon, a prosperous city in central Georgia. The train pulled into a tidy, bustling downtown area, with trolleys running through it; in another well-tended area stood the nearly century-old Wesleyan College for women. But southern Negro poverty awaited Lena again when Edna left her in her latest foster home. The child's new "street" was a fly-ridden, dirt alleyway lined by wooden frame houses. She recalled moving into a two-room shack whose walls were patched with newspaper. Washing clothes in a big iron pot out back was the lady of the house—"a very elderly mammy," said Horne— who presided over many boarders. Her daughter lived there with her two children, one a little girl named Thelma. The other, a boy, shared the mammy's bed, at the foot of which lay a cot for Lena. Others slept in the kitchen.

The old lady seemed to sense Lena's loneliness, and treated her caringly. Now ten, Lena noticed how the poorest people she met were usually the kindest, for they understood struggle better than anyone. The daughter, who cooked for a white family, brought home scraps of fine southern food, and made sure Lena never went hungry.

Edna was broke on a regular basis and struggled to afford Lena's upkeep. For all her mother's flightiness, Lena still yearned for her, and refused to see her as a villain. "She tried hard to take care of me," said the singer in 1952. Lena would later observe that a black woman of the day was "apt to be a whore" when times got rough. Since actresses were already deemed loose women, prostitution proved an easy segue. A journalist who knew Horne well recalled her mentioning that Edna had sold her body, at least briefly. It wasn't surprising; Horne also spoke of her mother's prostitute friends, with whom she'd stayed.

For all the squalor of the child's southern life, she was reminded every now and then of the grandeur a Negro could achieve. In November of 1927, her schoolteacher in Macon stood before the class and announced that Florence Mills—dubbed the "Queen of Happiness"—had died at thirty-one. Tuberculosis had felled the winsome songbird, reportedly due to an exhaustive run in *Blackbirds of 1926*, the show that had sealed her fame. "We've had a great loss," stated the teacher. Horne never forgot his sadness. "I think that was probably the first time I was conscious that we looked upon certain people as *ours*," she said, "with this kind of pride." If Mills could scale such heights and evoke such devotion, then maybe Edna's ambitions weren't so far-fetched.

She was still far from Lena in December when the child's uncle Frank paid a surprise visit to the house in Macon. It wasn't clear who in the family had sent him there, but he was in a unique position to help Lena. Frank worked thirty miles southwest in Fort Valley, a largely black Georgia town. There, the dapper, wavy-haired young man served as dean of students at Fort Valley Normal and Industrial School, an all-black college.

Frank moved Lena to Fort Valley. There, she roomed in the dorm with his flapper fiancée, Frankye, a teacher. The child felt uneasy living among a bunch of college-age women, but they went out of their way to treat her sweetly. That wasn't true of her classmates at a nearby elementary school. Observing that Lena's parents were nowhere in sight, and that her skin was much lighter than theirs, they lashed out at her. In her first memoir, Horne recalled their jeers. "Yaller! Yaller!" they chanted. "Got a white daddy! Shame! Shame!" They linked arms and danced around her, calling her a "little yellow bastard." Lena cried out, *"I am not!"*

Their words haunted her. She tried to darken her skin by lingering in the sun, but she wasn't sure how she should talk. At her grandmother's home, to use anything but textbook English was grounds for punishment. But the Fort Valley locals talked in thick southern accents, using Negro dialect. A confusion overtook her that she never quite lost. In 1965, she called herself "two or three people," depending on her company. Her accent kept shifting: "I hear it happening and still I go ahead and do it."

But as she soon found, switching identities could be helpful. In the auditorium of Uncle Frank's college, the child watched a rehearsal of *Romeo and Juliet.* Lena had been around the theater as long as she could remember, but as she neared puberty, the notion of acting struck her in a whole new way. To escape one's self and take on a dramatic new persona—better still, to be applauded for it—took on a great mystique for the young Lena. There in Fort Valley, she recalled, the yen to act hit her for the first time. She began reading plays in the library and imagining herself in various roles.

When Frank and Frankye wed, Lena got her own room in their new house. Life hadn't felt so normal in years. But it was shaken up by a rare appearance from Teddy Horne. Lena barely knew her father, but Edna and Frank had told her stories of his dastardly ways, which, combined with his absence, had turned him into a magnetic, mysterious figure in Lena's mind.

Teddy didn't disappoint her. She watched in awe as he pulled up to the house in a big black car. Out came her smooth-looking, fashion-plate daddy, dispensing presents like Santa Claus.

Lena was awestruck. Teddy stayed for weeks—their first extended time together in her memory. In recent years, Teddy had only moved up in the world. He'd relocated to Pittsburgh, a city with a bustling black population and cultural life. It also had a thriving underworld, and Teddy made the best of it. He'd gone to work for Gus Greenlee, the city's premiere racketeer. A Negro from North Carolina, Greenlee had grown so rich—largely through illegal gambling interests—that he'd bought the Pittsburgh Crawfords, one of the city's two black baseball teams, and built his own field.

As Greenlee's treasurer, Teddy had grown well to do himself. He'd opened a restaurant that bore his name, and acquired a small hotel for blacks, the Belmont. It was actually a front for gambling, which took place in a back room called the Bucket of Blood. Teddy acquired a Jewish partner, along with a piece of the Crawfords. Then he got involved in the career of John Henry Lewis, a black world-champion boxer whom Greenlee managed.

For Lena, who felt increasingly victimized, her father seemed dazzlingly free-spirited. He laughed at authority and spouted hard-boiled pearls of wisdom: "Ask for no mercy and give less," "Don't trust no bush that quivers." In this brief attempt at fatherhood, he schooled his daughter well on surmounting the hard-knock Negro existence. "Because he knew how loathsome life was, he taught me a lot," said Horne in the late eighties. "He gave me all the street knowledge I needed to survive."

But with his toughness came an inability to show much love, a family trait he passed on to his daughter. No amount of bluster or expensive gifts—including a fur coat—could disguise the fact that he'd deserted her. In 1986, Horne told writer Glenn Plaskin that the father she'd adored had never hugged or kissed her. Instead he, like Edna, teased her with affection, then snatched it away. Suddenly Teddy's visit to Fort Valley was over. He drove off, leaving her to wonder what she'd done wrong. Later she contemplated another sad legacy he'd left her, "a willingness to accept the fact that some of the greatest things just couldn't happen for me." Foremost among them was the comfort of knowing that people she cared about would stay.

At least Fort Valley had brought her some stability, as had the love of Frank and Frankye. Lena didn't welcome the letter that Edna sent her in the spring of 1928. Its familiar promise—that soon they'd be together for keeps—brought only dread; now Edna seemed like a stranger to her, and not to be trusted.

Soon her mother arrived with a friend, known to Lena as "Aunt Lucille." Excitedly, Edna told Lena she'd found a house in Atlanta. The cost would be covered by a wealthy beau of hers from Miami, where Edna was again spending a lot of time. According to *The Hornes*, Edna's flame had agreed to foot the bill as long as this new house wasn't in Florida; apparently he didn't want a little girl around.

Lena said a reluctant good-bye to Frank and Frankye and departed with her mother and "aunt." Before they left Fort Valley, Lucille insisted they stay with a relative of hers who lived in town. Lena found him fat and repulsive. But Edna and Lucille saw no harm in going off and leaving eleven-year-old Lena in his care. She recalled the consequences in her second memoir. "Back in Macon, those good women had told me: 'Don't be a bad girl. . . . Don't let a boy touch you.' . . . But you haven't been told whether you're to blame or it's the other person's fault. All you know is that if somebody touches you it's bad." Horne did and said nothing. But many years later Marcia Ann Gillespie, a writer and editor who worked with Horne on an aborted third memoir, could see the scars of that childhood trauma: "So much of her behavior was that of someone who's been abused."

Lena's relationship with Edna had grown so strained that she feared confiding in her. Grandmother Cora's upbringing came into play: At any cost, she had to be seen as a good girl—one who never got involved in anything unsavory, even if it wasn't her fault. Privately, though, she despised the man, and the incident drove a further wedge between her and her mother—in fact, between her and the world. "I became very secretive," said Lena. "I became very suspicious of everyone."

Once they'd reached Atlanta, Edna tried, in her fumbling way, to be a good parent. Thanks to her moneyed suitor, she enrolled Lena in dancing school. At her eleventh birthday party on June 30, 1928, the girl gleefully demonstrated the snakehips, a dance created by Earl "Snakehips" Tucker, a famed black vaudevillian. Lena walked to grade school, encountering some southern-style friendliness on the way. Years later she told of passing white men on Peachtree Street; they patted her on the head and said, "What a cute little nigger you are!"

As usual, any sense of home she may have felt was soon dashed. Edna's career had petered down to almost nothing; now she seemed more interested in living as a kept woman. Off she went to Miami with Lucille, again leaving her daughter in foster care. One of her guardians was the mysterious "Aunt May," who belittled Lena for the slightest infractions. Two other caregivers, a black couple, passed her off to their housekeeper. She made Lena perform punishing chores, and nothing the girl did was good enough. After Lena had stepped out of the bathtub, wet and shivering, the housekeeper beat her with switches cut from a backyard tree.

Lena lived in dread. Once more she avoided telling her mother of the abuse. But neighbors heard her cries and informed Edna when she came back. Instead of offering comfort, Edna scolded her. According to Gail Lumet Buckley, "Lena felt that Edna was embarrassed about the neighbors knowing something she did not."

In early 1929, Lena finally escaped the South and its violence. Edna gave up on trying to manage a preteen girl on the road, and she sent her daughter home to Brooklyn for good. Lena was relieved. Immediately she began a semester at P.S. 35, a junior high school, then progressed to the integrated Girls High School, one of the city's most prestigious institutions. Lena played basketball there and gradually made new friends. The Great Depression had come, but its worst effects passed over the privileged Horne household.

For all its dark side, her grandmother's training had helped Lena survive the last few years; forever after she would speak of Cora with a certain awe. But now that she was a young woman, she found Cora more stifling than ever. In the parlor and at the dinner table, Lena heard her rail on about the "silly, foolish" Edna. "You must be stronger than your mother," she declared. "She's weak and she's illogical."

Cora wanted to help Lena buttress herself against the cruel outside world. But her haranguing stirred up a protective impulse in the girl. For the first time, Lena struck back at her grandmother; she recalled "battling" with her in Edna's defense. Lena didn't dare reveal that she, too, wanted to be an actress. Cora had already made it clear that she wanted her to become a teacher, like others in the family. Lena went along with her grandmother's wishes in word but not in deed. She loved dressing in grown-ups' clothes and enacting plays she'd devised. The now-adolescent girl signed up for more dancing lessons, and starred in a play for the Urban League.

In 1931, Cora left on an around-the-world trip, financed by her son Teddy. Lena was left in the care of a cherished family friend, Laura Jean Rollock. "Aunt Laura," as Lena called her, directed the dancing and acting groups at the Lincoln Settlement, a Negro community center. She wasn't at all discouraging of Lena's ambitions. They spoke for hours about the stage, and movies, too, for Lena had become an avid filmgoer. When she appeared in a revue at Girls High, Laura offered sympathetic advice. The theater gave Lena a much-needed sense of belonging; it was no wonder that in 1942, when she supplied information to M-G-M's publicity department, she would answer a query about her childhood ambition with the simple phrase: "To be on stage."

Lena joined the Junior Debs, one of a slew of social clubs for members of the black bourgeoisie. "We were the 'best bunch in town'—and we knew it," she said; no other girls in Brooklyn had such classy breeding or looked so good. Lena had never thought much about singing, but she tried it at the group's tea parties, and had fun. A prominent black newspaper, the *New York Amsterdam News,* took notice of the teenager, calling her "'tops' among the younger set."

Eventually her grandmother came home, but she wasn't the same. Cora had turned sixty-seven, and her stony fortitude was starting to crack. Bronchial asthma ran in the family, and she'd begun showing signs of it. Cora feared her days were numbered—the likely reason that Teddy had bought her a world cruise. Lena began to hear hacking coughs in the night. As usual, nothing was said the next day.

Another homecoming occurred in 1932. Edna had recently gone to Havana; now she'd returned to Brooklyn, and she wasn't alone. With her was her new husband, Miguel Rodriguez, a former army officer. White and Cuban, Mike (as Edna called him) struck Lena as a "fierce little man." He had a stocky build, a thick mustache, and dark, blazing eyes set off by bushy eyebrows. What English he knew was obscured by a thick accent. He seemed to worship Edna, but Lena loathed him on sight, and his color had much to do with it. Her bouts with southern racism, combined with her family's hatred of whites, had left a mark. If the Hornes had disliked Edna before, her marriage to a white man now made her a pariah.

Mike had his own reservations. He was skeptical of a lot of the blacks he saw, for he couldn't understand why they tolerated such abuse. He saw no point in the cautious resistance advocated by groups like the NAACP. And the cold shoulder he got as the husband of a Negro made him angry. But he had a more pressing concern. He was a skilled machinist, and had to somehow find work in the depths of the Depression. He and Edna pooled what funds they had and found an apartment near Chauncey Street.

Lena moved in with them, but the damage her mother had wrought on her could not be fixed. Edna, she felt, had kept her dear father away from her, while making her feel as though she were just "a nuisance and an interruption" in her mother's career. Cold as Cora seemed, undoubtedly she cared for her granddaughter. During her cruise she'd sent letters home, voicing affection for the "dear little girl." And if her own weakness showed through in her inability to speak a loving word to Lena's face, she still represented home. When a violent asthma attack killed her in September 1933, Lena was shattered.

Edna's hatred of Cora remained. In a story Lena told often, her mother forbade her to go to the funeral. Hysterical with grief, Lena ran there anyway. Edna pursued her and made such a scene in full view of the family that they disowned Edna permanently.

Within months, Grandfather Edwin died too. He took with him the last vestiges of real security Lena knew. But there was still Laura Rollock, who kept nurturing her dream to perform. Lena quit Girls High and, for practical purposes, enrolled in secretarial school. Meanwhile she joined the Anna Jones Dancing School, whose members, according to the *New York Amsterdam News,* were "a group of pretty New York and Brooklyn debutantes."

In 1933, the Jones girls took the stage of the Lafayette Theatre, the place where Edna Horne had gotten an intoxicating but short-lived taste of stardom. Now her daughter was dancing on its stage and on another just as grand, that of the Harlem Opera House, a home for lofty drama and music since 1889. White Broadway headliners like Edwin Booth and Lillian Russell had played that shrine, but lately black attractions had become welcome there, too. The Anna Jones ensemble brought something suitably high-flown: a piece that Isadora Duncan, the mother of modern dance, had choreographed to "Stormy Weather," Ethel Waters's show-stopper in the current show at the Cotton Club.

That year, Rollock directed an annual benefit show held by Brooklyn's Junior Theatre Guild. She cast Horne as the lead in an original-book musical, *Marriage Versus Contract.* Playing a Broadway star wooed romantically by a producer, she sang "I've Got the World on a String," another Cotton Club hit, and Cole Porter's "Night and Day."

Chic white audiences adored those songs, and if Horne sang them amateurishly, her looks made up for it. The young woman had grown to five foot six and a half, and her beauty had flowered. She had elegantly high cheekbones, her dark eyes glowed expressively, and her broad smile was just as disarming. Visually, she eclipsed her mother. In a bathing-suit photo taken of them on Jones Beach in Long Island, Edna looked squat and homely. Lena was wide-hipped and a bit chunky, with skinny legs, but her stunning face caught the eye. Clearly she knew it. Another picture showed her in a one-piece swimsuit, arms crossed behind her head in a sexy movie-star pose.

Writer Alfred Duckett grew up in her Brooklyn neighborhood, and saw Horne on the street every day. Wearing sunglasses, she would leave Girls High and head to the library, walking out shortly after with a book. Years later he recalled her as "the most desirable, the prettiest girl God had made and permitted me to see . . . She had a few brown freckles on her clear bronze skin. She carried herself like a princess. . . . I remember that she walked with a swaying walk and that there was southern warmth and depth in her voice." He and his pals whistled and shouted out, "Hey, baby!" at the sight of her. "The regal way she sailed past our united insolence only spurred us to greater efforts. 'What say, Stuck-Up?' we called out to her."

But when he met Horne in church, Duckett saw another side of the teenager. He found that "Miss Stuck-Up wasn't really stuck up." She would chat warmly and politely, he said, "if you only acted decent and tipped your hat." From then on, he remained smitten with her. Around 1933, he sat in the balcony of the YWCA, where an amateur musical took place. Its star was a white-gowned Horne. "I was awed to realize that I knew such a beautiful, talented girl," said Duckett.

Once home with her mother and stepfather, though, Horne reentered a web of hostility. To her, Mike seemed arrogant and unsympathetic to what black Americans had to endure, and she resented her mother for marrying him. All Mike knew was that this was the Depression, and everyone had it bad. He couldn't find work, and his marriage to a black woman didn't help. Edna found a way to minimize the fallout. Her light skin and Portuguese blood enabled her to pose as Latin. But Lena knew too well that they couldn't pass for white with a child of her coloring.

The family went on government assistance. They moved from Brooklyn to a less expensive apartment in the Bronx, then to an even cheaper one in Harlem. In later years, stinging from numerous career disappointments, Horne would claim that she'd turned to show business only to support her starving parents. Edna, she claimed, was ailing and unable to work, and had pressured her to step in as breadwinner.

But in her obscure first memoir, Horne told a different tale. With the family in need, she begged Edna to let her quit school altogether and find a paying job on the stage. The answer was no. The teenager persisted. By the fall of 1933, she had joined the chorus line of the Cotton Club, the most prestigious nightclub in Harlem. No one there noticed Edna's illness; every night she stayed glued to her daughter's side until the wee hours.

CHAPTER 2

FROM 1923 through the late thirties, the Cotton Club was a promised land, attained by few. "If you were a black person, that was a very, *very* important gig to get," said Bobby Short, the singer-pianist who began as a child vaudevillian and wound up as the prince of café society. "As colored people in Illinois, all we dreamed about was New York and the Cotton Club. *That* was glamour."

A job there meant victory over brutal odds and applause from the white elite. It also gave pretty young black women a chance to play Cinderella—for every season a handful of unknowns were decked out in glittering finery and added to the club's world-famous chorus line. They danced among the stars—Duke Ellington, Ethel Waters, Cab Calloway, Adelaide Hall, Bill "Bojangles" Robinson.

All these giants embodied the heights a talented Negro could attain in Harlem, the most stylish, vibrant ghetto America had ever known. The area stretched from 110th to 155th Streets and swept all the way from the Hudson River to the East River. During and after World War I, it filled up with migrants from the South, who'd come East to seek a better life. Cleo Hayes, a Cotton Club and Apollo chorus girl who eventually made it to Hollywood, had moved to Harlem from Greenville, Mississippi. She never forgot her first glimpse of her new neighborhood: "You couldn't believe what you were looking at, it was so different."

Photos taken in the thirties near the crossing of Lenox Avenue and 125th Street show a minimetropolis, teeming with energy. Hoards of urban blacks hurry past storefront beauty parlors, locksmiths, and greasy spoons; purpose and direction are on every face. On Sundays after church, Lenox Avenue turned into a year-round Easter Parade, as locals gussied up and went strolling. Trumpeter Doc Cheatham, who played in Cab Calloway's orchestra, recalled the sight: "Everyone tried to see how nice they could dress—necktie, jacket, clothes pressed, nice hair, cap." It was a display of community pride and a demand for respect, at a time when the rest of the world wanted to keep black people "in their place."

Certainly few parts of Manhattan held more architectural beauty than West Harlem, whose brownstones gleamed like copper in the sun. As for intellectual life, the twenties had spawned the so-called Harlem Renaissance—a cultural explosion of writers, thinkers, and artists whose work collectively explored what it meant to be a black American. Actor Ossie Davis, who was born just before it started, called the Harlem Renaissance an effort to show the rest of the country "that we had a command of the arts that qualified us as human beings." Behind it was the dream that their art could improve the lot of all black society.

They knew well the trials faced by Harlem's less fortunate: squalid tenements, rent gouging, shoddy health care and schooling, police brutality, and other forms of homegrown discrimination. A revolt was brewing. Even so, most Harlemites seemed to feel that God was smiling down on them. Exultant voices praised the Lord at Sunday mass, but compared to what some of them had known down South, many residents felt they'd already found heaven.

Its doors opened widest at night. Chorines, jazzmen, bartenders, flashy pimps and whores—they emerged after dark and reveled until dawn. "At five o'clock in the morning the streets were alive," said Cleo Hayes. "Breakfast balls" with champagne and dancing hopped at an hour when schoolteachers were getting dressed for work. Louis Armstrong or Fats Waller might show up after playing at Connie's Inn, a cabaret at 131st and Lenox whose floor shows overflowed with skimpily clad dames and hot jazz. Further up Lenox, on the entire block between 140th and 141st, stood the legendary Savoy Ballroom, "The Home of Happy Feet." The world's greatest Lindy Hoppers crowded the shiny mahogany floor, legs flying in a blur. Inside the cellar saloon known as Small's Paradise, waiters twirled their trays and danced the Charleston. Even in the Depression, Harlem brimmed over with a slap-happy, live-for-the-moment glee.

To young blacks who could sing or dance, the district's nightspots offered a ray of hope—a ticket out of poverty and struggle and into a world of recognition. In the late thirties, three girls often camped out on the fire escape behind the Apollo Theater. They craned their necks, straining for a glimpse of the headliners as they walked on and off stage. Those youngsters were Doris, Hortense, and Audrey Bye. Later they would bill themselves as the Bye Sisters, three slick and perky close-harmony singers and hoofers.

Doris also danced in the line at Small's. The view from its stage was similar to those found inside numerous other high-class Harlem joints—many of which, like Small's, were white-owned. "All our clientele at Small's Paradise was white," Bye explained. "It was jammed—people with their furs hangin' down, diamonds and everything. They'd be coming in their big Duesenberg cars."

To them, venturing uptown meant entering a barely civilized world: mocha-skinned, near-naked dancing girls; streets perfumed with the pungent smell of reefer; and jazz, at a time when the music formed a sound track for decadence, and "jazz me" was a lewd invitation. Much of the public's fascination with Harlem had begun with *Nigger Heaven*, the controversial hit novel of 1926. An interracial love story, it unfolded against a torrid backdrop of the Harlem netherworld. The author, Carl Van Vechten, was a gay white photographer with blond hair, delicate features, and a fetish for all things Negro. He named his book after the uppermost rear balcony of many theaters, the only place most blacks could afford (and often were allowed) to sit. But the title's double meaning was obvious.

Van Vechten's book celebrated the allure of the New Negro, the type on display in clubs all over Harlem. In his book *The Harlem Renaissance*, Steven Watson described the change. "Racist images of the Negro as a barbaric jungle creature transformed into those of the noble savage, the natural man exuding animal vitality . . . an uninhibited, expressive being." Only a few observers at the time saw that this new persona had its own racism.

For well-heeled whites in search of kicks, Harlem was irresistible. They flocked there at night with bulging pockets; in turn, gangsters seized upon the area as a prime place for bootleg liquor sales. In 1922,

Owney Madden, the city's most dreaded Irish mobster, went searching for a place to sell his "No. 1" beer. He came upon the Club De Luxe, a huge second-story ballroom on the northeast corner of Lenox and 142nd. Its boss was Harlem hero Jack Johnson, a slave's son from Texas who in 1908 had become the world's first black heavyweight prizefighting champion. By the fall of 1923, Madden had forced Johnson out and turned the Club De Luxe into the Cotton Club—a place of such unending mystique that, sixty years after it opened, Francis Ford Coppola directed a film about it.

Madden wanted the moneyed swells to feel right at home, so he furnished a club that harked back to slavery days in the Land of Cotton. Each detail was carefully planned, starting with the small sidewalk entrance, which replicated a log cabin. A flight of stairs led to a cavernous, white-columned room, designed like an old southern mansion. Images of slave quarters were painted on the walls behind the stage, a slightly raised platform up front. Black waiters in red jackets milled through the tables, pouring champagne and bowing like slave butlers.

Once the lights dimmed, tuxedoed and bejeweled revelers sat in a sea of tables and watched a parade of entertainers who had no apparent care in the world besides making their white "masters" happy. To the latter, those singers and dancers seemed plugged into some magical high-voltage socket that only Negroes could access. The great Bill "Bojangles" Robinson tapped in machine-gun-fire jazz rhythm. Princess Orelia, an "untamed and terrific" dancer (as the program touted her), offered a "lesson in savage rhythm." Norton, an oiled jungle boy clad only in a dance strap and feather headdress, stood with knee uplifted, spear thrust into the air, before breaking into an interpretive dance. The Nicholas Brothers (dancers Fayard and Harold) "defied the laws of gravity" with their acrobatic leaps and twirls. Leitha Hill titillated listeners with such risqué songs as "You Sure Don't Know How to Shake That Thing." Whyte's Hopping Maniacs furiously danced the Lindy Hop; the Tramp Band, in bowler hats and raggedy plaid, grinned toothily as they strummed guitars. The club's supremely elegant bandleader, Duke Ellington, was introduced as "the greatest living master of jungle music."

"Reefer madness," that naughty Harlem delight, wasn't neglected. It went on manic display in the person of Cab Calloway, the singing jive-hipster bandleader whom the Cotton Club had made a star. A gangly giant in a canary-yellow zoot suit, Calloway swept across the stage as though controlled by some crazed puppeteer. His moves were loose-limbed and jerky as he flung his arms through the air, flashing a demented grin. Calloway's trademark song, "Minnie the Moocher," was full of coded drug lingo and scat phrases; he sputtered them out as though high on some weird jungle cannabis.

Throughout the show, one could ogle the finest flesh in Harlem: that of the Cotton Club girls, a line of smiling beauties who were billed as "tall, tan, and terrific." (Hardly any were darker than café au lait.) "We'd have twenty-four girls on stage at once," said Wilhelmina Gray, a chorine and exotic dancer better known as Tondaleyo. "And maybe a jungle in the background and six drummers. It was very tight, precise staging."

The shows flew by in a dizzying hour and a half. George Ross of the *New York World-Telegram* warned potential customers to "take a strong sedative for your nerves" before entering. As if any more spice were needed, patrons got to rub elbows with real-life gangsters. One of them, George "Big Frenchy" De Mange, worked as the club's manager and greeter, until fate intervened in a spray of bullets—an act of revenge by enemies of Madden.

The three-dollar food and drink minimum would have shut out most black customers, but even among those who could afford it, hardly any were allowed inside. Certain black moneymen or celebrities, such as prize-fighter Joe Louis, were placed at the "family table" in the back, near the kitchen, where relatives of the cast sat; ordinary blacks who tried to enter were coldly (and sometimes forcibly) turned away. "You know better than that!" some were told, as though they were children who'd stepped out of line. White swells wanted to be amused by blacks, not necessarily to be in their company. Cotton Club habitué Jimmy Durante offered reassurance: "You don't have to mix with them if you don't want to." Herman Stark allowed the beloved Nicholas Brothers to enter and exit through the front door, but Fayard admitted that they were the exceptions.

The club's biannual shows—which ran approximately from March to July and September to January—were assembled largely by whites. Lew Leslie, the impresario known for his all-Negro *Blackbirds* revues, produced several Cotton Club shows; emcee Dan Healy introduced the festivities in his rat-a-tat-tat, Damon Runyon delivery. Years before he wrote the score for *The Wizard of Oz*, Harold Arlen—a composer with a passion for jazz and the blues—penned dozens of the Cotton Club's best songs. A gifted Jewish lyricist, Dorothy Fields, wrote lyrics (set to Boston-born Jimmy McHugh's music) about the New Low-Down and the Black Bottom, two Negro dance crazes.

Nowhere were the color lines drawn more bluntly than on opening night, when Harlem locals crowded the sidelines and fought for a glimpse of the white celebrities who stepped out of chauffeured limos: Franklin D. Roosevelt, Tallulah Bankhead, Mary Pickford, Bing Crosby, Eleanor Powell, Cecil B. DeMille, Johnny Weissmuller, George Raft, Milton Berle, Charlie Chaplin, Gloria Swanson.

Such luminaries weren't only there for the photo op. The Cotton Club shows *were* spectacular; their mixture of beauty, sex, and exoticism, pulsing with energy and polished to a diamond's gleam, was as potent as any drug. The chorus girls' high Harlem style—yard-tall feathered plumes, trailing chiffon scarves in tan and silver and gold, huge sequins shimmering on satin skirts—made it clear that black was bigger and more fabulous than anything downtown. "The Cotton Club discriminated, but none of us seemed to mind," declared Billy Rowe, the *Pittsburgh Courier*'s gossip columnist. "Its fame brought us glory all over the world. Guess we looked up to it because the folks, the rich, the near-rich and the poor, on a one-night spree, had to pass our way and drop some of that loot to get to it."

In the early months of 1933, before her sixteenth birthday, Lena Horne took her first steps toward joining the club's line of beauties. According to the story she traditionally told, her mother, Edna, phoned an old friend, Elida Webb, dance captain of the Cotton Club, and asked if her daughter could audition. Eighteen was the age limit for employment. Nonetheless, Webb took her to an early (10:00 P.M.) show so she could see what the chorines did. The twenty-second edition of *Cotton Club Parade* had recently opened, and Webb sat at the family table and watched it with a wide-eyed Lena. The teenager thought it was "fantastic," and longed to be part of it.

One number made a searing impression on her. Near the end of Act I, the evening's star, Ethel Waters, entered singing a bluesy torch song that Harold Arlen and Ted Koehler had written for her. "Stormy Weather" was a cry of frustration by a woman whose sky had caved in; her man had gone, taking all hope with him. "Life is bare, gloom and mis'ry everywhere," sang Waters, and there was no escape in sight. It "keeps rainin' all the time," she wailed, and only the dream of a brighter day kept her alive.

To Waters, this heart-rending cry of frustration was about a lot more than love gone wrong. Lena didn't know of the horrors that this front-rank star had survived as a black entertainer in the teens and twenties. "When I got out there in the middle of the Cotton Club floor I was telling the things I couldn't frame in words," said Waters in her autobiography, *His Eye Is on the Sparrow*. "I was singing the story of my misery and confusion, of the misunderstandings in my life I couldn't straighten out, the story of the wrongs and outrages done to me by people I had loved and trusted. . . . Only those who have been hurt deeply can understand what pain is, or humiliation. Only those who are burned know what fire is like. I sang 'Stormy Weather' from the depths of the private hell in which I was being crushed and suffocated."

Waters had brought a rare moment of pained introspection to the Cotton Club stage, and nothing could follow it except intermission. Lena was so "scared" by the song, she said later, that she never wanted to hear it. She never imagined she would one day sing it herself—indeed, that she could ever reveal herself the way Waters had. Her grandmother's mandate—"Never let anyone see you cry"—was too firmly in place.

That summer, Horne went to an audition for the chorus line of the September show. (She was sixteen, not eighteen, but the Cotton Club wasn't known for following the law.) Edna accompanied her. By day, the glamorous nightspot was a seedy-looking place, with tattered upholstery and walls stained by smoke. Horne found it frightening. "Instead of being bright and glittery," she said, "with beautiful appointments at every turn, it was dark and barn-like." She joined an intimidating number of young black women who were there to vie for two openings. "Black women at the time were supposed to be red-hot and sexy," Horne explained later, and the candidates knew it. One by one they stepped to the center of the dance floor and did frantic kicks and shakes while a pianist played. Everyone had to lift her skirt high and show her legs.

Presiding over the audition was Clarence Robinson, the ex–Cotton Club dancer who staged the shows. A suave, salt-and-pepper-haired charmer in a suit, he fancied himself the Ziegfeld of black beauty. "Many were called but few were chosen," he noted in 1949. "Why, we'd even bring girls from California and Texas and have to send them back, because they weren't right, in terms of looks, dancing ability, or both."

In fact, dancing ability was low on the list of requirements. *Ebony* later published those requirements:

1. Beauty
2. Height: 5'5" or more
3. Weight: 120 pounds or less
4. A little rhythm and knowledge of body movement
5. Age: Not over 26

By the time she was called, said Horne later, she was almost paralyzed by fear. She "stumbled" forward, thinking she couldn't even walk, much less dance. Horne heard a laugh, and felt sure it was directed at her rail-thin, flat-chested figure.

Horne did a time step. Although in later years she laughed off her early abilities—"I had no talent; I had nothing but looks"—Horne was surely better than she claimed, for she'd diligently studied dance under Anna Jones, a former ballerina with a Russian troupe. Clarence Robinson was impressed: "A likely prospect, thin, but beautiful," he called her.

Another aspirant, Winnie Johnson, was a year younger than Horne, but had already appeared as the child dance partner of Bill Robinson. Breaths were held as the chosen two were announced—Winnie Johnson and Lena Horne. A groan rose from all the others, who packed up and turned to shuffle out.

Both mother and daughter rejoiced. Immediately Lena joined rehearsals for the twenty-second *Cotton Club Parade;* it would star Adelaide Hall, one of the nightspot's grandest headliners, along with the Cab Calloway orchestra, singers Aida Ward and Leitha Hill, and a dozen more. In that company of seasoned troupers, Lena couldn't help but feel terrified. A sunny smile covered up her vulnerability. Hall found her "very shy" and as "nice and polite as you can imagine." Song-and-dance man Avon Long thought her "very sweet."

But with so little experience, she had her work cut out for her. Elida Webb knew her chorines would be judged more harshly than those in any white show, and she functioned as a stern but loving taskmaster. Webb had a tough job, because it wasn't talent that had gotten most of her girls in the door. Still, she wanted the club's show-me, white audience to see a line of top professionals, the equal of any Ziegfeld chorus line. More than that, she wanted them to exude class. "She was very interested in us, and the way we conducted ourselves," said Isabel Washington, who had danced there in 1931.

To be surrounded by Harlem's finest beauties, all of them vying for attention, brought out Horne's every insecurity. "You should have seen the girls at the club," she said years later. "Now *they* were beautiful! I was nothing more than average." Fayard Nicholas disagreed. "I saw this gorgeous girl," he recalled in 2004, "and I said to my brother, 'Look at her!' He said, '*Wow!*'"

But Horne was sure the club kept her on only because she was thin enough to fit in the costumes. She was just as self-conscious about her dancing; the teenager had so little coordination that she kept falling. The teenager vowed to get it right. Horne rehearsed strenuously, and continued to study with Anna Jones. Almost immediately, the Cotton Club brass singled out the lovely teenager for special attention. The preferential treatment began with manager Herman Stark, an ex–army sergeant. Gruff and heavyset, with a stogie in his mouth, Stark looked like a thug, but he wasn't; he only worked for thugs. As a tough guy with taste, he proved an ideal front man for a mob-owned cabaret.

Stark asked the big-sisterly Hyacinth Curtis, a senior Cotton Club girl, to look after Horne. Cab Calloway did his part, too. On the rare occasions when her mother wasn't watching, Horne would descend shyly from the dressing room to hear his band rehearse. When Calloway saw her he would shout, "Jail bait, don't you come down here, you stay upstairs! I don't want any of these men getting fresh with you!"

Clarence Robinson and Elida Webb extended their own helping hands. Noting how hard the young woman was trying to master her moves, they took her aside and patiently guided her. According to her colleagues, she loved the process. In a bit of newsreel footage from a Cotton Club rehearsal, the camera scans the chorus girls, all seated on benches as they wait to get up and dance. Horne is there in short shorts, hands clasped between her long legs, wearing a glowing smile. One can see no hint of the inner turmoil she recalled so often in later years.

Ambitious as she was, Horne still felt conflicted. Years hence, she would tell the author and photographer John Gruen that she saw the job as an escape from a miserable home life. But she knew that Cora Calhoun would have been mortified to know that her granddaughter was cavorting in scanties for a roomful of white voyeurs, in what the *New York Amsterdam News* called the Cotton Club's "most undressed revue in years." More troubling was the response of her beloved dad, who "objected violently to his daughter's career on the stage," wrote the same paper.

Edna didn't care. She saw herself as the mother of the happening new girl, and if her own career had ended almost before it began, she could now bask in Lena's reflected glow. Henceforth, Edna lived to make it brighter. She muscled her way into the packed dressing room and planted herself on a corner chair; from there she kept a close watch on her daughter and everyone else. "She was always there, every night," said Ruby Dallas Young (then known as Ruby Allen), one of the Cotton Club's most stunning showgirls. "Whatever we did, she was seeing." The older woman listened in on their conversations and asked prodding questions about their love lives. Meanwhile she corrected anyone who addressed her as Edna—"Call me *Mrs. Rodriguez*."

There were many snickers from the girls, who finally barred her from their quarters. She was relegated to the "family" table, but more often she stood in the wings, getting in the way. One night "the brown Valentino," dancer Paul Meeres, half of the boy-girl team Meeres and Meeres, came offstage and knocked Edna to the floor—"accidentally," said Ruby, who was there.

Once Lena left the dressing room, she was seldom out of Edna's sight. "There was no doubt in her mind what white swells and hoods wanted from a pretty little chick like me," Horne told reporter Robert Wahls forty years later. "Her forebears had been slave women. It happened to them." For the rest of her Cotton Club tenure, the youngster's rare dates were all approved, begrudgingly, by Edna, who hoped to save her daughter's virginity for a man of means. Edna's overprotectiveness was maddening to the increasingly boy-crazy teen, but not without cause: Harold Nicholas referred to Horne as the only girl in the chorus he didn't "get to."

Edna was just as fussy over who her daughter picked as pals. According to historian Delilah Jackson, an expert on the Cotton Club era, Edna discouraged Lena from getting too friendly with the room's tap-dancing virtuoso, Ernest "Brownie" Brown, because he wasn't handsome enough. Years later, Horne would describe her young self to Gruen as "the most frustrated sixteen-year-old you'd ever want to see!"

The new *Cotton Club Parade* opened, and Horne acquitted herself nicely. But Edna was impatient. She kept her ears open for word of performers who had called in sick, then rushed forward with a solution: "My daughter can do it!" Lena could learn any dance on the spot and sang beautifully, she insisted. In truth, the teenager had no illusions about her voice. "I couldn't carry a tune in a bucket," she said. According to reporter Rosemary Layng, Horne would "sing in the dressing room, with the girls kidding her, but never in public."

But Edna's pushiness paid off so soon, and so often, that Horne got the reputation of teacher's pet. "Lena was *never* just a chorus girl," said Cleo Hayes. "She could be put in a chorus line, but before too long she would be taken out of the line and given something else to do." And that's what happened only weeks after she'd first set foot on the Cotton Club stage. One night, Aida Ward took ill, and a sub was needed to cover her solo, "On a Steamer Coming Over." The club took a chance on Lena Horne. A quick study, she learned the number with little problem. After hours of drilling by Edna, the trembling girl stepped out to sing her first song for a Manhattan audience.

The results were competent and unmemorable, and soon Horne returned to the chorus. She knew she had no rhythm, so between dancing spots she stood in the wings, studying the blues singing of Leitha Hill, the crooning of Ward, and the airy swing of Adelaide Hall. Even if she couldn't come close to their finesse, Horne had a perky likability to go with her looks, and got singled out for further solos. In the same show, she won a featured spot in a number called "Lady with the Fan," written by Cab Calloway in honor of a famous Cotton Club fan dancer, Amy Spencer. A fan dancer, he explained later, "is a lady who comes out on the stage with her legs and arms and shoulders bare and only a fan in front of her. You're never sure whether she's wearing anything else." Horne would have to enter on a bare stage wearing just a G-string and two pasties and holding the fan demurely in front of her; she would warble a quick chorus, then the showgirls, including Ruby Dallas Young, would parade out one by one, all holding the huge, unwieldy feather fans.

On opening night Horne made her entrance. "I promptly paraded out and fell," she recalled. Her stint as the Lady with the Fan lasted one night. And still she kept grabbing center stage. Fayard Nicholas recalled a number he and Harold performed with Cab Calloway, "Keep Tempo." Calloway "had to go on the road with his band," said Fayard, "so they asked Lena Horne to take his place and sing this song with the Nicholas Brothers. And she did. And it was beautiful."

Backstage, the resentment increased. "Whenever I would be picked, I sensed the flak," Horne told Gruen. "You don't always like it if you're chosen. It's not always a comfortable position to be in, especially if you know that it's unfair. But anyway, I got noticed."

Determined to improve, she paid close attention to the work of the headliners. Several were forming a new show-business tradition; it challenged racist notions of how a black entertainer should sound and act. This new breed stressed cultivation and refinement and pandered to no one; without ever raising their voices, they demanded respect. Leading his orchestra, Duke Ellington maintained a cool smile that implied control. His manner was aristocratic, his clothes more elegant than those of almost anyone in the audience. Ellington's band was no freewheeling hot-jazz ensemble, but an impeccably arranged and rehearsed concert unit that burned at a low simmer. Unlike the risqué songbirds and near-nude showgirls on the Cotton Club stage, Adelaide Hall was a lady—demure, vocally trained, hands clasping a white chiffon scarf in front of her. But at select moments, Hall—a soprano from Brooklyn—would get hot. Her high voice broke into nimble scat, then she hiked up her skirt to do some tap dancing—a graceful kind, not the sort that begged for approval.

Avon Long garnered respect in a more aggressive way. Born in Baltimore, Long had studied to be a preacher, but he moved his evangelical fervor to the stage. His feisty singing and dancing skills earned him star billing at the Cotton Club and then on Broadway, where he played Sportin' Life in a revival of *Porgy and Bess*. Long knew his worth, and at the Cotton Club he didn't hesitate to inflame his employers. When a patron called him a "black nigger," Long snapped back, "Oh yeah? Well, you're a white nigger!" He was so outspoken that he was "fired from every show and rehired for the next." Onstage, he and other cast members gave their jolly repartee a sarcastic edge, peppering it with inside digs at the audience. "Such applause would come out," Long said. "We could survive on so many things of that particular nature." After the show, when he and the other entertainers were sometimes called upon to sit at tables and amuse customers, they would glimpse the society folk on the dance floor, attempting such dances as the black bottom. "We'd go upstairs and crack up," said Long.

Many of his colleagues already had illustrious pasts. Elida Webb had danced on Broadway in *Lucky,* a Jerome Kern musical of 1927, and in a 1932 revival of *Show Boat*. Isabel Washington, born in Savannah, Georgia, had played the part of a coldhearted temptress who steals Bessie Smith's man in a now-historic film short of 1929, *St. Louis Blues,* the only existing footage of the Mother of the Blues. Washington also appeared in two all-black Broadway revues. Hyacinth Curtis had traveled to Europe in a Florence Mills show and joined Elida Webb in *Lucky.*

But in their attic dressing room, Webb's chorines faced the tawdry realities of show business seven nights a week. They were crowded into a long, narrow space, one side occupied by racks of costumes, the other by dressing tables and mirrors. The dingy walls were hung with mirrors, and the dancers sat elbow to elbow, budget cosmetics and overflowing ashtrays spread out in front of them. Outfits were slung over chairs, and the air reeked of perfume, cigarettes, and sweat. It was a typical backstage chorus-girl scene; dancers at most of the big white nightclubs had it no better.

The Cotton Club, though, brought its own indignities. Most of the performers—even Ethel Waters and Adelaide Hall—were barred from using the restricted white street entrance, and had to come and go through a back door. The customers' bathrooms were off-limits; the chorus girls didn't have one at all, and had to relieve themselves in a basin.

"Now it seems awful," said Ruby Dallas Young in 2007. "But at the time it never occurred to me to complain."

Indeed, most of them thought themselves lucky to be employed at the legendary nightspot and did their best to shrug off the conditions. "It was a real distinction to belong to the Cotton Club line," said chorus girl Carolyn Rich Henderson. The job, she said, brought "good pay" throughout the Depression, and ensured future work. "Wherever you went," she added, "people pointed you out as the highest type of glamour."

Even the most talented chorines would never have gotten that job had they not been "high yaller." Blond, blue-eyed mulatto Marian Egbert could have easily passed for white, her sister Christina for Mexican. Peggy Griffiths ended up marrying a New Jersey judge and living as his "white" spouse. Webb, like Harold Arlen, fought for the inclusion of darker-skinned girls, and in 1932 she was allowed to hire the club's first, Lucille Wilson.

But hardly any others followed. "That's the way things were in those days," said Doris Bye, whose skin was unusually fair. "You just had to take it the way it was, and be glad that you were lighter or brown. They used to say back then, 'When you're white, you're all right. When you're brown, you can hang around. When you're black, stand back!'" Bye laughed and clapped at the memory. "So we knew we were all right!"

For many of the so-called lucky ones, fair skin was a key to advancement and a point of pride. Elida Webb's daughter, Druscilla Dawson, termed the chorines and showgirls "a snobbish group, because they were light." Class elitism ran high in their circle. Dawson recalled one dancer's snickering comment when a colleague of hers whipped out a curling iron before the show: "I don't see why people don't go to the hairdressers and get their hair done!"

Money and hardship were the great levelers. All the girls were earning the same pay, twenty-five dollars a week. While the club could surely have afforded to pay more, that salary lay in the top third of Depression-era incomes—this at a time when a decent apartment could be rented for fifteen dollars a month. The dancers worked hard for every cent. They had no night off, and performed two strenuous shows a night and three on weekends. They often doubled at theaters, for which they received a welcome bonus. But Bessie Dudley, a snakehips dancer from the club, told David Hinckley of the New York *Daily News* that she and her colleagues had to appease the cops by offering them free shows.

Cleo Hayes, a green-eyed, tawny-blond beauty, rallied for changes when few others would. She gathered her fellow Apollo Theatre chorines to go on strike for a raise of a few dollars—up to what the Cotton Club girls were paid. "That was about the best you could get," she recalled in 2006. "They worked us very, very hard, but we were never reimbursed for what we had given of ourselves. That was here, that was in California in the movies, I don't care where you went—if you were a chorus girl you had to fight for everything."

If funds ran short, the dancers did what they had to do to get by—including, in some cases, a little prostitution. Getting near a Cotton Club girl wasn't easy, because the mobsters guarded their investment strenuously; male admirers sent gifts upstairs, but couldn't enter the dressing rooms. Decades later, most of the chorines denied strenuously that they'd traded their favors for cash, or that the gangsters had ever had their way with them, as people assumed. But Hayes acknowledged that it had happened sometime: "A couple of those girls, I guess that's what they wanted." Hyacinth Curtis even admitted to Delilah Jackson that she turned the occasional trick.

In most cases, "marrying up" was the goal, and Cotton Club girls were seen as trophy wives for even the loftiest of men. Isabel Washington met Adam Clayton Powell, Jr., there and gave up show business to wed him in 1933. Duke Ellington added Bea Ellis to his succession of girlfriends. Hyacinth Curtis became Mrs. Clarence Robinson; Winnie Johnson married Stepin Fetchit, the black comic actor of Hollywood fame.

How Lena Horne really felt at the time about her life amid mobsters was hard to discern; she smiled a lot, did a pro's job, and otherwise kept quiet. She told reporter Glenn Plaskin that her grandmother's hardness had rubbed off on her, enabling the girl to keep smiling and hide her fear. She recalled "an ability to keep myself to myself, and not let anybody see that I was really frightened." Only years later did she talk of how she had felt onstage, when she would look out and see the club's cigar-smoking thugs, brassy-looking babes at their sides. She felt their eyes burning into her. "I *hated* this exposure of them looking at me this way," she said. The clientele offended her too: "I sensed that the white people in the audience saw nothing but my flesh, and its color."

In the sixties, she began denouncing her launching pad as a "pigsty." The so-called "Aristocrat of Harlem" was a "*dreadful* place," she said, which exploited its talent in every possible way. The club's veterans, she said, "were full of stories about how white people had drawn on their experience, taken their ideas for individual numbers—even for complete shows—and given them nothing in return."

The owners did make some effort to reach out to the Harlem community. They sponsored outdoor soup kitchens to feed the Depression-era hungry; they booked their acts into the Lafayette Theatre, where anyone could see them. But according to Langston Hughes, the neighborhood wasn't appeased. "Harlem Negroes did not like the Cotton Club and never appreciated its Jim Crow policy in the very heart of their dark community," he wrote.

Cab Calloway didn't disagree, yet he looked back on the club with a practical eye. "The money was good, the shows were fine, and the audiences and the owners respected us and our music. What else can I say about it? I don't condone it, but it existed and was in keeping with the values of the day. It couldn't happen today. It shouldn't have happened then. . . . But on the other hand, I doubt that jazz would have survived if musicians hadn't gone along with such racial practices there and elsewhere."

Horne, too, made the best of things. For all her later protestations that she "didn't want to be onstage," her fellow chorines remembered her as one of the most driven of them all. Horne's appearance in another Cotton Club film clip reveals a fast and determined learner. The girls, all clad in white and wearing matching flowers in their hair, are shown dancing in a whirlwind production number. Horne and her radiant smile are easy to spot. She doesn't miss a step; she moves much more capably than she ever admitted she could.

In the dressing room, she confided her dreams to Hyacinth Curtis: "Someday I'm gonna be famous and I'm gonna have a big house. I'm gonna be nice to my children."

Horne wasn't feeling much warmth at home. She recalled Edna's promise, after her marriage to Mike, that they would be a family at last.

"But it was too late," Horne said. "I was no longer a child. I was working in the line at the Cotton Club in Harlem and that kind of life grows you up fast."

Her stepfather remained clueless as to the traumas of racism, and Horne's resentment kept growing. "He couldn't understand why we came in the back door of the Cotton Club, and you couldn't come and see your children in the act if you were black," she told John Gruen. "I'd want to punch him in the eye. And it caused a constant friction because somebody had to earn a living." The fact that Mike, a foreigner, could go places in New York that she couldn't galled her. It didn't matter how good she looked, or that white big shots salivated over her. Nothing would override the fact that Horne was black and would be treated accordingly.

But there were compensations, for news about the Cotton Club's gorgeous up-and-comer had started to spread. Horne's Brooklyn admirer Alfred Duckett recalled the excited buzz about the local girl who'd made good; there in the old neighborhood, she'd turned into "a misty, distant, and fabulous legend." The Anna Jones Dancing School held a class recital in February 1934, and Lena was proudly billed as a star attraction.

She was still sixteen when she moved officially into the spotlight. It happened in the twenty-fourth edition of the *Cotton Club Parade*, which opened on March 11, 1934. The show starred Adelaide Hall and Harlem favorite Jimmie Lunceford, whose orchestra teemed with flamboyant showmen. Avon Long was also in the cast.

Harold Arlen and his lyricist, Ted Koehler, had written a lilting sequence entitled "Spring Breaks Thru." The show's centerpiece, it opened with the dancing of Meeres and Meeres, then segued into a sprightly new song about eternal love, "As Long as I Live." Long would sing it with a soubrette in the cast.

That now-forgotten cast member quit the show on short notice. Avon Long thought Horne could fill the spot nicely. Not everyone in charge agreed; as much as they liked her personally, nobody thought she was much of a singer. But Long fought for her, and since time was short, he got his way.

Horne would serve mainly as decoration; she would stroll out on Long's arm, smiling sweetly, and sing just the eight-bar bridge. Arlen gave her some quick coaching, and Long walked her through her steps over and over.

In years to come, he chuckled as he described the response. Walter Winchell, the most influential columnist of the day, singled out the exciting new girl who sang "As Long as I Live." He didn't even mention Long, who marveled, "All she needed was eight bars!" Apart from getting featured billing, Horne had graduated from chorine to showgirl. This less strenuous role was reserved for the finest of Cotton Club beauties, who merely paraded on and off as decoration. In the spring of 1934, Winchell's rival, Ed Sullivan, singled out Horne and Winnie Johnson as the two outstanding lookers of the group. All this attention made Horne believe that the Cotton Club "might be more than a job."

In the dressing room, raised eyebrows and snide remarks greeted her. "You sure didn't get that song on your *voice*," said one of the girls. According to Horne's first memoir, Edna demanded endlessly that she try harder. Good diction was paramount; so was feeling. "You're telling a story in your song," Edna explained. "Make the audience live it with you!"

Ultimately Edna's wise advice became the hallmark of her singing. But for now, the struggle to "put feeling into that song" was so intense that it was making her hoarse. "I would sing one night, then the next night it would be gone. I couldn't open my mouth!" Edna sent the teenager to a vocal coach in Harlem. Even after the *Cotton Club Parade* had closed, there was no rest for Lena. A pared-down version of the revue went on tour; along the way the girls were loaned out for various events. On every payday, Lena handed Edna her envelope, unopened. Having built her daughter up, the failed actress seemed all too ready to take her down. "If I had your opportunities," she said, "I'd be the biggest star in the world."

The warmhearted Ruby Dallas Young saw "a very unhappy person" in Lena. "I remember her sitting on my lap, and I told her, 'Don't worry, someday a Broadway producer will see you and make you a star.' I should have hung out my shingle. I knew she would be somebody."

Confirmation of that appeared in a 1934 Paramount movie short, *Cab Calloway's Jitterbug Party*. It includes a glimpse of Horne in her first film appearance, apart from Cotton Club newsreel snippets. The short's last song, "Call of the Jitterbug," is set at a house party, where smartly dressed Harlem revelers play instruments and gleefully dance the Shim Sham. One can spot Horne twirling in a man's arms, then standing in a line and tossing up her hands in exhilaration. Even in those fleeting moments, she outshines a roomful of uptown glamour girls.

The twenty-fifth edition of the *Cotton Club Parade* opened that September. "As Long As I Live" had been reprised, and Horne received even more prominent billing in the ads. Young's wish for her younger colleague proved prophetic. Just after the opening, producer Laurence Schwab came to the Cotton Club in search of a girl for his new Broadway play, a voodoo thriller called *Dance With Your Gods*. The show would costar Rex Ingram, a strapping, handsome black actor of stage and screen, as the "first lieutenant" of a voodoo tribe. Schwab needed someone light enough to play a "quadroon girl"—the quarter-black offspring of a mulatto and a white—who becomes a voodoo sacrifice. The prettier, the better. From a stageful of fair-skinned beauties, Schwab chose Lena Horne.

She accepted eagerly. In a typically kind gesture, Herman Stark allowed her to skip the early (10:00 P.M.) show at the Cotton Club so she wouldn't feel overworked. She would rush back in time to do the midnight and 2:00 A.M. shows.

Written by Kenneth Perkins, a white playwright, *Dance With Your Gods* told the convoluted story of a Yankee reporter who visits New Orleans in hopes of seeing a voodoo ceremony. Jacques Boyean, a young Creole, helps him concoct a scheme. The two men will ask a local witch doctor, Mam' Bouché, to curse an imaginary man for raping the daughter of a friend of theirs. Boyean gives the culprit a fabricated name, Amos Juvenal; he doesn't know that an Amos Juvenal actually exists, and comes from a respected New Orleans family. Bouché discovers the ruse and wreaks revenge on Boyean for daring to toy with voodoo. She wills the spirit of Black Jack, a Negro just hanged for murdering his white rape victim's husband, to invade the body of Boyean.

Once possessed, Boyean turns into what John Chapman of the *Daily News* deemed a typical Negro: "Swaggering, twirling a razor and talking like a longshoreman." But Bouché's curse backfires, and the now-apelike Boyean carries off the lovely virginal daughter of Amos Juvenal and tries to make her his voodoo bride. In the play's pivotal scene, a voodoo wedding ceremony, drunken Negroes undulate and chant while six black musclemen pound drums. A girl is plucked out of the gathered crowd to become Boyean's victim in effigy. That was Lena Horne. Chapman described the scene: "In a wild scene of drum-beats, shouts and orgiastic dances she is married to the recently hanged corpse of Black Jack."

Over fifty years later, Horne recalled her part as "very silly"; it required her "to do nothing more than go into a sort of voodoo dance, lots of drums throbbing and me being caught up in the hysteria of voodooism." But after the indignities of the Cotton Club, Broadway was a relief. Compared to the competitive uptown chorines, the cast of this show felt like family. "I liked getting away from dancing through the tables," she said, "having men look at me and blow smoke through my face."

Dance With Your Gods opened on October 6, 1934. Panned by critics, it folded after nine performances. The play's racist stereotype of black men as voodoo-obsessed rapists of white women went uncriticized in its day. Instead, Arthur Ruhl of the *Herald Tribune* voiced disgust at the gay audience members who went to see the "animated pornography" of the shirtless, muscular black actors.

Short though its run, *Dance With Your Gods* had put Lena on Broadway. It earmarked her more than ever as a girl on the rise. Black newspapers began keeping a close watch on the youngster and cheering on her every move. Her greatest booster, the *Pittsburgh Courier*, reported that she "had worked her way up from the chorus ranks to one of the best-liked entertainers ever to grace the floor of the 'Aristocrat of Harlem.'" Others, recalled Horne, deemed her "too sophisticated for a colored girl."

The Cotton Club didn't think so. September of 1935 found her there again for the nightspot's twenty-seventh revue. Horne's stage time had grown considerably. The show paired her in several scenes with her fellow Brooklynite Emmett "Babe" Wallace, a handsome, burly singer with a booming bass-baritone voice. But *Variety*'s review was a valentine to Horne. "The champ looker in the outfit is Lena Horne, a beaut in any shade of color, who makes it so tough for the rest of the company that she's purposely eased on and off quick after her numbers, otherwise they'd be still looking at her."

Billy Rowe, a columnist for the *Pittsburgh Courier* and an enraptured champion of Horne's, took credit for suggesting to her that it was time to leave the Cotton Club behind. She agreed. Even before *Variety*'s review had run, the *New York Amsterdam News* reported, "Lena Horne, the Cotton Club pretty, is planning a dramatic career in earnest."

Horne wanted out, and Edna agreed. That was around December of 1935. A few years later, Lena started telling a tale of how she'd "escaped" from the mobsters' clutches. It sounded like a scene out of a gangster film, and in repeated tellings it grew into a symphony of victimization—by her mother, by the mob, by show business, by whites in general. The trouble began, she said, when Edna managed to land her a job singing with Noble Sissle, a thriving black society bandleader of the day. Edna announced to her daughter's employers that Lena would be leaving the Cotton Club. They were enraged, for Edna had signed her to a "lifetime contract" with the hoods, at twenty-five dollars a week. Under those terms, Horne complained, she would have remained in servitude there indefinitely. "That was my introduction to the white world," she recalled.

When her stepfather showed up at the club to demand Horne's release, "they did terrible things to him," she said—including dunking his head in the toilet—and refused to let Horne go. Mike and Edna had to take emergency measures. "Actually they had to kidnap me," she told Gruen. "When we wanted to leave, we literally had to flee in the night." They headed for Philadelphia, where the job with Sissle awaited her.

It's likely that her resignation did anger her employers, for Horne was a promising girl. But little evidence existed to back up her account. The Cotton Club girls knew one another's business, but not the toilet story, until Horne began telling it years later. Ernest Brown, who was very much on the scene then, was surprised to hear it decades later. "I don't think nothing like that happened," he said. But by the time Horne popularized the tale, all involved parties had died. "If *Lena* thought the Cotton Club was a hellhole, God, I don't know what anyone else would think, because they just adored her," said Cleo Hayes.

As for the "lifetime contract" Horne's mother had signed her to: "We didn't have any contracts!" said Ruby Dallas Young. Even headliner Ernest Brown couldn't recall ever signing one. It was hard to imagine the club binding in perpetuity an unknown who'd started out as a "*bad* dancer" who "couldn't sing." Once or twice Horne explained that this "lifetime contract" was actually a simple statement of terms, with no closing date of service.

It wasn't even Edna who secured the job with Sissle. Reporter Rosemary Layng wrote that it was Flournoy Miller, a Cotton Club comedian and the coproducer of Sissle's Broadway revue *Shuffle Along*, who offered to try to get Horne a job with the bandleader. According to Layng's article, the youngster told Miller, "What would a band do with *me*? I can't sing."

"Are you willing to learn?"

"Oh, *yes*! But I don't think my mother'd let me go . . ." She went. In unguarded moments, Horne told interviewers that it was indeed Miller who had set her up with Sissle.

Fictionalized as her story seems, its basic charge—that the Cotton Club exploited the race it purported to glorify—was hard to deny. Unlike her colleagues, she made no allowances for the bigotry of the times. To her the Cotton Club embodied all the indignity her grandmother had taught her to revile. She walked away with a lifelong disdain for night-clubs, which nonetheless became the focus of her career.

By the time she left it, the Cotton Club hadn't far to go—largely because Harlem itself had imploded. In March of 1935, word spread that a black teenager had been beaten and killed by police. He'd stolen a pocket knife from Kress & Co., a white-run racist department store. In fact, the youth was Puerto Rican, and after his arrest he was released unharmed. But the rumors were enough to trigger a firestorm in what Alain Locke, the Harlem Renaissance writer and philosopher, called a "dark Harlem of semi-starvation, mass exploitation, and seething unrest." Riots broke out that nearly destroyed the community; there were three deaths and an estimated two million dollars in property damage.

Mayor Fiorello La Guardia responded nobly. His WPA renovation project included numerous apartment buildings that lower-income blacks could afford to move into. But Harlem no longer seemed like a carefree playground for pampered whites; now most of them were too frightened to go. The Cotton Club moved to an address where whites felt safer, Broadway and Forty-eighth Street, near Times Square. A less discriminatory nightspot, the Plantation Club, took over its old location.

In September 1937, the new Cotton Club opened with many of the past headliners. It softened its racist admission policy; now the room welcomed Negroes of "the better class," as *Ebony* would report. But its magic couldn't be recaptured downtown, and profits sagged. In 1939, the IRS nailed Herman Stark for tax evasion. That year he began cutting corners; his revues were shorn of their grand costumes, sets, and chorus members, like a fallen general stripped of his medals. The club finally closed on June 10, 1940. It soon became the Latin Quarter, an all-white emporium of legend.

The Cotton Club girls would prove more durable than the landmark they'd helped make famous. Those who weren't lucky enough to marry well became nightclub hostesses, secretaries, switchboard operators, salesgirls. Cleo Hayes worked as a barmaid for decades, while continuing to dance; in 1985, when she was past seventy, she teamed with three other Harlem chorines of her day and formed the Silver Belles, a song-and-dance act. Ruby Richards invested in Harlem real estate and made a fortune; Ruby Dallas Young had a much-touted affair with Joe Louis before marrying a businessman, then a politician. Hyacinth Curtis worked as a dental assistant and lived to age 104.

Nearly all of them looked back on the Cotton Club as the pinnacle of their lives, when they reigned high among the most desired women in Harlem. But Lena Horne had no nostalgia for that show-business landmark. "She was not thankful for what the Cotton Club had done for her," said Isabel Washington. Horne only viewed it as a hotbed of abuses and saw no reason to be grateful.

CHAPTER 3

AT A TIME when café society had dozens of pet bandleaders to politely score its charity functions and debutante balls, Noble Sissle was unique; no other black maestro belonged to that soigné circle. Through his impeccable refinement, Sissle—forty-six when Horne met him—had climbed farther up the social ladder than any Negro musician of his day, including Duke Ellington. Even his name suggested royalty. Sissle's band entertained at highbrow white functions in Paris, London, and New York, thrown by such society kingpins as the Rothschilds and Elsa Maxwell. The Duke and Duchess of York danced to Sissle's music; so did the Prince of Wales. He'd even played the Kentucky Derby. The Indiana-born preacher's son stood in tuxedo and tails, head held high, as he gracefully wielded a baton. A cool half smile never left his "lean aristocratic face," as Horne remembered it.

To the black bourgeoisie and the blue-collar alike, Sissle was heroic. He employed Negroes of all shades, each one a nattily dressed symbol of politesse. Sissle believed they could wield a strong influence on conditions for their whole race—*if* they behaved themselves at all times. It was essential, he felt, that white observers see them as figures of high cultivation. That meant no smoking onstage, no raised voices or swearing anywhere near the job. No matter what insults they faced, every band member, said Horne, had to be "exemplary and demure so the white society types Sissle worked for wouldn't say, 'There go those black people messing up again.'"

If he struck some observers as a snob, high-handed, and "very opinionated," as Cleo Hayes found him, Sissle had earned it. He'd graduated from Butler University, a bourgeois black college in Indianapolis. During World War I, he'd risen to the post of second lieutenant, and worked for his role model, James Reese Europe, a black society bandleader whose massive Clef Club Orchestra had introduced jazz to Carnegie Hall in 1912. Sissle and his partner, pianist Eubie Blake, cowrote Broadway's first black musical smash, *Shuffle Along*. In 1937, he helped found the Negro Actors Guild.

As a conductor, Sissle had higher-minded goals than fine music. He led a competent dance band, polished and professional. Barely any "hot" jazz influence colored its orderly lines; that would have seemed unmannerly. Cleo Hayes, who danced in a USO tour with Sissle, had heard better. "Noble had good musicians," she said—one of them was saxophonist Sidney Bechet, a star of traditional jazz—"but he was not an artist. I never saw him do anything but wave the baton. 'Cause he could not sing, he could not dance, and if he played an instrument, he hid it from me."

January 1936 found the band playing in Philadelphia. Sissle needed a girl singer, and Flournoy Miller had convinced him to audition Horne. Off she went by train, Edna beside her, to sing for the princely conductor. She chose a favorite of the day, "I'm in the Mood for Love." He didn't think much of her voice, but he liked what he saw, including her decorum. He offered Horne the job. She jumped at it, but her mother came along with the deal. As Lena was only eighteen, Edna couldn't leave her unguarded.

Before her first appearance, Sissle sat Horne down and instructed her firmly, "You must be a lady!" By that he didn't mean some pampered socialite, but a woman who countered every black stereotype. Horne recalled his rules: "One must be neater and cleaner and more genteel in attitude so that one will be accepted *for the sake of helping other Negro people!*" Over and over, Sissle reminded her, "You are not a whore—don't let them treat you like one."

Then the real grooming began. He taught her how to walk onstage, how to speak and carry herself with that all-important dignity. She studied movement at the Harlem studio of Henry LeTang, a tap dancer who would one day choreograph such Broadway hits as *Sophisticated*

Ladies and *Black and Blue*. Obviously her singing meant less to Sissle than her presentation. In one number, Horne would do a tap dance while wearing white gloves and a top hat. Her outfits—such as a dress suit with sequined tailcoat—were eye-catching, all the better to distract from her vocals.

One of her earliest jobs with Sissle was in February 1936 at the Howard Theatre, a prestigious black venue in Washington, D.C. Apart from Horne, the leader had ornamented his band with two dance teams and a boy singer, Billy Banks, who took some of the pressure off Horne by singing several duets with her. Every time she rose from her chair at the front of the bandstand, her knees shook with fear. Sissle was a star, and even though a blizzard was raging, his fans packed the Howard all week. Timidly as she sang, his lovely songbird was a treat for the eye. "Sissle's new find, Lena Horne, made a tremendous hit," wrote Jesse Mann in the *Chicago Defender*.

Horne was a dutiful student, but the adult world she'd been thrust into felt stifling. She missed school and the company of people her own age. The teenager was grateful to meet Cleo Hayes when Sissle's band came to New York, and they stayed friends for years. Horne's sweetness touched Hayes's heart. "Lena was just a young girl, laughing and talking," said the dancer. "You were so glad to see her. She always made me feel special."

Soon Horne would learn why her employer had tried so hard to bolster her self-respect. The band would sweep into this or that town by bus to play at a white ballroom or social function; invariably they had to enter through the back door. Often they had no idea where they'd be sleeping. Sissle and his musicians would scout ahead for black families who were willing to take in a player or two; the rest of the musicians stayed in black hostels on the outskirts of town. Sometimes they drove around in the middle of the night, combing the streets for a place to stay. Everyone, including Horne, grew used to sleeping on the bus. Only there were they safe from the racist slurs they heard from some of the bluebloods they entertained, or from employees in white shops and diners.

Edna stuck to her daughter's side; for a time, the unemployed Mike Rodriguez joined them, and Horne's salary supported all three. If the bandmembers found Edna annoying, they hated Mike, who railed loudly about what he perceived as Sissle's hypocrisy. How could the maestro insist his stepdaughter be a "lady" when he brought her to work in places she had to enter through some alleyway? Horne's sympathy went to the band; Mike, she felt, could never have realized that racism had to be fought. "How could he understand?" she said. "He was a foreigner." Mike and the light-skinned Edna could stay in almost any hotel they could afford. Eventually Sissle threw him off the tour.

The worst night she could remember occurred in Terre Haute, Indiana, where no hotel wanted them. The bus ended up parked on the grounds of the Clyde Beatty Circus. The din of the howling animals made it almost impossible to sleep, and Lena was traumatized. "Ladylike" treatment didn't matter to her anymore; she would have settled for some basic humanity. But Sissle demanded they keep their chins up. Dignity was all.

Horne wanted more. Once again, she knew she hadn't been hired for her talent, and she vowed to improve. Tirelessly she practiced her vocals. She dreamed of sounding as effortless as Orlando Roberson, who sang with the Harlem bandleader Claude Hopkins. As a Cotton Club chorine, she'd appeared on several bills with Hopkins; once she and Roberson teamed up on a schmaltzy hit of the day, "Cocktails for Two." Her partner had such a high, light voice that when he sang on the radio, many listeners thought they were hearing a woman.

For Horne, singing was hard work and not much fun. But by March 11, 1936, Sissle felt she was ready to make her first record, and that day she cut two sides with his orchestra for Decca, a top label. The title, "Vocal by Leana Horne," used a spelling she adopted briefly. In years to come, only the most discerning of ears could recognize the girlish voice on that platter. "That's What Love Did to Me" found her doggedly trying to express the misery of a world-weary woman for whom "love put the clouds in the sky above."

One can hear the lump in her throat as she struggled to connect with the words, to give them feeling and meaning, just as Edna had insisted she do. Horne gave them everything she had, and if that still wasn't much, her obvious desire to tell a story set her apart from most of the generic band singers of the day. She also had a basic musicality; every note was in tune. She sounded more comfortable on the B-side, the flirty love song "I Take to You." Horne sang it like a breathless high school girl on a date, full of spirit and hope.

But she seemed to lack any black-music influence at all, and Sissle's musicians weren't impressed. Neither were the members of one of Harlem's favorite bands, Andy Kirk and His Twelve Clouds of Joy, who were in a studio down the hall on March 11. Kirk's pianist was Mary Lou Williams, a fiery and versatile player who became one of the most influential women in jazz. To her, Horne was just another shallow beauty who couldn't sing. In her diary, Williams recalled seeing Dick Wilson, Kirk's tenor saxophonist, and the other musicians running outside between takes. Wilson had spied Horne and told his colleagues how gorgeous she was. They hurried into Sissle's room to hear her sing. "In one voice they said, 'Yeah, she's beautiful'—and came back to our studio, where they stayed," wrote Williams.

But among the black public her fame kept spreading. Her looks made her eminently photographable, and Horne posed eagerly for glamour-girl pictures. One of them showed her wrapped in the fur coat her father had given her; in another she grinned while twirling an umbrella.

In the spring of 1936, following the release of her 78 with Sissle, the teenager accepted a deal for the first of many print endorsements she would do in her life. The ads ran for months in the major black papers, including the *Pittsburgh Courier* and the *Chicago Defender*. The product, which came from Atlanta, was of a type popular until the sixties. Its name: Dr. Fred Palmer's Skin Whitener Ointment. Beside a large photo of Horne's face, a cartoonlike bubble pointed to her mouth. "Girls!" it said. "Here Is the Fastest Way to Really Lighten Skin!" The copy explained, "When surface skin is ugly, dark, Dr. Fred Palmer's Skin Whitener Ointment lightens and brightens. Medium? It lightens and whitens. Light? Keeps it bright. . . . There is only one way to skin beauty, and to know the joy and happiness and better times that lighter, brighter skin will bring."

The magic ingredient wasn't specified. But typically, such creams used bleaching agents (sometimes lye) or hydroquinone, a chemical that inhibits melanin production. Given Horne's eventual reputation as a symbol of fierce black pride, it seems jarring that, at eighteen, she agreed to endorse a skin lightener. But skin bleaching was long an accepted practice among blacks, and the fee, whatever she got, was surely appealing. To Horne's friend of the eighties, the lawyer and activist Vernon Jordan, her appearance in those ads meant "nothing. She was young. She got paid."

Edna, who had no qualms about passing, might easily have encouraged her daughter to take the job. Racial identity had long been a tangled issue among the Hornes. For all of Cora Calhoun's committed work for Negro causes, she and her family lived lives that were patterned upon the white middle class. Fair skin was synonymous with upward mobility. Among women, said the actress Ruby Dee, "the impression was that if you were almost white, somebody fine would come along and take care of you and sweep you off to Germany, or wherever."

At least Horne got to tour the country. The band had a packed spring and summer agenda in 1936. Slated for June was an important first in their careers, a run at the Moonlite Gardens, a white Cincinnati ballroom where no black band had ever performed. Sissle was proud. Two weeks before the opening, he and some of his men were in a car near Delaware, Ohio, heading to another job. They never got there, for another car crashed into theirs on the highway. Several of the musicians were injured, and their forty-six-year-old leader, who seemed like such a rock of invincibility, almost died. He sustained multiple fractures and a concussion.

Obviously, he wouldn't be healed in time to open at the Moonlite Gardens. Horne visited him in the hospital. As she sat at his bedside, he gave an order: She had to step in as leader. Horne panicked. She only knew how to sing and dance a little, certainly not how to conduct. One of the musicians could take over, she said. "No!" declared Sissle. This job was crucial, and his group could not cancel. They needed a fetching presence out front with the right manners and the right look; otherwise they'd lose the job. Horne had no choice but to agree.

Word of Sissle's accident had spread instantly, and his forthcoming gigs were canceled. But as soon as people learned about the amusing novelty he'd dreamed up—"a cute little girl swinging around in front of the band," in Horne's words—every employer hired them back. The orchestra fulfilled its booking at Coney Island, the Ohio ballroom to which Sissle and his men had been driving on the night of the accident. In front of a packed dance floor, the club manager read a wire Sissle had sent from the hospital, saying that although he couldn't be there in flesh he was certainly present in spirit. Everyone cheered.

Horne smiled bravely as she stepped out and began moving Sissle's baton through the air. "After the first awful moments, tension relaxed," wrote Rosemary Layng years later. "She got her first laugh; the words started coming easy." Horne sang a little and made the appropriate announcements. Instead of merely dancing by, white couples stopped to gape at the beautiful creature onstage who was doing a man's job. Over sixty years later, Gene Mikell, a member of the reed section, described the results. "She was supposed to be directing, but we all knew what we were doing," he said. "She was just a figurehead, a decoration. But she looked good, and she had a nice personality."

Far from damaging business, Sissle's accident and the stepping in of Horne proved a cause célèbre. On June 19, 1936, opening night at the Moonlite Gardens, customers packed the ballroom. Horne "took the patrons by storm," wrote one of her cheerleaders at the *Pittsburgh Courier*. "She is being widely acclaimed as the new hit personality."

The reporter added that while Horne was "intensely interested in her work," she told him that she and her mother felt "a little lonesome" on the road, so far from home. If she felt pressured at having to carry the band's immediate future on her young shoulders, she didn't mention it. On the very first night of the Moonlite Gardens engagement, America's greatest black hero of the day was in the boxing ring, risking far more than a few nightclub engagements. At twenty-two, Joe Louis—known as the "Brown Bomber"—was on his way to becoming the world's second black heavyweight champion, after Jack Johnson. The match was hugely symbolic. Louis's opponent was Max Schmeling, an iconic German prizefighter whom Hitler deemed an ultimate example of racial superiority. Though not a Nazi himself, Schmeling typified the growing Nazi threat, and many Americans hated him for it.

Among his people, Louis was godlike. And while a large portion of America was as racist as it was anti-Nazi, this sharecropper's son from Alabama had even captured the white man's fancy. That year he'd knocked out three white champions, Primo Carnera, Max Baer, and Paolino Uzcudun. In an age when Negroes were barred from many competitive games, notably major-league baseball, his achievements were unprecedented. Black youths had never had a role model like Louis, a simple man of superhuman reflexes, who embodied the most decent of Negro values. Unlike the incendiary Jack Johnson, who married white women and made his penis look even larger in his boxing shorts by wrapping it in gauze, Louis was groomed to be the ultimate credit to his race. Black men who felt castrated by whites saw him as a sign of hope.

David Margolick, author of *Beyond Glory: Joe Louis vs. Max Schmeling, and a World on the Brink*, detailed the process. Louis "would always be soft-spoken, understated and polite, no matter what he accomplished. He would not preen or gloat or strut in the ring. . . . He would always conduct himself with dignity. . . . When it came to women, he would stick to his own kind. . . . The press would be saturated with stories of Louis's boyish goodness, his love for his mother, his mother's love for him, his devotion to Scripture." With his bulldog face and pug nose, he looked like a slightly oafish guy on the street, easy to identify with; in the ring he acted deadpan, robotic, and invulnerable to blows. Newspapers quoted him on his social responsibility: "If I ever let my people down, I hope to die."

On June 19, millions of black people in America and countless more worldwide sat by their radios, listening to the fight and praying for Louis to win. During every break at the Moonlite Gardens, Horne and the musicians ran backstage to hear the broadcast. Their hearts sank in round four, when Schmeling knocked Louis down with a right jab to the chin. The Brown Bomber had never hit the canvas before. With each round he suffered new blows. Louis was losing.

Horne burst into tears, and the normally unflappable musicians were heartsick. Then they had to stroll back onstage, looking cool and regal. Only Edna was unmoved. She barely knew who Louis was, and had no idea why anyone should care so much about a boxing match. When Edna asked her why she was crying, Horne said, "He's being beaten!"

"You don't know this man."

"But I do—he's mine, he's ours!"

Louis lost, but his race was counting on him to make good. One year later, he knocked out boxer James J. Braddock in Chicago and became world heavyweight champ. Then on June 22, 1938, Louis flattened Schmeling in a rematch. "For one night, in all the darktowns of America, the black man was king," wrote British journalist Alistair Cooke. By that time, according to the vaudeville hoofer Leonard Reed, "blacks throughout the country generally had three pictures in their homes—the president's, Jesus's, and Joe's." A few years later, Louis and Horne would be carrying photos of each other in their pockets.

The memory of that first Louis–Schmeling match never left Horne: "I was identifying with the symbol that we had of a powerful man, an impregnable fortress, and I didn't realize that we drew strength from these symbols." Nor did she know she was becoming one of them. The Sissle band returned to the Howard Theatre in Washington, D.C. Nearby was an all-night, black-owned drugstore and diner. A student at Howard University's School of Pharmacy, James E. Jackson, Jr., worked the graveyard shift. Before graduating from Howard, he would help found the Southern Negro Youth Congress, a historic forerunner of the civil rights movement. With that he began a long career in the trenches of the movement; he also held key positions in the Communist party.

After she got off work with the band, Horne would come to the drugstore with Edna for sandwiches. "This was a thrilling moment for James!" said his wife and fellow activist, Esther Cooper Jackson. "He was so honored to have Lena Horne come in. There were several people behind the counter but he always wanted to be the one to serve Lena Horne."

Sissle rejoined the band on July 21 for another weighty engagement; this would be the first appearance of a black orchestra at Boston's Ritz-Carlton Roof. Horne stayed with the band throughout the fall. But the rapport between her and her lofty father figure had "cooled," reported the *New York Amsterdam News*. Sissle wanted his spotlight back, and the paper reported that he "shifted Lena to a secondary role, and hired [singer] Edna Harris and lifted her above the former Cotton Club favorite."

Now eighteen, Horne remained frustrated in many ways. She continued to don the smothering mask of a lady, and felt her girlhood slipping away. Men showed interest in her everywhere—and she in them—but her mother was there to extinguish any budding romance. Edna, said Horne, "was as rigid on the subject of sex as a nineteenth-century Victorian," and warned her that "if I didn't marry the first man I had, I would go to hell." For a "virtuous though hot-blooded" girl, as she called herself, the situation was maddening.

According to the *New York Amsterdam News*, the tension between Lena and Edna exploded around Christmastime 1936. The teenager fled to Pittsburgh to visit her father, whom she longed to know better. Horne would give a more romantic account of their reunion in her biography *Lena;* there she claimed that Teddy drove down to Cleveland, where the Sissle band was playing, and took her back to Pittsburgh. One thing was sure—she wanted away from Edna.

Teddy Horne had never approved of his daughter's career on the stage. That may be why he introduced her to his friend Louis Jones, a Baptist minister's son. Among young black men of his generation— he was then twenty-eight—Jones stood out. He'd attended a southern Negro college; after that he'd worked for the Young Democrats in Pittsburgh. Now he did publicity for the Cleveland Indians while hoping for a career in politics. Along the way he'd honed a suave, man-about-town veneer much like Teddy's. Early photos show an attractive, light-skinned man with straightened hair, parted and slicked back, dressed in an elegant double-breasted suit.

To Avanelle Harris, a young dancer who would appear in several of Horne's films, Jones was a "snob." Pittsburgh locals knew him as a playboy. And despite Horne's description of him as "very handsome and very black" and quite the catch, Doris Bye wasn't impressed. Jones would later operate a nightclub in Ohio where she and her sister Hortense danced. "He was peculiar-looking; he wasn't no nice-looking fellow," said Doris.

But Horne was smitten. "He charmed her," said Cleo Hayes, who had met Jones before Horne did. "I didn't like him, not really." Hayes never forgot his grand, chilly "How do you *do?*" when Horne reintroduced them. But Jones was striving for the high polish and confident air that an ambitious black man needed in a white world; it hardly differed from the façade Noble Sissle ingrained in his musicians. Jones had big ambitions to enter politics, and he wanted the proper wife on his arm. His courtly manner impressed her, and she couldn't get over how nice he seemed. "I don't know if he really respected me," she said, "but he seemed to." In early January, approximately three weeks after they'd met, Jones proposed. Though she hardly knew him, Horne said yes. "Why wait?" she told the *Pittsburgh Courier*. "We love each other and that is all that matters."

Edna was incensed to see her throwing away her chance at stardom. "It's the end of your life," she declared. But Jones promised her a stability she'd barely had since childhood; marrying him would also get her away from Edna, and closer to her father. There were many naysayers, wrote the *Courier's* scribe. "But love ruled, and darling Lena shook her head. 'It's love and a home,' she said, and no amount of persuasion could change her decision . . . She is contented to be a wife . . . the greatest and grandest place a woman can occupy."

Louis Jordan Jones and Lena Calhoun Horne filed for marriage in Pittsburgh on January 6, 1937. A week later came the wedding. Reverend B. S. Mason of the St. Luke Baptist Church officiated. In attendance were Teddy and Irene Horne and several of Jones's relatives, including his two brothers. But not Edna. "Mother sends 'blessings,'" wrote the *Courier*. Louis's father, the Reverend W. Augustus Jones, wasn't there, either. To him, girls in show business were virtually whores, and he felt his son had married down.

Lena moved into Louis's home at 2709 Breckinridge Avenue. Disappointment on both sides came quickly. Horne had dreamt of the pleasures that came with a marriage certificate, but sex with Jones proved a crushing letdown. "Lena said he was like an animal," recalled Elle Elliott, her stylist in the seventies. Horne faulted herself, too. Edna, she said, had taught her "that sex is dirty," and it had left the young woman uptight and insecure.

Bigger problems awaited them outside the bedroom. "My grandfather wouldn't have won any kindness contests," said Samadhi Jones, who was born into the life of Ted Jones, Louis and Lena's son, in 1967. "He was a very charismatic character but he could also be very harsh and disapproving—a dyed-in-the-wool male chauvinist. He was almost medieval. He came from an era in which women kind of submitted to men and were satisfied in almost a servant role to their husbands."

Horne was hopeless in that regard. She'd grown up with a grandmother who thought cooking and cleaning beneath her, and a mother who had spent all her time training her daughter to become a star. "Here I was, Miss Cotton Club—didn't know how to cook, didn't know how to wash clothes," she admitted later.

Very soon into the marriage, more information about Jones came out. Behind his grandiosity was an embittered young man. His family expected great things of him, but he'd married before he could gain his college degree, which embarrassed him greatly. Jones's refinement hadn't taken him far; he'd lost every hoped-for job to a white applicant. Finally, he became a clerk in the county coroner's office in Pittsburgh. He hated the lowly post, and left it each day in a foul mood. "I thought that he should come home and be warm and loving," said Horne, "and he would try, but he had been treated so cold himself he just didn't have nothing left over." His anger started to mount. Jones tried to teach his young wife to drive, but she couldn't get the hang of it, and the car kept stalling. "You dumb bitch!" he finally yelled. "Dumb" was a word that hit a nerve in Horne; having come from a college-educated family of teachers and intellectuals, she already felt inferior. She took Jones's swipe to heart; never again would she sit behind the wheel of a car.

After just a few weeks of wedlock, Horne decided she'd made a terrible mistake. She contemplated leaving, but that became impossible. In March, she learned she was pregnant. Now she felt trapped, and yearned ever more for her daddy to take care of her. People in the neighborhood recalled seeing her sitting on the steps of her father's hotel in the Hill district, waiting for him to arrive. She looked sad and very young.

Despite its complications, performing had given her a center; without it, life felt empty. Movies provided escape. She saw at least one a week. Her pulse beat a little faster if the star was Charlie Chaplin or Bette Davis, her favorite actors. But watching other entertainers only made her miss the career she'd tossed aside. Louis Jones had gained membership in the Loendi Club, where well-heeled black men came to socialize; even Duke Ellington went there on occasion. Horne showed up on Jones's arm and impressed the regulars, who knew of her show-business history. In the summer of 1937, a visibly pregnant Horne began singing there for free. It seemed to give her some of her identity back.

After many lonely and confused months, she went into labor. Her trusted black doctor took her to the delivery room of a white hospital, but his color prevented him from tending to her himself. Horne was frightened to be left there without him, but the doctor told her not to worry. "You're in excellent hands," he said.

In fact the delivery was long and excruciating. The white doctor and nurses handled her roughly; she recalled being stuck with needles. On December 17, 1937, she gave birth to a baby girl. Horne named her Gail. Jones had wanted a boy, and he treated his newborn daughter indifferently; once more, Horne felt alone.

Once more she grew desperate for some sort of escape, and in February of 1938 she got it. Unexpectedly, a call came from a white agent in New York, Harold Gumm. Actor-dancer Ralph Cooper, a handsome peacock who emceed at the Apollo, was looking for her. Cooper had become a partner in Million Dollar Productions, a company that made very-low-budget, all-black films. He wanted Horne to star opposite him in a musical, *The Duke Is Tops*. She would play a beautiful young singer asked to leave a chitlin-circuit touring revue—and the good-natured shyster who runs it—and star on Broadway.

Horne wasn't Cooper's first choice. He'd hoped for the beautiful Nina Mae McKinney, the sassy star of dozens of musical shorts and *Hallelujah!* (1929), the first all-black full-length feature from a major studio (M-G-M). McKinney was known as the "Black Garbo," and since people called Cooper the "Dark Gable," it seemed like a perfect match. McKinney wasn't available, though, and Cooper thought of the singer whom the *Pittsburgh Courier* called the "Prettiest Girl in Show Business." He offered Horne six hundred dollars for a ten-day shoot. The opportunity excited her, and she prayed that Jones would let her go. Because they had a toddler and needed the money—and he wasn't making much—Jones said yes.

The Duke Is Tops fell into a genre known as race movies: all-black, poverty-row efforts made for Negro theaters. Most of the films were painfully ill produced, sometimes in as little as two days. But they provided a crucial first step in the acceptance of Negroes by the film industry, and preserved the work of hundreds of black performers. The race-movie tradition stretched back to 1909, when the first Negro depictions appeared on celluloid—grinning, apelike figures singing, dancing, and clowning. Six years later came the explosion that inspired the race-movie revolution, director D. W. Griffith's legendary and reviled *The Birth of a Nation*.

The three-hour epic—a survey of pre– and post–Civil War America— dealt a crippling blow to the fragile cause of race relations in the United

States. It sparked a firestorm of race hatred by portraying blacks as killers, thieves, and rapists. Because the film was hailed as a masterpiece, its theme of white supremacy was taken very seriously; after its release, the Ku Klux Klan flared up with renewed fervor.

Nationwide protests against *The Birth of a Nation* had little effect, and Hollywood would perpetuate many of the same clichés for thirty years. In *Hallelujah!* director King Vidor tried to extol Negro culture by showing fervid riverside mass baptisms and gospel congregations. But the film bowed to every stereotype. Darkies joke and sing "Swanee River" as they pick cotton; little black boys tap-dance their hearts out and bounce on the knees of women who look like Aunt Jemima ("I b'leeve yoo sho is right, mammy!"). In the 1933 Vitaphone short *Rufus Jones for President,* Ethel Waters plays a rural mother who cradles her little boy (the seven-year-old Sammy Davis, Jr.) to sleep, promising him a bright future. "Yessuh, honey, you *shaw* is gonna be presi-dint!" Rufus dreams of the campaign. Banners trumpet a slogan—VOTE HERE FOR RUFUS JONES, TWO PORK CHOPS EVERY TIME YOU VOTE—and he wins by a landslide. At an assembly of swaying, bug-eyed senators, Rufus appoints a "watermelon investigator" to "plant the watermelon vines near the fence, instead of in the middle of the patch." Later, in "Underneath the Harlem Moon," Waters extols the joys of being black, singing, "It ain't no sin to laugh and grin/That's why we *schwartzes* were born."

Socially conscious, forward-thinking blacks were appalled by such portrayals; out of their disgust, race movies were born. Most of these films aimed to present positive, nonstereotypical images of blacks; some were merely mindless fluff to divert viewers from the hostile world outside. Tedious, illogical plots, bad acting, and technical chaos were common. But for James Thomas Jackson, a poet and writer raised in Houston, even the shoddiest race features tossed out crumbs of hope. "Just seeing a black in a movie was ever an inducement to save our money for the day when a film 'with some of us in it' would come to our segregated movie houses," he said. The major studios depicted blacks in the most subservient roles, but there were exceptions. The sight of Bill Robinson "wearing his favorite dancing shoes and that ingratiating toothy smile . . . keeping in step with those magic dancing feet brought joy, great joy," Jackson wrote.

In 1938, *The Duke Is Tops* gave black film audiences their first look at Lena Horne. Ralph Cooper had sent Horne the money to fly to Los Angeles, where she would begin shooting on February 14. When he met her at the plane he was dismayed; Horne was still chubby from her pregnancy, and looked like no leading lady. But Avanelle Harris, who'd been cast as a chorine for the film's nightclub scenes, remembered how much everyone seemed to like Lena. The dancers were nearly all southern California locals; some had toiled in the film industry for years without getting too far. Harris, who came from St. Paul, Minnesota, and had grown up in L.A., was a child when some filmmakers recruited her for her screen debut, a silent, all-black short, in *Our Gang* style, with the dancing Berry Brothers. Harris played one of a group of rambunctious boys and girls who ride a trolley through town. The director and crew felt she didn't look dark enough. "They wanted to paint me black, and my mother wouldn't let 'em do that. But they put some white stuff on my lips."

Harris might have easily been jealous of this ex–Cotton Club girl who had grabbed the lead in her very first film. But once she and the other dancers met her, she said, "we welcomed her. She was a doll." Harris recalled Horne's sense of wide-eyed wonderment. "It was all new to Lena. Most of the girls that were raised in California had worked at the studios; Lena had no idea what was going on." Harry Levette of the *Atlanta Daily World* came to the set to interview her; he found Horne sitting on a toolbox in between takes. He asked her how she liked the West Coast. "Oh, fine, but . . ." She hesitated. "You see, I have a husband and Gail, my six-weeks-old baby girl, back home in Pittsburgh."

Still, she seemed to be having a ball, both on the set and in the California sunshine. Horne was determined to learn how to act for the camera. Contrary to her later claim that she'd taken the job only to support her baby, Harris remembered Horne as "*very* ambitious."

But this was a humble screen debut. Cooper made *The Duke Is Tops* in ten days, using a run-down lot in Temple City on the outskirts of L.A. There was hardly any rehearsal time; he couldn't afford it. The title seemed like an effort to fool audiences into thinking they'd see Duke Ellington; Horne's character, Ethel Andrews, was surely named to remind people of Ethel Waters.

The story concerned a small-time impresario, Duke Davis, and his

Sepia Scandals revue, which toured the "chitlin circuit" of low-grade black vaudeville and tent shows. Every member of *Sepia Scandals* is outshone by headliner Ethel Andrews, who dazzles audiences. A big-shot agent offers to make her a Broadway star. Out of loyalty to Duke she declines, but he insists she go: "It's your chance, kid! Take it!" Ethel leaves in tears, and Duke is sad, too, as he sees his show flounder without her. Out of desperation he becomes a scam salesman, selling his cure-all Magic Elixir to bumpkins and fleeing the cops. Ethel isn't doing so well, either; her big musical has flopped. Duke rushes to New York, rebuilds his show around her, and all ends happily.

Horne is a sweet but unformed presence in the film; her singing is generic, her acting flat. But she conveys a high-class image, and tries so hard to sound expressive that she wins the heart through good intentions. One can see, in *The Duke Is Tops,* the first glimmers of her budding star quality.

By the end of February, Horne was home in Pittsburgh. Her Hollywood experience had ended sourly. Cooper had run out of money, and wound up shortchanging her and other cast members. But the black newspapers were eager to build her up, and they announced the upcoming premiere with much fanfare. *The Duke Is Tops* made its bow in June of 1938 at Pittsburgh's Granada Theatre, a movie house chosen in Horne's honor. An NAACP benefit, the event sent waves of excitement throughout the city's black community.

But the outcome proved scandalous and was splashed across the pages of the *Pittsburgh Courier:* REFUSES TO APPEAR AT PREMIERE OF OWN FILM. According to the paper, Horne had gone downtown to see a white movie instead of attending *The Duke Is Tops.* That day the theater manager had received a telegram signed by Horne: PROFESSIONAL APPEARANCES SHOULD BE MADE ON A PROFESSIONAL BASIS, it said.

"The 'professional' angle emphasized by Miss Horne hinted strongly of compensation, a thing unheard of at a premiere of a star's own picture," wrote the *Courier's* reporter. "I think Miss Horne has been ill advised," added the manager. A pall hung over the crowd that night. "A group of fashionably dressed patrons saw Lena labor through one of the saddest pictures of the season. It was as 'plotless' as a 1908 vaudeville show . . . the beautiful Miss Horne should stick to her soloing before an orchestra. As an actress she is no Myrna Loy." The next day her absence was "the talk of Pittsburgh," added the *Courier*.

Horne later claimed she'd wanted to go, but that Jones wouldn't let her—due, she supposed, to a macho need to dominate her, and his disdain for showbiz. It was he, she said, who made her demand a fee. The *Atlanta Daily World*'s Harry Levette tried to compensate for the mess. "Lena Horne, gifted both with a beautiful face and voice, is very successful with her debut in films and is sure to make future triumphs." he wrote. But *The Duke Is Tops* only left Horne feeling cheated. Cooper would later brag that he'd "discovered" Horne; after M-G-M had signed her he rereleased *The Duke Is Tops*, passing it off as a new film, *The Bronze Venus*. But he never gave Horne the rest of her money.

Having known a brief taste of movie stardom, she resumed the role of housewife and mother. But according to a now-forgotten black celebrity of the time, Horne began to stray. Leonard Reed was a vaudevillian, impresario, and former pimp; in the fifties, he produced a series of popular movie shorts, *Showtime at the Apollo*. A smooth operator with a huge ego, Reed assembled touring black vaudeville revues and had his own career as a song-and-dance man; because he was only a quarter black, with wavy hair, he could pass for white when it suited him. After Joe Louis's boxing career ended in the late forties, he partnered with Reed in various business ventures, including restaurants; Louis invested the money and Reed did the wheeling and dealing.

In a memoir cowritten with Bill Reed (no relation), he boasted of many things. "Starting in the mid-1920s," Leonard declared, "I doubt that many men were fucking any more than I was. I wouldn't even go into a show unless there was somebody I could screw." The showman claimed an affair with Horne that took place in 1938. If true, it would most likely have occurred during the filming of *The Duke Is Tops*, when she was safely far away from her husband. Leonard left the circumstances, locale, and length vague, but not the denouement. Months earlier Reed had nearly died in a car crash; well after his release from the hospital he still bled. One day, said Reed, "she saw on the bed blood comin' from my . . . Shit, she got scared and she ran and I can't blame her. I look over and see some son of a bitch bleeding, I'm going to run, too. That was the end of Lena and me."

Did it happen? A friend of Horne's from the eighties heard no mention of Reed, but didn't doubt the possibility: "It was clear from my conversations with Lena that she was a *real* wild child, honey." Horne's fellow Cotton Club chorine Hyacinth Curtis didn't disagree. "Lena *loved* to make love," she told her friend Delilah Jackson. Leonard gave Bill Reed a photo of himself and Horne taken in the late thirties; it shows the two of them standing close, flanked by unidentified friends.

Horne did admit that her husband thought her "flighty," and that their marriage was turning increasingly hostile. As the spouse of a rising entertainer, Louis Jones was having ego issues. Gene Davis, a black filmmaker several generations younger, understood why. "Black men at that time felt they were not achievers," said Davis. "To be married to a black woman of status was very, very difficult." Rather than pursuing his own political career, Jones was helping campaign for white candidates who wanted an in with the Negro community. He came home each day spewing antiwhite venom.

Horne, meanwhile, had begun singing at white social events in Pittsburgh, some hosted by the Mellons, the exorbitantly wealthy family of financial and industrial moguls. The training of Cora Calhoun, Noble Sissle, and others had paid off. In the most well-to-do company she seemed demure and sweet, and whites embraced her wherever she sang. Horne, in turn, observed the relative ease of white show business, especially when people of power were in one's corner.

As Horne kept performing, Jones watched her interest in their marriage crumble. "The lure of show business got the best of her and she was off to the footlights again," he said in 1954. "She was never the same person to me."

The actress and dancer Fredi Washington—whose sister, Isabel, had danced at the Cotton Club—had befriended Horne and vowed to help her. Washington recommended the young singer to Lew Leslie, a Jewish impresario who served as the kingpin of the all-black revue. In the fall of 1938, Leslie was seeking a leading lady for the sixth edition of *Blackbirds*, his celebrated series. Soon Horne got a message from Leslie, asking her to come to New York and audition. Jones didn't stop her; they needed money.

In Leslie, Horne encountered a tireless bundle of nervous energy, all of it aimed at exalting black talent. Since 1926, the former Lew Lessinsky had persuaded white investors to finance his revues, which he mounted on Broadway and in London. Having coproduced shows at the Cotton Club, Leslie took pride in plucking gifted black artists out of segregated settings and presenting them in splendor on the theatrical stage. Ethel Waters, Bill Robinson, Adelaide Hall, and the Nicholas Brothers had all starred in *Blackbirds*. But Leslie's prize discovery was Florence Mills, whom he'd groomed into a poised and ladylike star. Thanks largely to Mills, Leslie's premiere 1926 edition of *Blackbirds* was a smash.

Leslie had been trying to survive the Depression as a producer. But funding had dried up, and the black revue had waned in popularity. By 1938, Leslie was fifty and floundering but not ready to give up. He had been at the Cotton Club when Horne stepped out of the chorus and into the spotlight. Reminded of her by Fredi Washington, he called her in. Soon he told the *New York World-Telegram* that he had found his new Florence Mills: "She can sing, dance, and read lines with great comic spirit. In addition to all of this, she has youth and beauty."

Horne thought the show would make her a star and enable her to pay off her and her husband's debts. Jones, in turn, could quit his job and become her manager, which he seemed willing to do. It was better than having white men pass him at work and assume he was the porter.

In New York, Horne began preparing for a show that had no backers. Leslie had hired most of his cast; it included two name comics, Hamtree Harrington and Dewey Markham, and two former Cotton Club chorines, Joyce Beasley and Cleo Hayes. They rehearsed without pay, fueled only by Leslie's assurances that funding—and a long run—were right around the corner.

Meanwhile, he drilled Horne relentlessly to get her in shape. She would have to sing three solos and several ensemble numbers, all without a mike, and her meager lung power wasn't up to the task. Horne was petrified; and Leslie, who saw his own future resting on a more or less unproven twenty-year-old, pushed her almost to the breaking point. He made her sing with the show's choir and try to project above it. Endlessly, he goaded her to sing the song once more, until she wound up hoarse and exhausted. He kept moving farther back in the theater and shouting, "Louder, Lena, I can't hear you!" All the while he invoked the name of

Florence Mills, who had strived hard for perfection and never lost her cool. Finally Horne screamed at Leslie, *"I'm doing the best I can!"*

Cleo Hayes, who was among the show's "large number of pretty colored chorus girls," as the cast list billed them, saw Leslie's point. "Lena should never, ever forget Mr. Leslie," she said in 2005. "He was a real Svengali. He took her and he walked up and down on that stage with her, and treated her like she was a big glamorous star. He would have a chauffeur pick her up and bring her to rehearsal, then drive her home."

He also gave Horne a little money to keep her going. The backers' auditions continued for weeks, seemingly in vain; the opening was postponed again and again, until no one but Leslie seemed to think it would ever happen. Louis Jones fought rabidly with Horne on the phone. His friends must be right, he yelled. All of them were chiding him about his stagestruck wife, who had deserted him and their child to go chase her career. It humiliated him every time he saw them, he said.

Horne pressed on. November 8, 1938, found Leslie's cast of nearly a hundred onstage at Boston's Majestic Theatre, where they played their first out-of-town tryout. Critics found the show "woefully short on humor" and starved for "punch and drive." Horne fared somewhat better: One reviewer praised her "extraordinary beauty," but faulted her "lack of professional poise."

A key backer pulled out, and Leslie's dream of Broadway seemed doomed. But at the last moment, a stroke of luck occurred. Belle Baker, Leslie's ex-wife and a renowned vaudeville and Broadway star of the twenties, showed up at a rehearsal. Baker pawned her jewels and gave Leslie the money he needed.

Finally, on February 11, *Lew Leslie's Blackbirds of 1939: A Harlem Rhapsody* opened at Broadway's Hudson Theatre. After all the turmoil, the results reeked of haste and desperation. The show looked like a bus-and-truck version of a Cotton Club review. Its dancers executed a cyclone of punishing moves, but the sketches seemed pale and clichéd. There were a few entertaining songs by the team of Johnny Mercer and Rube Bloom (who would soon write "Fools Rush In"), and some memorable scenes. In the opener, "Children of the Earth," hands pushed up through the ground and wriggled like snakes. "Frankie and Johnny," the old folk song about a murderous woman, was spun into a fully staged courtroom scene; this time Johnny was tried for shooting Frankie, and jurors, lawyers, and defendant sang their testimony.

Leslie stood in the orchestra pit, frantically waving his arms and dripping with sweat as he pushed the tempos ever faster. "All the performers must be limp with exhaustion by the time the show is over," wrote Brooks Atkinson of the *New York Times,* "and the audience has been blown into a state of coma by the shrill sounds that assault the defenseless house." He found the material and most of the performers second-rate, but liked Horne. Despite the mediocrity of her three numbers ("You're So Indifferent," "Thursday," "Name It and It's Yours"), Atkinson singled her out as "a radiantly beautiful sepia girl . . . who will be a winner when she has proper direction."

But Horne couldn't save a revue that critics had savaged. Louis Jones attended opening night, then went home, sure that *Blackbirds* would close soon. It did, in a week. Leslie's inability to pay his cast got him into trouble with the labor unions; he ended up penniless, and never produced another Broadway show.

Horne returned home heartbroken, while Jones felt more like a failure than ever, having just seen his wife on Broadway. Needing to prove his worth, he announced a new plan. He would quit his ill-paying job and run for local office against a popular black candidate. The already debt-ridden couple sank further into the red as Jones borrowed a substantial sum for his campaign. She demanded he reconsider.

"What kind of man had I married?" she wondered in her first memoir. "Was he too selfish to consider anyone or anything but what he wanted?" Jones had a family; he should have gotten a civil service job, maybe as a mailman. But he refused to listen to her. "I waited in vain for him to say he'd give up politics for some kind of work in which there was more security."

Horne's objections, realistic as they were, struck her husband as hypocritical. Hadn't she, a new mother, thrown caution aside and run to New York to pursue a life on the stage? In May 1939, the marriage took on an even greater strain as Horne found herself pregnant again. It was a troubling development for a woman who secretly planned a divorce.

On February 7, 1940, Horne bore the son her husband had wanted. They named him Edwin Fletcher Jones. Thereafter he would be called

Teddy, after her father. For a few months, Horne seemed happy as a young mother. Pittsburgh residents long remembered the sight of the twenty-two-year-old Lena holding Teddy in her arms at the local baseball games; she came to root for the town's beloved all-black team, the Homestead Grays.

But tension kept building at home. "It was a pretty bad scene," she admitted. For her, the final insult came when Jones, ignoring their debt, spent a bulky sum on a new wardrobe for his latest job, as official escort to a female Democratic official on a lecture tour.

Horne called her mother, who was in Cuba with Mike, and told her the marriage was over. She begged Edna to come look after the children so she could go to Manhattan and get a singing job. Edna refused. Mike had pneumonia, and she had to stay in a warm climate and tend to him. "That was a hard blow," said Horne, "but I dared not let it stand in my way." Years later, she gave a rare and candid summation of her ambitions. "My husband wanted to be my manager," she said, "but, honey, back then no black man could walk into a café and book a black woman. The marriage couldn't last—he tried to stop me from working. If I had been older, I would have realized it was the only way he thought he could assert his masculinity."

Her lack of confidence in Jones hurt him. And when his latest political dream collapsed, he saw no choice but his clerk's job at city hall. He found it unbearable, and the marriage reached a violent pitch. Later Horne commented obliquely, "His personality was just too strong for me." The eventual divorce papers would suggest he'd beaten her.

She had to escape. On August 2, 1940, Horne took the children from her husband and put them in a neighbor's care. Before she boarded a train for New York, Jones grumbled, "You'll come back."

CHAPTER 4

ONCE SHE REACHED Manhattan, Horne headed straight to Harlem. There she checked into the Theresa, a towering, white-exteriored hotel at 125th Street and Seventh Avenue. The Theresa had opened in 1913, but only in 1940 did it start admitting black guests. It became a haven for Negro celebrities of all sorts; Joe Louis could sometimes be seen waving to fans from a balcony.

Once settled, Horne went downtown in search of a singing job. Harold Gumm, the agent who had booked her into *The Duke Is Tops* and *Blackbirds*, began setting her up on auditions; Horne made other calls herself. She'd asked Lew Leslie for help, but *Blackbirds* had ended his career, and he had nothing for her. She tried out at George White's Gay White Way, a nightspot on the former site of the Cotton Club, and auditioned for a new version of *Shuffle Along*.

Horne found that in the black show-business world outside of Sissle's rarefied cocoon, the dainty grooming he'd given her was no help. Not even her Broadway and Cotton Club credits impressed people. Later she told Ralph J. Gleason of the *San Francisco Chronicle*, "I was just about at the end of my rope. . . . They all said, 'You don't sing colored enough.' And they wanted me to sing the blues. But I didn't sing them very well. I tried everywhere, but I had no luck."

That December, Horne sang a few songs for free at the Apollo, in an all-star benefit for Harlem's poor. Sissle was on the bill. He greeted her with customary grace, but when she asked if she could work for him again he declined. Desperate and nearly broke, Horne tried to fall back on her dancing skills by auditioning as a chorus girl for the Latin Casino, a three-thousand-seat showroom in Cherry Hill, New Jersey. She tapped to "I'll See You in My Dreams," a mellow swing-band hit of the day. The Latin Casino didn't have an integrated company of dancers, and in 1982 Horne related the bosses' response to Dick Cavett. "They said, 'Why don't you pass as Latin? You don't *look* colored.' That was meant to be a big compliment."

In her first memoir, she told of wanting to scream, "What difference does it make what color I am?" As rejections piled up, she sank into a hole of depression. Meanwhile, the black newspapers continued to proclaim her a starlet on the rise. She went to Chicago to visit her second cousin Edwina. The *Defender* showed Horne—the "sensational Broadway 'It' girl"—dolled up for a nightclub opening. Columnist Billy Rowe, the singer's champion from Pittsburgh, reported in the *Courier* that "Lena Horne . . . has her heart set on a permanent location in Manhattan." She didn't yet know how much rope she was giving to the angry husband she'd left behind.

Horne had more pressing issues on her mind. Her account of what happened to her in December of 1940 fit in with the most sugar-spun fairy tales of her career, but the man who ended up hiring her that month corroborated at least some of the story. A despondent Horne had wandered down to the Loew's Victoria movie house on 116th Street to lose herself in a movie. She settled into her seat and watched *The Sin of Madelon Claudet*, an early Helen Hayes talkie about a French country girl sprung from jail after ten years. Needing to support her child, she turns to prostitution. "I remember thinking resentfully that with all her troubles she didn't know what real heartache could be," declared Horne. "She was white, wasn't she?"

The singer had stayed in touch with Clarence Robinson, who had moved to the Apollo after the closing of the Cotton Club. According to Horne, Robinson had gotten a call from Charlie Barnet, conductor of a chart-topping swing orchestra. Barnet led what *Metronome*, a key journal of the jazz world, had called "the blackest white band of all." He worshiped Duke Ellington, and had broken a reverse color line by becoming the first white bandleader to play the Apollo. The Barnet band was booked to play the Casino Theater in the Bronx. His usual singer had taken ill, and he needed a replacement fast. Did Robinson know anyone?

Yes, he knew a great one—but she had just gone to the movies. He would try to find her. Robinson rushed from theater to theater in Harlem until he spotted Horne. He urged her to come with him: "I've found you a job!"

Robert Rice of the *Daily News* detailed her response: "She didn't want to miss the end of the movie. She was fed up with false hopes, and besides, she was enjoying the show." Robinson insisted she go. In her first memoir, she claimed she was miffed to learn that a white bandleader was her potential employer. Horne recoiled at the thought—even though she hadn't hesitated that fall to call Lew Leslie and to audition for a string of white club owners.

Still, off she went to the Bronx. If she really felt that "a white man is a white man," she had to admit that Barnet was unique. Born of a rich family in Manhattan, Barnet had quit Yale in order to play saxophone and lead a band. "Cherokee," his 1939 hit, had the smoldering, low-down sound of Harlem. The handsome maestro was also a notorious Lothario and would rack up ten marriages, some lasting just a few months. Barnet once took three prostitutes on the road for his band's pleasure, and treated his men to nights in their favorite brothel in Ohio. He had a much-publicized affair with the film star Dorothy Lamour, and was also known for bedding (and sometimes wedding) his girl singers.

He met Horne between marriages. She recalled adopting a stiff, cold demeanor as she walked into the basement of the Casino Theatre to meet Barnet. She hadn't even grabbed a moment to gussy up. Barnet's regular boy singer, Bob Carroll, recalled his first glimpse of Horne. "I remember she had long, straggly hair, and her dress wasn't especially attractive."

She felt sure that Barnet would reject her. Only two black singers had come aboard white swing bands—June Richmond (with Jimmy Dorsey) and Billie Holiday (with Artie Shaw)—and prejudice had forced them away. But Horne's color didn't faze Barnet; he found her stunning and a fair-enough vocalist. He told her that Ford Leary, his singing trombonist, had a sore throat, and he needed a sub. Barnet talked her through Leary's songs for half an hour, and that night she went on. "Somehow, they liked me," Horne told Robert Rice. "I don't know why." But according to Barnet, she "tore up the place."

Before chancing the risky hiring, he tested the waters. Barnet had her sing with him at the Paramount Theatre, then at a weeklong engagement in Newark, New Jersey. Finally she played a New Year's Eve dance with him at the Golden Gate Ballroom in Harlem. All went smoothly. On January 2, 1941, Barnet signed Horne to a six-month contract with an option for renewal, at a salary of $125 per week. It was the best money she'd ever made. She recalled crying with relief.

The ever-loyal *New York Amsterdam News* reported that Horne "brought down the house" in her official bow as Barnet's vocalist. But the flak started fast. Horne called her family in Brooklyn to tell them of her break; they were aghast to hear she would even consider taking a job with a white bandleader. She phoned her father to ask him for money to buy a gown, and he raged at her. How could she think of working for a white man? Horne claimed that even the NAACP protested; a black woman, they said, didn't belong with a white band.

She found herself in a dilemma she would come to know well: Should she please herself, or do what controlling forces in the black world thought correct? Horne saw no reason to leave Barnet. For one thing, she needed the money. For another, the band embraced her, making her feel that not all white men were suspect. Whereas Sissle's men had seemed constantly tense and on guard, Barnet's musicians were having fun—especially their bad-boy leader.

But Horne sat on the bandstand with a frozen smile, feeling isolated and very conscious of her color. White couples danced by the bandstand and stared at her. In her first book she recalled their remarks, which she felt were voiced deliberately loudly. "How do you suppose *she* got the job?" she heard. As she left the bandstand one night, someone said, "Did you see the way that nigger singer throws herself at the men?"

In many ballrooms and colleges, Horne wasn't allowed to sit on the bandstand between numbers, so she hid in a ladies-room stall. At a prom in a New England girls' school, she overheard the matronly, white-haired dean inform Barnet, "We can't have that colored girl sing here." Horne fled to her dressing room, with Barnet running to console her. Most of the white restaurants where the band ate refused to serve her. Barnet would shout for all to hear, "She eats here, or none of us eat here!" Usually they ended up storming out, threatening to trash the joint, as Horne followed in tears. When a restaurant did feed her, she worried that they'd spiked the food.

It was easier to sit alone in the dark on the band bus and let the musicians bring her something to eat. But she was sure they'd lose patience, so she began avoiding them as much as possible. She waited in the dressing room, reading magazines until the men had left for dinner. "Then I'd sneak out alone to find a newsstand or cigar counter where they sold apples and wrapped sandwiches."

Hotel desk clerks were apt to turn her away, and rather than let her sleep on the bus, Barnet would introduce her as Cuban. Horne herself considered passing for Latin or European, but didn't go through with it. Calling her children at home made her loneliness all the worse. She recalled praying, "Give me the strength to resist the temptation to take revenge for my hurt on the men in this band. Help me to forgive . . . and keep me from hating in return."

The battle weighed on her, and it was affecting her personality. Around this time, Doris Bye of the Bye Sisters met Horne. "I thought she was nice, but a lot of people in show business were saying she was very persnickety. They said she was moody. One minute she's happy and talking with you a lot, the next minute she don't have nothing to say."

Horne tried to rise above the flak by proving herself as a singer. Whenever possible she stood in the wings, singing along with the instrumentals. During breaks she'd slip into a quiet hallway and practice. Barnet had enough faith in her to feature her on four recordings. "Good-for-Nothin' Joe" was a daring choice. In it, a street whore reflects on her love for a coldhearted pimp. Rube Bloom and Ted Koehler had written it for the twenty-sixth edition of the *Cotton Club Parade,* Horne's next-to-last show there.

Someone else had sung it, but the song touched Horne, and she struggled to do it justice. On that 1941 recording, she sounds innocent and sweet; her naïveté, as she portrays a trusting, victimized girl of color, is moving. She ponders every phrase, stressing the meaningful words: "Guess I'd *die* if good-for-nothin' Joe / Ever tried to leave me flat." Her delivery lacks even a hint of black-music influence; she sings with elocution school diction, clean and neat. "She was a white singer," said Artie Shaw, the star bandleader and Horne's soon-to-be lover.

Horne's "hot-blooded" side, as she termed it, got nowhere near "You're My Thrill," a declaration of lust, with erotic moans and sighs written in. She did better with a perky children's novelty, "The Captain and His Men," in which she sounded like a young mother trying to make her baby laugh.

Barnet saw promise in those early recorded efforts, and later in January he asked his arranger Billy May—one of Frank Sinatra's future conductors—to write something for Horne. May went to work on "Haunted Town," a torchy confession of loneliness in the big city—something Horne understood. But in public, her turmoil couldn't puncture her smiling façade.

In the winter of 1941, the band prepared to tour the South. Barnet didn't dare take Horne, so he gave her several weeks' pay and told her to stay home. Now she could return to Pittsburgh and take care of some family business. It wasn't pleasant. She hadn't seen her children in six months. According to Gail Lumet Buckley's *The Hornes*, the singer had a "traumatic reunion" with Louis Jones. They fought about the children. She could have Gail, he declared—not Teddy.

But as a traveling band singer, how could she care for a little girl? Lena's father came up with a solution. She should ask her cousin Edwina, who had recently lost her husband, to pitch in; Edwina could stay with Gail in the Horne house on Chauncey Street, which he'd inherited.

On February 13, Horne was still in Pittsburgh, but not living with her husband, when an officer of the court knocked on her door. He bore a subpoena. Louis Jones was suing her for divorce. The order stated, "Lena C. Jones has committed willful and malicious desertion, and absence from the habitation of the injured and innocent spouse, without a reasonable cause, for and during the space of six months and upward; to wit from August 2, 1940, which desertion still continues." Horne was summoned to appear in court on April 7.

Two days after the subpoena came, the *Courier* shouted out the news: DESERTION CHARGED HERE IN LENA HORNE DIVORCE SUIT: FAMOUS SINGER SUED FOR DIVORCE. The *Chicago Defender* chimed in. "This marital crack-up resulted from quarrels over the resumption of her theatrical career, according to intimates of the couple." According to the *Courier*, Horne had refused the subpoena; that night she left town and returned to New York. It was either on that day, or soon after, that she claimed her daughter and took her to Chauncey Street. "I remember being dressed up in my pink coat and hat," wrote Gail, "and I remember being surrounded by grown-ups' knees."

Edwina arrived in Brooklyn, and Horne rejoined Barnet. The racist slights on the road continued; meanwhile, more than one black publication hinted that the relationship between her and the bandleader had become an affair. It was a dangerous situation, for Horne was facing a nasty divorce and a custody battle.

The singer ignored her court date. Instead she filed a countermotion against Jones, accusing him of "cruel and barbarous treatment" and of perpetrating "such indignities to the person of the Libellant, the injured and innocent spouse, as to render her condition intolerable and life burdensome." Now Jones got a subpoena, commanding him to appear in court a month later to finalize a divorce. He didn't show. The date was postponed to July, then to September; he answered none of his subpoenas. The cat-and-mouse game would drag on for three more years, prolonged by Horne's travels, an increasingly nasty war over Teddy, and sheer spite. "I didn't want no singer," said Jones years later to Clint Rosemond, his son's best friend. "Peggy Lee sings all the songs that I need. I wanted someone to stay at home and cook my grits."

In April 1941, Horne sang with the Barnet band in its return to the Paramount. The *Chicago Defender* noted the "many rumors in and out of the profession" about a clash between singer and maestro. Horne was anxious to leave, and she sought the help of John Hammond, a young record producer with a staggering array of credits. Hammond was responsible for Billie Holiday's recording debut; he'd also brought the Kansas City–based Count Basie orchestra to New York for the first time. Horne barely knew Hammond, but she came to him "practically in tears," he said, begging him to get her a solo job. "I asked her what the matter was and she told me she was sick and tired of being chased around by Charlie Barnet's band. I made a few calls."

In turn, the city's most controversial nightclub impresario went to hear Horne at the Paramount. Barney Josephson was a former shoe salesman from Trenton, New Jersey, with a stubborn dedication to social justice. Racism made his blood boil; in response he'd created Café Society Downtown, Manhattan's first nonsegregated cabaret and an oasis for the liberal cognoscenti.

Watching Horne from his seat in the cavernous Paramount, he wasn't sure what color she was. But he didn't care. "I was impressed," he recalled. "Not so much that she was a great singer. She had so much else going for her. Looks alone. The way she handled herself at the mike. I thought, 'I could work with this one.'"

In the dressing room, he introduced himself. She greeted him curtly, but grew warmer as he spoke. "Now, people coming into this theater, they don't know who the hell you are," he said. "You're a singer with Charlie Barnet. What are you gonna get with that? How would you like to come into Café Society, where you'll have no less than the great Teddy Wilson at the piano for you? And you won't have to go on the road with one-nighters. If you're good with me you can stay on forever."

"Fine," said Horne. "I'd like that."

Horne allowed that she and Barnet were feuding, but said she had no contract with him and could leave anytime. In fact, the six-month deal she'd signed had several weeks to go. But Josephson urged her to finish out her engagement. On April 15, *Down Beat* reported that Horne had left the Barnet band by "mutual agreement." She had already begun a ten-month run at Café Society Downtown. Her seventy-five-dollar-a-week salary was a dip from Charlie Barnet; still, Horne would call her Café Society gig "the sweetest job I ever had"—one of the few she remembered with pleasure. It also helped trigger the leftist connections that would eventually get her blacklisted.

Josephson himself feared nothing. In his club, Billie Holiday stood in a pin spot and introduced "Strange Fruit," a bloodcurdling lament for lynched Negroes down South. Paul Robeson, who sang there too, was photographed dancing on the Café Society floor with Julie Gibson, a white Warner Brothers starlet. Josh White, a country-blues guitarist and singer, detailed the hard-knock lives of rural blacks in his haunting story songs. The Jewish comics Jack Gilford and Zero Mostel were both devoted to left-wing causes; the FBI had its eye on Mostel, noting his attendance at Communist party meetings.

Progressive politics were Café Society's heart, and any hint of racism on or off its stage was verboten. Josephson passed on the still-obscure black singer-comedienne Pearl Bailey, finding her too much of an Uncle Tom. And he fired an equally unknown Carol Channing for parodying Ethel Waters.

On the club's small dance floor, white and black couples couldn't avoid brushing arms. Josephson had hired cutting-edge WPA artists— Anton Refregier, Adolph Dehn, Abe Birnbaum, Gregor Duncan—to paint the walls with scathing murals that lampooned the upper crust. One of them showed a fat, blustery roué with a walrus mustache, wearing red underwear and dancing with a fan.

Even the club's name jabbed at uptown hypocrisy. Josephson loathed the Stork Club's owner Sherman Billingsley, an anti-Semitic snob who admitted Jews only if they were celebrities. Barney wittily called his cabaret "The Wrong Place for the Right People," and hired a doorman to stand beneath the canopy in topcoat and cap, the standard garb of the snooty gatekeepers uptown.

It all added up to a stinging slap in the face of bigotry. As Josephson told the *New York Post*, "I was sick of discrimination, had seen too much of it. I was determined to come to New York and do something about all this." He was born in 1902 of Jewish-Latvian immigrants; in their adopted home of Trenton, his father set up a shoe business. Social consciousness ran in the family. Barney's brothers Leon and Lou, both avowed Communists, became lawyers for the working class. In 1934, Leon was arrested along with twenty-nine others in a reported plot to assassinate the recently appointed Adolf Hitler.

In junior high school, Barney was assaulted for befriending a black student; at fourteen, he and his brothers picketed a Jim Crow movie house in Trenton. Later, he joined the family business and asked a client to take him to the Cotton Club. The segregation there repelled him, and he saw it mirrored everywhere in society. In bars, he watched a ritual that greeted the rare black men who were served—as soon as they finished their drink and turned to leave, the bartenders smashed the glass they had used in front of them and everyone else. "All these white guys would guffaw," explained Josephson. "That was saying, 'No white man'll ever drink out of that glass again!'"

He knew hardly anything about the saloon business, but set out to create New York's first fully interracial nightclub—audience, entertainers, and staff. In 1938, Josephson borrowed six thousand dollars and took over the basement of Two Sheridan Square, in the heart of Greenwich Village. He asked John Hammond for advice on whom to book. Hammond built the club's first band, which starred "trumpet-tootin'" Frankie Newton. He called in Billie Holiday and gave Café Society a sprightly background of boogie-woogie twin pianos, played by two masters, Meade Lux Lewis and Albert Ammons.

Josephson sent out press releases to black newspapers, inviting them to send their writers—none of whom would have gotten past the door of the Stork Club or El Morocco—to the December 18 opening. There would be no cover charge, and the minimum—a dollar Monday through Thursday, a dollar fifty on weekends—conveyed a message of come one, come all. Quickly, however, Café Society filled up with notables from Manhattan's liberal and intellectual community. "It drew an elite crowd," said actress Madeline Lee, who became the wife of Jack Gilford. "All kinds of celebrities were at the bar every night." They included Duke Ellington, Orson Welles, Errol Flynn, writers Langston Hughes and Richard Wright, caricaturist Al Hirschfeld, even Franklin and Eleanor Roosevelt.

Whenever Josephson discovered a promising young girl singer, he arranged for vocal coaching as well as a makeover. He loved watching the faces of saleswomen at the snooty Bergdorf Goodman department store when he walked in with some pretty young black girl. "I'd like this lady gowned," he would say, as jaws dropped. He knew what they were thinking: Here was a rich white daddy with his whore.

Just before he opened his doors, Josephson prepared to do battle. He gathered his waiters and instructed them on what to say to anyone who uttered a racist remark, including one they heard quite a bit—"What are you running, a nigger joint here?"

The rebuttal: "Mr. Josephson wants you to leave." When asked why, the waiters responded, "Because you used what he says is a dirty word in Café Society." The acts didn't always have it easy. "Hoodlums waited outside the club and threw eggs at them," said Madeline Lee Gilford. "And Jack was heckled from the floor." But after the slew of press that greeted the club, including a nine-page spread in *Life,* troublemakers tended to stay away.

They missed getting intimate glimpses of a barely known Sarah Vaughan; of Billie Holiday's instrumental counterpart Lester Young, the gossamer-toned tenor saxophonist; of Imogene Coca, the future costar (with Sid Caesar) of TV's *Your Show of Shows;* of the black jazz pianist and fashion plate Hazel Scott; and of Helena Horne—as Josephson renamed her—in her solo cabaret debut.

Before she opened, Horne ran through her material for Josephson's scrutiny. He found an oddly disjointed singer with little sense of identity, who sang with her eyes closed, face turned to the ceiling. "I noticed that all her movements and routines were done in Latin rhythms, which were very big then," he said. If Horne didn't intend to pass, she certainly seemed in hiding. Josephson challenged her: "Lena, are you a Negro?"

She bristled. Yes, she said, adding, "I don't dig you."

"Lena," he continued, "there are dozens of nice Jewish girls from Brooklyn doing the Latin rhythms. Let me present you as a Negro talent." He bluntly asked her if she was afraid to look white people in the eye. And he gave her "hell," she later said, for choosing to sing "When It's Sleepy Time Down South." He said scoldingly, "How can you sing that? Look at how your people were treated there!"

Josephson sat at ringside and studied her as she sang. "When she looked at the ceiling I'd make signals," he said. "And I went over the lyrics of her songs, pointing out their meanings." She recalled another of his suggestions in a 1981 interview with radio host Jonathan Schwartz. "Barney said, 'You've got to try to sing a blues.' He knew I couldn't sing the blues. He said, 'Nobody expects that a man is gonna desert you and you're gonna be mistreated, look at the way you look! The audience will think it's very amusing if you sing a blues.'"

On opening night, a slightly chubby Horne adorned her long, straight hair with a white flower, just as Billie Holiday did. Teddy Wilson, who had recorded extensively with Holiday, played for her. Her segment on the bill would last about fifteen minutes. "There were so many famous people there," she said. "I was thrilled, because I had never been in an atmosphere that was so mixed—white and black people together. I had only seen it in an adversarial way."

Paul Robeson, Jr., who was then about fourteen, sat and watched the young beauty. "The first time I heard her at Café Society, frankly, she was terrible," he said in 2006. For all of Josephson's coaching, Horne felt dead inside as she sang, and it disturbed her. "I had a lot of show tunes to do then, and things that had no real meaning for me. Nobody thought I was a great singer. I didn't either. But I had a sense of . . . romance, I guess. And I was literate. I respected the song." For some observers, Horne's looks were enough. The comedy troupe The Revuers shared a bill with her; two of the members, lyricists Betty Comden and Adolph Green, would figure substantially in Horne's future career. "Oh, God, she was unbelievable!" said Comden of Horne's short act. "She was so beautiful!"

Expressively, though, she had far to go. Between acts, Horne sat amid a spellbound audience and watched Holiday bare her soul in "Strange Fruit." Horne felt emotionally crippled by comparison. That made it all the more unnerving when people kept asking her to "sing some Billie Holiday songs." Horne loved telling the story of a conversation she had on the subject with Holiday. "'Miss Holiday, I've come here to tell you that they keep asking me to sing your songs, and I don't want to do it, because I *can't do them!*' And she said, 'Lena, you have children, don't you? You have to pay your rent, you don't have a husband. You have expenses. Do anything they ask you to do.'"

The results were pale, but her looks carried her. For many people, her color alone earmarked her as a blues artist, because few blacks sang show tunes. "Blues Singer Brings Uplift to Village's Café Society," read a newspaper headline. Josephson wasn't through grooming her. "I got her teeth fixed," he said years later; when he'd first seen her, he'd cringed at how crooked they were.

For Horne he functioned as a combined Svengali and Santa Claus. About two weeks after she opened, Horne joined a company of Café Society regulars in a concert Josephson presented at Carnegie Hall. In June, the white Dixieland trumpeter Henry "Hot Lips" Levine asked her to guest on his Victor album *Birth of the Blues,* a tribute to the father of the form, W. C. Handy. Levine and his band headlined a hit radio show, *NBC's Chamber Music Society of Lower Basin Street.* It treated Dixieland in tongue-in-cheek highbrow fashion. Horne's ladylike delivery was just what Levine wanted.

Nevertheless, on her four tunes she strained to sound like a salty blues singer. "Beale Street Blues" describes the low-down shenanigans on a legendary Memphis thoroughfare. As the players mimic a raunchy blues band, Horne seems like a refugee from a finishing school. With her perfect diction and demure air, she comes off as almost comically girlish, with no feeling whatsoever for the blues. Her Noble Sissle training had outlived its welcome; singing of drunks and pickpockets, Horne sounded as though she'd never dirtied her hands. When Jonathan Schwartz played the record for her in 1981, Horne exclaimed, "That is *horrible*—I never heard anything so flossy, la-di-da, in my life!" She discovered another vocal shortcoming: "I had this terrible postnasal drip, and it interfered terribly with my singing. Always some vocal glitch would happen. I said, 'Well, I can't ever be a singer.' I had all these psychological hang-ups. It was always very difficult for me, singing."

She became all the more determined to get it right. Teddy Wilson gave her pointers, and she studied the delivery of one of the most respected jazz vocalists of the day, Mildred Bailey, whose light, sweet voice floated with an easy lilt. Deep in the night, after the late show had ended and the crowd had thinned, Horne would sit at a table with Barney Josephson, sipping cognac and talking about music and life. Sometimes Bailey dropped by, or Billie Holiday, who'd taken a liking to the young singer. Horne remembered her as a big sister. If Holiday spotted her in a club with someone she deemed inappropriate, she'd chase Horne out.

The club gave her a great education. Years later she told Joanne Stang of the *New York Times* that "cabaret was kind of freak show business. It wasn't theater; it was whisky, wine, and women and fellas ... But you can learn everything about show business in cabaret, and that was where we had to work; there wasn't anyplace else."

Like everyone else who performed at Café Society, Horne marveled at the chance to share a stage with Paul Robeson, the black community's most inspiring Renaissance man. He struck her as a god—the huge shoulders and hands; the handsome face that exuded purpose and strength; the bass voice that thundered "Let My People Go" as though it could move the earth. Now here he was, singing in a café, with the ringside customers close enough to touch him.

Robeson had flown above every roadblock in the life of an early-twentieth-century Negro. At Rutgers University, he was a Phi Beta Kappa student, football star, and champion public speaker; he delivered the commencement speech for the class of 1919, then earned a degree from Columbia Law School two years later. He put it aside to pursue acting—and in 1924 made his Broadway debut as the majestic star of Eugene O'Neill's *The Emperor Jones*. Robeson went on to play Othello in London and to sing "Ol' Man River" onscreen in *Show Boat*.

All the while he fought politically, rallying blacks to organize, boycott, and fight for the vote. "He had a profound impact on all of us young activists who wanted to make a contribution," said Esther Cooper Jackson, who in 1961 would found *Freedomways*, a prominent quarterly of the civil rights era. "He helped mold our character, what we wanted to do with our lives, by the very fact that he had the courage to say, 'I'll give up my career if I have to. This is what I believe.'"

It was Horne's looks that initially caught Robeson's eye. Then, when he learned that she was the granddaughter of Cora Calhoun, he sat with her for hours at the club, regaling her with stories. He knew more about her family heritage than she did. "Paul came to me and said, 'Your grandmother was a fiery little woman who chased me off the street corners of Harlem,'" recalled Horne. "Really?" she answered. "Nobody ever told me that!"

He reminded her that, by virtue of her color and her history, she had a great responsibility. She heard the same thing from NAACP executive secretary Walter White, to whom Josephson introduced her. Both of them explained that unlike her white colleagues, she couldn't work merely for her own gratification. Instead, she had to think about how she could help pave a way for her race.

More immediately, she had to support her daughter, who was staying with her at the family house in Brooklyn. Six nights a week Horne left Gail in cousin Edwina's care and rode the BMT into Greenwich Village. On the seventh, she entertained in the upscale white neighborhood of Fifty-eighth and Park, where Josephson had opened a second club, Café Society Uptown. Sometimes she managed to wrest Teddy from her husband. Doris Bye, who then danced in the chorus line of Small's Paradise in Harlem, used to see Horne holding Teddy's hand as they strolled past the club. "He was a pretty little boy; he looked just like Lena," she said. "And there was Lena, walking with them pants on. She looked good in pants because she had no shape. Skinny legs, you know?"

The thought of marrying up, preferably to a white man, was growing in her mind. According to Madeline Lee Gilford, a flirtation had arisen between Horne and Jack Gilford, who was still a bachelor. "She lived near him in Brooklyn, so he used to take her home after the 2:00 A.M. show, and then they began dating. He thought he was in love with her. Everybody did."

In the spring of 1941, she graduated to an affair with the biggest catch in jazz. Clarinetist Artie Shaw reigned among America's three or four top swing bandleaders—a reputation sealed in 1938 by his record of Cole Porter's "Begin the Beguine," a number-one hit for six weeks. Attractive and highly literate, Shaw had hung around with Ernest Hemingway, F. Scott Fitzgerald, and Thomas Mann. Women found Shaw irresistible, and he married eight of them, including Lana Turner and Ava Gardner.

One night in June, Horne looked out from the stage of Café Society, and there was Shaw, listening at John Hammond's suggestion. "I'd had a crush on some music that he played, for instance his great recording of 'Star Dust,'" Horne noted. Shaw held another powerful attraction—he was fiercely antiracist. Having taken Billie Holiday on the road, he knew the obstacles a black entertainer faced.

Shaw was a curmudgeonly ninety-four in 2004 when he recalled his dealings with Horne. "She was a very pretty girl; everybody was after her," he said. "I liked her looks, and I thought her singing was OK. Nothing wrong with it. Lena was not really an artist; she was a girl singer. But she sang in tune, so I put her on a record."

On June 26, 1941, Shaw joined several Café Society musicians and thirteen string players in a New York studio; they backed Horne on a fluffy novelty, "Love Me a Little Little." The B-side was a pretty torch song, "Don't Take Your Love from Me." Horne sounded sweet and playful on the former; on the latter she tried, none too successfully, to dip into the song's pained desperation. Her vocal was the side's "only weakness," wrote *Variety*. The platter sold poorly. Shaw had told reporters that he was considering taking her on the road, but he changed his mind.

Later, Horne told deejay Ray Otis that she was "terrified" to record with Shaw, whom she termed a "difficult, complex man." Their relationship had turned more than professional. Asked in 2004 if they had dated, Shaw replied, "That's not the word for it!" Their affair, he said, lasted for months. "She wanted to marry me, and I told her it would be the end of our careers. Paul Robeson wanted her, but she didn't want to go with a black guy." When Horne and Ava Gardner became friends in the late forties, they traded digs at Shaw "and his mental domination, which drove both of us crazy. We laughed because he liked his women to read a lot of books."

Given Horne's raging conflict over whites, her romantic history with them would become one of the great ironies of her life. But after her experience with Louis Jones, she seemed to sense stability, as well as career potential, in her involvement with white men. "She knew that her career was very limited," said Shaw. "She was very ambitious, but she wasn't clear about what she wanted." Her pursuit of white show business and its men of power brought dangers, but it was taking her into places where blacks normally didn't go.

One of them was *Harper's Bazaar*, the elegant fashion and cultural magazine. A review there in 1941 called Horne "the reigning queen of Café Society Downtown. . . . Helena's voice is like dark honey in Gershwin's 'Summertime.' She makes 'Daddy' sound as though she were a modern Delilah bent on the ruin of a Wall Street Samson."

All this attention had raised the hackles of her Café Society rival, pianist Hazel Scott. Known for jazzing-up the classics, Scott was a diva: "very ambitious, very beautiful, tall, big bust," said Madeline Gilford. *Lion's Roar*, a magazine published by M-G-M, put it like this: "Patrons jammed Café Society Uptown to watch this lush, coffee-tinted Tondaleyo, spotlighted behind a grand piano, her golden skin luminous against an oyster white evening gown."

The more attention Horne grabbed, the more Scott resented her. "Hazel Scott *hated* Lena," said Delilah Jackson. "Jealous, I guess." Horne didn't try to deny it. "In the beginning Hazel and I had problems. She was queen uptown; I was queen downtown. We always got a crush on the same men." Horne envied Scott's jewelry, furs, and fashion flair; it annoyed her when people asked why she didn't dress like Scott.

But as the summer of 1941 ended, there were more pressing matters afoot. Horne had "borrowed" her son, Teddy, from his father and placed him, Gail, and Edwina (now the children's nanny) in an apartment in Harlem. On August 30, Maurice Dancer of the *Chicago Defender* reported that Horne had rushed to Pittsburgh "to join the hunt for her two children reported kidnapped." Louis Jones was the suspected culprit. Horne quickly denied the abduction story. "She says her husband took the children back to Pittsburgh with her consent," wrote the *Defender*'s Al Monroe. "Miss Horne was due to take a plane to Chicago about the same hour"; hence she couldn't accompany them to the train.

As the chaos in her personal life mounted, her career kept rising. On September 16, Horne cut a side for Columbia, the king of record labels. Teddy Wilson's sextet, which backed her at Café Society, accompanied Horne on a ballad of the day, "Out of Nowhere." Horne was making strides. She phrased thoughtfully and sang with careful musicianship; moreover, her months of cabaret singing had given her an intimate, purring-in-your-ear quality.

Around that time, she caught the attention of a group of left-wing hell-raisers who hung around Café Society, and who were set to make a short film. *Boogie Woogie Dream* would be a black Cinderella story set inside a facsimile of the club; it would preserve some of the only moving images of a Café Society show. The filmmakers had wanted Billie Holiday to star. But they couldn't get her, and Horne seemed a worthy second choice. She more than earned the part: *Boogie Woogie Dream* captures on film the Lena Horne who would outshine all other black starlets of her day.

The history of that short was probed by author Konrad Nowakowski in the eighties. Its associate producer and director, Hans Burger, had released several bold political documentaries, including *Crisis,* a Nazi exposé. Writer Herbert Kline, an avowed Communist, had attacked racism in 1933 with his play *John Henry—Bad Nigger*. Karl Farkas, who played a waiter, was an incendiary political cabaret writer and performer in thirties Austria; the Nazi occupation had sent him fleeing to New York. Producer Mark Marvin, Kline's older brother, had worked with left-wing theater groups; some of his work attacked racism.

On the surface, *Boogie Woogie Dream* seemed merely like a fun little film made for the race market. Although the set evoked Café Society

Downtown, the shooting occurred elsewhere, probably at a studio in Long Island City, New York. The plot was simple. It's closing time in a cabaret, and a well-to-do white couple is wandering out. Horne, a dishwasher in a drab white dress, is polishing glasses; Albert Ammons is a paperhanger, Pete Johnson a piano tuner. When the latter sits at the baby grand and noodles some boogie-woogie, the white couple drifts back in; Horne moons wistfully and polishes to the rhythm. Then the dream begins. Teddy Wilson's sextet materializes, along with a second baby grand. Through clouds of smoke, Horne emerges in a white evening gown. Ammons and Johnson play two-piano boogie-woogie, then Horne sings a blues, "Unlucky Woman," with the Wilson group.

As everyone knew, she was no blues singer. But with her long, shiny hair and radiantly beautiful face, she looks breathtaking. And as she wails a first-person account of a woman who manages to send her no-good lover packing, Horne captivates. She's feisty, flirtatious, and sexy; she grooves to the band and leaves no doubt that she deserves to sing with them.

Then the smoke clouds reappear, and she's back to housekeeping. But it turns out that the male half of the white couple is in the movie business. "Hey there," he says. "How'd you like to come over to my office for an audition?"

Even though it shows a black woman doing menial work—it had to, as part of the Cinderella theme—*Boogie Woogie Dream* finds Negroes mixing with whites, just as they did at Café Society. Unlike nearly all the black characters in white-produced films of the day, the ones in here reveal not a hint of stereotyping. Instead, the film treats jazz and the blues with reverence, and the offer posed to Horne at the end is voiced with respect.

Unfortunately, Mark Marvin could never find a distributor to place his short before white audiences. *Boogie Woogie Dream* premiered at the Apollo in 1944 in a show headlined by Ella Fitzgerald and bandleader Cootie Williams. Its historical value would become clear only in later years, after Horne had found fame and Café Society had acquired the glow of legend. In its time, though, the film exposed at least a few thousand more people to Horne, and offers kept coming in.

One of them startled her. Felix Young, a Hollywood nightclub impresario, invited her to come west and take her place among an all-star black cast at his soon-to-open cabaret, the Little Trocadero. The show, *Sepia Symphony*, amounted to a mini–Cotton Club revue. Young planned to present the Duke Ellington orchestra and the Nicholas Brothers along with Horne. He'd also engaged Harold Arlen and Ted Koehler, who wrote "Stormy Weather," to contribute six new songs.

But Young's headline act would be the acclaimed troupe of Katherine Dunham, who unearthed native African and Caribbean dance and adapted it for the stage. A beauty to rival Horne, Dunham would eventually be showered with honors. She was a trained and fearless anthropologist; Dunham had lived in Haiti and become a voodoo priestess, and traveled to Jamaican villages to observe (and step into) sacred dance rituals. She took her findings back to the States and turned them into elaborately costumed, erotically charged theatrical events.

By 1941, she was primed to conquer Hollywood. There was talk of a film version of a Broadway musical comedy, *Cabin in the Sky*, in which Dunham had originated the role of Georgia Brown, a diabolical temptress. She had shared the show's choreography with the Russian pioneer of modern ballet, George Balanchine. Understandably, Dunham—who had pioneered a unique art—saw herself as a higher being. "It was very hard to say that you knew Miss Dunham," said Cleo Hayes. "She was not from show business like we were from show business, you know?"

So far, however, her work was mainly a succès d'estime. She thought nightclubs beneath her, but accepted the Trocadero offer for the money. Dunham took charge of the show, which needed a singer, she felt. She recalled the young woman whom Noble Sissle had taken her to see. Afterward, she visited Lena Horne backstage. "I was struck by her beauty," said Dunham, "but frankly, I didn't think she was great, in the same sense as one would think Ethel Waters was. I never really admired her voice very much." Still, she thought Horne would make a good soubrette for the show, and certainly wouldn't provide much competition.

Barney Josephson wasn't pleased. Did she think Hollywood was going to make her a big star? She told him she wouldn't be staying long, and hoped he'd take her back. Josephson walked away without another word. But the men in Teddy Wilson's band told her she had to make the trip. Finally, she said, she "got talked into going out there" by her agent. That reluctance wasn't borne out by her M-G-M questionnaire, completed just a year later. "Had a hunch to leave New York and come to Hollywood," she wrote, "then landed a better job."

On Sunday, October 19, Horne played her last night at Café Society. From then on, Helena reverted to Lena. In two weeks she would open at the Little Trocadero. Before leaving, she went to Pittsburgh to see her son. The *Pittsburgh Courier*'s Billy Rowe reported excitedly that she and Louis Jones had reconciled. If so, it didn't last; Horne wouldn't return from Hollywood for a long time. She later revealed to Shonte Penland of the *Los Angeles Sentinel* that she'd gone there with greater ambitions than singing in a nightclub. Walter White of the NAACP had urged her to make the trip; he had a plan in mind. Before she left, Horne called her father and asked him to advance her some money so she could go to Hollywood. He asked her what she wanted there. "I told him I was going to be a movie star," recalled Horne in 1982. "He said, 'Lena, I'm going to buy you a house and most of all a maid, 'cause that's the role you'll be playing, so you might as well know what a real maid does.'"

CHAPTER 5

IN NOVEMBER 1941, Horne was amused to find herself living at 1228 Horn Avenue, off the Sunset Strip in West Hollywood. Felix Young had paid the train fare for her, Gail, and Edwina, then left them the keys for his spare apartment.

Neighbors saw a "rather Oriental-looking" child, as her mother described her, and a woman (Edwina) who could have been Italian or Mexican. Then Horne arrived—and some people thought she was Latin. "The questioning glances we kept receiving did not exactly make us feel welcome," she recalled.

Nonetheless, her new home brought a Hollywood-style thrill. Horne had recently seen *The Maltese Falcon;* now she learned that next door to her was the character actor Peter Lorre, who played one of his trademark foreign scoundrels in the film. The lead, Humphrey Bogart, lived down the street.

For the moment, no one was asking Horne to make a movie. And as she waited for Felix Young's club to open, there wasn't much to do except feel homesick. "When I got there I had no friends, and every place was a million miles away," she explained in 1989. "You couldn't walk anywhere and get somewhere. . . . There was no feeling of a city; it was just a *place* sitting there." She passed few pedestrians on Sunset Boulevard, where she took long, solitary walks. Thoughts of her far-off little boy tugged at her; he remained with his father, and Horne feared she would lose him when the divorce happened. Sometimes she woke up feeling so discouraged that she started packing a suitcase, determined to go home. Edwina would stop her, advising, "Give it time, honey."

Cleo Hayes, who moved to L.A. around the same time as Horne, offered another caring shoulder. "I used to go up there and stay with her, because she was so lonely," said the dancer. "We had some nice times together. The California girls didn't like either one of us." Then a common friend gave Horne the phone number of Alice Key, a red-haired, fair-skinned, intellectual beauty. Key wore two hats: one as a chorine in nightclubs and films, the other as a UCLA-educated journalist with a fierce civil rights conscience. Ahead of her lay a celebrated career of activism in Los Angeles and Las Vegas. Some of her stands got her jailed; others inflamed unions such as the American Guild of Variety Artists (AGVA), where she helped secure fair treatment of black chorines.

She took the timid Horne out on the town. "She was very warm, very friendly," said Key. "We had some good times together. Lena was very insecure around men; I don't know why. But when her daddy came out to visit she was the happiest I ever saw her. He was jovial, and very proud of her."

Duke Ellington was in town, and he knew Horne was there, too. He'd had his eye on her since the Cotton Club days; eventually he got what he wanted. But apparently the suave titan intimidated even her. More than fifty years later, Horne told the president of Blue Note Records, Bruce Lundvall, "You could never get to know Duke Ellington. He was only about music. Well, you could get to know him carnally."

Friends of Horne's speculated that Ellington wanted to keep her out of other men's hands—hence the "kindness" he showed her in November. The bandleader sent her a single ticket to a show of his, *Jump for Joy: A Sun-Tanned Revu-sical*. A variety spectacular with an anti–Jim Crow theme, *Jump for Joy* had played that summer at the Mayan Theatre in downtown L.A. Alice Key danced in it. "*Jump for Joy* was really the joy of my life," she said in 2006. "I loved that show because it was making people aware of racism, and they did it with skits and numbers." It closed after a three-month run, but got a one-week reprieve just in time for Horne's arrival in town.

She took a bus to the theater and sat alone as the curtain rose. "It was such fun to see this good, witty all-black show," she said. At intermission she stayed shyly in her seat. A voice said, "Miss Horne?" She ·looked up and saw "this boy" in tortoiseshell glasses. He introduced himself as Billy Strayhorn, and said he worked with Mr. Ellington. "He was charming to look at," recalled Horne. "Wise look, like a little brown owl. He said, 'Mr. Ellington was worried that you may not be comfortable. Are you comfortable?' I said, 'Yes. I'm enjoying the show.'"

"Well, would you mind if I come and see the second act with you?"

"Of course not!"

He sat next to her and they began to chat. "Immediately I knew he was bright. I was always looking to be with somebody smarter than I, because not having gone to school, I only wanted to be around bright people." She felt her guard loosening. "All the while we were talking, this thing between us was happening," she said. "There are people around you who are *you*, you know?"

Thus began the one true soul-mate relationship of her life. It was so strong that, decades after Strayhorn had drunk and smoked his way to an early death in 1967, Horne kept his picture by her bedside.

In the 1997 biography *Lush Life*, author David Hajdu brought Strayhorn forward as a vastly undersung jazz composer, as well as the heartbeat of the Ellington orchestra. William Thomas Strayhorn—known as "Swee'pea"—stood only five-two, but on his small shoulders rested much of that ensemble's eminence. He joined the band as an arranger in 1939; from there he became its maestro's best friend, alter ego, and the often-uncredited author of many Ellington signature tunes: "Day Dream," "Satin Doll," "Chelsea Bridge," "Take the 'A' Train." Classically trained, he brought the orchestra a degree of harmonic sophistication that took it even further beyond the realm of a swing band.

In the macho arena of jazz, Strayhorn had another distinction: He was a gay man who lived with a rare openness and ease. At sixteen, he had written his masterpiece, "Lush Life," an old soul's expression of ennui. It depicted a jaded bon vivant left high and dry by too much empty carousing and love gone sour. That impressionistic piece of melodrama bespoke a pained artistic soul of high refinement. Indeed, when he wasn't at the piano or hunched over sheets of staff paper, Strayhorn steeped himself in high art; he also studied French.

Horne would often say she wished she could have married him, but that wasn't about to happen. Strayhorn often had a boyfriend; Horne preferred not to know too much. "I was very jealous of him with everyone," she said. She'd known gay men since she entered show business; feeling like their fellow outcast, she found a natural rapport with them. Later, she spoke of how the men and women she liked the most had a "sense of being both sexes."

With Strayhorn by her side, Horne forgot her loneliness. "I was just greedy for him," she said. He took her down to Central Avenue, the Harlem of Los Angeles—an all-night party of jazz and blues clubs, honky-tonk bars, and soul-food joints. On Strayhorn's arm, Horne ran into many familiar faces: guys from Duke's band; Cotton Club alumni; the *Jump for Joy* dancer Avanelle Harris, whom she'd met in *The Duke Is Tops*. Strayhorn also took Horne on many trips to Brothers, perhaps the city's first black gay bar. The "brothers" were a lesbian couple who liked to wear men's clothes. They ran a dimly lit after-hours lounge, with pillows scattered on the floor, incense, and low-down music. "It would be crowded and hot and funky," said Horne, who loved it.

On Sunday morning, December 7, she and Strayhorn were at a friend's house working on songs—some for her New Year's Eve opening, others for an album she was set to make for Victor. Elsewhere, Katherine Dunham and John Pratt were having brunch with Felix Young and talking about the show. Mood music played on the radio. Suddenly an announcer's voice cut in: The Japanese had just bombed Pearl Harbor. "By the next morning," recalled Dunham, "Los Angeles and its environs were in a state of siege."

Word had spread that California might be bombed as well. Eleanor Roosevelt flew to L.A. to discuss protection strategies with the mayor. A quickly drawn-up rule prohibited gatherings of more than a hundred people in one establishment, or sixty in one room. Felix Young's club— built to accommodate hundreds—could not open.

Young acted quickly. He leased a much smaller space farther west on Sunset Boulevard; as before, he engaged John Pratt to decorate it. Now there would be more waiting. But Horne had her first album to occupy her. On December 15 and 17 she recorded the eight sophisticated torch songs that formed *Moanin' Low*. Some were favorites in Manhattan's poshest cafés; others were bluesy show tunes by white theater composers, notably Harold Arlen.

In time, Horne would rerecord many of them with fangs bared and fists clenched. But for now, she sang of gut-wrenching heartache in the voice of an ingénue who kept her troubles, if any, discreetly hidden. *Moanin' Low* contained her first recording of "Stormy Weather," the song Ethel Waters had sung so powerfully at the Cotton Club. Though she tried hard to bite into the words as Waters had, one would never guess that Horne had known a single dark cloud.

Over fifty years later, Jonathan Schwartz, in a radio interview with Horne, would play Arlen and Koehler's "Ill Wind," another track from *Moanin' Low*. "I *hate* hearing myself sing in those days!" she exclaimed. "I was like a child, singing a nice, pretty song that I heard somebody in the Cotton Club sing. But I knew nothing, I felt nothing about the song.... It's funny, because at that time I should have been feeling quite a lot, and I was."

In January 1942, with the world at war, the Little Trocadero had its grand opening. By now Duke Ellington had departed, leaving only the Dunham group and Horne on the bill. John Pratt had turned the club into a rococo jewel box of velvet and lace, with portraits in antique frames hung on the walls. But the small stage could barely hold Dunham's three drummers and eight dancers. As their skirts billowed out, the contents of the ringsiders' tables went flying.

The club's size worked much better for Horne, who didn't need a microphone there. Wearing a white dress, she sang eight songs, including "The Man I Love" and "Stormy Weather." The singer's failings on record seemed to melt away. Horne had poise and a radiant smile; her beauty, seen up close, overwhelmed the eye. Skitch Henderson, a goateed pianist and conductor who had worked with Judy Garland at M-G-M, heard true musical potential. "She blew my mind," he said. "Everybody in those days sang the melody. Careful. She could improvise with great taste. And she had a very white way about her. This was a time when blacks were still thought of as undertakers or housekeepers." Lyricist Buddy DeSylva showed up to hear Horne sing his hit song, "Somebody Loves Me." Later he raved: "She's the best female singer of songs I've ever heard. It's how she sells them. She puts something into a lyric that even the author didn't know was there."

Hoping to keep the buzz going, Felix Young arranged for Horne to attend her first Hollywood party. Cole Porter was the host. Horne smiled self-consciously and mouthed pleasantries as white celebrities milled around. One of them was Georgia-born Miriam Hopkins, the petite blond actress who wielded a "ladylike bitchiness" (as critic Richard Sater termed it) in dozens of films. Hopkins engaged Horne in conversation; as they talked, the young singer turned to steel. To her, the actress's honeyed drawl sounded "so gracious, so condescending. It was both a put-on and a put-down." She left enraged. The next day she told Young not to invite her to any more parties.

After just a few weeks in Hollywood, Horne began to sense resentment in many corners. Women in the business disliked her, she thought; she was sure they saw her as nothing more than a loose-moraled temptress who wore sexy clothes and purred come-ons like Cole Porter's "Let's Do It."

The suspicions were understandable. But they only served to raise her mystique. A memo about Horne reached the desk of Steve Trillin, a casting director at Warner Brothers. It came from Hal Wallis, the head of production.

In one of our proposed pictures, *Casablanca,* there is a part now written for a colored man who plays the piano in the night club. I am thinking of making this a colored girl, and when I was in New York I saw Hazel Scott. She would be marvelous for the part. I understand that there is a colored girl out here now appearing in a Felix Young night club and I wish you would see her and tell me what you think. The one out here is Elena Horn.

The part stayed male. But in January 1941, another cinematic opportunity walked through the door of the Little Troc. Roger Edens worked for M-G-M as a musical director and vocal coach. Born in Texas, he possessed a southern courtliness and a resonant, drawling voice. Edens held a high place in M-G-M's Freed Unit—the division, led by producer Arthur Freed, that created most of the studio's greatest musicals. Edens left his mark on many of them. It was he who devised the famous "doodle-de-doo" vamp that Gene Kelly sang while swinging an umbrella in *Singin' in the Rain;* he also molded the Judy Garland persona, according to her daughter Lorna Luft. "It was Roger who gave Mama the courage to let the softness, the vulnerability that was part of her, into her singing. Without Roger, we might never have had 'Over the Rainbow,' at least not the way we all remember it."

A few months earlier Edens had heard her at Café Society, and he sensed possibilities. Now he arranged for Horne to meet Arthur Freed.

Her arrival was well timed. Since 1940, Walter White, executive secretary of the NAACP, had been after M-G-M and other top-rank studios to revolutionize the black image in Hollywood. What he wanted seemed simple—an onscreen view of the Negro as "a normal human being and an integral part of human life and activity." But Leonard Bluett wondered if this would ever happen. A dashing, six-foot-five black dancer, Bluett won ensemble roles in a string of films. Amid hundreds of black extras in *Gone With the Wind*, Bluett was singled out for a brief on-camera exchange with southern belle Scarlett O'Hara, played by Vivien Leigh. Scarlett would ask him if he knew the whereabouts of Big Sam, her trusted field hand.

In 2006, Bluett recalled the rehearsal. "The director said, 'Lennie, don't answer her, just shake your head like you don't know, because if you answer her I've got to pay you three hundred dollars—otherwise you're getting your thirty-nine.' That was actually good money then." Though just an extra, Bluett wasn't afraid to speak out, and he "raised a lot of funk" about the WHITES ONLY signs above most of the toilets. "I knocked on Clark Gable's door and I said, 'They gotta get those signs down or we're all gonna walk. You can't get four hundred Mexicans out here to look like black people.'"

Bluett observed endless Hollywood bigotry. "If the part called for a black person, you had to be rather homely, with big lips, which we called soup coolers, and nappy hair, and you had to be very subservient in the role. 'Yes, mistuh.' 'Would you like another piece of pie, sir?' 'Can I shine your shoes?'" Most of the time, he said, a black actor would get cast only as a "jail fiend, or someone sitting on the docks and singing darkie songs. But I was pretty lucky because I was tall and very handsome, and a decent dancer, and I had a nice presence, and they used me a lot in films."

The big studios had signed some Negro contract players, but their images made White's blood boil. The three black actors under contract to 20th Century Fox had made the best of their limited opportunities. Louise Beavers typified the character most black film actresses at some point had to play, that of the grinning, maternal, benevolent maid. She did it with charm—and on rare occasions got to show some depth. In *Imitation of Life* (1934), she played a housekeeper caught in a painful family issue. Her fair-skinned daughter (played by Fredi Washington) is so ashamed of her race that she tries desperately to pass for white.

Hattie McDaniel looked like a classic southern mammy, and had long since resigned herself to playing servants. As she reasoned, it was better to play a maid than be one. But McDaniel did no bowing and scraping; she was a sassy, gritty-voiced firebrand who eagerly gave her white employers a piece of her mind. Usually she came across as smarter and more authoritative than they did. On February 29, 1940, McDaniel received an Oscar for her role as Mammy in *Gone With the Wind;* it was the first Academy Award ever claimed by a black actor. "I sincerely hope I shall always be a credit to my race and to the motion picture industry," said McDaniel through tears. The actress had been seated all the way in the back of the theater, as though it were a segregated bus.

Comic actor Stepin Fetchit (born Lincoln Perry) would go down in history as one of the embarrassments of black show-business history. Fetchit personified the "Laziest Man in the World," as he was called, a drawling numbskull who did little except loaf around and screw things up. "He made Hollywood comfortable and Hollywood made him rich," wrote actor Ossie Davis, who saw Fetchit onscreen while growing up in Waycross, Georgia. White audiences loved to laugh at him, and Fetchit clones (such as Willie Best) began to dot the screen.

What made Perry seem all the more exploitative of his race was his identity offscreen. The actor was an intellectual who spoke eloquently and wrote for the *Chicago Defender*. But on-screen he played the "Dumb Darkey," noted Davis—and therein lay his power. "Just think of what would have happened if all the slaves had been smart enough to be as dumb as old Stepin Fetchit . . . slavery would have had to go out of business in a couple of weeks. Well, that's what we thought. And anyway, nobody ever got lynched when Stepin Fetchit pictures were in town. He made everybody feel so comfortable and so superior that they didn't need to go out and hurt anybody."

Other black actors scored small victories. Eddie Anderson was a star thanks to his role on radio and TV as Jack Benny's valet, Rochester. But like McDaniel, Anderson had found a way to put a prickly skin on his persona. His beleaguered "*Yeeeess*, boss," murmured with rolled eyes, made Benny seem like the buffoon; Anderson shot out barbed one-liners that kept the white man in his place.

For a time, it seemed as though Nina Mae McKinney would ascend to the place that Lena Horne eventually reached. But she'd come along too soon. Comparably light-skinned and beautiful, McKinney had an elegant, acerbic presence; her big eyes sparkled, and the camera loved her. In 1929, she had lived her own Cinderella story. McKinney was nineteen when director King Vidor discovered her and gave her the lead in M-G-M's *Hallelujah!*. Thereafter McKinney was signed to a five-year deal. No black actor before her had ever signed a long-term contract with a major company. (That distinction would later be credited, inaccurately, to Lena Horne.)

But M-G-M gave her only one feature-film appearance, a small role in *Safe in Hell* (1931). Otherwise she played servants or immoral women in a variety of low-budget features and musical shorts. In *Pie, Pie, Blackbird* (1932), McKinney portrayed a cook sitting in the kitchen with her two young sons—the Nicholas Brothers in their film debut. "Don't you remember that song I used to sing for you when you were a little pickaninny?" she asks in a twang more exaggerated than the one she'd acquired as a child in South Carolina.

All these actors had reached the apex of their profession in the 1930s. To Paul Robeson, the industry was a sad mirror of the nation. "I am through with Hollywood until it changes its attitude toward the Negro," he said in 1942, when he made his last film. That didn't apply just to actors. "I remember writing a column in the *Los Angeles Tribune* saying that there were no blacks employed in movies," said Alice Key. "I was talking about electricians, grip men, people behind the scenes. There was definitely segregation and discrimination rampant."

Walter White was on the case. He hardly looked the part of a civil rights champion; White was one-eighth Negro and had blond hair, blue

eyes, and skin lighter than some of his Caucasian friends'. But the racism
of Hollywood so disgusted him that he'd been campaigning against it
for years. In 1940 he'd found an ally in Wendell Willkie, a wealthy lawyer who'd just lost the presidential election to Roosevelt. Willkie coun-
seled the movie industry, and he introduced the NAACP head to Walter
Wanger, a top independent producer. Over lunch, White argued that the
mighty film business—the fifth biggest industry in the country—was
"perpetuating and spreading dangerous and harmful stereotypes of the
Negro."

To his surprise, Wanger—a liberal and politically gutsy hell-raiser—
offered to help. Immediately he began finding ways to put White in
the faces of key moguls. White found most of them, especially M-G-M
president Louis B. Mayer, surprisingly receptive to his arguments.

Their cooperation couldn't all be chalked up to social conscience. Reports indicated that American Negroes were a greater commercial force
than anyone had imagined. They spent seven to ten million dollars per
year, a good slice of it on entertainment. There were an estimated four
hundred black newspapers, crucial to guiding their readers into movie
theaters. A huge Negro radio audience existed too, ready to respond to
ads for movies that spoke to them.

What Hollywood lacked was a shining black figurehead onscreen,
someone to help recast the Negro image. White remembered the beauty
he had heard at Café Society Downtown. Everything about Lena Horne
flew in the face of stereotypes. She wasn't a mammy or a whore; she
didn't growl the blues or speak in Negro dialect. Instead she sounded like
an educated, well-bred young lady, one whom a few white families might
even welcome in their homes. All her training, by Cora and Edna and
Noble Sissle and Lew Leslie and Barney Josephson, had prepared her for
the role White had in mind. The way she looked held crucial importance.
While Horne's skin was obviously that of a Negro, her features were
Caucasian enough to compare to Rita Hayworth's or Hedy Lamarr's.
The *Los Angeles Times* quoted Walter White, who said Horne would be
an "interesting weapon" against Hollywood racism.

In mid-January, less than two weeks after she'd opened at the Little
Troc, Edens greeted Horne at the M-G-M lot in Culver City, California. Two agents, Harold Gumm and Al Melnick, accompanied her.

Within minutes Horne was in Arthur Freed's office, singing the Vincent Youmans love song "More than You Know" while Edens played piano.

Freed was impressed, and asked her to sing for Mr. Mayer. Before they were called into the president's office, in walked Vincente Minnelli, an admirer of Horne from Manhattan. A former Broadway director, Minnelli had come aboard the Freed Unit. "I was so happy to see a New York face," explained Horne. Soon she was ushered into Mayer's office. There she beheld a "short, chubby man" with spectacles; contrary to his harsh reputation, he gave her nothing but warmth. His secretary, Ida Koverman, sat silently, taking notes as Horne sang. Mayer listened attentively, with a broad smile. After she stopped singing, he excused himself. He returned with a visiting M-G-M alumna, Marion Davies, the adored leading lady of silent comedies and early talkies. As a film buff, Horne couldn't believe her eyes. Everyone present seemed excited about their new find.

That night, recalled Horne, she phoned her dad in Pittsburgh. Thus was born the tale on which Horne hung her film career. Its characters were a distant but loyal father ready to stare down the M-G-M lion to protect her; a megamogul whipped into subservience; and a reluctant young singer caught in the cross fire of Hollywood wheeling and dealing. "I said, 'Would you come out here? These people are crazy, they're talkin' 'bout putting me in the movies!'" The next day, she claimed, Teddy Horne marched into Mayer's office "looking sharp," with a diamond pin on his dark suit. In 1981, Horne quoted her father's words to talk-show host Dick Cavett. "He said, 'Mr. Mayer, it's a great privilege you're offering my daughter. But I can buy my daughter her own maid.' He was just jivin', you understand." Nevertheless Teddy set down the rules: Lena would not play a maid or a jungle maiden. "I don't think Mr. Mayer had ever been approached by a black man like that," explained Horne.

Mayer, she said, insisted that M-G-M had the utmost respect for her and special plans, although he didn't go into detail. After the meeting, Horne told her father that Mayer would never hire her.

Variations abounded in Horne's many tellings of the Mayer–Ted Horne encounter. In her second memoir, Horne said her father met with Freed, not Mayer. Sometimes she was present, sometimes not. Teddy's sudden show of fatherly devotion smacked of wishful thinking; until then he'd been a shadowy figure in her life, sending her gifts but seldom there when she needed him.

He swore that M-G-M would never come through. But the gangster-playing movie star George Raft, who had met (and ogled) Horne at the Cotton Club, felt sure she belonged in the movies. Raft arranged a screen test for Horne at Universal. It happened in late January and led to nothing. For all her charms, the studio didn't know what to do with a black girl who seemed so white.

The day after she filmed that test came momentous news: M-G-M wanted her. On January 31, 1942, the *Pittsburgh Courier* announced Horne's signing. The studio didn't need Teddy Horne to set the ground rules for his daughter's hiring; Walter White had seen to that. Her breakthrough deal, according to *Motion Picture* magazine, stipulated that Horne "would sing in pictures or play legitimate roles and not have to do 'illiterate comedy' or portray a cook, roles customarily assigned to colored performers." She would make her debut in *Panama Hattie,* the film version of a Cole Porter musical.

Days later, M-G-M released a photo of Horne signing a seven-year contract in Mayer's presence. She was dressed tastefully in a simple black dress and pearl necklace. The studio would pay her $350 a week in the first year and $450 in the second. Her deal included other standard terms: The studio had control over her radio and nightclub appearances, and her weight could not exceed a certain number of pounds (in Horne's case, 122). A morality clause threatened suspension or firing if she displayed unseemly personal behavior.

For Walter White, this was a moment of triumph. But Horne revealed her feelings in the questionnaire she filled out for the publicity office. This break, she admitted, was a dream come true. If Hollywood hadn't called, she would have pursued theater and radio. But her childhood had left her reluctant to trust anyone, especially whites. Did she have any superstitions?

"Never hope too hard," wrote Horne. "Never pans out."

Horne came to feel that talent had played little part in the signing. In 1985, she told Kathy Larkin of the *Daily News,* "The NAACP saw me as a wedge . . . going where blacks had never been allowed before." She put it more succinctly when she called herself a pawn. As for M-G-M,

Horne was sure the studio had chosen her for her looks, certainly not her ability.

Panama Hattie wouldn't begin production for several months, but M-G-M had a plan in the meantime. Work was starting on *Cairo,* a spoof of espionage pictures. It starred Jeanette MacDonald as a movie star whom a reporter suspects is a Nazi spy. In the ensuing comedy of errors, her black servant, Cleona Jones, is thought to be her accomplice. Along the way she gets to sing a couple of songs.

M-G-M thought Horne might make a pleasing Cleona, and so did Horne—thus belying the myth that neither she nor her father nor Mayer would have ever let her play a maid. Years later, the singer informed MacDonald's biographer Sharon Rich that she was ready to take the part. "It was a good role," said Horne. "The maid was to be just as flippant and fresh as anyone. She was a human being, not a stereotype." There was even talk of giving her a love interest, Eddie "Rochester" Anderson, in the part of MacDonald's manservant.

He and Horne were screen-tested together in February. The studio's confusion as to how to handle a fair-skinned black beauty became instantly clear. It was decided that she and Anderson should share a similar hue, so Horne was darkened with makeup. "And then," she said, "they had a problem in lighting and photographing me because they said my features were too small." ("Small" seemed to mean non-Negroid.)

All the while, said Horne, "poor Rochester had to stand around and wait while they fussed over me. It was embarrassing to me, though they were very pleasant about it. In the end, the test was a disaster. I looked as if I were some white person trying to do a part in blackface. By the time they kept putting Rochester's makeup on me, I disappeared; there was nothing left but teeth!" The studio must have seen the futility of all this; they passed on her and gave the part to Ethel Waters.

As Horne moved her nightclub act into Hollywood's cushy Mocambo, M-G-M struggled to adapt *Panama Hattie,* a recent Broadway hit. It had starred Ethel Merman as Hattie Maloney, a brash saloon singer in Panama who tries to fit into her society fiancé's snobbish world. Arthur Freed had cast Ann Sothern and Red Skelton as the mismatched couple. The production was in chaos, and after the dismal response to an early screening, Freed called for a complete refilming.

Horne's role was incidental; she would play a sultry café singer and perform two songs. She began rehearsing in April. In his first M-G-M assignment, Vincente Minnelli directed the musical numbers. One of Horne's songs, "The Spring," would be choreographed by its cowriter Jeni LeGon. A black dancer from Chicago, LeGon had worked in Hollywood for years but her rewards fell short of her talent. Acknowledged as a masterful tapper, LeGon had danced with Bill Robinson in the 1935 RKO musical *Hooray for Love*. Like Nina Mae McKinney before her, LeGon signed a deal with M-G-M. She was slated to appear in *Broadway Melody of 1940*. But allegedly her tapping abilities so threatened the film's star, dancer Eleanor Powell, that M-G-M yanked LeGon's role and bought out her contract. Two years later, as minor recompense, they used "The Spring" as Lena Horne's debut number and let LeGon stage it. In that novelty rumba (its title a cross between "Spanish" and "swing"), Horne would be joined by the three tap-dancing Berry Brothers. Her other song, "Just One of Those Things," was borrowed from another Porter show to give Horne a second showcase.

For three weeks that spring, LeGon and her fiancé, Phil Moore, an M-G-M rehearsal pianist and arranger, painstakingly guided Horne through her number. Her dancing "wasn't very good," said LeGon. "She moved awkwardly. She was a better singer. But I taught her what to do."

On shooting day, Horne reported to the hair department. Her assigned hairdresser turned to stone as soon as she saw the black singer. Costume designer Helen Rose, who had just left 20th Century Fox for M-G-M, recalled the moment in her memoir, *Just Make Them Beautiful*. "This woman was hard as nails and refused to work on Lena," wrote Rose. "She said it was against union rules (which I doubted) and that we would have to send out for a black hairdresser. I blew up. I couldn't believe what I was hearing. Lena never lost her composure. She just sat quietly, never saying a word, behaving like the lady she is."

Rose recalled doing Horne's hair herself, but the singer detailed a much more elaborate wave of rejection. None of the hairdressers, she said, would touch her, and they made that clear to the department's aristocratic head, Sydney Guilaroff. Tall, slender, and natty, with a thin mustache and faux-British diction, Guilaroff—a native of Montreal, not London, as he liked to claim—was a master at creating ornate looks.

Marilyn Monroe, Elizabeth Taylor, Judy Garland, and Ingrid Bergman all sat beneath his long, fussy fingers and emerged looking as though they belonged nowhere else but on the silver screen. He also gave Claudette Colbert her bangs and Lucille Ball her red hair.

According to Horne, Guilaroff listened to his staff's ultimatum and answered imperiously, "*I* will do Miss Horne's hair." Guilaroff "sort of dismissed them, speaking to them like they weren't there. He said, 'Now, Miss Horne, do you know a lady who can come in to help assist me so that when I'm busy on another set, she will know what I want done and will come and tell me?' I said, 'Yes, I do.'" This was Horne's black friend Tiny Kyle, who would later become her assistant and her children's nursemaid. "Sidney said, 'Bring her in.' And he made the union accept her."

In the finished film, Horne appeared as an island girl in a Trinidadian nightclub. Costume designer Robert Kalloch had garbed her in a white skirt and halter top, with a West Indian headdress. While singing "The Sping," she dances a modified rumba, backed by the Berry Brothers in top hats and white dinner jackets. Silly though the song is, Horne comes off as glowing, sexy, and assured. Her dancing is elementary, but she sways and shimmies with grace. In "Just One of Those Things," Porter's brittle playlet about a fling that proved "too hot not to cool down," Horne showed viewers a black woman they'd never seen in a Hollywood film. Behind her smile is an edge of hauteur; it demanded respect, while keeping her distance. Every cliché of the Hollywood Negro is absent.

Panama Hattie opened in September 1942 to mostly poor notices. Given the usual splendor of the M-G-M musical, this one was seen as grade B—"tired and tedious," said critic Howard Barnes. But to nearly every reviewer, the film had one saving grace. Edwin Schallert of the *Los Angeles Times* called Horne "spectacular"; to *Time* she was "the high point of a dull show." In the *New York Post,* Archer Winstein heralded great things for the young starlet: "She demonstrates beyond any doubt that she is the one who should have been given all those half-caste roles for which they use dark makeup on lily-white stars."

For black viewers, Horne's performance was an epiphany. Dancer Leonard Bluett saw the film at a Hollywood theater. Horne, he said, was "like an angel—peaches and cream. She was so gorgeous. A white man in front of me said, 'What a beautiful woman. She can't be black!' I touched him on the shoulder and said, 'Yes, and she and I are related!'"

Historian Delilah Jackson's father, who had lived through the racism of the twenties and thirties, saw Horne as a shining hope. "When Lena was in *Panama Hattie* he went crazy," she said. "It was playing at the Harlem Opera House, and all the men on the block talked about '*our* Lena Horne in *Panama Hattie*.' It was like, Lena's our sister. Our daughter. She's *us*. Oh, she was so fabulous. Of course she really couldn't dance, but she had the Berry Brothers doing all those fancy steps, fitting right in with her."

For now there wasn't a ripple of dissent among white moviegoing bigots, even down South. Because Panama was a generically exotic locale in most viewers' minds—and because Horne was singing a rumba—she could have been Spanish or Caribbean.

"Everybody said, 'Who's the new Latin singer?'" she recalled. "Some people even suggested that I develop a Spanish accent so that I could be passed off as a Latin type . . . Some Negroes charged that I was trying to pass. That hurt." But her reviews staggered the studio's top brass. By that time, Horne had finished shooting a screen adaptation of the 1940 all-black Broadway musical *Cabin in the Sky*. This time she was the costar, not just a lovely but incidental brown bauble.

CHAPTER 6

TO STEP ONTO the grounds of M-G-M in the forties was to enter a fantasy world so enveloping that it could make one forget what reality meant. A filmed overhead view of the lot revealed a storybook town unto itself, complete with bungalows, a bank, a post office, a schoolhouse for child actors, police and fire departments, trees and lawns, and an artificial lake. M-G-M actress Betsy Blair recalled another detail in her autobiography, *The Memory of All That:* "There was a section the size of a city block filled with freestanding staircases leading nowhere except to the sky—it was Daliesque and fantastic."

The king of this demimonde was Louis B. Mayer, who had over three thousand people on his payroll. Mayer's thin white hair, glasses, slight double chin, and gruff expression made him look like a small-town high school principal. No one liked being summoned to his office, where he sat behind a big desk, ready to scold the uncooperative. Helen Rose, who created most of Horne's M-G-M costumes, recalled how Mayer left his office each day and "strode pompously about" the studio grounds. He "thundered and roared like the lion he was," she said.

Born Lazar Meir in what is today the Eastern European country of Belarus, Mayer had spent his boyhood picking scrap metal off the street for his father's recycling business. While still a teenager he'd moved to Massachusetts; there he entered the infant movie business by opening a string of movie houses. When D. W. Griffith finished *The Birth of a Nation* in 1915, Mayer paid a then-unheard-of fifty thousand dollars to give the film its New England premiere; reportedly he earned five hundred thousand dollars. He took the money and moved to California; there he founded Louis B. Mayer Productions. In 1924 it became M-G-M.

For the next twenty-seven years, the onetime junk dealer reigned as a guardian of American family values. "His favorite product," wrote Betsy Blair, "was an idealized story of small-town life, the Andy Hardy series, with Mickey Rooney as the freckle-faced, devilish but good-hearted, Norman Rockwell American kid and his mom and pop and his wise old grandpa. L.B. truly believed the myth he was creating—and he loved the money it made for Metro."

In his musicals, Mayer seemed determined to show the endless possibilities of the American imagination and pocketbook. Arthur Freed was his mastermind. Outwardly, he seemed no more refined than Mayer; he had a doughy face and the gruff voice of a gas-station attendant. Yet Freed, who came from Charleston, South Carolina, had written poetry as a child; he adored Jerome Kern, collected art and antiques, and tended orchids. He also penned the words to songs, like "You Are My Lucky Star" and "Singin' in the Rain," that made love seem like a perpetual walk on air.

His handpicked Arthur Freed Unit conjured up living dreams. In *Ziegfeld Follies,* dancers pirouette balletically over hills, weaving in and out of mounds of multicolored soap bubbles. *Million Dollar Mermaid* finds M-G-M swimming star Esther Williams ascending like Venus out of a massive blue pool surrounded by billowing clouds of red and yellow smoke. She plunges back in as yellow-suited swimmers form kaleidoscopic rings around her.

But Freed's movies weren't all froth. He gave Gene Kelly the chance to direct *Invitation to the Dance,* a plotless tapestry of ballet and pantomime with a cast of real ballet stars, including Igor Youskevitch and Tamara Toumanova. And he offered almost boundless rein to the creativity of Vincente Minnelli. In *Yolanda and the Thief,* a story by the children's author and illustrator Ludwig Bemelmans, Minnelli whipped up a Dalí-inspired dream ballet, whimsical Bemelmans paintings that spring to life, and a convent full of singing nuns.

The studio's starlets were turned into princesses. Gloria DeHaven recalled the thrill of walking onto an M-G-M soundstage to prerecord her songs and feeling swept away on a billowy wave of strings. When

Helen Rose and Sydney Guilaroff got through with her, the results, she said, seemed like "looking into a magic mirror and seeing someone that you didn't even know existed, and saying, 'That's *me*! Look at *me*!'"

The publicity department worked overtime to ensure that its stars remained fantasies. "Harmless items for the gossip columnists were supplied, interviews for fan magazines were written at the studio," said Betsy Blair.

But Almena Davis viewed M-G-M through a darker lens. Davis wrote for the *Los Angeles Tribune,* a black newspaper based in South Central L.A. Invited to M-G-M in 1942, she found self-aggrandizement everywhere: "from the fifth assistant publicity director" to Mickey Rooney, whom she saw "swaggering around like he owned the place. . . . And the ghost that prods them all is reflected in their treatment of you, if you're just an ordinary guy, a nobody who fails to impress them with either the fact or fiction that you're somebody."

M-G-M, of course, was in the business of selling deities. But what to do with Lena Horne, its first black starlet? If the makeup and hair departments hadn't a clue as to what constituted black beauty, neither did most of the country. "Assembly-line M-G-M," as she later called it, made her look "exactly like everybody else there, except I was a bronze swan."

Onscreen, every female bore a lacquered perfection. "M-G-M had the most elaborate makeup system imaginable," said Betty Garrett, the comic actress and singer who joined the Freed Unit later on. "There was a mimeographed chart of a generic face that was used by every makeup man, who marked it according to corrections he felt should be made. The studio spent forever trying to make everybody's face conform to a certain kind of look, a certain idea of what beauty was."

No white woman's foundation would have worked for Horne, so Jack Dawn, the head of the makeup department, commissioned one from Max Factor Cosmetics. It bore the quizzical name of "Light Egyptian." Years later Horne would turn that makeup into an object of both scorn and ridicule; she made it sound as though Light Egyptian were akin to blackface. But according to Dawn's assistant (and later successor) William Tuttle, "it more or less matched her coloring" and, like all other foundations, hid every freckle and blemish.

From there, Horne found herself made up and coiffed to look like Hedy Lamarr, M-G-M's Viennese femme fatale. An early publicity photo showed Horne in a white satin off-the-shoulder dress, clutching a pillow and looking seductive. The image helped inspire a title that irked her, the "Negro Hedy Lamarr." Flaws concealed in that photograph—slightly crooked front teeth, a pug nose with flared nostrils—would be gone by the time she left M-G-M.

But the makeover didn't succeed in making her think she was Cinderella; there were too many reminders to the contrary. One day in the forties, Horne sat in a New York hotel suite putting on makeup; keeping her company was Sy Oliver, a swing arranger and bandleader. "I'd known him since I was seventeen," she explained later. "He saw my naked face for years. He said, 'Damn, for somebody as plain as you to do whatever you do to your face and look pretty, I'll never understand it.' And that's exactly me. I *am* plain. I had learned to do my makeup that way at M-G-M. You know—making me what I wasn't."

Philip Carter of the *Chicago Defender* found her in the same frame of mind when he interviewed her in her first months at the studio. "Lena has remained extremely modest, and a little bit scared," he wrote. As the first black girl to reach such a peak, she knew she'd be closely scrutinized. Walter White reminded her that she could never simply revel in her career; "remember your position," he told her in letters. Dutifully, she obeyed. Horne advised Carter, "If it is within my power there'll be many more Negro girls getting similar breaks in the movies."

As much as she told herself to hope for little, Horne couldn't help but feel excited. She'd long wanted to act, and Freed and Mayer were busy seeking out projects for her. Newspapers kept touting her, but almost always as a novelty. Horne was the "sepian songstress" or the "beauteous bronze"; *Time* called her the "Chocolate Cream Chanteuse." At white showbiz parties, guests didn't know how to treat her—or pretended they did, to embarrassing effect. At one gathering, Horne was thrilled to meet her favorite stage actress, Tallulah Bankhead. But her heart sank as Bankhead tried to flatter her by comparing her to the house slaves her Alabama grandfather, a senator, had employed. Horne would later mimic Bankhead's slurred southern twang as she declared, "My dear, you aren't a typical Negro, with your patrician features. To me the dearest kind of Negro is the coal-black girl down on Daddy's plantation—so natural, so gay."

Horne smiled and said nothing, but inside she fumed. Increasingly, she felt misunderstood and isolated; at the studio, she said, virtually the only other Negro she saw was the shoeshine boy. Only weeks after M-G-M had signed her, Horne felt let down. She heard about the imminent filming of *White Cargo*, an exotic drama set in the Congo during colonization. It told of two white men's lust for Tondelayo, a jewelry-craving Egyptian-Arab vixen. The role included unintentionally campy dialogue ("Tondelayo no go!") and all the *Tarzan*-style jungle clichés that Horne had vowed to avoid. Tondelayo ran counter to every intention of M-G-M's, and Walter White's, in signing Horne. Yet she thought the part should be hers—and resented the studio for giving it to the actress she resented the most. When she heard that the makeup department "took *my* Light Egyptian" and used it to darken Lamarr, she was incensed.

But there in Hollywood, Horne would see rejection and alienation in almost everything—the legacy of a childhood marked by both those feelings. Although she spoke of having "no friends" in Hollywood, Eddie "Rochester" Anderson was a close one. And in her first year as an M-G-M starlet, she grew intimate with director Vincente Minnelli. Horne saw him as another "displaced New Yorker" and felt an immediate kinship. In his years as a set designer and director for the New York stage, Minnelli had shown a flair for lush visuals—bright colors; surreal, dreamlike lighting effects; eye-catching geometric patterns; highbrow allusions to art, ballet, and France. All of that made him immensely attractive to Freed, for whom he was now apprenticing. Minnelli began twenty-six years as a full-fledged director at M-G-M, a run that yielded such milestones as *An American in Paris, Father of the Bride,* and *The Band Wagon.*

Minnelli had many of the qualities that had drawn Horne to Billy Strayhorn—a soft voice, a refined air, a love of books and fine food. She raved about him to Irene Thirer of the *New York Post:* "He is so wise, so ingenious, so sensitive." Among the many misfits on the M-G-M lot, Minnelli seemed as much an oddity as Horne. The yellow jacket he wore at parties drew the eye to a strange-looking man, with popping eyes, bushy eyebrows, a guppy mouth, and "those lips pursing every two seconds," as playwright Mart Crowley recalled. "It was both funny and embarrassing." People snickered at his feyness. Years later, Ann Miller, the M-G-M dancing star, joked to author John Fricke, "Honey, you had to close the window, or he'd fly right out!" Clearly he had some heterosexual leanings, though, for he later married Judy Garland and sired a daughter, Liza Minnelli.

In 1942, while both of them waited for the next project, he and Horne spent a lot of time together. Rumors circulated throughout M-G-M that, improbable as it seemed, the two were more than just friends. Horne never acknowledged it outright, even to Richard Schickel, who coauthored her 1965 memoir. She and the director often dined at each other's houses, said Horne, with neither one exerting any pressure. But in her interviews with Schickel, she hinted that her feelings went deeper. "I believe she had an affair with Vincente," he said. So did Butterfly McQueen, who appeared with Horne in *Cabin in the Sky*. She saw Horne as "frustrated, because at that time she wanted to marry into the white race and she was afraid people would talk against it and she didn't know what to do."

The director, too, recalled their relationship discreetly. Minnelli wrote little of her in his autobiography, *I Remember It Well*. He and Horne were "very friendly," he noted, and he "took her out to dinner several times." He always phoned the restaurant first to announce the identity of his date—an M-G-M starlet, but a black one. "I didn't want any incident or embarrassment," he explained. Sometimes he was asked not to bring her. Often they invited a third party to derail suspicion.

Minnelli wasn't going to marry her, but he offered her something else that made her spirits soar. M-G-M had acquired film rights to the recent Broadway musical comedy *Cabin in the Sky*, an all-black Faustian moral fable. Horne was assigned the role created by Katherine Dunham: that of Georgia Brown, a siren sent by the devil to lead a faltering man astray. She would get to sing songs from a glittering score by Vernon Duke and John Latouche, and Minnelli would direct. The news thrilled them both.

Cabin in the Sky held great significance at M-G-M. The studio hadn't released an all-black musical since *Hallelujah!* in 1929. Since then only one other, *The Green Pastures* (1936), a Warner Brothers biblical saga rife with stereotypes, had come out of Hollywood. *Cabin* would give M-G-M the chance to do right by the NAACP and to blaze a new path for race relations in Hollywood. Freed voiced magisterial hopes for the film: "Upon its success or failure will stand the future of the race in the greatest medium in the world."

He'd chosen a vehicle with built-in perils. Set in a small, unnamed southern town, it portrayed blacks as childlike and unsophisticated. The lead character, Little Joe Jackson, is an illiterate, lazy, but likable gambler; his wife, Petunia, is a pious mammy with endless patience. Struggling to mend his ways, Joe gets a job running an elevator. But temptation lurks everywhere, and outside church he's taunted by crap shooters to whom he owes money. A scuffle ensues, and Joe is shot. Lucifer waits to snatch away Joe's soul. Petunia prays to the Lord (known here as the General) to save her dying husband, and he complies. Little Joe gets a six-month trial reprieve, during which he must live immaculately or else.

But that's not easy, for Lucifer teases Joe with forbidden fruit—notably in the form of Georgia Brown, a bombshell who sings at Jim Henry's Paradise, a local nightclub. Lucifer arranges for Joe to win a sweepstakes, knowing he'll gamble the money away at Jim Henry's. Petunia gets wind of the plan and rushes there to save Joe. A fight breaks out and they're both shot dead. The General says that Petunia qualifies for heaven; Joe, alas, is "in the red again." Still, he lets them trudge together up the white staircase that leads to the pearly gates. "Can I make it?" gasps Joe.

In the end it was all a dream; Joe wakes up in bed, recovering from the delirium of fever. His nightmare has put the fear of God in him. He makes Petunia burn his dice and dominoes; once more, he's determined to be good.

"If I was going to make a picture about such people," wrote Minnelli in his memoir, *I Remember It Well*, "I would have to approach it with great affection rather than condescension." He vowed to give them a touch of Hollywood élan. "My feeling was that blacks of that time wanted to see themselves as glamorous as possible," he said. Minnelli "raised hell" when the art department set the action in squalid rural surroundings; he wanted the settings to look "as livable and attractive as possible."

Once word got out that M-G-M had started an all-black musical, telegrams flooded Freed and Minnelli from black performers and their managers. Stepin Fetchit offered his services; so did Butterbeans

& Susie, a popular duo on the chitlin circuit. But the studio was aiming big. Paul Robeson was asked to play Lucifer, but he refused. Cab Calloway wasn't available either. Finally the role went to the man who'd held it on Broadway, Rex Ingram, a husky giant who spoke and sang in a Robeson-like, rumbling bass. Among black actors, the southern-born Ingram had gone far; he'd acted in over a dozen films—notably M-G-M's *The Adventures of Huckleberry Finn*—and had worked on Broadway for years; Horne had known him in *Dance With Your Gods*.

For the part of Little Joe, Minnelli had wanted Dooley Wilson, the saloon singer-pianist in the film *Casablanca* to whom Humphrey Bogart had said, "Play it, Sam." ("It" was "As Time Goes By.") But M-G-M preferred Eddie "Rochester" Anderson, another in the handful of black actors who were under consideration for contracts. The part of Lily, Petunia's churchgoing friend, went to Butterfly McQueen, the actress who, as Prissy in *Gone With the Wind,* had drawled the famous line, "I don't know nuthin' 'bout birthin' no babies!"

No one but Ethel Waters could play Petunia, a role she'd originated. John Bubbles, the original Sportin' Life in *Porgy and Bess*, was signed as bad guy Domino. Duke Ellington and Fats Waller would appear in a nightclub scene.

It was a stellar cast. Freed wanted to do everything right, and to anticipate flak. From the beginning, he was treading on eggshells, hoping not to offend. *Cabin* was no race movie, he announced; instead it would be "produced on a par with any major film under the M-G-M label." That wasn't quite true; *Cabin* was a modestly budgeted black-and-white feature that looked more like a filmed stage play than an M-G-M fantasia.

But in 1942, it was a progressive move, as well as a risky one. The producers, director, librettist, and songwriters were all white. The liberal black press had pounced on *The Green Pastures* for its racist images, and Freed feared more of the same with *Cabin*. He knew the risks of trying to tell a story about rural black folk: Retain their dialect and the characters would seem like clichés; have them talk in perfect English and realism would crumble. John Latouche had opted for the former in his lyrics, using "dat," "de," "ole," "you is." Screenwriter Joseph Schrank did the same. Albert Lewis, Freed's technical adviser, gave a copy to Hall Johnson, a choral director who played himself in the film. Johnson responded diplomatically. The dialect, he said, was "a weird but priceless conglomeration of pre–Civil War constructions mixed with up-to-the-minute Harlem slang . . . all adding up to a lingo which has never been heard nor spoken on land or sea by any human being . . . the script will be immeasurably improved when this is translated into honest-to-goodness Negro dialect."

Then Freed showed the script to Charlie Sands, who led the all-black Motion Picture Study Club. Sands railed in his response letter, "When is Hollywood going to give us a film in which the Negro is not depicted as a faithful 'Uncle Tom' retainer, a comic of the rudimentary sort, or an exponent of jazz or spirituals? Considering the short time the Negro has been freed from slavery, he has made remarkable strides. They're not all clowns or menials."

Rewrites began. Not even Sands, however, could quibble with the casting of Ethel Waters—in the twenties a sleek, salty jazz-singing pioneer and purveyor of raunchy blues; in the thirties a Cotton Club and Broadway star. Bobby Short remembered her as "the greatest black performer I'd ever seen," with a "matchless command of the stage. . . . Everything about her told you that you were in the presence of a star."

As a vocalist, she had towered above almost everyone in her field. The documentary producer Gene Davis credited Waters with many breakthroughs: "Ethel was the first black female performer to make the transition from rural blues to the urban experience. She was the first black singer that the Jewish songwriters of the day trusted to sing their sophisticated material. She was the first absolutely articulate black female voice. To me, she was the beginning of the track that includes Lena Horne."

In 1994, Susannah McCorkle, the jazz-cabaret singer, explored Waters's versatility for an article in *American Heritage*. To her, the star combined "the sexual swagger of Mae West, the subtle humor and immaculate diction of Mildred Bailey, the spontaneity, poignancy, and rapport with musicians of Billie Holiday, the vibrancy of Ella Fitzgerald, the jazz feeling, swing, and timing of the Boswell Sisters, the throwaway humor of Pearl Bailey and Eartha Kitt."

But her high spirits masked a lot of darkness. Waters would certainly have agreed with Short's comment that "Ethel survived things that Lena never dreamed about." Still, she and Horne had a lot in common. Waters's 1950 memoir, *His Eye Is on the Sparrow*, begins:

> *I never was a child.*
> *I never was coddled, or liked, or understood by my family.*
> *I never felt I belonged.*
> *I was always an outsider.*

She was born in Chester, Pennsylvania, a town outside Philadelphia, to a twelve-year-old girl raped at knifepoint. She grew up in rat- and bedbug-infested shanties along with her grandmother, mother, and two drunken, abusive aunts, one of whom hurled a hatchet at her head on Christmas Eve. Along the way she nearly died of typhoid fever and double pneumonia. Like Horne, she knew no fixed home; her mother, an itinerant live-in servant, dragged her from town to town, often leaving her with relatives. At thirteen, Waters tried to escape her home life by marrying; her husband abused her verbally and beat her, and the union died in less than a year. She became the foul-mouthed leader of a children's street gang; then came the day she nearly died in a car crash as a white onlooker laughed. All this happened before she was eighteen.

Her grandmother saved her by placing her under the loving care of the nuns at a Catholic school; to keep the girl off the streets, she let her go to a respectable dance hall. There she dazzled the crowds with her shimmy shaking. Nicknamed Sweet Mama Stringbean, she began touring in vaudeville as a dancer-singer. With her innate sophistication, she became a darling of the white theater circuit, and made many hit records. The Cotton Club never had a more beloved star.

But Waters was full of anger, and the higher she rose, the more demanding she became. She berated the Duke Ellington orchestra onstage for not playing her music "the way I like"; she terrorized chorus girls with her imperious glance and cutting remarks. "I was scared to death of her," said Cleo Hayes. "She was a very evil woman, Miss Waters. Everybody stayed as far away from her as they could."

Yet white theatergoers flocked to see her in one of the biggest hits of 1933. Irving Berlin had cast her in his show *As Thousands Cheer*, a Broadway revue with songs and sketches based on newspaper headlines. Before a sign that read UNKNOWN NEGRO LYNCHED BY FRENZIED MOB, Waters sang "Supper Time," the lament of a woman who can't find the words to tell her children some very bad news. Broadway had never made such a powerful statement against racism. In 1939, she starred in *Mamba's Daughters* and became the first black actress ever to play a dramatic Broadway lead.

But nothing could still her demons. By the time she returned to Broadway in *Cabin in the Sky,* she'd eaten her way to twice her weight. Having owned buildings in Harlem and lived in a ten-room penthouse, she now owed the IRS a fortune in back taxes.

By the time M-G-M cast her in *Cairo* and *Cabin,* Waters had burgeoned into a 250-pound mammy, laughing raucously and dispensing godly platitudes. As the civil rights movement began to form, Waters became a symbol of everything its proponents were trying to fight. Blacks, she felt, should be happy in their place. "It's a joy in being colored, because we have a peculiar sort of happy outlook on life," she told Jinx Falkenburg, the radio hostess. Waters cared little about the growing aspirations of the Negro. "If I can do good by acting, or by scrubbing and ironing, I'll do it," she told *The Lion's Roar,* M-G-M's promotional magazine. "I can do anything the good Lord sets out for me."

Avanelle Harris, who danced in *Cabin in the Sky* and several other M-G-M musicals, cringed at Waters's attitude: "She always had a bandana on her head, like 'Yessuh, boss.' I didn't go for that *at all.*" Meanwhile, said Harris, Waters was "very haughty, very 'I am the star.'" Her attitude toward her colleagues was anything but godlike. In 1940, she told columnist Earl Wilson, "I'm the kind of woman, if I was mad at you I'd just as leave kill you as look at you." Waters hated most of the white Jews who ran Broadway and Hollywood, and resented younger singers for copying her. Soon her wrath would be aimed at the svelte and gorgeous Lena Horne—the starlet who appropriated "Stormy Weather," Waters's signature song, and would later be credited with breakthroughs that its originator had helped make possible.

After reading the script of *Cabin,* Waters demanded changes. She wanted to play Petunia as a strong woman, not as the hapless wife of a good-for-nothing. The irreverence toward the church offended her; Petunia had better be shown as profoundly religious, or else. The actress began rewriting her role to depict the Ethel Waters she wanted people to see. She also made it clear that she wasn't particularly open to direction. (The same issue would arise in 1950, when Waters re-created, on film, her recent Broadway turn as an all-knowing servant in Carson McCullers's *The Member of the Wedding*. During rehearsals, director Fred Zinnemann asked her to stand elsewhere onstage. The star announced in high dudgeon, "*God* is my director!")

It was hard for *Cabin*'s cast and crew to reconcile the foul-mouthed volcano they came to know with the holy servant she pretended to be. In her dressing room Waters set up a little altar, complete with holy figures and a votive candle. Periodically she went there to have a one-to-one with the Almighty. "Ethel was on quite good terms with God," said Minnelli.

Shooting began on August 31, 1942. Horne's early scenes did not involve Waters, so for now a happy camaraderie infused the set. Though still a neophyte at moviemaking, she found that she loved the process. Minnelli and the crew marveled at how professional she was. "Before the camera she is tireless," wrote a visiting reporter. "No amount of rehearsal bothers her noticeably." Horne's explanation: "I don't mind the camera. I like to pretend the lens is a whole audience of eyes, rolled into one. And the people you work with in a studio are the nicest I ever met."

All except for the one she met at lunchtime. A group of *Cabin* cast members, including Horne, showed up at the studio commissary. They encountered Frances Edwards, the tough, heavyset woman who ran it. Many years later, the M-G-M producer Samuel Marx recalled what happened. Edwards, said Marx, had received a rule from above that black people were not allowed inside. As the actors stood before her and protested, there appeared Louis B. Mayer. He introduced himself and, according to Marx, he invited them to join him at his table in the executive dining room. Over lunch, he promised they would have no more trouble entering the commissary. Avanelle Harris confirmed that he kept his word. "You could sit right down in there and Clark Gable would be at the next table," she said. Meanwhile, Mayer reamed out the executive who had brought Jim Crow to the commissary. It was Mayer's brother.

Horne resumed having a ball. She became pals with Leonard Bluett, who made a memorable impression in *Cabin*. In one of Minnelli's long, sweeping overhead shots, Bluett danced Vivian Dandridge gracefully into Jim Henry's Paradise. Horne loved hearing stories of the films he'd appeared in, from *Gone With the Wind* to *A Day at the Races* (with the Marx Brothers) and *Ali Baba Goes to Town* (with Eddie Cantor). After a day's shooting, Bluett would sometimes drive Horne home. He even invited her to dinner at Humphrey Bogart's house, where Bogart's mother cooked and Bluett, a pianist-singer, often entertained. To her disappointment, Bogart wasn't there.

Once Ethel Waters came to work, the jollity on the set froze. Chorus members had warned Horne that the older star hated her. Waters looked at her and saw an upstart who was threatening her hard-earned turf. Bluett felt the friction immediately. "My God, she was very jealous of Lena," he said. "Lena was slim and beautiful and young. And Ethel was more or less on her way out, although she still had that great talent."

The unpleasantness only grew. "All through that picture," admitted Waters, "there was so much snarling and scrapping that I don't know how in the world *Cabin in the Sky* ever stayed up there." She fumed at the special attention Minnelli seemed to be giving Horne. Leonard Bluett recalled seeing the director "down on his knees fixing Lena's gown to make sure that when the camera said go, it looked beautiful. People kept wondering, 'What is he doing down there?' And I'd say, 'He's making sure that the creases in her gown are perfect!'"

Waters decided that the studio had hired Horne as part of a conspiracy to humiliate her. She made no secret of her assumption that the young singer had gotten the part by sleeping with the director—an appalling notion to her, given the gossip about Minnelli's homosexuality. Waters, recalled Horne, had loudly insisted that "sex had gotten me there—even though it wasn't true."

As a sometime lesbian, Waters could hardly have been startled at the idea of sexual fluidity, but her hatred of Horne held no mercy. Butterfly McQueen proved equally judgmental. She referred mockingly to "the *beautiful* Lena Horne"; and as for Minnelli, she told author Richard Lamparski: "When I read that little what's-her-name"—Judy Garland—"was gonna marry him, I said, 'If you don't have any better sense than to marry a man like that I'll never weep another tear for you.'"

Horne and Waters had only one scene together, a rollicking ensemble sequence set in Jim Henry's Paradise. Eddie Anderson would drive

Horne there in a Cadillac, then dance her inside the crowded club. Waters would sing one of her showstoppers from the stage version of *Cabin*, "Honey in the Honeycomb," while Horne danced.

The final rehearsal for the complicated scene took place on Wednesday, October 13, the day before filming. As Horne and Anderson practiced their entrance, Horne landed hard on her right foot. She heard a snap. Then she fell. Anderson picked her up, then Minnelli rushed over, followed by a crowd of cast members. Horne had broken a bone in her ankle. The director turned around—and there stood Waters several feet away, arms folded like an all-controlling schoolmarm—"as if she had prayed for it to happen," said Bluett. Waters was heard to say, "The Lord works in mysterious ways, his wonders to perform."

Her composure cracked when a prop man scampered over to Horne with a pillow for her ankle. At that moment, Horne wrote later, "Miss Waters started to blow like a hurricane." The tirade that followed encompassed a lifetime of racist blows, exploitation, and bad luck. Years later, Horne's daughter, Gail, offered more details. Waters had spewed out "a semi-coherent diatribe that began with attacks on Lena and wound up with a vilification of 'Hollywood Jews.'"

Minnelli canceled filming for the day. In the studio hospital, doctors placed Horne's whole leg in a cast and told her she couldn't walk or dance for up to two months. Nevertheless, she returned to the set on Friday. When she hobbled in on crutches, the cast and crew rushed over, bearing flowers and presents marked "Sweet Georgia Brown." Minnelli had rushed to do last-minute reblocking of the scene; due to Horne's infirmity she would sing "Honey in the Honeycomb" while sitting on a bar, and Waters would dance.

In order to make sure that Horne stayed deferential in her brief dialogue with Waters, Minnelli directed the young singer to address her in a kittenish fashion. It worked, and all went smoothly. Off camera, though, the two women exchanged not a word.

Somehow all this conflict stayed hidden from the press; *Cabin* was too important for M-G-M to risk word of infighting. Hardly anyone doubted Arthur Freed's sincere wish to contribute to Walter White's cause. But he was a businessman, and knew how to manipulate the press to M-G-M's advantage.

During the filming, Freed invited Billy Rowe of the *Pittsburgh Courier* to visit the set and interview everyone involved. He picked the right man. "Billy was intrigued by Hollywood," explained his friend Alice Key; and he looked as though he were always ready for his close-up. Rowe wore snazzy suits and a movie-star smile, set off by his pencil mustache; a white bowler hat topped his straightened, pomaded hair. Many found him arrogant, but few black columnists were more widely read. Off he went to Culver City to research not one, but a series of articles about *Cabin in the Sky* and M-G-M's plans for the Negro onscreen.

The studio treated him royally. Rowe met everyone, from Freed, Mayer, and Waters to grips and gofers. He basked in the glamour of the hothouse Shangri-la that was M-G-M. Rowe dined in the commissary, where he ogled Judy Garland, Fred Astaire, and Mickey Rooney. And he sat in Freed's office and heard the producer talk of signing Waters and Eddie Anderson to long-term contracts. Freed and his colleague Sam Katz also spoke proudly of "the wonderful plans they had in store for Lena Horne . . . and the great number of Negro actors and technicians this film had benefited, artistically and financially." Freed looked ahead to "that fast-approaching day when the screen, like the stage and concert world, will utilize the great histrionic talent that is the Negro."

Rowe went to his typewriter. He wrote a series of articles that were so lavishly pro-Hollywood, and was so impressed by its welcome of the Negro, that his liberal black colleagues were up in arms. Earl Dancer, the manager who had pushed Waters into the white radar, accused Rowe in print of accepting payoffs from Freed. Reporter Evelyn Cunningham, his *Courier* colleague, acknowledged that Rowe's loyalties were suspect: "He had great connections, especially with the whites. They were wonderful news sources for him. He made a lot of enemies, no question. And he didn't always tell the truth. He made deals at the drop of a hat—hustling deals. He could be had."

But Rowe stood firm. In that time of war, he declared, "there would be something very wrong" with the Jewish Freed "if he were not on the side of any oppressed group of people."

In November, the columnist sent lofty thank-yous to Howard Strickling, M-G-M's publicity director, and to Freed. The word "friendship" appeared in both. "You may rest assured that I will do everything in my power to bring about the success of *Cabin in the Sky*," he told Strickling.

In truth, Rowe had witnessed perhaps the most respectful treatment of black artists to ever occur in the movies. Waters and Anderson never got their extended deals, but Leonard Bluett and Avanelle Harris shared the opinion that *Cabin* was a refreshing change from the Hollywood they'd known.

Almena Davis, the black journalist from the *Los Angeles Tribune*, wasn't buying it. She, too, had visited the *Cabin* set, where she had observed "the arrogant Ethel Waters, the adored Lena Horne, the pompous Rochester." Not much impressed her. As soon as "Cut!" was yelled at the end of a scene set in Jim Henry's Paradise, she wrote, "Duke Ellington wipes that special camera smile off his face, the one where he tucks his upper lip under to make his lips thinner and show off his strong teeth better."

> Everywhere you have been impressed with the complete absence of race prejudice as such, on the set . . . but all the while the consciousness that there *is* something wrong with Hollywood (Billy Rowe to the contrary) faintly disturbs you. . . . You try and match the continual parade of stereotypes: the crap shooting scenes, the dialect, the traditional ignorant, superstitious celluloid darky, with the camaraderie which the director displays with the colored actors. . . . And it doesn't match.

One of *Cabin*'s prickliest issues involved the censors' reaction to the depiction of Georgia Brown. Before filming had even started, Horne's character stirred up controversy. While reading various drafts of the script, Joseph I. Breen, head of the Production Code Administration—Hollywood's chief body of censors—fired off a series of memos to Freed and Mayer. "Please avoid any improper exposure of Georgia when she crosses her legs," read one. Another declared, "Please change the line, 'she sho' looks hot.' Also, at the bottom of this page, this underwear which Georgia shows off should be a slip and not panties."

Such orders were nothing new from Breen, a staunch Catholic who forbade any hint of what he deemed "indecency." Mayer himself was the most moralistic of studio heads. Good taste meant everything to him. In an interview with Richard Lamparski, actress Ilona Massey recalled one of Mayer's rules: "A kiss couldn't last for more than one second, and never on the mouth."

During rehearsals, his watchdogs kept close watch for any content that might offend. Esther Williams told of practicing the Frank Loesser tune "[I'd Love to Get You] On a Slow Boat to China" for the movie *Neptune's Daughter*. "This young fellow there said, 'You can't sing that song.' I said, 'Why not?' He said, '"Get you" is a synonym for the f-word.' I said, 'You guys are sick! "Get you" is a game that kids play in the street. Tag. Where in the world did you get such a dirty mind?'" She lost. The song was cut.

For *Cabin in the Sky*, most of the controversy surrounded Horne's first scene, in which she took a bubble bath while delivering "Ain't It the Truth," Harold Arlen and Yip Harburg's sassy defense of all-out hedonism. Heaven didn't exist, sang Horne; "life is cash and carry," so better to kick up your heels and indulge in forbidden fruit before you were "laid horizontal in that telephone booth."

Vetting the script, Breen advised Mayer: "There must, of course, be no exposure of Georgia's person in this scene where she is shown in the bubble bath." Minnelli obeyed, but he pushed the limits. Horne's bare shoulders shimmied teasingly, and the bubbles lay thinly on her breasts; she grinned and winked in true sex-kitten fashion. Beneath the bubbles, a flesh-colored one-piece bathing suit did the necessary concealing.

Certainly M-G-M's cameras had revealed female flesh before. The year before, Lana Turner had stepped into a bubble bath in *Ziegfeld Girl*, while Hedy Lamarr's halter tops and wraparound skirts in *White Cargo* exposed more than Horne did in her bathtub. But the prolonged look at a near-naked black actress, singing a song that many would find blasphemous, couldn't help but cause discomfort. Later on it became a mini-scandal. But for now, Minnelli and Mayer had every intention of leaving the number in.

Shooting ended on October 24, 1942. Horne had no further film work until January, so she returned to a cabaret, the setting that had become her refuge. There she could be left alone to experiment as she chose, and to work on her acting, at least in song.

The *Pittsburgh Courier* would later call her next New York engagement a "historical debut." Hollywood's new "sepia eyeful," as one newspaper termed her, had been chosen as the first black entertainer to play an extended run in an upscale white hotel, the Savoy-Plaza, at Fifth Avenue and Fifty-ninth Street. Its Café Lounge presented stars whom international swells loved. These included "The Incomparable" Hildegarde, the Milwaukee-born, piano-playing songbird who charmed almost everyone into loving French chansons and high-class show tunes; and Jean Sablon, Paris's answer to Bing Crosby.

Horne's six-week engagement would open on December 3, 1942. According to *All Around the Town*, a going-out guide of the day, the booking of a black singer into that "snooty" club "was not without some internal managerial discussion." Just how much dissent it caused would become clear only after she opened.

On opening night, Horne stepped onto the middle of a small dance floor with tables all around her and a bar to the side. She was gowned in white, with a matching flower in her hair. Her movie reviews had helped pack the room. According to the *Pittsburgh Courier,* she was "surrounded by a sea of white faces," including "international celebrities of the theatrical world"—Ethel Merman, opera star Grace Moore, comic George Jessel.

The room had a small orchestra, and Phil Moore, her M-G-M rehearsal pianist, accompanied her. She needed no microphone, thanks to the projection skills she'd learned from Lew Leslie. Horne sang tasteful standards of the day—"I Can't Give You Anything but Love," "I Get a Kick Out of You," "Blues in the Night," "Embraceable You."

Arthur Laurents, the Brooklyn-born screenwriter and playwright, came to Manhattan one weekend from Ithaca, New York, the home of his college, Cornell University. Seeing a poster that advertised Horne, he made a reservation at the Café Lounge and took his place among the posh crowd. The lights dimmed, and out walked Horne. "She came down the corridor in a flame-red chiffon dress. She had long hair, and she was the most beautiful thing I'd ever seen. She sang—sweet. There was absolutely nothing, as you'd say in those days, Negro about her at all. I don't know if she was good or not; she was just so beautiful that you lost every bit of your head. After the show, I intercepted her and said, 'Oh, Miss Horne, I drove all the way from Ithaca to see you.' It was a little exaggerated, but she was very gracious, very charming. And very white."

Every critic raved about her beauty, and some liked her singing. *All Around the Town* touted her as "a looker of arresting order, with gleaming white teeth and a fetching smile, who croons a song competently if not extraordinarily." Another reviewer praised "the café au lait–hued delineator" for fitting well "into the strange atmosphere." After each show, customers traded awestruck remarks on Horne's looks. Singer-actress Diahann Carroll would grow used to similar comments when she launched her career in the fifties; she sensed the condescension in them. "What they're really saying is, 'Not all blacks are beautiful, but you are. And we're much more accepting of you, because you are beautiful.' Never mind the fact that Lena was breaking her back trying to become a good singer."

Down Beat's Mike Levin acknowledged this, albeit awkwardly. He noted a widespread fallacy "that colored people are essentially limited when it comes to any intelligent activity." Not so with Horne, who delivered a fashionable repertoire "in a fashion that arouses admiration not only for the singing but the consummate art in the way she does it. . . . The so-called smart crowd has discovered a new idol."

Newsweek announced that Horne had outsold even Hildegarde at the Café Lounge. Anticipated protests over the booking were few. But while the management loved having the profitable singer in its cabaret, they preferred she not live among the hotel guests. The Savoy-Plaza gave her a room for dressing, but wouldn't let her sleep in it. Each night after work she went home to the Hotel Theresa.

Horne didn't argue. If the Savoy didn't want her to stay there, she would just as soon go someplace else. But two weeks into her run, some staff members reportedly decided that they'd rather not be around her at all. On January 23, 1943, the *Pittsburgh Courier* wrote that the hotel's managing director and press agent had resigned "due to the booking of Miss Horne" in the ultra-swank Café Lounge. Allegedly the men had quit because the board wouldn't support their views. "The directors felt that the employment of a sepia songstress was not in keeping with the dignity of the Fifth Avenue house, though the star was a terrific financial and artistic success and received the unanimous support of all the New York newspapers."

The unwanted attention made Horne feel even more self-conscious than she already did. Harold Gumm issued a denial of the story, claiming the two directors had resigned "over something else." But the news blew over, and capacity crowds continued to stare at Horne in wonderment. Robert Rice of the *Daily News* saw a timid but unfolding presence. "She claims she doesn't know what gestures she makes at all, except that sometimes she suddenly notices her hands waving in front of her, and says to herself, 'What do I think I'm doing?' and puts them behind her back."

Offstage Horne seemed bewildered by reporters who wanted to know everything about her. "I haven't got any voice," she told *Time* magazine. "I don't know anything about music. I feel like the fellow who was dreaming: All he could say was, 'Don't wake me up.'" *PM* reported that Horne had received a letter inviting her to talk about a possible Broadway role. Horne "never had heard of the guy who sent it—feller named George Abbott." She cared more about "a group from her alma mater, Girls High School in Brooklyn, who came to the club to proudly see the local girl who had made good."

Horne had managed to hide from everyone the fact that she'd been ill since opening night. But one night she collapsed on the floor during her show. Hotel staff helped her up to her room, and a doctor came. The management had a change of heart, and asked her to sleep in the hotel for the rest of the run.

She didn't want their charity, and insisted on going home to Harlem. The next night she was back at the Savoy. The praise hadn't gone to her head. "I knew I was not a great talent," she said later. "But I had a brain and I had used it in performance to keep me from being too amateurish, because I had no one but me to depend on."

CHAPTER 7

AS *CABIN* in the *Sky* reached the editing room, M-G-M once more didn't know how next to use Lena Horne. Apart from all-black musicals, what could a white studio do with a "sensational colored chanteuse"?

They solved the problem temporarily by loaning her out to 20th Century Fox for another all-black extravaganza. Its working title was *Thanks, Pal,* but before release, Fox renamed the film for a song Horne sang in it, *Stormy Weather.* On January 21, 1943, she flew from New York to Hollywood and began work, bursting with pride and excitement. Her costar was the great Bill Robinson; the cast also included Cab Calloway, Fats Waller, the Nicholas Brothers, Dooley Wilson, Babe Wallace (Horne's Cotton Club partner), and the Katherine Dunham company. The wisp of a screenplay, coauthored by "Stormy Weather" lyricist Ted Koehler, found Robinson playing a facsimile of himself; the movie approximated his stellar career, which flourished between the World Wars.

Once rehearsals began, Horne found cause for unhappiness. As onscreen sweethearts, she and Robinson had a gaping age difference—twenty-five to sixty-four. She noticed that every black leading man on Hollywood's roster was a "Negro character" like Eddie "Rochester" Anderson or Bojangles; the studios seemed unwilling to groom anything approaching a black Tyrone Power or Errol Flynn.

Robinson, of course, towered in other regards. Having hoofed for pennies as a child in Richmond, Virginia, he earned a reported three thousand five hundred dollars a week as a vaudeville headliner. Unlike other Negro tappers, the plaid-suited, bow-tied Robinson never seemed desperate for approval. He danced with a master's ease, letting his feet and endearing grin do the work. Lew Leslie showcased him on Broadway in *Blackbirds of 1928,* and from then on he charmed a multitude of white and black fans. Hollywood cast him in a series of stereotypical roles— an antebellum butler, a farmworker. In several films, though, he played opposite Shirley Temple. Their tap dance together on a staircase in *The Little Colonel* gave a striking boost to race relations in 1935 Hollywood.

But Robinson, who could barely read or write, seemed as bitter as Ethel Waters. "He broke a lot of barriers but he was mean," said Delilah Jackson. The dancer was also known as lecherous—"he jumped all the girls," added Jackson—and notoriously ill tempered; according to legend, he pulled a gun on Benny Carter, *Stormy Weather*'s musical director. Still, he never tried to upstage Horne on camera. "He was a pro," said Gene Davis. "I understand he was also a terror, but he didn't overdance her while she did her little step."

Elsewhere, Horne was surrounded by warm, familiar faces. Clarence Robinson, the former Cotton Club dance director, made his Hollywood debut as *Stormy Weather*'s choreographer. The dance ensemble included Leonard Bluett, Avanelle Harris, and Cleo Hayes. Chosen to shimmy frenetically on a drum was Wilhelmina Gray, who called herself Tondelayo—the character from *White Cargo,* a hit Broadway play long before M-G-M adapted it for Hedy Lamarr. A longtime Cotton Club and Apollo shake dancer and nightclub hostess, Tondelayo was a spicy Harlem character. Her "provocative, orgiastic, snake-like dances have been described as wanton," wrote one reporter. She loved acting as grandly as Lamarr; when entering one of the low-down cabarets she fronted, she dragged a mink coat behind her, sweeping the sawdust off the floor.

Stormy Weather unfolded in flashback. In his sixties, tap-dancing star Bill Williamson recalls his post–World War I rise and his romance with a lovely young singer, Selina Rogers. The plot was mere connective tissue; much of the action took place in a nightclub, where one production number followed another. Except for *Cabin in the Sky,* Hollywood had never turned such a spotlight on the highest ranks of black show business.

But few of the cast members received red-carpet treatment. "Some studios were just great, like M-G-M and Paramount," said Avanelle Harris. "But not Twentieth Century-Fox. When we made *Stormy Weather*, we had to go to the moon to get to some little cafeteria they'd thrown together for us." The dressing rooms were just as remote. Typical of Hollywood in the forties, there were no black crew members.

The dancers were used to grueling hours, but Clarence Robinson pushed them almost to the breaking point. "He had never done movies before," said Cleo Hayes, "so he did not know that you don't go out there and dance for eight or ten choruses. Sometimes we'd be up on that floor two hours dancing, perfecting a routine, and the California girls used to tell us, 'God, he's gonna kill us, we never worked like this before!'"

The film's pivotal moment, of course, was Horne's performance of "Stormy Weather." Robinson staged it in what would become the defining image of Lena Horne. She stood on a nightclub stage alongside a simulated apartment window; rain thundered outside. Selina had left the Robinson character to pursue her career, but her heart ached, and she poured it out in song. Since recording it a year or so earlier, Horne had avoided "Stormy Weather." Decades later she told *Newsweek*'s Charles Michener that she had been "terrified" to sing it onscreen—"because it was Ethel's."

The prerecording in February 1943 proved an ordeal. Accompanied by Benny Carter's orchestra, Horne sang Harold Arlen and Ted Koehler's gut-wrenching lament as though she were a naïve schoolgirl. There on the soundstage was Andrew Stone, the film's white director. Stone's résumé listed a sprawling but mostly undistinguished string of B-musicals and thrillers. "He was the wrong one to do *Stormy Weather*," said Alice Key, who danced in it. "He didn't know how to work with black people." Horne disliked him on sight, and didn't welcome his prodding her to "feel it" in blues-singer fashion. He "thought that most of us could sing that way," she said resentfully. But her real frustration was with herself. "I'd always been taught not to show my feelings," she said, and she couldn't drop the Horne family reserve.

Stone told his side of the "Stormy Weather" session to reporter Frank Nugent. "Lena sang it all right, but there was no warmth, no emotional quality. I did everything I could to break her down. I spoke to her about her mother, her kids." A day later he tried again, to no avail. Cab Calloway took the singer into a corner and lectured her. "Girl, what are you gonna do, ruin the thing, and this is your chance? Sing it with some passion, some feeling! Bitch, you know what we've gone through. . . . Think about somebody in your family that's died and sing the song."

Even that didn't work. Finally, said Stone, Calloway "whispered two words in her ear. I never saw such a change in a person. She was wonderful! Real tears in her eyes, a sob in her voice." He wouldn't divulge the two words to Stone, and neither would Horne: "Cab just said something to tease me. He got me mad, that's all." Only years later did the bandleader reveal what he'd said: "Ethel Waters."

For all her recent success, Horne was feeling lost in Hollywood and "very unhappy," as Avanelle Harris observed. Many insiders viewed her with suspicion—as a none-too-gifted pet of the NAACP; as the girl who was sleeping with the director and maybe the producer (Freed), who was known for having black mistresses; as mere "decoration" no matter how hard she'd worked; as "professional," not inspired. "Everybody was jealous of Lena," said Cleo Hayes. "Because she walked in where they'd already been, and took over. And was not doing anything that any of them did. She was Lena."

Louis Jones was still intent upon suing her for divorce, but Horne tried her best to ignore him. A few months earlier he had moved to a town near Columbus, Ohio, taking Teddy with him. There he hired a new lawyer. When the latest batch of papers arrived Horne "paid it no mind," according to the *Pittsburgh Courier.* One can only guess why; perhaps she wanted to put off facing a messy custody battle that might rob her of Teddy.

Her personal issues weighed on her heavily during the shoot. Wardrobe test photos show a young woman whose seesawing weight had risen. With little makeup on her then-chubby face and her frizzy hair uncoiffed, Horne looked far from glamorous. Helen Rose, who designed the costumes, recalled how she and a depressed Horne bonded for moral support. "At that time we were both rather timid and not too experienced in studio procedure or politics," Rose said. "To keep our sanity, Lena and I talked about everything under the sun, except the studio. We talked of our families, our beliefs, our hopes and dreams."

On the set, Horne told a reporter from the *Chicago Defender* that her future film contracts would demand "only romantic leads." She didn't want to play another Georgia Brown vixen. "The menace girl gets a fat acting role, all right, but the romance girl gets her man. And I'm a girl that wants to get her man—and keep him—pictures or no pictures."

That ambition hadn't gone well. Within two years, several beaus had come and gone from her life—Charlie Barnet, Duke Ellington, Artie Shaw—while her estranged husband was pursuing a divorce. According to Avery Williams of *Tan* magazine, Horne had also dated Kenny Washington, all-American halfback at UCLA, in 1942. She was having trouble keeping her personal life out of the papers, largely through a surprising lack of discretion. Around the time of *Stormy Weather*, Horne became involved with two of the most-talked-about men of the day.

On March 6, 1943, the *Chicago Defender* ran a photo of her and Hollywood's feistiest renegade: the actor, producer, director, and screenwriter Orson Welles. They clasped hands and looked into each other's eyes. Years later Horne told her friend St. Clair Pugh, "I never had anything to do with any of those Hollywood guys. Except Orson."

Horne met him at an especially risky time. Aside from her imminent fight to retain custody of Teddy, she had just signed a coveted deal with a studio that wouldn't have welcomed a scandal about its touted black starlet's interracial flings. For Horne to endanger her contract would have let down Walter White's revolutionary cause.

But her affairs may have represented an early stab of rebellion against White and all those who sought to use her for their own means. Horne had goals unrelated to the NAACP. Professional gain mattered to her, as it had to her ancestors. She seemed to view white men as protectors, sheltered from the slights that Louis Jones had suffered. And she wanted a lover of stature and purpose. By all those standards, Welles proved irresistible. He was whip-smart, politically progressive, and eager to shake people up. On Halloween night in 1938, the twenty-three-year-old and his acting company, the Mercury Theatre on the Air, had hit the airwaves with *The War of the Worlds,* an adaptation of the H. G. Wells novel about Martians invading Earth. The Welles ensemble performed the story as a faux newscast, and many listeners believed it was true. Terror swept the streets and homes of a country that was already queasy from the smell of impending war.

To Welles, America was flashing with red-light alerts, as all kinds of freedoms—political, racial, artistic—fell under fire. Defiantly he employed leftists and Communists, supported socialism, and didn't care whom he offended. Welles had recently taken on newspaper megamagnate William Randolph Hearst—known for his scandal-seeking yellow journalism—in *Citizen Kane*, a film inspired by Hearst. The epic proved so incendiary that Welles got booed at the Oscars; he was branded, inaccurately, as a Communist.

He began his liaison with Horne in the course of an exciting new film project. In 1942, the State Department had asked Welles to create a movie that would boost wartime relations with South America. The invitation came from Nelson Rockefeller, who had the job of keeping as much of the world as possible in America's corner. Why he thought the ornery Welles could help keep peace is a mystery. Nevertheless, Welles flew to Brazil to explore Carnaval in Rio. He found a land whose "tolerance and quiet decency," as he saw it, outclassed the ugly discrimination he saw in his own country. Dazzled by the samba, Welles thought of filming a segment in which he allied it to American jazz. Louis Armstrong would appear, along with Welles's friend Duke Ellington.

It was Ellington who suggested he add Lena Horne. Her tawny loveliness couldn't help but entice the Latinos, and she sang well, too. Welles never forgot the bandleader's showy praise of Horne, whose radiance, he said, could "suntan the first ten rows."

Ellington introduced them. Horne met a chubby, baby-faced intellectual with probing eyes and speech as regal as Laurence Olivier's. Welles saw an exquisite beauty whose careful manners and gracious smile couldn't hide an untrusting nature. Horne, he noticed, was "not at all show-businessy as a person," whereas every move Welles seemed calculatedly theatrical.

But in him, she found someone who felt as alienated as she. His charisma and smarts captivated her—but his bulldog social convictions may have pleased her the most. "Race hate is a disease," he declared in a magazine editorial. "In a people's world, the incurable racist has no rights. He must be segregated as he himself would segregate the colored and semitic peoples—as we now segregate the leprous and insane."

Unfortunately, his screen collaboration with Horne never occurred; Welles abandoned the jazz element of his film to focus on Carnaval. But the project, like so much else he did, grew mired in controversy; it crumbled before completion. Brazil's government turned suspicious and stopped cooperating; RKO, his studio, loathed the first rushes. "They see a lot of black people," he said, "and the reaction is, he's just shooting a lot of jigaboos jumping up and down, you know?"

Welles was ready to flout anyone. At the beginning of 1943, while starring in a film version of *Jane Eyre,* he took one more professional risk by starting an affair with Horne. Decades later, he hadn't left her thoughts. "She was crazy about him," said Marcia Ann Gillespie, her collaborator on an aborted memoir in the eighties. But Horne never discussed the affair—or any of her extramarital flings—in public. She described Welles coyly to British writer Clive Hirschhorn as her "only real friend," a title she also bestowed upon Strayhorn, Minnelli, Eddie Anderson, and others.

Like so many people, Welles found Horne "not easy at all" to get to know. In a 1984 BBC interview, he remembered her as "touchy and hard to approach," adding, "I did get the impression that she gave off sparks because she was deeply suspicious of the world." But at least on the surface, she seemed to rise above every slight. "Her reactions to being in Hollywood, not being terribly well-treated, were all those of an essentially aristocratic nature. And in that atmosphere, bathed with uncommon dignity."

If Horne was searching for her father in every man she dated, she didn't find him in Welles. A brat and a prima donna, he wreaked havoc during *Jane Eyre;* his leading lady, Joan Fontaine, found him "undisciplined," "always late," and "prone to melodrama on and off the set." But many thought him a genius, if a dangerous one. Horne, too, was living perilously, moving from fling to fling with high-profile whites. In this case, she'd chosen a braggart who loved to boast of his conquests. Horne kept the romance as secret as she could, but word of it reached Hedda Hopper, the reviled Hollywood gossip queen. Schoolmarmish and near sixty, Hopper was a self-appointed moral guardian who threatened to "out" gay actors (including lovers Cary Grant and Randolph Scott) and named names in the McCarthy era.

Of all Orson's rebellions, she felt, nothing was worse than his affair with a Negro. Hopper confronted him and announced she'd heard that he and Horne were keeping company, and he'd better put a stop to it. "I said, 'What do you mean, Hedda?'" recalled Welles. "And she said, 'You know perfectly well what I mean! You can destroy your career.' People really did talk like that in those days. I told her to go put her head in a bucket."

Yet by midyear the affair had ended, and in September Welles married Rita Hayworth. If Louis B. Mayer knew about Horne's affair with Welles, he didn't punish or berate her for it, as he threatened to do whenever one of his stars embarked on a romance that might harm the studio's image. Mayer couldn't shirk his commitment to the NAACP, which meant tolerating behavior from Horne that June Allyson and Gloria DeHaven would never have gotten away with.

Remarkably, Horne's affair with Welles had stayed relatively secret; one wonders if M-G-M took steps to keep it quiet. The studio had less success in hushing a romance of Horne's that had set tongues wagging. Joe Louis was married, and had become a father in February 1943. But the world champion of heavyweight boxing kept visiting the *Stormy Weather* set to see Horne, whom he'd reportedly met at Café Society.

Louis spoke openly of their on-again, off-again affair to his friend Alice Key; Horne flaunted the mink coat he'd given her. Cleo Hayes and Ruby Dallas Young—two other girlfriends—knew that the Brown Bomber had Horne on a string. On November 12, 1942, Billy Rowe had reported the widespread rumor that Louis—then an army sergeant—would divorce his wife to marry Horne. Both he and Horne issued vague denials. "I think that Lena is a grand person, on and off the screen, but that doesn't mean I want to marry her or vice versa," said the boxer. Added Horne, "Sergeant Louis and I have been friends for several years and to me, like fifty million others, he's a symbol of greatness. I can certainly admire him and be in his company without hopping off to the altar."

Meanwhile, numerous photos surfaced of Horne alongside Louis; one showed them on a lake together, sharing a rowboat. In his book *Joe Louis: The Great Black Hope*, Richard Bak wrote of how the boxer's wife, Marva Trotter, found a love letter he'd written for Horne. Louis was away, and an irate Trotter packed up his possessions and sent them to him.

Though married since 1935, Louis had never stopped womanizing. His reported girlfriends included movie stars Sonja Henie and Lana Turner as well as a bevy of former Cotton Club chorines. At the time of *Stormy Weather,* said Cleo Hayes, "he was my fella. But there was no one person that could put her name on that and say, 'Oh, that's mine!'" His worldwide eminence had made the pug-nosed boxer a trophy catch. Hayes described him as "a funny guy, a sweetheart, just as nice as he could be"; what's more, rumor had it that "his member was like a huge coke bottle," to quote Leonard Bluett.

It was over Louis that two good friends fell out. Horne was madly jealous of Hayes, and the tension grew so thick that Cleo quit *Stormy Weather*. Later she would claim she'd left because of Clarence Robinson's merciless whip cracking. "No, she didn't!" said Alice Key with a laugh in 2006. "She left because she didn't want to be there with Lena and Joe."

Louis's autobiography contained a dramatic account of his final round with Horne. When *My Life* was published, Louis was nearing the end of a long decline. By the time he lost his last match to Rocky Marciano in 1951, Louis had earned and spent almost five million dollars. In partnership with Leonard Reed, he tried all kinds of endeavors—restaurants, bars, even a nightclub act. After the IRS nabbed him for $1.2 million in back taxes, he foundered. Louis ended his career as a doorman at Caesars Palace in Las Vegas. Paranoid and addicted to cocaine, he spent his last years in a wheelchair before dying of a heart attack on April 12, 1981. He was sixty-six.

Two years earlier, the sensationalistic *My Life* had come out under his name, with Edna and Art Rust as coauthors. As the book told it, Horne had confronted him in a blind rage over his "cheating." She "started cursing me like nobody ever had," he said. "Before I knew it, I hit her with a left hook and knocked her on the bed. Then I jumped on her and started choking her."

Horne gave a poised rebuttal to *Ebony*. The only detail of his account that she confirmed was his description of her vocabulary: "Lena can cuss like any sailor wished he could." Otherwise she called him a friend, not a lover, and termed him a vulnerable, exploited man whose cowriters had probably concocted lies in order to attract sales. Louis, she felt, was incapable of treating a woman violently. Cleo Hayes and Alice Key agreed.

Yet both believed it was he who'd sent Horne packing. "That breakup was kind of unpleasant," said Hayes, "because I think that Lena thought Champ was gonna marry her. But he had made one mistake when he married Marva, and he was totally unhappy about that." Later, Key asked him about the split. "I said, 'Champ, what happened with you and Lena?' He said, 'She thinks she's too cute.' I said, 'I don't think that's true, because Lena is one of the least affected women I know. And if she does think she's cute, she has a right to; she's a movie star! She's beautiful!' He said, 'There's a whole lot of movie stars, Alice, but there's only one heavyweight champion of the world!'"

Horne eventually made up with Louis, but she never quite reconciled with Hayes. After returning to New York, the dancer got a chorus job at the Café Zanzibar. Horne dropped by. "It was the first time I had seen Lena in a long time," Hayes said. "She came down to see the girls backstage, and she saw me and wouldn't speak to me. What can I tell you?"

IN the spring of 1943, Horne had two big-league films awaiting release and others under way. Like nearly every Hollywood star, she devoted much of her spare time to the war effort. Horne had already begun performing in USO shows for blacks in the segregated military; as the war progressed, her role as an ambassador of wartime racial tolerance would grow ever larger.

Meanwhile, M-G-M sent her out on all kinds of goodwill missions. At a noontime ceremony on May 14, Horne stood in a shipyard in Richmond, California, ready to christen a liberty ship named after George Washington Carver, the great Negro agricultural chemist. The yard employed 6,112 Negro workers, and about a quarter of them gathered to watch. A cheer erupted as Horne, smiling broadly, smashed a bottle of champagne on the SS *George Washington Carver*.

Cabin in the Sky would open that month. Concerned about how their all-black effort would be received, Freed and Mayer had held test screenings around the country for weeks. The first had taken place in Dallas. According to John Rosenfield of *The Dallas Morning News*, "the sidewalks in front of the theater were packed and jammed for a solid block." Black viewers had to tolerate old-fashioned Jim Crow seating in the upper balcony. Still, they applauded *Cabin*'s abundance of Negro talent, so handsomely displayed. The film began with a foreword, intended to soften the heart of every black viewer.

> Throughout the ages, powerful and inspiring thoughts have been preserved and handed down by the medium of the legend, the fable, and the fantasy.
>
> America has such a story and is fortunate that its warmth and beauty are guarded by a people whose sense of true values is needed in a strife-torn world—the American Negro. This story of faith and devotion springs from that source and seeks to capture those teachings in their original and most beautiful form.

From there, Minnelli's seductive direction took over. He brought an air of Hollywood glamour to this tale of a mythical southern town and its simple inhabitants. It mattered deeply to him that *Cabin* be luscious to the eye, and just before its release, he and Freed added a beautifying touch. One of them—Minnelli couldn't remember which—suggested giving the black-and-white stock a sepia tint. "We experimented with a portion of it," he wrote. "The film was transformed . . . Sepia created a soft, velvety patina more flattering to the actors' skin tones."

And it enhanced the movie's storybook unreality. In the opening sequence, which shows a gospel choir and congregation in church, the sweeping overhead view takes God's perspective. When the wind rifles through the trees, it seems as though the Lord has waved his hand. Through such devices, Minnelli gave a sense of human lives controlled by the otherworldly.

His visual details incorporate objects from the South. After Waters has prayed for the dying Little Joe, she blows out a coal-oil lamp; it starts to glow again, casting a shadow of the devil on the wall. Later, Horne plucks a huge magnolia blossom off a tree and dons it as a hat.

The audience at Dallas's Majestic Theatre burst into applause as soon as she appeared onscreen in a bra with her back to the camera, pulling on her dress while the devil lies on the bed. As a siren who nearly leads a man to hell, Horne looked sexy but seemed like a near-innocent, play-dressing in high heels and halter top. As she cavorted in her bubble bath and sang about biting the apple of sin, she sounded more coy than worldly.

But as the long-suffering Petunia, Ethel Waters is the mother of experience. Her all-encompassing grin, her glowing eyes, her earth-mother warmth, her impish wit—they bespoke one of most luminous acting talents of her generation. Pulling the wash off the line and crooning "Happiness Is Just a Thing Called Joe," Waters is the forgiving older woman whose vulnerability tugs at the heart. But when she confronts Georgia Brown at Jim's Henry's Paradise, Waters transforms herself into a high-kicking vamp, saucier than Brown.

Well intentioned as he was, Minnelli let a number of racial clichés slip through. The eloquent Petunia slips into a black southern tongue during "Happiness Is Just a Thing Called Joe." The devil's henchmen, including Louis Armstrong, are clownish and pop-eyed. "At one point," wrote a reporter from the left-wing newspaper *PM*, "you get a peep of heaven, and sure enough, it's a Jim Crow heaven, pickaninny cherubim and all!" Throughout the film, evil is associated with blackness, white with good.

To Gene Davis, even those images came off with a flair. "I think that when Vincente was faced with a stereotype in the script, he stylized it. At the end, when Little Joe and Petunia walk the steps to heaven, Ethel is in that glorious white gown, lit to a fare-thee-well, hair done, strutting those stairs, all ready to meet her maker. He even softened Butterfly McQueen."

Every preview audience seemed to love the film, but it inflamed local censors. Demands for cuts swamped M-G-M. The studio was commanded to "eliminate" a "suggestive view" of Georgia Brown lifting her dress above her knees to tease Joe. Ohio's censorship board called for the excision of a scene in which Georgia jumps into Joe's lap and kisses him. Reporter Frank Nugent wrote that Horne had snuck into theaters to watch the effect on audiences of her "rhythmic-hipped, bubble-bathing Georgia Brown."

The "Ain't It the Truth" bathtub scene got cut before the premiere. No specific order had come from the Breen office demanding its removal. Minnelli thought he'd heard that Breen found the shot "indecent" and that there was also "some order from southern distributors" to drop it. The number didn't go to waste. Part of it appeared in a 1946 short, *Studio Visit*, about a backstage tour through M-G-M. Fifty years later, "Ain't It the Truth" reemerged in the M-G-M highlights anthology *That's Entertainment! III*.

Cabin premiered nationally in May 1943. Ads billed Horne over Rochester and Waters, and used a cheesecake photo of her as bait. The film was an instant hit, despite reviews even more mixed than Freed had anticipated. The *New York Post's* Irene Thirer called it "thoroughly enchanting"; Virginia Wright of the *Los Angeles Daily News* found it heavy-handed and pretentious. *Variety* praised Horne for her "feverish intensity," but the *Hollywood Reporter* deemed her acting "rather forced. . . . Her singing, of course, never even approaches that of Miss Waters." Horne made up for that with her "colored beauty," wrote the critic, "which will result in many 'Ohs' and 'Ahs' heard from any audience, white or black."

Many liberal viewers weren't pleased. *PM* called *Cabin* "a magnificent show of talent, dramatic ability, and irresistible charm and humor," but scorned its clichés: "The book is that same old, unchanging Darktown-strutter business, with special zoot-suits and high old-time religion added by Metro-Goldwyn-Mayer . . . in the overall, an embarrassing example of how *not* to fulfill a pledge such as Hollywood made to Wendell Willkie last year, to treat the Negro as a first-class citizen in films."

Ruby Dee thought *Cabin* "gorgeous, but it was in the context of what Hollywood allowed for black people. You could talk about the cabin in the sky. The subjects of concern for black people were carefully orchestrated. The battle to denigrate and declass minorities was in full force in Hollywood. Lena came along on the edges of that. At least she was allowed to be beautiful, she was allowed to sing romantic songs, and she could be a sexual object, unlike men, who were absolutely stripped of that. There were no Denzels or Morgan Freemans then; those kinds of men didn't exist."

Still, Leonard Bluett saw *Cabin* as a breakthrough; never had an all-black film been made so artfully. "For its time," said the dancer, "it was a foot in the door." But in 1969, Horne told Wayne Warga of the *Los Angeles Times* that she'd caught *Cabin* on the late show and "could have died from embarrassment. . . . There I was, acting the ingénue, a fluttery, pretty thing. It brought back a lot of memories, most especially that being a fluttery, pretty ingénue wasn't at all what I felt inside."

In time her opinion softened. "That's the only thing I ever did at M-G-M that I liked," she said in 1996. "And felt that I wasn't embarrassing." But Katherine Dunham, Georgia Brown's originator, never saw the film; it had so pained her to lose her part to Horne that she couldn't bring herself to go.

On July 21, two months after *Cabin*'s premiere, *Stormy Weather* opened at New York's Roxy Theatre to similarly conflicting notices. Jesse Zunser of *Cue* called it "probably the most intelligently conceived, and certainly the most entertaining all-colored musical show to come out of Hollywood." He noted a complete absence of the "bug-eyed, loose-lipped, yammering" caricatures "so often met with in films in which Negroes are employed." The *Hollywood Reporter* announced that Horne had made "the most of her richest film opportunity since she skyrocketed to stardom."

But to Charlie Emge of *Down Beat, Stormy Weather* showed blacks "not as what they are but as what the white bosses think the American white public wants them to be." Several numbers show the actors dressed and painted as savages. In a cakewalking scene, the women wear oversize sunflower hats that reveal pickaninny faces. But it was hard to know who had dictated the movie's clichés: the white studio brass, the white director, or Cotton Club graduate Clarence Robinson. "I think it's a lousy film!" said Alice Key. "I thought the lovers were mismatched, but there was great dancing in it; the Nicholas Brothers were just sensational."

Eventually *Stormy Weather* and *Cabin in the Sky* would go down in history as milestones in black cinema—stunning conglomerations of Negro talent, allowed to parade its artistry. The films were tainted, to be sure, by the sometimes misguided good intentions of their creators. But Horne walked away from *Stormy Weather* with a lifelong theme song— "I got stuck with it," she said—and a new level of stardom. In October 1943, she headlined with Duke Ellington at New York's Capitol Theatre and eclipsed the maestro in popularity. "More than a thousand people had gathered to try to gain admission to the opening performance as early as nine AM," wrote the *Chicago Defender*. "Dozens of policemen had to be brought up to keep the crowd in order. . . . At the end of each performance dozens of fans jumped into the orchestra pit, besieging Lena Horne for autographs."

Horne called it a "fantastic engagement." But back in Hollywood, she felt a cold wave from the black actors of the old school—the ones who'd survived by playing the roles that Walter White wanted to ban. Instead of seeing her ascent as a sign of hope, they felt threatened. Maid, servant, and shoeshine-boy parts were keeping them alive and feeding their children. Now here came the NAACP's pet princess, threatening the tiny cinematic foothold they'd gained.

As groomed by M-G-M, Horne struck them as a haughty presence, especially when placed alongside her senior black entertainers. "She was stubborn, glamorous, always wore high heels, and did not bow her head to anybody," said Gene Davis. "That represented a lot to black women who, like my mother, were in the workforce already, and not necessarily as maids."

The animosity she faced from other corners didn't surprise him. "In Philadelphia, where I'm from, all of us were considered to be 'uppity' Negroes. Uppity in the sense that we had education, we set goals." As Horne began to speak out against the bigotry of Hollywood, Davis recalled a common response within her race: "Who do you think you are? You should be thankful!" The black modern dancer Carmen de Lavallade, who grew up in Los Angeles during the forties, saw the disdain: "I mean, black people didn't particularly like Lena Horne. She was fair-skinned, and they thought she was trying to pass."

Many Negro actors felt just as angry at Walter White. His one-eighth blackness helped place him under fire. Many actors accused him of trying to give the Hollywood Negro an "acceptable" Caucasian image—and put them out of work. Clarence Muse, who played Pullman porters in a host of films (including Alfred Hitchcock's *Shadow of a Doubt*), led the protests. Antipathy rose when White denounced all-black films, which he felt did nothing for the cause of integration.

Many of the black dailies supported him in his campaign against the "despicable, disgusting Uncle Tom roles," as the *Chicago Defender* called them. But Billy Rowe, of all people, accused him of being enamored of white Hollywood. The leader held firm. He wanted stereotypes out of the movies. Some of the actors who played them had formed their own Fair

Play Committee to rally for better roles. But White wanted no alliance with them. Horne attended some of their meetings, she said, and listened to them rail against her. How ironic, she thought, that her foes were helping maintain the antiquated system that had held them back.

Hattie McDaniel epitomized the type that White detested. In her biography of McDaniel, *Black Ambition, White Hollywood*, Jill Watts wrote of the actress's contempt for White; he'd spoken to her, as McDaniel put it, "with the tone and manner that a Southern colonel would use to his favorite slave." Every actor caught in her position would "welcome better parts," she added; meanwhile she'd done her best to dignify the roles she had.

She might easily have resented Horne, too. But of all the afflicted actors, McDaniel alone showed her some sympathy. Years later, Horne told Dick Cavett of receiving a note from McDaniel, inviting the young woman to her home. "She said to me, 'You're a very unhappy girl and I understand why. Your own people are mad at you. . . . But let me tell you, I have worn two hats.'" Onscreen, said the actress, "I am a fine black mammy. But I am Hattie McDaniel in my house, and I have a family I have taken care of very beautifully." She gave the confused Horne some advice: "Darling, don't let them break your heart. We just haven't learned yet how to stick together."

Long after she'd left M-G-M, Horne began telling a story that summed up her early dismay in Hollywood. It was set on New Year's Eve or Christmas Eve, sometimes in 1942, sometimes 1943. With repeated retellings, it grew into a tangled web of victimhood, centered around the pressure she'd felt as the film industry's chosen one. Four months after she'd gone west, said Horne, she "ran away and came east for Christmas. I wasn't supposed to, but I did." In her second memoir, she explained that she'd returned to New York to sing at a benefit for Café Society Downtown. Escorting her that night, she said, were singers Billy Daniels and Billy Eckstine. After the show, they went to a club to see Count Basie, and Horne ran into Charlie Barnet and Billy Strayhorn. It moved her to tears to see so many old friends, and Horne became more homesick than ever for New York.

In a later version of the story, told to deejay Jim Harlan, Horne had "just gotten off the train" from Los Angeles, "and I ran to the Theresa

Hotel, changed my clothes, and it was *cold*, it was freezing in New York. And I went right to Birdland." There, said Horne, she found Barnet, Daniels, Basie, and singer Dinah Washington. "They all said hello, and welcomed me. I began to have some champagne, and I started to cry and I said, 'I'm never going back there again!'

"They said, 'Come on, we gonna get you outta here 'cause you're gonna get drunk.' I got on this mink coat, the first one that I had ever had, that I paid for. And it was swingin' open. We're walking down Broadway in this freezing cold, and the wind is blowing the coat, and I'm hangin' onto Basie, and Billy Daniels on the other side, someone, maybe Billy Eckstine, I don't know. I said, 'I don't wanna go back. I hate it out there, I love New York! This is my town! I have no friends, I'm lonely, and what am I gonna do?' And Basie said, 'Listen here. We all don't get many chances. And you've been given this kind of unique opportunity to represent us, and you've got to be exemplary because it means something for some of your sisters that may come after.' He had never been that serious with me." In her memoir, the latter exchange took place in the lobby of the Theresa. The denouement was the same: Horne returned to Hollywood.

So much of the story seems improbable that one wonders if the incident ever happened. The singer had moved to L.A. in October of 1941 and joined M-G-M two months later; the passage of four months could not have brought her to Christmas. The club known as Birdland did not open until 1949—and on Christmas Eve or New Year's Eve, the jazz stars she named would surely have been working or at home with their families. Furthermore, Horne had signed a seven-year deal with M-G-M and could not have simply walked away.

She would always exaggerate her lack of friends in Hollywood. Hers included Vincente Minnelli, her accompanist Phil Moore, Billy Strayhorn, Cleo Hayes, and Alice Key. Her romantic life in itself was enough to keep her busy. But her story of that cold winter night attests to how ostracized she felt after just a year or so in Hollywood. Her star had just begun to rise, along with her ambition. But by the time she'd finished *Stormy Weather* and returned to M-G-M, she was already feeling the weight of the mantle she'd adopted. As she told Rex Reed in 1981, "The blacks were criticizing me, the whites were criticizing me, and I was always expected to be a glamorous black sex symbol who sang torch songs."

CHAPTER 8

IN A profile for the New York *Daily News,* "She's Nobody's Mammy," writer Frank Nugent had this to say about Lena Horne: "She is the nation's top Negro entertainer, and not in any Uncle Tom or Aunt Jemima sense. Her working dress is an evening gown, not a Mother Hubbard." One of Horne's few luxuries was Tiny Kyle, her resident maid, hairdresser, nanny, and secretary. Otherwise, the singer continued to live humbly in her small, rented house in the Hollywood Hills.

Other reporters took heed of her unlikely success story. That October, Horne appeared on the cover of the magazine *Motion Picture*—the first time a black actress had achieved that honor. Her look was admittedly Caucasian: Horne's high, swirled hairdo, built up with a fall, recalled Rita Hayworth in *Cover Girl,* one of the year's hits. But Sidney Skolsky's article applauded her for rising gracefully to heights unscaled by any other woman of her race. "She is unique because she is the only colored person who has sustained a career in Hollywood movies without becoming a comedy character or portraying servants," wrote Skolsky. He reported Horne's "great ambition . . . to use her talent and her success to win respect for her people." She meant it, but decades later she stated: "I must admit that was not my main motive."

The fact that M-G-M had signed her largely due to political pressure didn't help her feel too worthy. Judy Garland and Eleanor Powell were there because of their abilities; Horne saw herself as a token. "They told me that they *had* to use black people," she claimed. "It takes no talent, nothing unique, to be a symbol. . . . 'Anybody could take your place' was, implicitly, what was said to me. So, watch your step, be grateful, be modest. I never liked the role, but I had gone with it."

She had to admit that Louis B. Mayer treated her warmly. Tales of his scariness preceded him; actors were terrified to walk into his office with a request or complaint. "He yelled at everybody," said Esther Williams. Declining a role could bring suspension. Horne seldom ran into him, but when she did he went out of his way to make her feel welcome. She recalled Mayer as "a jolly, stout fellow with twinkly eyes" who would "smile and pat me on the back and say something like 'good girl.'" Mayer loved a schmaltzy tune, and he asked Horne to record one of his favorites, "I'll Get By," with the M-G-M orchestra just for him.

Horne complied, smiling all the way. To almost everyone else in Hollywood she kept up her guard. "Lena is not a particularly simple soul, nor an easy one to get along with," wrote reporter Robert Rice. That assessment had come from Horne herself: "I'm terrifically moody and sometimes I don't want to talk to anyone for two weeks at a time." She seemed much more comfortable with books—preferably murder mysteries and historical biographies—than with people; likewise, Horne went frequently by herself to the movies. "She gets loads of invitations," reported *Ebony*, "but has found that too many of them are from patronizing film celebrities who think it's 'daring' to have a Negro girl at a party."

Motion Picture's glowing feature brought a deluge of responses. Most of them, said the editor, were positive. Future casting director Joyce Selznick, the niece of producing mogul David O. Selznick, praised the magazine for its "brilliant display of Americanism in demonstrating so clearly your unbiased recognition of talent and beauty. . . . She is a credit to the industry and to herself . . . a gift to the public."

There were protests, too. One came unsigned from Hawkins, Texas: "I consider Lena Horne a good singer, but I also think all colored people should be kept in their place. . . . You picture her as if she were the same type of person as other actresses. . . . Try to keep her publicity and pictures off the front of your books. Such publicity is the cause of riots and is going to cause more."

Faced with such insults, Horne had to rise above them and never utter an untoward word, lest she sully the cause of racial dignity. She didn't know what an impact that and other articles about her were making on a young black woman in Harlem, Ruby Ann Wallace, who would later become famous as Ruby Dee.

"As a youngster first wanting to be an actress, I would get movie magazines," Dee recalled. "There weren't many heroines and heroes of color then, but I remember staring at Lena's picture for a long time, thinking she was so beautiful. Most black people couldn't get in movies, but around that time I was so encouraged and thrilled by Lena's success that I wrote a letter to a studio, thinking I was gonna be the starlet from the stables. I daydreamed about that, but it wasn't to be."

Horne had her own high marks to meet. "The studio is always after me to keep my weight down as I have a tendency to get fat," she told the *New York Amsterdam News*. In *Panama Hattie*, Horne had gone four pounds over her contracted weight of 122, and was ordered to lose them. The M-G-M physician prescribed weight-reducing amphetamines; her daughter, Gail, would recall seeing prescription pill bottles in the bathroom.

Already the pressure was wearing on her. Horne revealed a recurring nightmare to Frank Nugent: Stepping onstage, she starts to sing—and the audience stamps its feet so loudly they drown her out.

Even during an actual cabaret performance, she had the feeling that no one was listening. "White people just thought I looked good, sexy and all," she explained. "It didn't matter how I sounded." She yearned to prove she was more. To enhance her singing, she took piano lessons. To move better, she tried ballet. Hoping for substantial roles, she found an acting coach, while wishing that M-G-M would enroll her in the drama school on the lot. During the filming of *Stormy Weather*, the studio had announced that Horne would "have an important part" in *Girl Crazy*, a musical with a Gershwin score and Judy Garland and Mickey Rooney as stars.

The film happened without her, but the studio promised her other chances to act. For the rest of 1943 she stayed very busy. M-G-M featured her in five films, as a radiant diversion to brighten up often dull proceedings. Early that year Horne showed up in *Swing Fever*, a B comedy about a nerdy composer with psychic powers. The film was an excuse to showcase several top bandleaders: Kay Kyser, Harry James, Tommy Dorsey. In a musical that flimsy, anyone could be inserted, and *Swing*

Fever included a number of "strays" with whom M-G-M didn't know quite what to do. Ava Gardner, a contract player since 1941, took the uncredited role of a receptionist. Appearing more prominently was Mantan Moreland, a black funnyman who lent buffoonish merriment to several M-G-M films. Audiences knew him as Charlie Chan's chauffeur in that popular serial; he was also a fixture in race movies (like *Mantan Messes Up*), all-black westerns, and poverty-row horror films like *King of the Zombies*. Nearly always he depicted a servile, bug-eyed clown who fell apart under pressure.

Compared to him, Horne in *Swing Fever* seemed all the more magisterial. Gliding onto a nightclub floor, she sang "You're So Indiff'rent," recycled from *Blackbirds of 1939*. The scene looked like an experiment in how best to film her. Horne is shot from a variety of angles, and looks stunning in all of them. Her modest bosom is padded, but her skin tone is unaltered. The lighting seems inspired by George Hurrell, an M-G-M photographer known for his shadowy, tempestuous portraits of film goddesses. To match that image, Horne sings with a bluesy group led by Phil Moore, the kind heard in mellow 2:00 A.M. sets on Central Avenue.

Swing Fever went little noticed. Before she filmed her appearance in the star-filled confection *Thousands Cheer*, Freed, Minnelli, and other creative forces conferred on how to present her. M-G-M crafted an image for all its discoveries; what would be Horne's? The studio had no black leading man to pair her with romantically, and still no clue how to mingle her with white actors. Horne's strengths—her looks and sultry singing—were obvious. With them in mind, the studio's creative resources came into play. The result was a star turn that took its place in M-G-M history. Aided by a sexy tune ("Honeysuckle Rose"), an arching row of mirrors, and Minnelli's direction, Horne created one of her signature moments.

Thousands Cheer bore no relation to the similarly titled 1935 revue that starred Ethel Waters. Its featherweight plot involved a circus acrobat (Gene Kelly) who gets drafted into the army; there he falls for the colonel's daughter, played by Kathryn Grayson, M-G-M's pert coloratura soprano. In the last quarter of the film, Mickey Rooney emcees a stellar camp show. He ushers on "a grand artist . . . the one and only Lena Horne, with Benny Carter and his band."

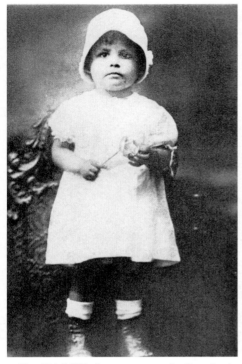

▲ The NAACP's "youngest member" made the organization's *Branch Bulletin* in 1919. She was fourteen months old in this photo.

▲ A sixteen-year-old Horne at the pool of Harlem's Colonial Park, 1933.

▲ The Cotton Club chorus line, 1934. Horne is fifth from left; her friend Ruby Allen (later Ruby Dallas Young) is third from left. *(Frank Driggs Collection)*

▲ In her first star turn, Horne had introduced "As Long As I Live" with Avon Long at the Cotton Club, 1934. They reprise it here at the Apollo. *(Frank Driggs Collection)*

▲ The king of black society bandleade Noble Sissle, hired Horne in 1935. *(Fra Driggs Collection)*

▼ Horne makes her Hollywood debut wi Ralph Cooper, the "Dark Gable," in *The Du Is Tops* (1938). *(Frank Driggs Collection)*

▲ An early Manhattan radio appearance, c.1941.

▶ Photographer-novelist Carl Van Vechten chronicled black cutural royalty, including Horne, shown in 1941 at the New Jersey training camp of her lover, boxing legend Joe Louis. *(Library of Congress)*

▲ Horne jams with her Café Society Downtown band (and guests) in 1941: (l-r) Don Byas, Buck Clayton, Red Allen, Tab Smith, Specs Powell, Count Basie, J. C. Higginbotham, Pete Johnson, Kenny Kersey. *(Frank Driggs Collection)*

▲ In this early M-G-M makeup test, the studio searches for the right look for Horne. *(Photofest)*

◀ Horne and the love of her life, her father, Teddy Horne, in Hollywood, 1942.

▲ Horne gets M-G-M's glamour treatment in 1942.

▶ "Who's the new Latin singer?" wondered some of those who saw Horne sing "The Sping" in *Panama Hattie* (1942). *(Stephen Bourne Collection)*

▼ Surprisingly, censors approved Horne's opening scene in *Cabin in the Sky* (1943), a presumably postcoital moment with the devil (Rex Ingram).

Breaking the color barrier at the Café ...unge of New York's Savoy-Plaza Hotel, ...uary 1943.

The film that made Horne an interna-...al star in 1943. *(Eric Kohler Collection)*

STORMY WEATHER

with LENA **HORNE**
BILL **ROBINSON**
CAB **CALLOWAY** AND HIS BAND
KATHERINE **DUNHAM** AND HER TROUPE
FATS **WALLER** NICHOLAS BROTHERS

DIRECTED BY ANDREW **STONE** PRODUCED BY WILLIAM **LeBARON**
SCREEN PLAY BY FREDERICK JACKSON & TED KOEHLER
ADAPTATION BY H.S. KRAFT
20th CENTURY-FOX PICTURE

From *Stormy Weather. (Eric Kohler Collection)*

▲ Gowned by M-G-M's Helen Rose, Horne purrs "Honeysuckle Rose" in *Thousands Cheer* (1943). *(Stephen Bourne Collection)*

▲ Horne was the sweetheart of the Tuskegee Airmen, America's first black pilots. In 1943, she made one of many visits to their Alabama airfield. *(Craig Huntly Collection)*

▶ During "Food for Freedom Month" (December 1943), Horne pitches in "to emphasize food's importance to the war," wrote the *New York Amsterdam News*.

▲ Horne's maestro from the 1940s, Phil Moore, accompanies her in "Trembling of a Leaf," an outtake from *Two Girls and a Sailor* (1944). Olinette Miller plays harp, Aaron Walker guitar. *(Tom Toth Collection)*

▶ In *Broadway Rhythm* (1944), Horne sang and danced the "Brazilian Boogie." *(Stephen Bourne Collection).*

▲ A vault fire destroyed an outtake of "Liza" from *Ziegfeld Follies* (1945). Avon Long did the singing; Horne's friend Avanelle Harris is fourth from left. *(Hilary Knight Collection)*

◄ Singing "Love" in *Ziegfeld Follies*. *(Stephen Bourne Collection)*

▼ Horne and Paul Robeson review plans in New York for a Madison Square Garden rally to combat African famine, June 15, 1946. *(Courtesy of Esther Cooper Jackson)*

◄ At M-G-M with ace vocal arranger Kay Thompson during the filming of *Till the Clouds Roll By*. (Photof

► Horne sings "Bill," the *Show Boat* torch song, in a lost outtake from *Till the Clouds Roll By* (1946). *(Stephen Bourne Collection)*

◄ In France for the first time, December 1947.

► Just wed in a secret Paris ceremony, Mr. and Mrs. Lennie Hayton dock in New York, December 22, 1947.

A smiling Carter appears, blowing his sax against a black background. His musicians, holding gleaming gold instruments, appear in a blossoming circle around him. The effect is of a black velvet jewel box opened to reveal its treasures. The camera pulls back to reveal a semicircular backdrop of eight full-length mirrors, separated by purple satin curtains.

From out of the center emerges Horne in a white toga-style dress. As she sings demurely of her "sugar" who makes "flowers droop and sigh," she sashays back and forth in front of the mirrors, which reflect eight Lena Hornes. Her movements are graceful, her sex appeal aloof—so different from the red-hot mama image of the black female entertainer. At the end, her face fills the screen—a vision of creamy skin, gleaming white teeth, and glowing eyes. Audiences had never seen such a sight before—a black woman as Venus, flaunted in full Technicolor glory. A *New York Times* critic wrote that Horne deserved a "bouquet" for her "haunting" performance.*

Louis Johnson, a choreographer of ballet and theater starting in the fifties, was a little boy in Washington, D.C., when *Thousands Cheer* hit the screen. He never forgot the tingle Horne gave him. "I had friends who would say, 'Lena's coming in a movie! Lena's coming in a movie!' There'd never been anybody like that. The look, the face, the body, the presentation. It touched us to see that kind of beauty and artistry in one of our own."

In May of 1943, before the film's release, Horne entered a screening room to watch the rushes of "Honeysuckle Rose." Several people were seated as Horne took a chair in the back and watched her sexy scene. At the end she heard a man's voice from out of the dark joking about the censors: "They'll raid the joint." She wondered who'd said it—and without quite knowing what he meant, she was offended.

The lights rose, and she saw Lennie Hayton, one of the Freed Unit's prize musical directors. At thirty-six he was clearly a man of the world; his graying Vandyke goatee and cool wit earmarked a figure whom many called "distinguished." On his head he wore a captain's cap, rakishly tilted. Arthur Laurents, who would later know him well, recalled Hayton's "very laid-back charm" as "captivating."

*The Broadway director-choreographer Michael Bennett acknowledged having used it as the inspiration for "The Music and the Mirror," dancer Donna McKechnie's showstopper in the 1975 musical *A Chorus Line*.

It wasn't Horne, at least not on that day. She admitted later that most men—especially white ones—aroused her suspicion, and she took an instant dislike to this one. "I had watched him walk around the studio lot with his nose in the air, and I thought, that's the most arrogant man I ever saw. And he thought I was too, obviously." Most of M-G-M had gone to see Horne at the Little Trocadero, but not Hayton. His indifference irked her; it also suggested some attraction. And his innocent wisecrack in the screening room had miffed Horne; did he think she was some kind of trollop? She had a typically defensive reaction: "I hated him."

Subsequently, Minnelli took her to one of the Hollywood parties she'd grown to dread. The hosts were Ella Logan, a Scottish-born singer-actress employed by M-G-M, and her husband, Fred Finklehoffe, who produced and wrote films for the studio. The Finklehoffes were firm liberals and became her friends. But as Horne walked into a roomful of white movie people, smoking, drinking, and laughing, she felt immediately ill at ease. She spotted Hayton at the piano, supplying cocktail music. Occasionally he chatted with his pal Rags Ragland, a burlesque comic on M-G-M's roster.

Ragland began entertaining the crowd with jokes, one of them racist. Horne turned to Minnelli and demanded he take her home. He led her out quickly. In the safety of the car she lashed out. Every time she went to one of these events, something like this happened; from now on she'd just stay home. Minnelli tried to soothe her, but Horne was shaking with rage. Lennie Hayton, she added disgustedly, was a friend of Rags. Now she loathed him even more.

On the lot, Horne groused about him to Kay Thompson, M-G-M's flamboyant wizard of a vocal coach and arranger. Thompson had sung on the radio under Hayton's baton, and she adored him; nobody, she insisted, played better piano for a singer.

Horne wouldn't listen. But her attitude changed about three weeks later during production of *I Dood It*, a fluff musical that starred Red Skelton and Eleanor Powell. Horne had one number, "Jericho," a biblical saga set to the hot sounds of Harlem. Vincente Minnelli placed Horne against a heavenly, star-filled sky. Hazel Scott played boogie-woogie piano, a gospel chorus sang Kay Thompson licks, and a trumpeter (Freddie Trainer) *wah-wah*'d in Louis Armstrong style.

The presentation was pure M-G-M, slick and whitewashed. Even so, it represented an attempt to salute black culture in a white musical, and Horne loved the song.

At the prerecording session on May 24, 1943, Horne surprised everyone by belting "Jericho" as fervently as though she were at a gospel service. But the session dragged on until nightfall, led by a conductor none of the participants liked. At one point Horne turned around, and there was Hayton in the corner, watching her. Thompson, playing matchmaker, had invited him. "If Lennie was doing this, we'd have been finished in two hours!" announced Thompson in her raucous voice. Finally they got a decent take, and everyone headed out to unwind at "this little joint that let me come in," as Horne called it.

Once settled in, she and Hayton got to talking. He wryly told her why he'd never come to the Little Troc. He'd heard such raves that he thought, "She can't be *that* good!" Horne's snap judgment of him began to soften: "I'd thought he was very, very snobbish and grand; he was just being quiet." She noticed how "civil" he was toward her. "If somebody was understanding and kind to me I liked them," she explained.

The club had a piano, and Hayton sat at it. "He played for hours and I sang," remembered Horne. "We got to be friends that evening." Soon they became more than that.

Try as she did, she couldn't find a hint of condescension in this white man. Hayton, she learned, had grown up in a liberal Jewish family that held artists in high esteem and lacked even a hint of bigotry. Born in 1908 of Russian-Jewish parents and raised on the Lower East Side, Leonard George Hayton entered the top ranks of jazz at a time when the art form was still young. From 1928 through 1930 he played piano with the nationally renowned "King of Jazz," bandleader Paul Whiteman. One of Whiteman's vocalists, Bing Crosby, left the band and hired Hayton as conductor; from there the musician's career soared. Hayton recorded with Bix Beiderbecke, the most esteemed white trumpeter of the day; he swung the baton on the most popular musical show on radio, *Your Hit Parade;* then he formed his own orchestra.

Horne's eyes widened when he told her he'd arranged a record she loved, Artie Shaw's 1941 version of "Star Dust." That year Hayton joined the Freed Unit. He helped create the studio's sound track style: "very glittery," as Horne described it, with clouds of strings and a larger-than-life Hollywood lushness. His colleagues called him a musician's musician, ever tasteful and meticulous; singers felt as though he'd wrapped them in a comforter. Eventually he won Oscars for *On the Town* (1949) and *Hello, Dolly!* (1969).

In a business full of flashy poseurs, Hayton was his own man, cool and assured, with nothing to prove. He played chess and treated social drinking as an art, knowing all about fine liqueurs and mixing a Martini with the same care he gave his arrangements. A Camel cigarette burned perpetually in his right hand. Horne learned that she and Hayton had the same taste in food and books; his refined piano playing reminded her of Billy Strayhorn's.

It was her most promising romance to date, save for a couple of issues. They were a mixed-race couple, working for a studio that shuddered at the faintest whiff of scandal. "When we knew that we were going to like each other it began to be uncomfortable," Horne said. Her affairs with Shaw and Welles had more or less escaped notice; now, to avoid inflaming M-G-M—and the public—she would have to be careful. When the couple ventured out to restaurants or jazz clubs, Minnelli came along as a beard.

A greater problem existed. Horne was still married, and Hayton was too, though none too happily. His wife, Helen "Bubs" Gelderman, was a former Ziegfeld dancer and the ex-wife of Ted Husing, a famous sports announcer who'd once numbered Hayton among his closest friends. Then the conductor married Helen just two years after the divorce. Husing never spoke to him again.

A tense situation grew messy on October 6, 1943, when Gelderman died suddenly at thirty-seven. Her death certificate listed "coronary stenosis and sclerosis"—a heart attack—as the cause. But gossip swirled around the M-G-M lot that Hayton's affair had so shattered her that she'd killed herself or succumbed to the trauma. Some people made even darker speculations. "It was the rumor at M-G-M that Lennie had knocked off his wife to marry Lena," said Hugh Martin, one of the studio's pet composers. "I don't believe it, of course, but that was what a lot of people thought, because she died mysteriously." Film actor Van Heflin, a friend of Gelderman's, reported the death. Where was Hayton?

Years later, a pal of the conductor's, columnist Gary Stevens, asked him what had happened. "I don't want to talk about it," snapped Hayton.

In years to come, Horne would doctor the chronology of their romance, inserting a year between the "Honeysuckle Rose" screening and the start of the affair. In her revised account, the two kept snubbing each other until Hayton passed her one day on the lot and said, "Hello, girl." At that moment, claimed Horne, "he looked at me and I looked at him and you know, the spark happened." At other times she described sitting in the commissary with a shifting selection of friends, including Vincente Minnelli and Lela Simone, a sound editor with the Freed Unit. Hayton wandered over to say hello—and then came the epiphany.

Resistance to the relationship began immediately, right in the singer's own home. Her dear Edwina, said Horne, was "violently prejudiced" against whites and told her this affair would end her career and leave her bereft. Hayton, she insisted, wanted just one thing. Horne tried to defend him, but Edwina wouldn't listen. Finally the older woman moved out.

For the time being no marriage occurred, but not because Hayton didn't want it. Horne doubted his sincerity, and feared for her professional life. The affair went on, but discretion was paramount, for Louis Jones had stepped up his divorce actions. Jones had moved to the Columbus, Ohio, area, taking Teddy with him. He got a job working in the ad department of a newspaper. In August 1943, on the day *Stormy Weather* opened in Columbus, he refiled his petition, suing her for desertion. As before, he insisted on keeping Teddy, but not Gail. The singer quickly filed a countersuit, charging him with cruelty and asking the court to drop his suit.

She lost, and the fight grew nastier. On November 13, 1943, the *Pittsburgh Courier* reported that Jones would now "seek an accounting of the screen star's earnings since she made her Hollywood movie debut." He would try to have her money declared community property, and demand his piece—unless she dropped her charges. Spite almost certainly drove his actions; it may have influenced Horne's, too, in not wanting him to have Teddy.

But Jones knew he had the upper hand. His wife dropped her charges, asking only for visitation rights. Still, the divorce would stay unresolved for months, and Horne put off Jones and his lawyers for as long as possible.

Reports of their war appeared regularly in the black newspapers. But for the public at large, Horne continued to play the part of a superbly diplomatic symbol. In October 1943, she told the *New York Amsterdam News* about life in Hollywood: "I do think there has been a tremendous improvement in the use of Negroes. I have been handled very well by my studio. And I hope the way I have been treated will mean more for all people."

Horne had just finished work on her latest film, *Broadway Rhythm*. Like *Swing Fever*, it offered a pastiche of production numbers strung together by a thread of plot. *Broadway Rhythm* starred George Murphy, a B-movie hoofer and future Republican senator, and Ginny Simms, a Dinah Shore–inspired radio songbird whom Mayer hoped, in vain, to launch as a movie star.

The script had included a small part for Horne—that of Fernway de la Fer, a society doyenne. She would work opposite her only available foil, Eddie Anderson. They made an odd couple onscreen, but affection showed in their eyes when they looked at each other. They prerecorded a comic duet. In "Tête à Tête at Tea Time," Horne, dainty as a debutante, invites the gauche Anderson over for crumpets and "a delicious spot of tea." But what he really wants is a heap of "solid po-*tay*-to salad ... mixed with *my*-o-naise, cole slaw on de side!" It sounds so good that Horne ditches the Emily Post routine and chimes in, "Let's stash this tea and talk about de spuds!"

The scene amusingly illustrated the clash between the accepted black guard in Hollywood and the new one led by Horne. The duet never made it to film, though, and no one could quite remember why. Was it due to space (the crowded final cut of *Broadway Rhythm* ran almost two hours) or a fear of how southern bigots might react to an "uppity" black woman showing a servant type how to act like a socialite?

Horne was still billed in the credits as Fernway de la Fer, but without "Tête à Tête at Tea Time" the name meant nothing. *Broadway Rhythm* showed her once more as a nightclub singer. Her polite version of a Tin Pan Alley standard, "Somebody Loves Me," made little mark. Not so "Brazilian Boogie," a Latin-style novelty. In tropical attire, including a midriff-baring yellow halter top, Horne slinked around in front of a male trio of black dancers (including Leonard Bluett) and sang of a new dance craze that was "twice as nice as a samba or a rumba."

Like "The Sping" in *Panama Hattie,* the scene might have been aiming to make Horne seem vaguely (and safely) Latin. But the young Gene Davis and his family never doubted that Horne was one of their own. "Every time Lena was in a movie we went to see it, as did every black person that I knew," he said. "She was the most beautiful creature we'd ever seen in our lives. Imagine, a generation of black women now seeing themselves as more beautiful than Greer Garson, more beautiful than Lana Turner."

No one had quite understood what black beauty meant; now Horne was in a position to define it. Geoffrey Holder, the dancer, choreographer, and director, recalled the "strong impact" Horne had on his country—Trinidad—during World War II. "She was a revelation," he said. "Lena was so stylish, so beautifully dressed in *Stormy Weather* and *Cabin in the Sky,* that everybody's daughter wanted to look like her." In a sense, he said, they already did, "because everyone in Trinidad is multiracial. They're Creole, Indian marrying Chinese, Chinese marrying blacks, blacks marrying Portuguese."

In the States, the standards of beauty were far more rigid, most of them applying to Caucasian features and ignoring other races. Jeanne Noble, a black feminist scholar who grew close to Horne in the sixties, wrote of a "Lena Horne syndrome" that emerged early in the singer's career. It involved "white preference for a black woman who was as much a carbon copy of a white female beauty as possible, with a few exotic quirks thrown in." That look became widely and sometimes harshly emulated in the black community. Skin-bleacher ads continued to fill the rear sections of magazines such as *Ebony* and *Our World;* so did offers for hair-straightening hot combs, creams, and gels. Flat, lustrous hair like Horne's was known as "good hair"; the coarser, more Afro-like kind was called "nappy," a term generally accompanied by a grimace. In 1992, Karen Grigsby Bates, a black correspondent for NPR, had told the *Los Angeles Times* of how a Negro woman of the fifties typically avoided going out in the rain without her head covered tightly. "The one thing she did *not* want her hair to do was get wet and 'go back'—as in back to its natural, unstraightened state."

In those days, black female performers who didn't "look like Lena Horne," wrote Noble, "were pushed into the background unless pure talent and a wide acclamation by blacks stormed through and demanded that attention be paid."

Early on at M-G-M, a sense of all this began to creep into Horne's consciousness. She knew she was the white person's "daydream" of a black woman, and again, it had nothing to do with her talent: "It was because of the way I looked."

By the end of 1943, M-G-M still hadn't found another role for her, so the studio kept groping for creative ways to showcase her in cameos. Like "Ain't It the Truth," some of these numbers took chances. Horne showed up in *Two Girls and a Sailor,* which starred Gloria DeHaven and June Allyson as singing sisters who launch a wartime canteen. At one of their USO shows, Horne is announced in a manner that demanded respect: "*Miss* Lena Horne." Out she glides onto a bare dance floor to sing "Paper Doll," a hit of the day. A white soldier, played by Tom Drake, gazes spellbound from the audience—a daring sight in an age when the Breen office threatened to ax any scene that even hinted at miscegenation.

Somehow the shot escaped the censors, perhaps because *Two Girls and a Sailor* itself wasn't much of an event. *Stormy Weather,* though, had made her internationally known. To further the diplomatic spirit that had made M-G-M hire her—and also, no doubt, to help entice black ticket buyers—the studio made her its goodwill ambassador for the Negro people. Sent out to sing in USO shows and army hospitals, Horne plunged into the war effort. For a time she appeared weekly—even on Christmas Day—at the Hollywood Canteen, a nightclub for servicemen founded and staffed by movie stars. *Lion's Roar* touted her efforts: "Lena goes anywhere, anytime, at the lift of a telephone receiver, if it's to entertain servicemen or workers in vital industry."

Those patriotic trips revealed how famous she'd become. On *Mail Call,* a weekly all-star cavalcade produced by the Armed Forces Radio Service, actress Ann Rutherford introduced Horne as "a gal who really keeps the APOs and FPOs [military mail services] working overtime. The poor postmen may be a little worn out, but it's your letters that keep bringing her back to GI microphones over and over again." Bing

Crosby and Bob Hope ushered her onto another starry AFRS variety show, *Command Performance,* by chanting, "We want Lena! We want Lena!"

Letters poured in by the sackful when Horne became a regular on *Personal Album.* On each fifteen-minute installment, a sexy-voiced girl singer flirted with the boys from afar and sang their requests. Horne's many appearances on the show embodied a bold step forward. Here was a black woman romancing soldiers of all races, with no apparent controversy. She teased them at the top of each visit with "Paradise," a come-hither love song full of orgasmic sighs. "Fellas, this is Lena . . . Lena *Hawwn!*" she purred, her slight drawl bespeaking a wide-eyed, eager-to-please southern belle. Never commercially issued, those performances show her in a more playful, freewheeling mood than anything she'd recorded commercially. Her Cotton Club star turn, "As Long As I Live," found her improvising with a swinging beat; though not a jazz singer per se, Horne had begun absorbing the influence of the jazzmen behind her.

Mike Jackson, an AFRS engineer, recalled her polite formality in the studio; she called him Mr. Jackson—"although I was an unranked sailor"—and he addressed her as Miss Horne. From the moment the recording began, he said, Horne "put such warmth, intimacy, and sex into her voice that you had to smile. But when we signed off at exactly fourteen minutes, fifteen seconds, she shed one personality to take on another. She seemed tired and worried. But Miss Horne was not a woman to invite confidences."

If Hollywood often depressed her, and her marital life was a shambles, the war gave her a cause she embraced. In 1942, M-G-M had begun sending her to black army camps around the country. There she entertained the troops with a more open heart than she could ever muster for a white cabaret crowd. To these beleaguered servicemen, often decried by bigots as inferior to the task of defending their country, Horne meant more than a sexual fantasy. They saw a determined fighter, a young Negro who had forged her way to the top, and who signaled change for the future. They named guns and planes after her, christened an Italian mountainside path Lena Horne Lane, made her an honorary sergeant.

She became their wartime pinup girl; they taped her picture to the inside of their footlockers or carried it in their knapsacks. Richard Kenyada, the son of a black World War II soldier, recalled how his father, known as Buddy, loved to boast of having danced with Horne at a servicemen's club in Fort Lee, Virginia. Richard and his brother laughed. After their father died, Richard looked in his wallet, where he found tucked away a folded-up, yellowed slip of paper. On it, "written in beautiful script," he said, were the words: "To Buddy, save the last dance for me. Love, Lena Horne."

Horne made regular visits to Fort Lee and to another predominantly black camp at Fort Huachuca, Arizona. But her favorite military base was in Alabama, where the newly formed Tuskegee Airmen were making military as well as racial history. These were America's first black flyers, all of whom had enlisted in a segregated military. A four-million-dollar training complex and airfield had been built for them at Tuskegee, in part so that white pilots wouldn't have to mix with black ones.

"They were a group of young men like all other young men: cocky, ambitious, very sure of themselves," said Horne to Charles Hillinger of the *Los Angeles Times*. "They had this impossible dream of becoming pilots, fighting for their country." But it wasn't impossible. Between 1942 and 1946, nine hundred and ninety-two pilots graduated from the Tuskegee Army Flying School. Its squadrons set an unprecedented record of flying all its bomber missions without losing a single plane to enemy aircraft.

Horne had met the first airmen before they went to war and identified with them so powerfully she kept returning to Tuskegee for mutual morale boosting. She rose each day at six and stayed up until past midnight. Horne liked to eat lunch with the cadets rather than in the officers' mess hall; she crawled inside planes for lessons in how they worked. Each night, to the accompaniment of an army orchestra, she fox-trotted with one airman after another until her feet had blisters.

When he met Horne, Bill Broadwater was an eighteen-year-old Tuskegee cadet. He and two fellow soldiers had gotten the job of driving Horne in a jeep from the cafeteria to the officers' club, which was some distance away. "What impressed me about this beautiful woman was how calm and in control she was of everything," said Broadwater in 2007. "I grew up in a little country town in Pennsylvania, and I held her in complete awe. She was so natural, chatting away with us, answering all our dumb questions."

In her darker moments, she had trouble accepting the servicemen's adulation. The only reason the military had given her this job, she reasoned, was that it didn't want black soldiers ogling white pinup girls like Betty Grable. "The men who fantasized about me, M-G-M gave me to them; they didn't choose me," she insisted.

Nonetheless she sometimes paid her own way to visit the airmen. In February 1944, Horne served as guest of honor at a Tuskegee graduation. One morning at 3:00 A.M. the singer landed in a cold, mostly deserted Alabama airport; there she would board a connecting flight. Exhausted and shivering, she spotted an all-night diner. She sat timidly at the end of the counter. The waitress passed back and forth, ignoring her. Finally she asked the singer what she wanted. Just a cup of coffee, Horne answered. "I'm sorry," said the waitress. "I can't serve you."

Silently, Horne rose to leave. Then a teenage boy ran out of the kitchen. Excitedly, he asked if she was Lena Horne. She nodded. Would she sign a menu for him? Eyes lowered, Horne scrawled her name, then walked off as quickly as she could. The moment pointed up one of the painful ironies of her life. She was an M-G-M star, with more fan mail than she could answer, but couldn't order a cup of coffee in a southern airport. No amount of Hollywood pampering could ease the sting of rejection.

But the Tuskegee graduation helped. As she entered the mess hall, the airmen formed a tunnel of crossed swords for Horne to pass through on the way to her seat. The flyers had a white cocommander, Lieutenant Colonel Noel Parrish, who had earned their respect. At the time they joined, most of them heard tell that as Negroes they would "automatically be mistreated," as Broadwater said. But Colonel Parrish made good on his vow to look out for them. "He was gonna make this work," said Broadwater.

After Horne was in her chair, Parrish took his place at the podium. "I've given wings to a lot of you boys," he announced. "You've proven that, granted the opportunity, courage and gallantry—the will and the power to learn—aren't confined to one group of people. In her way, Miss Horne proves the same thing: that the charm and beauty of womanhood are not confined to any one race." He turned to Horne and asked her to stand. Then he pinned a pair of silver wings above her heart. She remembered thinking, "This is the payoff. I'll never be prouder."

Once home in California, though, she faced the renewed vengeance of Louis Jones, who wanted their divorce resolved. No more could Horne avoid him. "He was prepared to air all the dirty linen," recalled a friend of the singer's. "You know—'You do this, I'll go to the press with a list of all your lovers.' I think there was also a question of paternity in his mind. She couldn't have a big, messy divorce with a lot of headlines, so a deal was struck."

A hearing took place in May 1944. Horne didn't attend, but sent her lawyer. Both sides drew up a formal separation agreement. Jones won custody of Teddy, Horne of Gail. Each parent had visitation rights "and temporary care, custody and control" of the other child "for such periods of time as the parties may mutually agree." On June 15, after nearly four years of estrangement, Jones got his divorce. "The court finds that the defendant is guilty of WILLFUL ABSENCE for more than three years," read the decree. Horne, wrote a reporter, "did not contest the action."

Many years would pass before she publicly accepted her share of the blame. "I was a lousy wife for my first husband," she told writer Alan Ebert in 1973. "But, then, my mother was a lousy wife for her husband. She, too, didn't know how to cook, or do anything." Later, in an interview with *Family Circle*'s Glenn Plaskin, she claimed that Jones had effectively blackmailed her. Occasionally, said Horne, Jones turned over their son— "but when he got angry or wanted more money than I had he'd take Teddy back."

By 1947, she'd stopped fighting. Until his late teens, Teddy saw his mother only on certain holidays or during school vacation. The scars he bore from so much upheaval would take their toll. His mother couldn't shake her guilt. She wished she'd tried harder to keep him, but that wouldn't have helped; she couldn't dispute Jones's charge of desertion. "My son grew up as a partial stranger to me," she explained. "I kept up with his progress in school through lawyers and accountants."

After Edwina walked out on her, Horne had found a replacement nursemaid and companion. Ida Starks had a child of her own, but her husband had entered the army, and she shared Horne's loneliness. Starks and her young daughter moved in with Horne and took care of Gail (and sometimes Teddy). For years she would remain a source of "great, quiet strength," as Horne put it.

In the Christmas season of 1944, the singer left them all behind to go on a USO-sponsored camp tour of the South. She visited army bases and veterans' hospitals, and all went well. Everywhere she went, segregation rules were lifted so she could sing to interracial audiences.

Near the end of her journey, Horne set out for Camp Joseph T. Robinson in Little Rock, Arkansas. Her plane was grounded in Jackson, Mississippi, and in the airport lounge fans crowded around her, asking for autographs. A reporter from the *Atlanta Daily World* interviewed her briefly. Horne, he said, "lived up to her reputation as a lovable and gracious person," while "stating in her own words a deeply felt sense of responsibility to her own race."

No connecting flight was available; in order to get to Little Rock, Horne would have to travel in a segregated train car. She went. When she reached Camp Robinson, she encountered all the racism she'd thus far been spared. Both the *Chicago Defender* and the *Pittsburgh Courier* reported the details. The commanding officer's behavior toward her was "rude" and "unforgivable," she said; he even slammed a door in her face. Everywhere else, she felt a chill. Later, while singing in the military theater, Horne noticed someone at the entrance, charging admission for what should have been a free show. She delivered her songs to a sea of white faces.

Horne was angry. After the show, she demanded to know what had happened to the Negro soldiers. There were only fifty on the post, she learned, and nobody had informed them of her appearance; they weren't allowed in the theater. "The next day she insisted that a piano be sent to the mess hall of the colored troops," wrote the *Courier*, "and she put on a full show for them at breakfast." As she sang, she saw German prisoners of war crowding into the tent—"to the annoyance of the colored soldiers," the *Defender* noted. Horne was enraged. She stopped singing and called for the removal of the POWs. Her request was ignored, and she stormed off, wondering what kind of democracy this war was achieving.

According to the *Defender*, the army sent a plane to fly Horne back to California. But the singer told a different story. First, she said, she wired the Hollywood branch of the USO to tell them she was quitting the tour. Then she gathered up her bags and demanded a ride to the nearest NAACP office. One existed in Little Rock. There she received a warm greeting from Daisy Bates, an elegantly dressed woman of thirty. Bates managed to soothe the tearful singer; she certainly understood how Horne felt. As the publisher (with her husband, L. C. Bates) of the *Arkansas State Press,* a fearlessly outspoken civil rights newspaper, Bates witnessed racism at a level Horne had barely known: lynchings, bloody police brutality, unpunished murders of Southern blacks. Her own mother was a murder victim; she had died trying to resist three white rapists, all of whom went free. In 1957, Bates would suffer death threats and find herself hanged in effigy when she led the fight to integrate Little Rock's Central High School—a milestone in the civil rights movement.

Horne poured out her heart to Bates, then begged her to arrange a ride back to L.A. She took the first one available: "on a sort of cattle car," said Horne, "with a lot of black guys, soldiers on their way out west." Once home, she hurried to the local USO office and to the Hollywood Victory Committee and filed complaints. The USO, Horne claimed, reprimanded her for stepping out of line. For the rest of the war, she visited only black camps, and paid her own way.

PERHAPS to counter the publicity about its growingly angry young star, M-G-M's press department ground out puff copy about her, replete with fabricated quotes. A piece about Horne in *Lion's Roar* found her rhapsodizing about the Cotton Club in terms that ignored her true feelings. "So much fun and so much excitement went into those years that I am the happiest and most grateful girl in the world," the article read. *The Milwaukee Journal* published another studio-generated write-up, "Leapin' Lena Just Can't Stay Still." It read: "Lena Horne is a one-gal jam session. She dances or sings practically all the time she's awake."

In April 1945, Horne made the rounds of radio interview shows, reading sunny copy about her latest film project. "It's titled *Ziegfeld Follies,* and it should be swell!" she effused. "Working with me on the *Follies* are Fred Astaire, Judy Garland, Red Skelton, Gene Kelly, Esther Williams . . ."

Produced mostly in the latter half of 1944, but years in the planning, *Ziegfeld Follies* was Arthur Freed's brainchild. Its premise: The late Florenz Ziegfeld, the greatest Broadway producer of them all, grows wistful in heaven as he dreams of mounting one more of his legendary revues. Thus bagan an extravaganza of skits and production numbers—a wartime buffet of Hollywood treats that made every other studio pale by comparison. Lucille Ball, Fanny Brice, Van Johnson, Cyd Charisse, and William Powell appeared, too. "More stars than there are in heaven!" trumpeted *Lion's Roar*. "Melodies made immortal by world renowned composers—costumes of fabulous beauty—settings with all the magic of fairyland—plus the most beautiful girls in the world!"

Horne performed one number, "Love," which cut through the film's confectionary excess with the pungency that became her trademark. The song listed all the madly conflicting qualities of love; it could be "two hearts that flower as one," but just as often it was a "moment's madness" and a "dirty shame."

"Love" gave Horne a dramatic tour de force, and she vowed to make the most of it. She still suffered from an agonizing inferiority complex about her singing. Sometimes on the radio her voice cracked in midphrase; she cursed herself each time. "There are many great, great singers who can just naturally burst into song," she said later. "I couldn't do that."

Horne sought out coaching from a battery of pros, including the song's composer, Alabama-born Hugh Martin. He and his partner, Ralph Blane, had written the score for the M-G-M classic *Meet Me in St. Louis* (1944), in which Judy Garland introduced "The Boy Next Door," "The Trolley Song," and "Have Yourself a Merry Little Christmas." Martin was also an M-G-M vocal arranger held in high esteem. He adored Horne, and sometimes attended her recording dates at the studio. But his southern twang made her wary, and she kept a cordial, chilly distance.

She still wanted his advice. In their first meeting, Horne picked some sheet music off the piano and said, "Let's try this one." It was Martin and Blane's "That's How I Love the Blues" from their musical *Best Foot Forward*. She read through the lyric. "I'd had the stupidity to write this line: 'Like a darkie loves cornbread,'" said Martin in 2005. "Can you believe I was that ignorant? I had heard all these songs like 'That's Why Darkies Were Born,' and I thought that was an accepted word. She got to it and choked on it, and of course I could have killed myself. But she just said very politely, 'Do you mind if I don't sing this lyric?'"

Horne knew how much she had to learn before she could even approach Garland's robust vocal ease. Hayton tried to give her some confidence. "He played music for me, every kind," explained Horne in a 1981 TV interview with Gil Noble. "He explained music structurally and architecturally, which was a help to me. I was beginning to be a little brighter, and I could understand. I was always literate with the lyric. But he laid the cushion down, which all fine musicians do, and you don't have to worry about doing anything but what you do."

Horne studied the records of Ella Fitzgerald, and arranged frequent sessions with Kay Thompson, whom she later called "the best vocal coach in the world." Thompson had a strong influence on Garland, and tried to do the same for Horne. Seated at the piano, she guided her through a series of vocal exercises while trying to comfort the anxious singer: "It's there. We just have to bring it out."

Thompson had certainly dragged a lot out of herself. "The girl with rhythm to burn," as *Your Hit Parade*'s announcer had introduced her, was a live wire—a breathless bundle of high chic, over the top and effortlessly stylish in all she did, be it nightclub performing or her breakneck, syncopated vocal arranging. Blond and angular, she blew through the M-G-M lot like "a living tornado," as the Broadway conductor Buster Davis recalled. "She was a walking and talking *Vanity Fair* of the twenties and thirties," he said, "yet very shiny and new." In 1957, she would portray a character based on *Vogue*'s fashion doyenne Diana Vreeland in M-G-M's *Funny Face,* but she emerged as pure Kay Thompson—a role she devoted her life to playing. Even her most famous invention, Eloise, the precocious brat whose antics inside Manhattan's Plaza Hotel would sell millions of children's books, seemed like a junior alter ego of the author.

If Horne was in the process of self-creation, Thompson had such a tough veneer that few ever saw the woman underneath—the former Kitty Fink of St. Louis. Buster Davis found her "always on," lest anyone glimpse her in an unguarded moment. She even referred to herself in the third person. "Do you think that ending is right for her?" she once asked

Davis. "I think she needs a slower build before we hit the ride-out." But Thompson's know-how was for real, and to a young woman as uncertain as Horne, she offered an object lesson in barreling past one's fears. "I liked being around her and her husband, Bill Spier, who was also very bright," Horne said. "I was always trying to soak up other people's minds, you know?"

According to Hilary Knight, the illustrator who brought Eloise to life in four books, Thompson was "filled with admiration" for Horne, and "probably jealous." Thompson was "obsessed," he said, with her self-perceived homeliness, which included a long, mannish face and a badly altered nose. "Dressing bizarrely was a routine for her," explained Knight. "You couldn't miss her. When we were in Russia together she brought all these fezzes, and a vicuna coat; it was a big fluffy orange thing. She had a black knit dress and black stockings, covered with hair from her dogs. The Russians were just stunned by her; we'd walk down the street, and they'd never seen anything like this."

Thompson had a field day ridiculing almost every female star at M-G-M, even Garland. But in a 1945 interview with the fan magazine *Movieland,* she called Horne "sweet, generous, modest, considerate, gentle, wise, and cooperative." For years, rumor had it that her bond with Horne exceeded friendship. But Knight doubted that Thompson would have acted on any lesbian feelings, "Kay was a *complete* prude," he said.

Horne, whose sexual history marked her as anything but, remained in awe of her flashy friend. For her big number in *Ziegfeld Follies,* she had the support of M-G-M's best: Thompson, Hayton, Vincente Minnelli, arranger Conrad Salinger, and costume designer Helen Rose. This was the first M-G-M assignment given to Rose, who went on to outfit Elizabeth Taylor, Lana Turner, Doris Day, and many more in some of the studio's most sumptuous clothes ever. Enhancing a woman's legs was her specialty, and Rose did so repeatedly for Horne, who felt terribly self-conscious about hers. The rest of her body was problematic, too. She had "no tits and a fat ass," as she put it, and her waist was high. But Rose's wizardry spun the illusion that Horne had one of the best bodies on the lot.

It certainly looked that way in "Love." The scene took place in a West Indian bar, with hanging palm fronds and caged birds. An ensemble of exotic beauties is there to drink and cavort. One of them fights with her lover then flees, distraught. Out steps Horne from behind a slatted door—a tropical vision in a green-and-pink off-the-shoulder blouse with matching flowers in her hair. The bongos pulse, and she glides from table to table to tell everyone what love really is: a roller-coaster of high hopes and letdowns, all too beguiling to resist.

"Love" shows the breakthrough of a promising actress in song. Moving from cool to sarcastic to fiery to pleading, Horne voices the only cynical sentiments in the film, that love and sex are maddening and fantasies don't come true. Gene Davis called the direction "pure Minnelli—it's such an intricate minidrama, right down to the subtle light behind the bar and that live parrot."

Only studio insiders ever saw her other scene, a production number based on the Gershwin song "Liza." It found Avon Long serenading Horne as she smiled down from a veranda in nineteenth-century New Orleans. Nearly the whole set was made of white paper; black chorines surrounded Long as he danced and sang. Horne merely posed, smiled, and twirled a parasol. With the first edit of *Ziegfeld Follies* running approximately three hours, "Liza" was deemed dispensable. Subsequently the footage burned in an M-G-M vault fire; only stills survive.

The cutting of "Liza" devastated Long, who had helped give Horne her first big break at the Cotton Club but who couldn't get far in Hollywood. Neither could Avanelle Harris, one of the number's beautiful extras. In an autobiographical cover story for *Ebony*, "I Tried to Crash the Movies," she poured out her disappointment as she tried to reach beyond ensemble work. At twenty-eight, Harris had danced in dozens of films at Paramount, Fox, and M-G-M—quite an achievement for a black chorus girl of her day. Each foray onto a soundstage stoked her lifelong fantasies about Hollywood and its possibilities: "Hundreds of movie magazines. Glamour! Super-colossal! Everybody had a chance! . . . I was going to be a movie gal, a movie queen!"

But as she neared thirty, the calls grew fewer; roles that required the "exotic" look she offered tended to go to white actresses who were darkened with makeup. By the time she shot *Ziegfeld Follies*, Harris had given up. "I don't know why I keep hanging on for calls, knocking myself out for two days here, three days there," she said. "It looks like making a living in the movies is pretty much out." She never did another film.

Harris and every other black performer in Hollywood could only envy Lena Horne, whose success seemed unimaginable to them. Over a thousand letters filled her M-G-M mailbox per week—almost as many as June Allyson received. "I never thought I'd need a secretary, but this is getting beyond me," the singer told Frank Nugent.

Much fan mail came from the South, where she was known to have lived. Vernon Jordan was a child in Atlanta during Horne's movie hey-day. "In my little segregated elementary school we had Negro History Week," he explained. "And so you learned about Paul Robeson and Joe Louis and Booker T. Washington and Lena Horne." Hers, he said, "was just a name you knew. There was this great sense of pride in her accomplishments." Before the war ended, serviceman Hilary Knight peered out the window of a troop train as it barreled through the South. "I saw what was literally a shanty-shack movie house with a billboard reading LENA HORNE IN THE BRONZE VENUS," he said. *The Bronze Venus* was *The Duke Is Tops*, re-released by its producer and star, Ralph Cooper, to cash in on Horne's renown.

Others had similar ideas. Around that time, Edna Rodriguez made a jarring reappearance. When marriage took Lena away from show business there seemed little reason for Edna to stick around, so she moved to Cuba with her husband, Mike. Interracial marriage had posed no problem for her; Edna's fair skin had long enabled her to pass for white or Latin.

Edna had long abandoned her own ambitions; in their place was a bristling resentment of her daughter's success. Lena, she felt, owed her—and the allowance the young woman sent wasn't enough. One day, she called her daughter from a white hotel in downtown L.A. She demanded a meeting, but wouldn't say why. A nervous Horne had Lennie Hayton drive her to the hotel. Horne would not have been allowed inside, so she sent Hayton to fetch her mother and bring her to the car.

There ensued a brief, unpleasant reunion. Edna stated bluntly that she'd created Lena's career; now it was payback time. She wanted her shot at the movies, too, and insisted her daughter pave the way by phoning some producers. Horne refused. She had no clout, she argued, and few connections. The older woman wouldn't back down. Lena could help; she just didn't want to. Edna stormed out of the car.

Soon after that, Horne went on a singing tour. Ida Starks phoned her on the road with distressing news. Edna had come to the house and demanded her daughter's address book so she could call the producers herself. Starks refused, and Edna turned nasty. In her next conversation with Lena, she made her position clearer. If Lena didn't cooperate, she would sell the press a story about a selfish girl who'd climbed to stardom on her mother's shoulders, then tossed her aside. Edna was set to reveal other dirty secrets, too. Such an exposé would not only have hurt Horne's career, it would have shamed her in the face of the NAACP, the Urban League, and the public.

Edna would never have a film career, but she got a payoff in exchange for her silence. Horne noted tersely in her memoir, "I worked out a solution with a lawyer."

Her mother returned to Cuba, but by no means had Horne seen the last of her. Years after Edna's death in 1976, her behavior left a sting. As Horne told writer Marcia Ann Gillespie, "I understood my mother, but she didn't want to understand me. She in some ways was younger than I, in that she just wouldn't compromise; she was thwarted in what she wanted and nothing compensated. She didn't approve of the way I handled my career. She said she would have done it better."

Walter White was certainly proud of Horne, and of his own efforts. Dignified black characters had appeared in such films as *Sahara* (which starred Humphrey Bogart), *Crash Dive* (with Tyrone Power), and *The Clock* (directed by Vincente Minnelli). But less than two percent of the industry's 30,000 technical employees were black, while the clichéd figures—mammies, porters, dim-witted servants—remained on-screen.

The actors who played them continued to resent M-G-M's sole black star. Only her friends knew how frustrated Horne was, too, as dramatic roles eluded her. Her zooming popularity suggested that audiences wanted to see much more of her, but M-G-M still didn't know how to proceed. "Metro in the past has talked of finding the right part for her," wrote Frank Nugent, "but it isn't as simple as it seems. Pictures with all-Negro casts, like *Green Pastures, Cabin in the Sky*, and *Stormy Weather*, have relied on music or the plantation motif or both. Neither fits Miss Horne's bill."

Quite often someone at M-G-M posed an idea that made her hopes rise. For a while there was talk of having her star in a biopic of Florence Mills. Horne wanted it badly. As she humbly told a reporter, "Of course Miss Mills was a great natural artist, and I'm not. But how proud I'd be to play her, if only because my people loved and admired her so." The film never happened. But early in 1944, the studio hoped to star her in a grand-scale, Technicolor feature based on *Uncle Tom's Cabin,* Harriet Beecher Stowe's bestselling novel about plantation days, published before the Civil War. The book argued powerfully against the slave system, but it also romanticized a gallery of stereotypes: the doting mammy; the pickaninny children; the title character, a humble slave. M-G-M had cast Lewis Stone (Judge Hardy from the *Andy Hardy* film series) as Uncle Tom's master. Child actress Margaret O'Brien would play Little Eva, an angelic waif whom Tom saves from drowning.

Leon H. Hardwick of the *Atlanta Daily World* decried the project to its producer, Simon Hornblow. "We tire of seeing ourselves depicted constantly as bootblacks, porters, maids, and now—of all things—as slaves." Hornblow countered that *Uncle Tom's Cabin* had the historical relevance of *David Copperfield.* The film, he said, would make a strong case for freedom.

Soon he realized the futility of his effort. Horne turned down the role of Eliza, a fugitive slave; Paul Robeson refused to play Uncle Tom. News of the movie had brought a stinging backlash from the liberal black community. Hornblow had to admit defeat: "We just presumed that, because *Uncle Tom's Cabin* is such a wonderful classic and so popular, even today, that a film version of it would be widely accepted by all people."

Having filmed a half-dozen nonspeaking appearances, Horne had begun to fear that M-G-M would never award her a serious part. She vented her frustration to David Hanna of the *Daily World:* Why couldn't a Negro girl be cast as a doctor's assistant, an elevator operator? Why couldn't she be written into a mystery? A detective could come to her home to question her; through her answers, Horne said, "one could note that her home and business life are normal, decent, and intelligent."

Stymied executives asked Horne for ideas. She proposed films based on George Washington Carver, or Harriet Tubman, or Toussaint L'Ouverture, the slave who led a revolution to drive Napoleon out of

Haiti. All were considered, none filmed. Several announced roles had already vanished. "The same thing happened to every star," explained John Fricke, the author and M-G-M expert. "Countless projects were rumored or purchased or went into development or scripting and were then abandoned. It was rougher on Lena because *comparatively* so little evolved."

In her case, of course, M-G-M had special worries. Foremost among them was the frequent clash between what would sell versus what would serve the cause of social justice. *Cabin in the Sky* was a starrily cast musical, nonoffensive to the masses. But the studio feared what might happen to a film's distribution—especially down South—if a nonstereotypical black were mingled with whites. "I suspect she might have heard a lot of talk around the Freed Unit: 'Oh, we're gonna get you this part, you'd be perfect for that part,'" said film critic Richard Schickel. "They got her hopes up." The executives, he felt, meant no harm. "They were kindly and supportive. They had an investment in her, right? But Lena was preternaturally touchy. Things that M-G-M would have thought meant nothing, she took personally."

Several times a week she sat in movie theaters, watching white starlets of lesser esteem get the chances she craved. She found it hard to contain her anger. After interviewing the singer in September 1944, a *New York Amsterdam News* reporter called her a "victim" of M-G-M. The studio, she complained, rented her out to nightclubs or to other film companies for four-figure weekly sums; she received $450. That was the deal Horne had made, and it differed little from that of most of her peers. But "the songstress . . . feels she has been sold down the river," announced the *Amsterdam News.* "Miss Horne . . . is doing a quiet burn wondering if this Hollywood is worth the effort."

Kay Thompson's husband tried to help. William Spier produced "Radio's Outstanding Theater of Thrills," *Suspense.* The award-winning CBS series had drawn the likes of Cary Grant and Orson Welles as stars, and Thompson had convinced Spier to give Horne a chance. On November 9, 1944, she starred in *You Were Wonderful,* a tale of overseas espionage. Horne played Lorna Dean, a black singing star who visits Buenos Aires and accepts a fee in order to spy for the Germans. When Dean sang a certain line on a broadcast, an enemy submarine would bomb an American fleet. The surprise comes at the end: Dean has tipped off the Allies, who sink the deadly sub just in time.

"Her performance should open the eyes of the casters at the M-G-M studios," announced the *Atlanta Daily World*. But rather than displaying a gifted and neglected actress, *You Were Wonderful* exposed Horne's weakness at delivering lines. Racism has made Lorna Dean a "coldhearted little dame," as another character calls her. "I'm an entertainer, because I like it," she tells a fellow spy. "It's the only way I can make enough money to live halfway like a human being. With money I can do what I want to . . . more or less. I can live where I want to, go where I want to, and be like other people . . . more or less. Do you know what even that much freedom means to somebody like me?"

Voicing those defiant words, Horne—with her lifelong training in politeness—could only sound like the ingenue she'd never wanted to be. She attempted sarcasm; it came out with a vampish tinge of Mae West. The show suggested what the years bore out—Horne was a compelling actress in song, but not with a script. M-G-M could have trained her at its acting school, but didn't. Instead, Freed kept searching for the part he thought would suit her. In early 1945, he found what seemed like a perfect fit. He announced it with pride. That year, Horne would star on Broadway in *St. Louis Woman*, an all-black musical that he would produce. Set in the bars, racetracks, and dance halls of turn-of-the-century St. Louis, the show would boast a score by Harold Arlen and Johnny Mercer, the tunesmiths who had recently penned "That Old Black Magic." Horne would play Della Green, a femme fatale who sparks a love triangle between L'il Augie, a lovable jockey, and saloonkeeper Biglow Brown.

The role scarcely differed from Georgia Brown. But Horne could handle its modest acting demands, and she would surely stop the show with Arlen and Mercer's songs. What's more, the book came from two distinguished children of the Harlem Renaissance, Arna Bontemps and Countee Cullen.

Freed was so sure he'd found a hit that he and Sam Katz, an M-G-M vice president, formed an outside company to mount the show. They teamed with Edward Gross, a top Broadway producer, and raised money based on Horne's name; Freed even invested some of his own.

He moved forward based on Horne's consent. But he also wanted to obtain the blessings of the key black organizations, to avoid any possible embarrassment or bad publicity. Freed sent the script to Walter White—and the response stunned him. White called the project "sordid," and lashed out his opposition. The story, he wrote, "pictured Negroes as pimps, prostitutes, and gamblers with no redeeming characteristics." Lena Horne could never stoop to such a vehicle.

The Interracial Film and Radio Guild agreed. Apart from the "atrocious dialect" employed by Cullen and Bontemps, the script was "an insult to Negro womanhood," declared the reader, "in that it depicts the principal character of Della as a good-looking but loose woman of the sporting variety whose chief ambition is to have and be had by the gambler with the most money." To star in such a debacle would do grave harm to Horne, who had "become something of an idol to her people, a symbol of the highest type of Negro womanhood."

Cullen and Bontemps, of course, were anything but bigots. To them, *St. Louis Woman* stood as an honest portrait of a moment in history. The show, added Bontemps, "has nothing to do with the weightier problems of our day. It is a love story. Its theme is the struggle of simple people to add a note of grace and beauty to the dark tones of life as they know it. I hope this subject is still admissible."

But in that hot-button time of extreme sensitivity to the depictions of blacks, the show had danger written all over it. With so much pressure to decline the part, Horne faltered. Aspects of the script offended her, but *St. Louis Woman* had clear assets, and a young black actress of the day couldn't have hoped for a better star turn. To say no would prove terribly painful. Horne resisted giving a definitive answer for weeks. M-G-M's executives asked her if the reluctance was hers, or if the organizations were pushing her around. Horne answered vaguely.

According to the *Chicago Defender,* she went to New York to meet with Cullen, Bontemps, and Edward Gross, maybe to discuss a way to salvage the script. But Walter White remained dead set against the project, and Horne knew she could not cross the NAACP.

The *Defender* reported that her Manhattan conference didn't happen; at the last minute, apparently, she had "refused to see any of them." In September 1945, newspapers announced her decision on *St. Louis*

Woman. Her words, as quoted, were startling. The show, she said, "sets the Negro back a hundred years"; it was "full of gamblers, no-goods, and I'll never play a part like that." Walter White would later state that he'd "defended Lena Horne's refusal to play in it."

Horne had done her civic duty, but she'd hated it. M-G-M wasn't happy, either. After all of Freed and Mayer's efforts to glorify Horne on-screen, her printed comments had made them look like racists. Years later, Harry Levette, theater editor for the *Los Angeles Sentinel,* interviewed Freed in his office about Horne and *St. Louis Woman.* The producer was so dismayed he talked for an hour. After word of her refusal had hit the press, Horne, said Freed, had come to his house to talk. "She actually cried," said Freed. Horne told him that activists had been writing her letters calling her a "harlot" for wanting to star in *St. Louis Woman,* and telling her she was shaming her people. According to Freed, Horne said she would have loved to do the part, which she didn't find especially distasteful. Freed quoted Horne's words: "But it looks like I'll have to give it up."

In October, Walter Winchell wrote that M-G-M had placed Horne on suspension—standard practice when a contract player refused an assignment. It's unlikely the item was correct. Horne had turned down a Broadway show that Freed would produce himself, independent of M-G-M. Possible plans to adapt it for the screen had never passed the talking stages. What's more, Mayer knew he couldn't suspend Horne for taking such an ostensibly valiant stand. If he did, the wrath of the black community would be upon him.

But White only knew what he read. He sent a wire to Mayer and released it to the press. "I'm loath to believe you would permit action of this character," he wrote. "Would you care to advise me?" Mayer sent a swift denial: "We are most anxious for Miss Horne to succeed and that is why we have her under contract."

In less than two months she would start another movie, *Till the Clouds Roll By.* A loosely biographical salute to composer Jerome Kern, it would feature Horne in a scene from Kern's musical *Show Boat.* A Broadway revival of that show was in the works. For many years to come, Horne would claim that Kern himself had requested her for the key role of Julie and that Mayer had refused to let her do it. That, she felt, was part of his punishment for her refusal to play Della Green.

But *Show Boat* would open on January 5, 1946, thereby clashing with the production of *Till the Clouds Roll By*. While making that film, she thought longingly of Broadway. In the winter of 1946, *St. Louis Woman* began there without her. Ruby Hill, a promising newcomer in the Lena Horne mold, had gotten the lead. Pals of Horne's—Rex Ingram, the Nicholas Brothers—took other roles. The cast also featured Juanita Hall (the future Bloody Mary in *South Pacific*) and a still-obscure Pearl Bailey.

The show opened to a mixture of raves and pans. Critics faulted the muddled plot and called the score tricky and unhummable. Time proved them wrong on the latter issue: The songs included "Come Rain or Come Shine" and "Anyplace I Hang My Hat Is Home," two future standards sung by Della Green. And Pearl Bailey's cheeky performance as a saloon girl helped make her a star. But the naysayers won: *St. Louis Woman* closed in three months.

Before it closed, Betty Garrett saw it repeatedly. "I don't really think it was stereotypical," said the future M-G-M mainstay. "It showed a culture of its time, built around nightclubs and racetracks. I guess black people were fighting such a battle against stereotypes that anything that sort of smelled of that was objectionable to them." The *St. Louis Woman* dispute, like that of the proposed film version of *Uncle Tom's Cabin*, brought up a heated sticking point in the quest for racial equality: how to truthfully convey Negro life of a bygone time and place when it evoked images considered harmful.

Freed persisted for years in trying to film *St. Louis Woman*. For a time it seemed as though Frank Sinatra would star, joined by the love of his life, Ava Gardner. Freed also held discussions with Sammy Davis, Jr., and Diahann Carroll. But the film never came to be. No one regretted it more than Horne, who had declined a star vehicle—both on Broadway and possibly on-screen—with a score she termed "glorious." Long after White's death in 1955, Horne groused about how the NAACP had blocked her from doing a show written for her—and how the Urban League had "come down hard" on her "for thinking about doing an all-black musical."

More and more she'd come to view herself as a "pawn," and after *St. Louis Woman* she took her first of several public jabs at the NAACP. By now Horne had stepped up her own civil rights involvement. She and Rex

Ingram had joined the board of the Screen Actors Guild as spokesmen for black actors, and in January 1946, White met with a group of members to discuss the Negro onscreen. The leader took his usual hard line against actors who earned their living by playing undignified roles. In an interview with the *Los Angeles Sentinel,* a black newspaper, Horne called White "a bit undemocratic" in his attitude. It was a gentle rebuke, yet it began a rebellion that would grow much angrier in the years to come.

CHAPTER 9

EVEN BY M-G-M's lavish standards, *Till the Clouds Roll By* felt historic to its participants. Twenty years after the film's release, Kay Thompson's friend Mart Crowley, the playwright, recalled how Thompson loved to tell stories about it. Conceived by Arthur Freed, who worshiped Kern, *Clouds* offered some of the greatest Kern standards—among them "Look for the Silver Lining," "All the Things You Are," "The Last Time I Saw Paris," and "Ol' Man River"—performed by M-G-M's finest: Judy Garland, Frank Sinatra, Tony Martin, June Allyson, Angela Lansbury, Cyd Charisse, Kathryn Grayson, Van Johnson, Lena Horne. Each number was a show within a show. For a segment based on *Sunny,* Kern's circus-themed 1925 Broadway smash, a tent was made from over three thousand yards of white China silk; trapeze artists, horsemen, jugglers, and gold-painted elephants cavorted inside.

But sadness hung over the shoot. A few weeks into production, Kern collapsed on Park Avenue from a massive stroke. He died on November 11, 1945. The opening of the film commemorated his greatest triumph. In a capsule version of *Show Boat*'s first act, Horne sang Julie's heartrending "Can't Help Lovin' Dat Man."

Ebony visited her on the set. She smiled her way through "candid" photo ops, lighthearted chitchat with Arthur Freed, a commissary break with studio arranger Conrad Salinger, a fitting with Helen Rose. But Horne told *Ebony*'s reporter that she wished she were back at Café Society. "I'm very gratified that people accept my singing," she said, "but I really wanted to be an actress." Horne managed only a halfhearted statement of gratitude: "Hollywood has been very nice to me and has presented me to the best of its ability."

That was certainly true in *Clouds*. Just after the opening credits, the film shows a gray-haired Kern—played by Robert Walker—in a nostalgic mood. His mind drifts back to 1927, when *Show Boat* opened on Broadway. The curtain rises to reveal an almost comically whitewashed glimpse of slaves on the banks of the Mississippi. Dozens of black extras burst into song, but they carol the whitest of sounds, singing "Here we all work on the Mississippi!" as though it were "Whistle While You Work." Handsome baritone Tony Martin plays gambler Gaylord Ravenal; Kathryn Grayson is Magnolia, his sweetheart. As Joe, a weary stevedore, Caleb Peterson intones "Ol' Man River" backed by the swaying throng.

The scene's plastic perfectionism foretold the way M-G-M would eventually handle its full-length remake of *Show Boat*, a property it owned. But Horne is showcased exquisitely. Flowers and a purple bow adorn her hair; a plunging yellow gown makes her glow like a sunrise. She had no lines to recite, but "Can't Help Lovin' Dat Man" reveals the continued emergence of a mesmerizing actress-in-song. With probing concentration, Horne confides the story of a woman so enraptured by her shiftless man that nothing he does can sway her. Her eyes flash with defiance, glisten with tears, and finally beam in gleeful surrender. She draws viewers into her complex inner world, aided by the hocus-pocus of Vincente Minnelli. When she sings of her grief at seeing her man depart, the camera pulls back, and Horne appears small and distant. A moment later she tells of how his return has brought the sun out—and the camera draws in again as a yellow spotlight illuminates her face.

Studio employees crowded the projection room to see each day's rushes. Howard Strickling, the head of publicity, recalled the response to Horne's number. "When Lena Horne came on the screen, one could have heard a pin drop. She was ravishing.... Everyone was overwhelmed by this beautiful star." Horne had clearly outdone herself in what many would perceive as an on-camera audition for a full-fledged portrayal of Julie. "In fact I hoped it was," she said.

Horne reappears in the finale, a sprawling medley of Kern hits, sung one after another by the film's stars. They stand positioned on a set that reached to the sky—a veritable Mount Olympus. Gowned in white, Horne sings an anguished torch song, "Why Was I Born?"

Bosley Crowther of the *New York Times* would pan M-G-M's "hackneyed and sentimental" telling of Kern's story, but his grousing didn't stop the film from earning a fortune. Crowther, Archer Winstein (the *New York Post*), and Lee Mortimer (the *Daily Mirror*) all pointed to Horne as one of the highlights.

But 1946 sealed her disillusionment with M-G-M. For at least two years, the studio had promised her a role in *The Pirate,* a swashbuckling Caribbean extravaganza based on a Broadway play. Judy Garland and Gene Kelly would handle roles originated by Lynn Fontanne and Alfred Lunt; Vincente Minnelli—now Garland's husband—would direct. M-G-M had enlisted Cole Porter to write the score.

Several writers had tried and failed to produce a satisfying script. All along, Minnelli had pressed for Horne's inclusion. The latest version, by Anita Loos and Joseph Than, would feature Horne as a native dressmaker who serves as Garland's best friend. Porter even wrote a song for her, "Martinique," about the "very smart and very chic" local mores. But the Loos-Than script was nixed, too, and Horne's part went with it. The Nicholas Brothers were luckier; they got to share the showstopping number "Be a Clown" with Kelly.

At least Horne could look ahead to the April 1946 premiere of *Ziegfeld Follies*. Once more the critics singled her out. Edwin Schallert of the *Los Angeles Times* wrote that Horne, with her "Love" number, "comes off the best."

The film went south to Birmingham, and Hugh Martin, who had composed the music for "Love," flew there for the premiere. At the Alabama Theatre, Martin—a Birmingham boy—sat proudly with his entire family, eager for them to hear Horne sing his song. "And the number was gone," he said. Puzzled, he asked the manager what had happened. "He said, 'Oh, down here we don't want to see a lot of niggers writhing around.' I was absolutely horrified." Storming out with his relatives, he shouted that he would never set foot in that theater again.

In Durham, North Carolina, the *Morning Herald* ran an ad for the movie's local premiere. It listed Horne among the players. Scores of black patrons bought tickets for the first showing—and saw a jagged splice where "Love" should have been. Many of them complained angrily and asked for refunds. Within twenty-four hours, Horne's name had vanished from ads. Word of the scandal reached the *Pittsburgh Courier,* which tried to investigate. No one would take responsibility.

"Love" got chopped in Knoxville, Tennessee, too. Theater manager Emil Bernstecker explained that Horne's song "might prove objectionable to some people." Posters for the film hung around town with Horne's name blacked out. Meanwhile, *Down Beat* and the *Chicago Defender* reported the excision of "Love" in Memphis, the town with the most bigoted censor in the country. The septuagenarian Lloyd T. Binford declared: "No film shall appear in a Memphis theater as where a Negro is shown mingling with whites. Unless, of course, the Negro is in the role of maid or butler, and then their every spoken word must be prefaced with 'Sir' or 'Madame.'"

In 2008, Michael Finger recalled Binford in a profile for the *Memphis Flyer.* The censor, he wrote, held an iron grip on "the morals and welfare of our city"—so much so that he banned *Curley,* a United Artists comedy with an interracial classroom scene. Wrote Binford to the distributors, "The Memphis Censor Board . . . is unable to approve your picture with the little Negroes, as the South does not permit Negroes in white schools nor recognize social equality between the races, even in children." Binford axed a scene in M-G-M's *The Sailor Takes a Wife* that showed Robert Walker tipping his hat toward Eddie "Rochester" Anderson. For all that, he denied charges of racism. "I love old niggers," he insisted.

Binford held wide influence. *Our World* reported that of 6,350 U.S. movie houses, 31 percent were in the South or in border states. Many of these theaters admitted blacks only for midnight showings or barred them altogether. Others provided a "colored entrance" at the side of the theater or down a back alley; blacks climbed a rear staircase and sat in the "Balcony for Colored." All-black houses such as the Palace—a New Orleans cinema whose marquee billed it as the "South's Finest Theatre for Colored People"—offered sanctuary, but such places didn't aid the cause of desegregation.

It was no surprise that the royally presented "*Miss* Lena Horne" inflamed southern censors. Yet none of the major black newspapers, including the *Atlanta Daily World,* reported deletion of her scenes from any film after *Ziegfeld Follies*. (Before it, only "Ain't It the Truth" from *Cabin in the Sky* had possibly incurred southern wrath.) In 1945, Mart Crowley, who grew up in Mississippi, began making annual Christmas-time visits with his family in New Orleans. Whenever he could escape from them, Crowley—who later wrote a groundbreaking gay play, *The Boys in the Band*—rushed to the city's Loew's State cinema. There he gazed at the gods and goddesses of M-G-M. Crowley saw every film Horne made for the studio, starting with the December 1946 release of *Till the Clouds Roll By*. Not once, he recalled, was Horne cut out.

Even so, said Hugh Martin, "you can see that when Arthur Freed made a movie he knew what he'd be up against, and he'd have to be a little bit practical." Certainly M-G-M wasn't encouraged to integrate Horne into their expensive musicals. The cutting of "Love" had distressed Mayer, but he declined public comment. Horne felt abandoned. She assumed—and eventually told a rash of interviewers—that her songs were cut automatically as soon as the films went south. Then she began claiming that M-G-M, not the local distributors, coldheartedly did the hacking. The notion was outlandish; her studio had no desire to see those costly segments go unseen by anyone. But Horne felt rejected by both the South and Hollywood, and no show of kindness from M-G-M could compensate. Soon she would wreak revenge.

It happened on the night of July 20, 1946, when Freed produced a lavish memorial to Jerome Kern at the Hollywood Bowl. Two huge or-chestras would accompany a galaxy of M-G-M stars, including Horne, in reprises of their songs from *Clouds*. Robert Walker narrated the show, which Frank Sinatra would close with "Ol' Man River."

Eighteen thousand people waited eagerly to see an M-G-M musical come to life. But as the musicians struck their first chord, Horne hadn't shown. Twenty minutes later, word came that she was indisposed. The news threw Roger Edens into a panic; Horne's songs had been woven into a long medley and couldn't be cut. He rushed to Judy Garland's dressing room and told her she would have to sing "Can't Help Lovin' Dat Man" and "Why Was I Born?" Garland didn't quite know them, but she and Edens scrambled to find a piano. A famously quick study, she mastered both ballads, and sang them to wild applause. But there were murmurs in the crowd: What happened to Lena Horne?

Freed, Mayer, and others at the studio concluded that she'd skipped the show out of spite. Horne remained under contract but didn't make another film until early 1948—her punishment, she believed, probably correctly. Later she claimed that Mayer had also exercised a clause in her contract by blocking her cabaret appearances. Undoubtedly, he could be spiteful to troublesome stars; sometimes he yanked promised roles or made them sweat out their next assignment for months. It was Joan Crawford, Horne said, who advised her on how to handle Mayer. A former M-G-M contract player, Crawford had frequently crossed swords with him. She urged Horne to "kiss his big fat ass" if necessary to get her way. Reluctantly, Horne did. As she later told Rex Reed, "I went to him and asked him to please let me work, if they didn't want me in the movies, 'cause I'd go and sing in cafés. He was, um, rather intimidating, but he liked to be appealed to very humbly."

Mayer agreed to revise her contract. Now Horne would be on studio call for just ten weeks per year, with another five reserved for promotional engagements. Back she went to nearly full-time cabaret work, and to increased parenting.

Louis Jones had temporarily entrusted Teddy to his mother, and she enrolled him and Gail at a public school in Los Angeles. It was ostensibly integrated, but only one other black student—Ida Starks's daughter—attended. Soon the children were called "nigger," pelted with rocks, and chased home from school by innocent-looking classmates who played hopscotch at lunch hour.

They learned much of that hatred at home, where "nigger" was a common word in white households. Children saw cartoons like *Coal Black and De Sebben Dwarfs*, which showed Negroes as bug-eyed, thick-lipped, jive-talking grotesqueries. And they found negative reinforcement at school. In an emotional interview with *Datebook*, Horne said that although her children "knew they were Negroes," they had "never heard . . . the other word." She struggled to find a way to explain it to them. "I told them the truth. That this word is used only by unknowing children of ignorant parents. That some people don't respect other people as human beings, that the only way they can make themselves feel bigger is to make somebody else feel smaller."

Her poise crumbled as she sat across a desk from her children's teacher and confronted her about the harassment. Back came an evasion. Prejudice was a fact of life, and the school was overcrowded. What was she supposed to do? Horne called the teacher a bitch and stormed out. "Don't worry," she snapped. "Our kids aren't coming back."

She'd found one more reason to hate Los Angeles. Only in the New York area, she felt, might her children stay safe. Cab Calloway told her about St. Albans, a mostly black neighborhood in Queens, New York. Its upscale section, Addisleigh Park, served as home to Count Basie, Jackie Robinson, and later Ella Fitzgerald and James Brown. Calloway helped Horne find a house where Ida would look after Teddy, Gail, and her own daughter. The children were enrolled in a local private school. Horne would later admit that she'd barely lived in the house at all.

The singer had plunged into a growing wave of civil rights work, independent of the NAACP or any other controlling faction. Life in Hollywood had left her angry; increasingly she identified with the oppression of her race. Evelyn Cunningham, a journalist who chronicled some of the toughest moments in the fight for equality, witnessed the star in action: "She was very, very good about her responsibilities. She wasn't flamboyant about it, but she understood that she had power, and that it could help."

Horne had joined the National Council of Negro Women, an organization started in 1935 by a friend of her grandmother's, Mary McLeod Bethune. A venerated educator and activist, Bethune had cofounded a black Methodist college in Daytona Beach, Florida, that would eventually become Bethune-Cookman University. In all her work, she fought to empower the black female. Horne named her as one of the two women she admired most.

Her other idol was Eleanor Roosevelt. In October 1944, during an engagement at the Howard Theatre in Washington, D.C., Horne went to the White House to meet Mrs. Roosevelt for the first time. They spoke of matters they both held dear. The first lady believed democracy couldn't exist without racial tolerance, and fought against segregation in housing, jobs, and schools. Horne left tearfully, calling Roosevelt "just the grandest woman ever." She had found a new mother figure. From then on, Horne eagerly joined any organization that Roosevelt championed.

Before a subsequent appearance at the Howard, Horne called an interracial press conference. "Besides beauty, she has brains," wrote a journalist for the *Los Angeles Sentinel*. "This correspondent was amazed at the
fluent manner in which she intelligently discussed unions, politics, race
relations, social welfare." Most of the white journalists, said the *Sentinel's* reporter, "had never come in personal contact with members of the
Negro press before—or with any intelligent Negroes, for that matter."

Horne adored Franklin Delano Roosevelt, and had helped campaign
for his fourth-term reelection. In August 1946, after Harry Truman had
succeeded him, Horne joined a civil rights rally at Hollywood's Masonic
Temple. She and the other participants pleaded for President Truman to
investigate the Ku Klux Klan and do more to protect southern blacks.
The *Atlanta Daily World* reported on Horne's speech: "With deep seriousness . . . she read a list of the recent lynchings, murders, and other
outrages against Negroes." Horne voiced a desperate call. "When such
things are going on," she announced, "I no longer feel that here is a place
of refuge for us in the United States."

The gusto of her commitment surprised many. Until now, most of
the public had viewed her as a demurely sexy glamour-puss. But Phil
Moore, her traveling pianist and conductor, felt otherwise. Born in Port-
land, Oregon, Moore met Horne in 1938, when he provided musical
direction for *The Duke Is Tops*. He'd already worked for M-G-M—an
early example of the studio's effort to integrate its staff, if modestly. The
studio had signed his wife, the black dancer Jeni LeGon, to a contract
that went nowhere. But Moore's career thrived. He arranged for Duke
Ellington, Louis Armstrong, and Count Basie; and in years to come he
would coach a stellar array of singing beauties, including Marilyn Monroe, Dorothy Dandridge, Hazel Scott, and Abbey Lincoln.

Short and stout, with a bulldog face, Moore had an air of fatherly
authority. He dressed sharply, smoked a pipe, and knew how to soothe a
starlet's ego. In 1943, he'd tried to calm a frustrated Horne during a rehearsal. "Shoo shoo, Lena, shoo shoo!" he said. He turned that expression
into "Shoo Shoo Baby," a number-one hit for the Andrews Sisters.

Over the next two years, he accompanied Horne on some singles
for the Victor label. "One for My Baby (and One More for the Road)"
nipped at the top twenty; the others were barely noticed. Her careful

singing reflected the Horne on longtime display—polite, smiling, afraid to show too much. The black music world had little use for her; not only couldn't she sing the blues, she had no apparent reason *to* sing them. Few musicians saw her as anything more than a movie star who could carry a tune.

But Moore sensed untapped potential. After Victor dropped her, he brokered a deal for Horne at Black & White Records, a family-owned enterprise in Los Angeles. Black & White issued mostly R&B and country music; for an M-G-M star it might have seemed a comedown. But at Black & White, she and Moore could experiment freely. In 1946, they made two 78-rpm albums of laments, *Little Girl Blue* and *Classics in Blue*.

Moore assembled a chamber orchestra and arranged it with artful details: a cascading violin, a wailing saxophone. The drama of his backings worked; Horne set down her genial pose and revealed darker colors. In Rodgers and Hart's "Little Girl Blue," a celeste twinkles like a child's music box; it cranks up the pathos as Horne sings of drowning in loneliness: "No use, old girl / You may as well surrender." "I Don't Want to Cry Anymore" finds her lashing out at the lover whose callousness is driving her mad. Moore even brought Horne a spiritual, "Nobody Knows the Trouble I've Seen," that slaves had sung on plantations and that Paul Robeson and Louis Armstrong had recorded. In her hymnlike rendition, one can hear the stifled pain of a woman who knew about racial woe, even if few who saw her on-screen could imagine it.

Her most-talked-about Black & White recording was a two-sided version of "Frankie and Johnny," the folk song based on an actual crime of passion in St. Louis. She performs it as a playlet with spoken dialogue, a choir that comments on the action in Greek-chorus style, and Horne as Frankie, the woman who fires three shots into the "hard heart" of her two-timing lover. That record, wrote a *Metronome* critic, "offers much in the way of moving singing. Lena really communicates her feelings, and her feelings are intense."

She certainly had a strong aversion to nightclubs. The fact that she played the top ones in the country didn't matter; to Horne they were second-class showbiz at best, sleazy at worst, and far inferior to movies.

Most boîtes had a thuggish atmosphere that reminded her of the Cotton Club. Nonetheless, Horne became a regular at New York's Copacabana, co-owned by mob boss Frank Costello. She headlined at Bill Miller's Riviera, a thousand-seat showroom in Fort Lee, New Jersey, "where the guys with the spread collars and the big necktie-knots go to dazzle their dolls with champagne and a stout check," as Robert Ruark wrote in *Esquire*.

If she had to earn her living in such places, Horne worked hard to build a protective veneer. Everything about her, from her posh repertoire to her gowns by M-G-M's Irene, signaled formidable high class. "Having started out working with Teddy Wilson, I couldn't have anyone less than he at the piano," she explained later. "Then I knew that I had to be well dressed, because even though I didn't have much to do at M-G-M, the best designers dressed me, so I began to get a style sense. The women from Hollywood who came to see me were all so well dressed, I just knew that I wanted to look as good as they did. For a long while those surface things helped a lot."

Sometimes her setting equaled what she brought to it. In the latter half of the forties, Horne appeared often at the Capitol Theatre, Manhattan's reigning cathedral of film. Located at Fifty-first and Broadway, the Capitol struck Bosley Crowther of the *New York Times* as "a temple, a pantheon," where up to 4,500 viewers at a time could experience "the magical illusion of unreality." They strolled through a cavernous lobby, and climbed marble staircases that led to dizzyingly steep balconies. The screen was so huge that it made the mortals projected on it seem godlike. All day long, stage shows followed the screenings. Mae West had danced the shimmy there in 1919; Clark Gable had stepped out to speak at the close of *Gone With the Wind,* which premiered at the Capitol.

It was a space for larger-than-life performers, but Horne didn't have to shout to fill it. On the contrary, she sang with her usual intimacy, commanding everyone to concentrate as hard as she did. Her trio used a musical phrase from *Show Boat*'s "Can't Help Lovin' Dat Man" to introduce her. She entered from the wings, clutching a handkerchief. From there she brought her Hollywood moments to life—"Honeysuckle Rose," "Love," "Why Was I Born?," "Stormy Weather." She sang her *Show Boat* number with half-closed eyes and burning focus, as though inhabiting the song with all her being might someday make the part of Julie hers. "Miss Horne's delivery is slow, deliberate, and as suggestive as it is possible to be in public," wrote columnist Bert McCord. "Her face is delicate enough to have been lifted out of an exquisite oriental print. There is a calculated economy about her gestures. Occasionally her manner is apt to become a bit affected, but even in such moments she maintains her hold over the audience."

Leading the Capitol orchestra much of the time was the pianist and conductor Lyle Russell Cedric Henderson, commonly called Skitch. Henderson had worked in M-G-M's music department before he was twenty; later he conducted for Frank Sinatra and led the first *Tonight* show orchestra. Having studied with Toscanini and Schoenberg, he brought a courtly grandeur to his role of a pop maestro.

But he felt humbled by the talent of Lennie Hayton, his idol, who accompanied Horne whenever he could escape from M-G-M. "I've watched a lot of people come and go," said Henderson in 2004, "but I've never seen anything as musical and professional as her act." Hayton prepped the musicians as carefully as a jeweler setting a rare and precious stone. He made them tune up one by one, stopping along the way to give them individual pointers. Hayton, marveled Henderson, "had the ability to get players of questionable quality to play like they were superstars." During the shows he stood in the wings, observing everything.

But Hayton's watchfulness couldn't shield Horne from the racism that lurked almost everywhere. Her Hollywood stature brought her entrée to the grandest venues, but often they housed the evilest bigots. The hotels in which she entertained reluctantly gave her a room, but black members of her band had to sleep elsewhere, and even Horne faced some humiliating rules—no using the main entrance, the front elevator, the dining room, the bar. She had a special loathing for Miami, where blacks could be arrested on the street after eight o'clock if they lacked ID showing employment by a white family.

But racism in her beloved Manhattan hurt her the most. In 1944, Horne had become the first black performer to play the Copacabana, but its seating agenda recalled the Cotton Club's. Blacks who phoned in their reservations and then showed up at that fashionable address—Sixtieth Street off Fifth Avenue—were coldly informed that their names weren't on the list. That policy helped turn Horne's opening night into an ordeal that left her shaking. According to the *New York Post*'s Ted Poston, Bill "Bojangles" Robinson had invited a Negro actress to join him at the show. The doorman turned them away. Robinson's enraged companion found a pay phone and called Horne in her dressing room just before curtain time. She attacked the singer for playing a club "where your people are treated like that" and vowed to tell everyone. Horne was "half-hysterical," reported Poston, as she phoned him and asked his advice. Could she cancel her contract? Poston told her to stay calm and do her show; tomorrow he'd be there at ringside.

The following night, he and his companion, a journalist from *Jet*, approached the reservation desk. The doorman blocked their way with his arm. "You can't go in here!" he barked. "You ain't got no reservation!"

"How do you know?" said Poston. "You don't even know my name."

The doorman pulled a bogus list from his jacket, kept handy whenever a Negro showed up. "See, you ain't got no reservation. There's Polinsky, Peretti, Pollard—but no Poston."

The reporter wouldn't leave, and a loud argument ensued. Along came Poston's other guest, Bill Robinson, with a cop in tow. Moments later Jack Entratter, the Copa's manager, stormed over. He took the doorman's side.

The cop turned to the black couple and offered loudly to arrest either the doorman or Entratter for discrimination. Thus flattened, Entratter let the Poston party enter. Later he tried to explain himself. What if a customer arrived from the South and found Negroes at the Copa? "Anything could happen," he said. If he let a black person in, the place would be flooded with them. Ridiculous, argued Poston. Why should blacks want to visit the Copa any more than whites?

He detailed his experience in the *Post*; Horne recalled the aftermath. NAACP and Urban League members picketed the Copa, and the singer herself took a feisty stand. George Evans, the club's publicist, recalled it later: "I admire Lena's loyalty to her people, but she can get difficult. She insisted I get her a suite at a hotel we both know bars Negroes. She also demanded that the Copa open its doors to people of her own race. I managed to get a few of her friends in, but not without some trouble."

It wasn't long before the Copa reluctantly lifted its ban on Negroes.

For all her dislike of the club, she kept appearing there defiantly, demanding ever-bigger salaries. She opened one engagement there in July 1947—"and no star ever received a more glorious welcome," exclaimed a radio announcer.

A month later, Brooklyn Borough President John Cashmore declared Thursday, August 21, "Lena Horne Homecoming Day." Thousands of locals jammed the streets to greet her like a princess. Famous as Horne was, she hadn't forgotten the names and faces of people she once knew. "She wasn't a celebrity, taking the bows and acting grand," said Alfred Duckett, her early Brooklyn admirer. "She was just a girl coming back to her home town and remembering how she loved it."

Wearing an elegant black suit and a white hat and gloves, Horne accepted a key to the city on the steps of Borough Hall. John J. Lynch of the borough president's office announced, "There will always be a welcome here for the girl who brought us great distinction through her outstanding artistic ability and her unceasing efforts to improve human relations." Then he pinned a white orchid on her lapel.

Horne took her place in the backseat of a convertible, and a motorcade took her through the streets of her youth. The car inched forward as a crush of admirers reached out to touch a beaming, waving Horne. Later on, Bill Robinson, then in his late sixties, honored her with a nimble tap dance, and her fans gave her a three-hundred-foot scroll full of inscriptions. Horne couldn't have gotten a more loving affirmation of how far she'd come. "Displaying a vivacious smile, Miss Horne told reporters that the occasion was one of the happiest moments of her life," wrote the *Amsterdam News*.

But some blow was always waiting to bring her down to earth. On the road, black teenage boys would approach her with lewd remarks or hurtful questions: "How's come you, a nigger, is able to get into the movies?" Some of them asked her how she made her skin so light.

Horne had guested on many of the hottest radio shows of the day, generally without incident. So she was unprepared for what happened before a scheduled appearance on *Duffy's Tavern*, a popular radio comedy about a goofy bartender. Staff members who saw the script told the show's star, Ed "Archie" Gardner, "You can't let that Negro woman call you Archie!" She should call him either "Mr. Archie" or "Mr. Gardner," they said. Horne refused. Gardner fought on her behalf, but achieved only a sad compromise. On the air, said Horne, "we just didn't call each other anything."

She didn't keep the story a secret. Horne's rage was obvious in an interview she gave to Nate Gross of the New York *Daily News*. "Almost every day I hear someone on the radio hailing America as the home of democracy," she said. "There are a few isolated cases of Negroes in broadcasting, but the lily-white policy is seldom violated."

The angrier she grew, the more outspoken Horne became. That year she began writing a column for *People's Voice*, a militant newspaper founded by Adam Clayton Powell, Jr., Manhattan's first black congressman, to fight what he called "Hitlerism" at home. In one essay, Horne berated the entertainment industry for continuing to depict Negroes as "silly, simple, shuffling types, laughing, dancing, and bowing their way through life. A great section of White America laughs at these characterizations, and accepts them as normal and true to life. . . . When will our entertainment be truly American in its scope and democratic in its treatment of Negroes and other persecuted peoples?"

Paul Robeson remained Horne's beacon of social justice, and she supported almost anything he endorsed. Horne helped him plan a rally at New York's Madison Square Garden to benefit his Council on African Affairs, which sought to aid South African poverty and famine. She and Robeson appeared at another Garden rally, "Join the Progressive Counter-Attack: Hear Henry Wallace." It spotlighted the burgeoning hero of the Progressive Party, a former vice president (under Roosevelt) turned secretary of commerce (under Truman) and impassioned civil rights advocate. The rally helped boost Wallace into the 1948 presidential race.

It was a tense but exciting time for liberal blacks. Their mission called for nothing less than changing the mind-set of a country, and they banded together in growing numbers. "We made it our business to become part of any force that was speaking out against this inhumane cruelty," said Harry Belafonte, a black singer with an angry dedication to change. "We were determined to force the issue of justice for everybody onto the public consciousness."

Many of the most influential human rights organizations had Socialist or Communist ties. "The Communist party was considered progressive then," said Gene Davis. "People who felt that they were downtrodden—and that included most blacks—joined the Communist party." So did the ragingly liberal Betty Garrett. "The more involved in the politics of the day I became," she said, "the more it seemed to me that the Communists, Socialists, and other radical groups were the only ones who were really *doing* anything about discrimination, better housing, Spanish Civil War orphans, and so on."

To widespread dismay, Negroes were becoming a political force. Their progress in Hollywood—some of it traceable to the success of Lena Horne—and in the theater signified their rising power. Ossie Davis, a young actor with his own deep commitment to civil rights, saw only in retrospect the danger he and other black freedom fighters had been under. In the late forties, he said, "we didn't know how thoroughly we were being watched."

Neither did Lena Horne, who continued speaking out candidly. Some of her comments were risky indeed. Echoing the beliefs of Paul Robeson, she announced at a press conference, "I like any group that makes democracy work, and so I have a feeling for democratic Russia." But since "we can't all run to Russia," she added, "we might as well make it work here."

As the Cold War burgeoned, Robeson and another man Horne knew well, Orson Welles, had come under close surveillance of the FBI. Their friendships with Horne were no secret. Neither was the admiring write-up she received from the Communist newspaper *The Daily Worker*. The FBI had found one more "threatening" entertainer to watch.

DURING her long hiatus from M-G-M, Horne enjoyed the company of her friends Ella Logan and Fred Finklehoffe. The couple lived in Brentwood, an affluent region of West Los Angeles, but shared none of their neighbors' prejudices. They hosted black guests like Horne and didn't care what anyone thought.

Logan's teenage niece, Annabelle, lived with them. When a teacher of hers phoned the house to warn that Annabelle had befriended a black schoolmate, Logan was disgusted at such bigotry. So was her niece, who grew up to become the influential jazz singer Annie Ross. In 1950, Ross bore the son of Kenny Clarke, a pioneering black bebop drummer.

She looked to Horne with awe. Years later, Ross remembered her from those visits in the 1940s as "very young and soft and warm," and almost unthinkably beautiful. "I remember my aunt Kathy saying, 'Have you seen her ears? They're like little shells.'"

Annabelle got a glimpse of how fearful the burgeoning firebrand really was. One day the teenager found her in the bathroom, crying. "I said, 'What's the matter?' She said, 'Lennie's asked me to marry him.'" Ross couldn't imagine what the problem was. "If you love him, marry him," she said. "You don't understand," said Horne.

She and Hayton had dated for four years, and while other men had drifted in and out of her life, he intended to stay. Hayton had proposed repeatedly, but Horne refused to believe he meant it. Edwina's and Cora's warnings still rang in her mind. A white man would use a black woman like a whore, but he would never marry her. Again and again, she accused Hayton of that in so many words. He responded with an unearthly patience, and gradually she began to soften; she wanted to say yes. "I always had that old-fashioned thing about *wanting* to lean on somebody," she explained. "A strong man, see?" And this one, she felt, "didn't have a bad bone in his body" or "an ax to grind."

It was clear she'd begun trusting Hayton when she took to calling him Daddy. "It was good for my ego to have someone really care," said Horne. Few of her friends doubted that they were in love. "He couldn't have been sweeter," said Arthur Laurents, "with whom she would soon become close. "He wanted her, and he had stature in her world. Let's not underestimate that. He was somebody."

Interracial marriage was then illegal in thirty U.S. states, including California. Hayton seemed unconcerned; they could marry abroad. But Horne had many worries. What would the NAACP, the Urban League, and all of black society think of this marriage? Would it be seen as a sellout to the white man? And would it hurt her career?

Until then Horne had taken reasonable care to hide the affair from the public, especially on tour. As Avery Williams of *Tan* magazine later reported, "They stayed at the same hotels but were always booked on the register under their separate names. Usually they occupied adjoining suites."

But their relationship was no secret at M-G-M. "We all knew pretty much what was going on," said Kathryn Grayson. Mentions of the supposedly hidden liaison kept appearing in the press. As early as January 1946, the *Los Angeles Sentinel* had confronted Horne over word that she was already Mrs. Hayton. "Is Lena Horne Married?" asked a *Chicago Defender* headline that September. "Whispers that the two have wed are becoming bolder daily," declared the paper. A few months later Earl Wilson wrote about Horne's "romance with a talented white man," adding, "it's an open secret in Hollywood." The *Chicago Sun* reported matter-of-factly, "Her husband is white."

Horne consistently denied the rumors, while admitting how hurt she was over some of the "ugly things" people were saying. "I was in love with him," she admitted later, "and I just had to find the courage not to care that people were wrong."

Defiance kept chipping away at her discretion. *Our World* published some intimate details she'd provided about her liaison with Hayton. She wore a bracelet engraved "To L.H. from L.H.," the magazine noted, adding that Hayton had "introduced her to Jewish foods like gefulte [*sic*] fish and kugel." If Horne wanted to inflame the organizations that sought to control her, this relationship would do nicely.

In 1947, the singer took an even bolder step: She left Horn Avenue and bought a home for herself and Hayton. Finding it wasn't easy. In dozens of U.S. cities, L.A. among them, "restrictive covenant" laws barred Negroes and Jews from buying any but a few select properties. The Supreme Court would soon declare such discrimination unconstitutional, but that didn't stop neighboring bigots from trying to harass minorities out of their homes.

Horne appealed to a Jewish friend to help her locate a house. "Something away, where I won't offend anyone," she noted ruefully. She wound up in Nichols Canyon, a mostly liberal neighborhood in the Hollywood Hills. Her new address, 2136 Nichols Canyon, lay on the winding road where Betty Garrett lived; Ava Gardner was close by.

The fallout came only weeks after Horne's arrival. While performing in May at Chicago's Chez Paree nightclub, she learned that a local real-estate agent was trying to push her out. Because restrictive covenant laws did not apply to her home, a local Realtor had founded "The Association for the Prevention of Gravel Snatchers"—a league intended, supposedly, to stop thieves from stealing gravel from driveways. But convoluted wording included an anti-Negro clause. The couple of "members" began knocking on doors and asking for signatures. Most people, especially Garrett, were furious and refused.

Even so, Horne told the *Chicago Defender* that someone had advised her "to return home immediately and prepare for the worst." She wouldn't back down, she said. "I like comfort and my home is comfortable and I do not intend giving it up without a struggle." She and Hayton took steps to protect themselves. They built a wall around their house and bought a gun, which Hayton taught her how to use. "I kept it in the corner, all handy," she said.

The attempt to banish Horne failed, and her opponents had no choice but to accept her presence. With so much tension in the air, it was no surprise that alcohol figured prominently in her household. Hayton, a devoted recreational drinker, found a book called *The Gentleman's Drinking Companion* and worked his way through all its recipes. "Every Sunday would be our day to try a new drink," Horne said. Friends joined in— Billy Strayhorn, singer Marie Bryant, Roger Edens, Gardner—and they would schmooze and imbibe until the moon rose. On many Mondays she awoke with a hangover.

Her social circle filled up with kindred misfits. She and Hayton made friends with a duo who lived across the street: "male impersonator" Tommy, a woman who donned a tuxedo and sang bawdy songs in clubs, and her companion, Olga. Betty Garrett and her husband, film actor Larry Parks, also grew close to the Haytons. Born on a Missouri farm, Garrett joined M-G-M in 1947. "I was either the kooky sister of the leading lady, the man-crazy best friend, or the tough gal with the heart of gold," she said in her memoir, *Betty Garrett and Other Songs*. Offscreen, she joined the liberal hell-raising of the day. Garrett had worked in leftist New York revues to support unions and integration; almost anyone organizing a benefit or demonstration for progressive causes could count on her participation. Like Garrett, Parks had entered the Communist party. The couple's fearlessness would soon end their film careers.

For now, however, they could laugh about their rebel behavior. Hayton joked that all of M-G-M's bad girls—Garrett, Horne, and Gardner—were neighbors. But one night it seemed as though nature were inflicting a nasty punishment on Horne and Hayton. Their house had a dangerous flaw; it stood on an incline in the direct path of mudslides, which heavy rainstorms provoked. Garrett's home had a drainage ditch out front, but not Horne's.

Well past midnight it started to rain, and water coursed down in sheets. Garrett and Parks woke up to a panicked call from Tommy. The Horne house was in trouble; could they come help? Hayton was there alone; Horne had gone on tour. Larry and Betty donned galoshes and raincoats, grabbed shovels, and trudged uphill. "The road was covered with mud," recalled Garrett. "It was almost like a landslide. Looking back I think, my God, we could have slid down into the canyon."

They found Tommy digging at the mud, which had risen to the middle of the French door that opened into the Horne living room. They spotted Lennie inside. His musician's fingers resisted handiwork, and he sat on the sofa with his head in his hands. "He was so distressed, he was absolutely helpless," said Garrett.

She and Parks used another entrance. They saw shelves of Hayton's precious record albums, all by the French door. "We said, 'Lennie, let's move these albums; if the mud comes in they're all gonna be ruined.' He just shook his head and said, 'I don't care!'" They lugged the heavy disks upstairs while Hayton stared. Then they helped Tommy shovel mud. Periodically they went inside and sat with Hayton, while eating the only food he had in the house: chocolate-covered cherries, washed down with brandy.

The ordeal lasted until dawn, when the rain finally stopped. Later Parks told Garrett, "I think we could have bought that house for fifty cents!"

In the fall of 1947, Horne prepared to leave on her first European tour, centered in England and France. Hayton would accompany her. Horne had finally said yes to Hayton's proposing. The couple had decided to wed overseas—exactly where, they weren't sure. Having paid dearly for past indiscretions, she took pains, along with Hayton, to ensure privacy. On October 22, they boarded the *Mauretania*, a Cunard liner bound for England. Hayton had arrived after Horne, to avoid any photographers who might have snapped incriminating photos of the duo setting sail. Luther Henderson, Horne's new musical director, joined them on the ship; so did her assistant, Tiny Kyle. Neither knew of her wedding plans.

The ten-day transatlantic journey, Horne's first, took them over rough seas and through bone-chilling cold. Their destination was in a state of dire crisis: Wartime bombing had destroyed three-quarters of a million homes, and those that survived could barely accommodate the returning servicemen. Coal and clean water were scarce, and most foods rationed. Like much of the British population, the *Mauretania* passengers subsisted mainly on potatoes.

They reached London during one of its most brutal winters in decades. But Horne and her companions warmed to the graciousness of everyone they met; years later the singer would recall that trip as the happiest time of her life. *Stormy Weather* and her M-G-M films had made her more famous there than she'd realized, and she felt swathed in respect. Ralph Harris, who would soon become her manager, called Europe "a great refuge" for Horne. Many Americans, he noted, still regarded a beautiful, cultured black woman as a "sideshow freak"; Europeans embraced her.

Various friends of distinction, including the poet Dylan Thomas and the actor James Mason, welcomed Horne and Hayton into their homes. The singer was slated for a three-week engagement at the prestigious London Casino, but whenever possible she rushed around town to soak up the culture. She visited Parliament and spent a whole day listening to debates in the House of Commons—"to see how real democracy ticks," she told an American reporter. In interviews, wrote the *Atlanta Daily World*, Horne "was not reluctant to denounce the kind of treatment that is meted out to the Negro in America."

At the London Casino she headlined a bill of British favorites, including Ted Heath, the country's favorite bandleader. But according to *Variety*, most of the ticket holders had come "to see and hear the sepia film star." Horne performed with only Henderson and two of Heath's musicians, bassist Charlie Short and Jack Parnell, a poll-topping drummer. She liked Parnell so much she used him in nearly every British appearance for the next twenty years. His swinging rhythm suited her, but she gave Short a talking-to in rehearsals. "Listen, Charlie. When you play, all I want is the time you see from my ass shaking. Keep your eye on my ass!"

Horne, said Parnell, "used to come in about two hours before every performance to start making up. She became transformed. And on the stage she was absolutely gorgeous to look at." Once the critics had raved, Horne relaxed. She and Hayton struck Parnell as a "great couple," fully at ease. "We used to have a lot of parties together, meals and chatting and carrying on," said the drummer. "They used to make me laugh. I remember going to see them for a drink, and Lennie used to make the most wonderful dry martinis, which he spent about twenty minutes preparing. She used to call for them: 'Drinks, Lennie?'"

They couldn't linger too long after closing night. On November 11, she and her entourage made another stormy trip, this one across the Channel to France. Horne was booked to play the Club des Champs-Élysées.

Their journey proved even grimmer than their first. They arrived at the ferry port in Calais on France's north coast. It was after midnight and raining torrentially, but their Parisian impresario had failed to send anyone to meet them. They walked through puddles along the dark docks without a franc in their pockets. Finally, said Horne, they found "an old cab and a driver twice as old." He couldn't speak English, but by repeating "Paris" and adopting a begging tone they talked him into driving them there. "Sleet was rattling on the roof," recalled Horne. They were hungry as they shivered in the unheated cab, but the driver munched on French bread, gulped red wine, and offered them nothing. He drove aimlessly, for he didn't know the way. Finally Horne blurted out from the backseat, "Just go straight!" with a karate-chop hand gesture, and that set them on course.

Around noon they reached the Hotel Raphaël—"blind from exhaustion and starving," said Horne. Staff from the cabaret "were hysterical when we did get there," asking what took them so long.

Having felt like vagrants, the weary travelers found themselves in a five-star, crystal- and marble-laden hotel near the Eiffel Tower, the Arc de Triomphe, and the Champs-Élysées. Soon Horne and Hayton would meet Yves Montand, Simone Signoret, and Edith Piaf. Whenever possible, Horne stayed in her room, poring over a French phrase book and fretting over how locals would receive her.

According to *Time*, which covered her French debut, Horne needn't have worried. Though "obviously nervous," the singer "flashed her magnificent teeth in the spotlight and curtsied demurely," then "slithered cozily up to the mike and began to sway." Horne tore into Cole Porter's "Just One of Those Things"—and "the French found Lena's English perfectly translatable," declared *Time*. On its front page, the newspaper *France-Soir* deemed her Paris debut "a triumph."

Others voiced their disappointment. Horne seemed nothing like France's iconic American expatriate Negro, Josephine Baker, who had conquered the country in the guise of a bare-breasted, banana-wearing, untamed jungle native. The image seemed as racist as any American stereotype, but the French regarded it with awe. As different as Horne was, she felt so at home in Paris that she thought she'd found heaven. Not a frown greeted her and Hayton as they strolled arm in arm down the Champs-Élysées or when they left and entered the same hotel room. This, they decided, was where they would marry.

Horne's best friend there was Auren Kahn, a San Franciscan who worked for a Jewish relief agency. Kahn helped arrange an afternoon wedding at the Paris city hall. Only the night before did Horne break the news to Henderson and Kyle; she needed them as best man and maid of honor.

After the ceremony, everyone piled into a cab. With the sun setting, they cruised down the Champs-Élysées. For years to come, Horne rhapsodized about the fall of 1947; never again would she know such a magical time.

The morning after the wedding, Horne called her nine-year-old daughter in St. Albans, Queens, and explained that Mommy had a new husband. She made Gail swear to keep it a secret.

CHAPTER 10

AFTER A RELATIVELY peaceful journey on the SS *America,* Mr. and Mrs. Lennie Hayton docked in New York on December 22, 1947. Nervously, they began phoning other family members, telling them of the wedding and begging them not to breathe a word.

The responses were worse than anticipated. Except for the interracially married Edna, who wasn't in a position to sneer, the family forgot its mixed-blood history and attacked her choice to marry outside her race. Most of them stopped speaking to her. That included her beloved father, whose disgusted response broke her heart. And while Horne claimed that Hayton's mother and sister were "wonderful" in their open-mindedness, Judy Davis, the daughter of Horne's friend Elois Davis, recalled otherwise: "Lennie was Jewish, and his family never accepted Lena, really. She and Lennie would joke about it, but it was a source of resentment."

No matter what, the couple had each other. Gloria DeHaven saw a pair of newlyweds who were "very much in love, and very touchy-feely. They held hands."

Hayton had returned to a full schedule at M-G-M, but on the job he left his wife in the best of hands. "She always had people of great taste playing for her," said Skitch Henderson. "Lennie saw to that." The best man at their wedding, twenty-eight-year-old Luther Henderson, remained her maestro. Born in Kansas City of two teachers, Henderson grew up in Sugar Hill, Harlem's upscale oasis. The Duke Ellington family, who lived nearby, became their friends. After graduating from

City College, Luther gained a rare distinction: The prestigious (and almost exclusively white) Juilliard School accepted him as a music student. Degree in hand, he spent the World War II years arranging for a navy band; then Ellington hired Henderson to perform the same duty for him. Duke and Billy Strayhorn recommended him to Horne. Once he passed muster with Hayton, Henderson was in.

He and Horne launched a love-hate collaboration that endured into the eighties. By now she'd gained a lot of take-charge confidence, and after years of manipulation by higher forces, she wasn't so eager to be mentored. Henderson, with his Juilliard and Ellington pedigrees, had an ego of his own. "Luther really loved working with Lena, but they always fought," said actress and director Billie Allen, whom he wed in 1980. "He was organized and methodical, and she was very bright and could get right to the conclusion. She didn't need to take the steps. And she didn't like being told what to do."

Her band grew even stronger with the addition, in early 1948, of Chico Hamilton, a rising young drummer. At twenty-six, Hamilton had already played with three aristocrats of jazz, Lester Young, Lionel Hampton, and Count Basie. Tall and rangy, with a caramel-hued handsomeness, Hamilton was a street-smart youth who had grown up boxing on the streets of L.A. Yet he played the drums with uncommon delicacy. "I kept good time," said Hamilton, "and I had a touch that was very soft and gentle, and yet it popped. Lena dug that." His brush and cymbal work gave her a subtle kick. For a singer who once described her early sense of time as "nowhere, no way," a drummer like Hamilton was essential.

She wanted his beat in her ear, so instead of keeping him in back of the band, she placed him right behind her. "She was one of the most challenging singers to play for," he said, "because you never knew what she was gonna do." Horne had learned to sense the mood of a room; if the energy dropped she signaled him, with her hand behind her back, to boost the tempo. "With me being right behind her," said Hamilton, "I could see how her ass moved, the cords in her neck, her body language. She sang the hell out of the arrangements. This woman knew rhythm, and her intonation was very good."

Hamilton had previously worked as house drummer at Billy Berg's, a Hollywood jazz club. Now his life changed: "All of a sudden I'm in show business, and not just a jazz player. Man, I'm meetin' movie stars. Lennie taught me how to eat a lobster, how to drink Cognac. He was a dynamite dude, man; I had a tremendous amount of respect for him. Smooth as silk."

Hayton often couldn't travel with Horne, and he worried for her safety on the road. She needed a new manager, and he called on a man he'd met in the thirties. Horne would later credit Ralph Harris with enabling her to go on as a black woman in show business. Once the vaudeville partner of lyricist Jimmy Van Heusen, he knew all about dealing with seamy hustlers and scuffling for a buck. But Harris—a white man who'd grown up in a melting-pot neighborhood in Syracuse, New York—was a gentleman. He fought Horne's battles with diplomacy for nearly forty years.

The job wasn't easy. In a racist era, Horne would not be pushed around. She worked in places owned by thugs and patronized by high-rolling white snobs, some of whom could turn drunk and abusive. She needed protection, and no black man in the late forties could have demanded such respect on her behalf.

But Harris couldn't get her what she wanted most. Throughout her M-G-M hiatus, Horne kept brainstorming for dramatic roles she might play. *Picturegoer* reported her desire to portray "a famous colored woman abolitionist" from the Civil War. No such project materialized. Carlton Moss, a filmmaker and journalist who attacked discrimination, asked testily in print, "Why is it that Lena Horne is never allowed to do anything but sing? Why aren't Negroes ever a part of the story?"

Moss didn't know something that M-G-M producer Samuel Marx mentioned to the *Los Angeles Times* many years later. Louis B. Mayer's authority went deep, explained Marx, but even he had people to answer to, notably the company's sales department. Its staff knew the financial risks of integrating a black woman into white musicals. Time and again the moneymen shot down Mayer's attempts to do just that.

Still, he hadn't given up on her. In April 1948, he renewed Horne's contract for two more years. From an initial $350 a week, her salary zoomed to $2,000. But her welcome-back project only sank her spirits further. *Words and Music* put a sentimental gloss on the story of Richard Rodgers and Lorenz Hart, the legendary songwriting duo. Tom Drake and Mickey Rooney starred, while a parade of luminaries—Judy Garland, Gene Kelly, Perry Como, Mel Tormé—made singing cameos as themselves. After some interoffice correspondence about how they might weave Horne into an all-white cast, executives reverted to the familiar way: She would sing two songs on a nightclub set.

Rather than garbing her as a femme fatale, Helen Rose designed a prom-girl fantasy. Horne wore lavender ribbons in a pageboy hairdo; matching flowers trimmed her high-necked white dress. She dutifully smiled and sashayed, but her glance told another story. "The Lady Is a Tramp" found her ladling sarcasm onto the story of a simple girl who snickers at the pretensions of high society. Charles Cochran, a movie-loving singer-pianist who would later befriend Horne's daughter, Gail, never forgot his first viewing of that scene. He was eleven at the time. "She scared me," he said of Horne. "Those flashing eyes."

Critics panned the film as pretentious and overblown. "There's just no taking this picture seriously as biography," wrote Archer Winstein in the *New York Post*. But almost every review called Horne outstanding. *Variety* praised her "superb work . . . without benefit of any production behind her." Rodgers himself loved her performance, and wrote to Freed to tell him so.

Horne couldn't relish the praise. If she was so great, why wouldn't M-G-M entrust her with a real part? Wasn't she sexy enough? "I began to feel depressed about it, wasted emotionally," she revealed.

She didn't realize that all those sumptuously produced scenes—in which she stepped into view, sang seductively, spoke not a word, then vanished—had spun a mystique around her that would serve her well for decades. Her anger, too, had brought her work a fiery new dimension. No more the ever-smiling, eager-to-please songbird of the Savoy-Plaza, Horne now wielded a tantalizing aura of look-but-don't-touch.

Arthur Laurents saw the change. In the spring of 1948, he joined the crush of fans and industry bigwigs who attended Horne's debut at Slapsie Maxie's, a club on Hollywood Boulevard. "The moment she came to life as a performer for me was that opening at Slapsie Maxie's," said Laurents. "That was a Lena Horne that *no one* had ever seen. It transformed her into this kind of sexual tigress, with humor. It was dazzling. It wasn't polished. That's what made it so exciting."

The *Atlanta Daily World*'s Lawrence LaMar agreed. "Regardless of how much the public has appreciated the singing ability of Lena Horne," he wrote, "the Horne heard here Wednesday evening will truly dwarf that appreciation into insignificance." He found her "oozing with confidence." If Horne felt powerless over her film career, on the nightclub floor she was queen. And she insisted contractually that the black press be invited to her first night. "We were royally treated," wrote Eddie Burbridge of the *Los Angeles Sentinel*.

Subsequently she took her act to the Mayfair Room of Chicago's Hotel Blackstone. Exclaimed a reviewer: "One can almost imagine fire emitting from her nostrils as she wrings full meaning from every lyrical phrase. . . . In short, perfection."

The "astute and somewhat icy Miss Horne," wrote another critic, had turned visibly more calculating. "The Horne operating technique calls for her to appear totally unaware of her listeners while totally wrapped in the 'message' of her song. The technique works wonders." In an interview with *Look,* Horne explained who was in charge. "Most of the time I'm not singing to the people out there. I'm singing to myself. But I'd like the people to come along, if they do it quietly."

For all her insistence that she stayed aloof from the Hollywood crowd, Horne ventured out to parties, restaurants, and clubs, Hayton by her side. The singer shunned premieres and other splashy public functions in favor of such insider hangouts as the Café Gala, a Manhattan-style cabaret on Sunset Boulevard. The Gala had a tony and gay-friendly clientele; Roger Edens, Cole Porter, and Billy Strayhorn went there, while a boyishly exuberant Bobby Short entertained at the piano.

Within her professional sphere, Horne's secret marriage "was not a secret at all," said Artie Shaw. She seemed to be daring people to object, and almost no one did. "I never sensed that anybody felt peculiar about it," said Betty Comden. "They just seemed like a great couple." To the ultraliberal Betsy Blair, prejudice toward them would have been unthinkable. "In our circles, any kind of relationship—homosexual, mixed race—was accepted."

The Haytons gave regular dinner parties, and every few weeks André Previn attended. Still in his teens, the Jewish, Berlin-born wunderkind had joined the Freed Unit in 1947 as a composer-arranger. His European suavity and erudition helped him fit into the most sophisticated crowds. Previn recalled those dinners in Nichols Canyon as "fun and raucous and irreverent." Sometimes Horne sang with him at the piano. "It was all very friendly," he said, "and you met some very interesting people." They included Gene Kelly and Betsy Blair; actresses Sylvia Sidney, Olivia De Havilland, and Jane Greer; songwriters Harold Arlen and Ira Gershwin; and Hayton's colleague in the music department, Conrad Salinger. "Democrats, mostly," said Horne. "We were all in political organizations."

In the bosom of like-minded people, said Gloria DeHaven, "she could be herself. She was much freer; she was very funny." So it was at the fabled all-weekend open-house parties held by Kelly and Blair at their house on Rodeo Drive, the most fashionable stretch of Beverly Hills. There one could glimpse Hollywood with its hair down. Kelly bartended; Peter Lawford played Ping-Pong; Noël Coward or Leonard Bernstein played piano; Judy Garland sang "The Boy Next Door" accompanied by its composer, Hugh Martin. With only the slightest prompting, Betty Comden and Adolph Green tore into a whole show of their old club material. Maurice Chevalier, Kay Thompson, Previn, and Bob Fosse joined in the revelry.

There beside the pool on many a sunshiny day sat Lena Horne and Lennie Hayton. Blair remembered Horne as "very vital" and "having fun"; even among Hollywood's most charismatic stars, she stood out. "There was always a slight aura around her that the beautiful have," said Blair. Hayton seemed happiest noodling at the piano or shaking up his famous martinis. "He has almost no small talk," explained Horne later, "and when he talks the dry wit comes out more barbed."

Arthur Laurents was a sometime guest at the Kellys', and Horne would later tell him how out of place she'd felt behind her smile and gracious air. "Lena was very perceptive," he said. "She could see through all the bullshit." Even in that liberal enclave, reminders arose that she couldn't truly fit in. One Sunday the housekeeper was off, so Blair and Horne went into the kitchen to fetch more lemonade. A southern showgirl, there with her Texas husband, followed them, chatting all the way. Blair asked her to get some glasses out of the cabinet. Glancing at Horne, the showgirl asked, "Why doesn't *she* get them?" Blair angrily asked Kelly to escort the offender and her husband out the door.

Horne watched in silence. Later, as she and Hayton were leaving, she paused and grasped Blair's hands. "Betsy," she said, "if you're really going to be a friend of mine, you must treat me exactly—and I mean exactly—like any other friend. But thank you."

"I think she meant she could fight her own battles," concluded Blair in her memoir. "I never asked, but I never forgot."

AS 1949 began, it seemed clearer than ever that Walter White's campaign to destereotype the film industry had borne fruit. "Hollywood Digs 'Black Gold,'" exclaimed the *Chicago Defender*. M-G-M had begun work on *Intruder in the Dust*, an antilynching drama. It starred Cotton Club headliner Juano Hernandez as an elderly Negro who goes to jail for murdering a white man—a crime he didn't commit. Shooting took place in Oxford, Mississippi, and featured one hundred and fifty black extras. The Arthur Laurents play *Home of the Brave*, an indictment of racism in the military, became a movie, produced by socially conscious young filmmaker Stanley Kramer. The independently produced *Lost Boundaries* starred Mel Ferrer, a newcomer of Cuban descent, in the true story of a gifted black doctor who is compelled to pass in order to find work. Bosley Crowther of the *New York Times* led the raves when he hailed the film's "extraordinary courage, understanding and dramatic power."

Movies about Negroes who passed became a vogue in the late forties. Cast with white actors, such films helped a fearful Hollywood present black stories in a safe way. But Negro activists showed little patience for the trend. Richard Durham, a young black playwright from Chicago, decried Hollywood's self-righteous "masturbation" as a sham of liberalism.

For the first time in years, however, Horne felt optimistic. She talked excitedly to the *New York Amsterdam News* about what "a long way" Negroes had come in the film industry, and how "encouraged" she felt. Maybe Hollywood could find a place for her at last. Her hopes zoomed even higher when she learned of a movie in the works at Fox. *Pinky* would tell the story of a light-skinned young black woman who passes in order to enter a discriminatory nursing school in Boston. Race hidden, she starts an affair with a white man. The term "pinky" was a popular put-down in the black community for those who passed, but the film looked sympathetically at its lead character's plight. In its script, a dying spinster (played by Ethel Barrymore) spoke about the plight of "fine, young, sensitive" blacks. "We give them political freedom without its meaning. We give them education and withhold its rewards. Dignity and pride can be more important than food and shelter."

Before shooting began, *Pinky*'s producer, Darryl F. Zanuck, contacted Walter White and requested he read the script. The NAACP leader assigned the job to his daughter, Jane. A gifted actress and well-read intellectual, Jane knew the complications of life as an extremely fair-skinned Negro. Her coloring, inherited from her father, had confused casting directors and left her frequently unemployed.

Jane flew to Hollywood to serve as technical adviser. She met with Zanuck, screenwriter Philip Dunne, and other members of the *Pinky* team. "Everybody involved was white," she recalled, "except me." Later she learned that Zanuck had told Dunne in private: "Don't let her sell you anything!" Nonetheless, he installed her in a hotel with a secretary and had her write an assessment of each scene. "It was a *highly* dubious script in many regards. I was terribly aware, as my father had inculcated in me, of what impression a thing that seemed to be innocent might give. There was a scene where somebody in the black community raised up her skirt and pulled a razor out of the top of her stocking. I said that this was a bad idea and should be cut."

Zanuck and Dunne heeded most of her suggestions, if not that one. A classic stereotype remained—Ethel Waters, in full mammy regalia as Pinky's grandmother. Not long before, the breakthrough star had hit bottom. In her memoir, she wrote of living in a friend's basement in Harlem; there, in Norma Desmond fashion, she sat singing aloud with her old records. Surprisingly, some of her best moments lay ahead of her, notably a lead role in the Broadway and film versions of Carson McCullers's *The Member of the Wedding*. And with the 1950 premiere of *Beulah*, she became the first black actress to star in a TV series.

But Waters unashamedly played a maid. All around her, black artists had joined the struggle to upgrade the Negro image, but Waters stood back. "I'm not concerned with civil rights," she declared. "I'm only concerned with God-given rights, and they are available to everyone!" Her attitude made her a pariah among many progressive-minded blacks, but they couldn't dispute her luminous acting, which would earn her Oscar nominations for both *Pinky* and *The Member of the Wedding*.

The presence in the former of her onetime nemesis didn't deter Horne. Knowing little more than the film's premise, she told herself, "Lena, *you* are going to be Pinky! There is *no way* they can deny you this part!" She hopped a train to Hollywood, marched into M-G-M, and begged executives to recommend her for the part.

It was an impossible dream. Even if she'd worn lightening makeup, Horne was too famous as a black star to portray a woman fair enough to pass. What's more, Fox had its own lead in mind: popular contract player Jeanne Crain, a blue-eyed beauty from Southern California.

Horne called Crain's casting "the last straw." She felt further insulted by the young actress's Oscar nomination for *Pinky*. The *Pittsburgh Courier* reported that Horne had "given up all hope that the vicious Hollywood code that restricts opportunity for Negro stars will be broken."

The rejection she felt in Los Angeles was proving unbearable. Years later she told Marie Brenner of *New York* magazine: "Over and over I kept saying to everybody, 'I hate this fucking place.'" Why would no producer give her a proper chance? By then even a maid's part would have been welcome. Speaking to Darr Smith of the Los Angeles *Daily News*, Horne denied that she'd ever categorically shunned such roles. "I've just refused to play certain kinds of maids," she explained. "If a maid is an integral part of a picture, if there's a reason for her being there and she has something to say, let me at her."

Her patience had shattered; now Horne set out to shame her studio. "She is a little tired of being kicked around because she happens to be colored," wrote Smith—adding word that Horne planned to leave M-G-M as soon as her contract expired. Frank Eng of the same paper scorned "the type of polite obeisance to Jim Crowism that finds Metro making all of Miss Horne's cinematic contributions in single separate episodes that can be cut from the film for Southern exposure." A *Life* feature declared her "The Girl Whom the Movies Buried." The magazine noted that she'd left a promising career as a singer in order to be "gobbled up" by M-G-M and "plunged into a stultifying series of small roles in what she calls 'pork-chop-in-the-sky' films." She hoped another studio would do better by her, the reporter noted.

Her mood is obvious in an M-G-M short filmed in the commissary that spring, during the studio's twenty-fifth-anniversary luncheon. Dozens of stars file in and sit down. The camera pans the long tables, where actors laugh and chat gaily. Katharine Hepburn looks especially delighted as she talks with a friend to her right. On her other side sits a silent Lena Horne—chewing gum and glaring at her. "I was the only one of us there!" said the singer later. "After a while, I would read in the paper that I should've been more grateful because they did permit me to sit in the commissary. Every time I think of it I get mad."

It brought her little comfort to hear how many blacks saw her as victorious. "Being a successful Negro artist is an unenviable position to be in," she told Ira Peck of *PM*. "I'll never forget how frightened I was for Jackie Robinson—because we knew that if he made the normal mistakes that any ballplayer made it would be a reflection on his race. We felt, oh God, he must perform magnificently or those white people will scorn him. Well, I'm in the same sort of position. You can never forget you're a Negro. You're reminded of it at every turn. I want to think as an artist. Jackie wants to think as a baseball player—not as a *Negro* artist, *Negro* ballplayer. It's our burden."

Yet on June 12, 1949, a radio play extolled Horne as the "Negro Cinderella." That was the name of an episode of *Destination Freedom*, a Chicago series that dramatized the lives of outstanding blacks, from George Washington Carver to Nat King Cole. The ninety-one scripts came from Richard Durham, a Mississippi-born dramatist. Durham sought to bust through "the camouflage of crackpots and hypocrites" that had led millions to think that most Negroes were like Stepin Fetchit or Amos and Andy. His show ran on Chicago's NBC affiliate from 1948 until 1950, when it died for lack of a sponsor.

Negro Cinderella depicted a stagestruck girl's "search for the golden slipper." Her quest was "rocky," explained Janice Kingslow in her role as Horne. "I was a Negro. I was Cinderella. My stepsisters were greed and bigotry, backed by those who make profit out of prejudice." A salesman forces her to pay for shoes she tries on but doesn't want. After a screen test in Hollywood, a producer gives her the bad news: "We had in mind more of a Negro type." Even after she becomes a star, a restaurant won't serve her. But her struggles would surely help bring on a brighter day.

"I knew there was a new generation, Negro and white, growing in the South—unafraid, unintimidated by bigotry and race superstition. They would furnish the princes who would put the golden slippers on tomorrow's Cinderellas."

At the end, Lena Horne herself offered words of reassurance:

Every American girl has her own Cinderella story. It springs from the rather human need to find a way to live free from persecution and insecurity. The great American dream is in itself a Cinderella story. The great American dream which Thomas Jefferson, Crispus Attucks, John Brown, Frederick Douglass, Harriet Tubman, and hundreds of our forebears brought closer to reality in their day, must be brought to reality, not in some distant and dim future, but in our own time.

That August, the real-life Negro Cinderella had to fight to sleep at St. Louis's Chase Hotel, where she was performing. Management barred her from the dining room. A month later in Chicago, Caruso's restaurant stopped Horne and an interracial group of friends at the door, demanding they show their "membership cards." *"Are you discriminating against Negroes?"* asked Horne twice. She filed a suit against the eatery and announced it to the press; later she agreed to drop it in exchange for a written apology, to be printed in Chicago papers. Around that time, Gloria DeHaven saw Horne at the Eden Roc hotel in Miami Beach. "She wasn't allowed to walk through the lobby. And she couldn't go down in the elevator."

At the swanky Cocoanut Grove nightclub in Hollywood's Ambassador Hotel, Ralph Harris stood alongside the maître d' to make sure no Negroes were refused. As a test, he invited black acquaintances to drop by posing as strangers. He also demanded that Horne and the band be given rooms in the hotel. "I'd like to be treated like everybody, not like a freak," Horne told Earl Wilson. But she continued to encounter "one nasty little fight after another" as she and her band worked a national circuit of highbrow supper clubs. This was the career she'd struggled to achieve, but after fifteen years in cabarets, the view from the bandstand hadn't changed. "Wherever we went, it was nothing but white people," said Chico Hamilton.

• • •

AT M-G-M, Horne continued to hear of projects the studio had in mind for her. In December 1948, columnists reported that Horne would costar in *East of Broadway*, a movie with Jimmy Durante and a black teenage discovery, singer Toni Harper. A month later, the *Los Angeles Sentinel* revealed that Horne might be sharing a film with Billy Eckstine.

The one she made proved far less interesting. *Duchess of Idaho* was an insipid B-musical; it starred Esther Williams as a swimming star who helps her lovesick roommate snare her rich boss. Horne's presence in the film seemed like an afterthought. She appeared, as usual, in a night-club scene, introduced in the familiar way—"Ladies and gentlemen, *Miss Lena Horne!*" Wearing silver-blue chiffon, Horne emerges from behind shimmery curtains and finds her spot on a dance floor. She sings "Baby, Come Out of the Clouds," a cynical antilove song, unmemorable except for her performance. She weaves and glides as gracefully as ever, but the hallmarks of her new style had taken over—the clenched smile, the blazing eyes, the feral gestures. A second number, "You Won't Forget Me," fell to the cutting room floor.

"Ole Nosey," a *Chicago Defender* columnist, had his say about *The Duchess of Idaho*. "The Horne songs are independent units, as usual—so the studio can CUT THEM OUT when they reach such Negro hating sections of the country as Memphis, etc. where this beautiful and charming star is not allowed to be seen on the screen because she is a NEGRO."

Around that time, a *Los Angeles Daily News* reporter told the story of his lunch with Horne in the M-G-M commissary. A little girl walked by with an autograph book and stopped at their table. "Are you an actress?"

Horne hesitated. "Well . . ."

"Because if you are an actress, I've got to get the signatures of an actress and an actor today."

"Maybe I'm better known as a singer," said Horne wistfully.

The girl frowned, but handed her the autograph book anyway. Then a friend of the singer's walked in. "There goes Gloria DeHaven," Horne said. "*She's* an actress. Why don't you get *her* signature?"

Horne thought she might find a home on television, but that dream, too, was naïve; the infant medium would prove just as discriminatory as film. TV brought its personalities into the living rooms of millions of Americans; many of them would only have allowed blacks in the kitchen. Even so, in 1949 Horne shot a talk-show pilot with two white friends, Tex McCrary and Jinx Falkenburg. Radio's most popular married sophisticates, Tex and Jinx hosted an interview show that welcomed achievers of all races, including Horne.

The pilot sank. She mentioned it to a reporter. "The people we were trying to sell were delighted with it, but they turned it down and said it would have its 'limitations.' Yep, *I* was the limitation."

If her studio couldn't do much for her acting-wise, at least it tried to utilize her singing. In 1949, M-G-M's namesake record label issued the last of a dozen sides that Horne had made since her return from Europe. With Luther Henderson conducting, she recorded a stylish repertoire in a variety of settings. For "The Man I Love" and "A Foggy Day," she sang with just piano. Horne revived Harold Arlen and Ted Koehler's "I've Got the World on a String," her favorite song from the Cotton Club revues; she performed it with a trio, as she did in cabarets. An Ellington rarity, "Take Love Easy," came from his short-lived Broadway musical *Beggar's Holiday*. Strings swirled around her in Cole Porter's dreamy beguine "Love of My Life," written for a film in which she almost appeared, *The Pirate*.

The sides marked her once more as a class act; she handled complex lyrics with grace and phrased intelligently. But the feistiness of her live shows was absent. In the businesslike climate of the recording studio, with the politest of backings, carefulness took the place of passion. Sometimes she broke the placid surface. In a swing-era standard, "Sometimes I'm Happy," she improvised playfully over a funky trio. "Is It Always Like This?," a tender account of first love, stirred some passion in Horne. Alec Wilder, a snob's-snob composer of café ballads and chamber music, had written it for Mabel Mercer, the doyenne of cabaret singers. But *Down Beat* declared that the highbrow single would go nowhere; Horne had to be seen, not just heard.

Indeed, all these sides were far from jukebox material; only "Deed I Do" made the charts. Horne spoke sourly of her recorded efforts to reporter William Peper. "They didn't sound like me. In fact, they didn't sound like anything. No wonder they didn't sell."

Away from the studio, her defiance kept growing. She wore a Star of David, a reflection of her union with a Jew. Horne also stepped up her activism. *Ebony* reported that Horne traveled the country to support liberal causes, from desegregation to veterans' rights. Nearly any group who requested her participation got it. She'd become a fervid speaker, and often took the podium. "I try not to be a screaming soapboxer," explained Horne, "but there are so many things to be mad at that I feel it my duty to tell the people we must fight."

Some personal appearances delighted her. At Ebbets Field, home of the Brooklyn Dodgers, Horne thrilled America's number-one black baseball hero when she made the feature presentation at Roy Campanella Day. Beaming with pride, Horne walked over to the guest of honor and handed him the keys to a car. Campanella would call that moment a highlight of his life.

For all her disillusionment with her own career, Horne still clung to a vestige of her Hollywood dream. She told reporter Lowell Redding, "There isn't a nightclub entertainer in the world who wouldn't give his right eye to appear in a movie—no matter how small or insignificant the part." Her contract would expire in April 1950, but she'd agreed to extend it by twelve months—"only for one picture a year," reported *Ebony*, "and with the understanding that she is free to perform wherever and whenever she wants the rest of the year."

The studio consented. Horne remained the only Negro star on its roster; to let her go when Hollywood was striving to atone for its racial sins would not have looked good.

Horne had a strong incentive for wanting to stick around. In 1949, her fantasy vehicle, the long-awaited third screen adaptation of *Show Boat*, entered the planning stages. M-G-M had held the movie rights to the Kern-Hammerstein masterwork for over a decade. *Till the Clouds Roll By* had given viewers a tantalizing foretaste of the Technicolor *Show Boat*—and of Horne singing one of the musical's greatest songs. After her glowing reviews, Horne couldn't imagine that M-G-M would deny her the role of Julie.

The character fascinated her. Julie is the beautiful wife of Steve Baker, the lead actor of a troupe who perform on a show boat that comes to

Natchez, Mississippi. She holds a dangerous secret, and Steve knows it. So does Pete, his rival. One night during a rehearsal, Julie and Steve learn that a sheriff is coming to arrest them. Pete has leaked the truth: Julie is one-eighth Negro and married to a white man, which is against the law. Before the sheriff arrives, Steve cuts her hand with a pocket knife and sucks her blood, so that he too will have Negro blood in him.

Ever since *Clouds,* people in and around the Freed Unit had told her she was a natural for the role. "I thought I was gonna be the hot lady in *Show Boat,* I was gonna be Julie," Horne told Johnny Carson years later.

But from the start, Freed and director George Sidney knew who they wanted. "There's no question that it was being scripted and sculpted as a major showcase for Judy Garland," said Garland authority John Fricke. With the news reported in columns, Horne had to have known of the studio's intentions. "M-G-M did not want her for the part," added Fricke. "I don't think it was ever even a remote possibility." George Sidney confirmed it. "She was never considered," he said in 1982.

Horne would later admit that executives had told her why. An obviously black actress could not play an octoroon who had survived in turn-of-the-century Mississippi by passing for white. They didn't mention a comparable obstacle: Horne's acting skills were in no way up to such a serious role.

Even if M-G-M had chosen her, Horne would have gravely endangered a costly film. Until 1952, the Hollywood Production Code barred miscegenation on-screen—not in scripts but in casting. The previous *Show Boat* film, released in 1936, had passed muster because even though Julie had mixed blood, the actress who played her (Helen Morgan) did not. The distinction seemed hypocritical, yet the studios were powerless to fight it; no wonder Hollywood cast white actresses as characters like Pinky, who falls for a white man.

Horne turned a deaf ear to every rationale. "Lena wanted to play Julie more than life," said Gene Davis. The loss of that part struck her as M-G-M's cruelest punishment for her refusal to star in *St. Louis Woman,* for her activism, maybe even for her color. There seemed no hope left for her in the movies. On March 17, 1950, the *Hollywood Reporter* broke the news: "Lena Horne and M-G-M yesterday agreed to a cancellation of the singer's contract which had thirteen months to go. The parting was amicable, Miss Horne and the studio agreeing that there was a dearth of top spots available for her."

In a *New York Amsterdam News* interview, Horne tried to sound philosophical. "I learned long ago not to want anything too hard. Then you're not too disappointed when you don't get it." M-G-M, she said, could give her only musical cameos "that won't be missed when southern movie houses cut them out. And they always do. They even black out my name in the advertisements."

Perhaps because she spent so little time on the lot, Horne seemed unaware of ominous stirrings within the Freed Unit. That extravagant division had dominated the studio, and it was bleeding money; furthermore, M-G-M hadn't earned a major Oscar in years. Nick Schenck, president of M-G-M's parent company, Loew's, Inc., felt the time had come to uplift the studio's frothy tone. Mayer tried to appease him by hiring an ambitious young writer-producer, Dore Schary, as production chief. Mayer lived to regret it. "I was a sheep who invited a hungry wolf to dinner," he said later. The "wolf" didn't care for musicals; message films, he felt, had far more bearing on the times. Gradually the Freed Unit's stars disappeared. "When Dore Schary came in, we were all let go—anybody that Mr. Mayer liked," said Kathryn Grayson. In 1951, Schenck fired Mayer.

Schary would seemingly have had little use for Lena Horne, who served a mainly decorative function on-screen—and who had a reputation as a troublemaker. But for all the friction, both he and Mayer liked her. They may have never officially dissolved her contract, for M-G-M continued to seek projects for her. In 1950, reports persisted that Horne might be cast in *The Man on the Train*, a film about an early effort to assassinate Abraham Lincoln. There was also talk of starring Horne with Billy Eckstine in a musical based on the Cotton Club, "provided she approves the script."

As usual, the ideas fizzled. But all she could think about was *Show Boat*. On the day the *Hollywood Reporter* announced her exit from M-G-M, Horne set sail for France with Hayton and Gail. The singer would play the Club Baccarat in Paris, then tour Europe all spring and summer. Wherever she went, the public hailed her as Hollywood royalty. Horne made her debut at the venerated London Palladium, and every major reviewer came to see her. *The Daily Telegraph* found her startlingly raw: "She dilated with great emotional intensity on the miseries, the tortures and the cruelties with which a lover is beset. She sings with poise, passion, and strength." Theater critic A. E. Wilson called Horne a "great tragedy queen," but rued the sight of her "distort[ing] her beauty with such expressions and grimaces. The numbers she sings are hardly worth that sacrifice."

Horne moved from success to success, unaware that two of the biggest crises of her life were brewing back home. Warning signs had preceded both. During a recent engagement in Hollywood, Alvin Williams Stokes, a black investigator for the House Un-American Activities Committee (HUAC), had entered her dressing room. The organization was hot on the trail of Communist infiltration of the motion-picture industry. It cast its net wide, and any progressive activity was suspect. When Stokes identified himself, Horne responded with disgust. How could a Negro work for such an organization?

"I started to tell her I hadn't married out of my race, but I decided that wasn't pertinent," recalled Stokes in 1958. He went on to ask that Horne join "a number of prominent Negroes" in testifying at a Washington hearing against Paul Robeson. All of them, he claimed, had agreed to comment on a recent statement of Robeson's, that should America decide to attack the Soviet Union, no Negro would cooperate. Robeson had visited the country, and its seeming antiracism thrilled him. "Here, for the first time in my life, I walk in full human dignity," he said. His stance willfully ignored the Stalinist atrocities that had claimed untold lives. It earned Robeson a lot of enemies, even on the left, and made him one of the FBI's most wanted.

But Horne "refused flatly" to criticize him, said Stokes. She added that even though she didn't always agree with his politics, he was her friend—"and she would never testify for our committee because its chairman was a Southerner." Stokes left. He wrote down what she'd said, then shared it with his superiors.

Later Horne groused to a reporter, "I don't know if Paul was a Communist. What's more, I don't give a damn. If he sought my company, I was happy to avail myself. He taught me the culture of my people."

California had its own un-American activities committee. Its leader, Senator Jack B. Tenney, had his eye on Horne. His 1947, 1948, and 1949 reports had listed her as a "pro-Communist," along with Robeson, Frank Sinatra, Betty Garrett, her husband, Larry Parks, and actors Edward G. Robinson, John Garfield, and Fredric March, among many others. *The Chicago Defender* noted Horne's "indignation and resentment" at Tenney's accusation. But at the time, accusations such as his had seemed too silly to take seriously.

Soon that would change. On February 9, 1950, Joseph R. McCarthy, a Republican senator from Wisconsin, pulled out a sheet of paper during a speech in Wheeling, West Virginia. Here, he alleged, was a list of 205 Communists and Soviet spies employed by the State Department. Many Americans found it easy to buy McCarthy's claim. Alger Hiss, a State Department official, had just gone to jail, convicted for lying under oath about his Communist past.

The Red Scare was on, fueled by fear of a superpower that seemed poised for world dominance. With a push of a button, the Soviets might unleash a nuclear catastrophe, destroying America and possibly the earth. Tension invaded almost every crevice of society, in what seemed like a black-and-white case of the bad guys out to get the good guys. Throughout America, the words "Commie," "pinko," and "Red" would become almost as widespread as "nigger."

HUAC had become a household name, thanks to its ruthless attempts to ferret out suspected Communists or sympathizers. In *The Memory of All That*, Betsy Blair recalls the start of the Cold War, when the suspected were subpoenaed, questioned under oath, and prodded to rat on colleagues and friends. To refuse was to risk imprisonment.

"Suitcases were packed for emergency flight," wrote Blair. "People began to avoid everyone except close friends. . . . The accusations, the confessions, the lists of names given to the committee screamed in the headlines of every newspaper. Men and women who had become caring, involved, idealistic became cowards as a result of threats and intimidation—and sometimes out of selfish ambition—denouncing their friends to save themselves."

One informer had helped bring *Pinky* to the screen. Elia Kazan was the Oscar-winning director of some of the most important films of the fifties, including *A Streetcar Named Desire*, *East of Eden*, and *On the Waterfront*. A former Communist and continued Socialist, he succumbed to pressure from HUAC and by a terrified Hollywood hierarchy to name names.

The witch hunt had given the government an excuse to weed out other undesirables—anyone who had dared question the American system, with all its discrimination and oppression. To brand freedom fighters Communists proved a good way to snuff out their efforts. "Anything that was a step forward in organizing or advancing the causes of civil liberties and civil rights was dubbed Communist," said Esther Jackson.

More and more of the liberals Horne knew were coming under fire. In 1947, Leon Josephson, the brother of Café Society owner Barney Josephson, had gone to jail for refusing to answer questions posed to him in a subpoena by the newly formed HUAC. Westbrook Pegler, the Pulitzer Prize–winning right-wing columnist, wrote a devastating column about Leon. It closed with the fatal line, "And there is much to be said about his brother Barney."

Several of Pegler's peers, including Walter Winchell and Dorothy Kilgallen, joined in on the attack. Rumors engulfed Café Society Downtown: that it was a secret meeting place for Russian spies, that undercover FBI agents photographed everyone who came in. Josephson's high-minded bravado had caught up with him. Business crashed, and he had to close both his downtown and uptown clubs. In 1950, he took out a full-page ad in *Billboard*. It was a single line on an otherwise blank page: "My head is bloodied but not bowed—Barney Josephson."

For years, Horne's anger had made her a lot less careful about watching her tongue. Now she'd begun taking public jabs at the witch-hunters. She was also less than discreet about her marriage; clearly Stokes had known all about it. So did many reporters. But whenever they asked Horne if she were Mrs. Lennie Hayton, she said no. Many in the industry assumed that Louis B. Mayer had ordered her to keep quiet, but Horne never said he had. Now she and Mayer had parted ways, so she had nothing to fear from M-G-M. Her family and friends had known about the marriage all along. But what would the public think? Would they turn on her?

S. W. Garlington, a *New York Amsterdam News* columnist, sensed greater damage in her secrecy. He asked in an editorial, "Is Lena Wrecking Her Future?" Garlington noted her audience's loyalty: "It went along with her when she left her husband and kids to make a stab at personal fame. It stuck by her when she could neither sing nor act. It did all of this because she was a pretty girl who always behaved in a ladylike manner." Now her denials were casting a sordid shadow upon her virtue.

"Is she married?" asked Garlington. "The public deserves to know."

Louella Parsons, the motherly Hollywood gossip queen, kept prodding Horne for the scoop. The *Atlanta Daily World* dug just as persistently. The singer, wrote a staff reporter, "has publicly stated that she is not married to Lennie Hayton, musician who is her constant escort around town. But at intimate private gatherings the glamorous motion picture and stage star has on several occasions introduced Hayton as her husband." The journalist sleuthed out the name of a New York hotel where the couple had registered, and placed several calls asking for the room of Mrs. Lennie Hayton. "Miss Horne usually answers," wrote the reporter.

The *Los Angeles Sentinel* stopped waiting for Horne to come clean. In April 1950, the newspaper freely called Hayton her "hubby." Few in the press seemed ruffled by the intermarriage; it was Horne's dishonesty that annoyed them. Dissent came from a surprising and hurtful source. That year, a disapproving Noble Sissle snitched to a reporter that he'd heard Horne introduce her "husband" at a gathering. A whole article resulted.

Horne knew she could no longer sidestep the truth. In Paris, Billy Strayhorn urged her to level with the public. "We sat with Lennie," she recalled, "and he said, 'Well, we're gonna have to make this known.'" Doing so from another continent seemed safer. On June 21, she called Parsons, who had always treated her kindly. Then she cabled the *Pittsburgh Courier*. Asked if she expected trouble in Hollywood, Horne said no. The movies didn't want her anyway, so why should they care who her husband was?

Rosa Heppner, her publicist, wired the U.S. press services to announce that the Haytons had been married since 1947. Ralph Harris explained that the couple had hidden their wedding "for professional reasons," but had decided that it was "time that everybody knew." The first reports appeared on June 22. "And then, of course, the shit hit the fan," recalled Horne decades later.

In fact, the press showed no hostility. The *Los Angeles Times* carried the news in a tiny item headlined "Lena Horne's 1947 Wedding Disclosed." Without editorializing, the piece noted, "She is a Negro, he is white." *Newsweek,* too, carried the announcement matter-of-factly, as did dozens of other publications. Some black newspapers expressed relief that she'd finally come clean.

June 22 brought a far more worrisome published piece. That day, *Red Channels* hit newsstands and the mailboxes of hundreds of entertainment-industry executives. A cheaply printed pamphlet, it came from a savage group of red-baiters: Theodore Kirkpatrick, an ex–FBI agent who ran *Counterattack: The Newsletter of Facts to Combat Communism*; Vincent Hartnett, a right-wing TV producer; and J. B. Matthews, a former leftist and HUAC informant. The cover showed a red hand clutching a microphone. *Red Channels* named 151 alleged "Red Fascists and their sympathizers" who, it claimed, were taking over the broadcast and film industries. The book vowed a boycott of anyone who hired them. Lena Horne was on the list. So were many artists she'd met or known—Orson Welles, Artie Shaw, Arthur Laurents, Langston Hughes, Fredi Washington, Avon Long, E. Y. "Yip" Harburg, John Latouche. *Red Channels* also named a host of Café Society alumni, including Jack Gilford, Zero Mostel, Josh White, Burl Ives, Judy Holliday, and Hazel Scott.

Word of the book reached Horne quickly. "The beige lovely is so mad she almost blew a blood vessel in Gay Paree," wrote Billy Rowe. Horne saw the blacklisting as payback for her association with Robeson. But *Red Channels* noted her involvement in eleven "subversive" causes, not all related to him. The Civil Rights Congress fought legal cases of racial injustice. The American Committee for Protection of Foreign Born defended the unjust deportation of non-American activists. The Southern Conference for Human Welfare, a favorite of Eleanor Roosevelt, was an interracial coalition that fostered democracy in the South. The United Negro and Allied Veterans of America protected the rights of former black servicemen. Horne had also joined various groups in support of Benjamin J. Davis, a fearless civil rights lawyer and Communist. Liberal petitioners could count on Horne. "She signed everything," said Madeline Lee Gilford, who had earned her own *Red Channels* entry.

A 1998 documentary, *Scandalize My Name: Stories from the Blacklist*, deemed the pamphlet an "honor roll" of individuals who cared enough "to lend their names and their talents to help others." But the film, TV, and radio industries didn't see it that way. Fearful of losing ad revenue, they bowed to the witch-hunters and banned most, though not all, of the accused. Other blacklists sprang up; they destroyed countless careers and even led to suicides. Robeson may have been hit the worst. "So inspiring was he and so powerful was he that at all costs he had to be silenced," said Harry Belafonte. Branded a traitor to a country that had given him an education and a career, Robeson lost almost everything, including his passport. After regaining it in 1958, he fled to Europe and the Soviet Union.

For the accused, *Red Channels* had varying repercussions. People involved in the broadcast media had to find a way to clear themselves— typically by appearing before HUAC and denouncing their pasts. Naming real or suspected Communists could suffice. Rather than face that sort of pressure, some of the blacklisted, like Arthur Laurents, fled to Europe.

Horne would later claim to Arthur Bell of *The Village Voice* that M-G-M had given her an ultimatum. If she wanted to be considered for any future roles she had to write an apology to the Screen Actors Guild. She cooperated. "The letter said, 'I'm black. I have these friends. I didn't know anything about their politics.'"

She knew plenty, of course. For now, however, *Red Channels* had little effect on Horne. She made most of her living in nightclubs and theaters, none of which concerned the blacklisters. But a late-July column item by Louella Parsons suggested the toll Horne's recent troubles had taken on her. According to Parsons, the singer had suffered a miscarriage in Paris.

HORNE felt such disappointment in her own achievements that she wondered how she could have inspired anyone. Yet in 1950, while home in Los Angeles, she helped boost a stunning nineteen-year-old who would eventually become the muse of black modern dance. Horne saw Carmen de Lavallade at Lester Horton's Dance Theater, a groundbreaking interracial troupe in Hollywood. Her Creole heritage, combined with her lithe, serpentine body language, had given the down-to-earth girl an air of mystery. "A lot of people couldn't tell what my background was," she said later. "They thought I was 'exotic.'"

Horne saw her as class and responded eagerly to Horton's request that she sponsor her. That meant little more than shared photo ops and a press release, but Horne's endorsement of the teenager made a difference. *Our World* placed de Lavallade alongside Horne in its choice of the "10 Most Beautiful Negro Women" of 1950. Black newspapers hailed the ascent of a young beauty who danced "non-stereotypical roles" in Horton's works. Her "sponsor," wrote the *Los Angeles Sentinel,* hadn't been so lucky. "Miss Horne, who has consistently fought for equal opportunity for the Negro artist, has just won her freedom from M-G-M after nine years of being stereotyped in musicals."

It was a bitter victory. But the fall of 1950 found Horne newly hopeful, for Judy Garland was out of *Show Boat.* For fourteen years M-G-M had worked Garland mercilessly, and finally she'd cracked under the strain. She was on her second suspension, due to her unreliability on the set of *Royal Wedding,* a film from which she was dropped. Arthur Freed and George Sidney still wanted her as Julie, but by September 30, the day she would have returned to work, her weight had so ballooned that she was deemed uncastable.

Horne begged for another chance at the part. But Freed and Sidney were no more interested than before, and the blacklist had nothing to do with it. Sidney began testing numerous singer-actresses, all white: Dinah Shore, Lee Wiley, Ginny Simms, Julie London, Julie Wilson. One candidate stood out. Since 1941, Ava Gardner had appeared in twenty-two M-G-M features, most of them forgettable. Her career had gained steam in 1947, when she played opposite Clark Gable in *The Hucksters.* Soon a press campaign would tag her "The World's Most Beautiful Animal."

Gardner had grown up poor in rural North Carolina; Betsy Blair recalled her as "this uneducated, backwards mountain girl. But she had the greatest generosity and goodness in her." That mixture of qualities struck George Sidney as just right for Julie. It also attracted Lena Horne, who'd become one of her closest pals.

The director gave Gardner a Horne recording from *Till the Clouds Roll By,* and instructed her to memorize it for her screen test. The actress would lip-synch to her friend's voice. Horne later quoted Gardner at the end of that day. "Girl, I'm sick to death of you. They're locking me up in a sound booth all day and making me work my mouth to Lena Horne records so I'll learn to play Julie the way you would have played it. Why didn't they just give you the fucking part in the first place?'"

Gardner got the part. The choice of her best Hollywood girlfriend—a white woman—devastated Horne. "I know that it weighed very heavily on Ava, too," said Marge Champion, who would dance in *Show Boat* along with her husband, Gower. But Gardner had never gotten a showcase as grand as this—"and she wanted that part so much," said Champion.

She brought it an edge that no other actress had. Her Julie was no subservient, fragile flower; years later the director Peter Bogdanovich summed up Gardner as "the good-bad girl, the tough-soft, hard-drinking, straight-shooting beauty who could keep up with any guy." Off camera, she cussed like a longshoreman and rebelled against authority. Gardner, said Horne, "was *down*. She was Ava, not Ava the star. She never believed that the image they saw was what she really was. . . . And she had a big mouth like mine. We had no subtlety, no discretion, and before we thought we spoke, which in those days was not always the right thing to do." What's more, in an age of intense sexual repression, Gardner was a predator to rival almost any man, fearless about cavorting in public with black friends, including Sammy Davis, Jr.

Horne, who felt victimized by so many of the males she'd known professionally, admired her friend's brass. But it was largely a façade. "I'm just poor white trash," Gardner told Esther Williams, and she didn't consider herself much of an actress, either.

For all her dismay over *Show Boat*, Horne saw the actress as a true kindred spirit: someone as anti-Hollywood as she, and as insecure. Gardner lived up the street, and often she dropped by Horne's house after work. The women got "loaded," as Horne put it, on Lennie's martinis. Then they raucously bit the hand that fed them. Both of them felt "screwed" by M-G-M: "I for racial reasons," said Horne, and "she for being liberated long before it became acceptable." They had a field day dishing the men they'd had in common (like Artie Shaw, Gardner's ex-husband) and individually.

Much of their talk centered on the star with whom Gardner shared a fiery obsession. Her public affair with Frank Sinatra had tormented the

crooner's wife, Nancy, the mother of his three children. In 1950, she announced their separation; the next year he wed Gardner.

Sinatra was at his neediest and most wounded. His years as a bobby-
soxer idol seemed through, and his record label, Columbia, had dropped
him. Meanwhile, he and his "beautiful animal" tore into a marriage
marked by taunting, head games, and stormy jealousies. Gardner proved
untamable, and she drove Sinatra crazy; he even attempted suicide when
she left him. They finally divorced in 1957, but the impossible relationship would haunt them for decades to come.

Gardner vented her frustrations to Horne, whose sympathies hardly
lay with Sinatra. He knew it—and forever after, he was no fan of Lena
Horne. "We don't like each other personally," admitted Horne to writer
R. Couri Hay in 1972. "It started with Ava Gardner."

Sinatra seemed to see Horne as an accomplice in Gardner's rejection
of him; she was butting in on his business, he thought. "Ava was one of
the only women that told Sinatra to go fuck off," said Ray Ellis, Horne's
conductor and close companion in the sixties. "She'd say, 'Ah, you dumb
fucking guinea'—she'd put him down all over the place. And Lena was
a witness to this. With his ego, every time he heard Lena's name all he
could remember is that she watched him getting put down."

Much later a friend of Horne's, the choreographer Claude Thomp-
son, recalled the long-standing rumor that a paranoid Sinatra suspected
more than just friendship between Gardner and Horne. According to
Lee Server's 2006 Gardner biography *Love Is Nothing*, Sinatra had ac-
cused his wife of straying with her own sex. One night, wrote Server,
Frank burst into a Beverly Hills restaurant in which Gardner, Lana
Turner, and a third woman were having dinner. *"Lesbians!"* he screamed.
"You're a bunch of goddamned lesbians!"

The early fifties were miserable years for three of Hollywood's most
envied stars. Slumped on Horne's living room sofa, martini glass in one
hand and a cigarette in the other, Gardner poured out her heart about
Sinatra. At the same time, she couldn't help reminding Horne of the role
she'd coveted.

In *Show Boat: The Story of a Classic American Musical,* author Miles
Kreuger denounced the film's casting. "The role of the sweetly fragile,
highly vulnerable bird who is crushed by circumstances went to (of all

people) the voluptuous Ava Gardner, who appears strong enough to take on a cage of wild tigers." Marge and Gower Champion played a pair of small-time hoofers. In *Show Boat,* wrote Kreuger, they seemed "so urbanely polished, attractively groomed, and dazzlingly skillful that one wonders why on earth Frank and Ellie are not top Broadway headliners."

Realism scarcely touched this production. Gardner's earthy, untrained singing voice would have suited her role nicely, but she was forced to lip-synch to the liquid mezzo-soprano of Annette Warren, an accomplished dubber who sounded nothing like Gardner. In M-G-M fashion, Conrad Salinger orchestrated the songs into clouds of confectionary excess. Worried about how to handle a racially edgy drama, the studio opted to make it a fairy-tale romance, holding controversy at bay. In the pivotal blood-sucking scene, Steve daintily pricks Julie's finger with a pin below frame level, then lowers his mouth out of view. Many viewers had no idea what he'd done.

But *Show Boat* remained a feast of candy colors and soaring tunes, and audiences loved it. The film premiered on September 24, 1951, and grossed nearly four times its $2.3 million cost. Oscar Hammerstein II, *Show Boat*'s lyricist, wrote Freed an ecstatic letter of thanks.

Horne couldn't share in anyone's happiness. Instead she continued to see *Show Boat* as the stolen chance of a lifetime. "But she did Katherine Dunham's role in *Cabin in the Sky,* you know what I'm talking about?" said Geoffrey Holder. The loss of that part had so pained Dunham that she couldn't bring herself to see *Cabin.* Only privately did she voice her grief, but Horne trumpeted hers. In 1993, she told columnist Liz Smith, "I really didn't mind too much losing *Show Boat* to my friend Ava Gardner. I mean, I was a little mad—for about ten or fifteen *years*!"

Her rage, in fact, lasted far longer than that. Horne's 1981 Broadway concert, *The Lady and Her Music,* found her using *Show Boat* as evidence of M-G-M's mean and racist treatment of her, and audiences believed. In 1983, when the show took her to Hollywood, Horne aired her vendetta in a *Los Angeles Times* interview. There she declared that Mayer had vindictively blocked her from playing Julie. The claim incensed George Sidney. "Lena Horne was never, *never* up for this part!" he said. M-G-M's Samuel Marx was furious, too, and defended his former studio in a full-length *Times* article. For Horne to have played Julie would have been "monumental miscasting," said Marx. "It would have totally obliterated that poignant moment—the discovery of Julie's blackness."

Horne wouldn't listen. All she knew was that M-G-M had signed "somebody white made up to be me." Mayer, she insisted, was a coward. "When the first flak came from white audiences," she said, he backed down and lost the conviction that had made him hire her in the first place. Marx could sympathize with her disappointment, but not when she accused her old studio of racism. Not even Mayer could have controlled the likes of Lloyd Binford or forced the studio's financial heads to risk the southern distribution of expensive films by making Horne too prominent in them.

But for Horne, it all added up to a giant rejection. Her Cinderella fantasy, she insisted, was "all a lie. The only thing that wasn't a lie was that I did make money; if I didn't, they wouldn't have kept me."

In 1951, Erskine Johnson of the *Los Angeles Daily News* interviewed Horne in her dressing room at the Cocoanut Grove. Hayton and a number of acquaintances surrounded her. The mood stayed light—until Johnson asked if she would ever make another film. Silence fell over the room as she recounted her anger at M-G-M. "I begged for real parts and they assured me that they were looking for stories," she said. "They kept bringing me stories about South Sea island damsels or poor girls who kill themselves over the love of white men. That's not what I want to do on the screen. Or they came to me and said, 'Have you a story in mind?' Why should I have a story in mind? They're producing the picture."

Increasingly, M-G-M had made her feel unwanted. "Hollywood was beginning to make pictures about my people and these pictures were making money; even my own studio did one of them," she said. But there were no parts for her—"so I asked for my release." Since then, said Horne, she'd "had offers from producers in Europe, plenty of them. Hollywood can't find stories for me, but they can in Europe. Look, it's not as tough as they pretend it is."

A blond actress in a chair spoke up, saying Horne should have played the role of Julie. "I know how hurt you must have been not to get it," she said.

"I *wasn't* hurt at not getting it," insisted Horne. "It hurt only because the time hasn't changed as much as I had hoped. A Negro girl still can't play Julie. Even a fair-skinned Negro girl couldn't play Pinky. *Pinky* interested me not at all."

Over twenty years later, interviewer R. Couri Hay asked Horne which of her films she'd like to see again. "None of them," she said. "I hate them." Asked why, she explained, "I couldn't sing; I didn't act. I didn't know if I could act because I didn't get the chance."

In 1993, Horne would curiously agree to host a segment of *That's Entertainment! III*, the last in a series of feature-film montages of M-G-M highlights. Liz Smith asked her to reminisce about her old headquarters. "Well, they never did know what to do with me," Horne said. "So usually they just gave me a song, stuck me up against a pillar, and then cut me out when the movie played the South." Horne had been making the pillar remark for years; it caught on as a symbol of a black woman enchained by white captors and powerless to break free. In truth, Horne had never sung against a pillar. M-G-M had choreographed her to the hilt; she descended staircases, glided through Negro ensembles, slinked in front of mirrors.

None of that mattered to her; the fact that she couldn't interact with whites on camera made her feel second class. "The feelings of isolation were in her marrow," said John Fricke. "No matter what, she was always gonna be black. That was heavy-duty, even if she was being treated like a goddess." Even at the Cotton Club, Horne had refused to measure her achievements against the racism of the times; for her, discrimination was indefensible regardless of the era. She thought it unforgivable that a studio as prominent as M-G-M would keep only one Negro star under contract, and that in scenes with whites, black people could only sing and dance.

But if M-G-M couldn't single-handedly revolutionize racial attitudes in the forties, it made Horne an international star. Fifty years later, Horne was still known best for her movie musicals. Nearly all her colleagues remembered her glowingly. "There wasn't anybody there who didn't admire her," said André Previn. Gloria DeHaven agreed: "Everybody adored her. But she always felt like it was never quite sincere." As for the abuse she felt she'd suffered, "Lena couldn't have been treated better at any other studio," said Esther Williams. "She was really highly valued. She may not have known it, because she wanted more. But that's about the limit of what they could do for her at the time." Rex Reed, who got to know Horne much later, wondered if anything would have made her happy. "Let's face it," said the critic. "If M-G-M had given her twenty-five dramatic leading roles she would still have found something to complain about."

Horne tried to give herself a pep talk: "Forget this movie jazz. Go and do what you do best." That meant singing. The Hollywood she exited held painful memories—and for Betsy Blair, who was blacklisted, too, it would never be the same. "All the gaiety had left town," she wrote. "The blithe confidence went missing, perhaps forever."

After the death of Louis B. Mayer in 1957, Horne claimed he'd ousted her and Hayton from M-G-M because of their marriage. Yet she also admitted he'd known about it since the beginning. She stayed on board for two years afterward; Hayton remained until 1953. Betty Garrett, who kept her ear to the ground, never heard that the Haytons' union had upset Mayer. "Why would it have?" said Artie Shaw. "She wasn't carrying his films."

But in Horne's emotional recollections of that time, every slight, real or imagined, felt painfully reflective of a world that seemed out to get her, regardless of how she fought to do the right thing. "There were times in my life when I wanted to scream, 'To hell with being representative, what about *me*?' . . . It's awful stumbling through the years thinking people don't give a damn about the real you."

CHAPTER 11

IN OCTOBER 1950, as Horne sang her way through Europe, bookstores around Manhattan unpacked a pretty pink volume called *In Person: Lena Horne*. Earlier that year, she had been approached by her longtime champion Carlton Moss, the black filmmaker and activist. He and a colleague, Helen Arstein, convinced Horne to let them write an as-told-to memoir. The singer divulged her recollections; Moss and Arstein crafted a dramatic portrait of her thirty-three years.

Horne's radiant smile on the cover promised a happy ending. But with her heart still broken by M-G-M, she was at her lowest, and her seemingly triumphant life emerged as a raw wound. "It is very true," she conceded, "that I have much to be thankful for." Yet almost every memory was steeped in pain and struggle, from the childhood taunts of "Yaller! Yaller!" to her disgust with the Cotton Club and her letdowns in Hollywood. She summed up her time with Charlie Barnet by recalling a fan who hit on her after a show, thinking that Negro girls were an easy mark. Horne fled in tears, asking herself, "Color! Color! Why does COLOR mean so much?"

That question was very much in the air in 1950, as the budding civil rights movement sought to reverse centuries of wrongs. The curse of bigotry haunted another memoir published that year, Ethel Waters's *His Eye Is on the Sparrow*. Critics called it one of the great showbiz autobiographies. Waters had survived hideous hardships, including a 1917 car accident that maimed her as white onlookers laughed. But her vitriol stayed hidden from public view; Waters's toothy grin suggested a complacency that many liberal blacks found offensive.

Horne could hardly be accused of the same. And although P. L. Prattis of the *Pittsburgh Courier* applauded the candor of M-G-M's black princess—"Would it occur to you that discrimination has been an ugly ogre pursuing her all her short life?"—George Freedley of the *New York Morning Telegraph* wondered what the Negro Cinderella had to be angry about. "It is natural that she should be bitter," he wrote, "but a whole book of bitterness makes sad and frustrating reading." *In Person: Lena Horne* sat mostly untouched in shops. Looking back in 1983, Horne didn't mind. The young woman revealed in that volume—lost, confused, yet determined to grab the spotlight—didn't jibe with Horne's latter-day image as a selfless champion for freedom. When a reporter asked her about her early memoir, she disowned it. "I didn't really have much to do with that. It was done by somebody who knew me and was hanging around. I think they had some axe of their own to grind."

The blacklist had added one more dark cloud to her life, and for the first half of the decade Horne stayed mostly abroad. "Lena wanted to get the hell out of Hollywood," said Arthur Laurents. "And out of the United States." Horne gave the overseas public the movie songs they craved. When she walked out in a gown by Irene, wearing her *Words and Music* hairdo and flashing her Hollywood smile, people gasped: She was a living M-G-M musical. In Glasgow, Scotland's largest city, the response overwhelmed her—"stomping, cheering audiences that simply screamed their liking for me." Israel's minister of labor, Golda Meir, welcomed her as visiting royalty, giving a dinner in her honor and cooking part of it herself.

In Paris, her former lukewarm reception had heated into a frenzy of acceptance. "For the French, to whom sex comes without inhibitions, Lena exploded full blast with blockbuster impact," wrote an American reviewer. Fans like Maurice Chevalier ("She sings like a tiger!") and Edith Piaf crowded the dressing room.

France's reputation as an oasis of tolerance was somewhat deceptive. Josephine Baker had ingrained an image there of Negro women as wanton jungle creatures; blacks in general were revered as blues-shouting, gospel-singing, jazz-playing idiot savants. J. V. Cottom, a writer for the French magazine *Ciné Revue,* declared of Horne, "She sings to forget her troubles, just like the Negroes on the cotton plantations."

Visiting France for the first time, Chico Hamilton encountered a "*whooole* lot of hostility." His Caribbean look made many of the French think he was from Martinique—"which they hate," he said. "They treated me like shit, man. Once they found out I was American it was different." Arthur Laurents, who then lived in Paris, made a reservation for the Haytons at a favorite hotel of his near the Eiffel Tower. The couple arrived at the front desk, black musicians in tow. Later, he said, "the manager chewed me out—why hadn't I told them?" No one was refused, but nor were they wanted back. Horne so adored Paris that she never had the heart to tell her what had happened.

Whatever its biases, France made her feel far more welcome than her own country. But it wasn't her home. She and Hayton decided to sell the Nichols Canyon house and move to Manhattan, the city she'd always loved most. But the "queen of the box office," as *Our World* called her, now felt as unwanted below Harlem as any other Negro. Her marriage to a Jew didn't help. Joined by Ralph Harris, the couple went from building to building, "finding places which became mysteriously unavailable when we appeared eager to rent them."

Finally the couple took a suite at the Park Sheraton, a liberal-minded midtown hotel. Eleanor Roosevelt lived there, too, which made her feel safe. The former First Lady consoled her when Horne talked dejectedly of the blacklist. "Oh, darling, don't worry," she said with grandmotherly warmth. "I've been blacklisted, too, and I'm afraid that you and I are in the company of some very important, nice people."

But for most of 1951, Horne seemed magically untouched by *Red Channels*. On January 20, she made her TV debut at the top. NBC's *Your Show of Shows* was a milestone of sketch comedy that turned its lead players (Sid Caesar, Imogene Coca, and Carl Reiner) into stars. The writing staff included Mel Brooks and Neil Simon, who attacked racism in their later work. Aired live on Saturday nights, *Your Show of Shows* reached an estimated fifteen million viewers.

Horne was terrified. A photographer snapped her just before airtime, biting her nails as she stared at her script. Coca remembered Horne shaking as she waited to greet the studio audience. TV cameras—and much of America—would scrutinize her every move, and she had just one chance to make good.

Moments after the show went up at 9:00 P.M., out she sailed. *Variety* reported that Horne "seemed self-conscious" as she stood beneath the burning lights and welcomed viewers. But by the time she sang "Love" from *Ziegfeld Follies,* Horne had turned her nervousness into a seething outcry. She descended a staircase in a black cocktail dress with a flared hem. Her slow, sinewy movements recalled her M-G-M choreography; the icy hauteur was all her own. To *Variety,* Horne had "really smashed home." Arthur Laurents compared her version of "Love" to Judy Garland's: "Lena could kill. Judy is being killed."

On February 25, she sang on another of the biggest TV shows of the day, the *Colgate Comedy Hour.* Horne chose "Where or When" and "Deed I Do," and startled one critic: "With a gown cut so low that it was probably a good thing she didn't bend over for her bows, she demonstrated that TV is just as much her métier for that uniquely sexy singing as films or niteries." It seemed as though a whole new horizon had opened for Horne. Throughout the fifties, the racism on TV would easily rival that in the movies, but the former M-G-M goddess found more acceptance there than almost any other black performer.

NOTHING could replace movie stardom in her dreams, but around that time another intriguing project fell through. In his book *Billy Wilder in Hollywood,* Maurice Zolotow detailed the top filmmaker's plans to cast her in a black musical version of *Camille.* The singer would play a Harlem courtesan in love with a naval lieutenant whose father, unbeknownst to him, is black. Wilder wanted Tyrone Power and Horne to star, Paul Robeson to play the father, and Duke Ellington to write the score. The concept seemed too good to be true. And it sank.

The letdown galled her anew, as she saw black Hollywood blossoming without her. At 20th Century Fox, Darryl F. Zanuck had maintained his campaign to integrate film with the acclaimed medical drama *No Way Out.* It starred a twenty-two-year-old Sidney Poitier as a doctor accused of murder when a white thief dies in his care. Poitier established himself as a new role model for black America: a quietly intense, impeccably dignified figure who demanded respect.

Every time Horne saw such a film she ached inside, confronted by what she wanted but couldn't get. Despite her achievements on-screen, no producer, finally, seemed to regard her as an actress. But if Hollywood wouldn't touch her, the theater beckoned. Early in 1951 came news that Horne would appear on Broadway for the first time since *Blackbirds*. The show, *International Revue* (later retitled *Two on the Aisle*), was a vaudeville pastiche; its creators—Betty Comden, Adolph Green, and composer Jule Styne—had dreamed of building a show for Horne. This one would pair her with Bert Lahr, the blustery comic actor best known as the Cowardly Lion in *The Wizard of Oz*.

As the songwriters kept writing with her in mind, Horne had second thoughts. Deep into the process she withdrew, claiming conflicting nightclub bookings. In fact, she didn't think much of the raucous comic duets and M-G-M–style solos that Comden and Green had whipped up. Horne was replaced by Dolores Gray, a Broadway belter whose mellow trumpet voice helped *Two on the Aisle* run for nine months.

Horne would decline many subsequent stage offers, including a much-publicized musical written for her and based on the Queen of Sheba. Her pattern became familiar. She initially accepted, allowed the creators to do extensive work with her in mind, then quit, making excuses. The stringing along smacked of what M-G-M had put her through for years; it might have been a form of revenge. But Arthur Laurents saw another motive. "She wanted to be in the theater, but she was afraid she wasn't good enough," he said. "She knew she could do cabaret." Lonely as she felt on a nightclub floor, it was the only place she felt safe; there, she alone was in charge.

That year Horne returned to Bill Miller's Riviera. Columnist Radie Harris reported breathlessly: "Over 500 paying customers were turned away, while some 1,900 were lucky enough to wedge their way past the red rope." Horne was earning a reported ten thousand dollars a week— the near-pinnacle for a black entertainer.

MANY of her peers would have envied her next break, a spot on TV's gold-ring variety show. From 1948 through 1971, *Toast of the Town*— later retitled *The Ed Sullivan Show*—helped launch an untold number of stars, including Dean Martin, Jerry Lewis, Elvis Presley, Barbra Streisand, the Beatles, and the Supremes. Sullivan's influence didn't end there; as the widely syndicated gossip columnist for the New York *Daily News*, he had fearsome clout. His booking of Lena Horne startled many. Sullivan had joined the anti-Red brigade and sought the approval of Theodore Kirkpatrick before signing potentially dangerous guests.

The host loved talent above all, and he admired Horne, but he was also suspicious of her. In *Somewhere: The Life of Jerome Robbins,* author Amanda Vaill related a story that Robbins had let Horne use his apartment to host a party in support of Soviet-American relations. Sullivan, wrote Vaill, tried to blackmail the choreographer into naming the guests by threatening to proclaim to the world Robbins's homosexuality and alleged Communist leanings.

No proof ever surfaced that Horne had thrown that party. But before he booked her, Horne would have to convince Sullivan that she wasn't a Communist. In 1982, she told Arthur Bell of *The Village Voice* that Sullivan met with her to talk things over. Apparently she convinced him of her innocence, for that day, she said, he told her he wanted her on his show. Whether or not he'd gained Kirkpatrick's approval wasn't clear. Newspapers carried the announcement: On September 9, 1951, Horne would take part in a *Toast of the Town* tribute to Oscar Hammerstein II.

Then the trouble began. Kirkpatrick said nothing, but Horne found herself a pawn in a vendetta against Sullivan by Jack O'Brian, his archenemy. A heavily syndicated columnist and TV critic for the right-wing *New York Journal-American,* O'Brian was a bloodthirsty Red-basher. Variety-show host Steve Allen would brand him "rude, inaccurate, unchristian and vengeful."

Snidely noting "this latest display of Sullivan's booking genius," O'Brian waged a campaign against the host, his network (CBS), and his sponsor (the Ford Motor Company)—all to force Horne off *Toast of the Town.* When she saw her name vanishing from ads, she prepared to fight. "I'm not going to be intimidated by any one-man campaign," she told the press. Horne and her booking agency, MCA, threatened to sue CBS if they breached her signed contract. Sullivan chimed in loyally, predicting that Horne would "fracture" his Sunday-night audience. But until the last minute he kept a replacement singer on hand, should the protests get too nasty.

Horne went on. With *Show Boat* about to open in cinemas, she sang "Can't Help Lovin' Dat Man." Her blazing intensity left no doubt:

Horne was going to show Hollywood and the movie audience how badly M-G-M had erred by denying her the part.

CBS had won, but O'Brian wouldn't rest. In the *Journal-American* he reported "many complaints" about her appearance, and made it clear that big trouble lay ahead should the network rebook her.

Horne would have to take steps to clear her name. There were ways. The obvious solution, chosen by Jerome Robbins and Elia Kazan, among many others, would have been to rat on friends and colleagues. But Horne flat-out refused. Another option was to denounce one's sins in writing and go public as a born-again Commie hater. It helped to pay off the right people. One of them was Edward Bennett Williams, a politically connected trial lawyer on the side of Red-baiters; he would later defend Joseph McCarthy.

A biography by Evan Thomas dubbed Williams *The Man to See,* and singer Georgia Gibbs did just that. Years later, she shared the details with author Richard Lamparski. Around 1948, the rising jukebox star had sung at a benefit for Russian war orphans—an empathetic move, for she was an orphan herself. Her kindness got her targeted by blacklisters, who pressured CBS to yank her imminent appearance on the Sullivan show. Gibbs had a number-one hit, "Kiss of Fire," and couldn't afford bad publicity. After making some calls, her lawyer advised her what to do. Gibbs gathered five thousand dollars—a then hefty sum—and brought the cash to a tearoom at the Plaza Hotel. Williams met her there. After a few moments of strained conversation, he collected the envelope and left. From that point on, Gibbs performed on any TV show that wanted her.

Quickly after her own Sullivan appearance, Horne began the process of scrubbing the red off her name. She kept the process shrouded in secrecy, especially in her 1965 memoir. The episode had a "dream-like quality," Horne explained, and she knew "very little" about certain details. She did reveal one step she took. Tex McCrary (of radio's Tex and Jinx) helped Horne set up a meeting with George Sokolsky, a powerful arbiter of McCarthy-era guilt and innocence. Sokolsky wrote a column for the right-wing and frequently racist Hearst papers; he was also a McCarthy booster, and one of the last men to whom Horne would want to appeal. Yet she did—and to her surprise, she found him sympathetic. "He said he understood some of the pressures I must have had because he was once married to a Chinese girl—that kind of bullshit," said Horne. As for what else transpired between her and Sokolsky, the singer remained "necessarily vague."

But Sokolsky's forgiveness wasn't enough. Horne's book omitted reference to the conference that allowed her TV career to proceed. Before September ended, Horne met with Mr. *Red Channels* himself, Theodore Kirkpatrick. Subsequently Ralph Harris phoned the *Daily Compass* to report that Horne had "made her peace" with him: "He's given her a clean bill of health."

Kirkpatrick released a statement Horne had allegedly given him. On October 10, 1951, Ed Sullivan ran it in his column. It found Horne extolling the tremendous strides made by her race in recent years—but the progress would have been greater, she said, if not for a concerted attempt among the Communists "to stir agitation." She wished she could advise every up-and-coming black entertainer to not only shun but fight "Commie-front organizations," as she herself had vowed to do. "[Paul] Robeson, for whom I once had great admiration, does not speak for the American Negro," she declared—and if HUAC wanted more details she was ready to provide them. She closed by mentioning her recent encounter with "an unauthorized group of whites from AGVA"—the American Guild of Variety Artists, an actors' union under close scrutiny by the Red-baiters. They'd tried to persuade Horne "to start trouble in nightclubs which don't permit Negro patrons," she explained, adding, "I'll give you their names and you can check their Commie-front backgrounds."

Kirkpatrick had put Horne to convenient use as a black star on a soapbox against subversion. Her vocabulary did not include the word "Commie," and the Robeson denunciation—which Kirkpatrick likely forced on her—must have proven painful.

But those were the prices she paid for her freedom. The day the column ran, Ralph Harris phoned the *Daily Compass* and denied that Horne had offered to name names. He refuted nothing else. As for her civil rights work, Horne would "do exactly as she's always done," said Harris. "Whenever a situation comes up that requires her help—a question of discrimination or something like that—she'll do whatever she can. But she'll try to avoid groups which are called subversive."

Soon Ed Sullivan would do a public turnaround, attacking McCarthy and presenting a blacklisted comic, Orson Bean. He went on to give a long line of black performers—including Eartha Kitt, Nat King Cole, and Ella Fitzgerald—their first major TV exposure. He even hugged Sarah Vaughan and Pearl Bailey on the air, at a time when an interracial touch on the arm could make southern stations replace a show with a test pattern.

In years to come, Horne would claim repeatedly that the blacklist had kept her off TV for seven years. No matter what, she saw herself as a victim, not a victor. "First there had been M-G-M curtailing my stage and movie activities, now there was this blacklist business, just in time to hold me back in television." In fact, by the midfifties Horne had done a considerable amount of TV. She returned to *Your Show of Shows*, sang at least once on Steve Allen's *Tonight* show, and appeared as a mystery guest on America's favorite game show, *What's My Line?* Four masked panelists—Dorothy Kilgallen, Bennett Cerf, Arlene Francis, and Steve Allen—tried to guess her identity by asking questions. She answered yes or no in a disguised squeak. Horne seemed girlish, carefree, and delighted to be there. And when Francis identified her and the masks fell, Horne strolled over and shook the hand of each white panelist—a gutsy move that went unprotested.

WHILE fending off Jack O'Brian, Horne was dragged into one of the nastier racial scandals of the year. Josephine Baker, had charged the Stork Club with snubbing her on the night of Tuesday, October 16, 1951. Liberal New York rushed to her defense. Since the twenties, the society hotspot had thrived as a palace of exclusion, much as Studio 54 would in the seventies. A playground for the rich and spoiled, the Stork drew its own class lines based on wealth and social stature. Its owner, Sherman Billingsley, a former bootlegger from Oklahoma, was known to shun blacks, homosexuals, and noncelebrity Jews.

His club's VIP-only Cub Room hosted the "whitest of the white," to quote Fred Rayfield of the *Daily Compass*. Despite that, Baker and three friends—one black, two white—had sailed right in. According to reports, the star ordered filet mignon and a rare red wine, neither of them on the menu. After what she deemed an overlong wait to be served, she stormed out with her group. Baker phoned Walter White and informed him that the Stork Club had ignored her because she was black. What's more, she said, Walter Winchell—who was in the Cub Room that night with Jack O'Brian—had ignored her plight. Thus began a nationwide media firestorm that aimed to take down several accused bigots.

Years later, restaurateur Jean-Claude Baker, one of the star's gaggle of adopted children, interviewed every surviving witness of the Stork Club event he could find. In his book, *Josephine: The Hungry Heart,* Baker deemed the incident an exaggerated scam. At its heart, he explained in an interview, was the same rage that had sent her fleeing to France in 1925. "Josephine is too light for her own people, and she's a nigger for white America! So that's enough to fuck you up."

According to evidence gathered by both Jean-Claude and Ralph Blumenthal, the author of the book *Stork Club,* one of Baker's companions that night—the former Cotton Club chorine Bessie Buchanan—had plotted with the star to make trouble. Blumenthal quoted Buchanan's husband, Charles: "Bessie plotted everything." The true victim, said Jean-Claude, was Winchell, whose adoring support of Baker had helped bring her overdue acclaim in her own country. "Josephine didn't give a damn," said her son. "She was guilty, absolutely guilty." The star herself was known to be anti-Semitic (though she married a Jew), and so fixated on fame that she'd seldom done a thing for civil rights. Jean-Claude found it hard to admire his mother's sudden show of concern for "my people," as she put it. "For years she didn't give a shit about them, and suddenly it's *my* people. Many black people who become successful out of the ghetto, suddenly when it serves them they reembrace their 'people.' Where was she for the past twenty years?"

Baker took her story aggressively to the press. The following Monday a group of protesters, including Walter White, picketed the Stork. Some held signs emblazoned with angry slogans: FAMOUS NITE SPOT JUST A WHITE SPOT; Horne received a telegram asking her to sign a petition. She didn't bother. She thought the place a dump, and not worth the attention. But Baker took her silence as a betrayal. She'd long resented her younger and far more beautiful colleague; now she loathed her, and bad-mouthed Horne for ignoring the cause.

In fact, Horne was fiercely dedicated to a host of groups, not just her own. She flaunted her Jewish sympathies by joining B'nai Brith, the Hebrew service organization, and going to Israel with its members. Horne gave benefit shows in Israel for the United Jewish Appeal. As a committed Democrat, she supported Adlai Stevenson in his 1952 campaign for the presidency. She played benefits for cancer research and the March of Dimes, and served as a guest model in a Manhattan fashion show to aid the NAACP.

Dressing up could be challenging, given Horne's serious qualms about her figure. But M-G-M had taught her how to conceal each flaw—"and in a style that never went out of fashion," said Arthur Laurents. "I think you can relate it to being black. She was not going to be what everybody thought she was or should be. She had wonderful taste. I will never forget when she wore a violet or lavender cashmere top with a beige skirt. It was sort of a WASP outfit, but on her it looked exotic. The match of the color with her skin was no accident."

If her looks won more attention than anything else about her, her marriage to a white man also attracted close scrutiny. Horne told of pulling death-threat letters out of the mailbox and hearing obscenities on the phone. According to one story, Hayton opened a letter one day and pulled out a sheet of paper with two red-crayoned words: NIGGER LOVER.

There were blacks who thought her a traitor, and whites, like Skitch Henderson, who thought the marriage a "selfish" move on Horne's part. "I never understood it," he said. "They were never a couple to me. She was a whitey, and Louis Armstrong taught me later what whities were: someone who panders to a white audience. I thought she was trying to climb the ladder."

Horne had to show the skeptics that an interracial couple could thrive like any other. "We just couldn't afford to make the usual mistakes," she said. *Ebony* helped by featuring Horne and Hayton on its cover, in a portrait as dignified as that of any president and first lady. This was the image they had to meet. And in the beginning, at least, they radiated harmony. "When I saw them together they were *very* close," said Arthur Laurents. "It looked to me like they adored each other. But I don't think she was very sexual. The people who project sex usually aren't."

Onstage she felt vulnerable. "Lena performed in one of the toughest venues in show business: the middle of a nightclub floor," said Bobby Short. "Here she is, a beautiful black woman, singing songs of love. At ringside are egos and libidos being brandished quite openly. How could she help but notice the reaction she's eliciting? If it wasn't the men who were leering at her, it's the wives saying to the men, 'You'd like a little piece of that, wouldn't you?' *That's* what being in a nightclub is about. It is *hell*! People are not sitting there with their arms folded. They have their arms around somebody or their hands are in somebody's lap. And they're probably two sheets to the wind. You must come out in the first two minutes and grab their attention and hold it. You've got to have your act totally in tow. Never swerve from it."

She couldn't do it alone. As far as her small support team went, "Lena *demanded*," said Billie Allen, the future Mrs. Luther Henderson. "She was 24/7." In a "cold, ruthless" business, as Horne called it, she needed protection. Every night of an engagement, Ralph Harris—bushy-haired, half smiling, tuxedo-clad, and dabbed with cologne—watched over her. No matter what the strain or how frazzled her nerves, he calmly handled every crisis. Harris, wrote *Esquire*'s Robert Ruark, "sticks as close to her as a Seeing Eye dog, takes her shopping, fends off importunists, screens her mail, handles her money. . . . He drives her around, checks on her lighting and the seating arrangement, and performs any other little odd chores which might crop up. He also fights with her when she needs somebody to fight with. His vacation from the Horne career only starts when he delivers her safely back to her husband." For all his efforts, he took only a five percent commission rather than the usual ten.

Harris had wed his beautiful blond wife, Grace, in the early fifties, but for three or four months at a time he was off with Horne. "You could tell he was really miserable being away from her, but he had no choice," said his daughter Trygve. "He kept saying, just another couple of years. My mother always thought that Lena was in love with him. It's probably true. And she was jealous of my mother."

Meanwhile, Hayton saw himself as the real man in charge. Arthur Laurents noticed "a sort of jockeying over who would control her. But in the end, *she* controlled her. She would play little girl sometimes, and it was so believable they would fall for it." Since Luther Henderson's exit in 1950, Hayton had placed himself at Horne's feet. He took long leaves of absence from M-G-M in order to tour with her; by 1953, when he said good-bye to the Freed Unit, he was scoring only a film or two a year. For him, all was Lena. He worshiped her, and after six years the honeymoon glow hadn't faded. In photos with Horne, Hayton seems as proud as the schoolboy who'd landed the prom queen. With his unruffled hair and wry smile, he was her rock. "She called him Daddy," said Laurents, "and in a way, he was. Lennie was security for her. She was living in a white world. And Lennie knew music, which was very important to her."

Horne admitted to writer Alan Ebert that she was "nothing until his influence. He taught me to sing. . . . The truth is, Lennie taught me, period." As she explained to Seymour Peck of the *New York Times,* "I began to feel not only success as a singer but fulfillment as a woman. . . . I was loved. I was believed in."

Since Hollywood had seldom let her play scenes with other actors, Horne delivered them alone in song. Her 1965 memoir told of a drama class she'd taken in the forties. Horne so feared interacting that it was "torture" for her to share dialogue; she found herself shutting classmates out and turning inward. Her solo improvisations were much easier; there she could recall the most intimate of experiences and turn them into art.

So it was when she sang. Although she couldn't read music, she knew what she wanted, and her band had to accent the right words. She groused to Sidney Skolsky about an overly busy pianist: "The trouble with that cat is he knows too *much* music. He reads it, but he can't feel it."

Hayton, however, "was a *consummate* orchestrator," according to Skitch Henderson. "He knew what went with her voice. He knew what timbre the orchestra should have." Bassist George Duvivier auditioned for the couple in 1953. "They opened up a book the size of the yellow pages to the first tune," he recalled. "Lena's music was involved, to put it mildly." He got the job, and stayed a decade. Horne called him "the world's best bass player," which meant that even Milt Hinton—the most recorded bassist in jazz, and an alumnus of the Louis Armstrong and Count Basie bands—couldn't compare. Duvivier brought him in as a sub on a Long Island country-club gig. "Like most lady singers," recalled Hinton, Horne was "very temperamental." And he couldn't please her. "George was her security blanket, and no matter what I played, it wasn't going to be George. The next day I said, 'George, you and I are friends and you know I'd do anything for you, but no more Lena Horne gigs, please.'" Horne offered an excuse: "Listen. Playing in my rhythm section is like being married to me."

Her real husband didn't need any scolding, though he got it anyway. As an accompanist, Hayton listened to her so raptly, she said, that "if I ran short of breath at one point that I never had before, he was never caught short. You could float on the base that he laid down for you." But he preferred to conduct, playing only the odd song for her, like "The Man I Love." They searched for pianists who could measure up. Billy Strayhorn played for her whenever he could take time off from Ellington, but that wasn't often. Chico Hamilton brought in Gerald Wiggins, a top-rank musician who had played with Armstrong and Benny Carter. After a few months she "got tired of him," said Hamilton, and let him go. Soon she found her man. Brooklyn-born Gene DiNovi had accompanied two demanding singers, Anita O'Day and Peggy Lee, but Horne proved far more so. She rehearsed exhaustively, and DiNovi sat at the piano, lost in the fiendish scores. Horne would grab the music away from him. "She was more concerned with that link that goes on between accompanist and singer," he said.

DiNovi followed Horne often to her new frontier, Las Vegas. To her and other black stars, the city brought fat paychecks, prestige, and wracking prejudice. But the men in charge wanted Horne, and did what it took to get her. "Ralph Harris told me a wonderful story," said Richard Schickel. "Lena for a long time resisted playing Las Vegas because she didn't like working for mobsters. He was in Vegas, and a couple of guys knocked on his door, and they're carrying a small suitcase. They opened the suitcase, and they dumped $50,000 in cash on his bed and said, 'This is for you if you can get Lena to sign up.'"

In early 1953, Horne made her debut at the brand-new Sands Hotel. It was managed by Jack Entratter, her old boss at the Copacabana. The Copa Room, as he called the cabaret, become her Vegas headquarters. The space was nothing special: a shimmery curtain, a roomy hardwood stage separated from the tables by a bar. But to drive down the garishly lit Las Vegas Strip in the 1950s and see LENA HORNE emblazoned across a marquee as large as FRANK SINATRA or DEAN MARTIN or MAE WEST was to see change afoot. Horne even got to stay in the hotel.

Alice Key moved there around that time to write for the *Las Vegas Voice*. Seeing the racism around her, she worked with the NAACP to fight it. "When I first came to Las Vegas, they called it the Mississippi of the West," she said. The town's heyday as a showbiz Mecca had just begun. Hotel owners still wore cowboy hats. They paid Negro stars well, but their consideration ended there. Most blacks were barred from the major hotels even if they were singing in them. They could eat in few restaurants and got the cold shoulder, or worse, in bars. That even applied to Sammy Davis, Jr., who had to stay in a black dwelling across town, and to Nat King Cole, whose number-one hits had made him a superstar. Cole—a model of suavity and poise—told Short in 1953 that the town had shattered his confidence; he worried that back home in L.A. he'd still feel like the hired help.

Horne understood. Author Grange Rutan was twenty-one and living in Las Vegas when the star made her Sands debut. Standing in the lobby, Rutan spotted Horne nearby in a scarlet gown. "She could not walk alone through the casino. I could feel her breathing as she waited to be escorted—and those elegant fangs waiting to eat one up." Finally a uniformed security guard showed up—"and then they went." She remembered Horne's regal gait, head held high, with no eye contact. On another fabled night, Marlene Dietrich took Horne by the arm and marched her into the casino bar, defying protest. None came.

Horne had seldom shunned a job because of racism; rather than walk away, she went in there and fought. So did Harris, who insisted that Horne's children be allowed to swim in the pool and that her musicians sleep at the hotel and use the front entrance. All of that, claimed Bobby Short, set a Vegas precedent. Entratter tried to keep her happy. "The Queen Gives a Command Performance," declared the program for one of her shows. Within five years she was earning twenty-five thousand dollars a week. In a town where performers served mainly as bait to lure tourists to the gambling tables, Horne got attention; Robert Ruark wrote that he'd never seen a singer hold such a tight rein over an audience. But to her the town felt sleazy, and she eagerly told people she was there only for the money. She packed trunks of books to take along; they gave her a sense of home.

Horne missed the noncombativeness of France, and in 1954, after her Vegas gig, she lingered there during a six-month European tour. She'd yearned to make a stronger connection with Teddy, who barely knew her. Now she could share with both him and Gail the intoxication of the city she loved. When Billy Strayhorn joined them, Horne's family felt complete. They strolled along the tree-shaded streets of Saint-Germain-des-Prés and stopped at outdoor cafés, settling into wicker chairs and sipping coffee. Horne and family browsed through newsstands along the Seine; wandered through the Versailles forests; visited antique shops in Montmartre. On shopping trips, seventeen-year-old Gail watched, wide-eyed, as her mother "poured herself into Balmain's beads, Madame Grès' jerseys, Jean Dessès' chiffons, and Maggy Rouff's hats." Horne left time to hobnob in Capri with Noël Coward, Bea Lillie, and Gracie Fields. "When I settle down I'd like it to be on the French Riviera, at a spot I've picked out," she explained.

Family in France also meant Auren Kahn, who usually greeted them as they stepped off the ship in Le Havre, the port town closest to Paris. Bald, with big ears, he struck Arthur Laurents as "a man almost without personality, but ineffably sweet and relaxed and comfortable. His apartment was home for her. She didn't have to be Lena Horne. She knew she was loved as opposed to adored." But she got her share of worship, too, especially in Paris, where fans kept stopping her on the street and asking for autographs in fractured English. One day, Horne and Laurents walked into a shop together. The French clerk asked in a thick accent, "Aren't you Doris Day?"

"No, Doris Night," said Horne.

Years later she reminisced to Bobby Short, "You know, I was happy in those days and didn't have sense enough to realize it."

In May 1954, during a run at the fabled Moulin Rouge, Horne read about the U.S. Supreme Court's history-making desegregation ruling, *Brown v. Board of Education of Topeka*. Thirteen parents in that Kansas town had filed a class-action suit on behalf of twenty black children who'd been barred from various schools. Unanimously approved, the law forbade segregated schooling all over the country. Its effects in the most bigoted cities were slow in coming, and segregation lingered in places such as public bathrooms. But the news, said Horne, "changed my life and altered my attitude to my own country." Shouting with joy, she threw her arms around Hayton and told him it was time to return to the States.

But what she found when they returned seemed unchanged, particularly in Los Angeles. While Horne had always stepped tentatively into Hollywood parties, she and Hayton showed up at a promising one; its guests included France's gaminelike dancer and stage star Zizi Jeanmaire, an artist Horne loved. There, too, was Jack Larson, the boyish actor who played cub reporter Jimmy Olsen on TV's *The Adventures of Superman*. Larson watched as Horne and Jeanmaire sat on a couch, chatting gleefully. Horne spoke proudly of her children and their love for France. As she recounted amusing things they'd said and done, a Greek photographer spoke up. "Oh, pickaninnies can be so wonderful!"

Larson's heart skipped a beat, but Horne, he recalled, "let him off the hook very sweetly." Smiling, she said, "Yes. *Colored children* can be particularly charming."

No matter how angry she might feel, Horne still felt obliged to act composed. But she couldn't contain her rage in February 1955, when she went to Miami Beach for a lucrative stint at the Copa City nightclub. This was the South, and racism still abounded. Previously a local impresario had housed Horne in his spare bedroom when no decent hotel would take her. The musicians had to stay across town, in the black district. Horne had tolerated it.

Now, Ralph Harris insisted she be housed at a "beach hotel" near the club. Murray Weinger, Copa City's manager, booked a suite at the luxurious Royal York. But there was trouble brewing. The week before Horne opened, another hotel had ejected twenty-four black guests who'd come to attend a Lincoln Day dinner. Reportedly, the manager announced, "This hotel is for whites only." Nearly half of the four hundred white attendees walked out, too.

Three days later, Weinger phoned Harris with some news. The Royal York had canceled Horne's reservation, giving no reason. Weinger had booked her instead at the Lord Calvert, a black hotel across town. Within an hour Harris called back to tell him that Horne was canceling her engagement.

From there Harris phoned the *New York Post*. The newspaper asked Jack Low, the York's manager, to comment. He claimed that he'd checked the books, and Horne had never had a reservation. What, wondered the *Post*, was Low's policy on black guests? None, he said, "because the problem has never come up." Weinger took Low's side by denying that Horne's contract had called for a "beach hotel" reservation, just "first-class."

Jack Mitchell, a reporter for the tabloid *Hush-Hush,* learned of the scandal. He challenged Horne in a harsh exposé, "Lena Horne: Why Did She Run Out on Her Miami Date?" The real reason she'd canceled, Mitchell wrote, was that Weinger had wanted to retain his current head-liner, Sammy Davis, Jr., as Horne's supporting act. "With her popularity already at its lowest ebb in years," said Mitchell, she didn't want the competition. Horne's complaining suggested to him that "when you're in a tough spot, you can holler race discrimination and maybe get out of it." Josephine Baker had sadly proven that accusation true, but it couldn't be leveled at Horne, whose demands were set in ink.

Abe Aronowitz, Miami's first Jewish mayor, apologized publicly on behalf of the whole city, calling Low's actions "disgraceful." Through it all, Horne struggled to remain stoic. "What the hell, someday they'll learn," she told the *Post.* "I'm not really upset. I've been refused before. A lot of good things have been happening for Negro entertainers." Later that day, she said, she was returning to New York: "God's country," as she called it.

Certainly, Manhattan seemed a safehold in America's racial land-scape. As the civil rights movement gained steam, backlashes erupted in other cities. In August 1955, national notoriety came to Money, Mississippi, population four hundred. Tiny as it was, the Delta town had a savage history of lynchings. Residents snickered about the black corpses in the Tallahatchie River, which ran alongside Money. The latest was Emmett Till, who had just turned fourteen. Two white men had brutally maimed him after he'd allegedly flirted with one of their wives. An all-white jury acquitted his assailants. Months later, paid off by *Look* magazine, they arrogantly confessed the truth.

The Till tragedy galvanized the fight for equality. But a gentle show of disobedience in Montgomery, Alabama, spoke just as powerfully. On December 1, Rosa Parks, a department-store employee and NAACP vol-unteer, refused to budge from her seat on the bus when the driver insisted she rise for a white passenger. Arrested, she calmly held her ground, and the blacks of Montgomery banded together to follow her lead. Guided by a young minister, Martin Luther King, Jr., they staged a citywide bus boycott. Black churches were burned in response, and King's house was bombed.

Reading about such heroic figures, Horne began to question her own protests. She told journalist Mike Wallace she felt "obliged" to fight for her race. But did that equal true social commitment? "I'm not sure I *always* acted out of a feeling of obligation to the Negro people," she confessed. "Often, I guess, it was selfish." She didn't feel her efforts amounted to much, especially onstage. Horne commiserated with Marilyn Monroe on the frivolity of their images. Both of them, said Horne, agreed that "it would be nice if we could be strong enough in ourselves as women and weren't just there to make the male audience want to go to bed with us."

And her allure, she thought, was fading fast. Horne looked in the mirror with dismay at her prematurely graying hair; in 1952, at the age of thirty-four, she'd termed herself a "dried-up old broad." Over and over she threatened to quit nightclubs, even to leave show business, a clear indication of her unhappiness. "I don't think there's anything too attractive about an older woman singing about sex and romance," she explained. When a reporter asked her about that "sexy look" in her glance, she said, "Just astigmatism in one eye, nothing else. Then, too, I'm near-sighted."

Horne was painfully aware of the Hollywood breakthrough of Dorothy Dandridge, another fair-skinned black beauty who made the cover of *Life* on November 1, 1954. Dandridge had toiled in film since 1935, mostly in bit or uncredited roles or as cheesecake decoration in race movies. Now, as movies embraced the Negro, Dandridge was the right girl at the right time.

Her fortunes had turned in 1953 when M-G-M cast her in *Bright Road,* the story of a teacher at a southern school who takes an interest in a problem child. Harry Belafonte made his screen debut as the principal. The black-and-white, low-budget feature was no message film; rather, said Dandridge, it showed "that beneath any color skin, people are simply people." And in that regard, *Bright Road* was ahead of its time. Dandridge's fresh, appealing performance touched the heart and earned raves. A year later, at 20th Century Fox, she showed her sultrier side as the title seductress in an all-black version of Bizet's *Carmen,* directed by Otto Preminger. For *Carmen Jones,* Dandridge earned the first Best Actress Oscar nomination a Negro had ever received. And at that year's ceremony, she became the first black presenter in history.

It was everything Lena Horne wanted. Dandridge had crossed a bridge Horne had created; she had trouble applauding the younger star's success in roles she "would have killed to have," as Leonard Bluett observed. But how much had Hollywood really changed? *Carmen Jones* also boasted the screen debut of Diahann Carroll, a beautiful teenage singer from the Bronx. After that film, she told herself she never wanted to make another. "There was nothing more demeaning than the apex of my industry, the film industry, where *everyone* wanted to go. The rejection was so insidious, it was everywhere—in the cafeteria, on the lot, where we parked our cars. We were visitors. They knew we were there to do a film. Not an enormous amount of adjustment was made to make us feel warm and welcome. They knew in a matter of weeks we would all be gone and they wouldn't have to look at black people anymore."

Yet Carroll continued to rise, as did Dandridge. It seemed as though the latter had gained on Horne in the cabarets. Phil Moore, Horne's former musical director, had groomed Dandridge into another elegant minx. Top supper clubs, along with network TV, opened their arms to her. *Life* proclaimed Dandridge "the most beautiful Negro singer since Lena Horne," while *Ebony* asked in a cover story, "Is Lena Still the Queen?" *Our World* trumpeted the question, "Can Dandridge Outshine Lena Horne?" The magazine called Dandridge "the queen of the country's swank Supper Clubs," adding, "In the opinion of most columnists, she is fast moving into first place. . . . She has the voice, looks and sophistication to rival Lena's. And she has something La Horne lacks—pretty legs."

But for all its flash, Dandridge's act seemed a pale copy of Horne's; she was a competent but generic vocalist, one of a slew of songbirds whose main influence was obvious. "Lena in a way reinvented lady nightclub singers," explained Bobby Short. "And there were dozens and dozens of women who patterned themselves after her." Horne pretended not to care. "I'm easy to imitate, those actions and the voice and all that stuff," she told *Look.* "But those dames, they'll never really get on to me. They don't know what I'm thinking when I'm out there singing. No one does."

But Claude Thompson did. "She was mad as hell," said the dancer, who would soon become her close friend. "Those dames" were copying what she'd worked so hard to create, and Phil Moore had trained a number of them, including Carroll. Having proclaimed Moore a pianist to equal Ellington and Strayhorn, she omitted him entirely from her second memoir. Dandridge wasn't mentioned either. When *Ebony* had asked her opinion of the actress, Horne tossed out a chilly bone of praise: "She has shown that she is a fine entertainer and indicated that the theater is the medium through which she will best express her talent." Horne had forgotten an older pioneer, Ethel Waters, who had watched in pain as Horne came along and grabbed the spotlight.

Contrary to Horne's opinion, Dandridge had three more plum film roles ahead. *Island in the Sun* (1957) boldly depicted two interracial couples: Dandridge and John Justin, Joan Fontaine and Harry Belafonte. The lovers never kissed or even touched, but the film triggered heated protests. In *The Decks Ran Red* (1958), Dandridge kissed the white actor Stuart Whitman, a historic Hollywood first. The next year, she and Sidney Poitier led a stellar black cast—Pearl Bailey, Sammy Davis, Jr., Brock Peters, Diahann Carroll—in the long-awaited screen version of *Porgy and Bess*.

But the vulnerable Dandridge came to embody the black female entertainer as victim in a cutthroat field. "Whenever I hear Dorothy's name, the first thing that comes to my mind is fear," said Carroll. "She was always afraid. Show business came into her life because she was beautiful. I don't know if she would have pursued it had she not been beautiful."

Like Horne, Dorothy had grown up with a stage mother, Ruby Dandridge, who played maids in several films. Ruby's lesbian lover had abused young Dorothy sexually, creating one more femme fatale who was terrified of sex. She and her first husband, Harold Nicholas, bore a brain-damaged daughter. And by 1960, Dandridge's shining promise had dimmed. She got hooked on downers and alcohol; her second husband, a white gambler, beat her; managers swindled her money. She wound up bankrupt and hounded by the IRS. On September 8, 1965,

Dandridge became one more Hollywood fatality, dead on her bathroom floor of an overdose. She was forty-two.

In the public's view, Horne had risen above every blow. But as she told photographer Brian Lanker years later, "It was a damn fight everywhere I was, every place I worked, in New York, in Hollywood, all over the world."

AN exciting possibility did come her way in the fall of 1954, when RCA Victor, the label that had signed and dropped her in the forties, gave her another chance. On November 10, she went to Webster Hall, a Manhattan recording studio, to cut her first single in five years, "Men Are Boys at Heart" backed by "Unsuspecting Heart." Sweetened with sappy violins and an *ooh*-ing choir, the songs were blatantly aimed at the charts.

But this time she was determined to make good. After New Year's, she went on a press junket of radio stations. Instead of reciting canned and meaningless patter, she told deejays her dream: Even though she'd never quite succeeded on disk before, maybe the new hi-fi recording techniques would capture a missing dimension. "I think perhaps this will be the year for me," she said hopefully.

Sure enough, springtime brought Horne her highest-charting record in a decade. "Love Me or Leave Me" had reached number two on the 1929 charts as sung by Ruth Etting, a torchy songbird and gangster moll. Now it was hot all over again thanks to a hit film of the same name, which starred Doris Day as Etting. In the biography *Basically Speaking*, George Duvivier told authors Edward Berger and David Chevan of a rehearsal in which he and Horne, "just kidding around," had broken into the song. She sang it over his sly, prowling bass line, improvising with a jazz feeling that impressed him. "Lena said, 'Why don't we record it like that?'"

Her single of "Love Me or Leave Me" sounded nothing like other records in the 1955 jukeboxes. Instead of saccharine strings, it began with only bass and the tiptoeing cymbal work of drummer Louie Bellson, Pearl Bailey's white husband. The guitar of Mundell Lowe crept quietly in.

Horne's performance, which she reprised on the CBS TV series *Music 55,* showed America a Lena it had never quite seen. Any traces of her onetime sweetness were gone, replaced by a ferocity that called up her every disappointment. Horne's enunciation slashed into phrases; she left no *t* or *d* unpronounced. On TV her eyes burned, her lips curled into a sneer, she moved with the sinewy spareness of a cobra ready to strike. "I want no one unless that someone is *you!*" sounded more like a threat than a plea. Romantic words like "kissing" emerged with a hiss. Her use of a southern drawl, often the sound of subservience, could have only been meant ironically. In between phrases, Horne kept looking away in pain, giving hints of what lay beneath her anger.

It was a compelling and scary performance, and it got attention. Buoyed by the success of Day's film and a sound-track album that topped the charts for seventeen weeks, Horne's "Love Me or Leave Me" reached the top twenty. The jazz magazine *Metronome* called the single "Lena at her most exciting. . . . It's a daring presentation, and it takes an artist like Lena to carry it off so magnificently." The seething Horne overwhelmed the playful one heard on the comically salacious B-side, "I Love to Love," a piece of special material from her act. "When the iron is hot, strike it!" she purred à la Mae West, groaning, *"I like it!"*

"I could never take a sex song seriously," explained Horne, a singer who could seem like a lioness in heat. But CBS radio found the performance all too convincing and banned it from its airwaves as "offensive." England's prim BBC followed suit, deeming the side "unsuitable for broadcasting to general audiences." That didn't discourage the royal family from inviting Horne to give a command performance for Princess Margaret in London. A reporter there summed up the "new" Horne. "Lena can be as savage as a caged tigress fed on British railway sandwiches. She can be as hypnotic as a snake with Svengali's eyes. She can brew black magic from a voice which sounds like a mixture of honey, brown sugar, and opium."

With Arthur Laurents, she knew she wasn't on show. Laurents was no star-struck fan, having written the screenplay for Alfred Hitchcock's *Rope*, along with several Broadway plays. By the midfifties, he'd left Paris and settled in Manhattan; a milestone lay in his near future, the libretto for *West Side Story*. Horne loved his bitchy intellectual wit—"poisonous and fun," as she termed that style—and his spot-on, often withering assessments of showbiz figures they both knew.

He, in turn, found her "smart and funny." She joked with "a very deadpan delivery," he said. "Then she would giggle." One weekend she visited him and his lover, Tom Hatcher, at their oceanfront house in Quogue, a village in the fashionable Hamptons of Long Island, New York. There to greet her was Leona, their giant schnauzer. "Well, two black bitches are gonna sleep together," announced Horne.

"She could say that sort of thing there," said Laurents. "We had the most wonderful time. A lot of it, I admit, was drinking. And eating dinner at ungodly hours. She didn't have to dress up. It was enormous joy and laughing."

But no one, not even Lennie Hayton, made her feel safer than Billy Strayhorn. His voice, firm but soothing, calmed her when she was ready to break. They could finish each other's sentences or sit together for hours and hardly talk. Strayhorn stayed in the room while she put on her makeup; if there was a piano there he played it. They went to museums or cooked at home. All the while, the composer held forth on music, culture, and life. Even at his quietest, "boy, did he observe," said Laurents. "And he could talk to her and tell her what he saw." It amused her that Strayhorn had a mild crush on her husband. Robert Mackintosh, her dress designer, laughed for years at Horne's comment to Hayton: "Oh, Daddy, let him have it!"

Strayhorn held her hand every time her movie-star dreams fell through. Early in 1955, she announced that she would soon play the lead in a screen version of *The Street*, Ann Petry's bestselling novel about Harlem life. She cursed herself for speaking too soon; the film never happened. That same year, Sam Spiegel, the Oscar-winning producer of *On the Waterfront*, invited Horne to star in a film about Negroes living in England. The script, she told *Ebony*, was "tremendous." Spiegel abandoned it.

Given her rancor toward her former studio and the cameo status to which she'd been reduced, it seemed odd that Horne would return for one more guest spot. But in the summer of 1955, she sang as herself in the M-G-M musical *Meet Me in Las Vegas*. Other stars—Sammy Davis, Jr., Frank Sinatra, Debbie Reynolds, Tony Martin—also appeared briefly, spicing up a bland tale of a gambling cowboy (Dan Dailey) who finds good luck with a Vegas dancer (Cyd Charisse). Perched on a pedestal, on a set that simulated the Copa Room of the Sands, Horne sang a drab ballad, "If You Can Dream," scored with old-fashioned grandiosity by Hayton. A second, sexier number, "You Got Looks," didn't make the final cut.

The film premiered in Vegas. Horne remarked testily to Jack Pitman, a *Variety* reporter, that she hadn't seen it. Once more she went back to the supper clubs, to entertain high-toned white crowds. They cheered at the very sight of her, and lavished her with applause. But as she bowed graciously, right arm held across her waist in geisha fashion, more than one member of the band heard Horne muttering under her breath, *"Kiss my ass!"*

Her temperament was all too familiar to Chico Hamilton. Horne's drummer had taken a year off in 1952 to play for Charlie Barnet, then to join a history-making group, the Gerry Mulligan Quartet, which had launched the trumpeter Chet Baker. Hamilton had needed a break from Horne. "She had more good days than bad days," he explained, "but when she had her bad days she was a motherfucker, man." Hamilton kept getting caught in the middle of tempo disputes between her and Hayton. Sometimes she used him as henchman. "When she got tired of somebody in the band, she put that shit off on me to fire them.... Lemme just say this, man, I bailed her ass out a million times."

Horne finally pushed the drummer too far. "Chico had strep throat one time and couldn't come," said Billie Allen, who heard the details from Luther Henderson. "And there was no sympathy offered. She was *really* put out and expressed it in a very bad way. And Chico was angry as hell."

In 1955, he quit. The next year he formed the Chico Hamilton Quintet, a semiclassical formation of reeds, cello, guitar, bass, and drums. The band was acclaimed for pushing the boundaries of jazz; it even appeared in a hit movie, *Sweet Smell of Success,* for which Hamilton wrote some of the score. His solo career still thrived a half century later.

Horne's friends were glad to see her mood rise in 1956. She'd all but given up on finding a permanent New York apartment, but that changed when Harry Belafonte became her new landlord. He and Horne had a love-hate relationship that would span thirty years. Born in Harlem of a Jamaican domestic and a Caribbean seaman, Belafonte had kicked off a nationwide calypso craze in 1953 with "Matilda," his first single for

RCA. That year he costarred with Dorothy Dandridge in *Bright Road*, and made a Tony-winning Broadway debut in *John Murray Anderson's Almanac*.

Women of all races swooned over the handsome singer, with his tight black pants, open shirt, and soft, husky voice. His sex appeal, like Horne's, grew from smoldering black rage. As a boy, he'd suffered beatings from white neighborhood thugs; later he couldn't find a New York landlord who would rent him an apartment. Horne told writer Shirley Norman that he'd stayed with her and Hayton. "That was the start of our deep friendship," she said. "He's like my brother." But time and again their egos clashed so badly that they stopped talking for months, even years. According to arranger-composer Bob Freedman, who later conducted for both of them, "It was always obvious that he and Lena were constantly struggling with guilt because of their acceptance by the 'white world.' They were never sure where and what they were, so they couldn't stay with any kind of consistent persona."

Even after he'd become famous, realtors kept giving Belafonte the runaround. But by 1956 he'd become rich enough to fight back. Registering with two partners under a corporate name, he bought a marble-lobbied apartment building at 300 West End Avenue, at Seventy-fourth Street in the heart of the residential Upper West Side. Then he fired the bigoted gatekeepers. Belafonte went on to sell co-ops to various blacks, including Lena Horne. He lived on the fifth floor, she on the thirteenth.

Horne was thrilled. "It's the first time I've had a place of my own in New York," she told Gael Greene of the *New York Post*. Horne proudly gave journalists the grand tour, skipping down the hallways like a kid in a playground. "Come up front and see a piece of the river," she told jazz critic Leonard Feather. There were ten rooms, including a huge living room with a fireplace. On the hearth stood a three-foot bronze sculpture of her by a renowned English artist, Peter Lambda. At her service were Grant, a houseman, and Irene Lane, her live-in maid and dresser since 1951. A fair-skinned, white-haired black woman, Lane became, in some respects, the mother she'd never had.

For long stretches, Horne's children had barely had one, either. Gail had spent most of her teens away at private schools, including the

Quaker-run, all-girl Oakwood Friends School in Poughkeepsie, New York. Horne proudly told Feather that now her daughter had a home to come back to on breaks. But she worried that she'd neglected Gail and Teddy. Arthur Laurents couldn't disagree. "Lena was not a good mother," he said. One friend commented that Horne seemed available in that role only "at odd moments." Horne guiltily described her daughter as a "hotel baby." Oftentimes, Ralph Harris had pitched in as surrogate parent.

Distance had marred her relationship with Gail. Horne felt it acutely when she was asked to sing for her daughter's class. A star who had entertained British royals and sung on live TV for millions confessed to feeling "more frightened, more terrified than I've ever been in any performance. I wanted desperately to be accepted—for Gail and her friends to like me." Yet Horne's second memoir revealed a curious remove from her daughter. During one European tour, she said, "Gail was the perfect little girl, finding girl friends her own age all over and taking tea with them." The "little girl" would have been eighteen.

According to Judy Davis, who knew her slightly, Gail "had a lot of complexes and hang-ups, because she was a chubby girl." She also bore the burden of constant identification as "Lena's daughter." Nevertheless she struck most people as bright, ebullient, and polite—a model daughter for Lena Horne. Gail graduated from Oakwood in June 1955, then went to Radcliffe, the upscale women's college in Cambridge, Massachusetts. "Gail was brought up in a white world," said Laurents, and Horne kept her there even while they were apart.

Since the late forties, Ted had lived with his father in a Los Angeles apartment and seen his mother little. Louis Jones had done his best to withhold Ted from her. Jones would later tell his granddaughter Samadhi that Horne had done the same with Gail—and that he should never have let her go.

Ted had grown into a tall, lanky, and serious teenager, with blue eyes and skin darker than his sister's. Observers described him as "beautiful." Like Gail, he had excellent manners and exuded intelligence. Horne was exceedingly proud of him, and Ted seemed to feel the same about her. As evidence, she told a story from his childhood. "My son used to be teased a lot by his schoolmates—'Oh, your mother can't sing. She sings like a white woman.' He would say, 'My mother is making it possible for your mother to get out of the kitchen.'"

But Ted was stuck between two warring parents, and Chico Hamilton saw him as "a very confused guy." Francine Kahan, one of his closest high school friends, sensed the problem. "A kid doesn't understand custody battles. These are rejections. He sees his sister with the mother, and he can't be with the mother."

His home life seemed worlds away from Horne's upscale existence. He lived with Jones in the Cadillac Manor, a two-story development at Twenty-seventh and Arlington in a middle-class black neighborhood of West Los Angeles. The complex had a carport and pool, but looked like lower-income housing. Prior to that, the Joneses had lived with one of Louis's relatives. "She took them in," said Clint Rosemond, the young man's best friend. "They were basically homeless, as far as I can determine." It puzzled Ted's friends at Los Angeles High School that they had nicer homes than the son of Lena Horne.

To Rosemond, Jones's employment situation was "mysterious." At one point he worked as a railway porter; later he became a postman. His political aspirations hadn't amounted to much; overall he lived by his wits, along with the money Horne sent for Ted's upbringing. The situation crushed the ego of a man who struggled to show the world that he was more than the former Mr. Lena Horne. As ever, he hid his wounded pride with a flourish of pomposity. "Lou had a gift of gab," said Rosemond. "He was very self-assured, and he was dapper—nice suits, monogrammed shirts." He kept announcing plans to run for public office, but no one believed he'd succeed.

His paternal skills were also in question. Having been raised with punishing strictness, Jones employed the same methods of child rearing. His generation knew that black men had to constantly strive for respect, so he pushed Ted to wear a three-piece suit to school every day. He raised his hand to the boy if he talked back. "Yes, Ted loved his father, and his dad certainly loved him, and they were together all the time," said Francine Kahan. "But I think what was more important to Louis were his own ends."

It couldn't have helped his self-esteem to watch his son emerge as a young man poised for great things. Ted was a star pupil at Los Angeles

High School, and his famous mother had nothing to do with it. The city's oldest high school, L.A. High had a 10 percent black student body and a reputation for liberalism. Ted had begun there in 1953; by the end of his freshman year, he'd become captain of the debate team—an unheard-of leap for a student so young. Ted would lead his school to victory in a national competition. None of that surprised Rosemond. As class president of Manual Arts High School, he, too, was a young man of high intelligence. But he considered Ted "the smartest guy I'd ever met. He could take on any academic challenge and master it."

Just the sight of him inspired respect. He dazzled Francine Kahan, the debate team's secretary, and most of her female classmates. "He was a person of class, a person you were drawn to," she said. "He had a radiant smile. But he was a regular guy, and fun to be with." Ted rose to greater heights by becoming the first black student-body president in his school's history. His classmates voted him in "by an overwhelming majority," said Roland Jefferson, Ted's fellow player on the basketball team.

Most people knew he was Lena Horne's son, but he rarely mentioned her. "I'm sure it was a tremendous source of hurt," said Kahan. "We didn't go there." Her son seemed such a stranger to her that, when asked about him by interviewers, Horne could do little more than list his credentials. Ted, she said, could "take a car apart and put it back together again," and he was "*the* modern jazz aficionado" who loved the cool jazz of Chet Baker, Dave Brubeck, and the Modern Jazz Quartet. "He would love to be a drummer," she added.

Rosemond felt that Horne had "fabricated" most of that description, clearly at a loss for what to say. But Ted's love of jazz was no lie. He and Rosemond shopped together for records and listened to them at night, memorizing the solos and discussing them passionately. Still, Clint felt his loneliness. All of Ted's friends had stable home lives; he had a distant sister and two self-obsessed parents. "Lou was a good man and wanted the best for his son," said Rosemond. "But he was a politician, a businessman who always wanted to be in on the action. The result was that Ted often ate cornflakes for dinner and did not live in the kind of comfort that his sibling enjoyed." Rosemond and his parents tried to help by adding him to their dinner table, Monday through Friday. It comforted Ted to feel he finally had a family.

CHAPTER 12

TWENTY YEARS had passed since Horne had left the Noble Sissle orchestra, and one didn't read anymore about sepia songbirds or chocolate-cream chanteuses. The custom of presenting Negroes onstage as near-naked, spear-wielding savages had barely outlived the Cotton Club. Black singers of refinement—Nat King Cole, Billy Eckstine, Sarah Vaughan—were selling millions of records. For sophisticated white New Yorkers, black glamour was no longer an exotic curiosity; it was chic.

Bobby Short had played Manhattan as a child performer in the thirties. Returning in 1956 after years in L.A., he found the cold draft of bigotry eased. Short went to work in the midtown Hotel Beverly, performing the poshest of show tunes in his blithe, breezy style. He sang of flitting through the Riviera and slumming on Park Avenue, and trilled phrases with a French-style clipped vibrato. Swells flocked to his piano; he in turn visited their haunts. "I went to the Copa to see Frank Sinatra, and I danced one night with Dorothy Kilgallen at the Plaza. Then, of course, someone would suddenly say, 'No, we can't have you.'"

Horne had played a sizable role in that progress. But she couldn't shake the memory of so much condescension. "When performing," she told Alan Ebert, "my mind would wander to the back exits my black musicians had to use and to room service which never delivered what they had ordered. . . . Anger! Anger! Anger! . . . All those years of night-club appearances, those thousands of people, and never once did I feel the joy of entertaining. I conquered my audiences, and that's a whole other trip."

Her newest victory occurred on New Year's Eve 1956 and launched a golden phase in her career. That night, Horne opened at the Empire Room, inside New York's Waldorf-Astoria hotel. The aristocratic dwelling stood at Lexington Avenue and Fiftieth Street—one of the East Side's most upscale hubs. Horne would become synonymous with the Empire Room, which seated four hundred in a horseshoe configuration, arranged in tiers around a dance floor. Singers had to perform to a broad semicircle of viewers—no easy task.

Horne wasn't the room's first black artist; Dorothy Dandridge had beat her there, which she resented. Owner Conrad Hilton had taken the risk of booking Dandridge. "When Hilton placed this radical idea before some of his associates, all hell broke loose," wrote reporter Max Maxwell. "A Negro at the Waldorf? . . . It was unheard of!" Nonetheless, Dandridge opened on April 11, 1955, to a packed society audience. "She sang—and the chi-chi clique listened, quietly," noted Maxwell. "Nobody moved, much less walked out." As soon as the hotel knew that a Negro headliner could make money there, others followed: the Count Basie orchestra with vocalist Joe Williams, Pearl Bailey. Then came Horne with a six-week run.

On New Year's Eve, the Empire Room charged a twenty-five-dollar cover, one of the steepest in town. Its clientele didn't mind; the reservation book filled up so swiftly that a 1:30 A.M. show was added. Lennie Hayton conducted the Nat Brandwynne Orchestra, the hotel's starchy dance band. But all eyes stayed on Lena Horne. "I can't remember when I've so literally been swept off my feet by a feminine performance," wrote Robert Dana in the *New York World-Telegram & Sun*. "The woman is so stunningly gowned to accent a beautiful figure that this, in itself, would catch an audience's attention. But the ultimate hypnotic effect is the music, the arrangements and an intensity of delivery that finds its essence in eyes that seem to bore into you."

Horne wasn't impressed by her surroundings; she called nightclubs at any level "toilets." But like it or not, that first Waldorf engagement banished any doubt: Horne was now the queen of the supper clubs, an honor held previously by such white doyennes as Hildegarde and Kay Thompson. Everything M-G-M had taught her about how to dress, move, and command the spotlight—plus Hayton's instruction on pacing and delivery—reached full flower at the Waldorf. There she proved herself "the ultimate nightclub performer," said Bobby Short. "She had all of it going for her. Hauteur. Complete security. A little meanness. Clothes. She was so fucking pretty and elegant that people forgot the fact that she was a *damned* good singer." If her beauty had lured people in, Horne would taunt them with it, dangle it out of reach, just as film roles had been held out of hers. She found a way to use her torrid image as a weapon, not just an enticement.

Before making her entrance, she stood behind a pair of heavy doors that opened into the back of the Empire Room. Irene, her servant, stood by her side. After the customary introduction—"*Miss* Lena Horne"— the singer dropped her cape into Irene's arms and glided toward the bandstand. Jaws dropped. Arthur Laurents recalled her "geisha walk" and deferential bows. "She came out as a paradox," he said. "Then she looked at you, and, ooh, you reared back. This was a formidable person."

Posed at a stand-up mike, Horne opened with a recent show tune, "Today I Love Everybody." Its irony escaped most of the audience, but not Gene Davis, who sensed its subtext: "You can have all the fantasies you want, but don't you *dare* touch me." From there she took people on a forty-five-minute whirlwind tour of her M-G-M past, of Broadway and the East Side cabarets, of international hot spots—Harlem, Paris, Buenos Aires. Other chanteuses buckled at the knees as they sang of love, but not Horne. The demureness of her original "Honeysuckle Rose" had hardened; she ended it with a jagged pause after "suck" and a barracuda's hungry glance. Words like "sweet" were spat out; her diction was sharp as a scalpel. "It made people *sit up*," said singer Polly Bergen. Even in a song as downtrodden as Duke Ellington's "Mood Indigo," Horne refused to shed a tear; when she sang of feeling as down "as any poor fool can be," her eyes burned with resentment.

Between songs she hardly talked at all, save for a frosty "Thank you *varuh* much." But what little she said made an impression. Decades later, fans quoted her breathy intro of the show's centerpiece: "We'd like to do a group of . . . well, *ahhh* think they're the always suh*prahhh*sing Cole *Pawtuh* tunes." As she sang about jet-set lovebirds "going gaga in gay Paree" ("Ours") or savored the high-flown language of "Love of My Life" ("Never more need I implore you to miss me"), audiences felt chic by osmosis.

They also saw how funny Horne could be. In "How You Say It" she was a Latina lusting comically after a "handsome Yankee" but unable to say much more in English than a growled "*Wow*-EE!" People roared at her little-known silly side. She explained decades later: "It would have embarrassed me to say, 'I know all you men want me!'" So I turned it into comedy, and I used to get laughs, and I loved that!"

Still, the humor never pierced her aloofness. "They kept saying, 'There's so much mystery about her. What is she thinking? And she's so *sexxxy*.' Oh, God! I wasn't. I just didn't like them, really. I said, 'I'm not gonna let them know what *I'm* thinking about.' So I had this kinda grand attitude, which went very well in the nightclubs."

It certainly impressed her peers. Sammy Davis, Jr., sat ringside with a pad and pencil, noting everything Horne did. Martha Graham watched in fascination. "There is not one spontaneous gesture," she noticed. "It's as calculated as Kabuki or a Hindu dance." Stella Adler, the eminent acting coach, told her class that Horne and Judy Garland were the greatest singing actors. To a young man attempting a monologue from *Othello*, she recommended Horne as an example of fiery but controlled rage.

Polly Bergen revered her, too. In May 1957, the doe-eyed beauty from Tennessee would score a major breakthrough with her portrayal of the tragic torch singer Helen Morgan in a CBS teleplay. It won her an Emmy and made her a Vegas headliner to rival Horne. "But I could not touch the hem of her dress, honey," she said a half century later. "I have a couple of tapes of me singing in which I do all of her facial expressions. It's truly embarrassing when you see them. You say, 'Why is this white woman trying to be Lena Horne?' Lena walked on a stage and grabbed every man by the balls. It was absolutely mesmerizing. But there was something unapproachable about her sexuality. And I think women saw that, and didn't feel threatened by her." In fact, Horne empowered women, because all her sexual innuendo involved what *she* wanted.

On several nights, an illustrious guest sat in the shadowy far reaches of the Empire Room. Now sixty-five, Cole Porter lived in a suite upstairs. He was confined to a wheelchair—the result of a horseback-riding accident years before. To see the legendary bon vivant in this diminished state, with pain etched on his face, tugged at the heart—especially as Horne stood onstage, singing tunes he'd written in his globe-trotting prime. Irritable and depressive as he could now be, Porter retained his old-world politesse, and thanked Horne graciously afterward. "He had this old-fashioned attitude toward women—with me, anyway," she said. "You felt that you were a delicate creature."

Yet Porter was struck by the change that had come over Horne since he'd first admired her in 1942. He saw it in her brittle up-tempo version of his song "It's All Right with Me." Porter had conceived it as a poignant scene between two lonely souls who seek comfort in a one-night stand. According to Stephen Citron, author of *Noel & Cole: The Sophisticates*, Porter had declared that the song was "not to be played too fast" and that "you should cry when you sing it." But Horne's arrangement—borrowed from her equally veneered friend, Kay Thompson—wasn't like that. Cold and cynical, it suggested jaded urbanites using and discarding each other without a backward glance. George Eells, Porter's biographer, wrote that the songwriter "hated" her rendition. But Cora Calhoun's command held firm: Nobody would see Horne cry.

In February, Horne performed a chunk of her act on *The Ed Sullivan Show*. As she sang one of the saddest of saloon songs, "One for My Baby (And One More for the Road)," she played to the cameras with the mastery of a lion tamer. "I learned it at M-G-M," she explained. Horne made no eye contact with the viewer; though the song's protagonist bares her soul in a deserted bar, Horne's guard stayed put. Billie Allen sensed "a frightened woman, with no idea who she is. She'd manufactured this persona—tough, that wall up. She's *sexy*, 'cause sex sells, but she doesn't really know what sexy is. She can't accept her own beauty; she feels she has to be Mata Hari."

Sullivan's audience didn't see the remarkable encore section of Horne's act. After a half hour she would walk off in what nightclub singers called a "false exit." Horne took several. She made the cheering crowds beg for one more song, then another, then another, holding out the longest for "Stormy Weather." Only then did she take her final bow, smiling with hands clasped before her. She switched off the charm as soon as she stopped offstage. Allen saw her do it many times. "It's like, 'Now I've got to go. You've had enough of me. And I've had enough of you.'" Irene met her with her cape, and into the elevator they went, back to the safety of Horne's suite.

Upstairs, Irene or Hayton answered the door as celebrities knocked. In walked Katharine Hepburn, Marlene Dietrich, Edith Piaf, James Mason, Ava Gardner, Harry Belafonte, and many of her former colleagues at M-G-M's Freed Unit. She and Gardner embraced merrily. With other guests, said Arthur Laurents, Horne "acted up a storm—'Oh, thank you, thank you.' She might say something else after they were gone, but she was always terribly well behaved."

Occasionally she found it hard to keep her cool. Night after night in the Empire Room, whoops and shouts came from her biggest fan, Johnny Mathis. Twenty-one at the time of her first engagement, Mathis was a new star; his choirboy tenor, afloat on a magic carpet of strings, had scored him his first hit record, "Wonderful! Wonderful!" For all his success, he nearly genuflected at the feet of Lena Horne. Onstage he began aping her mannerisms and even borrowed her special material. "Any minute he's gonna show up in one of my gowns!" she told a friend of theirs, dancer Claude Thompson.

"I wanted to be her," Mathis admitted. "I wanted to love her and hug her and tell her how much I worshiped her. She got annoyed with me, and I don't blame her. Because I thought nobody could appreciate her as much as I did. I'm afraid I made a fool of myself, but I couldn't help it. And she treated me as a naughty little child."

Idolatry like his made her squirm. After devoting hours each day to her hair, makeup, jewelry, and clothes, Horne resented it when people gazed in awe and called her beautiful, as though she had nothing else to offer. But for years she'd wondered if she had. As far back as 1943, William C. Payette, a Hollywood reporter, was amused at her nervous self-effacement. "Lena Horne can't sing, can't dance, can't act, isn't good-looking, and people are going wild over her. She's terrible. Told us so herself. She makes herself sick, she's so bad." Now the package had been buffed to a blinding gloss, the better to keep people from looking too closely.

They did anyway. Almost as enamored of her as Mathis was Gail's friend Charles Cochran, a budding singer-pianist from a well-to-do East Side family. Though barely of drinking age, he haunted Horne's shows at the Waldorf; soon Gail had invited him upstairs. One night, they waited for Horne to emerge from the bedroom so they could accompany her downstairs for the late show. "My blood pressure was way up there," said Cochran. "I was aware of every sound emanating from the next room. Finally she came out, looking drop-dead gorgeous." He was visibly entranced, and as they stepped into the elevator, he couldn't help staring. "Lena saw me looking at her and she stuck her tongue out—knowing that I would drop dead. And I almost did."

Gail later told him that when she brought home boyfriends who didn't quite know (or care) who Lena Horne was, and they hugged her and talked to her simply as Gail's mom, she became a different person. "She was like a kitten lapping up cream; she loved it!" said Cochran.

Horne also relished the company of Elois Davis, her West Coast pal. Elois was married to a Negro surgeon, and the couple lived among the black elite of Los Angeles. Later, she headed the L.A. chapter of Delta Sigma Theta, an organization of educated black women, but for now Elois was mainly a "spoiled socialite," as her daughter, Judy, laughingly recalled. "She did not work outside of the house. It was about accumulating cars and furs and doing the social things." Horne, with her tireless work ethic, needled Elois about her "stuck-up friends," and Elois gave it right back to her.

At home in L.A.'s Wilshire district, teenage Judy saw a Horne far removed from the detached creature on the nightclub floor. The singer still wore the "Light Egyptian" foundation that Max Factor had made for her, "but in the house she'd take it off and let her freckles show," said Judy. Horne's southern accent faded, her finishing school diction softened into something down-home, and she became Lena, not "*Miss* Lena Horne."

When work took her to L.A., Elois and the Haytons passed happy days at the horse races or on shopping sprees. They searched for Cuban black beans, a favorite of Horne's, or stopped at a soul-food joint and bought chitlin tamales. Sometimes, but not without a fight, Horne allowed Davis to show her off at a social function. One night the singer, along with Hayton, accompanied the Davises to a Christmas party full of those "stuck-up" friends. Judy had the house to herself, and sat in the living room with a young beau. They talked in a corner, hidden by the Christmas tree.

The front door opened, and in came her mother and the Haytons. "They were really, really wasted," recalled Judy. Thinking she was alone,

Horne let loose a stream of invective about the boring party Elois had dragged her to. "Lena took off this corsage they had given her and threw it, and it went all the way across the room and landed right on top of the tree. They all cracked up. Lena was the first one to see that I was sitting there with this guy, and they tried to straighten up and say, 'Oh, oh, excuse me, I didn't see you had company!' So I said to the guy, 'I'd like to introduce you to my mother, Elois Davis, and Mr. and Mrs. Hayton.' As they were walking up the stairs to go to bed, he said, 'That lady looks just like Lena Horne!' I said, 'Oh, she hears that all the time!'"

Amid the tipsy late-night laughs, Horne's despair came out. "She always kicked herself for missing out a lot on the early part of her children's lives," Judy recalled. Horne lamented her blacklisting and all she'd gone through to escape it, and cursed her aborted film career. Elois offered words of comfort; Lennie rose to shake up more martinis. Finally everyone said good night.

Her Waldorf run closed on February 23, 1957, and left her covered in glory. But in her second memoir, the Empire Room earned half a sentence. "I think it was just a job to her," said Gail. To Horne, nightclub performers bore "the naked, flesh-peddling, dirty title of cabaret artiste." She felt trapped. As she told reporter Aline Mosby, "Nothing is harder than singing all the time in clubs."

Her new album hardly revealed a woman in distress. *Lena Horne at the Waldorf-Astoria* boasted a *Vogue*-like photo of Horne in a coral sleeveless dress, jewels flashing. Her hands clasped her head, framing her face as though it were on display at Tiffany's. Horne's smile revealed dazzling white perfection—a change from her youthful photos, which showed a slightly chipped and crooked front tooth and spaces between some of the others. Her nose, too, had changed; years ago she'd had it streamlined at a Harlem hospital recommended by Billy Eckstine.

After years of disappointing record sales, Horne's album made a two-week appearance in *Billboard*'s top forty. *High Fidelity* judged it an exception to the "you have to see her" rule applied to her recordings. "One of the marks of the first-rate recording artist is the ability to triumph over invisibility. For Lena Horne, whose stunning appearance is an important ingredient of her success, this would seem quite a handicap. But in her latest record . . . she completely puts across the thrilling sensuality, without vulgarity, for which she is famous."

There was talk of Horne starring opposite Nat King Cole in *St. Louis Blues,* an all-star biopic of W. C. Handy, the legendary "Father of the Blues." She declined it, and the role went to Eartha Kitt. After all her longing for a Hollywood lead, her failure to accept this one was puzzling; her friend Claude Thompson wondered if her insecurity about acting had made her too scared to even try.

But finally a stage offer had come that seemed right. Just before she closed at the Waldorf, Harold Arlen and Yip Harburg had dropped in. After the show, they offered Horne a lead in their new musical. Set on the mythical Pigeon Island in the Caribbean, *Jamaica* would exploit the 1950s calypso craze. As producer they had David Merrick, an up-and-coming Broadway hotshot. Arlen and Harburg, alas, were on the skids. For all his success as a Hollywood songwriter—most recently in 1954, when Judy Garland introduced "The Man That Got Away" in *A Star Is Born*—most of Arlen's Broadway efforts had flopped. He still smarted over Horne's withdrawal from *St. Louis Woman*; she had also declined the lead in *House of Flowers,* his all-black Caribbean musical of 1954 with book and lyrics by Truman Capote. "I'm too old to play an ingénue," she'd grumbled.

The part launched Diahann Carroll, but Arlen slipped into a creative drought. Harburg's heyday, too, seemed mostly in the past. Ten years had passed since *Finian's Rainbow,* his last Broadway hit. The show's interracial chorus line and social outspokenness had made its liberal author proud. But his views had also gotten him blacklisted, and he needed a break.

In the beginning, he and Arlen didn't tell Horne that she wasn't their first choice. They'd written *Jamaica* for Harry Belafonte, whose calypso hits had made him big box office. But having shown interest, Belafonte refused to commit. He hoped his touring concert musical, *Sing, Man, Sing,* would reach Broadway. It didn't. Then he claimed a detached retina and conflicting bookings. When he asked Merrick to postpone the opening for almost a year, everyone gave up on him. Arlen and Harburg needed a comparable star to save the show and their futures.

Horne seemed amenable. After all, Arlen had written "As Long As I Live," the song that had thrust her into the Cotton Club spotlight. And she'd loved Harburg's lyrics for *Cabin in the Sky*. She went to Arlen's New York apartment, where he, Harburg, and colibrettist Fred Saidy performed the material for her. Horne liked the male lead, a bighearted fisherman, happy with island life. But his fame-hungry girlfriend—the role they wanted her to play—struck her as "a stupid broad who has somewhere gotten hold of a TV set and believes that the only place where things are really happening is New York." Horne had always felt the same way, but that wasn't the problem; the fisherman was the star, not she. The writers agreed to make some changes. On February 24, 1957, Horne signed on for *Jamaica*.

By the time it opened a seventeen-month run in October, the show had shifted into what Arthur Laurents called a "glorified nightclub act" for Horne. It was so tailored to her persona that people couldn't mention it without adding her name. But *Jamaica* had other assets. Hunky Mexican film star Ricardo Montalban played her frequently shirtless love interest. Adelaide Hall, a Cotton Club headliner, returned to Broadway as Horne's Grandma Obeah. The ensemble of near-naked island natives included a fledgling Alvin Ailey. But everything in *Jamaica* was outshone by the name above the title: LENA HORNE.

No sooner had she taken the lead than the jitters began. "I had such an inferiority complex when I started in *Jamaica*," said Horne. "I thought, I'm just a saloon singer—how can I act?" At home she vented her worries to Hayton. He tried to reassure her, but she warned journalists to expect the worst. "I have a terrible figure and only my best friends say I can act," she told William Peper of the *World-Telegram*.

In the revised script, she'd have to. Now her character, Savannah, was a seamstress who dreamed of New York stardom—even though her fisherman sweetheart, Koli, cherished Pigeon Island. That little oasis would embody big issues—mortality in a nuclear age, racial repression, the folly of fame. Experienced actors would surround her. Montalban had leapt to stardom that year as Marlon Brando's equally handsome costar in the film *Sayonara*. Though *Jamaica* had him and Horne playing West Indians, in reality they were Broadway's first interracial lovebirds.

Savannah's best pal, Ginger, was played by Josephine Premice, a flamboyant actress and calypso singer of Haitian blood. An obscure but promising stage actor, Ossie Davis, won the part of Cicero, a brainy island native. Ten-year-old Augustine "Augie" Rios made his Broadway debut as Savannah's wide-eyed scamp of a kid brother, Quico. Audiences had seen Pigeon Island's governor, Erik Rhodes, as a mustachioed dandy in Fred Astaire films.

Merrick didn't skimp on his creative team, either. Robert "Bobby" Lewis had cofounded the prestigious Actors Studio, where he taught method acting to the likes of Marlon Brando. Jack Cole had choreographed Rita Hayworth and Marilyn Monroe in Hollywood, while on Broadway he pioneered a slinky, intricate style known as jazz dance, which drew from ethnic influences. Set designer Oliver Smith's résumé included *My Fair Lady.*

Compared to all of them, Lena Horne was a theatrical upstart. No one knew it better than she. For years, Horne had sung into microphones, and in rooms, not halls. In the first orchestral run-throughs she could barely be heard. Horne demanded that Merrick fire the conductor— a sticky task, for he was Jerry Arlen, the composer's brother, and had signed a run-of-the-show deal. Merrick would have to pay him off until *Jamaica* closed. In came Jay Blackton, who had conducted *Oklahoma!* Horne didn't like him, either. One wondered why she hadn't insisted upon Lennie Hayton.

Eventually, the job went to a veteran Broadway maestro, Lehman Engel, who knew Horne would be hopeless without amplification. To extend her comfort zone, she made him add her nightclub trio—DiNovi, Duvivier, and drummer Jimmy Crawford—to the pit band.

Her flare-ups continued, some of them aimed at her costars. For Adelaide Hall, Harold Arlen's invitation to join the cast had come as a godsend. Hall had lived and worked in England since the thirties, but jobs had dried up and she'd fallen into debt. Arlen sent her the script, and she flew excitedly to New York. There she found that her part had been severely reduced. In his book *Underneath a Harlem Moon: The Harlem to Paris Years of Adelaide Hall,* Iain Cameron Williams related Arlen's apology to Hall. The producers had insisted on the expansion of Horne's role, and something had to go. "Adelaide was far from happy," wrote Williams, "and was convinced Arlen was not telling her the whole truth."

Stephen Bourne, author of *Sophisticated Lady: A Celebration of Adelaide Hall,* did his own research. In rehearsals, he said, "it became evident that Adelaide was going to steal the show. Lena, as the star, was alarmed, and had Adelaide's part cut. Perhaps the star felt 'threatened' and protective of her own role, and this is understandable, considering the pressure on Lena in her first attempt to carry an entire Broadway musical."

Hall refused to utter an ill word about Horne. But her pride was hurt. In 1934, she'd headlined a show in which the young woman had appeared as chorine; now Horne, who called her "my Auntie," seemed to be pushing her out of the spotlight.

Horne, of course, wasn't the first Broadway star to make demands. And in an arena that knew its share of Jim Crow, some of the stands she took broke ground. *Jamaica* employed the first black stage manager in Broadway history, ex-dancer Charlie Blackwell. Both she and David Merrick were credited with demanding at least five black crew members from the stagehands' union. They got their way. "Isn't it sad that you have to be grateful for something like that?" said Horne to a reporter.

Of all the company members, *Jamaica*'s young black chorus members intrigued her the most. Horne would recall them as "some of the most beautiful, talented, committed dancers I had ever seen." As she stood wrapped in mink on the sidelines and watched them rehearse, her face glowed; they, meanwhile, were dazzled at the presence of the great Lena Horne. "What a gorgeous creature she was!" said Alvin Ailey, who had worshiped her since high school. "We couldn't close our mouths, we were so awestruck."

In them, Horne witnessed the flowering of black modern dance. During breaks, she approached them shyly and asked them about their lives. The lead duo, Ailey and Cristyne Lawson, showed special promise. Born in Texas in 1931, Ailey was a student of Lester Horton, the founder of a fearlessly integrated Hollywood dance company. When Horton died in 1953, Ailey took over its leadership. He was twenty-two and rife with star quality. "When Alvin took off his shirt, both men and women died," said Lawson, who danced with him for years. "Alvin was like a truck driver who moved lyrically. He was not a dancer, believe me. He had absolutely no technique. But his movement was so supple, with this massive body, that it just took people in."

A reedlike, intellectual beauty, Lawson had grown up in Santa Monica, California, raised by a mother who played classical piano. As a child, she'd struggled in vain to find a dance school that would take a Negro. But Horton's welcomed her. From there she danced in many films, including *Carmen Jones;* she also studied at Juilliard—formidable achievements for a young black woman of her day. No less impressive was Claude Thompson, a dancer from Los Angeles who'd amassed several Broadway credits, including a long run in *Mr. Wonderful,* a showcase for Sammy Davis, Jr.

Some *Jamaica* dancers had hard-earned technique; others, like the handsome Nat Horne, had barely studied but moved with innate grace. Born in Richmond, Virginia, Nat had moved to Manhattan in 1954 with a burning desire to dance; expecting little, he competed with hundreds at a *Jamaica* audition. "I think I got the job because they thought I was related to Lena Horne," he said.

But he mastered Jack Cole's choreography, which required punishing precision and stamina. Masses of bodies moved in prowling, synchronized motion, often low to the ground. "My feet were bleeding and my knees aching," said Ailey, but Cole screamed if anyone fumbled. Broadway gossip had it that the *Jamaica* dancers weren't up to their task; that made them try all the harder. Horne was touched by their striving. She saw "those young people, without money, without encouragement, going to class every day, torturing their bodies, and continually learning."

Their success, she felt, rested on her shoulders, which were already burdened by her own fear of failure. On the strength of her name, *Jamaica* sold out its first week of out-of-town tryouts, which began on September 16, 1957, at Philadelphia's Shubert Theatre. But the first feedback was distressing; critics pronounced the show a muddled mess. Robert Lewis had directed serious drama but never a musical, and he brought a heavy hand to *Jamaica.* The effort to shift it from a man's vehicle to a showcase for Horne had left many threads hanging; moreover, the show's slender premise couldn't accommodate so much weighty social subtext.

The reviewers liked Horne, but each night her stomach was in knots. Sensing the worst, she felt condescension, not love, as the audience cheered her. While frantic rewrites took place, she thrashed about for her own solutions. Ever self-conscious of her physical flaws, she felt that costume designer Miles White hadn't a clue how to dress her. His replacement came and went quickly. Finally she insisted on Robert

Mackintosh, who made her nightclub gowns. According to Merrick's biographer Howard Kissel, even that wasn't enough. "Horne, in her insecurity, was uncomfortable about appearing on Broadway as a poor little native girl," he wrote. "She insisted on turbans designed by Lilly Daché." Singer Thelma Carpenter, a graduate of the Apollo Theater, the Count Basie band, and East Side cabarets, suspected another step on Horne's part to prepare for Broadway. Years later she told her manager, Alan Eichler, of visiting Horne backstage. "Lena's face was so tight she could hardly smile," claimed Carpenter.

September 23 found the company in Boston for a second week of tryouts. The *Boston Herald*'s Elinor Hughes deemed the book "dreadful." The critics praised Horne, but nothing could calm her. Having longed for a chance to act, she was now sure she couldn't. *New York Times* reporter Seymour Peck interviewed her in her dressing room. He saw her with fists outstretched, crying, "*I hate myself!*" Just to hear her own voice onstage filled her with dread. "I know when I'm ruining a couple of laughs. Is my Jamaican accent right or does it sound southern? I'm depressed in a way I haven't been before." Bobby Lewis walked her through every method-acting technique he knew, struggling to give her some confidence. Horne, he said, wanted "to kill herself" whenever she flubbed.

Backstage, *Jamaica* turned into a battle zone. Harburg was furious at Merrick's desire to save the show by making it a vehicle for Lena Horne. She, in turn, was buckling under the pressure, and resented Bobby Lewis for what he couldn't draw out of her. Lehman Engel, *Jamaica*'s old-school conductor, was annoyed that his star needed a microphone. "I thought this business was going to be fun," said Merrick, "but so far I haven't had any."

With the Broadway opening a week away, the show needed emergency help. Merrick placed a call to Joseph Stein, an experienced New York librettist, to solicit his services as script doctor. Stein had *Your Show of Shows* in his background, along with the hit Broadway musical *Plain and Fancy*. A Tony Award for *Fiddler on the Roof* lay ahead.

Stein boarded a train to Boston and went straight to Harburg's hotel room. He found the writer lying on his bed, fully dressed. Harburg had fought so much with Merrick that the producer had barred him from rehearsals. "Yip said, 'Thank God you're here!'" recalled Stein. "He took the next train home. Ricardo Montalban was totally lost. He said, 'I don't know what the hell I'm doing on that stage.'"

That night, Stein sat alongside Lehman Engel and watched the show. "Can you follow what's going on?" he asked the conductor.

"I haven't the vaguest idea!"

Stein set his pen to the script. "I had to work the story around those numbers and make the relationships clear," he said. "And although I was just as liberal as Yip, I really felt that trying to make this show a big political statement didn't work. It just got in the way."

Little remained besides connective tissue between the songs, but at least the musical made sense. By now, the Broadway ticket sales had reached a staggering height. All eyes were on Lena Horne, and she girded herself for the worst. Two nights of previews took place at the show's home, the Imperial Theatre. Horne termed them "disastrous." Jack Entratter came, and he shook her confidence even further. "What the hell are you trying to prove? You can make more in a month in Vegas than you can make in a year in that damn show."

The big day—October 31, 1957—finally arrived. Horne, as she put it, "stumbled through" the afternoon rehearsal; the *New York Post* would later report that she'd sprained her foot but told no one. Afterward, she sat in her dressing room, numb with fear and blaming many. She summed up the experience in her memoir as a harrowing backstage story, replete with backstabbing, bickering, and personal agendas run amok. "You find yourself being used to ban respectable, creative, temperamental people connected with the show from the theater. . . . You learn to cope when you realize your leading man is finding it difficult to see you as a tender, loving ingénue."

Around 6:00 P.M. came a knock at the door. Horne opened it to find Charlie Blackwell bearing a huge bouquet of flowers from the dancers. In the card, addressed to Savannah, they said they loved her. By now, Horne had informed her friend St. Clair Pugh: "To hell with anything anyone tells me to do—I'm gonna go out there and be myself."

The first-nighters included Kirk Douglas, Louella Parsons, Walter Winchell, Dorothy Kilgallen, and Dolores Gray. Cristyne Lawson saw "a white cloud" in the audience—Marlene Dietrich, wearing a trench coat lined in chinchilla.

After the overture, the curtain rose on the imaginary Pigeon Island off the coast of Jamaica. This was no paradise; people lived in shacks amid the mango trees. But it was home to Koli (Montalban), a poor but happy fisherman. Out of the wings he bounded with a netful of fish. Koli was eager to grab a guitar and serenade his sweetheart, Savannah, and he didn't have long to wait. Four minutes into the story, with a clatter of shutters, Lena Horne emerged from a hut. The response overwhelmed her. According to Howard Kissel, she faced two minutes of thunderous applause. Such approval "inspired her to give the performance Lewis had so far been unable to coax out of her," he wrote.

Horne played a would-be sophisticate who yearned for the bright lights of New York. Singing "Push De Button," she rhapsodized about that "little island on the Hudson," a utopia of modern conveniences, with skyscrapers that towered "in the air-conditioned air." But Koli loved the tangerine-scented breezes of home and wanted her to stay put.

From there, *Jamaica* became a confection of exotic atmosphere, threadbare plot, and sex appeal. The show offered a feast of eye candy, exploited daringly by costumer Miles White. A sexy "underwater" ballet found Montalban behind a scrim, diving for pearls. The male dancers "walked around half naked, no shirt on, torn pants," said Claude Thompson.

A calypso beat ushered on the natives of both sexes, a sinewy, writhing pack of beauties with flashy smiles, snapping fingers, and arms that reached to the sky. A New York con man, Joe Nashua, arrives to coax them into trading fishing for pearl-diving, an enterprise he plans to milk for a fortune. Savannah sees him as a free ride to stardom. In a dream sequence, she stands in a nearly bare Manhattan nightclub, purring "Take It Slow, Joe" while two couples dance sensually in slow motion. But when Koli rescues her kid brother during a hurricane, she realizes that the love of a good man means more than her hollow dreams of fame, and they return to each other's arms.

The score retained a glimmer of social commentary. In her witty star turn, "Leave de Atom Alone," Josephine Premice begged world leaders to keep their fingers off a button that would hurl everyone into the heavens. In general, though, Arlen's and Harburg's best work seemed behind them. The calypso ballads, such as "Cocoanut Sweet," sounded drab and inauthentic. Besides "Push de Button," Horne had two out-

standing numbers, but neither was new. "Ain't It the Truth" had gotten
sheared from *Cabin in the Sky;* "Napoleon" was an outtake from *Hooray for
What!,* a 1937 Broadway musical scored by Arlen and Harburg. Savannah sang this clever decimation of celebrity near the end, after forsaking
her dreams of fame. The happy sound of laughter greeted Horne as she
surveyed what commercialism had done to history's icons: "Columbus is
a circle and a day off / Pershing is a square, what a payoff!

All evening long, recalled Horne, she'd had "the usual terrible sick
feeling, and I wanted to kill myself. I was sure I would never live through
the night." But her final ovation surpassed the first, and she let herself
wallow in the approval. Nearly fifty years later, Claude Thompson remembered that night as "better than sex."

Everyone trekked to Sardi's for the party. In an upstairs room at the
famed theatrical restaurant, well-wishers crowded around Horne, hugging her and gushing praise. But she felt "sick again" in anticipation of
the notices, which would appear within hours. "Let's get drunk and enjoy
ourselves," she told the dancers. The revelers did not include Yip Harburg, who had boycotted the opening. *Jamaica,* he said, had been "completely overhauled and commercialized for Lena Horne, with the soul of
creative intention raped and cannibalized . . . I will take the cash." Joseph
Stein had come, however, and Merrick told him he'd saved the day. "I felt
like I was on a sled going downhill very fast going into an oak tree," the
producer whispered. "And you came along and pushed the tree away."

After midnight, Horne read the reviews. She'd entranced the critics—and all but blinded them to the other principals, who were lauded in
passing. The revamped book was panned, the slick choreography mostly
snickered at. To Robert Sylvester of the *Daily News, Jamaica* was an ar-
duous triumph for Horne: "She has nothing to sing. She has nothing
to do. She has nothing to say. But to hear her sing it, do it and say it is
somehow enough . . . even our better actresses can learn from her . . . a
completely enchanting artist whose atrociously gowned slender shoulders are still rugged enough to carry an entire evening in the theatre."

Two theater insiders and friends of Horne were less kind. "*Jamaica*
was foolish," said Arthur Laurents. "It took place in Never-Never Land.
There were all these Disney World natives in frocks. Whatever success it
had was because of Lena, and because Montalban was a very nice man,

which came across. But it was a silly piece of nontheater. She knew. Bobby Lewis talked a big game, but he didn't know what to do with her."

In his November 17, 1957, diary entry, Noël Coward wrote, "On Monday evening I went to see a sorry spectacle: *Jamaica* with Lena Horne, Ricardo Montalban and an over-vivacious colored lady called Josephine Premice who carried on like a mad spider. Lena was brilliant and Ricardo Montalban's chest was lovely. Apart from this the evening was a loss."

But the most important critic in town, Brooks Atkinson of the *Times*, gave the show his blessing. "No one associated with *Jamaica* has anything in mind except an evening's entertainment," he wrote. And on that score, he deemed the show "delightful." Mart Crowley spoke for much of its gay audience: "I was knocked out! Ricardo Montalban was sexy as hell, with his shirt off all the time, in tight white Capri pants and a straw hat. And Lena was dynamite in those fishtail outfits."

During a boat scene, Horne shared an interracial kiss with Montalban. Madeline Gilford, Harburg's assistant, recalled hate mail and angry calls, but Horne's fellow performers recalled no upset. Before the opening, Tina Morris, a reporter for the tabloid *Whisper*, asked Montalban if he anticipated an uproar. "I am flabbergasted that in this day and age such a thing should cause any comment at all," said the Mexican-born star. "Where I was brought up it was unnecessary ever to say, 'All men are created equal'—because it was always taken for granted that they are."

Any dissent passed quickly; *Jamaica* seemed to herald a new age of racial tolerance in the theater. For the next year, Horne was continually in the papers. To the *Post*'s Gael Greene, she spoke gratefully of the show: "I don't feel so lonesome, having all that company up there." For all the backstage melodrama, Horne would recall *Jamaica* as "heaven." For years she'd sung to seas of white faces; now, she said, "we had an interracial audience that was beautiful. Asian people, white people, black people, it was marvelous!" Dancers who'd initially felt too awestruck to approach her now popped their heads into her dressing room and said, "Hi, Lena!" After each Saturday-night show they had a "big party," she said; they cooked for her or she for them. "I was very happy in those years," she added wistfully.

Her elation was uncontainable on March 16, 1958, when she and some of the dancers appeared on Steve Allen's Sunday-night show to do

"Push de Button." After a moment of conversation with Allen, the white host took off Horne's mink, revealing a white beaded gown. Five months into the run, any attempt at characterization had clearly fallen away. Savannah was now Lena Horne, who emoted as though the stagestruck island girl were really the toast of Manhattan. *What an isle!* she exclaimed, as the natives shimmied behind her. Her Jamaican accent came and went, alternating with her southern one. Sometimes she said "de," sometimes "the." It didn't matter. The segment was exciting, and it gave *Jamaica* a new boost at the box office.

As always, she embodied professionalism, arriving three hours before each performance. She missed but one due to laryngitis. For Hayton, however, a malaise was setting in. He'd become Mr. Lena Horne, and his wife's success on Broadway had left him at loose ends. That year, his only project of note was an instrumental album of *Jamaica*'s score. He came to the theater almost nightly to check up on things, but the musicians didn't need him. Most of the time he sat in his wife's dressing room, acting as security blanket and bartender. His own consumption revealed a man eager for escape. Though rarely drunk, he stayed in what Arthur Laurents called a "haze of goodwill and brandy." Gail Lumet Buckley wrote in *The Hornes* that "Lennie was devoted to the art of food and drink. . . . He daily consumed a cold beer (or two) at lunch, several martinis at sunset, a bottle of Bordeaux at dinner, and some Hennessy and soda after dinner—not to mention four daily packs of Camel cigarettes."

By now, alcohol had become one of the Haytons' main links. "Lena was drinking a lot during that time," said Cristyne Lawson. "There used to be a case of Cutty Sark in her dressing room. I don't mean that she was drunk, I just mean that she was slightly away from us." Interviewing her one afternoon, Robert Wahls of the *Daily News* found her longing for her first drink of the day. "Daddy gives me a martini or a champagne cocktail," she explained. "But not one minute before four." On matinee days, she stressed, "no drinks at all."

Anyone close to Horne knew she found it hard to stay happy for long. She continued to complain about her character, and the schedule was exhausting her. After decades on nightclub time, she struggled to stay awake for matinees. Her nerves still flared; the stomach medicine Gelusil, helped calm her queasiness.

Some of the stress came, no doubt, in response to the presence of Edna Rodriguez. Now a stout, double-chinned widow, Horne's mother had left Cuba and moved back to Brooklyn. She tended to reappear whenever Lena was getting the most attention; so it was during *Jamaica,* when she haunted the rehearsals and sat in Horne's dressing room. The singer posed dutifully with her for *Ebony*'s photographer in loving embrace, and Claude Thompson saw Edna often at the Haytons' dinner table. He recalled her as a "very sweet lady" and "very quiet." But she couldn't resist needling her daughter. "Every time she'd see me in something," recalled the singer, "she'd say, 'Darling, you're prettier than ever.' The kiss of death!" Horne could hardly stand it. "Her mother was a termagant if there ever was one," said Laurents. "Lena was afraid of her."

In 1958, Horne told cabaret owner Dick Kollmar, the husband of Dorothy Kilgallen, that when *Jamaica* closed she would move to Paris and come to the States only to work. No more, it seemed, did she find the show "heaven." Tensions had set in between Horne and some of her costars, including Josephine Premice. The French called Premice "jolie-laide" (pretty-ugly), and although she'd known barely a fraction of Horne's success, the star still seemed threatened by her. Born in Brooklyn of Haitian parents, Premice had studied dance with Katherine Dunham and Martha Graham. Later she took to the nightclub stage with a solo act of Haitian-inspired song and dance. Premice moved to Paris, where audiences adored her over-the-top vivacity, wildly agile limbs, and cigarette-stained rasp of a voice. But in the States she was tagged a "novelty," and largely shunted aside. Her friend Carmen de Lavallade recalled the "terrible frustration" Premice felt: "Where Lena lacked confidence in some ways, Josephine had the bravura—but she was not in Lena's position."

Premice's struggles figured prominently in *Always Wear Joy,* a memoir by her daughter, Susan Fales-Hill. She wrote of how David Merrick had auditioned her mother, then declared her "not pretty enough to play Lena Horne's best friend." Premice swallowed her pride and gave a dignified response. "Mr. Merrick, I'm going back to Paris to sing. And after you've seen every other actress in New York, I'll be the most beautiful girl you've ever seen."

Her performance in *Jamaica* helped win her a blue-blood white husband, Timothy Fales. Onstage and off, Premice wore several masks.

Claude Thompson saw her as "a beautiful, bighearted drag queen. Josephine had her hair cut short, and after the show we'd go to a gay bar. Well, all the gay children would hit on her, thinking she was a little boy. No tits, no hair, after the show no eyebrows. We loved hanging out with her because she attracted the *best* of company!"

In highbrow circles she affected a showy grandeur, mixed with a life-of-the-party excess. All of it covered the hurt that Premice refused to show the world. Certainly she never would have revealed the unease she felt about playing second banana to a goddess at this high point of her stage career. Nat Horne suspected a jealousy that went both ways, for Premice stopped every show with "Leave de Atom Alone." In *Revelations: The Autobiography of Alvin Ailey,* the dancer detected a "real sense of friction" between the two women. Opposing factions, he said, sprang up among the dancers. "We who were anti-Premice made up all sorts of wonderfully bitchy things about what she was wearing that day. 'Did you see that silver motorcycle jacket Josephine is wearing? Lena would *never* wear a silver motorcycle jacket!' . . . Lena would then come in wearing some exquisite dress from Yves St. Laurent. 'Now *that's* the way to dress,' we would say."

The backstage discord didn't stop there. Several company members, including Cristyne Lawson, observed a growing distance between Horne and Montalban. The former hinted at this in her book, when she wrote of her costar's inability to see her "as a tender, loving ingénue." Among the cast, gossip swirled. Harry Watson, Montalban's dresser, would later tell Delilah Jackson that the actor suspected Horne had designs on him. If so, she wouldn't have gotten far, for Montalban was happily married to Georgiana Young, the half sister of actress Loretta Young. Rumor had it that one night, as they kissed in the boat scene, Horne bit Montalban out of spite.

So gentlemanly was Horne's leading man that he never breathed a critical word about her, not even to his close friend Geoffrey Holder. "But from what I gather there was some tension there," said Holder.

It was hard to view their star as a happy lady. "We never saw her complain or get angry," said Nat Horne. "But whenever she came to the theater and walked straight to her dressing room I knew something was wrong." If Horne's pride in *Jamaica* seemed to be wavering, the dancers knew they'd helped usher in big changes. "I'd never seen so many beautiful bodies of color onstage—all different colors of black, tan," said Claude Thompson. "It was like a beautiful family. I couldn't wait to get to work every night." Cristyne Lawson felt the same elation. "The world was our oyster. We'd do eight shows a week, and on Wednesday night we'd all go to the Palladium and do the mambo and cha-cha until five in the morning. Then we'd have breakfast and watch the sun come up. We'd go to bed and sleep all day and get up and do the evening performance."

A special thrill came with the news of the 1958 Tony Award nominations. *Jamaica* would vie for Best Musical; Horne, Montalban, Premice, Ossie Davis, Oliver Smith, and Miles White all earned nominations. The show won no awards, but it ran longer than any black (or predominantly black) Broadway musical ever had.

Jamaica played the last of its 555 performances on April 11, 1959. Business had dipped, and, as Nat Horne added, "Lena needed a rest." Many of the show's young artists faced bright futures. In 1958, Alvin Ailey formed his first company, the American Dance Theatre. It included several of his *Jamaica* colleagues (including Cristyne Lawson), who pooled their money and ideas to make the group possible. Backstage during the run of *Jamaica*, Ossie Davis had sat at a typewriter between scenes, writing *Purlie Victorious*, a play about a preacher in the Deep South. It reached Broadway in 1961.

Josephine Premice had just two more Broadway assignments in store. One of them, *Bubbling Brown Sugar*, ran longer than *Jamaica*, and earned stronger reviews. But a mention of her Tony nomination for the latter opened her 2001 *New York Times* obituary. Premice, who was seldom without a cigarette, had died of emphysema.

Months after *Jamaica* closed, Claude Thompson sat in Horne's kitchen and shared his tale of woe. He'd just returned from Puerto Rico with a black troupe. They went unpaid, he said, and were treated contemptuously. Broadway remained almost lily-white, and he couldn't get another musical; neither could most of his *Jamaica* colleagues. When he, Carmen de Lavallade, and dancer James Truitt went to Las Vegas to open for Pearl Bailey at the Flamingo Hotel, de Lavallade's young son was barred from the pool. "I didn't realize that Lena was very moved by all this," said Thompson. Horne herself had recently run into trouble on Perry Como's TV show. Como had touched her arm on camera, and angry letters poured in.

Not until he read an interview she gave in the seventies did Thompson learn the depths of Horne's dismay. "I sat in my kitchen day after day wanting to do nothing but scream," she told Alan Ebert in *Essence*. "It seemed like nothing had changed, not one damn thing, and that we were still coming through the back door; that we hadn't advanced one lousy friggin' step. I was so angry I cried."

BACK went Horne to TV guest spots and engagements at familiar places, such as the Waldorf and the Cocoanut Grove. Hollywood's premiere supper club, the Grove boasted a starlit ceiling and huge potted palm trees. André Previn called it "that surreal club—it was so awful! The name gives it away. It was a fake South Seas environment."

Horne continued to take Las Vegas's hefty paychecks and run, but never without complaints. Charles Cochran recalled her saying, "Oh, it's a waste of time, but I'm going to Vegas." The comment startled him, for he'd worn out *Lena at the Sands,* a live album that even Horne admitted liking. On it she'd borrowed "Some People," Ethel Merman's showstopper from *Gypsy*, and made it her own. To that anthem of gut ambition at any cost, Horne added a smug disdain. When she sang "Some people can be content / Playing *bingo!* Paying *rent!*" she spat out "bingo" and "rent" as though anything so mundane revolted her. By contrast, Hayton's graceful piano on "The Man I Love" made that song a recess of calm. After a year and a half of near inactivity, Hayton was back at work.

Las Vegas had reached its peak, thanks largely to the frat-boy antics of the Rat Pack, the world-famous summit of cronies—Frank Sinatra, Dean Martin, Sammy Davis, Jr., Peter Lawford, Joey Bishop—who cavorted at the Sands and in a hit movie, *Ocean's Eleven*. But Horne, who'd long disliked Sinatra, wasn't amused, and the town annoyed her. She hated the air-conditioning necessary in that desert climate, and continued to shun the nightlife along Vegas's neon-glowing Strip. "She would never go out after the show," said Gene DiNovi. "It was all work. Do the gig and that was that."

Despite lingering racism, conditions for blacks there had somewhat improved. Alice Key and other activists had banded with the NAACP to integrate housing and employment. Key had even managed to score her own all-black variety TV show, proclaimed the first of its kind. And "Frank Sinatra raised hell," she said, whenever he encountered racism; his hefty clout had helped make life more bearable for black entertainers in Vegas.

But New York remained Horne's liberal refuge. It was a place where a new comic, Lenny Bruce, was lampooning every kind of prejudice in his routines—sometimes shockingly, often hilariously. In the late fifties, he added the following to his act:

> You have the choice of spending fifteen years married to a woman. A black woman or a white woman. Fifteen years just seeing, hugging, and sleeping real close on hot nights. Fifteen years with a black woman or fifteen years with a white woman!
>
> The white woman is Kate Smith . . . and the black woman is Lena Horne.
>
> So you are not concerned with black or white anymore, are you?

As often as Horne herself had spoken out, a lot of observers, especially black ones, still deemed her a showbiz socialite, hiding in a world buffered from discrimination. Looking back, Horne couldn't entirely disagree. She and Hayton, she said, "were this New York couple. And a lot of bullshit went into that." There in their "black ivory tower," as she called their Upper West Side apartment, the Haytons threw frequent parties; the guest lists comprised a high-flown crowd of black and white achievers. Up in the elevator came Richard Burton, Miles Davis, fashion model Suzy Parker, Alvin Ailey, Billy Strayhorn, Kay Thompson, detective novelist Rex Stout of *Nero Wolfe* fame. Horne flitted from room to room, wearing some new creation that inspired breathless praise.

Also there was Horne's noncelebrity court. Hayton showed Claude Thompson the proper way to hold a martini glass—with just a thumb and two fingers on the stem. Bob Mackintosh was a Broadway costumer on the rise, but he seemed proudest of his association with Lena Horne. Tall and wiry, with tortoise-shell glasses, he stood around chain-smoking and making dry, witty chitchat. Sydney Shaw wrote mock-sexy special material for Horne and other singers. White and Jewish, he posed as "a fin-ger-snapping kind of jivester," according to his friend Charles Cochran. Horne wrung gales of laughter from his songs, especially "Evil Spelled Backwards Is Live," in which she groaned, "Embargo spelled backwards means ... *O grab me!*"

Future gossip columnist Liz Smith attended many of Horne's par-ties; so did her later right-hand man, St. Clair Pugh, from North Caro-lina. As a ghostwriter for the "Cholly Knickerbocker" gossip column in the Hearst papers, the brashly endearing Smith kept her ears open for printable tidbits; Pugh was pipe-smoking, bow-tied, and professorial. "Lena said I was the only southern gentleman she liked," he recalled. In-deed, Horne welcomed the twangs of Smith (a Texan) and "Clay-uh," as she called him. "Lena would use Saint and me to practice and perfect her 'Southernisms,'" wrote Smith in her memoir, *Natural Blonde.* "She had a perfect Deep South accent when she wanted to have one."

Gazing at Horne in awe was her friend Kitty D'Alessio, a young fashion consultant for an ad agency. New Jersey–born, she would as-cend the ranks to become a top-rung fashionista, heading the American wing of Chanel. But no one enraptured her like Horne, whom she found "glamorous and wonderful" and "absolutely fantastic." For years she helped Horne choose clothes, showered her with designer merchandise, and served as a confidante of endless concern. "We did things together that she never did with anybody else," said D'Alessio. "We took the bus together, went shopping, things that she perhaps had been protected from before."

Horne was even more coddled in Paris. There she was a frequent guest at the home of Ginette Spanier, *directrice* for the couturier Pierre Balmain, and her doctor husband, Paul-Émile Seidmann. The couple held regular *salons* at their apartment on Avenue Marceau, the Parisian equivalent of Fifth Avenue; an international crème de la crème attended. "But Ginette always talked about Lena Horne, the wonderful Lena Horne," said Geoffrey Holder. On November 22, 1959, Coward noted in his diary that "there was a little gathering—Lena Horne, Lennie her husband, and Marlene—at Ginette's. Marlene made an entrance looking ravishing and was quite entrancing for about an hour. Then she became boring and over-ego-centric."

Such brittle world-weariness was losing its charm in the face of the upheavals that launched the sixties. By that time, nearly every black entertainer of prominence had joined the fight for civil rights. But few people felt Horne cared. In 1958, a British reporter reflected on her last appearance at London's Savoy Hotel, which, he said, had refused her a room years before. "Now Lena's with the snobs and forgetting the snubs," he wrote.

OF all her public roles, Horne was least known as a mother. But now her children were young adults, and their presence in her life had grown, too. At Radcliffe, Gail had blossomed into the perfect Horne daughter, eminently suitable for display. She was Ivy League–educated, spirited but always a lady, and seemingly very conscious of upholding the family propriety. Explained a friend of hers: "She had that beautifully behaved demeanor you saw in celebrity children. They were programmed: Don't let the parent down. Make nice."

According to Claude Thompson, Gail "knew all of Lena's friends and was very 'theater.'" She seemed to like bathing in her mother's reflected glow. At social functions she wore Horne's old gowns, handed down after just one use; it wouldn't do for the star to be seen in the same dress twice. "My mother always insists on beautiful clothes—and I get them very quickly," Gail informed a reporter. Acquaintances and strangers alike found her unusually eager to talk about Horne.

But according to Arthur Laurents, Gail and her mother "were at odds for a *long* time." Rex Reed recalled the "serious love-hate relationship" between the world-renowned mother and her somewhat aimless daughter.

Years later, Sidney Myer, a cabaret booking agent and club manager in New York, would reflect on the plight of stars' children when he presented Melissa Newman, the singing daughter of Paul Newman and Joanne Woodward. "I had always sort of envied the children of celebrities, thinking that things were handed to them, and that much of the time they did it the easy way. After I got to know many of them, I began to realize that these people were never to be envied. Most every sibling or child of a celebrity never trusted anyone. They always thought that people were using them to get to the famous member of the family. No matter what you told them about their gifts, they never truly believed they had achieved anything on their own. They thought it was only given to them because of family connections, and they never really felt that anyone even liked them for themselves."

At school, Gail had tried her hand at acting, and had won an award in the Yale Drama Festival for her performance in Molière's *School for Wives*. But she lacked her mother's gut ambition, and the pressure of being constantly introduced as "Lena Horne's daughter" didn't help. After graduating from Radcliffe, she moved in with her mother and Hayton; from then on she drifted from job to job. Writing and editing interested her, and in Paris, Gail had worked briefly for the women's magazine *Marie Claire*. Returning to the States, she edited the staff paper at Grossinger's, the Catskill resort, and sold ads for the Manhattan-based *Paris Review*. She also served as an off-Broadway production assistant. But her search for identity would linger for years to come.

Her brother, Ted, however, seemed aglow with promise. In 1957, the year he graduated from L.A. High, the *Los Angeles Herald-Examiner* had named him Teenager of the Year. That fall, he was slated to enter the University of Southern California on a seven-year scholarship. Ted would spend the first four studying political science and the last three working toward a law degree. A scholarship of that length "was very rare," said Nelson Atkins, who had played on Ted's basketball team at L.A. High. "Everybody kinda looked up to him."

No one admired Ted more than Teretta LaVelle Burton, his vice president in the L.A. High student body. She and Ted were a remarkable pair, two black youngsters who ran a primarily white campus's most auspicious organization. "I was one of those girls who were not very popular but I was a 4.0, you got it?" she said years later. A school publication described Terrie as "sweet, vivacious, kind, and cute." Like Ted, she had accomplished much in four years. Aside from her student-body position, Terrie modeled, sang in the choir, and joined numerous school organizations. She was surely envied, for she was seen constantly with Ted, and perceived as his girlfriend. Terrie didn't mind, for she'd fallen for him. "I always used to think Ted was so glamorous," she said. "French was my major in high school and college, and I would be so jealous when he'd fly off to Paris. I was very fascinated with him, and so was every girl on the campus. He threw some of us a piece of bread now and then."

But Terrie sensed a strange ennui in Ted. For all his intellect, she said, "he just underperformed," and she had to coach him before many an exam when she saw he hadn't bothered studying. And although he never talked about it, she saw the pain of his family situation. "His dad was *strange*, his mother was *strange*," said Terrie. "The fact that he was the son of a famous person and living in an apartment . . . In California, most people don't live in apartments."

Terrie's parents often invited Ted for dinner; sometimes he brought his dad. Louis worked hard to impress them with his charm and achievements, but his eagerness backfired. To Terrie, he seemed "taken with himself, and the conversation would be all be about him. There was no way he could keep up with Lena, but he was trying."

With another high achiever in the family, Jones had become more desperate than ever to prove his worth. In 1956, he had run unsuccessfully for an assemblyman's post in L.A.'s West Adams district, where he lived. The time had come, he felt, for one more push. Soon after the New Year of 1957, Jones took a one-year lease on a building there and made it his political headquarters. Presiding over his election team would be none other than L.A. High's shining black hope. Ted, decided Louis, would lead the West Adams Young Republicans, an organization of about a hundred of the young man's friends and classmates.

Jones was known as an impassioned Democrat, and people wondered why he'd swapped parties. The Negro majority had begun doing just the opposite in the thirties, and now less than a third of black voters were Republican. But Young Republican clubs existed throughout the country, and this was the first all-black one; to Jones, that was good PR. He alerted the local press, who announced Ted as the group's "newly elected president." It appalled his friends' parents to see their children identified as Young Republicans, but the most distressed of all was Lena Horne. "It kills me," she told Mike Wallace of Ted's supposed affiliation. "I'm the dreamer that's hoping that a great Democratic man will come for us, because I can't switch. I'm loyal. . . . But I see logic behind what my son is doing. In fact, I even think it's smart for him. I guess the Negro people are finally becoming opportunists. Well, there's no reason why they shouldn't. These are new times."

Ted's friends couldn't have cared less about his father's political ambitions; they joined the Young Republicans to support Ted. Their key duty was to hold fund-raisers at the Jones headquarters. Apparently, their efforts worked: Jones became the first Negro ever elected to his local assembly.

A day after he'd begun, Jones was arrested for fraud. A complaint had been filed by his white colleagues on the assembly, "who had bitterly opposed Jones's election to the group," wrote the *Pittsburgh Courier*. The district attorney's office reported that he'd registered to vote from 5320 West Adams, his headquarters' address, instead of his home address. The charge hinged on a minor technicality, and Jones gained acquittal by convincing the court that he truly lived at 5320. But his colleagues got their way, and Jones left the assembly. He never ran for office again.

The lease on his office had months to run. The Young Republicans turned it into an after-hours jazz club, complete with a bar, food, and gambling. Their lark proved far more successful than Louis's campaign. By the time the police closed it down, the makeshift nightspot had netted thousands of dollars.

Now in his late teens, Ted was strong enough to escape his controlling father and accept his mother's invitations. Christmas 1958 found him at 300 West End Avenue. Lennie and Ted, insisted Horne, were a perfect fit: "He loved my children and my children loved him." But unlike the bubbly Gail, Ted felt out of place in his mother's high-toned milieu, and kept largely to himself. Playing big sister, Gail took him with her to parties. Although polite, he seldom seemed comfortable. And friends sensed the underlying strain between him and his mother. "Teddy did love her," said Judy Davis. "But he wasn't impressed by stardom and money and glitz and glory. So there was that little tension."

Horne was eager to make up for all the years apart, and perhaps to show the world that Ted belonged with her. In April 1959, *Ebony* published "I'm Proud to Be a Mother," a first-person article. Horne appeared on the cover flanked by her children. She'd dressed deliberately plainly in a blue button-down smock. Gail, with her soft, wavy hairdo and sleeveless blue-green dress, seemed WASPy and collegiate. Ted wore a tuxedo and an enigmatic half-smile. He and his sister clasped their beaming mother's waist.

In the article, Horne offered a fanciful account of her relationships with her children. "I wouldn't exchange the experience of motherhood for anything in the world," she exclaimed. She glossed over the battles she'd fought with Louis over their son; instead she explained that the "brilliant" young man was "under the guidance of his father during the school year." Horne boasted of Ted's USC scholarship and his plan to become a California lawyer ("to focus on race issues," she noted). As for herself, she had entered show business only because she "had to": "I never wanted to become a star. I only wanted to be a good mother and to help support my children and prepare them for life."

Louis Jones read the article and privately went on a tirade, pronouncing it full of lies. But Jones revealed a genuine dignity in one key regard. No matter how much she enraged him, he avoided bad-mouthing his ex-wife to reporters. When they phoned to ask him questions, he refused to speak or answered discreetly. In the seventies, he would help raise Samadhi Jones, one of the children his son had left behind. She spent untold hours hearing Louis recall Lena Horne. "I really think that Grandfather adored her. No, he wasn't a terribly gentle person and wasn't the best provider or the most loving person. But he remained in love with Lena until the day he died."

HORNE was determined as ever to maintain appearances, and nowhere were the surfaces buffed to a higher gloss than on her albums. From the fashion-model cover shots to the Hollywood-style orchestrations to the ultrasophisticated repertoire, each production was tailored exquisitely. In 1955, RCA had released her first full-length LP, *It's Love*. The material by Cole Porter, Billy Strayhorn, and Arthur Schwartz didn't aim for the masses. Instead it evoked the cafés of New York's fashionable East Side, a place where lovers were "enthralled" by the "call" of spring and declared their passion in lofty terms: "I've a notion you're life's reward." Lennie Hayton's charts mixed a hotel-band politesse with the star-dusted string sound he'd mastered at M-G-M. Horne would recall his arranging in somewhat skeptical terms. "It was very glittery," she said. "But that was good, because people would hear the arrangement, then they'd hear what I did with it."

The formality of his work tended to stifle her jazz feeling. But vocally, she showed how far she'd come since the forties. After all her study and struggle to "get it right," Horne, said Gene DiNovi, "knew what she was doing every minute." André Previn called her a "lyricist's dream." In addition to her flawless diction and pitch, she never made a bad choice in phrasing, and the honeysuckle tang of her sound was unmistakable.

For all her progress, Horne spoke of recording as lonely drudge work. As she told Peter Reilly of *Stereo Review,* "I detest being in the bare studio, isolated from the orchestra with just that microphone." Without the presence of an audience to fire her up, Horne could sound overstylized and chilly on record.

She made a leap forward on her next LP, *Stormy Weather.* This was no exercise in East Side chic; the bluesy repertoire, much of it by Arlen, unleashed the wail in her voice. And the presence of several fine jazz soloists, including guitarist Kenny Burrell and saxophonist Al Cohn, helped ignite Hayton's orchestra.

Horne may have felt like a victim, but she wouldn't sing like one. Detailing "this dream that pains me and enchains me" in Noël Coward's "Mad About the Boy," she spat in the face of unrequited love. Her "Summertime" is no lullaby of hope to a sleeping child, but a rallying cry to an imprisoned people: "One of these mornings you're gonna rise up singing!" The decision to remake her trademark, and to name the album after it, might have been RCA's attempt to goose her sales. Horne would just as soon have never sung "Stormy Weather" again. "During the years I worked with her," said George Duvivier in *Basically Speaking,* "she grew to hate the song because she had to sing it so often. But she had to perform it to get off the stage; it was her encore, and the audience wouldn't let her leave without it." More than anything she sang, "Stormy Weather" evoked the frustration of a woman who felt shackled by forces beyond her control.

Murray Schumach of *High Fidelity* called *Stormy Weather* "one of the best pop records I've heard this year." Similar kudos went to two albums of the late fifties: *Songs by* [Johnny] *Burke and* [Jimmy] *Van Heusen,* Horne's tribute to the Oscar-winning songwriting team of the forties; and *Give the Lady What She Wants,* a tongue-in-cheek collection of musical come-ons. In the studio, Horne had begun using Ralph Burns, a dean of modern jazz arranging and a top Broadway orchestrator. With his revitalizing touch behind her, Horne sounded freer. While recording, she performed as though onstage at the Empire Room: fists clutching the air, back arching like a kitten on the prowl.

The sales brought a happy surprise. *Give the Lady What She Wants* reached number twenty on the *Billboard* album charts—higher than her Waldorf album, which had peaked at twenty-four. But overall, her sales lagged well behind those of such stars as Peggy Lee and Ella Fitzgerald, and couldn't approach Frank Sinatra's. In record stores, an iciness seemed to emanate from Horne's albums. The covers suggested a haughty black fashion plate, which proved off-putting to the average 1950s customer. And after "Love Me or Leave Me," every Horne single flopped.

One way to tackle the problem, RCA believed, was to unite her, in early 1959, with a heartthrob whose disks had sold millions. Harry Belafonte and Lena Horne should have made an ideal team. The project, a pop version of *Porgy and Bess,* followed a rash of other nonoperatic albums of the Gershwin folk opera. This one seemed timely, for it would coincide with the release of a long-awaited *Porgy and Bess* film, starring Sidney Poitier and Dorothy Dandridge.

Gershwin's soaring duets might have lit some sparks between Horne and Belafonte. Instead there was an unforeseen explosion. Claude Thompson had seen the growing unrest in their friendship. Horne had not forgotten that *Jamaica* was written for Belafonte; and the potential for rivalry went beyond that. "Harry was like a male Lena," said Thompson. "He was pretty, she was pretty; they both were considered sex symbols. And they had tremendous egos."

And tempers, for Belafonte's anger easily matched Horne's. "Harry was not a nice guy," said Polly Bergen, his costar in the Broadway revue *John Murray Anderson's Almanac.* "He treated everyone like shit. He hated white people and he married a white woman." A similar charge, of course, had been leveled against Horne, suggesting that she and Belafonte had more in common than either cared to admit.

Both singers were too busy to make the album. Horne was still playing eight shows a week on Broadway; Belafonte had a film in the works, *The World, the Flesh and the Devil.* In February and March, they made *Porgy and Bess* piecemeal, joining Hayton in the studio when they had time. Their duet parts were recorded separately, then spliced together.

Not surprisingly, Porgy and Bess's exchanges sounded artificial and chemistry-free. Hearing the tapes, Horne demanded they be shelved. RCA went ahead with the release. On May 4, 1959, the *Post* reported that Horne was suing to force the album's withdrawal. She also wanted one hundred thousand dollars in damages, claiming her contract had given her approval over her own recordings—and that the record (which she called *Porgy and Mess*) would cause "irreparable damage" to her reputation.

Belafonte refused to back her up, and in court, an RCA attorney testified that Horne had okayed the duets. The judge dismissed her case. *Porgy and Bess* went on to outsell every other Horne album, surely due to Belafonte. Then the 1959 Grammy nominations were announced; Horne had received one for Best Vocal Performance, Female. None of this changed her mind about the record. "I didn't speak to Harry for years," she told reporter Eliot Tiegel in 1989.

Horne still dreamed of hosting a TV variety show, but Ralph Harris couldn't interest a producer. "No network would take a chance on presenting a black lady," he found. Eager to promote her goal, Horne gave an interview to the *Herald Tribune,* entitled "I'd Love My Own Show." The woman who had conquered almost every show-business arena was now reduced to pleading for one that eluded her. "I feel I've got something to offer," she said, adding, "It's getting a little frustrating at this point." It didn't comfort her to know she wasn't alone. TV at the time lacked a single black host; in 1957, a star-studded series hosted by Nat King Cole had folded for lack of a sponsor.

As usual, she turned to Europe for an open door. Late in 1959, during a stay in London, Horne taped three half-hour installments of *The Lena Horne Show* for the British network Associated TeleVision. *Variety* pinpointed a problem: "Although the expressions of Miss Horne at full blast are a noted feature of her impact, the TV camera tends to magnify them into grimaces, sometimes uncomfortable to watch."

Indeed, the friendly smile she'd shown on *What's My Line?* in 1953 had changed. Against her copper skin, one saw a mouthful of white teeth and eyes that blazed. Whereas Como and Garry Moore came off as family friends, welcome in any living room, Horne seemed ready to pounce out of the set like a cobra. "She was not Dinah Shore," said Gene

Davis, and she knew it—hence her digs at the blond southern songbird, the medium's favorite hostess. ("I like money," said Horne on a radio interview, "but I'd like to make it as easy as, say, Dinah Shore.") With Shore setting that mold, what chance was there for her? "It's pretty clear why I've never had my own show," she told the *Tribune*. "So I won't go into it."

Closing out a decade of professional triumph, Horne felt anything but jubilant. The singer counted her letdowns. She couldn't sell records on her own, couldn't get a movie lead, couldn't do TV on the level she craved. At forty-two, she saw her looks and her chances fading. She felt burned out on cabarets, but trapped in them; the only place she could safely call home was a nightclub stage, where she kept audiences from getting too close to her—"someone they could touch and hurt." And the exhaustion of taking everything personally, of living constantly in attack mode, had begun to wear her down.

Worst of all, she felt more isolated within her own race than ever. A black singer swathed in white glamour, she entertained in places where few blacks could afford to go, or felt especially welcome. The songs she sang now struck her as brittle and shallow, at a time when Negro artists had more timely things to explore than a jaunt on the French Riviera.

Claude Thompson recalled witnessing Horne at her Waldorf dressing table before a show. A full house awaited her downstairs. As she touched up her makeup she snarled, *"Fuck 'em! Fuck 'em!"*

"She was sort of polishing up her armor," said Thompson.

The man leading the orchestra, of course, was her husband. A marriage intended to soothe and protect had become a source of turmoil—and in this case, the victim was Hayton. Arthur Laurents had seen the budding conflict. "I remember watching her and Lennie rehearse with the musicians. He was conducting. But she, with her hand behind her back, was giving them the tempo *she* wanted." Remarks she made ostensibly in jest held darker undertones: "I'm an excellent thrower, as Lennie will testify."

Horne had grown increasingly hostile toward the white man at home, who was dependent on her and beatifically patient. Just as she'd once challenged him to marry her, now she pushed his loyalty to the limit. "I felt he could take the crap I often pretended to handle," she told Alan Ebert. "Lord knows he took mine. I was such a bitch at times. When the white world bruised me, made me bleed, I took it home and did to Lennie what my black husband had done to me. It was so undeserved." The world-renowned sex symbol was not the woman he lived with. "He reads how I'm sexy and what he's got is a despairing, tired woman," said Horne.

The marriage had certainly not ended her rivalry with Louis Jones. "They had the most horrible relationship," said Samadhi Jones. He still didn't want to share their son, who seemed to be flourishing right where he was. Ted had a bright legal career in store, but Terrie Burton, like his other friends, sensed even greater potential: "I thought he was gonna be the first black president of the United States. He could come into a room and command it."

She and Ted had started dating, but he stayed at arm's length, and it hurt. The young man had inherited some of his mother's defense mechanisms. "He could be very cold, very distant," said Terrie. "I'm quite sure it was a difficult existence for Ted, and I think he tried to cope by being aloof. He dressed well, carried himself well, but he didn't know how to love because nobody had taught him that. And he was afraid, I think, to let his hair down and feel."

Lena longed for his acceptance. When he saw her perform, she waited for a word of approval. Sometimes he would say, "Mother, you were very good tonight." When he said nothing, her heart sank. "I think she was a beautiful, sad person," said Terrie. "I liked some of her movies and the fact that she had triumphed over all this stuff that was going on at the time. But I never really liked her style of singing. I found her cold."

One night, Ted brought Terrie to the Cocoanut Grove to see Horne. When they entered her dressing room, Ted introduced them for the first time. They found Horne chatting with Anna Magnani, who had just won an Oscar as Best Actress for *The Rose Tattoo*. Ted interrupted his mother. "This is Terrie," he said.

"She turned around and looked at me," said Terrie, "and I thought she was gonna keel over. Now I should explain that I am a dark-skinned black lady—by all accounts pretty, attractive." After a heavy beat of silence, Horne said, "*Hello*, dear." Her frostiness made Terrie shudder.

It wasn't long before Ted shocked the young woman with an announcement. His mother had arranged for him to leave USC and study at the famed Sorbonne in Paris. All his friends questioned her motives. Clint Rosemond suspected that Horne was trying to wrest Ted from his father; Jones, of course, was enraged. He'd transferred his failed political ambitions onto his son and felt that Ted could become the city's first black mayor if he stayed on course. He was sure his ex-wife wanted to move their son to a fashionable French school "for publicity reasons."

Another potential motive went overlooked. As Horne told *Stereo Review*'s Peter Reilly in 1982, she'd tried to give her children "a better life than I had had . . . I did all the proper things—fine colleges, fine educations." Maybe she felt that a stint at one of Europe's most expensive colleges would help compensate for her long absences from his life.

There was a graver reason, however, for Horne to pluck her son out of USC and America. Ted had started dating an attractive Italian student, Barbara Corradini. She came from a wealthy family and drove a Ferrari supplied by her father. An on-campus jock, recalled Rosemond, "didn't like to see this black guy getting so much attention from this very attractive white woman." One night, as Ted left her apartment, the bully attacked him. "Ted ended up with a few bruises. But more important, I think that incident helped set the stage for events to follow that would change the direction of Ted's life."

The beating might have been the last straw in a turbulent stretch of years. Louis and Lena's warring had left Ted with "the short end of the stick," said Rosemond, "and I suspect there was some motivation on Ted's part to be a beneficiary of his mom's fame and fortune." Francine Kahan suspected one more incentive for Ted to leave L.A. In France, perhaps, he would see more of his absentee parent; maybe there he would finally "feel the security of that mother love" that he'd so long been denied. Whatever his reason for agreeing to go, said Kahan, "it was his undoing."

CHAPTER 13

THE STORY of Ted Jones's year at the Sorbonne in the early sixties remained vague even to his best friends; he wouldn't share many details. But Rosemond knew this: "Ted left L.A. whole and returned a changed man." And not for the better. In Paris, they heard, Ted had begun experimenting with hard drugs, most likely heroin. Judy Davis saw his actions as a stab of rebellion against his punishingly strict father. But Ted knew an even greater pressure—that of playing the model son of an icon who had to maintain a respectable image at all costs.

Ted contracted hepatitis C, a frequent consequence of intravenous drug use. Horne grieved over the consequences to Elle Elliott, her stylist in the 1970s.

"She was devastated," said Elliott. "The doctor had given him some medication that killed his kidneys, that had some kind of sulfur in it." After he came home, Ted was diagnosed with glomerulonephritis, a disease that destroys the cells of the kidneys, and that sometimes results from hepatitis C. For now it proved controllable, but eventually he would need a transplant or dialysis in order to live.

News of her son's health crisis brought Horne a crushing sense of guilt, and her acrimonious relationship with her ex-husband turned even darker. "My grandfather was extremely angry at Lena for ever taking Ted over to Europe," said Samadhi. "In Grandfather's words, Ted would never have gotten sick if she hadn't dragged him there to show him off. He was doing just fine at an excellent school, USC."

Ted blamed no one for what had happened. Once back in New York, he moved in with his mother, sister, and Lennie Hayton, and enrolled at Columbia University. But he didn't want to stay. He relocated to Berkeley and entered the University of California. Later he went back to L.A. and returned to USC, where he finally got his diploma. His new major, Spanish, puzzled his friends; and though he hid it from some of them, his drug use continued. All the promise he'd displayed just a few years earlier was slipping away.

His mother's career surged forward, all-consuming as ever. In the winter of 1960, she went to L.A. to tape an appearance on *To the Ladies*, one in a series of specials sponsored by Timex watches and hosted by her nemesis, Frank Sinatra. The show found Sinatra singing, clowning, and chatting with a diverse set of women: sultry dancer Juliet Prowse, his future fiancée; singer-comedienne Barbara Heller; opera soprano Mary Costa; Eleanor Roosevelt, then seventy-five; and Horne.

It was hard to know why she and Sinatra ever agreed to work together. Their chemistry was nil, and though Horne kept her disdain private, Sinatra aired his. In a first-person article for *Life*, "Me and My Music," he dismissed her as "a beautiful lady but really a mechanical singer. She gimmicks up a song, makes it too pat."

Some time back, Horne had seen Sinatra treat Mrs. Roosevelt rudely, she felt, and she'd never forgiven him. But on the Timex show the former first lady displayed grandmotherly warmth, and the other women seemed to melt in his presence. Not Horne. They paired off in a long Harold Arlen medley, sung as they sat on a bench. Throughout the segment Horne ignored Sinatra, focusing instead on the camera lens. In "Stormy Weather" she turned on her eyeball-popping ferocity to such an intimidating degree that her host all but withered at her side. His macho swagger vanished, his shoulders sagged, the bravado left his eyes, and all one saw was Horne, devouring the screen and the songs.

The program's East Coast airing took place on Monday, February 15, 1960. It was Horne's day off from a two-week run at the Cocoanut Grove. Around midnight, she and Hayton dropped by the Luau, a faux-Polynesian restaurant in Beverly Hills. Mart Crowley recalled the place as "kitsch and camp—all these blue strobe lights and fake rain that came down over the bar." But it gained a touch of Hollywood cachet from its owner, Stephen Crane, one of Lana Turner's ex-husbands; and a showbizzy crowd found it an amusingly unfashionable place to hang out. The Haytons were shown to a corner table, then Lennie went to phone Kay Thompson from a booth to see if she were free. Horne waited alone, amid a soft murmur of conversation.

From the lower level, just a few feet away, a drunken voice cut through the quiet. It belonged to Harvey St. Vincent, the thirty-year-old vice president of an upscale engineering firm. He sat with a friend, Norman Wynne. St. Vincent shouted for a waiter. One of the staff promised to come soon; first, he said, he had to serve "Miss Horne's table." Wynne looked up. "There's Lena Horne," he told St. Vincent, who glared in her direction, then raised his voice for all to hear.

"So that's Lena Horne, huh? Well, she's just another black nigger . . . there ain't nothing they can do for me."

According to some reports, Horne leaned over the partition and responded with dignity: "I can hear what you're saying, and I want you to stop." Other versions had her answering much more bluntly.

"Well," he barked, "all niggers look alike to me and that includes you."

Horne remembered closing her eyes as a wave of fury swept over her. When St. Vincent went on to call her a "nigger bitch," her control shattered. Trembling, she rose from her chair. Spying an ashtray filled with cigarette butts, she hurled it at his head. Then she grabbed a hurricane lamp and threw it with all her might, followed by another. St. Vincent sat there stunned, blood dripping from a gash above his left eye. Horne stared him down, "all red in the face, and evil," she recalled. "I'd had enough."

Seconds later, she felt Hayton grabbing her from behind. "For God's sake, what happened?" he asked.

He called me a nigger!

Horne wasn't done fighting. She clutched another ashtray and was all ready to fling it. But by then the police had come, and they rushed to St. Vincent. "Why'd she hit me?" he blubbered. "I didn't do anything!"

Hayton was dumbfounded. "Did you hit him?" he asked. "*Yes, I did!*" she snapped, as though it were the dumbest question ever. Hayton headed for the man's table, but a policeman stopped him and said, "We're taking care of it." Another addressed Horne accusingly.

"He's bleeding!"

"What do you want me to do?" she sputtered. *"Apologize?"*

One newspaper claimed that St. Vincent confessed his slurs to a policeman; with so many witnesses he could hardly deny them. He refused to go to the hospital or file charges; he only wanted to leave as quickly as possible. While police led him to the door, Hayton rushed Horne out of the Luau, then home to the Ambassador.

The next morning, reporters gathered outside their suite. When she opened the door, they pummeled her with questions about the night before. "He called me a name I resented, and I reacted," explained Horne, now calm. Her phone rang all day with calls from the press. "I Don't Like Being Insulted!" read a headline the next day in the *Journal-American*.

"I am not the sort of person who goes about making these incidents," said the singer. "I'm sorry he had to learn in such a violent manner that people don't like to be insulted. But I don't go for that stuff." *Time* magazine publishing an admiring brief, noting that "few Negroes are inclined to take direct action when their race is slurred."

Horne later claimed, none too ingenuously, that she couldn't understand what all the fuss was about; whites had been insulting her for years and she often blew up at them. But the Luau episode gave her a sobering look at the truth. To her fans, she was a Hollywood star, the queen of the supper clubs, an intimate of Noël Coward and Marlene Dietrich, and an internationally renowned fashion plate. But to Harvey St. Vincent and others like him, she was "just another black nigger."

Her own race, realized Horne, had thought "just because I was me that I wasn't catching hell." Few of them, if any, knew that her grandmother and numerous leaders in the black community had drilled her to never stoop to the level of her oppressors. Horne had tried to take a cool-headed stand every time a hotel or restaurant had refused her, but compared to the hands-on activism of W. E. B. Du Bois, Rosa Parks, or even her grandmother, her own efforts had struck her as meaningless, even narcissistic. "My anger had nothing to do with any movement," she admitted to Rex Reed. "I had never made it everybody's battle, I was just busy thinking about me."

At the Luau, she still was. But the incident, like many in her life, resounded further. In an editorial, the *New York Amsterdam News* declared, "We submit that in losing her temper, Miss Horne was wrong. But we hasten to add that Lena Horne in this case had a right to be wrong."

That opinion captured a main point of conflict in the racial battles to come, the clash between violent and peaceful resisters. Horne's courteous request that St. Vincent stop insulting her had gone ignored; her bloodletting had not. As she groped to find a place for herself within the movement, Dr. Martin Luther King, Jr.'s formula for nonviolent reform left her cold, while Malcolm X's enraged militancy made him her hero.

Intentionally or not, there at the Luau Horne had forged her first meaningful bond in years with her own people. The feeling intoxicated her. She recalled opening stacks of letters from blacks, telling her they'd never known she cared. Her ex-lover Joe Louis sent her a telegram, joking that he wished he had a right hook like hers.

Reporters sought out Harvey St. Vincent, who tried to defend himself. In the *Los Angeles Times*, he called Horne's action "an apparent bid on publicity," and denied having insulted her: "I have no racial nor religious bias of any nature." What's more, he was thinking of suing her. "I'm sorry if he feels that way," responded Horne. "I could also sue him for defamation of character."

No suit ever happened. She closed at the Grove on February 27, then moved on to Palm Springs and Miami. On April 4, she would open at the Waldorf. For all the hostility the place brought out in her, she couldn't wait to get home, she said: "New York, at least, is pretty straight."

THE ELEGANT EMPIRE ROOM PRESENTS LENA HORNE, read a series of print ads that spring. Beneath the headline stood Horne, arms outstretched in a glamorous Hollywood-style pose. This new show, her first at the Waldorf since 1957, followed the same formula of brittle chic. There were smart show tunes by Cole Porter and Rodgers and Hammerstein, clever movie songs by Burke and Van Heusen, sexy special material. Sydney Shaw and the still-unknown composer Burt Bacharach gave her "Out of My Continental Mind," in which Horne breathily intoned, "Better say *yes* . . . better say *now!*" Horne took "Surrey with the Fringe on Top," a gently galloping, western-style love song from *Oklahoma!*, and turned it into a come-hither vamp. That performance, which floated on the sprightly piano of Lennie Hayton, became one of her trademarks. "When she did it," said Arthur Laurents, "you knew what you were going out in the surrey for!"

But all her songs of carefree jet-setting, of lovers toyed with then tossed aside, were getting harder for her to bear. Her fans continued to pack the Empire Room but that fifties smart set was about to become a quaint relic of the past. Outside the hotel's golden doors, the city streets were growing dark and threatening, and reality couldn't be shut out much longer.

Nonetheless, RCA tried to recapture the magic of Horne's first Waldorf album by recording her there on April 30, 1960. The tapes were shelved. On the earlier LP, explained George Duvivier, RCA had "used a minimum of equipment and got a real natural sound. For the second album, they brought in an unbelievable battery of microphones. . . . Whenever Lennie Hayton raised his arm to conduct, he hit an overhead mike. Lena herself didn't know which of eight microphones to sing into! It was an aural disaster."

As far as their marriage was concerned, Horne still felt the need to maintain an image of wedded bliss. *Ebony*, as always, was there to help. One item, "Lena Horne Picks an Easter Hat," described Horne's breezy shopping trips with husband in tow. "He likes to shop with me," she explained. The Haytons, wrote the reporter, "like a variety of colors, and she usually drapes her turbans herself."

Arranger Ray Ellis, who would soon become Horne's conductor, saw beyond the union's surface. "If they'd both been the same color," said Ellis, "they would have gotten divorced a long time before. But with her ego—and she had a tremendous one—she did not want to admit to the world that it was a bad marriage, and he didn't, either. They'd gone through so much bullshit in the beginning to get married."

In public, Hayton betrayed not a hint of trouble. "Lennie was wonderful," said Geoffrey Holder. "He could put on a poker face." Certainly his drinking helped mask whatever unrest he might have felt. But Horne had begun to see his composure as a form of emotional paralysis, and it troubled her. She found him "strange, mystic almost." Laurents saw how complacent the musician was, arranging and conducting one club act after another and seemingly wanting little more. "Lena was more ambitious than Lennie," he said. "Not about career, necessarily; I mean for what life was about. I think that's one of the reasons she didn't fully respect him." Friends recalled the familiar sight of Hayton in his bathrobe after noon, seated on the living room sofa behind a screen of cigarette smoke, a drink in his hand and a blank look on his face.

Horne's confrontation at the Luau had done little to cure Hayton of his "color-blind" attitude, as Horne called it. She couldn't believe that anyone could be so unbiased, and increasingly she tried to taunt him out of his malaise, to no avail. "I would come home evil from putting up with the outside world," she recalled, "and I'd bring it home to him, and he didn't know what I was talking about. He'd say, 'Oh, she's that way.'"

But several of Hayton's friends, including Luther Henderson, believed the marriage had drained the life out of him. "Luther told me that she systematically ruined Lennie," said Billie Allen. "She made it almost impossible for him to have that job. 'Prove to me you love me!' Really challenging him."

As Hayton slipped deeper into his funk, Horne's disillusion with her career rose. Announcing a West Coast benefit she was about to sing in for the education of underprivileged women, the *Los Angeles Times* noted that this show was "part of a farewell tour for Horne, who will retire from live performances." By now the threat had grown familiar, and, as before, nothing came of it. Aside from show business, Horne had little other life to fall back on. Although her children lived with her in the latter half of 1960, they were now adults, and she still felt distant from both of them.

That fall, Gail told her mother she'd decided to try her hand again at acting, her collegiate pastime. She landed a supporting role in an off-Broadway production of the British musical *Valmouth,* a saucy Edwardian spoof that had starred Cleo Laine in London. Her friend Gene Andrewski, a theater producer, had told her about his plans to mount *Valmouth* at the York Playhouse. "He asked me, 'Do you sing?' And I said, yes—a little. Then he said, 'Can you act?'" She mentioned her dramatic efforts in school, and he asked her to audition for *Valmouth.* She got the job.

The announcement of Gail's participation earned her a cover story in the arty magazine *The Theatre.* Interviewer Gene Wright met her at 300 West End Avenue. Gail discussed her college acting roles, but confessed that theater had never been her calling; in fact, she had never quite known what she wanted. Any happiness the twenty-two-year-old felt about acting again went unshared by her mother. "I really didn't want her to, but I didn't say anything about it," confided Horne to John Gruen years later. She wasn't around to hold Gail's hand. Horne was in Paris then, and Gail sent letters asking her to hurry home. "I'm terrified," she wrote. Horne promised she'd be there on opening night, while offering long-distance advice: "Just open your mouth and sing." Kay Thompson stepped in to coach her.

"This has been the first big thing that has happened to me," said Gail to Gene Wright. "I want so much to be a success; so many people have faith in me. I hope I can make Mother proud of me on opening night."

Ebony touted Gail's off-Broadway debut in a short article; it included a press-release-style quote from Horne: "I want Gail to be happy and successful in whatever she wants to do. If the theater is where she wants to work I am perfectly agreeable to her doing so and I hope she will find in it happiness and creative self-expression. Gail is old enough to know what she wants to do, pick her career, to decide how she wants to live her life."

Valmouth opened on October 6, 1960. Horne was there to applaud her daughter, who played her part barefoot, and in one scene wore a sarong. All seemed to go well. But the actors' hearts sank when they saw the *New York Times* review's headline: "Tired Musical." Critic Howard Taubman found "precious little charm" in the show or in most of its cast. Of one of its featured performers, he wrote, "Gail Jones is pretty, like her mother, Lena Horne, and may turn out to be a singer."

The remark seemed tailor-made to arouse her insecurities. And even though Whitney Bolton of the *New York Morning Telegraph* praised her for her "intellectualism and unusual beauty," Gail pursued acting no further. *Valmouth* closed after fourteen performances; from there she returned to the dilemma of what to do next. Years later, she told the jazz critic Leonard Feather, "I wouldn't have been a good actress. I have a small talent for comedy, that's all, and I wasn't ambitious." Soon after *Valmouth*, Horne told a reporter that Gail was "now engrossed in social work."

As pessimistic as she liked to seem about her own performing, Horne's excitement could spring up anew. That year she and Hayton flew to Rio to headline at the Copacabana Palace, the city's most expensive hotel, which faces the beach. Although Horne had never been to Brazil before, her films had been shown there, and they'd dazzled one of the country's most distinguished men. Vinícius de Moraes was a diplomat, poet, and playwright whose *Orfeu da Conceição* became the renowned film *Black Orpheus*. Starting in the late fifties, he and his writing partner, Antônio Carlos Jobim, penned many bossa nova classics, including "A Garota de Ipanema" ("The Girl from Ipanema").

In 1943, de Moraes had published a valentine to Lena Horne in the Rio-based newspaper *A Manhã*:

> I'm going to just write you a letter, my dear, because my position on the blackboard of society requires a certain discretion ... You and I are two electric poles, two cosmic particles, two microbes of malaria meeting each other in the green globules of love. You and I are a great mysterious attraction, and I believe in view of this, we should meet soon for tea—what an idea!—for a whisky or two or three in some quiet bar. Lena Horne, you are pure sin ... Your warmth, how marvelous! Your smile is Carnaval ... I love you, you know.

They never shared that whisky, but his and other bossa songs caught her ear. In New York, someone had given her the first LP by the music's pioneer interpreter, João Gilberto, a feather-voiced singer and guitarist. His airy, dancing style, set over a throbbing pulse, had seduced much of Brazil, and according to Ary Vasconcelos, a journalist for *O Cruzeiro*, Horne "went crazy" over its syncopations and dissonances. "Therefore," he wrote, "one of her first wishes, as soon as she arrived in Rio, was to meet the young singer from Bahia." *O Cruzeiro* arranged a surprise. During her rehearsal at the Palace she spied Gilberto, guitar in hand, ready to serenade her. Horne stopped everything and sat on the floor, virtually at his feet, as Gilberto sang and played. Always a great audience for music she liked, Horne snapped her fingers and tapped the floor. In a TV special made during her stay, she sang his "Bim Bom," a tune about the beating of an excited heart.

Back home, Horne longed for a showcase that might rescue her from saloon work. The year had taken her from supper club to supper club in city after city, and as she told one more reporter, "I'm getting a little tired of cabarets." She felt a ray of hope when Alexander Cohen, a rising theatrical producer, approached her in 1961 about returning to the Broadway stage. Cohen had begun mounting a series of cabaret-style shows, one of which, *An Evening with Mike Nichols and Elaine May*, had just closed a nine-month run.

Now Cohen would star her in *The Nine O'Clock Revue*, a two-act variety show. Comic Don Adams, close-harmony group the Delta Rhythm Boys, and dance team Augie & Margo would open for Horne, who would present an hour or so of her nightclub material. Hayton would lead a small band. Cohen planned a tour that would take them, starting October 16, 1961, from Toronto to Boston to New Haven to Pittsburgh, and then, on December 26, to Broadway's John Golden Theatre.

Early reviewers liked Horne but found the hour of opening acts a tedious wait. *The Nine O'Clock Revue* was only a slightly beefed-up, budget version of her nightclub show. Horne's interest sank, and in interviews she didn't bother hiding it; she admitted that the show presented "a not very different Lena Horne, I'm afraid." Her candor didn't encourage business. On the road, ticket sales averaged fifty percent capacity. Pittsburgh was canceled; so was the Broadway opening. After five weeks, *The Nine O'Clock Revue* closed at a loss.

Her album career wasn't thriving either. Horne's RCA contract ran out in 1962, seven years after her first LP. Most of the record-buying public just wouldn't warm to her, and RCA had offered no renewal. She viewed the situation as one more rejection. "I'm not a recording performer," she concluded wistfully. "I'm just me . . . live."

Yet the last LP in her RCA contract finished her run there in a small blaze of glory. The company teamed her with Marty Paich, a young arranger from the West Coast jazz elite, for an album of standards, *Lena . . . Lovely and Alive*. Paich had made his name with the Marty Paich Dektette, a ten-piece group known for its hip modern harmonies and cool, brainy sound. His albums with Mel Tormé had helped elevate that singer from a crooner to a jazz star.

Paich could also write lushly for strings and make a big band race. On *Lena . . . Lovely and Alive* he did both. Paich brought out the swing in Horne as Hayton never had; no wonder the gloss of her husband's arrangements now felt smothering to her. Certainly Hayton couldn't have generated the crackling excitement that Paich did in his updating of Cole Porter's "I Concentrate on You," a stately beguine about a face that overwhelms a lover's senses. For Horne, Paich stirred up a flurry of racing brass, set over a furiously walking bass and the propulsive drumming of Frank Capp, who had ignited Stan Kenton's orchestra in the fifties. Riding that express train of a chart, Horne churned up a rush of sexual energy. She growled, she hissed, she bit ravenously into words like "sweet" and "tender." And when she sang of "the light in your eyes when you surrender," it was the conquest of a panther devouring its prey. So much of Horne's sexy singing had been an eye-rolling put-on; this time it had the ring of truth.

So did her smoldering desperation in "I Surrender, Dear," a Depression-era torch song. As strings cascaded around her, Horne became a woman yearning to tear off her armor and let love in. Her impassioned pleading—"I may seem proud, I may act gay / That's just a pose—*I'm not that way!*"—suggested how deeply she infused the lyrics with her autobiography. Years later, at a Carnegie Hall memorial for Ella Fitzgerald, Horne pointed out the difference in their singing: "Her voice didn't make us sad, it didn't make us angry, because I think she never allowed her personal angst to get into the song. All that she sang was colored musically, not by somebody who puts a lot of other stuff in their songs . . . like many of us do!"

A critic for *Stereo Review* judged *Lena . . . Lovely and Alive* a breakthrough for her. "Repudiating the excesses that have frequently marred her performances before audiences, she emerges here a supreme technician with an unerring ability to extract meaning from her material . . . her interpretive art is so formidable that even the most ordinary lyric takes on special meaning."

Horne was surprised when the album scored two Grammy nominations. In the category of Best Solo Female Vocal Performance, Horne lost to Fitzgerald and her latest album with arranger Nelson Riddle, *Ella Swings Brightly with Nelson*. Fitzgerald had remained the strong seller Horne wasn't—partly because, just as Horne said, the First Lady of Song was a spirit-lifting bundle of joy, not a spiky, intimidating artist like Horne.

But no record by the dowdy Fitzgerald would have earned a nomination for Best Album Cover, as did the striking exterior of *Lena . . .*

Lovely and Alive. A photograph by Robert Jones showed Horne's face in close-up, scarlet silk draped around her head as she gazed, distant and mournful, over the viewer's shoulder. That cover got the Grammy. Once more, Horne's looks had won out over her singing—and the album sold weakly.

Its producer, Dick Peirce, left RCA around the time Horne did. He quickly formed his own label, Charter, and signed Horne to inaugurate it. Charter's first release, recorded in late 1962, was *Lena Sings Your Requests,* a midcareer retrospective. Marty Paich and a budding West Coast arranger, Bob Florence, revamped Horne's trademarks. Most of them—including "Love," "The Lady Is a Tramp," "Honeysuckle Rose," and "Stormy Weather"—came from her M-G-M years, the era that still defined her in most people's minds. Peirce, who adored Horne, might have thought a greatest hits package would outsell her recent efforts.

It didn't. Poor distribution helped sink the album. But *Lena Sings Your Requests* counted as another Horne milestone. The woman whom Paul Robeson, Jr., had thought "terrible" at Café Society—and who, in her own harsh words, "couldn't sing" in the forties—had surpassed every vocal goal she'd set for herself. The timid delivery of her early days had given way to a fiery confidence; her rhythm now equaled almost any jazz singer's. She probed unflinchingly into the words, making even banal phrases seem believable. After twenty-plus years of singing, Horne could claim a lot of songs as her property. And in *Lena Sings Your Requests,* she brandished them with proud authority.

Horne made the interesting choice of reviving "Good for Nothin' Joe," a song she'd sung as Charlie Barnet's unknown vocalist in 1941. Daring at the time, it was the confession of a streetwalker in love with her abusive pimp. Horne's original recording suggested a young woman who was determined to stay a lady at all costs. But in her 1962 version she hardly sounds like the same singer. Sensuality, fragility, and defiance collide in a portrait of a love so fierce it overrides every blow. Line by line, Horne delves inside the shifting feelings of a woman who wearily walks the streets looking for business—knowing that Joe's wrath awaits her if she comes home penniless. But the cost is worth it. "Lawd, he thrills me like nobody can!" she sighs—and how dare people disapprove?

The song touched on many aspects of Horne—her little-girl long-ing for a protector, her iron-clad inner strength, her dutiful fulfilling of her role countered by an irritation with anyone who told her what to do. "Good for Nothin' Joe" was a song Walter White would never have con-doned. But Horne loved it, and she brought such valiance to her character that one could only end up admiring that downtrodden whore.

Bob Florence watched her record. Dick Peirce had told him how ner-vous Horne got in the studio. "I know he stood in the booth with her the whole time, I guess for reassurance," Florence said. "But I listen to those tracks and I think, you can't tell me she's insecure—she just lets it fly!" *High Fidelity*'s reviewer praised her for "an absolutely stunning job ... the glacial veneer, which I felt so often spoiled much of her work, has vanished. It is replaced by warmth and a complete involvement in every number."

Horne offered living proof that the great singers and actors, far from being inimitable, were ripe for copying. The singing impressionist Sheila MacRae—who played Alice Kramden in a 1960s revival of TV's *The Honeymooners*—drew gales of laughter in supper clubs with her spot-on impersonation of Horne. Other women borrowed from Horne freely, as though her innovations had entered the public domain. "I'm always being told that some young singer is doing me these days and I'm not complimented," she admitted, "although my husband tells me I should be." She later told Dick Cavett: "I was never a copier; I didn't know how to copy anybody."

The Horne influence was clear in the black supper-club songstress Barbara McNair, whose Caucasian-style prettiness, glowing smile, and white-bread delivery—laced with Horne mannerisms—scored her the weekly variety show her idol craved. Singer Lainie Kazan became known as a zaftig comic yenta in such films as *My Favorite Year* (1982) and *My Big Fat Greek Wedding* (2002), but in the sixties she was a Horne-inspired, over-the-top sex kitten who took herself far more seriously than Horne ever did.

In 1962, Diahann Carroll won a Tony award for starring as a fashion model in a Richard Rodgers musical *No Strings*. Carroll was the new black Cinderella, but Horne didn't go to cheer her on. To her, Carroll was one more upstart who had gone far by copying her. As Carroll moved from coup to coup—several juicy film roles, her own sitcom (*Julia*), four Emmy nominations, an Oscar nomination (for the 1974 movie *Claudine*), and a side career in top-rank nightclubs—Horne gave her the cold shoulder.

The similarities between them were undeniable, and Carroll tired of hearing about them. Her singing drew comparisons to Horne's for its satiny tone, sleek diction, and feline attacks. And as a fair-skinned, designer-dressed clotheshorse, she carried herself with a posh aloofness. That quality served her well on a hit TV series of the eighties, *Dynasty*, where she played bitchy millionaire Dominique Deveraux.

All these were achievements Horne envied and resented. In time, Carroll knew why. "I didn't realize how much it had impacted me, to be in her presence a few times and not get this warm, let-me-give-you-a-hug attitude. There was a fear in Lena. She was very protective of her position, and she wasn't outgoing, she wasn't forthcoming. I understood that as I aged. I did the same thing. I was not warm and forthcoming. We were not supposed to be. We were to hold on to whatever position we had in the industry for dear life."

Barbra Streisand never seemed to doubt her own eminence, but Horne intimidated even her. Arthur Laurents detected Horne's influence in the young star's boldly individual singing. Streisand's 1962 Broadway debut had come in the Laurents-scripted musical *I Can Get It for You Wholesale*. Streisand, he recalled, looked to Horne with awe, and when he threw a Christmas party at his Greenwich Village town house, the ruthless young star was afraid to walk into the same room as Horne. Finally she mustered the courage, but the chat went nowhere.

Horne had mastered a defense tactic of freezing out anyone who (she felt) had hurt, disappointed, annoyed, or somehow threatened her. She looked right through them, and they knew they'd been rendered invisible. No wonder so many people saw her as cold. "She had this 'I dare you to talk to me' façade when she walked into a room," said Ray Ellis. "What caused that, I always thought, is that she was afraid. She didn't know how to handle people, so she just walked in with that 'fuck you' attitude, and she became unapproachable."

As she later admitted, that was a reflection of what lay inside her. "I examined myself very carefully in the early sixties," she told Dick Cavett, "and I said, 'What is this cold, killing feeling in me?'" Her persona was based largely on her unearthly beauty, and on mannerisms so calculated that she seemed less than human. And despite the response to her Luau outburst, she still felt disconnected to her own race. The incident was far from "heroic," she admitted; it was just a knee-jerk flare-up after a lifetime of similar moments. The more the civil rights struggle advanced, the more left behind she felt. At a time when the definition of "black" was being probed and tested as never before—and measured against one's dedication to the cause—Horne wondered if she had any racial identity at all. The one assigned to her by a string of mentors, from Noble Sissle onward, was a "lie," she felt. Horne had struggled for years to maintain a proper image, and what good had it done? Negroes everywhere were still denied many of their rights. Occasional privileges granted to her and other chosen ones, she decided, were merely "buy-offs for the white man's conscience."

Horne had chosen to ignore a legion of black victories—notably those of her erstwhile hero, Paul Robeson. And she'd overlooked her own influence—not just as a bridge to a more enlightened time in show business, but as a beacon of hope for those who followed. All she knew was that she was sick of acting the "good little symbol." She'd grown to sense one of the essential realities of the civil rights battle. Its role models had less freedom than normal citizens; they had to lead the masses from a pedestal and not falter, lest they seem weak. Now, she felt, symbols had outgrown their use. The black youth of the day didn't care to "behave themselves" in hopes that the white man would throw them a crumb; they were ready to fight for what they deserved. But where did that leave her?

So much confusion churned inside Horne that she didn't know what to do next. But someone new had big plans for her. Starting around 1960, a regular guest at Horne's parties on West End Avenue was Jeanne Noble, the young president of Delta Sigma Theta, the prestigious sorority for scholarly black females. Photos of Noble from that time show a very fair, primly dressed woman with a nondescript hairdo and pearls. But there was nothing demure about Noble. St. Clair Pugh found her "very imposing-looking," but this came more from her attitude than her appearance—for Noble had an almost militant devotion to freeing Negro women from the chains imposed on them by whites.

During *Jamaica*, Noble had begun a persistent effort to induct Horne into Delta. A letter reached the singer, inviting her to become an honorary member. She ignored it. But Noble would not give up, and kept sending letters and wires to the theater, trying to convince Horne to join. She explained that Delta comprised over thirty-five thousand college graduates, and provided scholarships and job recruitment and counseling for other black women. Noble's persuasion worked. In a ceremony held at the Empire Room on December 21, 1958, the singer had become an honorary Delta.

Horne lent priceless name value to the group. But Noble had personal motives in pursuing her, for the star had been her lifelong fascination. As a student of black female victimization, Noble saw Horne as a woman who'd been exploited from all angles. So did the singer herself. Noble ignored the choices—not all of them pretty—that her idol had made to get where she was. Horne was eager to erase them, too. At a time when the singer was squirming to escape the domination of black leaders, Noble, said Arthur Laurents, would prove a "*big* controlling force" in her life.

Jeanne Laveta Noble was born in 1926 in the rural town of Albany, Georgia, where few black women had high school diplomas. Years later, through Delta, she fought to desegregate her birthplace. "She was the most energized and energizing president the organization had had," said Marcia Ann Gillespie, the editor of *Essence* magazine and later of *Ms.* In 1962, Noble became one of the first black women to gain tenure at New York University, where she taught almost until she died. Presidents Johnson, Nixon, and Ford appointed her to posts that involved Negro education and the fight against poverty.

According to the actress, singer, and Delta member Novella Nelson, "To know Jeanne Noble was to know that she was a focused woman. A conscious, committed woman. Her way was *the* way." Noble believed strongly in black image control, which included proper decorum, cultivated speech, and an impeccable presentation. In her own case, that entailed complete discretion about her sexual preference for women. Noble kept her prejudices a lot less hidden. "She hated whites and she hated men," said Arthur Laurents. Under Noble's direction, Horne would rework her life and revise her past, all to make herself the black woman she thought she had to be.

. . .

ON February 4, 1963, Horne returned to the Waldorf's Empire Room to start a six-week run—her first engagement there since 1960. That pricey palace of 1950s chic seemed colder to her than ever; it matched her own chill. "I may be admired as an artist, but I wouldn't say that I'm one of those performers who necessarily evoke a loving reaction from the audience," she told the *New York Times*. "I sometimes think it must be fun to have that kind of hold on an audience, though. . . . Those lovable people—I envy them."

In many respects, she was floundering. Horne followed up *Lena Sings Your Requests* with a second Charter album, *Lena Like Latin,* a bongo-laden hodgepodge of standards revamped in popular Latin styles, from bossa nova to cha-cha-cha. Hayton led the arrangements of Shorty Rogers, a jovial West Coast jazz arranger. The kitschy lounge disc was a step down for Horne, and she walked through it halfheartedly; never again would she record with Hayton.

Sick of touring, she made Ralph Harris refuse most of her nightclub offers. Meanwhile, she kept making empty announcements of retirement. *Ebony* reported that Horne would withdraw from clubs "to devote herself to stage vehicles advancing integration"—a plea, perhaps, for someone to write her one, but nobody did.

To fill the time, she appeared for a week as a guest contestant on the prime-time game show *Password.* It pitted two duos—each consisting of a celebrity and a civilian—against each other to try to guess a key word. The partners exchanged one-word clues. Surely *Password* had never had a guest who took the game as seriously as Lena Horne. She acted out each clue with hand movements and grimaces, then glared in the direction of her cohorts, trying to suck the answers out of them through sheer force of will. At the same time, she avoided her white partners in the eye. When they (or she) missed, she scowled and turned away.

Hayton was exposed to more of her unrest than anyone, yet seemed to grasp it the least. Horne would later tell Rex Reed that her marriage "was in a mess, because I wanted Lennie to experience the same pain I felt as a black woman, and that was impossible." Privileged as she was, Horne felt a shiver when Roy Wilkins—who succeeded Walter White as executive secretary of the NAACP—spoke about the daily lot of the

Negro. "Suppose from the time you woke up in the morning and left your front door," he said, "until the time you came home at night, *every* step of the way, everything you did, on the job, everywhere you traveled, on a bus, that your color dictated how you were treated."

In 1963, the TV brought graphic coverage of one civil rights explosion after another. Horne sat home with eyes glued to the set, Hayton sometimes at her side. She hoped the reportage would somehow make him feel what she felt; yet he watched it with his usual glazed expression.

On May 3, the couple saw the most shocking news footage to date. A mass of nonviolent black student demonstrators in Birmingham, Alabama, had been forcibly silenced by fire hoses so powerful that some of the youngsters fell to the ground. Snapping German shepherds were set loose on them. All this came by order of Theophilus Eugene "Bull" Connor, the city's police chief and a Klan member. He proudly ordered police to let white onlookers step right up: "I want 'em to see the dogs work!" Black spectators flung rocks and bottles at the cops. Many of the youths were jailed.

For years, Birmingham had embodied the ugliest discrimination in the South; it proved so daunting that few of the blacks who lived there had the spirit to fight. In 1960, only ten percent of them had registered to vote. On average, they earned half of what whites did and stayed confined to the lowest of blue-collar or menial jobs. Klansmen and other racists kept them further "in their place" by bombing homes, businesses, and churches.

The black ennui he saw there and elsewhere profoundly troubled James Baldwin, whose plays, novels, and essays probed the problems of race in America. On the TV show *The Mike Wallace Interview*, Baldwin had recently declared, "The extraordinary silence of most Negroes is the most dangerous thing in this country now."

Now, more of them were speaking up. In Birmingham, students had begun organizing and staging protests in the city's bustling downtown hub. Bull Connor had tried to scare them off through brutality, and arrests, culminating in his actions on May 3. Clearly he thought this nationally televised horror show would deter black protesters everywhere, but it backfired. The spectacle galvanized the South, helping bring on the next year's Civil Rights Act, which banned segregation in schools and public places.

For now, though, Horne sat in shock, watching children nearly drown as they fought for basic rights. As a mother, she was especially shaken. And Hayton seemed indifferent. Since he couldn't "see color," as she noted with dismay, he didn't know the point of the conflict. "I suddenly felt a hatred for the man sitting next to me—a white man," she recalled. "It was no longer the man who was to be my husband for twenty-two years but 'whitey.' I just couldn't help it." Around that time she told a close friend that she'd taken to sleeping with her arms locked in front of her like bars, lest Hayton try to touch her.

The Birmingham incident made her feel even more selfish. Recently Delta Sigma Theta had asked Horne to fly there and march with them on Mother's Day, then to sing on the steps of a church. Horne had declined, giving the excuse that she was afraid to fly, and instead took trains and boats. Horne didn't mention how scared she was of plunging headfirst into a battle where she might not be taken seriously—would perhaps even be ridiculed. She spoke of celebrities who got involved in the movement because it seemed "chic"; would she be viewed as one of those? Moreover, Horne was leery of being used as a publicity-attracting name for social causes.

As it happened, the Deltas never made the trip. Because of the brewing dangers in Birmingham, they were warned to stay home. But Horne remained angry at herself. Later in May, she and Hayton left New York for the second home they'd bought a few years earlier in Palm Springs.

There she answered a phone call from James Baldwin, who voiced an invitation. Attorney General Robert Kennedy had asked him to assemble a group of prominent blacks for a private, imminent meeting about civil rights issues. Would she participate?

Baldwin explained that pressure was building on the Kennedys to strengthen a weak allegiance to racial equality. In two years as president, Robert's brother John F. Kennedy had done almost nothing to help the cause—in part because he wanted to keep peace with southern Democrats. Now the Kennedys faced a growing wave of resentment from black activists, the NAACP, and other civil rights groups. A backlash was brewing. Baldwin himself protested angrily that the president had "not used the great prestige of his office as the moral forum it can be." In a recent conference with Robert Kennedy and his aide, Burke Marshall, who led the Justice Department's civil rights division, Baldwin had helped shame them into action.

Hesitation was not in his character. Born in Harlem in 1924, Baldwin had begun publishing passionate essays on race in top magazines; much of his early nonfiction would appear in the controversial book *Notes of a Native Son* (1955). Later he would frankly explore his dual marginalization as a black homosexual. Rage had been implanted in Baldwin by his stepfather, a fire-and-brimstone storefront preacher whose cruelty terrified him. Then there were the cold realities that faced him as an American Negro in the thirties and forties: "the day in which you're trying to get a taxi and four cabs pass you," or the sting of entering a restaurant or bar and hearing, "We don't serve Negroes here."

Baldwin saw anger as his birthright. "There is, I should think, no Negro living in America who has not felt, briefly or for long periods, simple, naked and unanswerable hatred; who has not wanted to smash any white face he may encounter . . . to break the bodies of all white people and bring them low, as low as that dust in which he himself has been and is being trampled." It was the reverse of the victim attitude that Horne and many other blacks in America had adopted. "From my point of view," explained Baldwin, "to take such a stance would simply be to corroborate all the principles that had you enslaved in the first place."

Such outspokenness landed Baldwin on the cover of *Time* while he was touring the South in 1963, braving physical danger to speak about racism. As he'd told Mike Wallace, the black man had "nothing whatever to lose. No matter what happens to you wherever you go, it will not be worse than what is happening to you where you are. You can't lose anymore than you've lost already. Go for broke."

He was firm with Horne; she *had* to attend the Kennedy meeting. She hesitated, telling him she had to think about it. She didn't know if she had anything worth contributing, and once she took that step she would have to stay actively involved in the fight.

Within the hour, Jeanne Noble called. Horne asked her advice, and Noble urged her to go. So did Hayton, who knew that she would curse herself if she stayed home. On May 24, Horne was the first to arrive at the Kennedy family apartment at 24 Central Park South in Manhattan. Gradually, the other guests drifted in. Lorraine Hansberry had written *A Raisin in the Sun,* the first drama by a black woman to be produced on Broadway. Dr. Kenneth Clark, a psychologist and educator, had made an important study of the effects of racism on children; it had been cited in the Supreme Court's breakthrough 1954 ruling, *Brown v. Board of Education.* Jerome Smith, then twenty-three, had formed the New Orleans chapter of the Congress of Racial Equality (CORE); he'd come to New York so that the group's volunteer doctors could attend to jaw and head damage he'd suffered in beatings by white supremacists. June Shagaloff worked on school integration for the NAACP. Harry Belafonte was there, as was film actor Rip Torn, a white Texan and friend of Baldwin. Robert Kennedy showed up with Burke Marshall.

Once they settled in, Horne noticed that the whites had all gathered on one side of the room, the blacks on the other—not a promising sign. Clark began the meeting with a dry recitation of statistics on discrimination. From there, Kennedy proceeded to defend the government's civil rights efforts, including his own attempts to desegregate chain-store lunch counters in the South. Rather than seeking their advice, the attorney general seemed to want their assurance that he was doing enough.

Jerome Smith could no longer stand the meeting's strained politeness. Enraged, he told Kennedy he wanted to vomit at being in the same room with an official from a government that had done so little to help his people. As a CORE fieldworker, Smith had been brutalized and jailed for battling racists face to face; what had the white politicians done beyond making empty promises? Bloodcurdling stories of his hardships tumbled out of him. The realities of Negro life finally became clear—and the meeting's sociological lingo now seemed meaningless. All the other black guests took his side, engulfing Kennedy in a wave of hostility. Kennedy tried, in vain, to cut Smith off; finally he sat there almost speechless. By the close of the three-hour meeting, he was shattered. Now he knew he *hadn't* done enough.

Horne felt just as lacking. All *she'd* done, she felt, was shake her fist at those who had insulted or rejected her. But guilt pushed her forward, magnified by a black journalist who came to interview her shortly after the Kennedy meeting. He boldly taunted her for being afraid to go near the southern trenches of the struggle. With that, Horne phoned the NAACP and said she wanted to go south to show her support. How, she didn't know.

She learned about an upcoming civil rights rally in Jackson, Mississippi, to be led by Medgar Evers, the state's NAACP field secretary. Evers, who had never met her, would be thrilled, she heard, to have her participate. Again, Horne hesitated. She was sure that the Negroes of Jackson would reject her as some phony come-lately black celebrity. But at the urging of Hayton, Noble, and Billy Strayhorn, she agreed to go. Horne asked Noble to come along, and Strayhorn to accompany her in a song. She also invited her son, but not her husband.

On Friday, June 7, 1963, Horne, Noble, Strayhorn, and Teddy Jones got off a plane in Jackson. Evers had led a motorcade of six cars from the NAACP office to pick them up. A TV camera caught Horne at the airport making a Hollywood-like entrance. Wearing a white suit and dark glasses, she swept past the lens, grinning. Despite her nerves, it was a happy moment; everyone gathered in clusters, laughing and posing for pictures.

In Evers, Horne found a "very tall, very warm, very vital man," then thirty-seven. The city's leading black activist, he had helped organize a series of demonstrations—including an NAACP boycott of white downtown merchants—that placed him and his family under constant threat of death. Yet he carried himself with a preternatural calmness. Evers drove Horne to the house where she would stay. He apologized for not hosting her himself, explaining that a firebomb had been hurled at his home a few days earlier. He and his wife, Myrlie, were still cleaning up the mess.

Yet he moved about the town with no protection. Horne was shocked, and wondered why he stayed in the hateful Deep South. But Evers liked Jackson, he said, and refused to be forced out. More important, he was needed there. Everything would be all right, he told Horne. "I had never met such a strong man before," she said.

To many eyes, that pretty town, with its booming industries and population, seemed like a picture of southern prosperity. But until recently, Jackson had suffered from a disturbing resistance to racial growth. Terrorized by white bigots, who worried about losing control, most of

Jackson's black population dared not speak out. Only 3.75 percent of Mississippi's blacks had registered to vote—the lowest rate in the nation. To Roy Wilkins, Mississippi knew no equal "in inhumanity, murder, brutality, and racial hatred."

But Jackson was changing, thanks largely to Evers. While many younger black activists had lambasted the NAACP for taking too dainty a role in the war for civil rights, Evers was a fighter. Aided by Myrlie, who helped as his secretary, he organized voter registration drives and demonstrations, some with violent results. Myrlie would later tell journalist Karen Grigsby Bates what happened to black Jacksonians who signed up for the vote. "Their names would be published in the newspaper with their addresses and phone numbers, and they would be harassed by phone calls, people driving by, throwing rocks, eggs, firebombs. . . . People got fired from their jobs immediately." Others were dragged by lasso into cars and beaten.

A long-suppressed flood of black fury was unleashed, and many of Jackson's white residents feared for their lives. As Hodding Carter, a Pulitzer Prize–winning newspaper editor in Mississippi, wrote in the *New York Times,* "The hatred of the Negro for the white man is stark, naked and openly expressed to anyone to whom a Negro is willing to talk."

Many of the city's white men had a comparable hatred of Evers. In an effort to evade danger, he drove home in disguise and along different roads. He and Myrlie spoke in code on the telephone. They instructed their three children to stay on the alert for strange sounds outside their home, and to immediately drop to the floor—out of likely bullet range—if they heard one.

He and Myrlie knew that eventually he'd be killed. Yet there in Jackson, a teacher told Horne, "Medgar is our courage. He inspires us to be a little less afraid." Evers had certainly done so for Myrlie. "He's the one who told me to be proud of my large lips," she told Karen Grigsby Bates. "It was he who told me to stop straightening my hair and be proud of my kinky hair. It was Medgar who told me to stop using bleach on my face and to be proud of my blackness." He even eased Horne's terror. "I am a woman and I was afraid to go to that rally," she said, "but I didn't ever feel fear in his presence."

In her whirlwind stay, Horne would speak at an NAACP rally on

Saturday afternoon, then make a guest appearance that night in a church concert for the Southern Christian Leadership Conference (SCLC), a group originally run by Martin Luther King, Jr. In her spare hours, Horne, joined by Noble, got an up-close look at Jackson's civil rights warriors in action.

A class she attended there would haunt her for some time to come. Horne met a group of black youngsters who worked for dangerous causes, notably voter registration. They learned how to protect themselves from beatings. A knee-to-chest position, with arms around the head, would guard some of the body against kicks. The youths were drilled on how to fall safely should fire hoses be turned at them. One of their teachers was Willie Ben Ludden, an NAACP youth secretary. He coached them before a picketing of J. C. Penney, a Jim Crow department store. "Hold your flags high and wave them proudly," he said. "Walk near the curb, keep moving, answer no one. Provoke no quarrels and as you agreed, accept arrest with the dignity that is the Negro."

Horne remembered the children's questions. "How do we hold our heads when the club sticks us? How do we carry the flag so it can't be turned against us and hurt us in some vital part of our body?" Whatever her failings as a mother, the spectacle of young people risking their lives for the freedom of her race touched her deeply.

She seemed more fearful than they, however, as she approached a podium that afternoon and, for the first time, addressed a large audience on a subject many blacks thought she knew nothing about. Horne wore plain white and big sunglasses. Nervously fingering her pearls, she read for a few minutes from prepared notes. "Nobody black or white," she declared, "who really believes in democracy can stand aside now. *Everybody's* got to stand up and be counted." After several more minutes of talk, the attendees cheered their agreement, and Horne, for the moment, felt relieved.

But the prospect of singing that night in a black church brought a new wave of panic. Horne hadn't set foot in one in years; the public knew her as an expensively gowned supper-club star, not as a gospel singer. She fretted to Billy Strayhorn; what would she sing? She didn't know any church music. He assured her that her presence there was all that mattered. "He always had a calming thing to say," she recalled. They decided on a spiritual that Grandmother Cora had taught her, "This Little Light of Mine."

Hours later, Horne stood before a teeming black congregation. Fearing the worst, she began to sing, with Strayhorn on piano. Recalled Jeanne Noble years later in a Horne documentary on PBS's *American Masters,* "I never will forget the grin on Medgar Evers's face when Lena started singing." Instead of hostility, she felt such a heartfelt connection with her own people that she spoke of it for years to come. Horne was overwhelmed at their response. "It was the first time I believed I had any talent at all," she told photographer Brian Lanker in 1989. "I cried for the first time in many years."

On Sunday morning, Evers and his colleagues drove Horne and her entourage to their plane. For all its importance to her, the rally had gotten scant attention beyond Jackson. And over the next few days its memory would be swept aside by weightier events. That month, the University of Alabama tried to bar admission of two black students; it did so with the full support of Governor George Wallace, who had told a cheering crowd in his inaugural speech, "Segregation now, segregation tomorrow, segregation forever!"

This time, President Kennedy acted. He created a federal ruling that Alabama's government could not block James Hood and Vivian Malone from going to school. But Wallace wasn't through. On June 11, he stood at the door of the administration building to keep Hood and Malone from entering. Kennedy successfully ordered the Alabama National Guard and its commander, Henry Graham, to make Wallace step aside.

It was a coup in the movement, and a dramatic coming-out, on Kennedy's part, for civil rights. But Martin Luther King and many others wanted more. That same day, King told the press of plans for a civil rights march on Washington. That evening, every TV network broadcast the president in a forceful speech. He called for every American to examine his conscience and consider the right to equality. "If an American, because his skin is dark, cannot eat lunch in a restaurant open to the public, if he cannot send his children to the best public school available, if he cannot vote for the public officials who will represent him—if, in short, he cannot enjoy the full and free life which all of us want—then who among us would be content to have the color of his skin changed and stand in his place? Who among us would then be content with the counsels of patience and delay? . . . Now the time has come for this Nation to fulfill its promise." Kennedy announced that he would ask Congress to enact new antidiscriminatory legislation.

On the night of Kennedy's talk, Jeanne Noble was at Horne's home on West End Avenue. The president's words brought a new stir of national hope; they also heated up the opposition. Horne was scheduled to appear the next morning on NBC's *Today* show and air her views on the movement's progress. She consented, eager to tell of what she'd seen in Jackson.

Shortly before airtime, a staff member approached her in the green room and mentioned that Roy Wilkins would join her on the air, but that he hadn't arrived yet. He'd probably been delayed—"considering what's happened."

She asked what that meant. The employee told her that Medgar Evers had been shot the night before. Horne went so numb she didn't think she could do the show. Then Wilkins arrived. They stared at each other, speechless.

Evers had been shot outside his own home at around 12:40 A.M., roughly six and a half hours after Kennedy had made his televised call for compassion. The activist had spent all day Tuesday in meetings. After midnight, Myrlie heard the comforting sound of his car entering the driveway. Then came a gunshot. Myrlie flung open the front door and saw her husband sprawled on the cement, bleeding to death from a gaping chest wound. Neighbors rushed him to the emergency room. Fifteen minutes after he'd arrived, Evers died.

In the vicinity of his home lay a rifle covered with the fingerprints of Byron De La Beckwith, a forty-two-year-old white supremacist and fertilizer salesman. He publicly denied guilt, yet boasted of it at a Klan meeting. Despite condemning evidence, an all-white jury pronounced him innocent. It took Myrlie decades of struggle to have the case reopened; with new witnesses speaking out, De La Beckwith was convicted in 1994 and sentenced to life in prison.

But all that was far away, and on June 12, 1963, Horne and Wilkins had to face national TV cameras and sound calm when they were in shock. Their poise and eloquence proved so remarkable that host Hugh Downs kept them on the air throughout the show's second hour. Ever cool and rational in crisis, Wilkins said he hoped the killing wouldn't spark an ambush of violent revenge. Nevertheless, he said, Negroes were tired of waiting politely for change, and weary of empty excuses from the government.

Horne spoke far more emotionally, and her southern accent, on this occasion, was nowhere to be heard. After mentioning her day with him in Jackson, Horne called Evers "a casualty in what to me now seems to be a war. We are fighting a moral war. And that my life would be touched by his, only inspires me to try not to hate"—she let out a sarcastic chuckle—"and to try to be purposeful in the kind of battle I think we have to wage."

Downs asked a question that had occurred to many. Why her "apparently sudden interest" in civil rights? Out came her first flash of temper. "I've been associated with the NAACP for many years!" she declared. "But I'm not a loudmouth." Now, though, restraint wouldn't do. As she described the meeting in Jackson in which teenage protesters asked how to ward off harmful blows, Horne grew vehement. "When I hear young *American* children talking like this, I only react as a mother," she said. "Because those children are our future in this country. And there are white children in there in the movement, too. They feel they are good Americans. If they can stand up and be counted and suffer like this, it's asking for very little from our politicians and from our *president*"—she spat out the word with contempt—"that he *must* not let this keep on!"

Later that day, Horne went to a meeting held by the Gandhi Society in honor of Martin Luther King, Jr. There she met King for the first time. When he asked her to headline an Atlanta rally to benefit the SCLC, she couldn't refuse.

She and comedian George Kirby were the program. The evening failed to sell out; a disappointed Horne felt she'd been used yet again for publicity and ticket-selling value, not because she had any relevance to the event.

But she was eager to recapture the glow she'd felt in Jackson, and June 21 found her there again, speaking and singing at the city's Masonic

Hall in another NAACP rally devoted largely to Evers's memory. On that muggy summer night, Horne sang a spiritual that became one of the themes of the sixties, "We Shall Overcome."

It was a song to rouse the masses, and for Horne it was overpowering in its resonance. Later she told Arthur Unger of *The Christian Science Monitor* that Evers's assassination had made her go "crazy." She repeated her belief that every stand she'd ever taken against racism had involved no one but herself. Now she'd discovered a "broader picture," and all had changed. "I began a whole year of crying." she said, "For years I hadn't used my tears."

But she kept them private. And in a pair of public-service TV spots she made that year for civil rights, Horne seemed almost cheerful. She had joined a distinguished group of names—including Roy Wilkins and Jackie Robinson—in filming personal pleas for black equality. As Horne, wearing a simple sleeveless blouse, sat in an armchair, an off-camera voice asked, "Miss Lena Horne, what can the individual American do about civil rights?"

She talked good-naturedly as she peered directly into the viewer's eyes. "Well, I have to ask you: Whadda *you* wanna do about civil rights?" She shrugged. "What do you want to do about bad housing, job discrimination, about inequality of opportunity and education? Now if you want to pretend that it doesn't exist, or, quote 'that's the way the world is' unquote, well then, I think we're in a lot of trouble. But if you want—*really* want—to give every child born on this God-given earth a chance to stand up straight and tall and find his place in the sun, well then, I think you know what to do about civil rights. I *know* you do." In her other message, she called for "respect on each side. . . . And I think it might also help if there were some *kindness* and *love*."

In that last statement, Horne might have been speaking to herself. But kindness and love did not come easily to a woman who'd felt cheated out of both for most of her life. It was her daughter, she said, who confronted her most stingingly with the truth. Horne told Alan Ebert that one day Gail made a jarring admission: Although she believed her mother had been her best friend, she didn't think Horne had ever loved her. Hearing that brought Horne "the worst hurt I've ever known," she said. "I just didn't know what to say. How do you tell your daughter that you didn't just love her but you adored her? How do you say to someone you love, 'I don't show it because so little was shown to me'?" Rather defensively, she added, "Love was wiped out of most black people, and this black person is through blaming herself for seeming to be or having been unloving."

CHAPTER 14

HORNE WASN'T out to warm hearts on the fourth episode of *The Judy Garland Show,* the star-filled CBS variety show, which premiered in the fall of 1963. The troubled first lady of the M-G-M musical was having an artistic rebirth after years of public breakdowns, pill addictions, and weight gains. On April 23, 1961, when Garland gave a concert at Carnegie Hall that would soon be deemed historic, she'd shown everyone that she still "had it." CBS seemed to believe that Garland and a galaxy of top-flight guests could do battle with *Bonanza,* the Sunday night NBC hit. But *The Judy Garland Show* survived just one season; only years later would that memorable series become a minilegend.

M-G-M had caught Garland and Horne at the peak of their youthful sweetness, before dismissing them both in 1950. From there, Horne had turned harder and tougher, Garland more vulnerable. Like a lot of the fresh-faced "kids" who'd helped make M-G-M world famous only to be let go, Garland loved to tell dishy stories about the scary Mr. Mayer and some of her sillier colleagues. But while she did so mainly for laughs, Horne's anti–M-G-M stories had vengeance at their core; they amounted to an indictment of the studio as a racist institution. And Horne, who remembered Garland's panic-causing lateness and no-shows during the filming of *Words and Music,* would proclaim her "the height of unprofessionalism" during rehearsal week for their July 23 taping.

The two stars had tricky numbers to learn—a long medley in which they sang each other's trademark songs, and, with British comic actor Terry-Thomas, Noël Coward's tongue-twisting spoof of England's

weather, "Mad Dogs and Englishmen." For much of the week before taping, Garland was in Las Vegas with the show's producer, George Schlat-
ter. She saw no need to rehearse much; Garland learned material quickly,
and may have assumed Horne did, too. For several days of run-throughs,
a stand-in did her parts. Horne was so offended by the perceived brush-
off that she eventually exploded in rage. Mel Tormé, who wrote arrangements and special material for the series, recalled the blowup of Horne's
"fiery temper" in his book about the Garland show, *The Other Side of the
Rainbow.* "When Lena is angry she is even more beautiful, if that is possible. Her celebrated dimples deepen, stunning white teeth flash, impos-
sibly perfect and even, her eyes widen as if she were watching a horror
movie and she gets to you. She was hopping mad now, and the target was
Judy. 'God damn it!' she cried. 'Who the hell does she think she is? We're
doing this show *tomorrow*! I don't even know if we sound good together.
Man, in all my life, I've never seen anything like this!'"

Garland finally walked in on Thursday, and greeted Horne with an
embrace. She got a frozen response. Later, Tormé told her of Horne's
impatience. "Aw, screw her," said Garland. During the first run-through
with orchestra, she made an unnerving number of gaffes. "Dress rehearsal
was ragged," wrote Tormé, "and 'Mad Dogs and Englishmen' was disastrous." There was talk of canceling the show. That night, Horne fumed
to Hayton about how bad Garland was making everyone look. When
taping time arrived, the star seemed so tired and scattered that everyone
else braced themselves for the worst.

Horne got true costar emphasis on the show, which began with a
duet of a Johnny Mercer–Rube Bloom standard from her act, "Day In—
Day Out." She and Garland sang it shoulder to shoulder in matching
high-collared, white satin raincoat-style outfits. But whereas Garland
turns her full attention to Horne, gazing at her with puppy-dog affection and even locking arms with her, Horne yields no more than she did
to Sinatra. She stares straight ahead, stiff as an ice statue. At the phrase
"then I kiss your lips," she snarls.

There, and for the rest of the show, Garland made hardly a flub.
And her tear-jerking pathos, not to mention her knack for getting
things right once the camera rolled, softened even Lena Horne. By
the time they sat together on a pair of cubes and tore into each other's

signature tunes, she and Garland were whooping it up like girlfriends—clasping hands, laughing together, locking eyes. Such interaction had been Horne's dream back at M-G-M; now a black and a white star were touching on TV without fear of reprisal.

In her solos, though, she was out there alone, illustrating her confused connection with the word "love." From the then-new British musical *Oliver!* she chose "Where Is Love?," a reflection on how that elusive golden ring might become hers. Horne sang it with a frustration that had an emotional tug; the song's aching hope was replaced by anger at herself for what she couldn't feel.

After such shows of vulnerability, Horne tended to revert to steel, as though she'd shown people too much. She followed "Where Is Love?" with "He Loves Me," her feminized version of the title song of a new show by Jerry Bock and Sheldon Harnick. Singing about the heartstopping jolt of winning someone's heart, Horne glares at the camera. "I love it, knowing that he loves me!" she growls, treating the song's openhearted glee with mocking coyness. She can't hold a smile; rays of warmth try to peep through her thundercloud and are quickly doused.

Throughout the Garland experience, Horne reinforced her reputation for steely efficiency, low on heart. "Everybody said, she's so professional, she's so professional," she recalled. "I began to feel as if it was a filthy word." Diahann Carroll knew how that felt: "It made you believe that the white community didn't expect blacks to be professional."

Horne's view of show business remained so cynical that she couldn't view the progress blacks had made in it as anything more than commercial opportunism. "People have discovered that if they can make money out of somebody they don't always care what color their skin is," she told Herbert Feinstein, a white interviewer.

For now, Horne sang eagerly for any racial cause that might show the world she cared. On August 20, she returned to Atlanta, Georgia, for the first time since her childhood; there she starred in a benefit for the SCLC at the city's five thousand, five hundred–seat Municipal Auditorium. Eight days later, Horne joined an array of socially driven voices, both white and black, at the crowning rally of the civil rights movement. The March on Washington for Jobs and Freedom attracted over two hundred thousand concerned citizens from all over the country. They gathered to hear hours of pleas for equal rights. President Kennedy had introduced a civil rights bill on June 19, but everyone at the rally seemed to agree that it was far too moderate; no longer would they wait.

The idea for the march had come from A. Philip Randolph, a veteran black activist. He and the five contemporary fathers of the struggle—Roy Wilkins, Martin Luther King, Jr., John Lewis (chairman of SNCC, the Student Nonviolent Coordinating Committee), Whitney Young, Jr. (executive director of the Urban League), and James Farmer (national director of CORE)—had spent the last several months designing the march. Its chief coordinator, Bayard Ruskin, was himself a monument to liberation—an openly gay man, a Communist, and a peace-loving black freedom fighter.

On the Wednesday morning of the march, thousands began to pour in on buses and on foot. The masses marched toward the Lincoln Memorial, singing "We Shall Overcome." From the steps of the memorial, Marian Anderson intoned the national anthem; then came heartfelt freedom songs from Mahalia Jackson, Joan Baez, Bob Dylan, Odetta, Peter, Paul and Mary, and others. The movement's leaders spoke, demanding an immediate end to discrimination in public schools and workplaces, an increase in the minimum wage, a public-works program to combat unemployment, and strict government measures against any institution that failed to comply.

The day culminated in a history-making, sixteen-minute address by King. Delivered with the zeal of the preacher he was, King declared his dream for America's future: "I have a dream that my four little children will one day live in a nation where they will not be judged by the color of their skin but by the content of their character . . ."

Scores of black celebrities, including Diahann Carroll, had made the trek to Washington. "It was wonderful to be able to verbalize all this and not be afraid," she said, "because there were so many of us doing it." They had to show their support; to neglect the cause in 1963 was a mark of shame. During King's speech Horne stood behind him, among a throng of prominent participants. Earlier, she had made perhaps the briefest on-mike appearance of anyone. Welcomed to the podium as "*Miss* Lena Horne," she came into view dressed in the plainest white blouse and slacks she could find. She obscured her beauty with tortoise-shell glasses, a scarf pulled around her head, and a white cap. Stepping to the podium, she yowled one word at the top of her lungs: *"Freeeeeee-dom!"* Then she grinned and waved.

Esther and James Jackson observed her. "I got the impression that she felt very much a part of things and was very excited," said Esther. Some onlookers, however, still saw Horne as a pampered star, stepping from a cocoon of privilege to call for something she'd always had.

And Horne knew it. Eager to prove her seriousness, she decided to speak publicly about a side of her life that few people knew. That summer Richard Schickel, a freelance magazine writer, received a call from *Show,* the glossy New York–based arts magazine he had recently left. An editor asked him if he would consider meeting with Horne and ghostwriting a first-person article on her racial views. Horne, it seemed, had been encouraged to let loose in print by Louis Lomax, a fiery black journalist. Lomax had plunged into the trenches of the civil rights movement and documented it for major magazines and in books such as *The Negro Revolt.* After hearing Horne speak at a CORE rally, Lomax thought it was time for her to go on the record and pledge her dedication to the cause. *Show* would later report that Lomax helped her shape an early version of the article. But years later Schickel, who was white, recalled hearing that Horne was uncomfortable with the militant stand being pressed on her, and wanted to tell the story her own way.

She met with Schickel in her living room on West End Avenue. "I found her extremely agreeable," he said. "She was an obviously intelligent woman, and had a good ironic sense of herself and of the world. But she was enormously resentful of all the things that had happened in her life—the one hundred and one different ways in which blacks were openly discriminated against. She'd had a lifetime of suppressing those feelings. She felt like coming out on the subject of her life and the black experience as she knew it."

Horne liked him, and they went to work. In the fall of 1963, *Show* published the article as its cover story, called "I Just Want to Be Myself." The piece found her giving word that she would no longer serve as a puppet for the NAACP or anyone else; from now on, any choice she made would be that of an independent, freethinking black woman. But the title seemed less like a declaration than a plea, for Horne still had no idea who she was. The cover photo suggested her confusion. Taken by Melvin Sokolsky, it showed her standing behind a tear in a mural-size sheet of white paper; only half her face and a sliver of her body were visible. The image evoked a figure still partly in hiding.

In *Show*, she strove to give herself a new persona—that of an "exploited Negro woman" who'd suffered more than anyone understood. She'd been victimized, she claimed, by nearly everyone: the grandmother who had trained her to be a warrior but squelched the human being inside, the mother who had exploited her for selfish reasons, the Cotton Club hoods who had all but enslaved her. Show business at large, she explained, had pinned a series of images on her for its own purposes.

Meanwhile, who was she? The pride that she and her family had felt as a part of Brooklyn's black middle class, of course, stemmed largely from the white blood in their lineage—the result of slave women being raped by their white masters. She recalled the club owners who'd refused to hire her because she didn't look dark enough; the others who urged her to pass as Latin. Hollywood, she claimed, had made her up to look blacker. To protect herself, she crafted what she called "a sophisticated cover for hostility."

The career that followed had so hurt and disappointed her that she practically disowned it, calling it a path of survival, not ambition. The article introduced several revisionist stories that would take a permanent place in her myth. In a pat explanation of her first marriage's failure, Horne noted that she'd lacked the strength, or the wifely know-how, to shoulder the outrage that every black man of the time faced in the white workplace. Once home, he faced a young bride who hadn't a clue about housework. "We were divorced," she explained.

Though her marriage to Hayton was falling apart, Horne didn't mention that; instead she defended him as the ultimate nonracist. Why couldn't her critics understand "that when you look at people you love . . . you don't see *color*?" Horne, of course, did. But she'd mastered a tone of candor and self-effacement that, for the rest of her life, would make almost all her assertions believable.

Despite her anger, many took it for granted that she supported Martin Luther King, Jr., and his policy of nonviolent change. They'd forgotten how Horne had reacted to being called a "nigger" at the Luau. "I thought that his goodness was overwhelming," said Horne of King, but according to Ray Ellis she "didn't like him at all," and doubted his idealism could ever succeed. Harry Belafonte was a friend and staunch advocate of King, and tried to win her over to his side. Horne resented it. As she told Joan Barthel in 1968, she was sick of being asked to support activists who thought that great things could be achieved by blacks if only they didn't act in rage.

Instead she identified passionately with Malcolm X, the radical Black Muslim minister who defined militancy. A mass of fury, X believed bloodshed was not only permissible but essential in fighting back. "The time for you and me to allow ourselves to be brutalized nonviolently has passed," he declared. Born in Omaha and raised in Lansing, Michigan, X—born Malcolm Little—had lost several family members, including his activist father, to murder by white supremacists. Playing by the rules, he decided, was pointless. He lived as a hood in Harlem and Boston; after six years in prison he joined the Nation of Islam, a radical organization committed to lifting black America to its deserved position of power. The group members commonly referred to whites as "devils," and changed their last names to "X." The X, he explained, showed a rejection of the false last names that slaveholders had assigned to their new captives, who were frequently branded on the arm with an X.

As an enemy of white America and a champion of vigilante justice, X threatened the very bedrock of society. The FBI trailed him; death threats came his way regularly. He even clashed with the Nation of Islam, which allegedly ordered his execution. X's extremism frightened many blacks. For others, it brought about cheers of support; finally someone was brave enough to give voice to their deepest rage.

Horne would later call *The Autobiography of Malcolm X* her "Bible." It wasn't clear if she knew her admiration wasn't mutual. In 1963, Louis Lomax had interviewed X at length. He spoke scathingly about those in the movement who had desecrated it, he felt, by intermarrying. Robert Kennedy's civil rights meeting had been filled with such figures, he said, including Harry Belafonte, Lorraine Hansberry, and Lena Horne. "Now how can any Negro, man or woman, who sleeps with a white person speak for me?"

Lomax asked why. "Because only a man who is ashamed of what he is will marry out of his race," said X. These Negroes, he added, "are linking up with the very people who lynched their fathers, raped their mothers, and put their kid sisters in the kitchen to scrub floors . . . the Negro is nothing but an ex-slave who is now trying to get himself integrated into the slave master's house."

Horne might not have disagreed. Again she mourned the choices she'd made in pandering to a white world. By now, said Arthur Laurents, Horne was heavily "under the influence" of Jeanne Noble, whose theories had suffused the *Show* article. Noble had no higher regard for Hayton than X would have.

Horne had long felt emotionally estranged from her husband, but now she had ample encouragement to take the next step. Years later she told *Ebony*'s Ponchitta Pierce of a "desperate chance" she had taken. "I said, 'Lennie, I'm going through these changes as a black woman. I can't explain them . . . but I've got to be by myself to work it out.'"

Later on, Horne related a more unhinged version of that moment to John Gruen: "I said, 'Lennie, I can't stand it, I've got to go!'" Hayton, she said, "didn't fuss," and moved to their house in Palm Springs. Except for occasional projects, the collaboration was over, and the marriage lived on in name only. Hayton had long depended on her to make his living; now he would have to resume scoring soundtrack music.

Many of Hayton's friends, including Skitch Henderson, never forgave Horne for putting him out. But Geoffrey Holder understood. "Maybe it was necessary for her to sacrifice her marriage to Lennie," he said. "There was absolutely no way they could be compatible at that time." Yet Horne was too proud to let those who had scorned her interracial marriage think that they'd been right all along. For some time to come, she kept up the illusion that they were still a couple. "When they were together," said Ray Ellis, "she would act like he was the greatest. She'd say, 'Hey, Daddy,' and do a whole number, which to me was obviously just a put-on. He would stand there and smile like he was the great stud of the world."

Horne had to maintain a similar façade when she agreed to team with Frank Sinatra for a pair of Carnegie Hall benefit concerts, produced by Belafonte Enterprises. On Saturday, October 5, the show would aid an organization chosen by Horne, the Gandhi Society for

Human Rights, chaired by Dr. King. The next night's proceeds would go to the Foundation for International Children's Health, one of Sinatra's preferred charities.

The rift between Horne and Sinatra meant that there would be no duets at Carnegie Hall. Instead, at Sinatra's insistence, his costar would do the first half and he the second—a sequence that annoyed Horne, for it meant that she was opening for him. Her irritation grew when ticket sales for the Saturday-night show lagged behind Sunday's. Horne blamed the fact that the charity she chose was racially controversial and Sinatra's wasn't. She phoned all the moneyed friends and acquaintances she could and asked them to buy seats, the priciest of which cost one hundred dollars. It exhausted her, but it worked.

Determined, perhaps, to outshine Sinatra, Horne set out to make her half of the concert truly memorable. Harold Arlen and Yip Harburg wrote her a poignant song for the occasion. "Silent Spring" took its title from a bestselling book by Rachel Carson about threats to the environment, notably pesticides and pollution. Such issues grieved the liberal songwriting duo; so did the previous month's racial tragedy, in which four girls had died in the bombing of a black church in Birmingham. Harburg's lyric imagined a world deadened by acid rain, nuclear destruction, and discrimination; where "the rains of hate rust the garden gate."

Arlen agreed to accompany her in some of his songs, including "It's a New World," a ballad about the revitalizing powers of love. He and Ira Gershwin had written it for Judy Garland to sing in *A Star Is Born*. Inspired by the March on Washington, the lyricist gave the song a civil rights spin for Horne. She'd asked Jule Styne to write her something special, too. He called upon Betty Comden and Adolph Green, and the three of them penned her a feisty civil rights anthem, "Now!" Styne adapted the tune from the Hebrew song of celebration, "Hava Nagila." The new words preached wholehearted love from one race to another: "Just don't take it lit'ral, mister / No one wants to grab your sister."

Though Hayton would conduct for Horne (and Nelson Riddle for Sinatra), Ray Ellis arranged "Now!" at Styne's request. He came to Carnegie Hall for rehearsals, and felt tension everywhere. Ellis himself was scared of Horne, whom he'd heard could be "tough." But after the first run-through of "Now!," she walked over and gave him a big hug.

Saturday night came. Carnegie Hall felt like the Metropolitan Opera on opening night; tuxedoed and evening-gowned revelers filled the hall. Horne was annoyed to be going on first, and when her orchestral cue came she sailed onstage in full battle mode, wearing a plunging white sleeveless dress. Snapping her fingers, she tore through "He Loves Me," followed by one of her showstoppers after another—"I Concentrate on You," "Why Was I Born?," "Stormy Weather." But with the newly written songs, she reminded everyone of why they were really there. Horne "trimmed her normal output of sex and sin," observed *Variety*, and sang of "new worlds to come." Her fervent shouts of *"Now is the time!"* helped make "Now!" the hit of her set.

Sinatra, though, seemed to gain the edge. Martin Luther King, Jr., introduced the star. Singing his standard program—which included "Ol' Man River," his nod to the racial struggle—Sinatra triggered such excitement that the crowd kept clapping in the middle of songs. Critics pronounced the "competition" a draw. In the *Herald Tribune,* Robert Salmaggi called the concert "a truly memorable evening that fairly buzzed with excitement." But according to Dorothy Kilgallen, Gail was "infuriated" that Sinatra had made her mother open for him. At intermission, she remarked, "We all ought to go home now, but it would mean missing Martin Luther King."

The next day, William B. Williams, a Sinatra-worshiping deejay at WNEW in New York, raved about the show. "Now!" just had to be recorded, he said. Ellis was listening, and phoned Horne to share the news. He found her in a rare state of elation. After her shows, he learned later, "she usually put herself down." But this time she felt she'd scored. Ellis had begun producing for a new label, 20th Century Fox, and asked if she'd like to record "Now!" as a single. She leapt at the chance.

Within two weeks, cartons of promotional copies were ready. Ellis hand-delivered the record to Williams during airtime. He played it—and the switchboard "lit up like a Christmas tree," said Ellis. "Now!" was shipped to stations all over America. Finally, thought Horne, she had a hit.

Instead, "Now!" set off what she called another "big hassle."

According to Ellis, it seemed to center on the controversial line "No one wants to grab your sister." Late in October, newspapers reported that

Joseph Cook, program director for CBS radio, had banned the disk from all playlists. Questioned by Mort Young of the *Journal-American,* Cook explained, "It doesn't fit our music policy. We don't play rock and roll and we don't play wailers. This one's a wailer. Did you hear that steel guitar in there? I didn't ban it, I just didn't recommend it for use."

Other stations followed suit, including KMPC in Los Angeles. "KMPC would rather avoid editorializing through music," announced program director Russ Barnett. Budd Granoff, who owned the 20th Century Fox label, was appalled by the enduring racism in L.A., where he lived. "Seven out of eleven radio stations here have banned it, while one of eleven in New York is not playing it," he told the *Los Angeles Times.*

Undeterred, Granoff released "Now!" on October 28 with an initial pressing of sixty-five thousand copies. Horne announced that she would share the proceeds with the NAACP and CORE. Angry as she was, she spoke calmly to the press. Bernard Lefkowitz of the *Post* reported that Horne was "puzzled" by the ban. "It would be a shame if this hurt the record sales," she said.

The press reacted with such hostility to CBS's decision that on October 30, Cook lifted the ban. William B. Williams continued to plug the single. "I'm airing it as often as possible," he said. "I'm just wondering if it'll be played in Birmingham."

It wasn't played much anywhere. "Now!" rose only to a disappointing number ninety-two on *Billboard*'s pop chart. "It never quite became what we wanted it to be," said Betty Comden. "I thought the song was quite good, myself." Horne was disappointed too, and dropped "Now!" from her shows.

The single did have two happy consequences. "Now!" caught the attention of Santiago Álvarez, a radically political filmmaker from Cuba. Spurred on by the triumph of the Cuban Revolution in 1959, Álvarez went on to direct hundreds of documentaries on human rights in Cuba and elsewhere, many in a breathless newsreel style. In one of his best-known short films, Horne's recording of "Now!" set the backdrop for a violent array of images from the civil rights struggle—lynchings, police brutality, bloody demonstrations.

In the States, the single had spawned an album, *Here's Lena Now!,* conducted by Ellis. It stands as the most convincing statement of racial conviction Horne ever made. On November 20, 1963, just before the sessions, she'd made an inspiring visit to the White House to see President Kennedy, whom she'd come to respect. Love songs were not on her mind. "How can I go on singing about a penthouse way up in the sky when, with housing restrictions the way they are now, I would not be allowed to rent that place?" she wondered. "I can't get up in a nightclub in a thousand-dollar dress and start singing 'Let My People Go' . . . I never had the right. I didn't choose it to be that way, but it was the illusion that Hollywood gave me." Somehow she had to find a way to speak out and not sound ridiculous.

She succeeded. *Here's Lena Now!* gathered a dozen songs, mostly standards, that spoke to her of the quest for freedom. She raced through a Depression-era spirit raiser, "Great Day," belting with feisty assurance about bright new horizons ahead. For years she had sung "Wouldn't It Be Loverly," a cockney flower girl's dream of a better life from *My Fair Lady*. Now she saw a whole new meaning in this plea for the basic dignities of life, such as a comfortable place to live, safe from the "cold night air." Onstage, said Ellis, "she walked around like a little old black woman during the song. It was hysterical."

From *Bloomer Girl*, a 1944 Broadway musical by Harold Arlen and Yip Harburg, Horne revived "The Eagle and Me," which argued for the right to exist as freely as the sun shone or the river flowed. "Lost in the Stars" came from a musical of the same name. Its source was *Cry, the Beloved Country*, Alan Paton's tragic novel about a racial crisis in South Africa. In the title song of Kurt Weill and Maxwell Anderson's score, a Negro sang of feeling all alone in the universe, abandoned even by God. Horne told it with such noble urgency that William B. Williams compared her to Paul Robeson.

On November 22, 1963, while Horne was in the studio, word came that President Kennedy had been killed by a sniper's bullet in Dallas, Texas. Horne "was *very* upset," said Ellis. But she had to continue. Somehow, the tragedy didn't bring out her usual cynicism; *Here's Lena Now!* brimmed with a sense of possibility.

Among his hundreds of arranging credits, Ellis was best known for the sentimental string backing he'd provided for Billie Holiday on *Lady in Satin*, the torch-song album she'd made in 1958, the year before her death. Before that, Ellis had conducted a string of jukebox hits for the Four Lads, Johnny Mathis and others, and worked as head of the pop departments at RCA and M-G-M Records. His was a commercial style, but Horne didn't want sweetening. She'd outgrown the old-Hollywood sound of her husband's music—and as Ellis pointed out, for all his expertise, Hayton's music didn't swing. And it never changed.

But starting with "Now!," Horne had a transforming effect upon Ellis. *Here's Lena Now!* was full of high-voltage big-band arranging; it exuded an energy that she fed on. "When she'd stand there and rehearse," explained Ellis, "it made me think in another way. All of a sudden I started to write differently."

In Las Vegas, Ellis witnessed the growing power struggle between the Haytons. Horne, he said, could uncannily sense an audience's mood from the moment she walked onstage, and knew how to manipulate it. Hayton, understandably, had his own ideas, and the couple had fought over tempos for years. As Ellis recalled, "Lennie would say to the drummer, 'Now look. You follow *me*. All right? Even though she might want it another way—you look at *me!*'"

Her next Sands show began with "Great Day." An offstage voice welcomed her on: "Ladies and gentlemen, the Sands proudly presents . . . *Miss* Lena Horne!" Hayton counted the song off at a racing clip as Horne strode onstage, bowing. "In the meantime," said Ellis, "she's got her hand in back of her and she's trying to slow the band down. And Lennie's up like Adolf Hitler, with a beat going, and she's gonna kill him." An hour later, Horne finished "Stormy Weather," her closer, to a roaring ovation. "She took a gracious bow, then turned around, bowed to the band, and screamed at Lennie, *'Fuck you!'*"

Soon thereafter, Horne phoned Ellis from San Francisco, where she was about to perform at a theater in the round. "She said, 'I'm gonna kill him! You've gotta come and conduct for me.' I said, 'OK, I'll come out, baby, but I'll tell you what. If you give me any bullshit, I'll walk off the stand and leave you there!' She said, 'I'll be good!'"

For the next four years Ellis would arrange her albums and lead the occasional Horne show. Although both were married, their professional relationship grew into an affair. At the beginning of their relationship she gave him some guidelines. "She knew she could get people angry, and she said, 'If you ever get mad at me, don't ever hit me in the face or use the secret word'—which was 'nigger.'"

He didn't, but he stood up to her as Hayton never had. Ellis informed her that the first time he'd ever seen her up close was at an opening-night party at Sardi's. "She was uptight, and she didn't know how to talk to people, so nobody talked to her. I told her, 'You know, the first time I really saw you was at the opening of *Gypsy,* and you walked in and you were pissing ice water all over the place!' She died laughing. Everybody was afraid to talk to her like that, and I used to kid her all the time. I used to say, 'For an old broad, you still look pretty good.'"

Where her daughter was concerned, Horne was in no joking mood. Gail, who still lived at 300 West End Avenue, had been working as a magazine researcher; meanwhile she had struck up a romance with one of the rising young directors of the day. At thirty-nine, Sidney Lumet could already look back on an Oscar nomination for *12 Angry Men,* the first film he'd directed; four more nominations—for *Prince of the City, Dog Day Afternoon, Network,* and *The Verdict*—awaited him.

A Philadelphia-born, New York–based Jew, Lumet was short (five foot five), intense, and driven. He was also married—to Gloria Vanderbilt, Manhattan's most gossiped-about heiress and socialite. Even though the seven-year union had crashed, Horne seemed "horrified," according to Arthur Laurents, at the thought of her daughter dating a man with a wife. It was easy for her to forget that Hayton was no bachelor when they started their affair; twenty years later she seemed to be projecting her early suspicions of him onto Lumet. Horne vented to Laurents at a small dinner party in his home. "She'd been drinking some, and she lashed out at Sidney for taking out Gail, because he was a married man. She said he wouldn't have done that if her daughter weren't black. Which is nonsense." Her pique grew at the news that Gail and Sidney were engaged. Horne pleaded with Laurents to take Gail out for a meal "and tell her not to marry him."

He did—but it made no difference, and Horne continued to fume about the relationship. "Lennie felt the same," she insisted, "but naturally, they didn't pay any attention to me and Lennie."

Years later, she offered an explanation to journalist Marie Brenner. "I've always been so overprotective with Gail. I tried to compensate for the fact that my own mother ignored me." More unwelcome drama was stirred up on August 25, the day after Vanderbilt divorced Lumet. Exhausted and depressed, he sought a long rest by downing a combination of sleeping pills and vodka. Before drifting off, a woozy Lumet phoned Gail.

"What's the matter with you?" she asked.

"I took a couple of pills."

According to the *Los Angeles Sentinel,* she rushed to his Greenwich Village apartment. When Lumet failed to answer his doorbell, Gail called the police, who climbed a ladder to his window. Inside they found the director unconscious on the bedroom floor, wearing only underwear. They gave him artificial respiration and carted him to the hospital. The next day, stories of his suspected suicide attempt were all over the news. Lumet denied them, while calling Gail "a rather hysterical little baby."

Now Horne could believe that her daughter's beau was not only adulterous and perhaps racist, but nasty and unstable. Lumet told *Newsweek* that all he'd wanted was about fourteen hours' sleep. "And I would have gotten it, too, if I hadn't been bothered."

The incident blew over quickly. On November 23, 1963, the day after the assassination of President Kennedy, Lumet and Gail were wed at the New York apartment of a friend of hers, writer Walter Bernstein. A reception followed at the Waldorf. It was pouring rain outside, and somewhat gloomy within. A reporter from the *Journal-American* made note of the "stark black suit" Horne had chosen to wear. "Some friends assumed it denoted mourning for President Kennedy; others thought it indicated disapproval of the match."

A few months later, the couple acquired a home in London, where they spent most of their time. Horne spoke to Claude Thompson about how much she missed Gail. Once more, she and her daughter were far apart, and Horne felt a new wave of guilt; she told Thompson that she felt she'd pushed Gail away.

Horne felt no closer to her son. Ted now lived in Los Angeles with Marsha Hamilton, a young woman whom he'd met while attending a free-speech rally at the University of California, Berkeley. Marsha had planned to join a commune in San Francisco; instead she had moved back to L.A. with Ted, who had returned to USC in 1963 to pursue his much-delayed college diploma. Slim and pretty, with bobbed hair parted in the middle, Marsha struck Ted's friend Daniel Johnson as "a very soft-spoken, nice person." But according to others, Marsha shared Ted's propensity for self-destruction.

Her life had been troubled. "She came from some wretched, awful people," said Samadhi Jones, whom she would bear in 1967. Marsha's relationship with a black man had made them disown her. Ted himself remained a lost soul, clueless as to what to do next. "My father was the product of his environment and kind of bitter," explained Samadhi. "He could be rather not nice." And although Marsha had a job, Ted "didn't have a real good work ethic. He kind of floated on his allowances from his parents." The Joneses lived in a cheap apartment in Ted's old neighborhood, near L.A. High. According to some of his friends, drugs ran rampant at the Jones residence.

Terrie Burton, Ted's high school flame, lived around the corner. She'd married and become a teacher, but ill fortune had recently struck. On the already tragic day of November 22, Burton had returned home from the hospital, where she'd suffered a miscarriage. Approaching her house, she ran into the young man who'd broken her heart a few years before. Terrie hadn't seen Ted since that time, and she invited him in for a visit. "I asked him how he was, and he was spaced out," she recalled. Terrie was startled, and wondered how her razor-sharp beau could have taken such a downward turn.

Horne would blame much of it on Marsha, to whom she'd taken an instant dislike. Marsha, in turn, referred to Ted's mother as "Lena Horne." The star's disdain for the woman her son loved didn't help their relationship. All their separations of the past seemed almost impossible to bridge, and Horne grieved over what she felt she'd done wrong. Questioned in 1963 by interviewer Herbert Feinstein, she spoke about Ted as vaguely as ever. "He wants, I think, to be a writer," Horne offered. "I think he'll probably have a tough time becoming a good writer; but I hope he doesn't want to be a mediocre one. I don't know what to say. I admire him and I love him and I find that I'm friendly with him, which is a great deal." The fact that she would call being "friendly" with her son "a great deal" indicated what strangers they still were.

. . .

THE civil rights movement had begun to make a mark on the TV industry. Blacks were turning up not only as variety-show guests, but as characters in shows—and not just as household help. The 1963 season of the popular sitcom *The Dick Van Dyke Show* opened with an episode entitled "That's My Boy???" It found Van Dyke's character Rob Petrie in a lather, having decided his newborn son had somehow been switched at the hospital with another baby. He tracks down the couple who he thinks claimed his son; they turn out to be middle-class, attractive, and black. In 1965, two new shows, *I Spy* and *Hogan's Heroes,* premiered with black costars. The former starred Bill Cosby and Robert Culp as secret agents; in the latter, Ivan Dixon, an acclaimed film and stage actor, played the wisecracking Corporal Kinchloe, who worked in a German prisoner-of-war camp during World War II.

The networks weren't altruistic, of course; new statistics had revealed how many millions of Negroes owned TV sets, and advertisers knew that a lot of money could be made by pandering to a black audience. But a series with a nonstereotypical black female lead wouldn't appear until 1968, when Diahann Carroll starred as a nurse in *Julia.*

Horne could play endless guest spots, but she remained irritated that no network would give her a series. She'd turned down an offer to host a local New York nighttime show; she wanted national exposure. So desperate was she to win out that she offered to work for free as a summer replacement hostess on one series. The answer was no.

Ironically, Horne would later tell deejay Ray Otis that she didn't even like doing television; it made her nervous, she said, to have "this thing"—the camera—staring at her. When she saw the studio audience staring at her performance on the monitor above her head, "and I'm there not being looked at, I go berserk." She added that she had to drink two martinis before she could bear to watch herself on TV. "I get critical. I get nervous."

Nevertheless, she continued to accept invitations to guest on various variety shows. Horne spoke fondly of the nonchalant but superprofessional Perry Como, and made annual appearances on his *Kraft Music Hall* from 1962 through 1966. Her spots, which chart some of her darkest years of upheaval, document Horne at her angriest. Her eyes flash uncontrollably like those of a caged beast, her nostrils flare, her smile is so feral it seems almost sinister. Her growling sexuality veers on self-parody; so do her jerky, loose-limbed movements. Tender love songs like "I've Grown Accustomed to His Face" emerge steely and drained of romance.

Ultimately, those featured turns only served to remind her of what she'd been denied. "Why should I appear on other people's shows and wear out my material?" she asked a reporter. "If I'm going to do that, I'd rather have my own show."

Horne kept pressuring Ralph Harris to get her one, but every network said no, and he identified racism as the cause. Harris decided to pursue a special in England, where Horne was set to play a month at the London Palladium in the spring of 1964. He managed to work out a barter with Lew and Leslie Grade, two of Britain's best-known theater impresarios. They offered to supply shoestring funding for a Horne special if the singer would tour a string of English concert halls that they controlled. Horne accepted. Among other things, the trip would enable her to spend time with Gail, who had just found out she was pregnant.

Harris himself produced *Lena,* as the special was called. Produced for ATV, it was performed on an almost bare studio set, with Hayton playing piano and leading the orchestra of Horne's old drummer, Jack Parnell. James Mason, her friend since her first trip to England in 1947, appeared in a brief comedy spot; otherwise the show was an intimate survey of her career. Some of it was set in a simulated bar, with Horne and a trio in the middle of the floor. She recalled the Cotton Club with "I've Got the World on a String," saluted Billy Strayhorn with his famous torch song "I Got It Bad (and) That Ain't Good," and revisited her hit "Love Me or Leave Me." Maybe because her dream of a special had finally come true, albeit in a foreign country, Horne seemed uncommonly mellow, even pensive.

But discontent came through in a segment of her M-G-M songs. "I must have been in umpty-two thousand pictures in the forties," she explained. "And the one thing that I remember about them is that I was always posed very elegantly against a pillar or a column. Singing my heart out. 'Course, there were some great songs to sing, so it wasn't *all* bad." She skipped her civil rights numbers from *Here's Lena Now!,* offering instead a few quiet strains, a capella, of "This Little Light of Mine," the gospel number she'd sung at the Evers rally in Jackson, Mississippi. It led into "Come Sunday," a spiritual that Duke Ellington had written in 1943 for his *Black, Brown and Beige* suite.

Lena was aired to raves from the British press. Harris hoped this would help him sell the special to an American network, but none wanted it. "The advertising agencies responsible for the dearth of black performers during that long, dry period were both frightened and greedy," he explained. He had to settle for syndicated sales to local stations. U.S. critics praised the show unanimously. The *New York Herald Tribune* called Horne "someone TV could use more of"; other reviewers called *Lena* "spellbinding," "splendid," "magnificent." Horne knew she'd done well. "It was a damn good show, which made me anxious to do more." But for several years to come, only ATV would produce her.

Back home in the States, she began a month at the Cocoanut Grove on June 3, 1964. Harris told reporters that it would be her only American club engagement that year. Horne had instructed him once more to turn down all other requests, including Jack Entratter's at the Sands. "It's part of an overall aversion singer has developed of late toward nitery appearances," explained *Variety*. But the "aversion" seemed to go farther than that, involving a withdrawal from a scene she saw as frivolous and exclusionary.

For years Horne had shunned requests to write a new memoir. Columnist Art Buchwald asked her why, and reported her explanation: "because she hasn't lived a very interesting life." Certainly Horne felt weary and dissatisfied, and believed that little she'd done had made much of an impact. But ever since her article in *Show*, publishers had plied her with book offers. With more time on her hands than usual, she had a change of heart. In the fall of 1964, she phoned Richard Schickel to ask if he'd work with her on a memoir. He agreed at once. Doubleday would publish it. "We got very little money," he said, but generously, Horne offered him a fifty-fifty split.

For the next several months, Schickel sat with her in various locations—on West End Avenue, in London, in an apartment she'd rented to be near Ted in Los Angeles—and interviewed her on tape. He found her eager to talk and surprisingly candid. "A lot of stuff came out that she didn't want in the book," he said, "but she told it to me." Horne conveyed the off-the-record sense that her mother was "pretty monstrous" and that Louis Jones "was another leech. He was like the mother: They all came out of the woodwork and wanted a piece of her. And the official black community hovering over her shoulder, people like Walter White—*that* oppressed her. It came up a lot in our conversations. You can't get tipsy in public, and if you have a sex life that's slightly indiscreet, nobody could know this. You are our symbol. Boy, that rankled her!"

He began to realize why Horne would choose a white man as collaborator. "That was the enigmatic thing," he said. "Why wouldn't she go and get a black writer to do her book with her? Why would Ralph Harris be her manager? Why would she marry Lennie? Decent white people who would just accept her for what she was were terribly important to her. All these other people were hanging off of her with their agendas, which might be political, might be showbiz—whatever they were, they wanted something. Sure, Ralph got his percentage, but he was a good, decent man. And I was a good, decent man. I'd just listen to her and put down what she said."

Propriety, he found, meant everything to her. She forbade him to mention her affair with Joe Louis—particularly the day she'd strutted proudly in New York, wearing a mink coat he'd given her. Horne would never allow herself to be seen as a famous man's mistress. "You have to remember," said Schickel, "that Lena was born into privilege. She was a middle-class child, and there weren't that many of them. She was proud of that. Whatever she did in life, sexually or in other ways, she was always a member of the black middle class, and nothing would shake that. She was of the Hornes, and the Hornes were respectable people."

But when she invited him to accompany her to London for a return engagement at the Palladium, he saw a woman who was anything but genteel. "Her attitude onstage at that time was aggressive: 'Fuck you, here I am, I'm gonna sing, I don't give a shit if you like it or not.' It was that kind of angry, prowling performance. She was electrifying."

On November 18, 1964, Gail, who still lived in London, gave birth to her first child. Horne was there in the hospital. The birth, she recalled, was agonizingly drawn out, and threatened Gail's life. But soon Gail took home a healthy daughter, Amy Lumet. Horne was thrilled. She seemed to see the birth of her first grandchild as a chance to make up for her own failings as a mother. Later she told of sitting in the nursery of Gail and Sidney's house, staring down at little Amy and talking to her.

The glow remained as she returned to New York in time for Christmas. Horne told Joanne Stang of the *New York Times* that for the first time in her life she didn't feel alone. She recalled her wishful feeling of peace on November 18: "I suddenly had this feeling of *absolute* knowledge that everything was gonna be fine."

CHAPTER 15

IN 1964, more children entered Horne's family. Marsha Hamilton Jones gave birth to twins: William Augustus and Thomas Hamilton Jones. "One was beautiful pink and one was beautiful brown," said Claude Thompson.

Their parents hadn't married, and had no particular desire to. America's youth was in rebellion, and the couple were all for it—especially Ted, who yearned to wriggle free from the straitjacket of propriety into which he'd been born. But the sexual revolution was under way, challenging all ideas of traditional morality. Three years earlier, Helen Gurley Brown's bestselling book *Sex and the Single Girl* had challenged the "sinfulness" of premarital sex; now "free love" was a popular subject to debate and even more fun to practice.

But Horne did not condone Ted's situation. She could hardly boast to reporters about a son who was an unwed and largely unemployed father. Louis Jones disapproved just as strongly. "Grandfather told me they were living with him in L.A. at the time, and he insisted they should marry," said Samadhi Jones.

Ted's friend Daniel Johnson agreed. An established painter and sculptor, Daniel was happily married to Virginia Jaramillo, another artist, and they thrived as the parents of two. "That sort of inspired him," said Johnson.

Ted and Marsha planned a Las Vegas marriage, to take place on February 7, 1965. The date coincided with an engagement of Horne's at the Sands. The Johnsons had agreed to be witnesses. Daniel drove them all from L.A. to Vegas; Louis Jones spoken of having given him the gas money.

The soon-to-be newlyweds had evidently come to like the idea of marriage, and Daniel recalled the trip as a happy time. Once arrived, everyone checked into the Broken Arrow, a motel on the black side of town. Horne had bought it for her father, Ted, to manage. It was one of many gestures she'd made in her ongoing, but only partly successful, attempt to mend their years of estrangement. Then seventy-one, the elder Ted had long suffered from emphysema, but he remained a charmer. Around the pool, the youngsters lounged in the sun and listened to their host regale them with tales of a colorful past.

The two couples saw the Lena Horne show, but neither she nor her father attended the wedding. Soon the Joneses and the Johnsons were home in L.A., and all went on as before. Ted still saw little of his mother, who was spending much of her time in London. Her British career had grown; moreover, she missed her daughter and granddaughter. The singer told *Ebony* that Amy's birth had brought her and Gail closer. "Gail is very sympathetic toward me and my fumbling attempts at affection," explained Horne.

Although her family life had grown friendlier, her rage hadn't subsided. She continued to identify so profoundly with Malcolm X's militancy that she called him her "idol," and a "saint in the inspiration that he pushed out to us." By 1965, however, X had undergone a surprise turnaround. He'd spent several months in Africa, and there, he said, he "saw white students helping black people. Something like this kills a lot of argument. I did many things as a Muslim that I'm sorry for now. I was a zombie then, like all Muslims; I was hypnotized, pointed in a certain direction and told to march." Renouncing his longtime "sickness and madness," he now declared, "My mind is wide open to anybody who will help get the ape off our backs."

February 21, 1965, found Horne and Hayton at home, watching TV in the kitchen. She froze as the news broke—X had been shot at the Audubon Ballroom in Manhattan. He'd just begun addressing the crowd when a gun-toting man rushed forward, followed by two more. X took sixteen bullets and was dead upon arrival at Columbia Presbyterian Hospital. Three Nation of Islam members would be convicted of the crime, which X's "rebirth" had apparently provoked.

Horne burst into tears. But little sympathy came from Hayton, who like much of America had found X frighteningly extreme. In a seeming effort to comfort her, he said, "Those radicals, they're always killing each other off."

"Yes, but they're *my* radicals!" Horne sputtered. She stormed out of the room, fleeing from the man she'd gone to such lengths to marry. Again she contemplated with "revulsion" the life she'd chosen. Years later she recalled her turmoil to Rex Reed. "I tell you the truth, I had a nervous breakdown during that period and didn't even know it."

F O R all her mounting bitterness toward whites, Horne was leaning more and more on Ray Ellis. His frequent presence at 300 West End Avenue aroused the suspicions of her downstairs neighbor Harry Belafonte. "I used to come in there with her an awful lot," said Ellis, "and I'd bump into him in the elevator and he'd look at me like, 'What the hell are you doing here?'"

Eager to work more with Horne, Ellis had finessed a two-year deal for her at United Artists, a label founded by Max Youngstein, an executive at the film studio of the same name. Ellis decided to produce a live Horne album at the Sands, with Hayton conducting. Horne consented, and on the appointed night all the recording gear was in place. But she and Hayton were fighting, and Horne canceled the taping at the last minute.

Back in New York, she and Ellis made their first UA album. *Feelin' Good* gathered a batch of recent show tunes and easy-listening hits, such as the Beatles' "And I Love Him," its gender feminized. In one of the most agonized periods of her life, Horne sounded excited to be making music with Ellis, and the album earned strong reviews. The title song had especially struck her. Drawn from *The Roar of the Greasepaint—The Smell of the Crowd,* an imported British musical by Anthony Newley and Leslie Bricusse, "Feelin' Good" allied a Negro's social breakthroughs to the freedom felt by almost every animal in nature. In Ellis's slinky arrangement, Horne coolly proclaimed "a new dawn . . . a new day . . . a new life." Musically, at least, she seemed to believe it.

Working with Hayton had become an ordeal, but that summer she did so again when they met in England to tape her second ATV special,

Lena. They argued the whole time, and Horne returned eagerly to Ellis. In October they recorded *Lena in Hollywood*. It was a scrapbook of movie songs, but it served more as a portrait of Horne's madly shifting emotional state—jubilant, furious, forlorn, wickedly funny. "Never on Sunday," the plea of an overworked sex kitten, became a vehicle for self-parody. Horne prefaced it by purring: "For a whole lotta years I worked . . . seven shows a week . . . three and four shows a night and . . . I got a little tired. I think that *ev'reh*-body deserves at least one day a week off—even this lady!" The Jerome Kern–Leo Robin torch song "In Love in Vain" depicted a brokenhearted little girl lost; Horne's version found her piping mad at the fates that left you to "cry yo' eyes out/And wrack yo' brains!" In a rollicking swing arrangement of "Singin' in the Rain," complete with its rare verse, she exulted over the thrill of "living a life full of you."

Ellis recalled her drinking a lot during the sessions, which may have heightened her lack of inhibition. Because they were having such "a ball" in the studio, he said, he didn't realize how angry she really was. But he got a sense of it when he accompanied her to a civil rights–related symposium in New York, held before an audience. Horne sang briefly, backed by the orchestra of Eliot Lawrence. "Then she started to lecture, and I thought she was gonna start a riot," said Ellis. "She was putting down the black men in that audience, like, you better get off your ass and stop making excuses for everything."

In a 1965 appearance on TV's *Mike Douglas Show*, Horne talked frostily about the movement's efforts to narrow the gap between blacks and whites. "I don't think that we really need to love each other," she declared. "I find that hard sometimes. I would like to show more compassion and more love, but that's not necessary."

Horne knew she was starting to appear "more militant," and that it was making a lot of her old circle uncomfortable. Claude Thompson knew which people she meant. "Lena had always surrounded herself with piss-elegant white ladies. She said, 'They're my fan club.'" Arthur Laurents called them and their male counterparts "her slavies," adding, "Part of her liked it, and part of her did not." Some had watched her cast away Hayton; now they found themselves banished from her life.

"All of a sudden, Lena dropped everybody," said Geoffrey Holder. "It happened when black power came in, and she began to be the voice of her race." Horne began a process of publicly disowning her white past, particularly the phase set in 1940s Hollywood. "I had no social life with white persons," she told Joan Barthel of the *New York Times*. In her memoir *Natural Blonde*, Liz Smith recalled a splashy party that followed Horne's opening at the Fairmont Hotel in San Francisco. "I realized I was the only white person there," Smith wrote. "That night I knew what it was like to feel in the minority, and out of the mix."

The dissociation from Horne shocked many of those who had counted her as a friend. On first meeting, said Holder, Horne could seem so accessible and friendly that "you'd feel like, oh my God, she's my sister. Lena comes from a school of Hollywood. They are trained to smile. They never know what camera is gonna hit them." Then people found themselves banished from her life, without explanation. "We thought that Lennie was the heavy," recalled Holder, "but Lena was the heavy, you know what I mean? I'm not criticizing her for that. Everybody has to protect themselves. Many stars are basically shy. It comes across as aloof. The whole world is basically strangers to them, and they get invaded like gangbusters."

Smith eventually began to perceive Horne's turmoil. "We had extolled Lena for her great sex appeal, her divine gifts and her gorgeous glamour. We hadn't dealt with her as a black woman; we didn't want to, perhaps. We were simply thrilled to know such an international star, one who transcended her race. But Lena wanted us to love her *for* her down-home self, *and* for her race *and* to behave better toward her brothers and sisters instead of treating her always as 'special.'"

No amount of objectivity could lessen the sting of rejection. A number of pals, including St. Clair Pugh, blamed Jeanne Noble. "I didn't like her very much," he admitted. "Maybe I was just jealous. She didn't take to me—maybe because I was white. I think she was trying to help Lena get rid of her white friends."

The women's relationship had deepened, with Noble accompanying her famous friend to events and spending much time on West End Avenue. Horne, who yearned to be taken seriously as a conscientious black woman, let her determined new mentor guide the way. Unknown to the general public, Noble seemed intent upon remaking Horne as a mouthpiece for her own ideas. In 1966, *Ebony* published an article, "Three-Horned 'Dilemma' Facing Negro Women." The byline read "By

Lena Horne." But smaller type noted that Dr. Jeanne L. Noble had "collaborated" with her—an understatement, for the themes, research, and language were pure Jeanne Noble.

The scholarly treatise explored black women's problems on the job, at school, and in the voting booth. But it seemed to have a larger agenda—to redefine Horne as a powerfully committed woman focused on race issues, intent on "reaching into the slums" to help her poverty-ridden sisters. Horne defended herself against those who saw her as a spoiled celebrity trying to make amends. In the end, she was "still just another black woman who would be stopped at the next barrier created by white society." Photos of Horne at various rallies bore captions that declared her "prominence" at the March on Washington, and lauded "Lena the civil rights militant."

Noble helped further the rewriting of Horne's past by erasing the ambitiousness that had helped end the singer's first marriage. In politically careful phraseology, Horne explained, "I have come to believe my failure in my first marriage was not so much my inadequacy in the role of wife and mother, but rather that I did not possess the unusual resources and strengths needed to sustain a relationship fraught with pressures from a hostile society."

Like all their collaborations, the *Ebony* piece had enabled Noble to get to know Horne intimately—and perhaps to live vicariously through one of the most desired black beauties in America. Their closeness shone through in the largest photo that accompanied the spread. Taken in a Washington, D.C., hotel room, it showed them seated side by side on a single chair, both wearing sleeveless white summer dresses and beaming smiles. "She and Lena were joined at the hip," said a writer who knew them both. "I thought it was just a friendship. But I would hear people say they're really lovers." Claude Thompson believed it, and Tom Hatcher, Arthur Laurents's lover, referred to Noble later as "the woman she had a relationship with." Her sorority sisters, however, maintained a veil of secrecy whenever Horne and Noble were mentioned in the same breath.

Onstage, Horne controlled her persona as rigidly as ever. "The public profile of black female entertainers, especially Lena, involved great sex appeal," said Marcia Ann Gillespie. "And that meant heterosexual sex appeal. Lena was very frank about sex. She'd talk a lot about her affairs with men."

Yet behind the scenes, as Billie Allen noted, "There was a lot of sexual ambivalence about Lena." The same was true of a long line of Negro women of the stage—including Ma Rainey, Bessie Smith, Ethel Waters, Josephine Baker, and Billie Holiday—who had led bisexual lives. Over the years Horne was rumored, sometimes ludicrously, to have been involved with a stellar array of women, including Holiday, Ava Gardner, Kay Thompson, Marilyn Monroe, and Hattie McDaniel. In time, believed Gene Davis, Horne joined, at least temporarily, "a clandestine community of women who found safety with another woman. You turned to homosexuality as protection, not necessarily as a preference." Horne knew as well as any of her predecessors that show business was a "rough racket," run by men and rife with exploitation and abuse. In that milieu, she confessed, staying traditionally feminine was tough.

Whatever the nature of their relationship, there was no question that Jeanne Noble exerted considerable muscle over Lena Horne. Until the star pushed her away in the eighties, Noble affected much of what Horne said and did as the conscious black woman she hoped to be—or that Noble sought to make her.

DURING one of Horne's supper-club engagements in San Francisco, Herbert Feinstein interviewed her in her dressing room. Feinstein noted how far blacks had come since the days of Bessie Smith, the "Empress of the Blues," who had died in 1937. According to legend, Smith had perished after a white hospital refused to treat her following a car crash. Smith's biographer, Chris Albertson, later disproved the rumor, concluding that the singer had been hurt so badly that she had perished en route to a black hospital.

Horne responded to Feinstein's comment with sensitivity. "That's tragic because we lost a great figure," she answered, "but it's tragic if an ordinary Joe Smith Negro can't be admitted to a hospital, believe me. His family suffers just as much as we miss Bessie Smith. I no longer think in terms of artists, I'm sorry. I think that any one of those people that have been kneeling on the steps down in Albany, Georgia, is a towering figure. I haven't done that."

Neither had her daughter, who as Mrs. Sidney Lumet reveled in a life of luxury, untouched by the harsh realities of the sixties. As she wrote in *The Hornes,* "Somewhere people were protesting a war. Somewhere they were smoking marijuana cigarettes and wearing micro-minis." Gail, however, resided in an Upper East Side town house with a live-in staff of three; she and Lumet also had a home in East Hampton. Some of her time involved first-class travel through Europe and the United States as her husband directed films. At home, she wrote, "it was a 'tough' life— breakfast in bed and a car to take me to Bergdorf's. My greatest activity, besides shopping, was needlepoint. . . . I was a passionate dabbler—ballet, yoga, tennis, jogging, Transcendental Meditation, and Mind Control."

It was no wonder she felt so little connection with her brother, whom she depicted in *The Hornes* as a hippie kook. She called Ted "a very angry young black man indeed." Gail noted his "wire spectacles" and "faded safari jacket," and added that he was "bearded and gaunt and looked to me like a brown Prince Mishkin. . . . And whenever Teddy smoked marijuana cigarettes, I ran around the house cluck-clucking and raising windows."

Yet Ted lived by the hands-on principle her mother praised in her political idols. Ted's ambitions to enter law or politics were behind him; knowing, perhaps, that his kidneys would eventually fail him, he wanted to devote his life to work of purpose. In the heavily Hispanic, low-income neighborhoods of East Los Angeles, Ted gave free English lessons in storefront churches and community centers. The Watts riots concerned him. The first full-scale racial uprisings of the decade, they swept through that impoverished region of L.A. in August 1965. The catalyst was a young black man's arrest by a white cop for apparently driving while drunk. Hostile onlookers gathered at the scene, and when a second officer struck some of them with his nightstick, a volcano of pent-up rage exploded from a community that was sick of police brutality and racial oppression. Six days of looting, fires, and vandalism followed, aimed at white businesses and the police force. For the rest of the sixties, urban violence sprang up frequently.

Shortly after the riots, communitywide arts programs sought to empower Watts nonviolently. Ted helped set up the Mafundi Institute, a performance and educational center for artists, most of them black. It grew into a Watts landmark and gained nationwide support.

Proud as Ted was of these endeavors, they earned no money; for that he often relied on his mother, plus whatever Louis Jones could spare from his job as a postman. "Ted was not a good provider," recalled Samadhi Jones. "My mother had a job, but he lived off his allowances." On several occasions Marsha listened to Ted and his mother "fence verbally," as Samadhi put it. "She would question his ambition, what he intended to do with his life; he'd give her vague answers. I think there was a certain resentment he must have had."

When Horne came to their apartment to see her grandsons, she was "crushed," said Claude Thompson, "to see the condition of the place." Aside from the mess, the space was too small for four. Chico Hamilton's brother, actor Bernie Hamilton, owned several rental houses in Los Angeles, and Horne paid for her son and his family to move to one in Compton, a mostly black neighborhood. She also covered the costs of a washer, dryer, and milk and diaper delivery services.

Horne blamed Marsha for the disarray of Ted's life, but for his sake she tried to be helpful. One day Terrie Burton was shopping in the May Company, a department store in the nearby Crenshaw section. She spotted Horne and her daughter-in-law. "Lena was buying things for the twins. I said nothing, because I'd had enough of her by that time. But I stood long enough at a comfortable distance to hear the conversation they were having. She wasn't loving and kind. It was like she was a salesperson. And she had a fur on. I thought that was so out of place. She was wearing a fur in southern California in the department store?"

In her latest interviews, Horne called Ted a "potentially great man," involved in community service; sometimes she mentioned his sons, but never brought up Marsha. Much as she loved Ted, much about him still wasn't appropriate to the offspring of a symbol.

Gail, however, continued to perform that role impeccably. "She did all the right things," said Terrie Burton. "She married the right people." Horne boasted of her granddaughter, Amy, and spoke fondly of the celebrated son-in-law whom she'd fought to dissuade Gail from marrying.

Now Horne's own life—or a discreet version thereof—was about to become an open book. Her memoir *Lena* would reach bookstores in time for Christmas of 1965. Contemplating her past choices tended to depress Horne. Denial saw her through, as did deflecting the blame. Ray Ellis saw this when he dropped by her apartment just after she'd received advance copies of *Lena*. "She was sitting in her living room, and she was smashed," said Ellis. "I said, 'Jesus Christ, what the hell's wrong with you?'" Horne let loose with a string of attacks against Richard Schickel, whom she accused of changing some of what she'd told him. "She said, 'That son of a bitch!' She was ready to kill."

When Schickel heard about Horne's ire, he was mystified. "She had full control of the final manuscript," he said. "She read every word." The language and much of the content were no different from that of the book's blueprint, the *Show* article, of which Horne had seemed proud. After calming down, she admitted to reporter Mary Wilson that it had dismayed her to see her life laid out in a book. "The first time I read the whole thing through, I went into a hole for a week," she said.

Yet unlike her vulnerable first memoir, *Lena* held readers at a distance. Recalling painful episodes, such as the rejection she'd suffered on the road with Charlie Barnet, Horne adopted a tone of stifled indignation; she seemed more fearful and self-protective than ever. *In Person* had acknowledged the kindness of Barnet and other whites she'd known; *Lena* did not. Guarded as it was, the book had a theme of oppression—and her wrath blurred many facts. The man she had once called "my brother," but with whom she clashed constantly, received short shrift; Horne denied Harry Belafonte the credit for providing her with a New York apartment when no one else would. Instead she thanked José Iturbi, the Spanish conductor and pianist, who, she claimed, had given her his Manhattan lease to thank her for appearing in a benefit he organized. *Lena* made no secret of Horne's resentment of Harold Arlen and Yip Harburg, who had deceived her, she felt, by failing to deliver the role in *Jamaica* that they'd promised.

Most telling of all was her treatment of Lennie Hayton. She explored their wedding in detail, while depicting the marriage as a flourishing thing. Yet in a list of nine people to whom she dedicated the book—including "Kitty D'A." (D'Alessio), "Ginette S." (Spanier), "Robert M." (Mackintosh), and "Herbie B." (Baker, who wrote her sexy ditty "I Love to Love")—Hayton's name did not appear. Neither did those of her children or of the father she professed to adore.

Promotion for *Lena* included a party at the Waldorf and several TV appearances, including an interview on *Tonight*. Host Johnny Carson asked if she'd enjoyed creating her memoir. "No," admitted Horne. "It suddenly opened a can of peas I wished I hadn't." The book, she said, had created mostly strife. "Some of my family that didn't speak to me before are still not speaking to me, and all the friends I forgot to write about in the book have dropped me, and . . . it's a pretty lonely world, writing books."

Arthur Laurents raised an eyebrow at hers. "I thought it was a lot of baloney," he said. Publicity notwithstanding, *Lena* didn't sell much better than her albums. *Yes I Can*, a memoir by Sammy Davis, Jr., was published almost simultaneously and became a best-seller; *Lena*, said Schickel, "simply got blanketed."

Horne's collaborator went on to become a movie reviewer for *Time* and a renowned author on film, but his association with the singer went no further. The Waldorf party, he said, was "the last time I ever saw Lena Horne. I'd felt we were quite close. One might have expected the idle phone call, but no. Not even a Christmas card."

LENA had done little to clarify Horne's self-image. One of its final declarations—"Now I am free"—held an unintended irony, for in many ways she felt more trapped than ever. Near the end of the year she taped an episode of TV's *Bell Telephone Hour*, "Music in Manhattan." In a cast of ebullient Broadway singers (Gordon MacRae, Florence Henderson) and hale-and-hearty opera stars (Richard Tucker, Robert Merrill), Horne was a despondent presence. She'd never looked less alluring. Normally she struggled to keep her weight down, but now it had dropped too low, and her severe pageboy wig drew attention to her gaunt face.

Singing "On a Wonderful Day like Today," a jubilant showstopper from the Broadway hit *The Roar of the Greasepaint—The Smell of the Crowd*, Horne seemed mechanical and joyless; she frowned as she sang of feeling "so full of love and good will." Ray Ellis's strings enveloped her in "Moon River," Johnny Mercer and Henry Mancini's wistful Oscar winner. It told of a wanderer who sought "the same rainbow's end" to which the river itself seemed headed. But to Horne, "Moon River" was about peace unattainable. She shook her head sadly as she contemplated the road ahead. At the phrase "old dream maker, you heartbreaker," she flinched in pain. Watching Horne's performance forty years after it aired, Gene Davis remarked, "That is not a happy lady."

Jeanne Noble had tried to draw Horne more deeply into the work of Delta Sigma Theta, where Noble served as president until 1963. Now Noble was vice president of the National Council of Negro Women, and she persuaded Horne to spend part of 1966 touring the South as an NCNW spokesman. Appearing mostly at schools, Horne met numerous black, female civic groups. Their work fascinated her, she said—"much more than my so-called career."

But years later, Horne told Rex Reed that she had really undertaken those trips to try to reconnect with her childhood self—"to find if anybody knew me." She spoke of going in search of the older blacks who had taken her in, and the children who'd briefly become her friends. "Everything was like I had never left," she said. "It was a flashback."

Horne talked of standing in a drugstore in Georgia at night and feeling someone looking at her. It was a girl named Thelma, with whom she'd once lived in a rooming house. "I said, 'Thelma,' and she said, 'Lena,' and the tears came, and I was finding myself."

Again and again she told reporters that the "terrible coldness" inside her had "broken down"; that she'd finally begun "to let someone see inside me."

Musically, at least, she could express all she was feeling. Her first two albums for UA hadn't done well, though, and in March 1966 the label tried to up sales by presenting her in a style that was sweeping the charts. Arranged by Ray Ellis, *Soul* offered covers of such top-forty hits as "What the World Needs Now Is Love" and "A Taste of Honey," outfitted in the sounds of R&B—funky piano, tambourine, street-corner vocal harmonies. "It was not one of my better efforts," said Ellis, and on much of the album Horne sang like a sex-kitten spoof. At least she had fun. On "I'd Like to Hear It Sometime," she snapped her fingers to the beat as she hissed a demand for "a little affection . . . now and *then!*"

That summer Horne went back to London. There, she and Ellis cut a Christmas album, *Merry from Lena*. One might have expected her to put an edge on the music of the holidays. Instead she sounded wistful, and sometimes jolly. She swung her way through Ellis's bouncy arrangements of "Jingle Bells" and "Winter Wonderland" and began "Rudolph the

Red-Nosed Reindeer" with a monologue explaining that Rudolph "liked a little nip once in a *whaahle!*" Her tender reading of "White Christmas" gave no hint of the behind-the-scenes irreverence that attended its recording. During the first run-through, she stopped after singing the first line, "I'm dreaming of a white Christmas," and turned to Ellis. "I have to sing that, huh?" she said. Yes, he said, and the tape rolled. "Every time she sang 'white,'" said Ellis, "she'd look over at me and make a face."

Horne brought out the bittersweet side of Christmas as few singers had. Having known so many sad and lonely holidays as a child, she sang "Have Yourself a Merry Little Christmas" with the wistfulness of someone who wouldn't be having one herself. Her torchy version of a Frank Loesser ballad, "What Are You Doing New Year's Eve?," revealed a woman who couldn't imagine that the person she fancied would ever spend that evening with her.

She still dreamed of proving herself on Broadway in a real part, preferably one of racial significance. Some time back, Horne had asked Arthur Laurents to concoct something. He did. His idea involved a young black woman's journey through sixty years of the twentieth century, from plantation days through the civil rights movement. She would never age; the point was to show her evolution as a Negro through radically changing times. Horne's character, he decided, "would be kind of glitteringly angry and sexual, all the things she was at that time."

She responded excitedly. As for the score, Laurents suggested they aim for the top—Stephen Sondheim, Jule Styne's young lyricist on *Gypsy;* and Leonard Bernstein. In 1962, Horne and Sondheim had shared an evening at the apartment of Johnny and D. D. Ryan, a café-society couple. Sondheim took over the piano and sang songs he'd written for his forthcoming musical, *A Funny Thing Happened on the Way to the Forum.* Horne effused over every song, declaring that one of them, "Love Is in the Air," would make a great opener for her act.

She never sang it, and three years later she passed on Sondheim for Laurents's show. Instead she opted for Styne, Betty Comden, and Adolph Green, whose take on civil rights in "Now!" had once struck her as right on. Horne's rejection of *Two on the Aisle* had broken their hearts, and they were thrilled to have another chance to write for her. David Merrick agreed to produce; a respected director, Gene Saks, came aboard too.

By the end of 1965, Laurents had finished a draft of the book. Georgina, the Horne character, is a maid and aspiring singer determined to make it in the racist world of show business. Her mother, a beaten-down symbol of the old ways, tries to hold her back, telling her to stay in her place. But Georgina presses forward, seizing on the interest of a white theater producer and brushing off the black train porter, Clem, who loves her. By the fifties, Georgina is a star of the white supper clubs, but Clem challenges her for selling out. He prompts her to reexamine her role as a black woman, and by the show's end, Georgina has become a civil rights firebrand.

Laurents had clearly drawn on his insider's knowledge of Horne. According to Buster Davis, who was hired as musical director and vocal arranger, "Arthur wrote the book boldly and incisively, with no punches pulled." He sent Horne the script. And he waited. Weeks passed, and Horne would only respond evasively. "Arthur kept saying, 'She won't give me an answer, she won't give me an answer!'" recalled St. Clair Pugh. Claude Thompson imagined why: "That's just what the M-G-M executives used to do to her."

Jule Styne saw Ray Ellis as a voice of reason in her life, and the composer gave him a demo of the songs to play for Horne. Ellis brought it to her apartment, and they listened together.

Horne had expected the sizzle of "Now!", instead the score had the sunny exuberance of 1940s M-G-M. In Georgina's first solo, "My Own Morning," the young maid on a southern plantation pines for a better day: "I want a door that belongs to me / I want a bed that belongs to me . . ." The song could have been sung by June Allyson or Gloria DeHaven at the start of a Freed Unit film. In "When the Weather's Better," a cautiously hopeful Georgina voices her dream for a tolerant world. But the song's perky can-do optimism was as disconnected from the struggles of the day as Comden and Green were from Malcolm X. "Down the aisle / We're gonna go dressed in style!" they chirped on the demo as Styne played bouncy piano. Even the show's title—*Hallelujah, Baby!*—promised a whitewashed, old-school Broadway spectacular.

Ellis watched Horne grow livid as the tape kept playing. "She hated it. She said, 'He's gotta be kidding! I'm not gonna do that goddamned thing!'" She proceeded to tear Styne apart, calling him "a real cracker"—a southern term for a white bigot. And he hadn't even written the lyrics.

"Well, they want to know if you like it," said Ellis. "You better tell them."

"*You* tell them!" shouted Horne.

"I'm not gonna tell them!"

Ellis called Ralph Harris. "She's gonna back out of it," he said. "You better tell them." Harris dreaded breaking the news. According to Ellis, it leaked out in an unfortunate way. The arranger was sharing an office with Budd Granoff, who had produced *Here's Lena Now!* Ellis mentioned Horne's response to *Hallelujah, Baby!*, but made him promise to keep it secret. "So Buddy went to a party at Betty Comden's house and got drunk, and throws out a line like 'I don't think Lena's too happy with your score.' That's how it got out."

Her opinion of the book was harder to gauge, for she wouldn't give the author a straight answer. But Laurents again sensed the hand of Jeanne Noble, who found the show infuriating on principle. "There were a lot of black people who thought, what business do white people have in writing about blacks?" he recalled. In her 1978 book, *Beautiful, Also, Are the Souls of My Black Sisters*, Noble revealed a take-charge attitude toward Horne and her decision. "*Hallelujah, Baby!* was clearly not that relevant. In fact its story was too vague and the whole show was riddled with stereotypes. As much as she wanted to do a Broadway show, she was too committed to the black liberation movement to lend her name and talent to that one."

None of the show's team had realized it, but with the fight for black power at its violent peak, there would be "*enormous* resentment and resistance," as Laurents put it, in response to the old custom of white showpeople delineating the black experience. The fact that a few of them, like Harold Arlen, had done so to the enduring satisfaction of many blacks didn't seem to matter. But Laurents had a hard time accepting that; as a gay Jew, he considered himself "about as unprejudiced as a white American can be."

More time passed, as he and his colleagues waited desperately for a final answer from Horne. She kept delaying, and even Ralph Harris wasn't sure why. Was she reluctant to hurt her friends' feelings, or loath to let go of a dreamed-of Broadway lead, flawed though the vehicle was? Did it rankle her, as it had as far back as *St. Louis Woman,* to let black political forces steer her decision?

By January 1967, she could no longer evade the issue. Through Harris, she declined *Hallelujah, Baby!* "She gave one phony reason after another," said Laurents. The singer told him she needed an operation on her foot; she informed Styne's wife, Margaret, that she didn't want to do eight shows a week. "Then why did she get involved in the first place?" said Margaret. "It was just a polite excuse."

For years to come, Laurents insisted that Horne had "never read a word" or "heard a note" of the show, so fully was she under Noble's sway. Horne couldn't find the courage to call or see him to explain her choice, but finally, he said, "she wrote me a letter with the truth." Laurents would never divulge its full contents, but eventually he told author Jackson R. Bryer that Horne had decided that she shouldn't "do any musical written by whites." He did reveal the final line of her letter: "You know I love you."

"And I believe she meant it," he said. But their twenty-year friendship was over. Horne would tell Joan Barthel of the *Times* that she'd turned down the show because it was "old-fashioned" and "full of clichés"—the very criticisms she'd made of *St. Louis Woman* in 1945.

Her departure from the show caused it to nearly fall apart. Merrick had a change of heart; according to Margaret Styne, he decided that Laurents's book "was too radical." Both Merrick and Gene Saks "ran like thieves," said Laurents. Their exits left the show reeking of trouble, and financing proved hard to find. "Fortunately," explained Buster Davis, "whipping the bloodhounds on were that madcap trio, Betty, Adolph, and Jule." At the "sight of an open checkbook," he said, they unleashed their full schtick of "songs, funny sayings, and sunny smiles." On a CBS radio program, *The Lee Jordan Show,* Styne described the upcoming musical as a "charming comic fantasia." He and the lyricists gaily performed its songs, omitting any mention of the black theme.

Cast in the lead role was Leslie Uggams—a "beautiful star," exclaimed Green, "and boy, can she sing!" Then twenty-three, Uggams had made her name as a teenage regular on Mitch Miller's wholesome fireside TV series, *Sing Along with Mitch*. At six, she had played Ethel Waters's niece on *Beulah*. Laurents would call her "one of the loveliest people I've ever met in the theater," but "an innocent," far from his original concept of Georgina. "Well, it all had to be redone. And softened. I lost interest in it." So did Betty Comden. "There was no one like Lena; no one could replace her star quality. You don't just put another person in her place." Yet one had to wonder how Horne, who was almost fifty, would have been received in the role of a twenty-five-year-old.

The show had acquired two new producers, Al Selden and Hal James, and a director, Burt Shevelove. But many of the backers "were a little on the conservative side," said Davis, and Laurents's book fell prey to a new climate of extreme political sensitivity. In his biography *Jule*, Theodore Taylor described the "atmosphere of anger" that permeated the show from the first rehearsal. "The civil-rights movement shadowed the play," he explained, "and each line of 'black' dialogue was subjected to careful scrutiny."

Hallelujah, Baby! opened at the Martin Beck Theatre on April 26, 1967. In the *Times*, Walter Kerr called it "a course in Civics One when everyone in the world had already got to Civics Six." Reviewing a 2004 revival, critic Brad Hathaway explained that the original production "was seen as a slice of patronizing liberalism from its white authors." Laurents wished they'd abandoned it when Horne left. "The show was a turkey," he told Trey Graham of the *Times*. "I don't think it had much to say."

Nevertheless, it eked out a run of almost nine months. When it won Tony Awards for Best Musical and Best Score, Jule Styne—who had failed to win for *Bells Are Ringing*, *Gypsy*, and *Funny Girl*—seemed mystified. Clutching his gold statuette, he remarked wryly, "There comes a time when you say, 'We ought to be fair and give it to him this year.'" Uggams got her own Tony, which might well have gone to Horne had she stayed.

David Merrick would later offer Horne the lead in the long-running *Hello, Dolly!*—a role that had already been played by Carol Channing and Pearl Bailey. Horne was insulted, and grumbled to Marcia Ann Gillespie that she didn't want to "be in some warmed-over version" of an old warhorse.

· · ·

HORNE would never realize her hope of starring in a full-scale book musical; except for *Jamaica,* she walked away from every one offered her. Only on a stage by herself did she feel secure. Early in 1967, she taped her latest one-woman special in London. *A Very Special Lena* offered a survey of her nightclub and film material. The metallic harshness of her recent TV appearances had softened; now she seemed almost morose. Her occasional murmured comments sounded distant indeed; more than once she blanked out on the lyrics.

Starry-eyed ballads couldn't have seemed more frivolous to her then, for Billy Strayhorn was dying. Three years earlier, at the age of forty-eight, Strayhorn—a heavy smoker like Hayton—had learned he had esophageal cancer. Horne had been haunted ever since by the prospect of losing her soul mate. She saw him as the only person with whom she could drop every veil, who loved her no matter what, and from whom she could accept the truth.

Strayhorn's collaboration with Duke Ellington had dwindled, and although he'd undertaken some solo recording projects and kept writing songs, he had little public profile apart from his former boss. There was both safety and regret in living under Ellington's shadow. Now he had graver concerns. As his cancer advanced, he underwent a series of operations. According to his biographer David Hajdu, Horne was so busy with her career that she'd only been seeing him every few months. In the spring of 1967, Horne persuaded Strayhorn and his lover, Bill Grove, to leave their New York home and visit her in Palm Springs; there he could rest in the California sun. The singer sat by the pool with her weary friend who had trouble breathing and walking. Although Strayhorn didn't talk of death, he cried and vented for hours at a time.

Their reunion ended when Horne had to leave for Europe, and when Strayhorn decided he should attend to some business. "I think I'd better go back," he told Horne. Elois Davis drove him and Grove to the airport. Horne never saw Strayhorn again. "He went home and died," she said. It happened on May 31, 1967.

The loss of Strayhorn added one more cloud to an already darkened life. Horne's UA record deal was about to expire. "They were gonna drop

her because she sold almost nothing," said Ray Ellis. He hoped to move
her to Columbia, where he'd arranged many hit singles. But the label's
new president, Clive Davis, was too business-minded to sign a prestige
artist who didn't sell. "She got turned down all over the place after that,"
Ellis said.

To Horne, little security remained in the career that had been her
top priority since her teens. And the civil rights movement, which had
given her a fleeting sense of purpose, seemed to be crumbling before her
eyes. April 3, 1968, found Martin Luther King, Jr., in Memphis to speak
at a rally. King employed no bodyguard, even though he, like Medgar
Evers, lived under the constant fear of assassination. That day, a bomb
threat had delayed his flight. King checked into the Lorraine Motel.
The next day, at around 6:00 P.M., King stepped onto his second-floor
balcony. A bullet tore through his cheek and hit his spine. At 7:05, he
was pronounced dead. His convicted assassin was James Earl Ray, an
escaped convict. Many people, including King's family, doubted that Ray
had fired the fatal shot. Theories of a government conspiracy abounded
when it became known that the FBI hated King and had trailed him for
years—and that, on the day of the shooting, agents were observing him
from a hidden lookout.

The murder of this hero of nonviolent change sparked riots in over
a hundred cities. As little as Horne had agreed with his views, the assassination shook her deeply. More cynical than ever, she decided to attend
his funeral in Atlanta, to see if the sadness "would soften me up a little
bit," she said.

Horne sat among a packed congregation at the Ebenezer Baptist
Church, where King had been a pastor. Everyone heard the voice of King
in a recording of his last sermon there. Presciently, he had looked ahead
to his own funeral:

> I'd like someone to mention that day that Martin Luther King, Jr., tried
> to give his life serving others . . . I want you to be able to say that day
> that I did try to feed the hungry. I want you to be able to say that I did
> try in my life to clothe the naked . . . And I want you to say that I tried
> to love and serve humanity.

Afterward, Horne joined the three-and-a-half-mile procession to King's alma mater, Morehouse College. But she felt no easing of her rage. The prejudice she sometimes thought she'd lost came rushing back.

Speaking to an *Ebony* reporter, Horne railed against the "arrogance" of so many whites, whose money and privilege made them feel they could get away with anything. By now she'd more or less written the movement off. Horne felt as she had after *Jamaica*—that all the alleged progress had gone for naught. She'd begun to think that neither she nor her children would ever see much change.

It was a difficult time to look at the bright side, especially for a woman whose second nature was pessimism. Horne had diverged far from the thinking of her early mentor, Paul Robeson. After a long-time exile in Europe, Robeson had returned to the United States in 1963. He and his idealism had survived blacklisting, decades of FBI surveillance, violent demonstrations against his concerts, an eight-year revoking of his passport, and a 1961 suicide attempt. On April 22, 1965, shortly after his sixty-seventh birthday, the now-ailing Robeson attended a grand salute to himself at Manhattan's Hotel Americana. It was organized by Esther Jackson, the publisher of *Freedomways*. Ossie Davis, Ruby Dee, James Baldwin, and other luminaries saluted their idol, but the audience of two thousand saved their rapture for the guest of honor. In a closing speech, Robeson spoke inspiringly about "the remarkable progress of the freedom struggle here at home. . . . It is clear that the Negro people are claiming their rights and they are in every way determined to have those rights, and that nothing can turn us back!"

With growing fervor, he noted "the ever-increasing opportunities and widening horizons . . . for our artists in almost every aspect of the cultural life of our country." Now, he declared, "we must find and build a living connection, deeper and stronger, between the Negro people and the great mass of white Americans who are indeed our natural allies in the struggle for democracy."

But Horne could never embrace that spirit. Although she hoped that the movement had allied her with the larger black struggle, she still measured almost everything in terms of her private hurts and

frustrations. With her husband far away, his replacement white conductor became her substitute whipping post. Unlike Hayton, Ellis had
never shied from standing up to her, and their relationship had turned
combative. One night he came to her apartment to take her to dinner. Horne was dressing, and as he waited outside her bedroom he
heard her start to curse. She emerged, fuming, and he asked what was
wrong. She told him she'd just opened some mail from Los Angeles;
it included a bill for two suits that Hayton had charged to her. Ellis
couldn't sympathize. "I said, 'What the hell do you expect, he's working for you! He blew his whole career out there for you.' Which didn't
go over too well."

At the restaurant, her rage escalated. "She said, 'You white mother-
fuckers! I hate you whities!' Finally I said, 'For Christ's sake, if you hate
white people so much how come you married a white man?' She looked
at me with her beautiful brown eyes and she said real slowly, *To get even
with him!*'"

"I don't think it was true at the time," said Ellis, "but it sure turned
out that way."

In the coming months, Horne kept egging him on to blow up at her.
It seemed a passive-aggressive way of making Ellis so angry that he, not
she, would do the rejecting; the scenario replayed itself in many of her relationships. This one exploded by phone, when Horne was in California
and Ellis was in New York. The arranger had landed a lucrative deal for
a series of Campbell's Soup commercials. "She almost lost me the whole
damn account because of something she did," he said. "And she would
not admit she was wrong. I wasn't gonna let her get away with it. And we
had a screaming and yelling telephone call. I said, 'You know something?
When we first started to work together you said that if I ever got mad
at you, never to hit you in the face or to use the secret word. Well, you're
sure acting like one now!'

"She baited me into that. At that point I wanted to end the relationship, and I think she did too. And that was it. Five years."

They never spoke again. "It's funny," he said. "When it's over it's over,
and she won't even look at you." Ellis would continue to thrive as a composer and arranger for TV; eventually he retired on residuals from the
theme music he'd written for the *Today* show. Horne remained a bitter-

sweet memory for him. "Lena was one of the funniest women I've ever met in my life," he said in 2004, four years before his death. "She used to keep me in stitches. Plus, she was extremely bright and well read. She goes through the motions of caring about people tremendously, but except for her children, I don't think she ever really loved anybody. I don't think she was capable of it."

CHAPTER 16

HORNE NEEDED a new protector, and as soon as Ellis left she found one. In the decade since 1957, Sherman Sneed had worked for Harry Belafonte, first as a backup singer then as his assistant manager and press agent. Along the way, he'd maintained an occasional career as an ensemble member in shows. One of them was *Jamaica*. Belafonte still employed him; now Horne did, too, as a road manager.

Soon they became lovers, although Sneed had a wife and two children. "Lena told me she never had good sex until Sherman," said Elle Elliott. "And she was fifty years old." The lovers stayed discreet, but Horne couldn't hide the affair from several friends. "When I found out about it I was very upset," said Claude Thompson, who adored Lennie Hayton. "I felt that I was used at times." The dancer was Horne's frequent dinner companion; now he'd become a beard for two philanderers. "Lena and I would go to the Russian Tea Room, and who would show up but Sherman. All of a sudden we were a trio."

Whatever comfort she gained from the relationship was fleeting. On June 5, 1968, Robert F. Kennedy was shot; he died the next day. The assassination took place at the Ambassador Hotel, where Horne used to stay while performing at the Cocoanut Grove. Kennedy and Horne weren't friends, but since her first meeting with him she'd grown to respect his interest in black equality. The senator had just addressed a throng of supporters after winning the California primary for the Democratic presidential nomination. His assassin was a twenty-four-year-old Palestinian, Sirhan Sirhan, who later testified that he'd committed the crime "with twenty years of malice afore-thought."

After so many killings of political heroes whom she'd met or known, any gunshot-like sound terrified her. In September, Horne taped one of her five late-sixties appearances on *The Dean Martin Show*. She'd chosen to sing "Live for Life," the theme of a recent Oscar-winning French film. The song, by Francis Lai and Norman Gimbel, wed a fast-moving melody to a torrent of words about seizing the moment. Horne stood in a cagelike structure decorated with balloons. During the taping, the heat from the spotlights made them start popping. "I got hysterical," she recalled. "They had to take me out of there. It spoiled the whole gorgeous set. I just went to pieces. That must be a funny show."

Bing Crosby clearly wasn't amused by his encounter with Horne on her next Martin appearance, aired that November. Horne was no fan. It mystified her as to why so many musicians—including his early conductor Hayton—thought so highly of the legendary crooner, whose unflappably casual singing was the opposite of her fire-spitting approach. And as a die-hard Republican, Crosby repelled her politically. The Martin episode featured a long medley shared by Horne and the two men. They all sat elbow to elbow, but Horne snubbed Crosby on camera, turning her shoulder to him and focusing her attention on Martin. Crosby glared ahead, glum and pouting.

Her ability to freeze people into oblivion would never leave her. But no one, it seemed, suffered more from her hostility than Horne herself. Speaking to a reporter, she voiced a lingering desire: "God, please break down this terrible coldness within me." She saw cause for hope in the emergence of a singer who had so galvanized 1960s pop that she would soon be called the Queen of Soul.

For much of the decade, Aretha Franklin—the daughter of C. L. Franklin, a renowned Baptist minister in Detroit—had recorded R&B and pop-jazz albums for Columbia, with only modest success. Only in 1967, when a new contract with Atlantic allowed her to draw on her soul and gospel roots, did the moody artist burst through. That spring, she scored a number-one hit with "Respect," which became her signature song. Franklin's raw, melismatic flights were wrenched from a deep place; a traumatic childhood had taught her all about suffering. When Franklin cried out for a man to treat her right, she wailed with a roof-raising exultation that, to Horne, signaled the strength of a whole history of proud, invincible Negro women.

Horne never forgot the jolt of hearing her for the first time: "Oh, I cried! The first thing I thought was, how dare she be so free, and I'm not? I just saw her insides, her heart. I said, God, let me open myself up, because maybe that's there in me too."

She called Franklin her favorite singer, and raved about her to everyone. "I say, inside every black woman, there's an Aretha screaming to come out," she told poet Nikki Giovanni in a TV interview. In May of 1968, Horne eagerly accepted an invitation to an advance screening of the ABC News special *The Singers: Two Profiles*. The two were Franklin and Gloria Loring, "this girl I'd never heard of." A pretty blonde of twenty-one, Loring had sung at the Playboy Club in Miami, then made her film debut with a cameo in a rock-and-roll farce, *Once Upon a Coffee House*. ABC saw possibilities in Loring, who twelve years later would land a long-running part on the NBC soap opera *Days of Our Lives*.

Horne sat before a TV monitor with Ralph Harris and various executives. The first half of the show centered on Franklin, the second on Loring. Horne watched the latter with growing disgust. With Loring still on-screen, she leapt up and snarled, *"I think this is terrible!"*

The startled production staff asked her what she meant.

"I said, 'How *dare* you have this bland, long-haired, blond . . . *woman* who can't sing, on the same program, and on last, with Aretha Franklin, who is the world? A giant!' I was crying, I was screaming, and Ralph Harris was trying to quiet me. I said, 'I don't give a damn if they never put me on TV again! This is an insult! How dare they?' And he dragged me out."

Her anger obviously hadn't dimmed, but she was comforted to find that at last she was making a heartfelt connection with her son. Throughout their years of separation and conflict, none of Ted's friends could recall him speaking an ill word about her. "He wasn't that type of person," said Daniel Johnson. "What he didn't understand he didn't talk about."

But Ted's spirits were especially down. On December 7, 1966, Marsha had filed for divorce. He responded to the petition just as his mother once had to Louis Jones's—by ignoring it. The couple continued to live together, and in the winter of 1967, Marsha learned that she was pregnant. A question of paternity arose; some of Ted's friends reported that the father was, in fact, a friend of his. Soon after he learned the news, Ted moved out of the house.

That spring his L.A. High classmates held their tenth-anniversary reunion. None of them knew the whereabouts of their former student-body leader, who'd fallen out of touch with all of them. "No one could get ahold of Ted," said Francine Kahan. "Somehow I got a number." She told him about the reunion, but he resisted attending. Kahan had to nearly beg him to come. "I said, 'Teddy, we cannot have a reunion without you!'" Reluctantly, he consented.

Many members of that remarkable class had fulfilled their early promise. Nelson Atkins was a lawyer, Terrie Burton a teacher, Roland Jefferson a psychiatrist who, years later, would forge a second career as an author of thriller novels. On reunion day, the former students stood in groups, sporting their best suits and dresses. Ted was one of the last arrivals. He walked in wearing a beard and a dashiki, and seemed only semicoherent. "He wasn't the same guy," said Atkins. "He was a hippie type at that point. He looked pretty well gone."

One by one, alumni stepped to a microphone at the front of the room and spoke. Ted opted to do the same. "He was absolutely rambling," said Kahan. "I was so embarrassed for him, I wanted to crawl under the table. It was such a shock. He was wasted, just out of it." She flashed back to the teenage Ted in his three-piece suit, a debating champion with the best public-speaking skills in the school. "The kid had it all—leadership, brilliance, looks, polish, class. And he went down to the abyss. He felt worthless. He couldn't make it."

Ted's kidney problem had started to worsen. Scarred by sickness, drugs, and growing confusion, he'd begun trying to reach out to the woman from whom he felt so removed. Ted started writing letters to his mother. Each one, she said, brought her an "intense thrill." She found him telling her about events in his childhood that she knew nothing about. Horne spoke regretfully to *Ebony* about all the years he must have felt she didn't care about him. But finally, he knew she did.

On November 1, 1967, Marsha bore a daughter, Samadhi. Whatever her parentage, said Judy Davis, Ted "always accepted the child as his own. It didn't even bother him. Samadhi and the boys were always together;

they were raised like brother and sister." But Horne still despised Marsha, and refused to recognize Samadhi as a part of the family. "If there was anything that almost came between Teddy and Lena, it was that," remarked Davis.

Ted had moved in with another woman—this one black—named Faye. She bore his fourth child, a girl. He called her Lena. Within the family she became known as Little Lena. Ted had never answered Marsha's divorce filing, but in February 1968 the court made it official.

Horne's career at that point had gone somewhat fallow. That spring, however, she began a project that would keep her in L.A. and close to Ted for several weeks. She'd long ago lost hope of ever getting to act on film. But doors for black performers had continued to open in Hollywood, thanks in part to Sidney Poitier. After his lead performance in the 1963 movie *Lilies of the Field*, Poitier had become the first black to win an Academy Award as Best Actor. Dark-skinned as opposed to an "acceptable" café au lait and formidable in his strength, Poitier was an antistereotype whom not even Walter White could have anticipated. In 1967, the actor made three hit films—*Guess Who's Coming to Dinner, In the Heat of the Night*, and *To Sir, with Love*—whose success extended to the South. Finally, Hollywood knew that black stars could spell big box office.

Richard E. Lyons, a producer at Universal, sent Horne a script. His new movie, *Patch*, was a turn-of-the-century western about a stubborn, old-fashioned police marshal at odds with a town that wants him out. He wanted Horne to play the marshal's mistress, Claire Quintana, a local saloonkeeper and madam.

At first glance, the part might have seemed an affront to everything Horne had stood for in Hollywood—the black woman who wouldn't be anyone's whore, much less a white man's. Actually, though, Claire may have struck her as an appealingly rebellious choice of role. Horne liked the fact that Claire's brothel was integrated and that her race went unmentioned, even when she married Marshal Frank Patch. The idea of a white man who weds his black girlfriend interested her, too; not even her own marriage had disabused her of the belief that most white men would sleep with black women, but not marry them.

Still, Horne hesitated, as her insecurities about acting came rushing back. Richard Widmark, a respected actor and friend of Sidney Lumet, had agreed to play Patch, and flew to New York to boost her confidence. They read through the script together on her living room sofa. "Richard was a sensitive man, I think," recalled Horne. "He didn't frighten me." She tested his racial attitude in their conversation, and was relieved that he responded "in the correct way."

On May 10, 1968, the *New York Times* ran a small article headlined "Lena Horne Plans Return to Screen." *Patch* would be her first film in thirteen years, and her debut in a dramatic role. Horne enthused to Wayne Warga of the *Los Angeles Times* that finally she'd gotten the part of her dreams, and hoped she was up to the challenge. "I'm gonna learn if I can act," she told Sidney Skolsky. "And so is the audience."

Unfortunately, *Patch* didn't give her much to do except say a few lines and look beautiful; the part would rise or fall on the presence she brought to it. By June 4, when production began in southern California, Horne felt "scared to death," as she told everyone who interviewed her. "Sidney said to be simple, be still and don't act," she explained to Warga. "That sounds pretty easy, right? Well then, why am I pacing the floor at night and throwing up every morning? I can't stand it." Director Robert Totten "terrified" her, she told Skolsky, "because he was marvelous and fast and used to actors, not amateurs."

She ended up using a prolific film and TV actor, John Lehne, as her acting coach. "He is turning the disadvantage—my wall—to an advantage by finding use for it in the role," Horne explained.

The film starts with its denouement, as Claire, dressed for mourning, watches her new husband's coffin hoisted onto a train. She lifts her black veil, and her eyes—dark, heavy, and sad—promise an expressive performance.

Horne played Claire as a melancholy, distant creature, but for most of the film all she did was wander into and out of scenes, wearing bustled, lacy period gowns and speaking little. Only when Patch shoots a young man in self-defense does she have a chance to act; the killing occurs in their house, and Claire hides behind their bed, looking convincingly scared.

Retitled *Death of a Gunfighter,* the movie opened in May 1969, almost a year after filming. "It was distinctly a lesser work," said Richard Schickel, and the *New York Times* agreed. Horne, wrote critic

Howard Thompson, "has little to do beyond looking tense and sympathetic. . . . She does it well." *Gunfighter* ran in some theaters as the lower half of a double bill, then it disappeared quickly. Its main distinction had nothing to do with Lena Horne. During production, Widmark and Robert Totten clashed, and the actor insisted on a new director, Don Siegel. By the end of filming, Siegel was so embarrassed by the results that he asked to have his name removed from the credits. He was billed under the pseudonym of Alan Smithee—and for years to come, the Directors Guild of America would lend that name to any director who, like Siegel, was dissatisfied and demanded anonymity.

Years later, Horne watched *Gunfighter* on TV. "I wasn't that great," she said, "but it was intelligent, you know. I was treated well. And I've never forgotten Richard Widmark for that." Her "blue-eyed soul brother," as she liked to call him, was one white man who had gained her everlasting respect; it gave rise to a rumor, noted by the *New York Post* in 2002, that they'd had an affair.

One thing was sure: Horne's dream come true of an on-screen acting role had left her feeling mainly disappointed. It dredged up fears she thought she'd long conquered, and may have shown her that the world wasn't yearning to see Lena Horne act. Even before the cameras rolled, Horne had low expectations. She admitted to Ponchitta Pierce that sadness plagued her, and that anytime something went "half-well" she was surprised. For a long time she'd told herself it didn't matter when she died, because there wasn't much to live for. But now, she claimed, she was finally starting to feel some satisfaction. "I'm very happy, I guess."

Lennie Hayton might have said the same thing. Since Horne had sent him to Palm Springs, the conductor had pieced together a sketchy career of film and TV scoring; his contributions to *Star!*, a 1968 musical starring Julie Andrews, earned him an Oscar nomination. After *Star!* he'd graduated to a bigger plum, 20th Century Fox's adaptation of *Hello, Dolly!*, starring Barbra Streisand. Hayton found himself amid an M-G-M reunion: Gene Kelly directed, Roger Edens was associate producer, Michael Kidd the choreographer. Irene Sharaff, M-G-M's couturiere, did the costumes.

But Hayton's life in 1969 didn't quite recall the old days. For one thing, he and his wife were long apart. And even though Horne claimed to the press that they'd ironed out their troubles, she seemed perfectly happy for them to keep living on separate coasts. When she visited, she beheld a man quite unlike the one she'd met in 1943. A souvenir program for *Hello, Dolly!* showed Hayton in quasi-hippie garb, with love beads hanging over his white turtleneck. But at sixty-two he looked like a very old man, with a bush of pure white hair and reading glasses perched on his nose.

Horne, however, had remained as much of a vision as ever; to nearly everyone she was still, above all else, "the beautiful Lena Horne." Although she swore, for years to come, that she'd had no plastic surgery, photos of her throughout the years revealed a nose that looks ever more streamlined. She also had larger, rounder eyelids, the common result of a brow lift.

Her looks were still of crucial importance to her, yet she'd complained to Ray Ellis of feeling imprisoned by them. "She said to me one time, 'You know, everybody thinks I'm beautiful and sexy. I don't *wanna* be beautiful and sexy!'" When talk-show host Mike Douglas remarked on how beautiful she looked, the singer cracked, "I'm like that portrait of Dorian Gray. You know how lovely it was outside? You should see what's goin' on in here!"

Horne knew that her style of beauty had fallen somewhat out of favor. The phrase "black is beautiful" had entered the popular lexicon; it meant that, among socially conscious Negroes, glossy straight hair, thin lips, and fair skin were no longer necessarily the ideal. Jazz singer Abbey Lincoln had started her career in the midfifties as a Horne-imitating siren; now she and her husband, drummer Max Roach, had made civil rights the core of their music. Lincoln sported an Afro—a new in-look— and sang searingly about freedom. Miriam Makeba, a handsome singing star from South Africa, wore her brightly colored native clothes, including tall, majestic headdresses. Dashikis and African jewelry became fashion statements.

All of it spoke of a fiercely emerging black identity—something Horne had yet to find. But in the summer of 1969, she made an impressive public step in that direction. It happened on a milestone occasion in her life. On September 10, 1969, NBC broadcast the first U.S. network TV special of the fifty-two-year-old star's career. *Monsanto Night Presents Lena Horne* was the result of Ralph Harris's tireless, decadelong effort to get Horne what nearly every top-rank white singing star had already achieved. Pearl Bailey, Harry Belafonte, Bill Cosby, Barbara Mc-Nair, Duke Ellington, and Sammy Davis, Jr., had all headlined their own televised network hours; but except for Belafonte, who had starred in one back in 1960, those stars had waited almost as long as Horne. Wayne Warga asked her why the delay. "I don't know why, other than to say that you and I both know damn well why," she responded.

Conducted by Hayton, the special ushered Horne gracefully into an era of modern black music and fashion. She wore an Afro-like hairdo; in one scene, choreographed by Claude Thompson, she donned a fringe jacket and hoop earrings and did some tongue-in-cheek boogieing with six male dancers, all black. Joined by a Shirelles-style trio, the Honey-combs, she lit into the Blood, Sweat and Tears hit "You Made Me So Very Happy." In "Blackbird," by the Beatles, she prodded a broken-winged bird to seize its "moment to be free" and fly; Horne brought out the song's racial implications. For "Turning Point," a song recorded by Nina Simone, Horne turned herself into a first-grade white girl quietly asking her mother if she could bring home her new friend, a black schoolmate. Resignation, not anger, filled her eyes as she murmured, "Why not, oh why not? Oh . . . I see."

Her restraint suggested the emergence of a new Lena Horne. Hayton wrote an ethereal arrangement of "A Flower Is a Lovesome Thing," a Billy Strayhorn art song that rhapsodized about the wonders of nature: "azaleas drinking pale moonbeams, gardenias floating through daydreams." Horne sang it as delicately as though she were in a trance; her glance seemed to focus on some distant, imaginary garden. She and soul singer O. C. Smith embraced and locked eyes for a tender "Didn't We," Jimmy Webb's wistful look at two parted lovers who had "almost made the pieces fit."

A closing segment of her old nightclub material reignited her famil-iar fire, minus the hostility. Only Hayton's piano backed her on a slow, reconceived "Stormy Weather." Instead of shaking her fist at the injus-tices of fate, Horne seemed to look at the black clouds above her with helplessness and a tinge of fear.

She was proud of her *Monsanto Night*. "I had fun on that one," she said. In the next day's *New York Times*, Jack Gould announced that Horne had "conquered the lifetime of peculiar discrimination by American television." He noted her newfound restraint. "Last night her wattage was judiciously rationed so that it seemed the greater when it came to less frequency. A soft-spoken Lena Horne has all the charm of the more advertised bombshell."

Horne agreed. "I'm a better performer, since I'm more at ease," she told Kay Gardella of the *Daily News*. "I've got nothing to prove. People can take me as I am. I'm not trying to protect myself anymore." To Robert Higgins of *TV Guide*, Horne insisted, "*Now*, I can love people—openly."

That included Harry Belafonte. Their seesawing relationship was on the upswing, as they revealed on the *Tonight* show. Television's most popular late-night series used substitute hosts on nights when Johnny Carson was off; some of them, like Belafonte and Sammy Davis, Jr., were black—another sign of racial progress on TV. Belafonte invited Horne on as his guest. They fawned over each other: He exclaimed at her physical "exquisiteness at all times," even without makeup; she called him and fellow guest Bill Cosby her "wonderful little brothers."

She agreed to share a three-week run with Belafonte at Caesars Palace, the sprawling Las Vegas showroom, in September 1969. Horne had sworn off of Vegas and avoided singing there for over two years. But now the city was largely integrated, thanks largely to pressure from the NAACP and from Frank Sinatra, the Strip's biggest moneymaker. To choreograph their show, Horne brought in Claude Thompson, who had moved to L.A. to work in film and TV. During rehearsals, he sensed Belafonte's competitiveness, and Horne's resentment of it. "They weren't getting along too well," he said. The singers had chosen "The First Time Ever I Saw Your Face," a sensual ballad just recorded by Roberta Flack. Belafonte would enter, singing, from stage right; then Horne would do the same from the left. "They sang the song together," said Thompson, "but they stayed on opposite sides of the stage. I kept saying, 'This is ridiculous! This is a love song! Why don't you guys start coming together?' Usually the man would go to the lady. No! Harry was waiting for Lena to come to him."

Nevertheless, there was real chemistry between them onstage, and the engagement was a hit. It gave Belafonte the idea of producing a TV concert special for himself and Horne. This time they would put aside their club material; "both Harry and Lena feel they want to make a statement," said Chiz Schultz, the show's producer.

Harry & Lena was a nod to the consciousness of America's youth by two giants who, at forty-three and fifty-two, were old enough to be their parents.

An integrated audience of all ages surrounded the stars, who performed in the round on a multilevel stage. Belafonte shimmied into the audience again and again, even placing a young black boy on his knee; Horne, as always, kept her distance, yet showed the viewers a gentler side of herself than most of them had ever seen. Together the singers revealed such a loving rapport that one couldn't imagine they'd ever clashed. Spurring them on were the elegant pop-soul arrangements of Bob Freedman, Belafonte's white conductor and soon Horne's as well. Freedman had a distinguished history in big-band jazz, but could write in modern styles.

Most of the songwriters, too, were white. From Delaney and Bonnie Bramlett, a married duo who sang southern soul, Belafonte borrowed "Ghetto," a poor man's vow to move forward and "build the new Jerusalem." In David Ackles's "Subway to the Country," Belafonte became a struggling father who longs to show his children a brighter place than New York, where "there's so much dirt they think the snow is gray." Horne previewed a song from Judd Woldin and Robert Brittan's score for *Raisin,* a musical version of *A Raisin in the Sun* that wouldn't reach Broadway until 1973. "Measure the Valleys" found a mother commanding her daughter to show some compassion for human frailty, and to laud mankind for its slow social progress instead of scorning it for what remained undone. Horne's exultantly funky singing had all the optimism she couldn't muster in real life.

The show, in fact, had a notable absence of anger—a surprise, given its stars. And at a time when "soul" had already become a commercialized cliché, Belafonte and Horne exuded it in their spare, catlike movements, their effortless sexiness, their down-home street smarts and uptown polish. Jack Gould of the *New York Times* called *Harry & Lena* a "triumph . . . one of the most poignant, dignified, professional and touching presentations that the TV medium has known." Horne and

Belafonte, he wrote, had mastered "the precious art of subdued understatement, and the impact was shattering."

Off camera, Horne was involved in a battle so painful that, for the time being, it had ripped away most of her defenses. In the summer of 1969—near the time the first astronauts landed on the moon—Ted Jones's kidneys began to seriously fail. Although successful transplants were not unknown, the operation remained rare and highly risky, and donors were extremely scarce. Dialysis, too, was in its infancy. The cumbersome machinery existed in very few hospitals; waiting lists were long, and not all patients were eligible.

Ted was, but he could hardly handle the crisis financially or emotionally. "Against doctor's orders, he continued to lead a semi-high-speed life," remarked his sister, Gail, of whom he saw little. "He refused to stop trying to enjoy his youth."

Faye seemed powerless to help him; that left Horne—who felt racked with guilt over her son's condition—to somehow find an answer. Clamoring for advice, she called Ted's friend Daniel Johnson, who had survived the loss of a cancerous kidney in 1956. "She was going out of her mind," said Johnson. "Being famous doesn't mean anything when you're dealing with personal human emotions about your loved ones. She was just a very concerned mother." Because both of Ted's kidneys were bad, a transplant seemed the only lasting solution. Years later, a friend recalled that Horne had been ready to offer one of her own kidneys, but had learned that the match wasn't close enough. "I said to her, 'Of course not; the usual person they look at would be a sibling.' Lena said, 'Yeah, but Gail couldn't do that.' I said, 'Couldn't or wouldn't?' And she started to cry."

As she investigated a possible transplant from an outside donor, Horne's fame proved useful. "Lena really went out on a limb and used her influence, who she was, to get him high up on that list," said Judy Davis. A kidney did become available. "He was in kind of a get-ready situation at the hospital," recalled Clint Rosemond. "Then he looked around and saw all these guys who had operations, and they all looked like they had two weeks to live. He said, to hell with this. He bailed out."

The alternative was dialysis. It required an operation to implant a cow artery, called a shunt, in his arm. Several days a week, for four or more hours a day, Ted would have to sit in a hospital room with a thick needle inserted into the shunt; through it the toxins would be cleaned out of his blood. "We went to visit him in the hospital, and saw all the little children in that condition," said Kitty D'Alessio. "Their skin was so yellow. It was not a pleasant thing to see."

Ted agreed. Daniel Johnson came to visit him in the hospital. "Ted was lying in the bed with this cow artery in his arm. I remember he was looking at the machine. He said, 'Dan, do you believe this? The only way for me to live is to be attached to this machine.'" He balked so much at having to sit that way in a sterile hospital room that Horne bought him a dialysis unit, at great expense, to use at home. Ted's upkeep was proving highly costly. It was only a fraction of what she spent on family members over the years, which included helping support Ted's whole family, paying some of Hayton's expenses, and purchasing a motel for her father to run.

The singer was also known to give friends extravagant gifts from high-end retailers. Such generosity was a way, perhaps, for her to make up for what she deemed her failings as a mother, a daughter, a friend. But Ralph Harris told St. Clair Pugh that Horne had to net at least a million dollars a year to meet her expenses. She might not otherwise have chosen to do TV commercials for Schaefer Beer, Tang breakfast drink, and Skippy peanut butter. In 1969, she appeared in an ad for Blackglama minks as part of its "What Becomes a Legend Most?" photo series of fur-clad stars.

As if her son's situation weren't painful enough, Horne now had to watch her father fade before her eyes. He'd been diagnosed with emphysema in 1950; in recent years it had made him so weak and short of breath that he'd had to give up managing the Broken Arrow Motel. Horne had bought him a small house with a backyard in Arlington Heights, an upper-middle-class black neighborhood in L.A. She spent long stretches in the city to see him and her son; while there, she lived with her father for the first time since she was a toddler.

Their relationship remained puzzling. Horne had always spoken of her father as her great love, yet they'd stayed largely estranged. "We had drifted into that 'Horne silence' through the years and had not been really close for a long time," she explained, adding that "circumstances prevented" them from being together all those years. As a woman who constantly threw up walls to avoid getting hurt, Horne had experienced the same alienation with almost every member of her family. She told Jan Hodenfield of the *New York Post* that only in her father's decline did she find the courage to tell him she loved him. "I thought if I went to him he'd go away again." She was surprised to hear him say he'd always loved her, too.

Now he was dying, and as with her son she scrambled to make up for lost time. For moral support, she brought Claude Thompson with her to her father's house at 1200 South Arlington. Typically, the elder Ted sat in his bathrobe and stared at the TV, too sick to talk much. "That was the only time I ever saw a daughter attitude come out of her," said Thompson. "It was, 'Daddy this, Daddy that, what you want, Daddy?' She'd bring him his little tray of food."

Sometimes, to her delight, her son came, too. When Ted Horne had the strength, he talked at length with his grandson; Horne sat mostly quietly, learning things about them that she hadn't been around to see. She was thrilled to be with them, and crushed to know that these two men, nearly a half century apart in age, were both on the verge of leaving her.

At the start of April 1970, Horne made an emergency trip from New York to see her father, who had entered Burbank Community Hospital with pneumonia. The news overshadowed a joyful moment in Lennie Hayton's life. Some weeks earlier, he and film composer Lionel Newman had received an Oscar nomination for their work on *Hello, Dolly!* This was Hayton's sixth chance at the award; he'd won one in 1950 for *On the Town*. The ceremony would be held on April 7 in Los Angeles, but he wrote to the Academy to tell them he'd be unable to attend. Horne was in no mood to attend the Oscars, and Hayton didn't want to go without her.

The couple went to Elois Davis's to watch the telecast. All of them, plus Judy Davis, gathered on Elois's bed in front of the TV, while Hayton mixed martinis.

He and Newman were up against heavy hitters: Cy Coleman (for *Sweet Charity*), Nelson Riddle (for *Paint Your Wagon*), John Williams and Leslie Bricusse (for *Goodbye, Mr. Chips*), Albert Woodbury and Johnny

Green (for *They Shoot Horses, Don't They?*). Shani Wallis, a pert singing actress from London, presented the award. Hayton and Newman had won. Hayton, it was announced, had wanted to attend but couldn't. The Oscar was a crowning achievement of his forty-year career, but Horne's bitterness about Hollywood, and about her life, took over. Apparently she had no congratulations: She flung her glass at the TV; it hit the screen and shattered.

The next day she returned to the hospital, where her father lay dying. His lungs were filling with fluid; soon blood poisoning set in, along with hypoxia, a deprivation of oxygen. At 3:00 A.M. on April 18, 1970, Edwin F. Horne died. He was seventy-six. "The morning that my father died I sat there for a long while," she told the deejay Jonathan Schwartz. "I'd never been around someone dead. And I had this bliss. . . . Complete communication."

But the loss soon hit her. Claude Thompson accompanied Horne when she returned to the now-empty house on South Arlington. "We walked around the backyard and I hugged her and she was crying a little. . . . She couldn't believe it."

No sooner had she found the courage to reach out to her father than he'd gone away. The old sense of abandonment consumed her. Now she had to face her son's decline. After the reunion, Ted had again fallen out of touch with most of his classmates; Francine Kahan heard stories of him driving around Los Angeles in a broken-down Volkwagen, writing poetry. One day, Roland Jefferson pulled into a gas station. There was his old student-body president, the man they'd thought might even be the first black president, pumping gas. "He looked horrible. I hardly recognized him. But he recognized me. I'm sure he was embarrassed." After a few moments of strained conversation, Jefferson drove away. He never saw Ted Jones again.

At home, Ted spent five days a week hooked up, for hours at a time, to the dialysis machine purchased by his mother. He felt as shackled by it as she had by the imaginary pillar she had been "stuck" to at M-G-M. Horne, it seemed, was more desperate to keep him alive than he was to survive. Once while walking on the street, Ted went off his restricted diet and bought a slice of pizza. It made him pass out on the street and nearly die. "His attitude towards all that was happening to him was, *fuck this shit*!" said Daniel Johnson. "I would say to him, 'Hang in there.' I had felt the same thing after they'd given me five years to live in 1956."

But Ted wasn't encouraged. "I think he was looking to die as soon as he could," said Johnson, "because he was in a miserable state." Around that time, Ted dropped by Clint Rosemond's house to return all the books and records he'd borrowed but had been lazy about returning. "It didn't dawn on me then that this was classic presuicidal behavior," said Rosemond.

All his life, Ted had groped for a more meaningful existence than he found in the veneered, carefully controlled members of his family. He still hoped to do useful work while time remained. In 1970, he took a part-time job at KPFK-FM, a radio station located in Watts. A local branch of the Pacifica Radio public network, KPFK was a left-wing station devoted to free speech. Ted became involved in a program to train young blacks for radio positions. Despite Ted's frailty, Tom Reed, the station's director of training and production, found his leadership qualities undiminished; Ted, said Reed, was "an intelligent, outstanding writer, a progressive thinker, and very much into black art and culture."

But the thirty-year-old could scarcely enjoy any of it while chained to a life-supporting device. In August, Ted decided to stop dialysis. Horne, said Kitty D'Alessio, was "crushed," for without it Ted would not survive. He stopped seeing his doctor; instead he decided he would try holistic remedies. Marsha visited him often; she found him terrified of death but unwilling to go back on dialysis.

Late at night on September 12, 1970, Ted, at home, went into toxic shock. Almost at once, his body shut down. He was dead on arrival at Morningside Hospital. The main cause was uremia resulting from chronic renal failure. Horne, said Judy Davis, was "devastated." Louis Jones was angry. For the rest of his life, he would blame himself for having ever let his ex-wife move Ted from Los Angeles to Paris. The news of Ted's death spread quickly among his former school friends. "I cried so much when he died," said Terrie Burton. "I thought, what a waste!"

Most of his friends and family—but not his sister—attended the funeral, which took place at the Angelus Funeral Home in L.A.'s Crenshaw district. Judy Davis recalled the ceremony as full of people, and "very positive, calm, and philosophical." Clint Rosemond, who had done much of the planning, spoke of how Ted had spent his last years doing what he wished to do, helping the needy.

Marsha, the mother of Ted's children, never heard those words. She wasn't invited—"or even advised as to where the funeral would be," said Samadhi. "Her impression was that Lena did not want her there." Behind the scenes, Horne and Louis sparred as viciously over their son's funeral as they had over his custody. "He wanted to do this, and she didn't want him to do that, and it was crystal clear to me that Ted never had a chance with these people," said Rosemond. "For Christ's sake, come together where your children are concerned, even if you hate the hell out of each other. But they could never be adults where Teddy was concerned. They were always fighting."

Horne's guilt over her son's fate would never leave her. She made only rare public comments about him. In 1977, she told reporters Stephen Wilding and J. M. Weyburn, Jr., that she and her son had been "forcibly separated" early on. Yet it was her choice of showbiz over motherhood in the early forties that had cost Horne her son. "I think after all is said and done, Lena's career trumped everything," said Rosemond. "Some people stop their careers in the middle to raise families, and some people don't. Unfortunately, neither his mother nor Gail knew very much about him. They couldn't have. His formative years were spent with his father, and the rest of them with us here in L.A. His mother was just too involved in her career to be that much involved in the life of her son, who was at least three thousand miles away most of the time."

Horne performed little in the months after Ted's death. But on February 17, 1971, she joined her friend Alan King, the popular Jewish "rant" comic, on TV's *Kraft Music Hall.* "Alan King's Wonderful World of Aggravation," as the episode was called, contained one dark cloud, courtesy of Horne. She sang "To a Small Degree," a song from *Prettybelle,* a Jule Styne–Bob Merrill musical that had just opened and closed in Boston. Horne rarely chose a song that didn't somehow reflect her state of mind; this one evoked the unbridgeable distance between herself and the people who mattered to her the most. "I guess we loved . . . I think we did," it began.

• • •

LENNIE Hayton was now unemployed, and drinking to excess. His arteries had been hardening for years; doctors warned him off alcohol, cigarettes, and rich food, to no avail. Hayton had fallen out of touch with nearly everyone, and Skitch Henderson, like many others, wondered how he was: "None of us knew."

But Frank Sinatra had a house in Palm Springs as well, and he and Hayton revived a friendship that dated back to M-G-M. Sinatra worried about the conductor's sagging spirits, which he blamed on Horne. Whenever possible, Sinatra took him out to dinner. Often, though, Hayton sat in restaurants alone. One night he spotted Eileen Barton, a perky singer who had performed with Sinatra in the forties, then scored one of the biggest hits of the next decade with "If I Knew You Were Comin' I'd've Baked a Cake." Hayton practically begged her to have dinner with him. She agreed. "All he talked about was Lena," said Barton. "He adored her, he adored every ounce of her." At home, he wrote her long letters, telling her how much he missed her and needed her. But her visits were infrequent. "I never heard her say anything about Lennie that sounded at all sentimental," said Bob Freedman, who saw her use Hayton's *On the Town* Oscar as a doorstop.

On April 21, 1971, Sinatra and Hayton met at Ruby's Dunes, a restaurant in Palm Springs. They moved on to a gathering at the singer's house. Around 4:00 A.M., the phone rang in Horne's apartment. She picked up to hear Sinatra at the other end. He told her that her husband had suffered a heart attack and had been placed in the intensive-care unit of Desert Hospital. Hayton would probably require surgery, and they needed her permission. She consented, but Sinatra wasn't through. He insisted she fly the next day to Los Angeles, where his private jet would take her to Palm Springs. From there she would be rushed to Hayton's side. Fred Walker, who coproduced Horne's one-woman Broadway show of 1981, heard more about that call. "Sinatra said, you better get your ass on that plane. She wasn't gonna go."

Horne phoned her daughter and son-in-law, who were then in New York. They booked her a flight for the next day. By nighttime she was at Desert Hospital. A barely conscious Hayton lay in IC, hooked to tubes. His aorta had ruptured, and several arteries to his heart were blocked.

April 23, 1971, was his last full day with Horne. Dawn had just broken the next morning when he died at age sixty-three.

A modest funeral was held at the Hollywood Cemetery Chapel. Later, while talking to St. Clair Pugh, Horne angrily blamed her husband's demise on Sinatra, for giving him cognac against doctor's orders. But Claude Thompson found her "kind of calm," perhaps numb. "All the men in my life left me," she said. "I was surprised, and yet I wasn't."

At first, it was easiest for Horne to blame some cruel master plan. "I'm very fatalistic," she explained. "I believe in fate. And this powerful person who decides just the way your life is going to go." But after the losses of 1970 and 1971, she found safe harbor in the emotions she knew best. "I was furious. I was hurt. I was angry. And I was dead, too."

CHAPTER 17

"**ALAN, WE'VE** got to do something about Mother."

That was Gail Lumet's plea to Alan King in the days after Hayton's death. King had grown close to Horne in the sixties, and in his autobiography, *Name-Dropping: The Life and Lies of Alan King*, he writes that Gail had called to say that her mother had fallen into a deep funk. Horne recalled that time in *Family Circle*: "I couldn't get out of bed, couldn't work, didn't want to come out of my cave." She saw no hope: "Why am I here? I have no interests, really." King knew how to make her laugh with his cranky Borscht Belt–style quips, but even he couldn't cheer her up now. Whenever he phoned to check up on her, she brushed him off. King persisted, and Horne agreed to see him.

As she sat numbly on her living room sofa, he told her she couldn't do nothing forever. "You're too young, you're too great!" He was about to open at the Westbury Music Fair, a concert hall in the round located in Westbury, Long Island. King insisted she share the bill. "Are you crazy?" she snapped. "I can't work! Don't give me that old crap about work will ease your pain!" Anyway, she said, "Who wants to see an old broad like me anymore?" She couldn't be swayed, and finally King left.

The next day Ralph Harris called him. "I don't know what you did," he said, "but Lena says she's going into Westbury with you." They would open a two-week run on May 17, 1971. It hadn't taken her long to bounce back; Hayton had died just three weeks earlier. But that short stretch of inactivity was enough to make her feel that without work, she had nothing.

Horne and King proved a winning combination, and they toured together sporadically for more than a year. The comic was anti-chic; onstage he vented his irritation with airlines, insurance companies, and other foes of the hapless common man. Horne seemed uncommonly pensive. She and King performed separate sets, then came together to sing a medley of standards; by his side she became lighthearted and playful.

For years, Horne had told reporters of how one trauma or another—the Luau confrontation; the deaths of Medgar Evers, Malcolm X, Martin Luther King, Jr., Robert Kennedy—had opened her up and helped her connect with audiences, family, friends. But in the seventies, much of her "letting people in" consisted of ruminating to strangers who came to interview her, and who exited her life once the questions were asked. "I never really understood why they thought I was glamorous," Horne told Mary Campbell of the Associated Press. "I used to read that about myself, knowing what I was really like, and laugh." But her treatment of Lennie Hayton was no joke, and she brought it up apologetically to reporter after reporter. Wracked with guilt, she told *Sepia*'s Shirley Norman of how she'd failed him. "I guess I was not a very loving or open person," admitted the singer. "I didn't learn it in my family." Horne recalled Hayton's endless patience. No matter how she tested him, he wouldn't leave until she forced him. To Alan Ebert, a white journalist who profiled her for *Essence,* Horne was especially candid. "I owe Lennie a great deal. Wishes are only that, wishes, but I wish I had been less cruel to him—more able to separate the man from his color. He had such warmth, and when I allowed myself, I felt it."

Ebert had interviewed the singer a decade earlier for the NBC radio series *Monitor,* and she liked him so much that a picture taken at the time showed her beaming in his direction. She'd forgotten this by 1973, when she went to his apartment to answer questions for *Essence.* "No white man can ever understand a black woman or the black experience!" she declared.

"Then teach me."

As he questioned her calmly, the hostility faded. "I saw a Lena I had never seen on stage or television—warm, loving," Ebert explained. "She not only answered my questions but posed some of her own. She insisted I think. She demanded I walk a mile in her shoes back in the thirties, forties, fifties, and sixties when blacks, even the celebrated Lena Horne, took a lotta crap from white America. She took me under her wing and educated me, a white, middle-class Jewish young man from Brooklyn, on what it was like to be Lena Horne way back when."

The Horne of the seventies, however, seemed to be clutching for purpose. "I am determined to make a life for myself—other than just being another lonely woman singing her life away to strangers," she said. Horne mentioned that she'd been thinking a lot about an alternative path—possibly as a teacher, at least as a college graduate. "I mean, that has to be laughs for someone who has been so anti-intellectual all her life; who can barely spell and who isn't too together with higher mathematics," she said.

Before Ebert left, Horne invited him to come to the Lumet town house the next day and meet her granddaughters Jenny and Amy, who seemed so free of the defensiveness she'd inherited from Cora. "She taught me wrong," concluded Horne. "People can be strong *and* loving . . . strong *and* affectionate. I never knew that till Lennie."

Since 1967, Sherman Sneed had worked as Horne's part-time roadie. Harry Belafonte, who employed him for similar tasks, wasn't pleased. Sneed had a drinking problem that tested everyone's patience; in 1971 the two men came to blows in Las Vegas and never spoke again. Horne took him on full time. He relieved Ralph Harris of many mundane tasks and, once he conquered his alcoholism, proved himself an able frontman and troubleshooter. Sneed went to Horne's venues early to check up on details; his job also required constant soothing of a star who called herself "a real Cancer—sometimes sunshine, most times storm."

While she envied Sneed's parenting skills—"She said once, 'Your father has done such a great job with you, I wish I could send my grandkids over there,'" recalled his daughter, Sherri—Horne treated him as her property, and kept his family at bay. Sherri and her brother, Gregory, called Belafonte "Uncle Harry," "whereas Lena was pretty much 'I don't want to be bothered with the wife, I don't want to be bothered with the kids.'" Their mother, Frieda, was an independent spirit, but to have Horne on the scene, monopolizing her husband and acting as though she didn't exist, wasn't easy. Yet Sneed was under Horne's spell and catered to her dutifully.

Horne's relationship with her own family was still shaky. She'd traded her apartment on West End Avenue for one at 21 East Ninetieth Street, around the corner from Gail and Sidney. She talked of making regular trips there to watch TV with little Amy and Jenny. "They don't hate me," said Horne in amazement to a reporter. But she felt removed from them due to her fame. "My Jenny, when she was four or five years old, said to me, 'Are you Lena Horne?' I said, 'No, who said so? I'm your grandmother, don't you forget it.' They heard that I was Lena Horne from Michael Jackson, 'cause he used to go up in their room and sing to them and act like a child with them, and play with their toys with them, and they just adored him. And Michael Jackson told them that their grandmother was famous."

It had taken a long time for her to come to accept Sidney Lumet as her son-in-law. But as she told reporter Margaret McManus, "I respect a man who is decent to a woman, and he makes Gail very happy. . . . He's a good guy, very wise, and he works. . . . I respect people who work. We get along fine." Yet the strain had never quite left her relationship with Gail. If Ted had proven too sensitive to survive, his sister still led a quite insulated life. In April 1971, Judy Klemesrud, a *New York Times* reporter, noticed the contrasts between mother and daughter when she interviewed them for a feature, "On Reverse Sides of Generation Gap?"

As Mrs. Sidney Lumet, Gail occupied a four-story town house; Horne, who'd never cared for ostentation, had a small apartment. The two women sat together in the Lumet parlor. Klemesrud noted that they "somehow dress their parts." Gail wore "a prim white turtleneck and Gucci shoes"; her mother opted for mod bell-bottom pants and boots. Lena's hair was teased out to resemble an Afro, while Gail kept hers "longish" and "in a straight style." Gail seemed indifferent to almost every social concern of the day and confessed she didn't do enough reading or speaking out. "I have never experienced any overt indignities," she explained, while adding that she couldn't care less about women's lib. Her typical day, she explained, began by walking Jenny to the costly and exclusive Dalton School. Then she took an exercise class and shopped at Bendel's.

Her mother remained anything but complacent. To her the civil rights movement had been a bust, and in a repeat of 1959—when she had felt responsible for *Jamaica*'s failure to revolutionize black show business—Horne felt as though her activism hadn't meant a thing. "I can't bear to face my six grandchildren whenever I think about how little progress we've made," she told Klemesrud. "I get so impatient . . . I want liberation *now!*"

In place of the staunch black commitment she once knew, Horne saw mostly apathy. "Black symbols—who needs 'em?" she told another reporter, Mary Wilson. "Young black people don't require them anymore. What the hell, let's face it—unless someone comes along like Malcolm X or Martin Luther King, that leadership is gone."

Certainly she felt she'd long outlived her own usefulness in that regard. Her stardom, too, had dimmed; Diana Ross, Roberta Flack, and Gladys Knight were the black female idols of current pop, while Horne had become a venerated but hardly newsworthy elder statesman. "I'm sort of dwindling down; I don't work nearly as much as I used to," she admitted. To R. Couri Hay of *Interview*, she termed herself "an old lady who is still doing a little bit of show business."

Much of it was on television, the medium she professed to hate. In the first half of the seventies, Horne appeared four times on *The Flip Wilson Show*, the NBC series whose impish star had become America's favorite black comic. Wilson had reached that peak after years of club work and *Tonight Show* appearances. The country's racial climate had relaxed enough for him to have some nonoffensive fun with stereotypes. Wilson portrayed the money-laundering Reverend Leroy, the pimplike Freddy the Playboy, and the White House janitor Sonny, and made them all human and likable. His crowning alter ego was Geraldine, a wisecracking, take-charge "sister" decked out in a miniskirt, huge false eyelashes, and sleek flip hairdo. Swinging a handbag, Geraldine proclaimed, "When you're hot, you're hot!"

Singing or acting in sketches, Horne seemed more relaxed with Wilson than she ever had on TV. He gave her big bear hugs on camera, and her face lit up. She had the same affection for Redd Foxx, the bawdy, grizzled comic who starred as junk dealer Fred Sanford on *Sanford & Son*, another ratings smash. In January 1973, came Foxx's dream episode, "A Visit from Lena Horne," in which Sanford successfully schemes to get the star to come to his house. Foxx told the *Los Angeles Times* that he'd "been waiting for thirty years" to work with Horne. "I told the boys, don't just count on what the eyeballs see—she runs deep inside, that woman. And she speaks out."

Elle Elliott had gotten a taste of that when she joined Horne as traveling stylist in 1972. A Latin American from Los Angeles, Elliott had worked for years with the film star Jennifer Jones, but Horne checked for more than experience when she screened the young woman. "What do you think about the Chinese?" she asked.

"The Chinese?"

"Yes, do you think they all look alike?"

"Sort of," said Elliott.

"And what do you think about black people? Do you think *they* all look alike?"

"No, not at all."

"OK," said Horne. "That means you're not prejudiced against blacks but you are prejudiced against the Chinese." Horne grilled her with humor, but Elliott got the point. "Her thing was, if you felt that if members of a race all looked alike then you weren't viewing them as individuals." Starting with a Caesars Palace engagement, Elliott did Horne's stage makeup and hair on and off until the late seventies.

In that time, she marveled at how little deception was needed to create the Lena Horne that audiences saw. Horne worked hard to fight the ravages of time; she did floor exercises each morning, went on long walks, slept eight hours a night, and had cut back her drinking (at least on workdays) to a postshow vodka and orange juice. She needed no slimming undergarments, although she did wear two pairs of pantyhose under her stage garb—"so I don't jiggle too much when I'm shakin'," she told Elliott.

For now, Horne had cast aside wigs in favor of her natural hair, which was curly, mostly gray, and dyed dark brown. Elliott set it in rollers, then combed it out. Everyone chalked up her smooth, taut skin to cosmetic surgery; for some time Horne had noticed people staring at the perimeter of her face, trying to detect lifting. But Elliott saw no signs of it. "It's very difficult for black people to have plastic surgery because they keloid," she said, using a term that refers to a raised scar that results from a cut.

Offstage, said Elliott, Horne dressed stylishly—"either in black or beige, with some beautiful scarf, maybe by Hermès." But her stage clothes had changed drastically. The days were over when Horne had stood behind a stationary microphone, encased in gowns so tight she could hardly walk in them. Now handheld mikes were the norm, and as she roamed around while singing she needed outfits that wouldn't confine her.

Most of them were made by Giorgio Sant'Angelo, a flamboyant Italian designer whom David Colman of *New York* magazine called "a supernova of the seventies fashion world." Cher and Bianca Jagger loved his wildly flashy prints, fringe, and flowing, asymmetrical cuts, but for Horne he tailored a more classic look. Her friend Kitty D'Alessio, by then the president of Chanel's American branch, considered those dresses works of art.

"Giorgio had a way of mixing two colors together that shouldn't have gone together but did, brilliantly," D'Alessio said. "Maybe purple with green, or pink with a flash of khaki. The shape was always something Lena knew how to work—huge kimono sleeves or a jacket with an uneven end. The length was always long, to give a graceful line. It was all modern, and very different from those highly constructed things she wore in the movies."

Sant'Angelo's clothes helped Horne feel more at home in the 1970s, but her self-makeover didn't end there. By now she'd shed what a *Stereo Review* critic had called "her highly lacquered approach to popular song." The young singers she admired, notably Aretha Franklin and Roberta Flack, had a directness that to Horne constituted real soul, and she yearned to share it. The sophisticated standards she'd sung all her life now struck her as "uptight" and "unreal."

More young musicians admired her than she realized and happily took Horne under their wings. For some years, the star of her ensembles was Gabor Szabo, an expatriate guitarist from Budapest. She'd first laid eyes on him in the Chico Hamilton Quintet, which had backed her at London's Talk of the Town nightclub. He was dark-haired and broodingly intense, but played with a spare, silky touch, flavored by gypsy folk music. Szabo dazzled Horne. "He plays *fantastic* guitar," she told John Gruen. "Very *down,* very soulful guitar." From then on she hired him whenever possible; on many a TV show, Szabo sat by her side as she sang. "She was kind of in love with him," said his friend Ann Ruckert, a studio and jingle singer.

Szabo had cofounded his own record label, Skye, in 1967; three years later he immortalized his partnership with Horne in the album *Lena and Gabor*. A lightly funky nod to the songs of the day, it featured three in-demand session musicians—keyboard player Richard Tee, electric bassist Chuck Rainey, and drummer Grady Tate. They laid down an R&B groove, and Horne and Szabo explored ten recent tunes that had enough depth for her to sing them convincingly. They included the Beatles' "Something" and "In My Life," Michel Legrand's "Watch What Happens," and "Everybody's Talkin'," the Harry Nilsson hit from *Midnight Cowboy*.

After all her years of singing with orchestras of bountiful lushness, Horne loved Szabo's minimalist playing, and the spacious charts of acclaimed jazz arranger Gary McFarland made Horne feel unleashed. The affectations of her Waldorf singing would have seemed ludicrous here; instead she indulged in a dash of Harlem street-corner diction and sounded nothing but authentic. "That's the way I sing now," she told Gruen. "You're just used to hearing that airy-fairy Lena. I have grown; I sing young people's songs. I don't want to be around anyone older than me no more."

Lena and Gabor won raves, but her partnership with Szabo petered out by the midseventies, as he sank into the heroin habit that eventually killed him. A year after their album was released, Horne collaborated with another troubled young titan. Soul singer Donny Hathaway would jump to his death from a New York hotel window in 1979; he left behind many hits, notably "Where Is the Love?," a duet with Roberta Flack. Hathaway idolized Horne, and in 1971 he played piano on and helped arrange her pop-rock album *Nature's Baby*. The producer, Alfred V. Brown, cradled Horne in a huge ensemble, complete with strings, star jazz musicians, and a gospel-like vocal trio. "I was completely intimidated," said Horne.

The fare included hits by Elton John, Paul McCartney, and Leon Russell. But the piece that touched her most was "Bein' Green," drawn from the children's TV series *Sesame Street*. It was an outcast's reflection, written by Joe Raposo for Kermit the Frog. But Horne saw it as a racial metaphor, and delivered it with the patient warmth of a woman preparing her black grandchild for the world. With Richard Tee playing the sparest chords, Horne talk-sang about lives lived in the shadows, beset by self-doubt. Green, however, was "the color of spring" and held all the majesty of a mountain or a tree. Her conclusion: "I'm green, and it'll do fine! It's . . . *beautiful*!"

"Once in a while," Horne said later, "I'd think, yes—I know what I'm singing about."

In *High Fidelity*, Morgan Ames wrote of *Nature's Baby*: "Miss Horne is not trying to be a kid. She is simply responding to the musical seventies with fresh, open ears. . . . Lena Horne likes the kids and learns from them."

Nature's Baby made Horne "excited for a minute," as she put it, over the potential of this new Lena. "She did *not* want to be perceived as a nostalgia act," said her conductor Bob Freedman. But in her eagerness to break with the past, Horne faced a problem known to many of her peers. Their audiences were older, and generally hostile to pop-rock. After seeing her at London's Grosvenor House, critic James Green complained that she "indulges herself over-long with today's contemporary sounds . . . and too late, almost apologetically, tosses in past favourites like 'Stormy Weather.'"

Many promoters doubted her solo drawing power. For much of the seventies, she shared double bills with Danny Thomas (the star of TV's *Make Room for Daddy*), Billy Eckstine, and Vic Damone. From 1973 through 1975, Horne's main cohort was Tony Bennett. A former singing waiter from Astoria, Queens, Bennett had risen so high in the pop pantheon that he'd made Frank Sinatra nervous. But unlike Sinatra, Bennett hadn't a whiff of bad-boy surliness. He sang with a smile, flinging out his arms as though ready to hug the whole audience. His grainy tenor came straight from the heart, and he let no private angst cloud it.

But Bennett's career was far from its peak. His last hits, notably "I Left My Heart in San Francisco," had happened a decade before, and in 1972 his longtime label, Columbia, let him go. The sight of him grinning and singing Cole Porter, while wearing a tuxedo and an unflattering toupee, marked him as kitsch; offstage he faced a crumbling second marriage. A cocaine habit compounded his troubles. "That was a tough period for me, very tough," he recalled.

Bennett had taken to self-producing; inspired by his appearance with Horne on a Burt Bacharach TV show, he organized a duo tour. *Tony & Lena Sing* drew strongly. After several U.S. dates and a British special, the show headed for Broadway's Minskoff Theater, where it opened a four-week run on October 30, 1974.

In a musical era that had made Horne and Bennett's middle-age fans feel cast aside, the concert ushered them back to what seemed like the ultimate in class. This was no rote survey of the stars' hits; instead the show focused on the cream of the Great American Songbook, from Arlen to Bacharach. The singers barely spoke, save for a few words at the end: "Good night, Lena" . . . "Good night, Tony."

Critics saw a Horne they'd seldom experienced. "Gone was the cold, hard, professional, stylized, mannered, taut and tense singer of sophistication," wrote Jan Hodenfield. "Lena Horne was absolutely joyful, that non-refrigerated smile given way to exultation." The singer mesmerized Bennett. "I found myself watching her performance every night. I couldn't believe her consistency. To be able to stand next to her and watch her wonderful instincts on stage—she was riveting."

Few viewers, it seemed, noticed her subtle detachment from her co-star. During a long Arlen medley, Bennett gazed at her in awe; Horne fixed her glance carefully in the distance. Offstage, she wasn't overly friendly. "We were just respectful of one another, and it stayed like that," explained Bennett.

At the opening-night party at Sardi's, columnist Earl Wilson asked Horne about rumors of tension between her and her costar. Horne denied them. "Tony looks out for me like he really cares about me being happy," she said. But privately, she didn't hide her annoyance at her second-place billing, and at the fact that she opened the show for Bennett. Some of Horne's black friends, especially Jeanne Noble, were incensed, and chalked up the matter to racism.

The real cause was much simpler. "I put the show together," said Bennett. "The whole package and the expenses came out of me. Usually in the past if I worked with Count Basie or Duke Ellington, I put their names on top of mine, because I felt it would be incorrect for me not to play second fiddle. But that didn't happen with Lena. I realized the situation, but we never spoke about it."

Newsweek did. "Tony Bennett, 48, and Lena Horne, 57, are on Broadway together, sharing the billing and the plaudits—though not quite equally. His name came first on the marquee, in the playbill and in every press-release mention, but she won better notices from the critics." Wrote one of them: "Tony Bennett found himself in an all but impossible situation. He had to follow Lena Horne." Another praised Horne as "a genuine superstar" while terming Bennett "almost an afterthought." One writer who took the opposite side was Nat Hentoff, veteran jazz critic of *The Village Voice*. He praised Bennett's utter sincerity—"I've seldom seen anyone who so enjoys being a performer"—while damning Horne as artificial. He found her phrasing "exaggerated," her rhythm unswinging. "The stage Lena Horne needs to keep pushing her singing to help her voice impersonate buoyancy and passion." Where, he wondered, was the real Lena Horne?

The singer herself seemed as unclear about that as ever. The show proceeded to Toronto, and Nancy Collins of *Women's Wear Daily* came backstage at intermission to interview her. Greeting Collins was yet another "new" Horne, a self-consciously salty mama, seemingly bent upon tearing down the regal persona she'd just displayed. Opening the dressing-room door in a huge Turkish towel, the star announced, "Honey, I don't know why you want to talk to an old black broad like me, but come on in."

From there Horne dismissed her hard-earned "dignified" reputation. She should probably have become a "whore," she said; at least then she wouldn't have had to answer to anyone. Asked if she would ever remarry, however, Horne sighed; she'd always preferred older men, but they tended to want women much younger than she. She wouldn't mind "a young cat, but I'm very hip that a lot of that kind of attraction might be because he wants a little money or something, which is fine, as long as it's all right out there."

Clearly Horne had felt trapped in her overriding image as a lady. But she had to maintain it in the tightly directed *Tony & Lena*. Years later, Horne told Jonathan Schwartz about "this feeling" that struck her during certain performances, when she truly felt the magic happening. She could only remember it occurring during a performance once, with Tony Bennett at the Minskoff.

Bennett, whose enthusiasm for his audiences kept them packing his shows even when he'd passed eighty, couldn't understand Horne's pessimism. "If you're doing well, count your blessings!" he said in 2005. "This business of artists who are unhappy with their lives—it's just incorrect. If you get a break and connect with the public, what is the problem? Anger doesn't work; love is the only thing that works. And when you can arrive at that genuinely, and you learn forgiveness in the proper way, you have a more content life. The other way you're just hurting yourself."

Horne couldn't shake the sense that the world was out to get her. But after all the praise she'd earned for her newfound air of serenity, she wasn't about to admit discontent. She told Mary Campbell she'd never been happier. "I don't think I'm bitter, not even frustrated."

Elle Elliott did see her at her most carefree. In dressing rooms, the two women and Audrey Whitmore, Horne's dresser, laughed and clowned like old girlfriends. The star teased Elliott about Alan King— "Look, he's flirting with you again, what are you gonna do about it?"— and shared laughs at Johnny Mathis's expense. "He would walk through the door all starry-eyed, holding his umbrella sideways, and it would get caught in the door," recalled Elliott. Horne would smirk and whisper, "Now watch, he's gonna trip over that umbrella!"

Chatting backstage with celebrities and fans, the singer acted quite charming. But when *California Living* magazine interviewed her via questionnaire, Horne filled in the blank after "The worst part of my job" with the answer "Being nice to people offstage." Once the room had cleared, Elliott would hear her uncensored comments. "Did you hear what she said? That fat slob with the gray hair just told me that when she was a child she would listen to me sing! She has her nerve!"

In 1974, her friend Hugh Downs, former host of the *Today* show, had fought to help Horne attain her long-standing dream of her own talk show. *TV Guide* and other publications announced the imminent premiere of *Lena Horne's Grapevine,* to be produced by Downs. Targeted to a black female audience, the show found a sponsor, and many local markets expressed interest. But no station in the essential city of New

York signed on, and *Lena Horne's Grapevine* never premiered. "TV is a cold part of the business," said the star to reporter Gene Arceri.

To Horne, her beloved hometown had become just as unfriendly. Ten days before Christmas, her apartment was robbed. She reported the loss of over fifty thousand dollars' worth of jewelry, some of which had come from her father. This was the second theft she'd suffered. By the end of 1974, she decided she'd "had it with Manhattan."

The city still teemed with reminders of Hayton and his loving gestures. "I think now I'm having a delayed reaction to his death," she told *W*. "I'm more discombobulated now than I was when he died." Horne recalled a night in 1951 when he'd escorted her to a showing of M-G-M's newly released *An American in Paris*. Afterward they stopped by the Plaza, then rode through Central Park in a hansom cab as she held a bouquet of violets he'd given her. "I don't do that kind of stuff no more," said the singer.

One day in 1974, she rode in a car headed through Montecito, an upscale town near the California city of Santa Barbara. Horne spied a "real storybook house" two blocks from the Pacific Ocean and surrounded by trees. The three-story home had once served as an olive mill—hence the name of the street, Olive Mill Lane. In the distance were the Santa Ynez mountains. All seemed quiet.

In a "weak moment," Horne decided to buy the house, and in 1975 she traded New York for Montecito. "I was making some sort of gesture of good-bye," she recalled. "I had literally given up all my club dates. I was quitting." She'd made an isolating move. Other than her old pal Suzy Parker, the 1950s-era supermodel who lived in the area, and Parker's husband, actor Bradford Dillman, Horne had few friends in Santa Barbara.

For weeks and even months at a time she stayed home, reading murder mysteries and autobiographies. Family members and New York friends flew out to visit her; Sherman Sneed was often there to drive her around and do errands. At other times, Horne had only nature to keep her company. Outside her windows were woodpeckers, bees, and a tiny hooting owl. At night, the air turned chilly and fog rolled in from the ocean; the waves, she said, sounded like "soft voices."

The solitude fostered her depression, and when Stephen Wilding and J. M. Weyburn, Jr., reporters for *Black Star* magazine, came to interview her, Horne couldn't hide it. It was "silly" of her, she said, to have planted fifty trees on her property; she wouldn't live to see them grow. Her locale, she confessed, was making her lonely. "There are certain things that I just don't enjoy doing alone—like listening to music, or even seeing a pretty dog. I kinda want to nudge somebody and say, 'Hey, isn't that terrific?' but often there isn't anybody there."

She hastened to add that everything was all right. "I'm comfortable with myself," she said.

CHAPTER 18

HORNE'S LAST record, *Nature's Baby*, had sold little, and once more she gave up hope of ever having a successful album. But eminent musicians and producers still yearned to record with her. One of them was Michel Legrand, the brashly versatile jazz pianist, arranger, and film composer. Legrand was riding high on a string of hit movie songs, including "What Are You Doing the Rest of Your Life?" and "Pieces of Dreams," but he still had his idols, including Horne. In 1972, she had appeared on *The Michel Legrand Special*, a TV showcase for the Frenchman's talents. With Legrand at the piano, she'd sung a heartrending version of "I Will Wait for You," a song he'd composed for the movie *The Umbrellas of Cherbourg*.

Now he was a partner in Gryphon, a fledgling production company for jazz LPs, most of which appeared on Horne's old label, RCA. After seeing her in concert, he approached the singer about making an album with him. "She said, 'I don't believe in musicians, because every time a musician comes to me and asks me to make an album, it never happens.' I said, 'Miss Horne, it *will* happen.'

"'No, I don't believe you.'"

In February of 1975, Horne joined Legrand and an all-star group of young jazz men at RCA Studios in New York. This was no rehashing of standards; Legrand took her far from her supper-club image and thrust her into an of-the-moment funk-jazz setting. The players—including keyboardist Richard Tee, Ron Carter on electric bass, guitarist Joe Beck, and trumpeter Thad Jones—had accompanied almost every jazz and

R&B heavyweight in the business. The Howard Roberts Chorale added a lusty gospel sound to several tracks.

Legrand and his partners, Norman Schwartz and Nat Shapiro, gave her a repertoire of mostly new songs, half of them Legrand's, which Horne described as "hell to sing, but wonderful." They pulled her out of her recent malaise—and with so many masters in the band to spur her on, Horne pounced on every lyric as though it were a statement she'd been dying to make. She sang of her losses, her joys, and her quest for identity, and embraced them all victoriously.

Lena & Michel opened with "I Will Wait for You," whose words, by Norman Gimbel, expressed unshakable loyalty to an absent lover. The song's tenderness had vanished; now when she vowed to wait "a thousand summers," it sounded like a threat to anyone who might dare leave her. This was rage undisguised as feisty sex appeal; at last Horne was unafraid to sing the whole truth. Her guard was down, whether she sang of her solitary state in a song by Paul Williams and Kenny Ascher ("Loneliness takes the romance out of falling stars/Fills the wishing wells and fills the bars") or envisioned a blissful state of belonging in Bob Freedman's "Thank You Love."

That October, Peter Reilly of *Stereo Review* placed *Lena & Michel* among the best albums of the month—this despite the fact that the old "you have to see her" argument hadn't died. "Another has it that she may be a great and neglected stylist, but that just about everyone copied her unique phrasing and tigerish delivery for so long that it became impossible to appreciate the lustrous original, obscured as she was by garish imitations."

Hoping for big sales, RCA pressed far too many copies. The album apparently scared off Horne's mature fans, while failing to attract younger ones. *Lena & Michel* wound up by the boxload in cutout bins, selling for $1.99. It lost money for Gryphon Productions, but Legrand had no regrets. "It was beautiful to record with her," he said.

His colleagues at Gryphon weren't through with Horne. The spring of 1976 found her at the Olympia studios in London, where she made what some fans thought her greatest record, *Lena, A New Album*. If the Legrand album had seemed offputtingly modern, this one was as classic and extravagant as a Tiffany brooch. A collection of mostly famous ballads, it featured Phil Woods, a revered alto saxophonist, and the most sumptuous orchestra ever to back Horne. The arranger was Robert Farnon, a Canadian maestro who had spun ethereal settings for Frank Sinatra, Sarah Vaughan, and Tony Bennett. Farnon had long lived in England, and in the fifties the airwaves there were filled with his semi-classical "light music."

But lightness wasn't Horne's forte. A year after the fury of *Lena & Michel*, she now sounded so vulnerable it was hard to believe she'd ever been "packed in ice," as she liked to say. "I was going through a very interesting personal crisis then," said Horne later, without elaboration. "Strange things happened in my life, and I guess some of it comes out."

Gryphon president Norman Schwartz had coaxed a huge budget from RCA; it encompassed not just the production costs but apartments for the visiting participants, limousines, and a more than generous cut for himself. "Norman didn't mess around with cheap albums," said Phil Woods. "This way he could steal more, because he was a crook. It didn't end well between him and any of his clients, and I was one of them. But he made some great records."

In his liner notes, Ralph Harris explained that he'd given Horne a list of twenty songs, drawn from the nearly thirty years he'd managed her. Fearlessly, Horne chose some of the most oversung standards, then delved into them so incisively she made them her own. "My Funny Valentine" was a pledge of unconditional love to a plain-looking lover; Horne sang it with a defenselessness she'd seldom allowed herself in her personal life. Her final "Stay, little valentine, stay!" was the cry of a woman who couldn't face another desertion.

She took the reverse role in "Softly, as I Leave You," a ballad that had haunted her since the sixties, when she had recorded it with Ray Ellis. It depicts a woman who gazes at her sleeping lover before she heads into the dawn, never to return. Farnon's strings evoked an early-morning stillness; Horne's focus was so hypnotic that one could picture the bedroom and the head on the pillow. "It's a scene," she explained. "It's my set, and I see all these things happening in my head."

Other tracks, including a languidly sexy "I've Got the World on a String"—a song she'd chirped vacantly at the Cotton Club—teamed her with Phil Woods. "He had a lot of nice rawness," said Horne. "I was, like, on two sides. One side, I'd sing softly, then I'd get around him and I'd feel freer."

Woods sensed a rare synchronicity among the participants. "The musicians were all smiling," he said, "playing Robert Farnon's music." Horne, he added, "was shy, quiet, all pro. The personification of musicianship. Knew exactly what she was doing and what she wanted. Very attentive to the conductor's needs. Very kind to a saxophone player who was trying to find the holes." The singer was just as taken with Gordon Beck, the British keyboard player who added discreet fills on electric piano. "He raves about that session to this day," said Woods in 2005.

As an opulent finishing touch, Norman Schwartz engaged Richard Avedon, a giant among portrait and fashion photographers, to take the cover picture. Horne wore a Giorgio Sant'Angelo black silk dress whose jagged hem billowed out as though windblown. Having long hidden her legs, she made a brave statement by revealing one of them, in black mesh, up to the hip.

Even that photo, and the excitement implicit in the title *Lena, A New Album*, couldn't gain the record much attention. Reviews were few, and with disco now the rage, an LP of Horne singing standards was not perceived as news. It lost much of RCA's investment. But Horne, who took so little pride in her achievements, still felt proud of both her Gryphon albums, made when she was near sixty. "I guess I'm a late bloomer," she said.

In the fall of 1976, she appeared on the eleventh episode of *The Muppet Show*. She brought a song from *Lena & Michel*: "I Got a Name," a posthumous hit for singer-songwriter Jim Croce, who'd died three years earlier in a plane crash. Written by Charles Fox and Norman Gimbel, it told of finding an inner core as solid as anything in nature. Wearing a denim jacket with huge sleeves, Horne sang while surrounded by Muppets at a train station. She cut through the playfulness and turned that song into an anthem of black strength. With no less conviction than Martin Luther King, Jr., she told of having "a dream . . . and it's gonna make me free." In an oddly touching show of unity, she grabbed a Muppet dog and proclaimed, "If you're going my way, I'll go with you!" Later she explained, "I sang that song about my father."

Years after his death, Teddy Horne remained her fantasy hero—the gutsy free spirit who'd always known what he wanted. But just the thought of her mother could send her spirits plunging or make her see red. "Lena never talked much about Edna," said Claude Thompson, "but when she did it was usually with an expletive."

Edna's husband, Mike, had died years before; now she, too, was in declining health, and lived alone in an apartment in Brooklyn's Flatbush section. Lena paid most of her expenses, but visited as seldom as possible; Sherman Sneed, who had a home nearby, checked up on her regularly. When she did see Lena, Edna invariably groused about her daughter's "bad" career choices and personal flaws. "I did as well as I could, but she was a little unrealistic," said Horne to a reporter.

No amount of financial generosity could buy from Edna what Horne wanted the most. In 1973, she'd told Alan Ebert: "I always wanted my mama to love me . . . still do. Can you imagine? Fifty-five years old and still wanting to know that feeling before I die."

By the autumn of 1976, Edna was dying, and Horne knew it was her last chance to get some answers. "I had to confront my mother," she told journalist Marie Brenner. "I went to see her and I said, 'Mommy, do you love me?' and she said, 'No.' I just broke down. 'Lena, I wanted a career,' she told me. 'I wanted what you have. I wanted to be glamorous. To be famous.' I asked her, 'Why did you have me?' and she said, 'I only married your father because he was the best-looking guy in our set. We wanted a boy and we got you and you got my career.' 'Mommy,' I told her, 'I didn't want the career. I never wanted to be a singer. I only wanted you to love me. I would give you every bit of it if I could, if only I thought you cared about me.' My mother looked at me and said, 'It's over now, Lena. Just forget about it.'"

That October, Edna lay in a hospital bed. Horne came and found her mother uncommonly cheered by her presence. "She said, 'Lena's here. Now I know things will be all right.' She asked me to help her move to a better room. I felt good because she let me make a fuss over her. I thought it meant that maybe she did care about me after all."

After Edna's death, Sherman Sneed helped clean out Edna's apartment. She'd kept several mementos of her daughter's Hollywood heyday, including a Max Factor makeup case and a small M-G-M glamour photo of her daughter in an elaborate wooden frame. Horne didn't want them. She found no peace in her mother's memory, nor did she believe, finally, that Edna's final pleasantries had meant much. In 1977, Shirley Norman of *Sepia* came to interview her. "The agony is apparent these days in her haunted eyes, in the grim set of her lovely lips, and in the invisible wall she has built between herself and most of the world," wrote Norman. Horne summed up her career bluntly: "I hate this business and I always have."

Yet she also felt she had nowhere else to turn, and the touring went on. The mellower Horne of the first half of the seventies had begun to freeze over again, and she wore a new mask in a televised appearance with Arthur Fiedler and the Boston Pops. In that semilegit setting, Horne affected the grand posturing of an opera diva. Between songs she offered what would become a central element in her shows, a tart attempt to distance herself from the industry that had created her. "I had a *brief* career in the cinema a hundred years ago," noted Horne, drawing out the word "cinema" with sarcastic precision. "I am given a great treat now and then—treat is in quotes—by my friends who want me to see *Cabin in the Sky* or *Stormy Weather*. They don't know how it makes me feel to see this woman, a hundred years younger, and quite dumb." That didn't stop her from laying claim to "The Lady Is a Tramp," a song published ten years before she sang it in *Words and Music*. "Though my *darling* friends Mr. Sinatra and Mr. Davis [Sammy] have appropriated it through the years, I've decided to take it *back!*"

Back in her M-G-M days, Horne could never have imagined that blacks would one day became a powerful force in Hollywood. But it happened in the seventies, albeit in a manner that repelled her. This was the age of blaxploitation films, low-budget action features that found black people cashing in on their own stereotypes. It grew out of cynicism. After so much struggle for equality, segregation still pervaded the school system, and President Richard M. Nixon, whom Horne loathed, opposed busing. Other battles remained unwon, and with most of the great leaders dead, angry urban blacks found a new set of heroes—ghetto thugs, drug dealers, hookers, and wielders of vigilante justice. All of them knew about "stickin' it to 'the Man,'" as S. Torriano Berry wrote in his book *The 50 Most Influential Black Films*.

Hollywood pounced on their stories. The smash hit *Shaft* (1971) told of a private detective, played by Richard Roundtree, who joins the black underworld in waging war on some white Mafia blackmailers. *Shaft* was credited with saving M-G-M from bankruptcy; it also launched the blaxploitation genre. Films like *Foxy Brown* and *Cleopatra Jones* showed black women as gun-toting warriors who would have spat on an apron or a bandanna.

Empowering as these movies seemed to much of black America, they were a distressing step backward for many actors who had fought long and hard against stereotyping. Ellen Holly, who played a judge on the ABC soap opera *One Life to Live,* spoke her mind in the *New York Times:* "Law-abiding, tax-paying black citizens who are not gunslingers, dope-pushers, pimps or prostitutes have been rightly and understandably enraged that the prevailing black image in most films . . . is so grossly at odds with their own."

Some movies countered blaxploitation. *Sounder* (1972) starred Cicely Tyson and Paul Winfield in a serious drama about a Depression-era family of Louisiana sharecroppers. *Claudine* (1974) earned an Oscar nomination for its star Diahann Carroll, who played a single welfare mother and part-time maid in Harlem.

Lena Horne had passed the age of Hollywood marketability, and no one was offering her roles of substance. Ossie Davis had hoped to add her to the cast of a film he directed, *Come Back, Charleston Blue,* a 1972 comedy about a Prohibition-era hoodlum whose ghost runs amok in Harlem. Horne was offered the role of "some lady that had buried a gangster or something," as she described it to John Gruen. She called it a "nothin' thing," and turned it down flat. Horne saw an irony in the blaxploitation genre that had escaped almost everyone: "If you're makin' so much money for *that man* who's makin' that movie," she said, "and you ain't gettin' an equitable piece of it, then that blitz should be unblitzed, you know what I'm sayin'?"

But on June 15, 1977, *Variety* announced Horne's latest screen comeback, and the vehicle was no blaxploitation flick. The singer would appear in *The Wiz,* a lavish screen version of Broadway's all-black adaptation of *The Wizard of Oz.* Universal Pictures and Motown Productions were the coproducers; Sidney Lumet, her son-in-law, would direct. Michael Jackson would play the Scarecrow, Richard Pryor the Wizard. In a choice that raised eyebrows, Diana Ross, who was then thirty-three, had signed on for the lead role of Dorothy, a barely teenage girl who finds herself in an enticing but alien fairyland far from home. Horne was back to playing a cameo role, that of Glinda the Good Witch, who appears at the film's end to guide Dorothy home. Nepotism, of course, had helped in Horne's casting.

Lumet himself was second choice for director. The producers had initially wanted John Badham, the director of a soon-to-be-released smash, *Saturday Night Fever*. But when he fought the illogical casting of Ross, he was fired; her star power, it was believed, would carry the extravagantly costly film.

Lumet had to work around such compromises. He decided that Dorothy's age didn't matter—*The Wiz* should tell the broader story of a young black woman's search for identity. "Dorothy's trip to Oz is really her trip to self-knowledge," he told Tom Burke of the *New York Times*.

In September, filming began largely on location throughout Manhattan. But Horne's scene, like most of her old ones at M-G-M, kept her isolated. She sang an inspirational anthem, "Believe in Yourself," to Ross, whose lines were shot separately and intercut. Sherman Sneed took a tape of the orchestral backup track to Santa Barbara and offered some coaching. Horne went to New York to film. She was nervous, but ended up happy with her "little bitty scene," as she described it to *Ebony*.

Soon Horne had a full-scale chance to play and act the star. She'd accepted the female lead in an all-black West Coast revival of *Pal Joey,* the 1940 Broadway milestone that had helped launch Gene Kelly. Based on short stories by John O'Hara, *Pal Joey* dealt with a sexy cad who connives his way into the bed and bankbook of a married socialite. Rodgers and Hart's score included two future standards, "Bewitched" and "I Could Write a Book"; its music had kept *Pal Joey* a perpetually alluring vehicle, and in 1957, Frank Sinatra played Joey on the screen.

With the casting of Lena Horne, the show would have to be retooled to make Joey's keeper, Vera Simpson, the focus. The sixty-year-old star would also be thrust into an updated setting for the old musical— a disco-fied New York, replete with booty-shaking black musclemen, flashing lights, and a boogie beat.

Trouble was written all over this production. But the head producers, Robert Fryer and Ernest H. Martin, felt that with the iconic Horne reigning over the show, *Pal Joey '78,* as it was retitled, couldn't miss. After a preview run in San Diego, the musical would open on April 21, 1978, at the Ahmanson Theatre in Los Angeles. Then, Broadway.

What leading man could stand up against Horne? She wanted Ben Vereen, then the hottest black actor-singer in the business. Vereen had won a Tony as the star of Broadway's *Pippin;* he'd also appeared memorably in *Roots,* a history-making 1977 miniseries about the evolution of slavery. But Vereen proved unavailable, and a reasonable second-best got the job—Clifton Davis, a handsome, Tony-nominated Broadway and sitcom actor. Horne pronounced the thirty-three-year-old a "perfect" choice for Joey.

Little else about *Pal Joey '78* pleased her. Three decades after *Jamaica,* Horne was still insecure about carrying a musical. Everywhere she looked, she saw threats, even in her role itself. As originally conceived, it would require her to drop the mantle of "lady" and show a woman willing to be exploited in exchange for sex—and that was not something that Cora Calhoun's granddaughter could permit. In their revised script, Jerome Chodorov and Mark Bramble altered the part to Horne's specifications. Instead of a "frivolous, bored white woman who was married and had nothing to do but go around meeting young studs," as Horne put it, Vera would be a widow whose wealthy husband had left her a nightclub, Chez Vera, and a honky-tonk bar, the Golden Spike. Joey would happen by the latter and meet Vera by chance. "I'm playing her as an independent black woman who feels that if she wants a companion she has a right to have one," said Horne to reporter Leonard Gross. "She knows that she will eventually lose him to a young woman or his own stupidity, and she just feels that she'll survive. And *I* have."

Little of that psychology would come through onstage; the edge was removed from a sexually daring, emotionally complex character. As one reviewer commented later, "Vera used to be the kind of woman who kept men, and Joey used to be the kind of man women kept. Now she is a chic, Lena Horne–type lady, and he is an engaging lad in a leisure suit, maybe just a little pushy."

But Horne wouldn't be told what to do. She quickly came to blows with Gower Champion, the towering Broadway director who had joined the team of *Pal Joey*. Having won seven Tony Awards, two of them for *Hello, Dolly!*, Champion was a man of bullheaded confidence. He wasn't about to handle Horne with kid gloves, the way everyone else scrambled to do. At an early rehearsal, Horne recoiled at one of his commands. "I don't have to do that shit," she snapped. He related his answer to Marge Champion, his former wife and dancing partner. "Gower said, 'Nobody calls my work shit. Get yourself another director.' And he walked." By other reports, Horne had him fired.

In came Michael Kidd, a director-choreographer of comparable acclaim; his credits encompassed many M-G-M and Broadway classics. He clashed with Horne repeatedly, but the star invariably got her way. It was *Jamaica* all over again, as the show's initial concept fell away and everything was altered to make it a vehicle for Horne. In *Pal Joey*'s original script, Vera sang two solos and two duets. But in order to shine the longest possible spotlight on her, two more numbers, "This Can't Be Love" and "A Lady Must Live," were pulled from other Rodgers and Hart shows and given to Horne.

Even that wasn't enough to put her at ease. Other roles—particularly that of Melba, a brash newspaper reporter—grew smaller with each rehearsal. Cast in that part was Josephine Premice, Horne's Tony-nominated costar in *Jamaica*. In the two decades since that show, Premice had lived a pampered but frustrating life as the spouse of Timothy Fales, a Wall Street executive turned sea captain. Between raising two children and holding salons for Manhattan's black elite, acting jobs were few.

But when the call came for *Pal Joey*, Premice had just finished an almost two-year run in a Broadway smash, *Bubbling Brown Sugar*. As Melba, however, Premice would once more be in the shadow of Lena Horne.

She took the job. But she couldn't have known the extent to which Horne would try to shunt her aside. According to Claude Thompson, the show's choreographer, Horne had nearly blocked the hiring, then thought better of it. If Premice knew, she would never have stooped to mentioning it; she'd always struggled to rise above every slight. "When Jo came out to L.A. and joined Lena," said Thompson, "it was all 'Darling, darling!' and they were having their martinis together after rehearsals."

It didn't take long for Horne's insecurity to flare. Thompson had begun choreographing Premice's moves for the first-act finale, "What Do I Care for a Dame?," when Horne phoned him in his hotel room.

"She said, 'What are you doing, baby?' I said, 'Working on putting Jo into the finale.'" He heard Horne hesitate. "'Well, don't you think . . . I love dancing, and moving my big ass, people love seeing it . . .' She was trying to tell me not to put her in. She was worried that Jo would upstage her."

No matter what, Horne would get what she wanted. The producers, like almost everyone else, were afraid of her; as far as they were concerned she *was* the show. "Jo's part was cut, cut, cut," said Thompson. Perhaps as compensation, she was chosen as Horne's understudy. But the major blows were still to come. In her big solo, "Zip," newspaperwoman Melba recalls asking the famous stripper, Gypsy Rose Lee, what ran through her mind as she worked. While recounting Lee's hilarious wandering thoughts about Schopenhauer, Dalí, and Whistler's mother, Melba does her own bumping and grinding.

"Zip" was a surefire showstopper. But Premice received word that it would now be a duet with Horne—a dramatically senseless change, and one that robbed her of her key moment to shine. "That was just killing for Josephine," said her friend Carmen de Lavallade. A Rodgers and Hart song from another show, "I Wish I Were in Love Again," was given to Premice. It brought her roars of approval in the first two previews. Then the song was dropped.

By then, so much tension had spread throughout the production that many of those involved thought that only Horne's star power could save it. Talented and attractive as he was, success had made Davis "a bit arrogant, headstrong and outspoken," as he later told *After Dark*. It was no secret that he was also "fucked up," as Thompson put it, on cocaine. But Horne could intimidate almost any man, and company members watched Davis wither in her midst.

Sensing that Horne was more nervous than anyone else, Thompson took pains not to overtax her in his choreography. "I just took all her mannerisms and put them into steps," he said. "I didn't try to take her out of that image she had of herself."

During previews, one of the producers told him that the Act I finale, which centered around Horne, ran too long and had to be cut. Thompson made an appointment to meet her at the theater so she could approve his changes. She never showed up. Afraid to make a move without her, he told the assembled cast members that he would wait until she was there to proceed.

That night at intermission, the producer pulled him aside and told him he was fired—"because you don't follow orders." Thompson's chin dropped. He tried to explain that he didn't want to make any cuts without Horne's permission. "Sorry," said the producer. "You have to go."

He rushed to Horne's dressing room, and she acted surprised at the news. Later that night Thompson sat, dazed, in his hotel room. Sherman Sneed knocked on the door bearing a note from Horne. Thompson never forgot its contents: "I'm sorry, baby. At least you know you have a point in this show." (A point was a share of the royalties.)

Thereafter Horne cut off contact, leaving him baffled as to how he'd displeased her. Was it his closeness to Josephine Premice? The mystery went unsolved; Thompson only knew that a treasured twenty-year friendship had ended. "I never cried so much in my life," he said. "I'd seen this happen before with other people when she wanted them out of her life. I never thought it would happen to me. Geoffrey Holder, Johnny Mathis, everyone knew my relationship with Lena, and they were shocked." Thompson pleaded with Ralph Harris to intervene, "because we got along beautifully. He said, 'I don't want to be part of this, Claude. I'm sorry. It's ugly.'"

With the April 21 opening drawing near, the producers were at war. Robert Fryer, the Ahmanson Theatre's artistic director, had conceived this revival; now he feared a disaster in the making, and pressed for changes—including the replacement of Michael Kidd, who he felt didn't "know how to communicate" with the all-black company.

Nothing could be touched without the agreement of Ernest Martin, managing director of the Los Angeles Civic Light Opera, which produced all the Ahmanson's musicals. But Fryer wanted no meddling from Martin. "We're happy with the show the way it is," he declared to Sylvie Drake, a *Los Angeles Times* writer who reported on the squabbling. Evidently the show's $2.5 million advance ticket sales had made him feel he had a triumph on his hands. Horne took no sides; to her the show was "very real, very believable. Of course they got carried away, enlarging my role."

And that backfired. For the most part, *Pal Joey '78* met with pans. To Ron Pennington of the *Hollywood Reporter,* the show had been almost destroyed in the effort to make it a Lena Horne spectacle. The opening moments established that Joey had taken second place. From out of the darkness, Horne was heard singing "Bewitched." Then a spotlight shone on the star, who made her way forward in an evening gown, trailing a fox fur behind her. "This is where it all began," she explained, as the set of the Golden Spike slid into view.

Horne, wrote the critic, "looks and sounds incredibly good," but "appears to be doing a concert date—giving a blasé, throwaway solo performance and acting as if everyone else on stage were there only for her to have someone to deliver her lines to." He preferred Premice, with her flair for "bright, broad camp," and Marjorie Barnes, who as Vera's secretary ached with unrequited longing for Joey. But Clifton Davis seemed to be wandering around in confusion, said Pennington, who couldn't imagine what Horne's character would have seen in him. Said Gene Davis, "Onstage, I don't think she even looked at him once. They were catering too much to Lena. I thought it was awful. She just didn't get it."

In the *Los Angeles Times,* Dan Sullivan called the production "a sort of staged LP, with most of Rodgers' songs sounding faintly embarrassed to be caught trying to boogie." He cited the first-act finale, in which Vera "shows up at a construction site and throws all the guys into a dither of push-ups and hunky poses. My God, Bruce—Lena Horne!" The book itself, wrote Jim Johnson, leaned heavily on "jive talk," in an exaggerated "ethnic dialect," to give it its supposed soul.

No one was unhappier with the results than Michael Kidd. Marge Champion related the contents of a telegram he'd sent after the opening-night show to Gower Champion, the man he replaced: "Thanks a lot!"

With the production clearly a dud, enthusiasm waned on both sides of the footlights. Friends remembered Horne's snickering backstage comments about Clifton Davis, who began missing shows. Soon his understudy took over. Then it was announced that *Pal Joey '78* would be "suspended until Lena Horne recovered from a throat infection."

She escaped to Santa Barbara for several days, then returned to a show whose "adverse word of mouth," wrote one reporter, surpassed its bad reviews.

In September, the show moved to San Francisco's Orpheum Theater, where all involved hoped for a kinder reception. Instead, Stanley Eichelbaum of the *San Francisco Examiner* wrote a damning feature on the floundering musical. He quoted an unnamed Civic Light Opera spokesman, "who said the star insisted on doing things her way." Horne was furious, and in a published rebuttal she denied all published "innuendoes" about her "influence" on the radically updated musical. But nothing could save it. By September 30, when the show closed for good in San Francisco, the Civic Light Opera had lost a reported nine hundred thousand dollars. *Pal Joey '78* left in its wake a swirl of ill feelings, most of them centered around Horne. Team playing, it seemed, was simply not her strength.

AT least she could look forward to the October 24 premiere of *The Wiz*. It took place at the 1,440-seat Loews Astor Plaza in Times Square, but had the excitement of 1950s Hollywood. Mobs of fans packed Broadway between Forty-fourth and Fifty-fifth Streets to glimpse the arriving celebrities. In came Michael Jackson, Nancy Reagan, the dress designer Halston, New York State Governor Hugh Carey. Diana Ross made a star's late entrance on the arm of Motown founder Berry Gordy. But it was Lena Horne who received a queen's welcome. As she walked inside the theater to a storm of flashbulbs, everyone rose.

If viewers had expected a heart-tugging, naïvely hopeful fairy tale like the original, Sidney Lumet had a surprise for them. Known for somber psychological drama, Lumet tried to bring the same weightiness to *The Wiz*. Dorothy was now a repressed Harlem kindergarten teacher, living alone with her little dog. When the animal runs outside on a winter night, Dorothy chases it—and is swept away by a snowstorm to the mysterious Land of Oz, reimagined by Lumet as a decaying urban nightmare that looks "like an abandoned shopping mall," wrote Vincent Canby in the *New York Times*. Street people lurk in corners; crows, killer dolls, and flying monkeys supply constant terror; and the once-adorable Munchkins are graffiti-scrawling ogres. If Dorothy wants to go home, she must find the godlike Wiz, who allegedly holds the solution.

But he doesn't. Salvation comes only in the film's final minutes, when Dorothy tearfully beholds the Good Witch of the South, played by Horne. Glinda descends from a twinkly night sky wearing a silver-spangled gown with matching headdress. Around her, similarly dressed black babies float in the air. "Home is a place we *awwwl* must find, child," she explains soothingly. "It's not just a place where you eat or sleep. Home is knowing . . . knowing *your* mind, knowing *your* heart, knowing *your* courage. If we know ourselves, we're always home, anywhere." From there she launches into "Believe in Yourself." Admonishing Dorothy to "believe you can go home," she puts her old mannerisms on full display, and Glinda turns into Lena.

The Loews audience gave her a standing ovation. Soon after, a police-guarded, balloon-filled subway train took the VIP guests downtown to Windows on the World, the penthouse restaurant on top of the World Trade Center. Horne seemed elated by the film. "I loved everybody in it, and the energy was so marvelous," she said.

The reviews took her down. Vincent Canby called *The Wiz* a "mess due to the misguided efforts to turn the energetic, likeably dopey stage musical into what might pass for a ghetto fairy tale." Geoffrey Holder, whose direction and costume designs for the Broadway version had won him two Tonys, was even less enchanted. "If Diana Ross was to cry one more time you'd puke!" he said. Most critics mentioned Horne only as a footnote.

Lumet's interpretation was brave, but despite its abundance of star power, *The Wiz* flopped. Only years later would it be shown in England, Horne's professional second home. "I went to see it at the National Film Theatre, and people really enjoyed it," said a British journalist and author. "Then Lena came on and they all fell about laughing. Someone said, 'Why is she wearing a shower cap?' And those little black babies flying around—it was so kitsch."

The Wiz was Horne's last attempt to act in a movie. And the director who had given her the invitation had ceased to be her son-in-law. During the filming, Gail and Sidney Lumet had divorced after nearly fifteen years. Part of the reason, explained Gail, was her recent conversion to Catholicism. "Sidney and I were not on the same wavelength, religiously or politically," she explained. "I became a different person, and we had nothing in common."

If Gail seemed matter-of-fact about the breakup, Horne was "in shock," as she told the *Los Angeles Times*. She'd felt proud of her daughter's successful mixed marriage, for her own had fallen apart. Now Gail's had met the same fate, and Horne took it personally. "I realize that it's selfish on my part to want everything to be like a fairy tale," she admitted.

Whatever the true circumstances of the divorce, Horne would end up painting Lumet as the villain. In an interview with *The Village Voice*'s Arthur Bell, she termed the director "the bastard—and you can print it." In years to come, Lumet refused to talk about his ex-mother-in-law; John Gruen, who knew him, saw Lumet's face freeze at any mention of Horne.

His daughters, of course, still called her Grandma, and peace had to be kept. Yet Horne could not resist complaining about how Amy and Jenny didn't understand her. Speaking of her choice to do *The Wiz*, she told an interviewer: "My two grandchildren said to me, you gotta do this part so you'll have something to leave for posterity. Nothing I'd ever done before meant anything to them."

Her relationship with Teddy's children was far messier. Marsha had fled, leaving William, Thomas, and Samadhi with Louis Jones; Little Lena had stayed with her mother, Faye. Jones, who worked as a postman, was close to retirement age, and barely equipped to raise a brood of energetic youngsters. Samadhi felt neglected in the all-male household, and Jones's ironhanded style of discipline was alienating the boys. Meanwhile, his wrath toward his ex-wife hadn't left him. According to Judy Davis, "he started doing the same thing he did with Teddy—he sort of cut off their relationship with Lena."

It was already an awkward one, for Horne's refusal to recognize Samadhi as a member of the family annoyed William and Thomas. "Lena would sometimes send presents to the boys," recalled Davis, "and if she didn't include Samadhi they would send them back. They became very protective of their sister."

These tensions helped set the scene for the descent upon the Joneses of a female acquaintance of Ted's from his final days. Samadhi came to know her as "the sort of person who likes to attach herself to celebrity" and had the charisma and craftiness to pull it off.

Ted's best friend, Clint Rosemond, saw her as "a professional con artist," not to be trusted. Years earlier a local black newspaper had published her adoring obituary of Ted, with whom she seemed obsessed. The article implied great closeness between them, but nobody near him had heard from her since. Then, around 1977, she made a surprise reappearance in the Joneses' lives. "I think she was looking to attach herself to Lena through us," recalled Samadhi. The scheming that followed assumed almost psychopathic dimensions. It started, Samadhi said, when the woman gained Louis's trust by claiming intimate friendships with Ted and Marsha. Her looks and charm also got his attention. "Lou was always vulnerable," said Rosemond, "because his ego was so damn big. Any person with a sense of how to manipulate people could take him to the cleaners."

According to Rosemond, the woman began an affair with Jones. She became a familiar face at the house, and kept offering to take Samadhi on outings. "She would come and pick me up and say, 'Oh, let me get her away from all these boys.' It was great to have someone pay attention to me." Jones's growing friction with Thomas gave her one more chance to gain control. "He and my grandfather had a horrible exchange," said Samadhi, "and Thomas said he was leaving. Grandfather told him to get out."

Soon, said Rosemond, the woman "saw where she could make her move—and it was to present Lou as unfit, and her as concerned and able, and to get the kids away from him. Remember, they were worth a few bucks in Social Security survivor benefits. That's what she was after, along with whatever she could swindle out of Lena."

To Rosemond's distress, she gained access to Horne. "It didn't take much for her to get Lena over to her point of view," he said. "I tried to get to Lena, to tell her this woman was a crook and what she really wanted was to get her hand in Lena's pocket." But his effort failed, and the conniving grew more insidious. "She got a lawyer, " said Samadhi, "and lied to my brothers—vicious, horrible lies that my grandfather had abused me, which he never had."

The woman scored a bizarre triumph. "With a boost from you-know-who," said Rosemond, she gained custody of the children. Samadhi escaped by going to boarding school, then to college; from there she stayed on her own. Eventually the twins went their own ways, too. The woman, who had been involved in other shady business dealings, vanished.

Ted Jones's family legacy would become a shadowy part of the Lena Horne story. Like the circumstances of his death, much of it proved too painful to talk about; Horne dealt with the problem by saying as little as possible.

She and Arthur Laurents hadn't exchanged a word since her withdrawal from *Hallelujah, Baby!,* and the loss of their friendship gnawed at her. Laurents was still angry with her, but he had a thriving career to occupy him. It boomed in the seventies when he wrote the screenplays for *The Way We Were* and *The Turning Point,* two hit films based on his own novels.

One day he answered the phone at his house in the Hamptons. It was Gail, calling from the East Hampton home she shared with Sidney Lumet, whom she had yet to divorce. "She said, 'Mummy'—which is interesting, because it's the WASP version—'is coming for the weekend, would you come for a drink?' She said Lena wanted to see me."

Laurents told her he'd think it over. Finally he accepted. He showed up at Gail's house—"and there was Lena, looking absolutely as beautiful as ever. Gail and Sidney discreetly left us alone. We talked—friendly, polite. She said, 'Can we have dinner in town?' I said, 'Anytime, on one condition.'

"'What's that?'

"'That you're honest. If you're willing to do that, then call me.' She never called."

What was "honest" about Lena Horne had become harder to discern. For all her disappointment over the outcome of the civil rights movement, proud and distinctive black identities had emerged all around her. After forty-five years gearing her persona for mostly white audiences, Horne sensed new possibilities. The popular black culture of the day—sassy urban sitcoms like *The Jeffersons, Sanford & Son,* and *Good Times;* the comedy of Richard Pryor and Redd Foxx; even blaxploitation films, which she hated—now gave her the license to be what her career, up to then, hadn't allowed.

The latest Lena Horne went on display in 1977 at Caesars Palace. Her show included "A Fine Romance," Jerome Kern and Dorothy Fields's sexy rant about a courtship so chaste it was driving her crazy. Horne began the song as she'd sung it for years, beautifully articulated, with a slight southern drawl. But after a short announcement—"Now *this* is Lena"—she made it known that her "whiter" self wasn't really her at all. She switched to a grunting ghetto dialect: "Ah nev-uh git to muss de crease in yo' blue serge pants!"

The audience loved it, and soon that delivery overtook her shows. She added an explanation: "One of the great privileges of being a *lady* is that one's entitled to be as *trashy* as one wants *whenevuh* one wants!"

Some of those who'd known Horne for years were dismayed by the change. At the Westbury Music Fair, Billie Allen watched the singer "bumping and grinding, talking in this supposedly black English, swaggering and squatting and carrying on. Wearing somebody else's clothes, somebody else's hairstyle, not knowing who she was anymore. . . . Oh, it upset me. I cried."

But at sixty-plus, with her performing days seemingly numbered, Horne felt it was time to let loose. The comic actor and film star Danny Kaye had encouraged her to do so after a performance in San Francisco. "He said, 'It's absolutely marvelous when you open your mouth, because everybody's wondering what the hell you're thinking. And when you talk it's so fascinating, even though you're not saying anything much. Keep it in, because it lets them know who you are.'"

She more than complied. In 1978, Horne and Vic Damone played the South Shore Music Circus in Cohasset, Massachusetts. In a ten-minute monologue about M-G-M—"a really big outfit in those days," she noted sarcastically—Horne disguised her ill will with a shoulder-shrugging candor. "Now, all this I'm tellin' you is true," she declared, before explaining that the studio's executives had asked Max Factor to "create a makeup to make her look more colored! That's a euphemism we used to use in the old days before we got straight, see?"

He came back about a week later with a makeup that they had created *just for me*. They named it Light Egyptian. They took this Light Egyptian, they put it all *ovuh* Ava Gardnuh! Gave her a part I really wanted to play. The part o' this black-haired black woman in this movie musical called *Show Boat*, the role of Julie . . . Finally they called me into the big office again, they said, "We losin' money on you." Said, "We gonna have a scene where you stand up against these mirrors, look glamorous and sing these songs. 'Cause 'specially when we send the movies down South, summa the states *cut yo part out!*"

Horne was finally convincing people—and perhaps even herself—that she'd had a racial rebirth. But the "new" Lena couldn't seduce Paul Mooney, a critic for *The Plain Dealer* in Cleveland, where she shared a week with Billy Eckstine in 1979. Her "sour grapes" over Hollywood bored him. "Apparently it has never occurred to her that she just cannot act very well. In fact her moaning and groaning about this and that diminishes the impact of her performance." The "toughness under her taut, wrinkle-free skin," he added, "seemed rock-hard down to the heart."

Curiously, in England Horne felt no need to assume this jivey persona. Her June 1979 appearance on the TV special *Song by Song by Alan Jay Lerner* found her at her most touchingly unguarded. Performing "I've Grown Accustomed to His Face," the first track of *Lena, A New Album*, Horne sang with enormous tenderness and a newfound fragility. Signs of wear had crept into her voice, but they only enhanced its poignancy. For "I'm Glad I'm Not Young Anymore" from the musical *Gigi*, she sat on a thronelike armchair and preened with hilarious mock-hauteur as she lampooned her "ageless" façade: "The fountain of youth is dull as paint / Methuselah is my patron saint."

Horne seemed to have so much more to give, yet a sense of emptiness haunted her. While taping *Song by Song*, she told reporter Francesca Hare, "I would like to give it all up; I never thought my career would go on this long." During a week at the London Palladium, where she'd been performing for thirty years, Horne faced a disillusioning sight. "The theater was practically empty," said author Stephen Bourne. "It was embarrassing. She'd been forgotten."

If that wasn't quite true in the States, there she'd regressed even further into a haze of nostalgia. Now past sixty and startlingly youthful, she found herself making ever-more-frequent denials of plastic surgery—"I tell you, I've had nothing done to myself but having a mole removed"—and self-consciously apologizing for her age. After a March 1980 performance at the Fairmont in San Francisco, she told reporter Steve Warren, "I don't want to drag around and be an obscene old lady. I won't keep getting up on stage so people can say, 'The old bag's still hangin' in there.'"

On the twenty-fourth of that month, United Press International carried word of Horne's imminent good-bye to showbiz. The news had been announced to a "stunned crowd" at the Fairmont. Inevitably, the report spurred on a new wave of interest in Lena Horne, as people flocked to see her one last time. Delta Sigma Theta jumped in, sponsoring a twenty-six-city tour, some of whose proceeds would benefit youth organizations.

The sentimental response to those concerts had its effect on Horne. Her supposedly final show took place on June 16 at the Los Angeles Music Center, where Vincente Minnelli introduced her. That night, Horne told *Variety* that she wasn't really retiring, "just cutting down on club dates," and that she was booked through January. The show revealed a woman who wanted anything but to stay home. According to David Weiss of the *Herald-Examiner*, Horne "offered a whirlwind display of sound, movement and gesture that left a mammoth question mark hovering over the theater. Where in the world does all the age-defying energy come from?"

Despite Horne's semiretraction in *Variety*, the tour carried enough finality to garner her some retirement-style tributes. On October 19, she was the guest of honor at "To Lena with Love," a twenty-fifth-anniversary gala held for the Thalians, a Hollywood charity organization. Sammy Davis, Jr., saluted Horne in song; the Nicholas Brothers reminisced about her days at the Cotton Club. Her M-G-M colleagues—Donald O'Connor, Debbie Reynolds, Vincente Minnelli, Kathryn Grayson, Sydney Guilaroff—cheered her on. The *Herald-Examiner* quoted her "good pal" Harry Belafonte's story of how he'd once told his army superiors he was Horne's cousin so that he wouldn't "have to work too hard." Belafonte even promised that Horne would come and sing for them—"if his commander, who was a bit gay, didn't bother him too much."

At Howard University in Washington, D.C., James E. Cheek, the school president, held a "graduation" ceremony for Horne. In cap and gown, she accepted an honorary doctorate. After all her years of bemoaning her spotty education, Horne was visibly moved. Then she headed back to Santa Barbara, and ostensibly to semiretirement. In 1981, she recalled that time to Charles Michener of *Newsweek:* "I felt I was dying with a whimper. One day, I thought, I'm going to go home to New York and just *do* it."

CHAPTER 19

IN ALL of Horne's recent onstage rambling about her hard times in Hollywood, Sherman Sneed had heard glimmers of an autobiographical one-woman show. As usual, she fought him. "I don't want to do my story," she snapped. "I've lived it. It bores *me*."

But her ego wouldn't let her drift quietly into obscurity. If her career was almost over, as she believed, then she wanted to end it in a blaze of glory. As she later told John Corry of the *New York Times*, "I just had to make some sort of statement before I left."

Around June of 1980, Sneed had phoned James M. Nederlander, chairman of the powerful theater chain known as the Nederlander Organization, to see if he had some sort of vehicle for Horne—a musical, perhaps. Nederlander suggested teaming her in concert with the Italian pop tenor Sergio Franchi, a 1960s heartthrob. The idea offended Horne, who later fumed, "I can work by myself, you know?"

Sneed turned it down, while pressing Nederlander for an exploratory meeting. The impresario asked Michael Frazier and Fred Walker, two younger producers who worked in his office, if they were interested in meeting Horne. They jumped at the chance, even if they had no idea where it would lead. (Frazier had seen *Pal Joey '78*, and knew she was no actress.) Soon the men were sitting at lunch with Sneed and Horne. "She was totally charming," recalled Frazier. "She said, 'I don't really know what I want to do, but I want to do my swan song and I want to go out on top. And I want to do it on Broadway.'"

An original solo piece seemed the only possibility. All of Sneed's badgering had made Horne seem less resistant to the idea. Frazier suggested hiring an emerging black playwright, Samm-Art Williams, to work with her on the book. Williams had just earned a Tony nomination for his comedy *Home*. Horne consented. After the meeting, Nederlander handed the project over to Frazier and Walker. He had only one demand about the content of Horne's show: "No messages!"

The producers sent Williams out to Santa Barbara to interview Horne and fashion a script. Some months later, the producers received a draft, and Horne came back to read through it with them. It was heavy on the black experience, and not much fun. A few pages into it, Frazier could see the star's discontent. Williams was out. "I can tell my story better by singing," she explained, "and I'll fill in the spaces." Horne was adamant about not wanting to be seen as nostalgia; she also wanted to make people laugh.

Frazier and Walker scrambled to contact songwriters, asking them to submit new material. Horne enlisted the services of Luther Henderson, who had become a top-flight arranger for such Broadway hits as *Ain't Misbehavin'*. "Luther loved working with Lena, even though it was impossible," said his wife, Billie Allen. "She was exciting. But they'd always end up fighting." According to Allen, her husband wrote an outline for the show in which Horne would sing "Stormy Weather" twice, near the beginning and the end. "She said, 'I'm not singing "Stormy Weather" in the show at all!' He said, 'But that's your signature! You begin with the old Lena singing it as you did it then, then go to what you've progressed to and how you would do it now. And that ties the whole thing together."

"'*No*, I'm not singing "Stormy Weather," do you understand?'"

"Of course, she did what he suggested, because it was a marvelous idea," said Allen. "But she had to challenge him—'I'm not gonna do anything that anyone expects me to do, I'm tired of that!'"

She kept a Cotton Club sequence he'd devised, along with other ideas. But they couldn't cease their warring, and Henderson left. Sneed began drawing reminiscences out of her during rehearsals and helped her cobble them into a script. The scramble for wise input continued. Harold Wheeler, who had orchestrated *The Wiz* and *Dreamgirls*, came aboard as musical director; Arthur Faria, the choreographer of *Ain't Misbehavin'*, signed on to do staging. And although he didn't raise a dime, Sneed was made associate producer by Horne.

Everyone but him had modest expectations. Frazier and Walker had decided on a monthlong run, with a possible two-week extension. "We'll be here four weeks and that's all," the star warned Sneed, adding that probably only old folks would come. Ralph Harris knew the producers were taking a chance on a seemingly faded star, and negotiated a modest five-thousand-dollar-a-week salary, plus five percent of ticket sales—ten percent if the show recouped its costs, which came to a then-slim $360,000.

Still, by the winter of 1981, the producers had seen nothing of the show, and were getting nervous. Their dream director, Mike Nichols, had turned them down, and after Horne's clashes with Gower Champion and Michael Kidd (not to mention Robert Lewis in *Jamaica*), preferred to do the job herself. Walker called Harris every day for reassurance. "Ralph said, 'Fred, in all my years in the business, no one knows how to program a show better than Lena Horne.'"

Finally, Horne invited the producers and the press agent they'd hired, Josh Ellis, to a midtown rehearsal studio to unveil the results. She performed a rough version of the show. "We were just dumbfounded," said Frazier. When a friend asked him to describe it, he sputtered, "It's a fucking hit!"

Frazier took her to look at possible venues. They rode a cab to West Forty-first Street between Seventh and Eighth Avenues and stopped in front of the Nederlander Theatre. It stood on one of the seamiest stretches of Times Square, which was years away from its eventual cleanup and gentrification. At night, prostitutes hovered in doorways; garbage lay in gutters. Horne was incensed, "and she let us know," said Frazier. For a woman who'd been raised to think the theater was a pigsty and actresses were whores, West Forty-first brought back every bit of shame that show business had ever given her.

Still, she agreed to look inside the theater—and once there, she began to soften. The Nederlander seated 1,232 but had some of the intimacy of cabaret; the stage wasn't long, and the front row was right up close. The mezzanine, too, was near enough for her to see faces. Frazier also offered her the Brooks Atkinson, a house on West Forty-seventh, comfortably north of Times Square. But Horne preferred the Nederlander.

By now Sneed had sold her on a title for the show: *Lena Horne: The Lady and Her Music*. It was uncomfortably close to the name of a Frank Sinatra TV special of the sixties, *A Man and His Music*. But for Horne it served a special purpose: to remind everyone that no matter what happened onstage, or how shabby the street outside, Lena Horne was a lady.

Another one would be wielding the baton. Linda Twine, a young black musician from Muskogee, Oklahoma, had worked as assistant conductor on *The Wiz* and *Ain't Misbehavin'*; prior to that she'd accompanied Novella Nelson, a scorchingly dramatic black singer-actress, at Reno Sweeney, the Greenwich Village cabaret. Horne and Sneed loved the idea of having a black female maestro, and gave Twine the chance. With her Afro, glasses, and scholarly air, she cut a stately figure before the orchestra, nearly all of which was black. Horne made an exception for Mike Renzi, a pianist from Providence, Rhode Island, who had moved to New York and set the gold standard for pop-jazz accompaniment. Mel Tormé and Sylvia Syms had discovered him early; later on he spent years with Peggy Lee. Horne auditioned him and hired him on the spot. Renzi played for her on and off until the late nineties. He was a white man with a jet-black Afro and beard, and Horne renamed him Pinky, after the film character who "passed." Three black dancers—Clare Bathé, Tyra Ferrell, and Vondie Curtis-Hall—would hoof beside Horne in various segments.

Not long before the show opened, she appeared on *Good Morning America* to plug her return to Broadway. "Possibly this will be my last year to perform," she said, echoing a claim she'd been making for years. "I figured that since I started here, long time ago, I'd like to wind up here, hopefully with a big smash."

Sneed, and very few others, knew that Horne was terrified that no one would care. One of her show's press gimmicks involved the simultaneous descent upon Broadway of three veteran glamour girls from old Hollywood—Elizabeth Taylor in a revival of *The Little Foxes*, Lauren Bacall in the musical *Woman of the Year*, and Horne. "They named the season 'Liz, Lauren, and Lena,' with the commensurate pecking order," said Josh Ellis.

Indeed, Horne seemed to be drawing the least interest. After *Good Morning America* she proceeded to a rehearsal hall, where Ellis had invited the press to see her perform songs from her show. The turnout was modest; the reaction "good, not great," said Ellis. And Horne knew it.

She played the first preview on April 30. Sparsely attended, it ran almost three hours. The show's early promise had gone awry: The narrative wandered, and many songs got a pale response. An expensive new wig, paid for by the producers, didn't flatter her. Once offstage, Horne sped into action. She yanked the wig off her head and threw it in the garbage, vowing to wear her own hair, troublesome though that was. Next, she chopped out songs and started paring down the patter. This was her last chance, she felt; she *had* to make it work. During that time she spoke to writer Marcia Ann Gillespie for a *Ms.* profile. "Yes, I'm out to prove something," admitted Horne. "I'm going to show you that I deserve this attention. I don't fit the neat categories, never did, but I'm me and I've got to make myself listened to and noticed."

The press preview took place just before the May 12 opening, and Horne was ready. "She hit the bull's-eye on every single song," said Ellis. During intermission, critics rushed up to him and hugged him; some said they'd never spent a greater night in the theater. Act II began, and ushers who could have gone home stayed huddled in the back, eyes glued to Horne.

Success was in the air on opening night. *The Lady and Her Music* kicked off with a few strains of "Stormy Weather," played by an orchestra hidden behind a thin white scrim. Light flooded it, revealing Horne's signature in neon. One saw the silhouette of Linda Twine, conducting in grand gestures. The curtain rose and out charged Horne, singing Cole Porter's "From This Moment On." The statement-making that Jimmy Nederlander had warned her against came in the second number. Horne belted "I Got a Name" as though giving a sermon on the importance of relishing life: *"I ain't never gonna let it pass me by!"*

The next two hours incorporated some cursory musical biography; several of the songs came from her past, many did not. Audiences saw an emancipated black woman, electrified by her freedom. Author Linda Dahl was there on opening night. "The way she had access to whatever she was feeling and just thrust it out there—it was amazing. People were going absolutely crazy. Her claque was out in full force, and they were screaming for her. I remember the fierceness of her energy. I was almost scared."

The story began with a Cotton Club segment, choreographed by Arthur Faria. Horne depicted her teenage self as awkward and unambitious; as she fumbled through her steps, one of the dancers chided her: "Baby, you ain't in Brooklyn no more. This is the Cotton Club!"

In the next song she's in Hollywood, trying to sing "Where or When" as humiliating directions are hurled at her: "Now, Miss Horne, try not to open your mouth so wide when you sing! . . . Try to sing with a pretty mouth. You know, like Jeanette MacDonald." She steps reluctantly into a white fox fur held out to her. "Now, *smolder*!" demands the offstage voice. She finishes the song in a froth of anger, and M-G-M's imprisonment of Horne is complete. Sprawling anecdotes about the role she'd "lost" in *Show Boat* took a central place in both acts. The audience roared when she added a dig at Jeanne Crain, the "pretty little brown-haired, blue-eyed child" who got "her" part in *Pinky*.

The dishiness of Horne's memories, her stabs at the mean old movie execs, her turning of the last laugh on them—all these things left the audience overwhelmingly on her side. So did "Yesterday, When I Was Young," the showstopping moment of truth that came near the end of Act I. Written by the French *chansonnier* Charles Aznavour, the song recollected a life squandered frivolously and selfishly. Horne drew them out as though taking an agonized look at the mirror: "And now it's only me out here all alone on this stage waitin' to end my play!" She finished by crying out in pain: "*I have got to pay! Pay for yesterday! Yesterday, when I was young—young—when I was young!*"

"It's very difficult for me, that song," said Horne later. "It brings back too much. Every line has to do with my life. It talks about Paris and lovers I didn't have and maybe should have. And the way you don't fit in and you really suffer on account of it."

She devoted the rest of the show to displays of the emancipated Lena Horne. "Deed I Do," a flirty love song she'd recorded demurely in her M-G-M days, now became an excuse for the sixty-three-year-old star to do aerobics-style strutting and squatting to a strip-show beat. From *Pal Joey '78* came "A Lady Must Live," Rodgers and Hart's credo of sexual liberation. "Git on out dere 'n' git yo-self some *live*!" she rasped. Charlie Smalls, composer of *The Wiz*, wrote "That's What Miracles Are All About," Horne's earth-motherly promise of a rainbow at the end of every storm. The protagonist of Fats Waller's hit "I'm Gonna Sit Right Down and Write Myself a Letter" whimsically imagines the note he wishes his loved one would send. Horne turned it into a fist-swinging vendetta of revenge: "I'm gaw'n pull myself on up in fronta mah antique Chippendale desk—'cuz I done saved some money since I got ridda you, you turkey!"

Audiences cheered. She assured them that she loved them, too, black or white: "You are *awwwwl* my brothers and sisters and ah feel much healthier feelin' that way!"

By the time she reached her closer, "Believe in Yourself," she had almost everyone believing that faith and an open heart could transform their lives. The response was too thunderous to doubt. "I felt something coming in to me," recalled Horne, "and they were saying, 'Yeah, we don't hate you, we bought the ticket, we wanted to be here.' I let them know that I was gonna let 'em in, and, boy, it was fabulous."

Later on, Josh Ellis rode an elevator with her and Sneed to the opening-night party at Le Parker Meridien hotel. Ellis had received advance copies of several reviews, and gotten word of others. All were raves. In between floors, he gave Horne the news: "They're the best reviews I've ever seen for anybody, at any time, at any place." He started to cry.

"Baby," said Horne, "let's just have a good time."

She'd hardly been calm, of course. "I'm numb," she told *Newsweek*'s Charles Michener at the party. "I thought I was going to lay an egg." In the *New York Times*, Frank Rich called her show "an evening of generally undiluted triumph." Horne, he said, "was in transcendent voice and, at age sixty-three, as beautiful and elegant as ever." Her late-evening reprise of "Stormy Weather" captivated him. "Before she even hits the first lyric, she lets loose with a gospel cry that erupts from her gut with almost primeval force."

Other critics could do little more than gush. "Perfection!" wrote Jeffrey Lyons of WPIX-TV. "The most important show in town," declared Howard Kissel in *Women's Wear Daily*. "The season's best musical," exclaimed Douglas Watt of the *Daily News*.

The next day brought an avalanche of ticket sales. Many came from the black audience Horne had dreamed of capturing. Delilah Jackson, who'd followed her career for decades, glanced around at the Nederlander and saw a sight unlike any at the Waldorf or the Fairmont: "All the black people were hugging each other and saying, 'Our Lena!'" At the Sunday matinee, said Horne, "the buses would come in from churches, and the ladies would come in and they'd look so pretty, and they would say, 'Yeah, sister!' 'Preach, sister!' 'Tell it.' And I'm saying, 'Ooh, yes—they're *mine*.'" They whooped as she ground her behind at them during "Deed I Do"; they stomped and whistled at her Aretha-like wails and Tina Turner shimmies. "I can make people laugh," said Horne in amazement to John Corry of the *Times*. "When I hear the audience laugh, I think, 'Oh, my God! I'm funny!'"

Horne was on the high of a lifetime. So were her producers, as *The Lady and Her Music* became one of Broadway's hottest tickets. "I thought that show was a very smart piece of showbiz," said Marcia Ann Gillespie. "It served the purpose of Lena projecting the Lena she wanted people to know. People seemed surprised by how earthy she was, because there was the idea of this very aloof person."

The star made herself widely available to interviewers; each of them walked away feeling like her best friend. Rex Reed met her in the dressing room before a show. She sat wrapped in a towel, pasting on false eyelashes and speaking of her emotional epiphany: "Honey, I was packed in so much ice it took me thirty years to thaw out!" Tales of her hard times tumbled out of her. At last, said Horne, she'd earned the right to her trademark song. "I've had stormy weather all my life, and if anybody can sing about the trouble they've seen, it's this old broad."

The "symbol" in her had not died; if anything Walter White's old insistence that she remember her position had come back to haunt her. With so much of the black community now in her corner, she felt a need to explain many things, starting with her marriage to a white man. Having long talked about its grave risks, Horne now said she'd done it out of opportunism: "It was cold-blooded and deliberate. I married him because he could get me into places a black man couldn't." Hayton, moreover, was the musical Svengali she had needed. (No one asked her why she hadn't just hired him as her manager or conductor.) Horne justified her title of Mrs. Hayton: "I learned to love him because of how good he was to me, and *patient*. . . . I had a perfect marriage." In the sixties they'd separated for "just a minute," and when Hayton died on the heels of her two other great losses, Horne became the grieving widow: "I couldn't sing without Lennie," she declared.

Professional details were broadly revised. One story was crucial to uphold: "I wasn't gonna be a maid—not for the biggest star in Hollywood." It ignored her eagerness to play Jeanette MacDonald's servant in the 1942 movie *Cairo*, and her long-buried admission in the *Los Angeles Daily News* that she'd only "refused to play certain kinds of maids." The blacklist, she maintained, had ruined her American career for most of the fifties. And after the Luau incident in 1960, she'd become so entrenched in civil rights that she'd "stopped singing for three years." Sometimes she said five.

Almost every claim went unchallenged; Horne's self-effacing candor gave all her allegations a sincere ring. And as a long-suffering black icon, her word could and would not be questioned. But in her own mind, was she telling the truth? "I think any of those people who came out of the M-G-M factory were taught to lie," said Alan Ebert. "All their lives were myths. Then they started to believe the lies."

There was more to Horne's revisionism than that; her childhood and professional disappointments had led her to feel like the victim in every scenario. So had the grooming of Jeanne Noble. In her 1978 book *Beautiful, Also, Are the Souls of My Black Sisters*, Noble wrote about the black woman's strength and majesty throughout ages of white victimization. She used Horne as the perfect example. Responsibility to her race, she insisted, had forced Horne to surrender to white impresarios and become a symbol, miserable as that made her. M-G-M was the oppressor that had kept her "a butterfly pinned to a column," and forced her to sing a white repertoire. It had taken her civil rights involvement, and her survival of massive loss, to make her a black woman at peace.

That was the image the star felt compelled to uphold. She displayed it to millions of TV viewers in a profile on *60 Minutes*—the dream interview of segment host Ed Bradley, who adored her. A camera followed him and Horne on a walk through Central Park as she reminisced, sometimes tearfully, about her hard times. They continued the discussion in her suite at the Wyndham Hotel. There, Horne spoke of how her rebirth in the sixties had helped make up for "the dead years." Throughout them she'd had to work with a white manager; there were no black ones then, stated Horne.

Ralph Harris's daughter Trygve was at home watching. "I almost fell off the couch," she said. "He was the one who dealt with all the gangsters. He was the one who'd have to say he was gonna pull out of this or that contract if they didn't allow her to stay in the hotel or come in the front door. He was the one who had to go down to Miami Beach and get Lena and Lennie a house because blacks were only allowed out during the day."

Others besides Trygve were less than enchanted with the Horne of 1981. To Mart Crowley, the spicy candor of her show seemed "angry as hell. I knew those stories were either paranoia or deliberate fiction." Geoffrey Holder found her tales of black persecution hard to cry over. "It has been going on for centuries. Why is she now a martyr because of that?" It bothered him that the musician who had done more than anyone else to create Lena Horne wasn't even mentioned in her show. The only Hayton arrangement she used, "Surrey with the Fringe on Top," was cut in the course of the run. Amy Lumet certainly hit a nerve in her grandmother when she gave an uncensored reaction to her raunchy shenanigans: "Grandma, you embarrassed us!" Horne was so jarred she repeated the story for years. "Don't come, if I embarrass you!" she grumbled.

The most scathing assessment of *The Lady and Her Music* came from Arthur Laurents. "This was no Lena Horne I ever knew," he said. "You know, where she came from, Lena had *great* diction. Her speech was beautiful. That faux African-American jive that she was putting on was absolutely whipped up for the occasion. I thought it was grotesque. It was as false as the Waldorf." He watched Horne from the first row. "She was singing away, and suddenly she looked down and saw me. She did a take! I thought she was gonna kill me! Because I think she knew I was wise to her. That show was the greatest con game in years. And they all fell for it. Even she fell for it!"

Nat Horne, who had danced in *Jamaica*, was just as startled by her transformation. "In Harlem they didn't think she was soulful enough, and now she wanted to prove that she was black. She made a caricature of herself. I felt bad for her, and also bad for the people who helped her in Hollywood. I thought, why are you so angry? You are where you are because those people put you there. They made you look good, and they gave you good things to do. You bought into it, almost like selling your soul to the devil. Now you must live with it."

But with a standing ovation after every show, there was no need for Horne to change a thing. Truthful or not, *The Lady and Her Music* was masterful theater, and sent people away exhilarated. Horne did near-sell-out business even in the summer, despite the sweltering heat inside the Nederlander. Horne claimed an allergy to Freon, the refrigerant used in air-conditioning, and the system stayed off. Sweat poured off of her under the spotlights; audience members fanned themselves vigorously with their programs. And still they came. Horne repaid their loyalty by taking time afterward to greet almost every fan who wanted to meet her.

The show was a magnet for celebrities, but even the most stellar of them had to wait outside the dressing room as Horne showered, had her hair and makeup freshened, wrapped a white towel around her neck, and donned a plush dressing gown. Then, with a photographer poised, Sherman Sneed brought in the luminaries—Elizabeth Taylor, Barbra Streisand, Aretha Franklin, Miles Davis, Sidney Poitier, Ethel Merman, Sammy Davis, Jr., Rosa Parks, Shirley MacLaine, Cab Calloway, George Burns. Coretta Scott King came on the same night as Jacqueline Onassis, who arrived on the arm of Mike Nichols. "Henry Kissinger wanted to get into the picture with Paul Newman and Joanne Woodward," said Michael Frazier, "but Paul didn't want his picture taken with Kissinger."

The photos appeared in newspapers all over the country. In almost every shot Horne flashed a dazzling M-G-M smile, while gazing out as disconnectedly as though she were alone.

Though nearsighted, Horne could spot almost any familiar face from the stage. If a star failed to pay respects afterward, Horne was offended. One night, recalled Frazier, she saw Diana Ross in the audience. "Later on she said, 'That bitch didn't come back!' She was very annoyed."

Not all who ventured backstage, of course, received the warmest welcome. Diahann Carroll, whom Horne had always treated curtly, saw the show repeatedly; she always went to the dressing room. "And waited forty-five, fifty-five minutes each time, while she changed and showered," said Carroll. Then Horne would glance her way.

"You're here again?"

"Yes, and I may be here *again!*"

The grandest of admirers would be taken onstage after the house emptied; then Horne would greet them in front of a line of photographers. So it went on the night that Nancy Reagan came with her son, daughter-in-law, and a battery of Secret Service men. Told in advance of the visit, Horne was unimpressed. A month earlier she'd groused to Arthur Bell of the *Voice*. "I don't think it's about white and black anymore. I can sit down with white people and say, 'What the fuck's happened to this country? What have we got? President Reagan? That's a joke.'"

Yet she put on a polite face for the Reagan family. "Mrs. Reagan was very gracious, very complimentary," said Frazier. "She said, 'It's such a thrill to see you. I'm so happy you're having such a wonderful success.'"

After the first lady had gone, Horne turned to Frazier. "That bitch wants something!" she muttered.

"Oh, come on! She's just paying homage to you."

Two weeks later he got a call from the White House. The Reagans had asked that Horne sing at one of their state dinners. She could choose between guests of honor—the king of Spain or the chancellor of Germany. Before the show, Frazier poked his head into Horne's dressing room. "I hate to admit it, but you were right," he said. "That bitch *does* want something. She wants you to sing in the White House for the king of Spain or the chancellor of Germany."

"She said, 'No way! I've sung for the best. I sang for Roosevelt, I sang for Harry Truman, I sang for John Kennedy. I'm *not* gonna sing for Reagan.'"

But she approached her audiences with absolute devotion. Horne had to deliver six two-hour performances a week, without betraying a hint of what she told Rex Reed: "This Broadway schedule is killing me!" For the 8:00 P.M. show she was in her dressing room at five-thirty, creating the Lena everyone had paid to see. "She'd come into the theater looking like an old lady," said Fred Walker. "She had spots on her face. Then she made herself up, and when she opened the door this was the hottest woman who ever lived." Only after she'd returned home did Horne have a drink. On Monday, her day off, she stayed in bed and didn't speak.

Ralph Harris had stepped back considerably as her manager. Living in Montecito, he wasn't able or willing to stick to Horne's side during what promised to be a long Broadway run. In his absence, Sherman Sneed eagerly took charge. Horne hated dealing with business, and gave him broad rein to conduct her affairs, from handling fan mail to serving as her constant gatekeeper. "Sherman and Lena were together *all the time*," recalled Walker. "Nobody got near her. Lena didn't do the dirty work. If anything had to be done, Sherman did it."

He spread the word that everything involving "the lady," as he called her, fell within his control. "Sherman always made sure that we were aware of his stature in the Lena Horne pyramid," said Mike Renzi. In recent years, Horne had acquired an apartment at the Apthorp, a huge Upper West Side apartment building with a courtyard. But she liked staying at the Wyndham, and Sneed often lived there with her. He kept her both under his watch and on a pedestal, distant as possible from such lesser beings as her musicians. Some had known her for years, and fumed at having contact cut off. "I would call her to see how she was doing," said Chico Hamilton, "and this motherfucker wouldn't even let me talk to her! So it just got to the point where I said, 'Fuck it. I don't want nothing from this woman.'"

At least part of Sneed's protectiveness was justified. During the show's Broadway run, he and Horne had to deal with an unwanted pursuer. The *New York Amsterdam News* broke the news in a cover story, "Lena Is My Mom." Its subject was Annie Steele, a pretty, light-skinned black woman from Long Island. Steele, who had four grandchildren, claimed she'd been on a twenty-year quest to find her "mother," Lena Horne, whose real name, she said, was Ora Wiley. Steele's father, she believed, was Joe Louis, and the consummation had occurred in Alabama. But Horne had never visited Alabama before the sixties, and there were no Wileys in her family. Horne's lawyer and Sneed met with Steele and shot down her claims. Meanwhile, angry letters barraged the *Amsterdam News* over the story, which "was like peeing on the American flag," said Josh Ellis. The paper issued a profuse apology.

This was Horne's time to be compensated for past wrongs, not exploited. The Tony Awards Nominating Committee rushed in to do its share. *The Lady and Her Music* had opened too late to qualify for inclusion in the 1981 ceremony, but since Horne was toast of Broadway, the voting committee found a way to honor her. Just weeks after her show opened,

Horne appeared on the June 7 Tony telecast to accept an award for special achievement in the theater. She entered to a standing ovation, braless under a blue Giorgio dress. Her speech cleverly juxtaposed "the lady" with some mild shock value. Horne bowed as grandly as Eva Perón, then cradled her Tony in both hands while speaking. "I want to say thank you to the Tony Committee, and I want to say thank you to my peers . . . and the critics," purred Horne. Then she thanked her producers. Slowly she moved her hand up and down the statuette as though she were masturbating it. She teased out her punch line. "I can tell you that . . . sometimes you have to wait fifty years . . . and sometimes it comes in a year . . . but whenever it comes . . ."

Her hand froze, and she stared suggestively at the audience, which burst into applause.

She added: "I'm just so happy that I'm getting all of these flowers before I lose my teeth!"

A few months later Horne got word that she'd scored two Grammy nominations, for best original cast album and best female pop vocal performance. She couldn't attend the ceremony, for she had a show of her own to do. On the night of February 24, 1982, Sneed took her aside during intermission and tearfully told her she'd won in the cast-album category—her first-ever Grammy. Later on, as she took her closing curtain calls, Sneed walked onstage. "Lady," he announced, "you've won the Grammy!"

"I know, Sherman. We talked about this during intermission!"

No, he said—she'd gotten a second one. Horne had beat out Kim Carnes, Sheena Easton, Juice Newton, and Olivia Newton-John. Sneed started to cry.

Yet almost every salute seemed to pry open an old wound. Horne told Clive Hirschhorn how sorry she felt that her mother wasn't around to see her now. "She always used to say to me I'd never really make it because I didn't have star quality. *She* was the one, she used to claim, who had what it took. And who knows, maybe she was right."

Hedy Lamarr, her old M-G-M rival, came backstage one night to praise her extravagantly and reminisce. But Lamarr's starstruck reflections only dredged up more sour memories for Horne. "She said to me, 'Oh, Lena. Weren't those happy days? Weren't we lucky? We didn't have to think for ourselves. We didn't have to choose our clothes. We didn't have to choose our lovers. Everything was done for us.' I sat there with my mouth hanging open. I realized she liked that dream world. I didn't hurt her. I said 'Yes. Wasn't it wonderful.'" Back at her hotel, Horne imagined what would have happened to her if she'd lingered in such a cloud of unreality. Would she have ended up a short-circuited has-been, or a premature casualty like Judy Garland?

Horne still lived the life of a star, and that included a flock of acolytes. Jeanne Noble came to the theater frequently; so did Kitty D'Alessio, who poured out her heart to Horne in a letter. "The gift of our friendship—so meaningful—deep, comfortable, private, lovely, truthful . . . I value it very much—because we are both a bit complex and private and careful with each other."

Horne certainly showed no restraint at Christmastime. Her 1981 gift list was startling in its extravagance, and covered over sixty recipients, including most of the people involved in her show. The presents included caviar, champagne, Baccarat crystal, jewelry from Tiffany, and pricy clothing. For many others—including Audrey Whitmore, Greg and Sherri Sneed, Elois Davis's grandchildren, and nearly all her family members—the list indicated "$$."

For her son Teddy's children, who'd led far from privileged lives, Horne's largesse made an impact. William and Thomas thanked her with a handmade Christmas card: "From two guys who love you so much, our love could move a mountain." Twelve-year-old Lena Mary Jones wrote poems for her grandma, and by mail from Los Angles she confided her adolescent concerns about flat-chestedness and boys. "I love you grandmother and miss you a great deal," she wrote.

Even Samadhi, whom Horne had refused to acknowledge as a family member, seemed to benefit from Horne's generosity. Samadhi had attended Marymount, a private, all-girl high school in Hollywood, followed by a boarding school in Utah. Only later did she stop to ponder who had paid her tuition. Horne seemed the only possibility. "I can't imagine how else it would have happened," said Samadhi. "I would have to be very grateful to her. I also think it was a guilt tactic, because Lena was demonstrably not nice to me."

Thank-you notes aside, Horne still felt unappreciated. "My grandkids don't treat me like no star!" she told writer George Hadley-Garcia.

"They listen to my music—*if* they listen—and they make a face like they'd rather be out doing *anything* else!" Over and over she spoke of how Amy and Jenny thought of her as their "crazy old grandmother" and couldn't relate to her on any level. Only Jenny, she said, "lets me hug her"; as for the others, "a cold gust of wind can come from them in a minute." Even her daughter, she felt, didn't care much about her singing. She often quoted Gail's old comment: "Why don't you sing like Patti Page?"

Horne, in turn, felt she had little in common with any of them. Like their mother, the Lumet girls had grown up privileged, and Horne talked to them as though they were spoiled princesses. "I find with very, very young people now, a kind of lack of *passion* that I think is necessary to survive," she explained to Jim Hartz, a host of TV's *Over Easy.* "My generation, we were *hot* about everything. . . . I find that everything is so free now that one loses the sense that one has to be . . . in there, in it. Well, that's their generation, and mine is mine."

But her greatest regrets lay with herself. Horne's disappointment was so strong, it seemed, that no amount of success could ever make up for it. Oppression was the theme of her interview with Bernard Drew of the Gannett Westchester Newspapers; his feature bore the ironic title "The Rage Now Is Gone, and She's 'Free to Be Me.'"

"If I'd been born earlier or later," Horne told him, "I might have become a great musical comedy star on Broadway. My one show, *Jamaica,* did nothing for me, and of course, *St. Louis Woman* was written for me but the NAACP wouldn't let me do it." After Broadway, she planned to retire: "It's a question of too little, too late."

To Mike Renzi, the statement had a clear subtext: "If I were white this would have happened a long time ago." Jabs at her producers became a part of her show, and wound up in many articles. In the *Daily News,* Rex Reed wrote that her dressing room was so small she had to hang her gowns over the toilet. "This place is a dump, honey," said Horne. "That Mr. Nederlander, he don't spend money on nothin'."

She depicted herself as a woman alone, onstage and off. "I never had anyone in the beginning and now it looks like I'm ending up the same way," she said. "Nobody I adore is still living. And so when I sing 'I Got a Name,' I'm saying that I'm carrying on even though they're not here." Once home, though, music brought her little comfort. "There's not a great song I can listen to that doesn't remind me of something awful," she told Reed. "But I'm not bitter." After concluding that she'd "finally merged all the Lenas" and found peace, she contradicted her own words: "I've been through so many changes and projected so many images that sometimes I look in the mirror and I don't know who I'm looking at."

Her show reflected that identity crisis. Horne alternated among unaccented English, southern twang, and ghetto dialect. "Ah intend to keep movin' ahead!" she declared in "I Got a Name," but *The Lady and Her Music* evolved into a litany of score settling and miffed looks backward. Partly to rest her singing voice and partly out of boredom, Horne had added about twenty minutes of talk. Her eyes burned as she recalled Hedy Lamarr in *White Cargo,* "oozin' around in the jungle in my Light Egyptian!" The black soldiers of World War II, she said, had "really wanted Betty Grable's photo in their footlockers"; she also noted her "tiny little cameo part" in *Death of a Gunfighter.* Her greatest beef of all assumed a new edge: "I just naturally assumed they'd choose me to be Julie when they decided to film *Show Boat.* I told you I was crazy." Her second "Stormy Weather" revealed a woman whose frustrations were far from over. Shaking a fist, she yowled until she was almost hoarse.

In a 1994 interview, Horne confessed she'd grown "tired" of the show; what held her interest, she said, was scrutinizing viewers for their reactions. "To get to them was a challenge always," she said. One thing hadn't changed since her days at the Waldorf—Horne still viewed the audience more as adversaries to conquer than as fans to embrace. She'd grown to mistrust the applause, which she chalked up to "surprise that I haven't fallen apart. I hate the feeling that I'm a freak—you know, she can still do it, even though she's that old."

For Horne, her whole Broadway experience seemed to boil down to two women who sat in the front row and began whispering while staring out with alarmed eyes. Horne's story about them was as angry as it was hilarious, and it took up several minutes of Act I. Quiet as the women were, their chattering was driving her crazy, and as she sang she fumed over what the problem was. She even pondered having them thrown out. Finally, said Horne, "I looked down and I said, *'What's the matter? What is wrong?'*"

One of them sheepishly answered, "Your fur is on the floor."

As she quoted that line, the audience's eyes shifted to the white fox she'd used in her Cotton Club sequence, then dropped near the piano. "Never *mind* all this sweat I am washin' up this stage with," snarled Horne in memory of the women. "Never mind all this singin' I'm *tryin'* to do. *My fur is on the flo'!*"

She recalled her response. "That ain't my fur. It's Jimmy Nederlander's fur. Let him worry about it. *This* is mine." She took off her aquamarine wrap, then lowered it ever so gingerly on top of the fur.

After repeated extensions, a closing date was set for *The Lady and Her Music*—June 30, 1982, Horne's sixty-fifth birthday. A national tour would start only days later. The singer later told Joyce Eskridge, a fan she befriended on the road, that she would just as soon have stayed home, but Sneed had talked her into touring. To Arthur Bell of the *Voice*, the closing was overdue. "By the time she had reached the last night, we all knew the sermon by heart. Intensity was lacking from both sides of the pulpit." Audiences still rose after "Believe in Yourself," but Horne later admitted that singing it had become a trial. With each repetition, its promise of a happy ending to all who persevere felt more like a lie. "But if I let that song go I'm not gonna make it."

Still, the closing performance—her three hundred thirty-third—was unavoidably emotional. At the end, Horne brought Amy, Jenny, William, Thomas, and Lena Mary on stage with her as the audience stood and roared out its love for her.

Horne and family proceeded to the Roseland Ballroom on Fifty-second Street for a costly send-off, excitedly thrown by the producers and sponsored by Seagram's. David Gropman, her Broadway set designer, had trimmed Roseland with green ribbons and white lightbulbs. In her *Daily News* column, Liz Smith detailed the goings-on, which included an "orgy of food" and a five-hundred-pound birthday cake that read LENA in big black letters. The Count Basie orchestra played for a star-studded crowd of seven hundred. Smith helped shield Horne in print from the pique of the excluded: "Lena hasn't much bothered herself with the guest list but did insist that 'my people' be invited—meaning all the ushers and ticket folks from the Nederlander."

On that black-tie occasion, Horne wore a custom-made tuxedo-style suit. She sat at a table surrounded by family members. Distance, both spatial and personal, had touched them all. According to Lena Mary, the two sets of grandchildren had never met. She told John Corry of the *Times*, "It's not a family reunion, but a family getting to know each other."

Their grandmother greeted a parade of well-wishers and reporters. Horne seemed as delighted as she had on opening night. She told Dennis Cunningham of CBS News, "I think I'm leaving at just the right time. I want New York to miss me, and I hope I'll be back someday."

CHAPTER 20

ON THE Fourth of July, Horne launched her tour with two shows at Tanglewood, the Massachusetts festival that hosts the Boston Symphony Orchestra each summer. Then she returned to the Nederlander, where Showtime taped her performance for a cable special. The TV cameras offered a harsh view of Horne. She wore a copper-hued foundation that darkened her dramatically, and her eyes were outlined in black. Sweat poured down her face; onstage she blamed the lack of ventilation on the cheapness of Jimmy Nederlander.

But the audience responded as ardently as ever. An intermission featurette on the special showed attendees effusing over Horne. One young woman exclaimed, "I can't believe she's moving around so much! If I could do that at sixty-five!"

Back went Horne on the road. That September, her tour brought her to San Francisco's Golden Gate Theatre. The town had always greeted her fondly, but it was also known for its tough theater critics, especially where visiting New York productions were concerned. Horne didn't endear herself to them by holding a press conference in lieu of giving interviews. In San Francisco, she got the worst reviews of her life. Gerald Nachman, theater and cabaret critic for the *Chronicle*, led the naysayers.

> I'll take the old Lena Horne over the older new one. OK, maybe that wasn't the *real* Lena, but it was swanky, aloof, and irresistible. The new model on display at the Golden Gate is flashy and low-down, less a person than a proud personal statement about coming out from be-

hind the chic facade she assumed all the years we were adoring her for, which she now claims was a fraud. People love a reformed star. I can't tell what they love most: her about-face at sixty-five, her image as the world's most glamorous senior citizen, or the fact that at her age she's willing to let it all hang out and, as she says, "risk makin' a damn fool of myself," at which she succeeds too often. . . . Lena wants it both ways, regal and raunchy, a baffling act. . . . Her gittin'-down seems as much a mask as the old iceberg bit. In revealing her ethnic roots, rich artistic ones are choked. . . . If this is honesty, tell me lies.

In the *San Francisco Sentinel,* Michael Mascioli called the show a "slap-dash" attempt at autobiography in song, full of selections that had "no bearing on her life or career." Many of them, he wrote, were "small and tender and cannot withstand so brutal an attack. . . . Less interpreter than predator, she snarls, she growls, she bellows, but she does not sing."

After the unabashed love letters she'd received from the New York press, this critical reaction was a shock. "I don't make any apologies for feeling vital and angry," she told the *Chronicle*'s Ruthe Stein. "I'm talking about the fact that we should live." Nachman had admitted that the crowds went "bananas" for every move she made. But Horne looked out and sensed disapproval; later she complained to reporter David Colker that her audiences had been "fantastic" everywhere, "except there." She blamed it on the fact that the Golden Gate sold most of its seats by subscription, and that blacks couldn't afford to see her. The viewers who came, she felt, had been stuck with her. "They bought those tickets so they could see *Show Boat.* . . . Those people tend to be from the outskirts."

A grand homecoming lay ahead of her. In November, Horne opened a seven-week, forty-show run at the Pantages Theater in Los Angeles. Horne's loathing of M-G-M had long been a part of Hollywood lore; now, back in the town where she'd experienced so much hurt, the ill feelings crested. She gave Paul Rosenfield of the *Los Angeles Times* an earful of her old gripes, then did more of the same on the *Tonight* show with Johnny Carson.

Horne did record business, and after one performance, black mayor Tom Bradley awarded her a key to the city. "She has helped all of us in 1982 to dream these impossible dreams," he announced to a deafening ovation. But there on Hollywood turf her M-G-M bashing didn't go unchallenged. Samuel Marx, a producer at the studio during her tenure there, wrote a lengthy rebuttal for the *Times*. Marx was "outraged by her persistent attacks," he said, on the movie company that had essentially created her. "It was those nine or ten M-G-M movies, and the magic with which they clothed her, that started it all." She had Arthur Freed and Louis B. Mayer to thank. "Yes, Louis B. Mayer . . . super-target for the uninformed, the misinformed, and those who know better but enjoy target practice."

Elsewhere on the road, further controversies arose. Before Horne's January 1983 run at Dallas's Majestic Theatre, Elsie Faye Heggins, a black city councilwoman, publicly attacked ticket costs for opening night, a benefit for a local arts organization. Blacks, she felt, would be forced to sit in the balcony again. Horne was so infuriated by Heggins that she canceled the engagement. She issued a cool statement of explanation. "Charity is something which should be supported by people who can afford it, regardless of their color. . . . Ms. Heggins used my name to draw national attention to a local issue, and I was made a pawn of some local politicians. I do not want to be caught in the middle of a local dispute."

In New Orleans, another clash lay in store. Broadway producer Zev Bufman had booked Horne for a three-week run at the city's historic Saenger Theatre. When she stepped inside it, "she was fit to be tied," said Michael Frazier. The four-thousand-seat Saenger was over three times the size of the Nederlander. Horne's show had a supper-club intimacy; now she would have to retailor it to a space so massive that she felt lost on its stage.

She got through the engagement, but Bufman was no happier with Horne than she was with him. After she left town, he spoke out to the press. "I've noticed that the chip on her shoulder seems to have grown," he told *W*. "In the New York show she had a good balance of entertainment and social comment. Now her feelings about racial injustice have magnified to the point where her audiences are squirming in their seats. They still like her show, but there is too much anger."

During her marathon of tour dates came a persistent invitation from Quincy Jones, the pop-jazz arranger and star record producer. Jones had met Horne in the fifties, a decade in which he'd gone from playing section trumpet in the Lionel Hampton orchestra to arranging for the likes of Count Basie, Peggy Lee, and Sarah Vaughan. Jones went on to build a stunning career in the music business. His shrewdness culminated in his foremost commercial coup: In 1982 he produced Michael Jackson's *Thriller*, named the biggest-selling album of all time.

Horne remained his special idol, and he'd released her Broadway cast recording on his label Qwest, a Warner Brothers subsidiary. Now he dreamed of pairing her with Frank Sinatra for the recording event of a lifetime. He envisioned an "Ultra Deluxe Package," as he called it, of three LPs, with a lavish supporting cast of jazz luminaries and pop idols.

Long before Jones had dreamed up such a project, Horne had had her qualms about him. "Lena was very funny about Quincy," said Elle Elliott. "She would always say he was trying to make a career on her career, to produce one of her albums, that he would always send her huge bouquets of flowers. She felt that he was buttering her up *way* too much."

Persuasive as Jones could be, anyone who knew Horne or Sinatra well would have doubted the notion that either star would agree to sing with the other. Horne's latter-day treatment of Lennie Hayton had sealed their alienation. Sinatra refused to see Horne's one-woman show; his wife, Barbara, attended the Broadway opening without him.

If Jones knew of the friction, it didn't keep him from barreling ahead. Evidently, Horne had given him a vague show of possible interest; as with *Hallelujah, Baby!* she tended to avoid saying a final no until she'd raised people's hopes. Sinatra, who had recorded with Jones, apparently offered a similar response.

With no firm commitment from either star, Jones booked five sessions of late-February recording time in Hollywood—dates that fell smack in the midst of Horne's grueling schedule. His meticulously planned agenda was notable for its grandiosity. Jones had enlisted dozens of hotshot musicians, including George Benson, Dizzy Gillespie, and Gerry Mulligan, and a large string section. Burt Bacharach, Marvin Hamlisch, and Marilyn and Alan Bergman would write songs for the occasion; Michael Jackson and Lionel Richie would provide guest vocals.

The main gimmick of Jones's production involved having Horne and Sinatra sing each other's signature tunes. As he later told writer Will Friedwald, "We were really planning on a real big extravaganza there.

. . . We had a medley we were supposed to do where he would open up with 'Stormy Weather,' and then she'd sing a couple of bars from 'Angel Eyes.'"

But Horne had said long ago that she hated doing other artists' trademarks; certainly she didn't care to cover "Strangers in the Night" and "My Way," as Jones wanted. She was no happier when columnists all over the country began running announcements of the planned album, sent out by Jones's publicists. Not long before the February dates, Horne gave a prickly denial of involvement to the *Los Angeles Times*. "All I know about it is what I read in the papers. You probably know more about it than I do. When you find something out, let me know." Sinatra's representatives issued a firmer statement: "It's no more than just talk at this time."

Apparently Jones clung to the idea. According to Charles Pignone's book *The Sinatra Treasures: Intimate Photos, Mementos, and Music from the Sinatra Family Collection,* for which Jones wrote the foreword, "all that was left was for Horne and Sinatra to meet to discuss the album." Embarrassingly for him, no conference—and no recording—ever took place. Now he had to save face. Various excuses were given as to why the project had fizzled. Pignone noted that the proposed conductor, Don Costa, had died during preparations, "delaying the meeting" between the singers. In fact, Costa's death occurred on January 19, 1983, amid long-established tour dates that would have left Horne unable to attend a meeting in Hollywood. "Vocal problems" on her part were also blamed, yet no sign of them appeared in her engagements. "Then Sinatra had back-to-back gigs in Atlantic City and Vegas," wrote Pignone; these, too, would have been booked many months earlier, and could hardly have come as a surprise to Jones.

Ever resourceful, he found in the aborted project the seeds of a solo disk he produced the next year, Sinatra's acclaimed *L.A. Is My Lady.* But he continued to mourn the collapse of what "would have been a great album," as he told Friedwald. More likely there would have been no chemistry between its stars at all; they didn't even want to be in the same room, much less singing love duets.

Horne's tour was initially slated to end in May of 1983, but more and more cities got piled on. With each stop, her performance seemed to turn harder and more mechanical. "The road show should have stopped a lot sooner than it did," said Marcia Ann Gillespie. "But I think she wanted that attention. She's an entertainer. That's what they live for." After leaving the theater, she and Sneed got their main pleasure of the night. Their driver took them to Popeyes, where they ordered fried chicken, cornbread, and corn on the cob. They hauled it back to Horne's hotel room, where she downed a stiff drink.

By now Michael Frazier and Fred Walker had withdrawn as active producers, though they retained a financial interest. Both men believed that Sneed had been trying to phase them out in order to gain a controlling interest in the show, and according to Mike Renzi, Sneed had successfully alienated the producers from Horne. "He used to tell her they were jerks, and she believed it."

Walker had seen the process before. "Sherman tried to get rid of everybody," he said. "But I realized he was being allowed to do this by Lena."

It was hard not to feel sour, but Horne had earned the two producers a fortune. For the next twenty years, Frazier sent her flowers on her birthday and Christmas. He never heard a word of thanks.

On August 6, 1984, *The Lady and Her Music* opened a monthlong engagement at London's Adelphi Theatre. Only Sweden remained. The sparse turnouts that had greeted her at the London Palladium in 1980 weren't repeated now; Horne was showered with publicity, and played to packed houses. There in England, where Horne had performed since 1947, plastic-surgery speculation was rife. During one performance, wrote Irving Wardle of the London *Times*, Horne actually tried "laying rumors of a face-lift [to rest] by yanking her hair up."

In interviews, she didn't try to feign enthusiasm for the show. "Enough is enough," she told Clive Hirschhorn. "It's time to concentrate on my five grandchildren a bit. Not that they really care one way or another, though." The teenage Jenny Lumet was in London, Horne explained, and had asked her for a pair of opening-night tickets. "Not because *she* wanted to see the show, but, she said, because her friend Debbie did. Well, in a way that's a good thing, I guess. They're not impressed with their grandma and that's fine."

Horne's happiest moments in London were spent with Ava Gardner, who had lived there since 1968. Long a recluse, the actress came to the

Adelphi midway through Horne's run; subsequently Richard Young, a photographer, snapped their picture as they laughed together at Downes Wine Bar.

But Gardner was just as depressed as Horne; commiseration had always marked their friendship, and they looked back with equal disdain on their careers as Hollywood beauties. Horne quoted Gardner's response to a comment made about her "wonderful" time in the movies: "It wasn't wonderful. It was shit." Nonetheless, Gardner would go on to play a running part on the television series *Knots Landing* and to make two TV movies. In 1989 she suffered a stroke; the next year she died of pneumonia. Frank Sinatra paid her medical expenses.

Horne's crowning laurel awaited her back home in the States. She'd been chosen to receive one of that year's Kennedy Center Honors for lifetime achievement in the performing arts. That December she and the other honorees—Danny Kaye, Gian Carlo Menotti, Arthur Miller, and Isaac Stern—would go to Washington, D.C., to visit the Reagan White House; then they would attend a televised ceremony at the Kennedy Center.

The news had reached Horne in time for her London opening, and Clarke Taylor, a visiting reporter from the *Los Angeles Times,* asked her about it in her dressing room. Horne, he said, "spoke of the Kennedy Center Honor only hesitantly, and with coolness." She didn't mention her loathing of the Reagans, but shared another opinion: If it weren't for her hit show, the center would never have thought her worth honoring. "I have worked nearly nonstop for forty years," she explained, "but nobody seemed to pay much attention." It was "kind of sad," she mused, that people had taken this long to notice her—"but I'll take whatever I can get."

Lonely as she was, Horne had welcomed the attentions of Joyce Eskridge, a bank executive from Waxahachie, Texas, with whom she'd developed an unusual closeness. Then in her early fifties, Eskridge was entranced by Horne; two years earlier she had treated herself to an idyllic trip that included Horne's Broadway closing and a night at the Plaza Hotel.

Eskridge had been heartbroken at the cancellation of Horne's run in Dallas, and furious at Elsie Faye Heggins for prompting it. She'd fired off an irate letter to the *Dallas Morning News*, and sent a copy to Sherman Sneed, whom she hadn't met. Both he and Horne were so impressed that Sneed arranged for Joyce to meet "the lady" after a performance in Houston. In the dressing room, Horne met the banker, an attractive woman with glasses and a warm, efficient air. The star thanked her for the letter she'd written, noting that it had taken guts. Not guts, said Eskridge— "just a burning anger." Horne was pleased. Later on, in a letter to Joyce, Sneed commented on the "instant rapport" that Horne had felt with her, adding that she'd loved her sense of humor.

Horne had agreed to reschedule her Dallas appearances for October 1983, and Eskridge wrote to Sneed, telling her which night she planned to attend. After the show, he whisked her up to the dressing room. There, said the banker, Horne "grabbed me in a bear hug," greeting her as "my friend and fighter from Waxahachie." They chatted and laughed together for some time. Horne invited her to come for Sunday brunch; in her diary later, Eskridge noted a two-and-a-half-hour visit in the star's hotel room, with no one else present.

Ten months later, when Joyce could take vacation time from the bank, she and Horne reunited in London. Sneed had booked her a suite in their hotel, the Athenaeum. Joyce arrived to a red-carpet welcome— a fruit basket and champagne, free tickets to as many performances as she wished to attend, invitations to rehearsals at the Adelphi. The banker was elated. More royal treatment followed of a kind Horne had seldom, if ever, shown to a fan. Joyce was invited to join Horne and Sneed for a night on the town at Ronnie Scott's jazz club; in the dressing room, Horne introduced her to Ava Gardner, Rex Harrison, and Dyan Cannon. Her diary included the following entry for Thursday, August 30: "Rested in room at 2:00 P.M. 3:30 to 5:00—visited with Lena in her suite." After seeing the show again on Sunday night, Joyce noted: "Back to hotel in limo and to Lena's suite for a nightcap."

Then she returned to Waxahachie. She never heard from Horne again. But Sneed wrote on September 7, 1984, to thank her: "Your visit here was good for Lena. . . . It provided a break in what gets to be a tedious work schedule." Horne, he said, had been "delighted" by her company.

Shortly before she died of lung cancer in 2005, Eskridge had developed a correspondence with Wendy Munson, a Horne enthusiast who lived in Westchester County. Munson would inherit much of the banker's memorabilia. It included a detailed scrapbook of Horne's tour, all her correspondence with Sneed, and meticulous documentation of her time with Horne—save for certain details that were, in Eskridge's words, "personal and private."

LATE in September, after over two years away, Horne finally went home to New York. In addition to her Tony and two Grammys, *The Lady and Her Music* had earned her a Drama Desk Award, a special citation from the New York Drama Critics' Circle, and keys to nine cities. *Harper's Bazaar* had listed a sixty-four-year-old Horne among the ten most beautiful women in America. Over the years, many veteran songstresses tried to do what Horne had done at the Nederlander; the results ranged from disastrous (Peggy Lee) to celebrated (Elaine Stritch).

Horne, of course, would henceforth be seen as an unabashed victor. In 1984, *California Living* magazine had interviewed her by questionnaire. Under "Major Accomplishment," the star filled in, "Not having killed myself."

THAT December, accompanied by Sherman Sneed, Horne joined her fellow Kennedy Center Honorees in a front-mezzanine box at the center's Opera House. She had rarely looked more beautiful, and sat with queenly carriage, head held high, as tributes were heaped upon her. Dionne Warwick hosted her segment. "I call Lena 'Mama,'" explained the singer. "You made it possible for me and the rest of your children to be anything they wanted to be." Warwick narrated a biographical film montage, played over the song "Believe in Yourself." The script encompassed most of the familiar Horne myths. Lena had entered show business reluctantly, Warwick noted. In Hollywood she was "a butterfly pinned to a pillar"; during the civil rights movement "the hurt caught up with her . . . she couldn't sing." After the three big deaths, "the two Lenas—one private, one public—became one."

The emcee, former CBS Evening News anchorman Walter Cronkite, added the inevitable. "In the 1940s," he said, "M-G-M would not let Lena Horne star in the movie *Show Boat*"—he paused—"because she was black." He then introduced the young dancer-choreographer Debbie

Allen, who costarred in the M-G-M hit *Fame*. As Horne's recordings of "The Lady Is a Tramp" and "Can't Help Lovin' Dat Man" played, Allen danced a tribute to the star. Choking back tears, Horne joined in her own standing ovation.

She had succeeded abundantly in crafting an iconic self-image. Horne was on an untouchable pedestal; now, at sixty-seven, she had to figure out what to do with the rest of her life. Asked by Arthur Unger of the *Christian Science Monitor* if she wanted to star in another show, Horne groaned. "I'm too tired now," she said.

She certainly didn't need the money. If, according to Fred Walker, Horne had opened her show as a millionaire, she'd left it far richer. Another hefty payoff came with the sale of her Montecito home; she'd resumed living at the Wyndham Hotel. Soon she would describe herself as a "fucking recluse."

Her six-show-a-week schedule for over three years had taken other tolls. In 1985, gossip columnist Cindy Adams reported that Horne needed surgery on her toes. Her singing, too, had suffered. The ravages were clear that spring when she made a guest appearance on *The Cosby Show*. Horne had a genuine fondness for its star, Bill Cosby, who played Heathcliff Huxtable, a doctor and family man. "He is true and special," she said. "He never makes a wrong move on that show."

In the episode, Cliff's wife, played by Phylicia Rashad, arranges a surprise for his birthday and won't reveal it no matter how he tries to coax it out of her. Finally, she and their children lead him, blindfolded, into a little supper club. The emcee announces the evening's headliner— Lena Horne. Accompanied by Mike Renzi, she salutes him by singing "I'm Glad There Is You." Horne could barely sustain a phrase, and talk-sang her way through one chorus.

Frail as she sounded, the show made her realize that she did not want to retire. On May 26, a few weeks after the episode ran, Horne told Kathy Larkin of the New York *Daily News* that she was waiting for the green light on her own spin-off series from *The Cosby Show*. Horne, explained Larkin, envisioned a series in a café setting, where young guests would drop by to sing and chat. "Not just me being Mother Earth," she explained. "Nothing is more boring than an old broad trying to give advice to this generation."

The project fell through, and Horne was left to deal with a separate one she wished she'd never started. During *The Lady and Her Music*, Sneed had talked her into writing her third autobiography. "The fact is, I have a lot of trouble reliving all that crap," she told Cindy Adams. To ease the way, she and Sneed chose Marcia Ann Gillespie as cowriter. Gillespie had profiled Horne for *Ms.*, and Horne liked her. The pair signed a contract with Delacorte Books, which planned to publish the memoir in 1986.

Gillespie followed Horne on the road, recording their conversations. The effort dragged on for years, and the deeper Gillespie probed, the more she began to sense Horne's mounting reluctance. "There were so many demons she was wrestling with, so many. I think she wanted to get some truth said. But Gail was also writing a book about the family, and Lena didn't want to upset what I think had long been a tricky relationship with her daughter. We would have sessions where we were really starting to get at the bone of the thing, then she would clam up, and not want to talk to me. I knew what was going on. I knew it wasn't personal."

Finally, after several long silences, Sneed phoned Gillespie. Horne did not wish to go forward with the book. Gillespie never expected to hear from her again. Some months later she was startled to receive a call from Horne, asking her to drop by the Wyndham. There Horne offered a rare apology, while letting Gillespie know that she didn't want to upset her daughter by revealing any truths that could prove painful. "I knew she was saying to me, 'I'm gonna protect this family.' I couldn't argue with that. I liked Lena. I thought she was fabulous. It was an extraordinary experience on so many levels."

As Gail approached fifty, Horne thought a lot about their troubled relationship. "I wasn't what you'd call a storybook mother," she admitted. "I didn't have the time, the space, before; I missed that. But I'd like to know her, the woman she is now. Maybe I never will, yet I hope and I try."

Gail's religious rebirth had changed her life, and recently she'd married a man with "exactly the same ideas" as her own. Journalist and editor Kevin Buckley was a former Vietnam War correspondent for *Newsweek*. "He had lost his faith, as all good Catholics do," said Gail in the *Los Angeles Times*. "When he found it again he went to do a story at Lourdes." She would henceforth call herself Gail Lumet Buckley. The two weighty last names, along with her inescapable title, "the daughter of Lena Horne," brought her a triple dose of social pedigree—even if Kevin wasn't related to William F. Buckley, the renowned conservative political commentator, as some people assumed.

None of that seemed to have alleviated Gail's sense that although she'd come from a family of achievers, she herself "hadn't done much of anything." In the early 1980s she'd discovered a solution. Opening a trunk that had belonged to her maternal grandfather, she discovered a wealth of family memorabilia—photos, documents, artifacts. Out of that came her first book, *The Hornes: An American Family*, published by Alfred A. Knopf in 1986.

It explored the phenomenon of the black bourgeoisie, while exhaustively documenting seven generations of the superproductive Hornes. Gail reminded readers, "I am a Horne, too"—and in the latter half of the book she traced her own journey, which seemed at odds with that of her forebears. If the movie business had thrown her mother into turmoil, Gail had "lived the lazy Hollywood life to the hilt." Of her days as one of the few black students at Radcliffe, she reflected: "Personally, I found that tokenism could be 'fun.'"

The downside of life as the daughter of Lena Horne remained unshared, either in her breezy lines or between them. "Buckley chooses a policy of never apologize, never explain," wrote Melvin Maddocks in *Time*. "The story of Lena and Gail can be measured in privilege and recognition; what remains incalculable is the withholding tax that both women are still paying for their lives."

Nonetheless, all of Gail's striving for identity had ended happily, for now she was an author. In public appearances, she made a crisp, authoritative impression. Speaking to Boston TV interviewer Tanya Hart, Gail remarked, "I do feel that I've climbed my own mountain."

FOR her mother, however, the hurdles seemed unending. Toward the end of her tour, Horne had attracted a stalker. Letters had started arriving from Doris Newman, a woman of around forty from Tacoma, Washington. She rambled maniacally about how she and Horne shared psychic and biblical bonds; reportedly Newman claimed to be the reincarnation of Judy Garland. She begged the star for a meeting. The letters trailed Horne around the country; then Newman began leaving phone messages. Police arrested her on December 12, 1984, but after posting bail she left town. Horne filed a restraining order, but the letters kept coming. Sherman Sneed again called the police, and finally they apprehended Newman on May 2, 1985. She'd been in a Manhattan hotel, dangerously close to Horne.

The trauma of having a stalker might well have provoked the move she took that summer. On June 24, 1985, the *New York Post* carried the news. Horne had just bought an eleven-room condominium in Washington, D.C., and gave curious reasons why. In New York, she said "The price of real estate is so inflated . . . and the transportation system is so bad." She found the D.C. Metro a refreshing change from New York's IRT, she noted. No one, of course, had seen Horne in a subway car in decades, except for the night when one of them had transported her and other VIPs to a downtown party for *The Wiz*. Horne added that she was "getting old and am alone a lot." Presumably she just wanted to go away.

The *Post* article noted that she planned to spend time there with her friend Vernon Jordan, the lawyer, activist, and "ultimate Washington insider," as *Newsweek*'s Howard Fineman called him. Born in 1935 in Atlanta, Jordan worked as an NAACP field secretary before becoming the stern, formidable president of the National Urban League in 1972. His achievements in civil rights would pale, in the public mind, beside his role as a cultivator of the politically powerful. True celebrity came in his role as Bill Clinton's close friend and adviser before and during the Monica Lewinsky scandal.

But that was far away in 1983, when Jordan and Horne shared a memorable moment in New Orleans. The NAACP had awarded her its Spingarn Medal, given to the most outstanding black figures in the community. Horne requested that her friend Vernon Jordan make the presentation. In his speech, he placed her in a line of freedom fighters that included Harriet Tubman, Mary McLeod Bethune, and Marian Anderson. "To Hollywood's shame, her roles were limited," he said. "But whatever Lena did was done with pride, with taste, with total and irrefutable dignity. And being the Lena that she was—proud, stubborn, uncompromising—she helped us all walk a bit taller and smile a little broader."

In 1985, she called him in Washington, D.C., to announce that she wanted to buy an apartment there. "To this day I don't know what the motivation was," he said years later. Jordan helped her find a luxurious new address on Connecticut Avenue, not far from the White House. She went to great expense to have it designed. Jordan and LaSalle Leffall, the acclaimed black surgeon and former president of the American Cancer Society, threw her a grand welcoming party.

"And she never moved into the apartment," said Jordan. "She never actually lived in Washington. I don't know what that was about. I think she was in a state of flux about what she wanted to do."

The *Post* item had helped set off rumors of a romance between Horne and Jordan. If it were true, he would have had to be working overtime. Jordan was married when Horne arrived, but near Christmastime he lost his wife to multiple sclerosis. Months later, he wed Ann Dibble, a social worker and professor from Tuskegee, Alabama. Jordan invited Horne to meet her over dinner. She showed up with Sneed for what began as a tense gathering. Horne clearly didn't know anything about Jordan's new spouse, who was fair enough to be mistaken for white. "She was very cold to Ann," said Jordan. "She was just chilling. She thought I'd married a white woman and she wasn't happy about it." But then Ann started talking about her childhood in Tuskegee, and Horne melted. "It was all great after that," Jordan recalled.

Other relationships of hers hadn't fared so well. Friends noticed that Jeanne Noble had disappeared from her life. Given Horne's history of submitting to mentor figures, then resentfully pushing them away, the break was no surprise. The next to go was Ralph Harris. In 1986, a falling-out occurred that he refused to discuss even with his children. The only clue his daughter Trygve could find lay in a letter he'd gotten from his best friend in France, who wrote, "I can't believe that Lena said that. That's terrible."

"And all of a sudden—boom, it was over," said Trygve. "She wasn't around anymore. Never heard from her again."

Harris lived out his years in retirement at his Montecito home. In all that time, his daughter never heard him utter a thing about Horne. "I think I might have asked once and he just said, 'Oh, shit!'" His death in 1992 brought not a word from the star to whom he'd devoted his career. Harris's widow, Grace, who had long referred to Horne as "that bitch," was more incensed with her than ever.

Publicly, though, Horne's esteem had only risen. Now a semiretired grande dame, she continued to amass prestigious honors. The Radcliffe College Alumnae Association gave her its Radcliffe Medal for distinguished women. The United Negro College Fund chose Horne for its Frederick D. Patterson Award, named after the organization's founder. The Parsons School of Design in New York honored her for her contribution to fashion.

Horne had been away from her hometown for three years, but in the late eighties she sold her unused Washington, D.C., apartment for a reported million-plus dollars and took a small one at 211 East Seventieth Street in Manhattan. Her friend Kaye Ballard, the singing comedienne of stage and television, was her neighbor. During that period, Horne had made a separate windfall by singing at private corporate events, many for IBM.

She seemed intent upon making as much extra money as she could while her health permitted, perhaps to ensure that her family members would have no financial cares after she'd left them. Accompanied by Frank Owens, the pianist who'd taught her "Believe in Yourself" for *The Wiz,* Horne made occasional trips out of town. For staggering fees, she went to Bermuda, Vancouver, San Diego, and Phoenix to entertain businessmen. One tycoon hired her to sing for his birthday aboard the USS *Intrepid.* Horne also profited handsomely by hawking Sanka instant coffee and Post Bran Flakes on TV.

For years she'd enjoyed the generosity of one of her most loyal friends. Shirley Cowell, whom she'd met in the forties, had been born into three major fortunes—soybeans, starch, and oil. But unlike such heiresses as Barbara Hutton and Doris Duke, Cowell was painfully shy and terrified of the spotlight. Mostly in secret, she donated millions to hospitals, universities, arts organizations, and AIDS causes. The "Poor Little Rich Girl" fable applied to Cowell, who had battled alcoholism and depression for years. Once sober, she knew no greater delight than pampering her friends, many of them singers or musicians—Gloria DeHaven, Eileen

Farrell, Sylvia Syms, Johnny Mathis, Sandy Stewart, jazz pianist Barbara Carroll. Cowell doled out an endless stream of gifts, ranging from Beluga caviar to a condominium. "She was like a fairy godmother," said Stewart. Most of all, she loved financing albums for her pet songbirds; it thrilled her if they agreed to record one of the pretty love songs she'd written.

Horne, of course, stayed a bit apart from the rest of Cowell's flock. "Their relationship was very private," Stewart recalled. "Lena would visit her about once a year in Florida, and Shirley made sure she got treated like a queen. Shirley would tell me, 'Oh, I'm all excited, Lena's coming down to visit!'" It distressed some of Cowell's friends to see how offhandedly Horne treated the white heiress in return. "Shirley had a huge crush on Lena, who was not above using rich people to her advantage," said Rex Reed. Most annoyed of all was Gigi Carrier, the woman with whom Cowell had lived for years. "Gigi was jealous of Lena, *very* jealous," said DeHaven.

Horne hadn't released a studio album in over a decade, and Cowell urged her to make one, all expenses paid. Horne agreed. *The Men in My Life,* as she called it, was recorded in New York in the spring and summer of 1988. Owens and Mike Renzi did most of the arranging; some tracks were swathed in strings. On *CBS This Morning,* reporter Mark McEwen asked her what had made her do a new album. "Actually a lot of prodding from my grandchildren and my daughter and my manager," said Horne. "I don't think they like to see me not working—because they're not working. They said, 'You've got so much energy, Mama, why don't you do somethin'?' I said, 'I'm too old, I've been doing it too long!' 'No, you gotta, you gotta.' So to get 'em off my back I did it."

Aside from guest appearances by Sammy Davis, Jr., and Joe Williams, *The Men in My Life* had nothing more to do with men than any other Horne album. But after years of telling interviewers that she never wanted to remarry, the singer claimed otherwise. "I like to have a man in my life—*yes* . . . I would like to be married," she told Barbara Gordon. To Eliot Tiegel she declared, "It's boring for a seventy-one-year-old broad to sing about how bad she wants a man . . . even though it's true."

As comments of that sort piled up, speculation arose among some of her gay fans. Was Horne afraid of "outing," the new media phenomenon that had sent many gay or bisexual celebrities running for cover? Or was she just lonely?

Seldom had she sounded so morose as she did on *The Men in My Life*. Cole Porter's "Ours" harked back to her nights at the Waldorf, but now she couldn't feign excitement over its account of Mediterranean jaunts and gondola joyrides. Vernon Duke's "Round About" told of living on a treadmill, going nowhere. "She loved that song because she said it described her life," said Renzi, but her thoughts seemed to wander as she sang it. Upbeat songs like "A Fine Romance" had a somber air.

The vocal rest she'd given herself at that time had done Horne good; only a slight wobble betrayed her age. She'd dropped her affected street diction, and sang every song in the precise English she'd displayed in the fifties. A fan of hers from those days, Sammy Davis, Jr., had agreed to sing with her. The sight of him in May 1988 moved Horne deeply. At sixty-two, this most ebullient of song-and-dance men was physically and emotionally diminished. Davis had just attended his father's funeral; and after a lifetime of smoking, drinking, and carousing his own health had declined. Two years later, he died of throat cancer. He owed the IRS millions.

Sadness enveloped him, but he could still sing beautifully. Later Horne talked about their duet, "I Wish I'd Met You": "It's very difficult to make long-lasting friends in our business, because we go from town to town and place to place, and we don't form a lot of great friendships. That song said all that."

The Men in My Life scored a Grammy nomination in the female jazz vocal category; Horne's track with Joe Williams, "I Won't Leave You Again," earned one for Best Jazz Vocal Performance, Duo or Group. The trophies went elsewhere, but at the February 1989 ceremony Horne collected a Grammy for Lifetime Achievement.

Her satisfaction was short-lived. Three Cherries, the start-up record label that had issued her album, soon went bankrupt. After all her triumphs of the past decade, the failure of yet another album truly hurt. Unwilling to give up completely, she agreed to play a few more top-dollar corporate events, accompanied by Renzi. "She didn't really perform up to her standard," said the pianist. "She was just doing it for the bread."

Once home, Horne began having fainting spells. After collapsing at an antique show she was rushed to the hospital. The singer was diagnosed with heart disease, and learned she would need a pacemaker. "I fought it," she said, "because I hated the thought of something . . . not me being inside me, you know?" The operation took place in 1989. It left her "angry," she admitted later. "I feel like the bionic woman. But it's a lifesaver, so they tell me."

That year Brian Lanker, a Pulitzer Prize–winning photographer, released his book *I Dream a World: Portraits of Black Women Who Changed America*. Horne was included. Lanker's image of her revealed a strikingly sad-looking elderly woman. She sat on her bed in a plain dark suit; draperies behind her shut out the sun. Her chin rested on her hand as she looked wearily into the distance.

Horne wrote an accompanying one-page text of reflections on her life. They were as gloomy as the photo. To her, the future looked bleak. "I never thought I'd live this long to see this kind of ruin, decimation," she said. "My own people are so disillusioned, desperate, and angry. Angrier than in the sixties, I think, except they have no place to put this anger."

For the next three years, few outside her family and an inner circle of friends saw much of Lena Horne. She did receive a visit from Lena Mary Jones, her then-teenage granddaughter, but it didn't go well. Little Lena shared the details with Samadhi Jones. The young woman had brought a Polaroid camera, and at one point she ran into her grandmother's room to snap her photo.

"Lena completely flew off the handle and accused her of taking pictures so she could sell them to the tabloids," said Samadhi. "Little Lena was horrified. In her mind it was just something fun to do. That's how guarded Lena was about her image."

But Horne was in hiding, and wished to stay there. "I went into another one of those pits I go into," she explained. "I didn't want to do anything, I didn't want to see anybody. I just wanted to stay home and read a book."

CHAPTER 21

BY THE 1990s, Horne had moved into another new home. It was on the fifth floor of the Volney, an exclusive condo building on East Seventy-fourth Street. The Volney had a prior distinction: Dorothy Parker had lived and died there in the sixties. Horne's sprawling apartment was "very well appointed," said Mike Renzi, "with a lot of valuable stuff." But it felt homey, with plush carpeting and soft couches. Friends recalled seeing fresh flowers everywhere, along with loads of books, which Horne called her best friends. According to Sherman Sneed, a whole room housed her dresses, protected in plastic bags. Her own records were another story; Horne claimed she'd kept only one of them, *The Lady and Her Music*.

Almost constantly, she wondered why she was still alive. At the same time, she yearned for more. "I'm looking for something . . . *exciting,*" she confessed to an interviewer. "And that's so crazy at seventy-six! I don't even know what I'm looking for. A companion like Billy would be wonderful, but there are no people like that. There will never be another Lennie in my life. When I go out and do one of those parties sometimes, they're looking for Lena Horne, and I'm not . . ." Her voice trailed off. "So . . . I read a lot."

Her spirits were low, but vanity hadn't left her. Horne made a small admission to Ponchitta Pierce in *Modern Maturity:* "I had some loose flesh removed from under my chin when I was seventy-five. That was the best birthday present I ever gave myself."

It wasn't the action of a woman who planned to stay in seclusion. Horne had grown restless, and in 1993 she made a surprise reemergence.

She agreed to play herself on *A Different World*, a sitcom set in a black southern school. In the script, Horne is invited there when a scholarship is named after her grandmother. Initially the children dismiss her as some old lady, but they wind up enchanted by her, and stage a show in her honor.

Beautiful as she remained, this was a frankly aged Horne, wearing a salt-and-pepper wig and glasses and moving gingerly. But she seemed to be having fun. The same could not be said on March 29, when she appeared as a presenter at the Oscars. She and Quincy Jones would give the award for Best Original Song. Horne had only one line to recite, but according to Sherri Sneed, who was with her in Los Angeles, she was so nervous that she rehearsed incessantly. As they walked to the podium, Jones offered a steadying hand to Horne, who seemed slightly disoriented. He read all five nominees off a teleprompter; she stared out, looking lost.

That's how Horne had usually felt in the town she loved to hate. Sherri drove her around and kept her company. "She wanted to have some drinks, so we went to Trader Vic's and got trashed." On the way home, Horne asked her to pull over to the side of the road so she could relieve herself behind a bush. "I said, Lena, I don't think so!"

Horne's late burst of Hollywood activity peaked with an appearance no one had anticipated. George Feltenstein, the senior vice president of Warner Home Video, had conceived a third edition of *That's Entertainment!*, a feature-film compilation series of golden moments from the M-G-M musical. Executive producer Peter Fitzgerald suggested including Horne among the segment hosts: June Allyson, Howard Keel, Cyd Charisse, Ann Miller, Debbie Reynolds, and Esther Williams. "Ask her, but I'm sure she'll say no," advised Feltenstein. Remarkably, she didn't. Horne was allowed to tell her M-G-M story as she chose—even though Feltenstein knew this would entail "taking a little license with history."

The shoot went pleasantly. "She was in a wonderful mood that day," said Feltenstein. It brought her a nostalgic pang to have her hair styled by Sydney Guilaroff, who had worked on it in 1942.

Her twelve-minute section began with a clip of "Where or When" from *Words and Music*. The camera pulled back to show Horne today, watching herself on-screen as she stood on the soundstage where she'd filmed that number. She sang along briefly with her thirty-year-old self.

Then, shot from various angles, she turned on her old M-G-M camera technique and reminisced.

"I have many memories here, good and bad," said Horne. "I never felt like I really belonged in Hollywood. At that time, they didn't know what to do with me, a black performer, so I usually just came on, sang a song, and made a quick exit." What she'd really wanted, she stressed, was an acting role. She'd gotten one in *Cabin in the Sky,* but her sexy rendition of "Ain't It the Truth" had been cut. It was exhumed for *That's Entertainment! III.* "Studio bosses thought it too risqué to show a black girl in a bubble bath," she explained. Horne's *Show Boat* story was illustrated by her performance of "Can't Help Lovin' Dat Man" from *Till the Clouds Roll By.* "I was being considered for the part," she maintained, "but the production code office had banned interracial romance on the screen, so the studio gave the part to my good friend Ava Gardner—and she was wonderful in it."

Having agreed to appear in this M-G-M salute, Horne proceeded to thumb her nose at it. Before the premiere, a poster was circulated among the stars to inscribe for Feltenstein. Only Horne wouldn't sign it. She attended a screening of the film at the Museum of Modern Art in New York, and conspicuously walked out after her segment. Around that time, she appeared on TV's *Live with Regis and Kathie Lee.* When cohost Regis Philbin announced a clip from the movie, Horne rolled her eyes and said, "Oh, please!" The singer aired more of her true feelings in an interview for the M-G-M archives. There she quipped about the part she'd really wanted. "I'd love to have been a wicked cook in a rich, white antebellum family, who poisoned them all. You know, slip something in the peas and rice."

She spoke just as candidly to her old friend Liz Smith. "It's hard not to feel bitter, the roles that I lost," she said. "But I'm still here, honey. And so many others aren't."

A welcome tribute came her way in June 1993, when Horne was honored at the Essence Awards, which hailed a wide range of black role models. The presenter was twenty-six-year-old Halle Berry. A former beauty queen from Cleveland, Ohio, Berry had leapt to fame with her costarring role in Spike Lee's *Jungle Fever.* In 2002, she would become the first woman of color to score the Best Actress Oscar; she won it for

Monster's Ball. Berry sobbingly acknowledged a legion of black female predecessors, including Lena Horne. It didn't go unnoticed that Hollywood had bestowed this long-awaited distinction upon an even more Caucasian-looking black beauty than Horne. (Berry's mother, in fact, was white.)

Black actresses remained a neglected breed, and Horne still wondered if her struggles had changed anything. But no one at the Essence Awards doubted it. Berry lauded her—"for your artistry, and for opening the door to Hollywood for African-American actresses, and for the passion and pride you have displayed in your career and in the fight for civil rights and human rights."

The standing ovations at Horne's entrance and exit were nothing new. But as Aretha Franklin and Tina Turner tearfully applauded her, she herself turned misty-eyed. "I couldn't have made it without my grandmother and my great-grandmother and all the grandmothers that came before me," said Horne. "I learned a bit from all of them. . . . I love you all, and I thank you for hanging in there with me this long."

Horne rarely went to public events anymore, but in May 1993 she attended a black-tie benefit for Harlem's Studio Museum. When someone asked if she'd be singing after dinner, Horne bristled, "I'm too old to be singing! You don't keep a voice all your life. When I had to start lowering keys, that was the cue telling me to get out."

She didn't mention that she'd already decided to headline a June 20 concert for the JVC Jazz Festival in New York. *A Tribute to Billy Strayhorn: Lena Horne Sings for Swee'pea* would also feature Bobby Short, saxophonist Joe Henderson, and bandleader Mercer Ellington, the son of Duke. The festival's founder, George Wein, had been after her for years to sing at his fabled summer cavalcade, which he'd founded decades earlier in Newport, Rhode Island. "I'm not a jazz singer," Horne snapped. But this time she accepted, for the show would salute the man she missed the most. "Billy pushed me," she said.

Horne chose seven of his songs, some written for her. She and a group led by Mike Renzi rehearsed diligently for weeks, as Horne struggled to warm up her voice. June 20 came quickly. Backstage, recalled Renzi, "she was petrified. She said, 'I hate this! I don't know why I'm doing it.'" Worried about her pacemaker, Horne had brought along her cardiologist.

"Oh, I'm getting pains!" she told him as she waited backstage. "No, you're gonna be fine, Lena," he said. "It's just nerves."

Bobby Short had prepared a lavish spoken introduction to usher her on in the second half. Before he'd finished delivering it, out wandered Horne to an instant standing ovation. She began to sing "Maybe," which had opened her album *Lena at the Sands,* and the audience gasped. *New York Times* critic Stephen Holden marveled at her "rivetingly energized performances"; the concert, he felt, deserved to "become legend." Horne reveled in every moment, and the time flew by. "The audience was like something I never imagined," she exclaimed later. "They were *wonderful*! Young and old. I had such a ball."

Afterward she was exhausted—yet "walking on air," as Wein told Lisa Schwarzbaum of *Entertainment Weekly.* "She knew she had done something wonderful." The backstage throng included Shirley Cowell, who'd been trying to coax Horne into letting her finance a new album. "Are you ready to start rehearsing?" Cowell asked.

As ever, Horne put up a fight. "I don't just naturally sing, you know?" she argued. "I never sing in the house. I never sing in the bathtub. I'm not a singing, joyful person." Her voice now sounded distinctly elderly, and in an interview, a franker worry emerged. "I'm just so afraid of disappointing. I guess my mother did that to me."

With great trepidation, she agreed to Cowell's plea. Within days, she'd begun practicing with her band. Helene Greece, a New York publicist who had promoted nearly all of Cowell's CD productions, was aboard this one almost from its inception. She saw that Horne's reluctance was no pose. "In my dealings with her, she was very much concerned with how she would be remembered. She never wanted to sing past the point where she could give a performance she would be happy with. In order to get her voice in shape to record, she went into heavy training mode. I think it had taken her a long time to decide that she wanted to put in that kind of intense energy. She knew that when she said yes, what she was gonna ask of herself was enormous."

The musicians boosted her. "They keep my head full of ideas," she said. "I got to feeling good, and the guys said, this is an album." The focus, of course, would be Strayhorn. But as Horne and the band weeded through other people's songs, a larger theme of lost friends began to emerge. Mike Renzi and Rodney Jones wrote a ballad, "Forever Was a Day," inspired by a pal of Horne's who had died of AIDS. "It's not easy for me to make a friend," she mused. "I could walk in the park and talk to him. I was sorta like a mother to him, I guess. We were good friends. Good as I allow myself to be. And he died."

Without a label, Horne and her accompanists recorded in September and October of 1993. The site was Nola Studios, the midtown birthplace of some of the greatest recordings in jazz history. Shirley Cowell paid abundantly for everything.

At every session, Horne walked in and went straight to her isolation booth. She stayed there, behind glass, until the end, never even emerging to listen to playbacks. At the controls was Jim Czak, Nola's co-owner and head engineer. Born in Maspeth, Queens, the bearish Czak was a respected veteran at his craft; he was also a natural clown, expert at cutting through record-date tensions and making people laugh. His friend Renzi knew that these sessions needed Czak.

Early in the first one, Czak went into Horne's booth to adjust her microphone. Her long gray hair was pulled back; she wore a hat, glasses, and a white, long-sleeved men's shirt. "Hi, Miss Horne," said the engineer. "I'm Jim Czak, I'll be recording you."

"Lena," she said. He grinned.

"Jiiiiim?"

"Yes, Lena?"

"I hate my fucking voice!"

"I said, 'Hate your voice? Everybody loves your voice! They hate this band, but they love your voice.'" Throughout the sessions, as the musicians talked among themselves, Czak kept hitting the intercom and joking with her. "Everyone treated her like a star," he said. "And I did, too, but I would talk to her like I'd talk to anyone." She and Czak became instant friends.

Outside her booth were two musical directors, Renzi and Frank Owens, and Rodney Jones, a guitarist in whom Horne had taken an interest. "He was trying to become more influential in her life," said Czak, and Sherman Sneed clearly felt threatened. When Czak introduced himself to Sneed, the manager told him, during their handshake, that no matter what anyone might have claimed, *he* (not Jones) was in charge.

Horne put on no airs. "She did whatever she was told," said Czak. "She was great to work with. Easy." As soon as the recording light in her booth turned red, she went into full performance mode, just as though she were filming an M-G-M number. Renzi had written a swing arrangement of "Old Friends" from Stephen Sondheim's *Merrily We Roll Along*. "I love it, I love that song!" Horne exclaimed later. Her once high-gloss singing had loosened up dramatically; she swung as she seldom had in her youth, and improvised like a jazz singer. Of Renzi, she said, "Many times he reminds me of Lennie and Strayhorn in his chord choices. Not the cheap, easy chords, but the dissonant, the beautiful, the ones that make a singer think." She was delighted by saxophonist Houston Person's "talking to me" on his horn during "Havin' Myself a Time," an early Billie Holiday tune. "It's so wonderful when you have musicians like that," she said.

Horne had agreed to sing "Day Follows Day," one of Shirley Cowell's songs, as a duet with Cowell's longtime friend Johnny Mathis. Even though he recorded his part in California, for Mathis it was the treat of a lifetime. "To have someone you worship call you up and ask you sing with her—oh, wow!"

Most of the Strayhorn titles were rare, and spanned their entire friendship. She'd begun learning his early art song "A Flower Is a Lovesome Thing" when he died; it took her two years, she said. "It's difficult, but it's *so* beautiful," explained Horne. "The words he uses, his changes. I saw the whole picture."

Horne had recorded "I've Got to Have You," Kris Kristofferson's sultry bedroom reverie, on *Lena, A New Album*. It required her to sing about a lover whose touch and gaze so seduced her that time stood still. "I can remember days, lovely days, when I felt that kind of song," she said. Now that she was in her seventies, the song's images of erotic longing took on a new poignancy. Horne worried if people would snicker. "I thought, 'I wonder if they'll say, why would an old broad like that be singing with passion?' They don't know that people will *always* have passion and romance inside them. We don't become empty shells because we're older."

Everyone involved in the CD, even Horne, knew they had created something special. "She won't say so," remarked Cowell, "but deep down, she knows the album is good."

Normand Kurtz, a show-business attorney, took the tape to a venerated jazz label, Blue Note. Its president, Bruce Lundvall, knew he
wanted it after hearing half a song. "To me, Lena was a great jazz singer
who wasn't recognized as such by the critical jazz community," he said.
"She'd been taken for granted forever." Horne was happily startled that
he wanted her, but hanging over her were memories of a lifetime of poor
sales. "I have to remind you, I don't sell records," she warned Lundvall.
"Maybe you're in for a surprise," he said. "What category are you gonna
put me in?" she replied. "Old-Lady Listening?"

Lundvall invited her to Blue Note to meet his staff. She went from
desk to desk, shyly greeting each employee. She was old enough to be
their grandmother, yet they welcomed her like a pop star and enthused
over the plans Blue Note had for her. Their youthful excitement made
her painfully aware of her age. "I feel like an intruder," she said later. "I
want to say to them, 'Look, you're just children to me. I can't, and I won't,
try to be young for you.' They don't know anything about my generation,
and I don't think they understand what I'm saying and singing." And
at a time when power belters like Whitney Houston, Celine Dion, and
Mariah Carey defined the female pop singer, Horne felt all the more
alien. "It's very difficult for me to be . . . commercially emotional," she
explained. "I can't imitate anybody, I can just be me, and I'm sorry this
poor company's gonna have trouble!"

Yet she couldn't doubt the staff's faith in her. Blue Note produced
a music video of Horne in a downtown nightclub, lip-synching to
Duke Ellington's "Do Nothin' Till You Hear from Me," a track from
the album. The company poured time and money into publicity, even
issuing a deluxe promo edition of the CD, elaborately boxed and tied
with a red ribbon. "I'm in love with Bruce Lundvall and Blue Note!"
Horne said.

She tried to earn their belief in her. In March 1994, prior to her album's release, Horne agreed to ride a cross-country train to the National
Association of Recording Merchandisers convention in San Francisco;
there she would preview the CD for an industry crowd. Horne was by
far the oldest of the guest artists, who also included Jackson Browne.
Lundvall recalled how long she fussed in the mirror before performing,
to strive for the old knockout effect. It worked. Horne sang a couple of

songs, a video tribute was shown, "and the audience went insane," said Lundvall. "These were salespeople, they were hustlers. I think she was thrilled by the response."

Less eagerly, she went to Florida—where she'd known some of the worst prejudice of her life—to do two concerts with the Palm Beach Pops. Mike Renzi had gotten her the job. "I did it mainly to see if that joy I felt the night of Billy's concert would carry over," said Horne. In her first full-length performances in years, the flamboyant chattiness of her 1980s rebirth was gone, replaced by her reticence of old. "That's what I'm going back to," she said later. "I was in Florida, and I thought, 'I don't want to talk to these people!'"

She found them a blasé crowd. "They really didn't react as a New York audience would. Evidently they liked it. But I think that out of New York, you know, nothing is happening."

In Manhattan, Horne's reemergence was an event. Blue Note released *We'll Be Together Again* on May 9 to unanimous raves. Stephen Holden called it "one of the most heartfelt chapters in a recording career that has seen the singer thaw from a forbiddingly slinky nightclub chanteuse into a more emotionally unguarded, if still regal, pop-jazz legend." Two Carnegie Hall concerts were scheduled for September; then, after she'd had a day's rest, the Arts & Entertainment cable network would tape a performance at the Supper Club, inside New York's Hotel Edison.

Horne had typically mixed feelings. "The ego still wanted to be fed," said Renzi, "but the other half of her said, 'No, I have enough money, and I don't know if I really like this.'" And as always, she mistrusted the attention. "Too little, too late," she complained to Jonathan Schwartz. "Where were they twenty years ago? But then I wasn't as lonely and strange as I am now. I feel sad in a lot of it. I miss Billy. I'm angry with him. I'm angry with all of them that I loved who've died." Horne told Bruce Lundvall that she, too, would be dead soon, so what difference did any of this make?

Talking to Horne on his radio show, Jonathan Schwartz asked her about the album's closing track, "My Buddy," a sentimental old ballad about a departed soul mate. Horne recalled performing it in the forties at a meeting of her uncle's fraternity. She'd spotted a boy she'd grown up with in Brooklyn. Buddy was his name, and she sang "My Buddy" to him. "It was a very strange, loving moment in my life," said Horne.

Fifty years later, at the *We'll Be Together Again* rehearsals, she'd started singing the song unaccompanied, and the musicians urged her to record it. Accompanied only by Renzi and violinist Sanford Allen, Horne became so emotional that her voice cracked. The last of the old armor was gone, and Horne seemed uneasy about revealing so much. Schwartz played the track, and as soon as it ended she said in a trembling voice, "I'm gonna leave you now. I thank you for playing the, uh, the album . . . I thank you."

Interview requests poured in to her publicist, Helene Greece. She agreed to most of them, reluctantly. When Carol Rosen of *Theater Week* asked her how she could stand to do another interview, Horne answered, "Everybody's got a chore they have to do." She'd grown tired of talking about her life, and as Greece soon learned, she wasn't any happier being photographed. *Entertainment Weekly* had scheduled a shoot in conjunction with a Horne feature, and as it began, the star was uneasy. But having learned of Horne's passion for Aretha Franklin, Greece had brought along several CDs. "The minute they went on there was a transformation," she said. "Lena started to loosen up, she started to dance. She took off her wig and allowed herself to be photographed with her real hair. I remember her saying, 'I always wanted to be able to open my mouth and sing like Aretha Franklin. Now *there's* a real singer.'"

As the summer ended, Horne's tension rose, for she had Carnegie Hall and the Supper Club facing her. She rehearsed almost daily in the weeks before the concerts, which would take place on September 16, 17, and 19. True fear had begun to set in, related mostly to her age. She told David Patrick Stearns of *USA Today*, "I'm terrified to get up onstage now, trying to remember thirty songs." In what may have been a dig at Frank Sinatra, whose failing memory required him to use teleprompters, Horne added, "I can't afford to carry around those prompt machines."

Carnegie Hall was sold out on both nights, which only worsened Horne's anxiety. "They're waiting to see if I can walk across the stage," she said. Certainly her audiences saw a more sedate Horne than they'd witnessed at the Nederlander. Only flashes of the old ferocity remained in a program that scanned her whole career, from the Cotton Club to

M-G-M to the Waldorf to her one-woman show. Horne's moves were now slow and careful, her manner solemn. She seemed to lean on her musicians for strength, whether by standing close to Renzi, sidling up between sax player Donald Harrison and bassist Ben Brown, turning to face drummer Akira Tana, or clutching the hand of Rodney Jones as she bowed.

Her fragility was obvious, and the audiences showered her with a reverence reserved for distinguished elder statesmen. Their loudest applause followed "Yesterday, When I Was Young." Horne had dragged a stool to center stage, sat with her shoulders hunched, and sung to herself in a murmur that finally broke into a primal outcry. "I think that song belongs to a lot of us," she said once the standing ovation had died down.

By her encore, "Stormy Weather," she seemed tired. Then she reached the word "love" and spewed it out as though it were poison. The rage that had driven her for so long boiled up as feverishly as ever, and she finished the song at full tilt.

A bevy of colleagues, including Josephine Premice and Cicely Tyson, lined up to congratulate her after each Carnegie Hall show. Horne wasn't eager to see anyone; Sherman Sneed told some of her admirers that she'd lain down to rest before saying her hellos. She finally said her hellos, but barely had the energy. Her dressing room was "pandemonium," said Jim Czak. "Masses of people were trying to get to her." Horne sat slumped in a chair, towel around her neck, wearily greeting the throngs.

Two days later she repeated the program at the Supper Club. She won the same rapturous applause, but her fatigue showed.

Horne had told Czak that she'd wanted to end her recording career with *We'll Be Together Again*. Her enthusiasm had faded, but she seemed unwilling to let go entirely. Curiously, in 1994 she agreed to appear on *Duets II*, Frank Sinatra's last studio album. Nearly eighty and losing his memory, he could no longer learn new songs. In a stroke of commercial brilliance, his advisers had conceived a CD in which he'd revisit his most celebrated tunes in tandem with major pop names. *Duets* had brought Sinatra a bona fide hit album, and the inevitable sequel followed. No guests on either CD sang in the studio with him; the parts were recorded separately and pieced together. "That's probably why she did it," said Bruce Lundvall.

Mike Renzi coached an unenthusiastic Horne on "Embraceable You." Later, she was filmed lip-synching the song for a *Duets* special, an assemblage of videos in which old Sinatra footage was superimposed upon his partners' performances. Horne looked more like an old church lady than a glamour queen; she wore a plain black dress with a silver cross around her neck, round tinted glasses, and a net around her white hair. Asked on camera for her fondest memory of Sinatra, she could only stammer out a halting mention of their first meeting at M-G-M, where Lennie Hayton had introduced them. Her segment was left out of the show.

Now in his midseventies, Sneed had remained intensely protective of Horne, and she continued to lean on him heavily. But he'd had two heart bypass operations, and glaucoma clouded his vision. He hobbled like a run-down old man.

Rodney Jones was taking over much of Sneed's position. Jones had met Horne when he played in *The Lady and Her Music*. A slick talker who loved expounding on New Age spirituality—but was also quick with a put-down—Jones had made it to the front line of Horne's affections. "From what I could see," said Helene Greece, "she and Rodney had a great personal friendship. She trusted his musical judgment; she trusted him personally; she liked having him close to her."

In a replay of Sneed's selective gatekeeping, musicians who had known Horne for years complained of having their contact discouraged. When Frank Owens called her from Bermuda to wish her a happy birthday, Jones answered the phone in her apartment and wouldn't pass it over.

The guitarist urged her to keep singing, and Blue Note was all in favor of more recordings. That year the label released a CD of her Supper Club show. Without the visual element, Horne's vocal losses sounded all the more pronounced. But this was her time to be celebrated, and the album won a Grammy for Best Jazz Vocal Performance.

Requests and invitations kept coming in; Horne declined almost all of them. Mary Campbell of the Associated Press talked to her in that period. "Her smile is still dazzling, and her face wrinkle-free," wrote Campbell. Horne added more specifics. "My face has stayed, but my sight is gone. I can't see very well." Walking was getting harder; soon her pacemaker would need replacing.

She felt safest at home, visiting with family or with favored members of her musical circle—Jones, Ben Brown. Jim Czak took on the job of making her laugh, especially in her darker moments. He always phoned her with a cheeky greeting. "Hey, get dressed, come on—I'll throw you over my shoulder and we'll go out drinking." She loved his irreverence; with Czak she knew she didn't have to "be Lena Horne," as she was increasingly loath to do. Even so, said the engineer, "I felt a lot of hurt in her life." In her apartment one day, they stopped in front of a large framed photo on the wall. "Wow, who's that?" said Czak.

"That's my son."

"What a handsome man."

They stood together for some time, staring at the picture in silence. Czak asked for no more information, and Horne didn't offer any.

Talking about her past was a prospect she didn't relish. But when *American Masters,* the prestigious PBS documentary series, approached the star about profiling her for a pledge-drive special, Horne—a PBS lover—said yes. In 1996, she sat for a series of new interviews. She also recorded her own narration, for the show allowed her to tell the story her way, aided by an array of talking heads. Horne dragged out her familiar tales of victimization, with all the myths squeezed into one hour.

Broadcast on November 25, 1996, *Lena Horne: In Her Own Voice* teemed with other people's effusions—"I had never seen anyone so sexy!" "She was paying the dues for all those who had come after." Jeanne Noble pronounced Horne a "leading light" in the civil rights movement, then went from exaggeration to untruth: "We were the last persons to see Medgar before he was assassinated."

Josephine Premice spent hours primping for what would be one of her last appearances on TV. She ended up with five seconds on camera. But her comment, which referred to *The Lady and Her Music,* was the film's most profound. She called that show "Lena's truth." Horne had been telling conflicting accounts of her experiences for years, but there were hints that she was having trouble maintaining the illusions. When Sherry Carter, an interviewer for Black Entertainment Television, noted Horne's longtime assertion that she'd really wanted to be a schoolteacher, not an entertainer, the singer hesitated—then said, "Yes, that's right."

◄ Horne shows her "naked face," as she called it, to photographer Herman Leonard during a 1948 engagement at Manhattan's Copacabana. *(Herman Leonard Photography LLC/CTSIMAGES.com)*

▲ Meeting Edith Piaf in France, 1950.

◄ Louis and Teddy Jones at home in Los Angeles, c.1950. *(Courtesy of Samadhi Jones)*

▲ A petrified Horne sings for millions in her January 20, 1951, TV debut, on *Your Show of Shows. (Photofest)*

◄ With Sophie Tucker, "The Last of the Red [Hot] Mamas," at Ciro's in Hollywood, 1953.

▼ Starring in Las Vegas, 1956. *(William Clax[ton] Photography)*

▼ Onstage at the Sands' Copa Room. *(William Claxton Photography)*

Sands

LENA HORNE
GEORGE TAPPS & HIS DANCERS
CHUCK NELSON
THE MOST BEAUTIFUL GIRLS IN THE WEST
ANTONIO MORELLI AND HIS MUSIC

Continuous entertainment nightly on the stage

NAPOLEON BRO[S]
ERNIE STEWART TR[IO]
RUBEN AND THE GUADALUPES
BARBARA CARROLL [TRIO]

► Photographer William Claxton caught this glimpse of Horne and soulmate Billy Strayhorn in the Sands' dressing room, 1956. *(William Claxton Photography)*

◀ Emoting at Hollywood's Cocoanut Grove while Lennie Hayton conducts, 1956. *(Frank Driggs Collection)*

▲ With Lennie Hayton and pet at the Sands, 1957. *(Courtesy of St. Clair Pugh)*

▲ On TV's *The Ed Sullivan Show,* 1957.

◀ Ted's high-school sweetheart and student body vice president, Teretta LaVelle Burton. *(Courtesy of Terrie Burton-Charles)*

◀ On Broadway with Augustine Rios and Rica[ ]
Montalban in *Jamaica*, 1957. *(Photofest)*

▼ Horne and Montalban greet visiting sailors outs[ ]
the Imperial Theater, 1957. *(Courtesy of Claude Thomps[ ]*

▲ With son, Teddy Jones, and Lennie Hayton at the Cocoanut Grove, 1959. *(Jess Rand Collection)*

▶ Backstage at Manhattan's York Theater after Horne's daughter, Gail Jones, makes her off-Broadway debut in *Valmouth*, October 1960.

ew white journalists gained Horne's trust
Alan Ebert, shown with her here at NBC
o in 1963. *(Courtesy of Alan Ebert)*

▲ With son, Ted, and her close companion, the feminist
scholar Jeanne Noble, in Jackson, June 8, 1963. *(Schomburg Collection/New York Public Library)*

'Freedom!" shouts Horne at the March on
shington, 1963. *(Library of Congress)*

▶ Teddy Jones and Marsha Hamilton with
newborn twins William and Thomas, 1964.
(Courtesy of Samadhi Jones)

◀ Horne played a madam and the lover of a western marshal (Richard Widmark) in the movie *Death of a Gunfighter* (1968).

▲ Horne and Harry Belafonte tape their 1970 special *Harry & Lena* during an upswing in their thirty-year love-hate relationship. *(Billy Rose Theater Collection/New York Public Library)*

▲ Horne arrives at London's Heathrow Airport to tape a special with Tony Bennett, April 8, 1973.

▶ Singing Joe Raposo's "How Do You Do?" to Grover on *Sesame Street*, 1974. *(Children's Television Workshop)*

◄ With Tony Bennett in London, mid-1970s.

▼ *(Left)* Horne and Michel Legrand, the French master of movie music and jazz, at a Manhattan launch party for their 1975 album *Lena & Michel*. *(Schomburg Collection/New York Public Library)*

▼ *(Right)* Horne made a five-minute Hollywood comeback in *The Wiz*, a high-budget disappointment directed by son-in-law Sidney Lumet, 1978. *(Stephen Bourne Collection)*

▲ Backstage at the Nederlander with Cab Calloway and Elizabeth Taylor, 1981. *(Photofest)*

◄ The triumph of a lifetime: *The Lady and Her Music*, Nederlander Theater, New York, 1981. *(Photo by Nancy Barr, CATRESCUE@monmouth.com)*

▲ *The Lady and Her Music* earns Horne two Grammys, February 1982. Jazz historian and fellow winner Dan Morgenstern looks on.

▶ *(Right, top)* With fellow presenter Quincy Jones at the Oscars, March 1993.

▶ *(Right, bottom)* Eighty-year-old Horne receives Yale's Honorary Doctorate of Humane Letters, May 25, 1998.

▼ Mother and daughter at New York's Rainbow Room, 1998. *(Photo by Tom Gates)*

Lena Horne: In Her Own Voice was screened at the Waldorf-Astoria's Hilton Room, formerly the Empire Room. "It will be very hard for me to watch," Horne told the *Daily News*. She said she might stand in the back. "That way I can sneak out if it gets to be too much for me."

She did, in fact, stay to the end, and even spoke a few words to the crowd about the unabashed valentine they'd just seen. "I guess it wasn't such a tough life after all," she quipped, "and I'm sorry that maybe I didn't act like a lady about the whole thing."

The show did seem to give her spirits a small boost. If it was well received, she said, she might consider "rehearsing, singing a little bit, and seeing how badly I've deteriorated."

To the surprise of some who knew her best, Horne signed a new multialbum deal with Blue Note. This time her "heart"—as she called Rodney Jones—would produce. Horne began a new series of recording sessions in New York. Some were small-group dates with an R&B feel; others featured the strings of Jeremy Lubbock, a pricey commercial pop arranger from England. Such jazz stars as vibraphonist Milt Jackson and pianist Herbie Hancock were brought in to puff up the sessions further. Some of Horne's standbys, like Mike Renzi, Ben Brown, and Akira Tana, were there, too.

Renzi recalled those dates as "chaotic—and Lena was not really into it. She didn't like a lot of the stuff that was going on. And she hated Jeremy Lubbock, who was a pompous asshole." Lubbock's résumé glittered with big names—Barbra Streisand, Michael Jackson, Celine Dion, Sting. Hancock dazzled him, but he didn't act impressed by Horne. "He treated her like a band singer," said Jim Czak, who engineered those dates. "He was more interested in the cello line he wrote."

Lubbock had been hired to sweeten an array of standards, few of which seemed to mean much to Horne. After several takes of one song, Horne wanted feedback, and hit the intercom in her booth. "Jeremy?"

His attention was elsewhere. "He said, 'One moment, Lena, I'll be right with you,'" recalled Czak. "You don't do that in front of thirty-five musicians. That got her."

Seated at the controls, Czak heard Horne's voice on the speaker. "*Jim?* Did you like that?"

"At that point," explained Czak, "Lubbock was dismissed. As far as she was concerned, he was no longer in the room. I looked at him. He didn't look at me. I said, 'Lena, you're up to doing another one?'"

"'Do you think we need another one, *Jim?*'"

"I said, 'Yes, Lena, let's do one more.'"

Some of the Jones-produced tracks had their pleasures. Hancock showed up almost an hour late, blaming a delayed flight; then he made a fifteen-minute visit to the men's room while everyone waited. Once he settled in, he and the singer recorded a salty piano-voice duet of "Willow Weep for Me," an old pop-blues lament from Horne's past. She loved "Black Is," a children's song by Marissa Dodge, a white songwriter from Minnesota. Dodge wanted to explore the wonders of blackness in all its forms: "Black is writing on a page / Berries sweet and clouds that rain." Explained the writer: "Of course there was a deeper, more universal meaning."

In 1997 came a request for Horne to add her voice to a movie. Author-screenwriter Paul Auster wanted her and Tony Bennett to team on "Singin' in the Rain" for *Lulu on the Bridge,* a mystery about a famous jazz saxophonist (played by Harvey Keitel) who is accidentally shot. Bennett and Horne met to rehearse, and according to Bruce Lundvall, they clashed. By now Horne's delivery had slowed, and she wanted to sing that perky song as though it were a lazy stroll; the ever-chipper Bennett preferred to bounce along. Neither singer would budge, and Bennett solved the problem by not coming to the recording session. Horne wound up singing the song alone, her way.

HOPES that she might actually perform again were dimming. But as her eightieth birthday approached, it was time for her colleagues to serenade her. On June 23, 1997, Horne was fêted at Lincoln Center in a benefit gala thrown by the Society of Singers (SOS), a support organization for vocalists in need. A host of notables gathered on Avery Fisher Hall's stage to celebrate Horne, who would merely watch. Hollywood dancer Cyd Charisse introduced a montage of M-G-M clips. A plucky song-and-dance segment came from the Silver Belles, four veteran Harlem chorines; one of them was Cleo Hayes. Joe Williams, Cleo Laine and John Dankworth, Rosemary Clooney, Bobby Short, Leslie Uggams, Alan

King, Steve Lawrence, Eydie Gorme, Sidney Poitier, and Liza Minnelli gave their own salutes.

The guest of honor sat in her mezzanine box, watching other people sing her songs. "She looked like this frail little old lady," said Michael Frazier. Everyone expected Horne to stay put. But by the time the show was ending, she'd left her seat and headed backstage. She then emerged to a standing ovation.

Horne said her thank-yous, and announced that although she hadn't prepared a song, she and the band would try something. "Let's see what happens," she said.

Frazier was astounded by the results: "She took the microphone, the shoulders went back, and twenty years disappeared." Horne opened with a bit of "Come Rain or Come Shine" and segued into "As Long As I Live," the song that had launched her in the 1934 Cotton Club Parade. A cake was wheeled out, and everyone sang "Happy Birthday."

Another year of minimal activity followed. In May 1998, Horne accepted one more honorary doctorate, this one from Yale. Onlookers noticed her difficulty in standing. But Horne could still seduce a camera, and on the twenty-second of that month she made what would be her last TV appearance. It was on *The Rosie O'Donnell Show*, which employed Rodney Jones in its band. The occasion was the release of *Being Myself*, a Blue Note collection of her recent recordings. Horne wore a denim-blue silk suit, with her white hair pulled back, and looked like a glamorous granny. Rather than singing something from the album, she chose "Stormy Weather." The fire in her voice had burned down to a soft glow; she sounded distant and gauzy, and moved in slow motion. Jones stared at her adoringly as he played.

From that point on, Horne was ready to withdraw. A year and a half of near seclusion passed. Then, on October 18, 1999, she found herself back at Avery Fisher Hall for *Lena: The Legacy*, a benefit gala for a short-lived endeavor, the Lena Horne Youth Leadership Scholarship Awards Program for inner-city youths. More celebrities paraded onstage to sing and speak her praises: Laurence Fishburne, Bobby Short, Ed Bradley, Gregory Peck, Ossie Davis. In a replay of her eightieth birthday, Horne watched from a box, until close to the end, then unexpectedly appeared backstage, on wobbly legs. She told Carmen de Lavallade, the evening's director, that she wanted to sing, but feared walking out unassisted. Carmen arranged for Fishburne and Alan King to escort the star on each side, and out she went. Horne sang Billy Strayhorn's "You're the One" to predictably thunderous applause.

At the reception afterward, she stood and greeted a seemingly endless procession of well-wishers. They raved about her singing, and marveled at her energy. Carmen asked quietly if she wanted a chair. "No," said Horne, "because if I sit down I won't be able to get up."

Rodney Jones convinced her to make one more appearance. In May 2000, the upscale Manhattan Country School, which his daughter attended, held a benefit for its scholarship fund. Jones's ability to deliver Lena Horne had impressed everyone. She sang and spoke briefly; in return she received the school's Living the Dream mentor award. Mike Renzi played for her. "It went OK," he said, "but she was kind of frazzled. She didn't really want to be there, but she had promised Rodney."

She'd also agreed, halfheartedly, to sing at a Carnegie Hall concert to celebrate the release of *Classic Ellington*, an EMI CD. It featured the symphonic arrangements of Luther Henderson, conducted by Sir Simon Rattle. Horne appeared on that album in three oddly pieced-together tracks produced by Jones. For her *American Masters* documentary, the singer had rerecorded three Strayhorn songs from *We'll Be Together Again*. Jones had stripped away most of Mike Renzi's piano and replaced it with a flashy group, which included two Blue Note stars, pianist Geri Allen and saxophonist Joe Lovano; synthesized strings were added.

Horne sounded uninspired, and wasn't eager to promote the album. On short notice, she canceled her Carnegie Hall appearance. Singer Dianne Reeves filled in. From that point on, Gail Lumet Buckley told inquiring reporters that her mother was "one-hundred-percent retired."

AS Horne slipped out of view, Gene Davis wondered how much pride she took in anything she'd accomplished. "There are people who will look at a blue sky and find the one small cloud and stand under it," he said. "That's Lena. I think that deep down inside, despite all they've given and done, they don't think they deserve it. I think they believe they're not supposed to really be happy. Too much went down, and they're not going to find solace. No matter what the accolades are. No matter what the worship is."

She seemed to dwell the most on people she'd lost. The nineties had begun with the death of Ava Gardner, who succumbed to pneumonia. "How dare *she* go, too?" asked Horne. "She left me. She had a nerve dying." Subsequent casualties included Shirley Cowell, a victim of cancer in 1997. "I'm winding up just as I was—alone," reflected Horne. "Which is OK, because when I was a little girl I was alone all the time. It's so funny. Things come in one piece."

But for all the deceased, there were many more she'd pushed away. Bobby Short grieved privately to friends that Horne no longer returned his calls. Other intimates found themselves excommunicated after a minor disagreement, or for no apparent reason at all. Claude Thompson had been pondering Horne's ways ever since 1978, when he'd found himself abruptly fired from *Pal Joey '78*. "Was it defensiveness?" wondered the choreographer, who died in 2007. "Rejecting people before they could hurt her? Guilt over how she'd treated them? One thing I know is, Lena was not able to say 'I'm sorry.'"

And still he'd hoped for a reunion. One night he watched an elderly Horne on TV. She told an interviewer that she hoped her record of "Old Friends" would reach some of hers and let them know she loved them. "I saw that she realized she'd hurt a lot of people," said Thompson. "I thought it was a message to me. I sent her a telegram. I said, 'Don't worry, this is one friend who's still here. And we're friends for life.' I never heard anything back."

In 1994, Horne's early booster Fredi Washington died at the age of ninety. The extremely fair-skinned black actress had proved mostly uncastable in the Hollywood of her day. But she'd seen Horne's potential and offered a big-sisterly helping hand. She recommended Horne for jobs, loaned her clothes to sing in, and raved about her to people in the business. Fifty years later, when Fredi was ailing, her sister Isabel tried reaching out to Horne through Audrey Whitmore, the singer's longtime dresser. "Isabel would say, 'Tell Lena Fredi's not well,' and could Lena call her," said Fredi's friend Delilah Jackson. "Lena never did." Fredi was hurt, but Isabel was incensed. "The way she treated my sister after Fredi had been so kind and gracious to her, I didn't feel too kindly toward Lena Horne," said Isabel. "She just ignored Fredi on so many occasions. She'd already gotten everything she needed from her." Horne's side of the story, whatever it was, went untold.

Her volatile relationship with Harry Belafonte had long since vanished. "We were never friends," insisted Horne. "*Acquaintances*. His ego is different than mine." The man they'd shared in common, Sherman Sneed, had long suffered from failing health, and his wife, Frieda, wanted him home. In January 1997, she got her wish. Suddenly, Sneed and Horne were through. "That was it," said his daughter Sherri. "Not a call, not a card."

What had happened? Sherri related a story her father had told her. Horne traditionally funded a costly birthday for Gail, and in December 1996, said Sneed, she had asked him to give Gail a blank check. He refused, telling her he wouldn't do such a thing even for his own children. Arguments ensued. "Lena said, 'Well, why don't you just take the rest of the day off?' and my father said, 'Why don't I not come back?'" explained Sherri. "That's what my dad told me."

But for some time, friends claimed, Horne had suspected Sneed of handling her business deals in his own best interest. Then it was discovered that Sneed had placed family members of his on her payroll. And he was out.

Subsequently, said Sherri, he heard from the singer's accountant, Edward White. "He was trying to get my father to sign this paper saying that he would agree to not talk about her." A substantial check was offered in exchange. Sneed refused. "He would never have talked about Lena anyway," explained Sherri. "But he said, 'I didn't sign anything going in, why should I sign anything going out?'"

From then on, Sneed stayed home, watching TV with Frieda and helping her around the house. Once a month he donned his suit and cologne and hobbled out to meetings of the Society of Singers. On April 19, 2001, Sneed died of a heart attack. He was eighty. Not a word came from Horne, but Edward White, said Sherri, made a donation in Sneed's name to the SOS.

Sneed's absence cleared more room for Rodney Jones. In the late nineties, the guitarist spent countless hours assembling *Seasons of a Life*, a Horne CD that bore his name as producer. Jones had compiled it from Supper Club outtakes, unissued studio tracks like "Black Is," and the Strayhorn remakes from *Classic Ellington*. Much of the album revealed a painfully diminished Horne. *Seasons of a Life* was announced and then delayed several times; according to a Blue Note executive, Horne kept holding up its release.

It finally came out in 2005. By then she wasn't calling Jones her "heart." Bruce Lundvall recalled a telling comment from the guitarist: "Rodney said, 'Lena will do what you ask her to do, but then she'll never speak to you again.'" Through his connection with Horne, Jones had scored his own deal with Blue Note, as well as some impressive producer credits, tied to her name. But several recordings made her cringe—and when Horne suspected ulterior motives in anyone near her, the door slammed shut. Amid Jones's liner notes and extensive personal thank-yous in the booklet of *Seasons of a Life*, he related a question Horne had asked him at the start of their relationship. "Do you want to be my friend?" she asked him. He said yes.

"Then always tell me the truth."

At her Christmas party in 2006, Jim Czak asked her about Jones. "Oh, you mean the producer?" she said. "He's not around anymore."

THE purest joy Horne felt in her advanced years seemed to come from her great-grandson, Jacob. He was born in 1995 to Jenny Lumet and her then-husband, actor Bobby Cannavale. During the first airing of her PBS documentary, Horne had visited the studio to talk on air with Tom Stewart, one of the station's longtime pledge-break hosts. As a surprise, an outtake was shown of Horne singing "This Little Light of Mine" to baby Jacob. "That's my great-grandchild!" squealed Horne. "That's Jake!" Her happiness recalled how she'd felt in 1964 as she gazed upon her first grandchild, Amy Lumet, in her crib. Before Jake was out of diapers, she named him in an interview as the living person she admired most.

Horne's grandkids were adults now, and her relationships with them had remained complicated. They'd inherited the family good looks, but their seeming lack of ambition had driven her crazy. "I don't understand my grandchildren, but I love them," she concluded in 1994. "One of them in particular I love to death. And she likes me and *lets* me love her, you know?" Yet a wall still surrounded Horne, and they seemed to feel it. As a friend of hers recalled, "She always wanted them to call her 'Grandma' and they wound up calling her 'Lena.' It didn't make her feel good."

Amy eventually became a sound editor for films. The tawny-skinned, haughtily confident Jenny dabbled in acting, appearing in a few films—notably *Q & A* (1990), cowritten and directed by her father. After her 2003 divorce from Cannavale, she taught drama and pursued screenwriting. In 2008 Jenny's script about a dysfunctional family, *Rachel Getting Married*, made it to the screen, directed by Jonathan Demme.

Teddy Jones's youngest child, Lena Mary, had left home at sixteen and done her own drifting. Finally, said Judy Davis in 2005, "she went back to school and is thriving." So was Samadhi, who found a stable life in Florida as a mother and as deputy communications director for the Department of Juvenile Justice. Thomas was also doing well. After a stint in the Marines, he found his bliss by becoming a pastry chef and a teacher at New York's French Culinary Institute. Author and playwright Jim Piazza got to know him at a series of Christmas parties thrown by the TV writer-producer Paul Avila Mayer. "Tom was a very charming guy—seductive, sweet as anything, kind of edgy," said Piazza. "He was so light-skinned, I would never have known he was black. He was a sous-chef at a famous restaurant downtown, but his dream was to work with pastries. And here he was, this brawny, all-American guy, good-looking enough to be an actor. It kind of threw me."

Tom's equally handsome twin, William, lived aimlessly and often needily; of all the grandchildren, he seemed the most lost. Physically, said Samadhi Jones, "William was the split image of Ted. Louis and Lena saw so much of my father in him. He's almost a walking, talking reminder of the mistakes they made with their son." The nineties found William living in Los Angeles with his grandfather and fellow black sheep, Louis Jones. When Jones died in 1998, William, said Samadhi, "was almost incoherent with grief." Horne paid for the funeral, but neither she nor Gail attended.

Her history with Jones typified a past that Horne would have liked to bury with him. She balked at proposals that she write a new book; the prospect of a biographical film didn't thrill her either. Several people had tried to produce one. In 1994, Tim Reid, a producer and sitcom actor, shopped a Horne feature for TV. He was assisted by Sherri Sneed, the vice president of his company. Horne cooperated, with hesitation. The choice of an actress concerned her. "She didn't want Halle Berry;

she wanted someone who was the right color," said Sneed. "And she kind of wanted an unknown, because she didn't want someone else's persona to take over."

Unfortunately, there were no takers. "They said, 'If you get Whitney Houston to play Lena, we'd be interested.'"

In 2003, another possibility took wing. Roy Campanella, Jr., had produced an impressive list of TV movies and directed episodes of many a top series, including *Falcon Crest* and *Knots Landing*. He had inherited a fascination with Lena Horne from his father, a groundbreaking black baseball star of the forties and fifties. Roy, Sr., had said that the high point of his career had occurred during Roy Campanella Day at Ebbets Field, the home of his team, the Brooklyn Dodgers. An auto dealer had given him a free car, and Lena Horne had handed him the keys.

Over fifty years later, Roy, Jr., had interested ABC in his longtime dream of producing a Lena Horne biopic. Horne and Richard Schickel agreed to the option of their book *Lena*. It helped that Campanella was the son of a black hero whom Horne respected, and that, Roy, Jr., idolized Horne and vowed to treat her with respect. That included seeking her views throughout. Gail would benefit, too. Horne appointed her as representative, and her opinions would be sought. No star had been chosen, but Campanella hoped for the beautiful R&B singer Alicia Keys.

All looked promising, especially as the script took shape. Campanella wanted Horne portrayed "as a victor, not a victim," and he hired Shirley Pierce, a black screenwriter who worked for Disney, to carry out that theme. Her script focused on 1941 to 1943, and delved surprisingly deep into Horne's youthful conflicts.

What ABC really cared about was a star in the lead. They got one, thanks to Neil Meron and Craig Zadan, partners in a production company called Storyline Entertainment. Specialists in TV-movie musicals, Meron and Zadan were known for delivering names, with an emphasis on gay icons. They'd gotten Bette Midler to star in *Gypsy*, Whitney Houston in *Cinderella*, and Diana Ross in an original musical for television, *Double Platinum*. They'd also just produced the film version of *Chicago*, which won a Best Picture Oscar.

ABC's Horne project interested them, and they offered the network a package deal—themselves as coproducers, and Janet Jackson, who wanted to play Horne. "She is someone I've admired my whole life," Jackson said. ABC jumped at the offer. Jackson had little acting experience and a small, weak voice; nonetheless, she would do her own singing. At the end of August 2003, Campanella's new colleagues announced their coup to the press. "I can't think of more ideal casting," said Quinn Taylor, ABC's senior vice president in charge of TV movies. "Janet Jackson and Lena Horne—it's like peanut butter and jelly." The news spread through the media, without comment from one key player. "No word on what Horne, who is eighty-six, thinks of ABC's sandwich plans," wrote Gary Susman in *Entertainment Weekly*.

Horne had spoken well of Jackson in years past. But of all the participants, only Richard Schickel seemed to grasp her deep disdain for Hollywood and its ways. Having felt so abused there, Horne was ultrasensitive to any hint of cavalier or self-serving treatment. That would certainly have included barreling forward on a film about her life without asking her opinion. The trade announcements alarmed Schickel. "I said, 'This deal is gonna go south, Roy. Lena, in her mind at least, has some kind of casting consultation on this. Did they consult her?'"

Campanella was worried, too. Horne hadn't signed her contract, but the business-affairs department at Sony—which had come aboard the project—wasn't too concerned. They had a verbal agreement; to them that was sufficient. "Before they got Janet Jackson, I told all of them, 'Let's close the deal before we take any other steps, especially publicity.' And I made it very clear that I wanted to consult Lena on key creative matters."

Indeed, after news of the film broke, so did the trouble. Horne's business manager phoned Campanella, demanding a boost of her fee along with other changes. "He said he could stop this project unless he got a better deal," said Campanella. Horne had the power; she still hadn't signed. Those who knew her best might have foreseen a reoccurrence of her longtime pattern—halfhearted cooperation with a project that didn't quite please her, then sudden withdrawal.

Both Sony and Janet Jackson gave Horne an out. February 1, 2004, was Super Bowl Sunday, and CBS broadcast a halftime show. Justin Timberlake sang his hit "Rock Your Body" with Jackson. Near the end of the song he yanked off part of her bustier, giving viewers a momentary, distant view of her right breast. Many suspected that the stunt had been planned. The incident exploded into an embarrassing cause célèbre; Timberlake's attempt to pass it off as a "wardrobe malfunction" made him a laughingstock.

Later that month—just as *Vanity Fair* published a photo of Jackson in a facsimile of Horne's *Stormy Weather* gown—came a bombshell. The Horne camp had announced that no contract would be signed unless Jackson left the film. The young star consented. In support of Jackson, Zadan and Meron withdrew. ABC lost interest, and the project died.

Neither Campanella nor Schickel doubted that the Super Bowl prank had offended Horne. "I believe she was only, at the most, reluctantly approving of Janet anyway," said Schickel. "But here you come back to the most basic thing about Lena—that middle-class gentility. She doesn't want scandal or lowlife stuff swirling around her. This lack of respectability on the part of Janet Jackson just blew her mind, or somebody's mind."

Jackson suspected there was more to the story. She made a public statement: "In my deepest heart of hearts, I don't think the decision came from Lena. I think maybe it came from her daughter or the people around her. But that's OK. I still have to respect that, and I still admire her to the fullest." According to Schickel, Campanella suffered the most; the film was his dream, and he'd poured years of effort into it. "I feel Sony business affairs could have closed the deal," he maintained in 2008. "If they had, we could have gotten this done even with Lena's reticence. If they had just taken my advice." He had to wonder how much the people in business affairs even knew or cared about this iconic black figure.

HORNE'S final role was that of recluse. After a lifelong love affair with Manhattan, she'd grown mistrustful of what lay outside her door. "I used to love to walk in this town," she said. "Just a few years back everybody knew me, but the new New Yorkers, they don't know me, they don't know anybody. They don't like anybody. They're unknown people to me. I don't feel I *can* get to know them."

By the time Roy Campanella, Jr., had found her, Horne avoided leaving the house, except to go to the doctor or hospital. Family members and an ever-shrinking inner circle of friends visited her. But there was nothing left to experience. "I've seen it all," said Horne, "from the stage, from the bandstand."

Her disappearance didn't surprise Geoffrey Holder. "The key to Lena is that she's a Cancer. A crab. If you understand Cancers, they are wonderful shining lights. But when they feel enough is enough, they crawl into their shells."

Arthur Laurents's reunion with Horne in the nineties had gone unrepeated. But after Knopf published his memoir, *Original Story by Arthur Laurents*, in 2000, she gave him a surprise call. "I had to read your book to find out how happy I was back then," said Horne. With that conversation, they briefly resumed a phone relationship. He summed up her mood: "She's bitter. She's angry. There is no optimism. I'm curious to know why she goes on."

But rage, admitted Horne, was probably keeping her alive, whether she wished to be or not. An old acquaintance, the radio producer and jazz filmmaker Jean Bach, quipped in 2007 that Horne lived to hate George W. Bush; another pal reported that Horne would fling objects at the TV when a Republican appeared. Still, her sense of humor hadn't left her. It shone through in one of her last interviews, granted to *Vanity Fair* for its "Proust Questionnaire" series. The format allowed her to fill out her responses at home.

What is your current state of mind?
Addled.
What is your idea of perfect happiness?
Eating chocolate.
What is your greatest fear?
Running out of chocolate.
What do you dislike most about your appearance?
Big backside.
What is your most treasured possession?
My teeth.
Where would you like to live?
It's too late now.

The last question—"How would you like to die?"—brought a practical response: "In bed—asleep."

Asked about her mother's condition, Gail stressed the positive. In 2007, she told Clarence Waldron of *Jet* that her mother was "mentally great," and "in good health" considering her age. She mentioned Horne's arthritis and bad eyesight, "and she is on her fourth pacemaker. But what do you expect for ninety?"

There was more. Horne's knees had so degenerated that she could barely walk. According to Laurents, Horne had refused surgery; wheelchair and walker were kept handy. Starting around 2004, a rumor began circulating on the Internet that she suffered from multiple sclerosis. Gail denied it, as did others who visited her thereafter. Laurents wasn't among them. "I was always going to go see her," he said, "and she was always putting it off. My interpretation of that is, she didn't want me to see her looking as she looked. Beauties are like that."

Jim Czak could break through her melancholy like almost no one else, and during the Christmas holidays of 2006 he paid her a visit. He brought a black cashmere scarf, beautifully wrapped. Horne sat in a chair in her bedroom and gingerly removed the paper. "She liked the scarf," said Czak, "so she put it around her neck, then twirled it up one side of her head and down the other, then she wrapped the end across her face. And she said, 'Look! I'm a Muslim!' I fell on the floor."

On July 1, 2007—a day after the family party for Horne's ninetieth birthday—Czak and Mike Renzi were invited to drop by for champagne. Horne awaited them in a living room chair—"gray hair pushed back in a bun, but still pretty," said the pianist. "She had thick glasses on, but she certainly recognized me." Having brushed him off years before, she now seemed grateful to see him. Horne was in a reminiscing mood, and as they talked about past friends and events, a bittersweet glow came over her. "She was like the old Lena," he said. "Not the cold Lena."

After all the years of tension, she and Gail seemed "mother-daughter close," Renzi observed. Now approaching seventy, Gail had become caretaker, press rep, and manager of sorts for her mother. She reported that they ate lunch together daily. Horne had had ample time to ponder her flaws as a mother, and her latter-day bond with Gail confused her. "Someone once said to me, 'Why didn't your daughter write *Mommie*

Dearest? She writes about you like she's a fan.' And I had to stop and think about that for a long time. I told my daughter, 'Write *Mommie Dearest* about me if you want.'

"She said, 'I don't want the public knowing what I feel about you, or what you're like. And besides, they'll think I have nothing to write about but you!' I said, 'Well, if it'll make a lot of money for you, go ahead and do it.' She said, 'You're crazy.'"

Many of her fans expected her to voice a public statement in support of Barack Obama. But Horne had long ago stopped speaking out, and remained silent even after his election. The world had closed in on her. As her eyesight faded, she lost her ability to read—her lifetime refuge—and had to settle for watching TV. On one of her birthdays Hilary Knight, who hadn't seen her in years, called the apartment to congratulate her. The Turner Classic Movies cable channel was airing a Horne marathon; the illustrator had it on as he phoned. "I got a nurse or someone and said, 'It's Hilary Knight, do you think she could come to the phone?' I could hear the television. She was watching the same thing. So she couldn't blot out the past entirely."

For some time, she'd lived in a world of memories—many about her son, whom she missed more than ever, she said. "The men in my life all left me," Horne had explained, "and I feel them pulling at me." Her father had visited her in her sleep, she said; so had Billy Strayhorn and her Uncle Burke. "They're *happy* dreams. It's like they're saying, 'Come on.'"

Horne had been raised Catholic, and more than a little of that teaching remained. A few years earlier she'd told Jonathan Schwartz how firmly she believed in a great beyond where she would reunite with her departed loved ones, including Lennie Hayton. "I don't care whether they're in heaven or not," she said. "I'll just take them back down to the other place that I'm gonna wind up in, I have a feeling." And who, among the dead, would she like to see walk through her door? "Well, I'd like to talk to my mother, because I had some unfinished business with her. And next, my father. I *loved* him, intensely."

Efforts continued to bring her story to the stage or screen. In December 2007, Oprah Winfrey had announced plans to produce a Horne biopic starring Alicia Keys. There were also hopes of finding a Broadway home for a fanciful book musical, *Stormy Weather: Imagining Lena Horne*, that played out of town. Leslie Uggams starred in the show; its author, Sharleen Cooper Cohen, had written such novels as *Marital Affairs* and *The Ladies of Beverly Hills*. Reported Cindy Adams in the *New York Post*: "Lena Horne knows about this life story but, wheelchair-bound, is receiving no one connected with the project."

Having grumbled so often that her story was too wearisome to tell, Horne had come to feel otherwise. "I had a very interesting life, actually," she mused. "It's not all music, but it comes out in the music." She was regarded as a symbol of ultimate class, whose fighting spirit had inspired many lives. But whatever anyone said about her, some variation of the word "beautiful" always came first.

By the time she'd reached ninety, Horne was free of the pressure to live up to that word. Almost no one except her family got to see her. But she still welcomed Jim Czak, who honored a tradition of theirs and dropped by for a Christmas visit in 2007. Horne felt no need to primp for him, and he found her in a chair inside her bedroom, gray hair hanging down, wearing a T-shirt and no makeup. She and Gail were watching TV. Czak grinned at Horne and announced, "You look like shit!"

Smiling, she called out to Gail, "This is the only honest man I know!"

Of all her regrets, one had pushed its way to the top. "I should have realized that maybe I was more loved than I thought, you know?" Horne resisted giving worldly advice; she'd made too many mistakes to do that, she felt. But she'd certainly reached some conclusions. The singer had told Rex Reed in 1981, "Pain is what makes you live!" Several years later, she'd expanded that thought into a philosophy. "Don't be afraid to feel as angry or loving as you can," she warned, "because when you feel nothing, it's just death."

ACKNOWLEDGMENTS

TO EVERYONE WHO agreed to be interviewed for this book, my heartfelt thanks for your time and candor. For generously sharing photos, recordings, and other materials, or for providing valuable contacts, further gratitude goes to Joan Archdeacon, Jean Bach, Ron Brewington, Barbara Brussell, Cheryl Buchhalter, Roy Campanella, Jr., Alexis Caydam, Charmaine Clowney, Evelyn Cunningham, Barry Dennen, Will Friedwald, Tom Gates, Michael Krauster, Carmen Fanzone, Barry Farber, Joe Gilford, Bruce Goldstein, Mark Griffin, David Hajdu, Devra Hall, Jane Harvey, Billie Allen Henderson, Eliot Hubbard, Craig Huntly, Daniel L. Johnson, Peter Jones, Hilary Knight, Eric Kohler, Sondra Lee, Herman Leonard, John Lewis, Annette MacDonald, J. Fred MacDonald, Reggio McLaughlin, Novella Nelson, Stephen Paley, Michael Panico, Preston Powell, St. Clair Pugh, Bill Reed, Cynthia Sesso, Whit Strub, the late Robert Tracy, Bob Waldman, Stan Walker, and Iain Cameron Williams. As always, thanks to Michael Mascioli of www.allmusicservices.com for helping me track down rare and essential recordings.

Without the Schomburg Center for Research in Black Culture (Harlem), the New York Public Library for the Performing Arts, the Margaret Herrick Library of the Academy of Motion Picture Arts and Sciences (Los Angeles), the Institute of Jazz Studies at Rutgers University (Newark, New Jersey), and the Cinematic Arts Library at USC (Los Angeles), it would have been much harder to write this book. Deep appreciation to the staffs of all those libraries—especially to the remarkable Dan

Morgenstern (Rutgers) and Ned Comstock (USC), whose helpfulness and expertise are nonpareil.

This book was written not just in Manhattan, where I live, but in the homes of out-of-town friends, whose hospitality and encouragement helped keep me going. For all that and more, I'm indebted to my Brazilian "family": Zuza Homem de Mello, Bartolomeo Gelpi, and Ercília Lobo (São Paulo); Juan Weik and Fernanda Koprowski (São Paulo); Alan Eichler and Ralph Ziegler (Glendale, California), Jim Key and Jim Walb (Fire Island Pines); Harry Locke (Nashua, New Hampshire); Rebecca Parris, Marla Kleman, and Paul McWilliams (Duxbury, Massachusetts); Darren Ramirez (West Hollywood, California); Yvans Jourdain (West Hollywood), Joel Thurm (Los Angeles, California); and Paula West (San Francisco, California).

Several key sources took special pains to help me tell this story by letting me grill them for hours, giving me broad access to their collections, or both. Enormous thanks go to Stephen Bourne, Terrie Burton-Charles, John Fricke, Delilah Jackson, Samadhi Jones, Harry Locke, Wendy Munson, Jess Rand, Clint Rosemond, and Tom Toth. I'm equally grateful to Alan Ebert, John Gruen, and Rex Reed, all of whom let me quote lavishly from their probing interviews with Lena Horne. Jane White's insights helped greatly in enhancing several chapters. A special thank-you to Gail Lumet Buckley, who graciously led me to several individuals who might never have spoken to me otherwise.

For their all-around loyalty, cheerleading, and wisdom, I'm indebted to Polly Bergen, Lisa Bond, Baby Jane Dexter, Jim DiGiovanni, Tom Evered, Alan Eichler, Danny Fields, Bob Freedman, Freeman Gunter, Robert Hicks, Richard Lamparski, the late Peter Levinson, Arthur Lubow, Shannon McCarty, Jan McCormack, Mark Murphy, Gerald Nachman, Ted Ono, Jacqueline Parker, Ned Rorem, Ann Ruckert, Spider Saloff, Liz Smith, and Mike Wolf.

To my editor at Atria Books, Malaika Adero, my eternal thanks for allowing me to write the Lena Horne story and for showing so much patience and care along the way. You're a class act. Thanks to assistant editor Todd Hunter; ace copyeditors and proofreaders Anthony Newfield, Doug Johnson, Lynn Anderson, Anne Cherry, Eva Young, Toby Yuen, and Nancy Clements; indexer Nancy Wolff; production editor Isolde Sauer;

my inspired jacket designer, Janet Perr; text designers Nancy Singer and Esther Paradelo, and Meghan Day Healey; Christine Saunders, Atria's deputy director of publicity; Malaika's former assistant Krishan Trotman; and the rest of Simon & Schuster's staff for doing their jobs wonderfully. To Mitch Douglas, the agent who turned my life around: This never would have happened without you. Buddy Thomas and Tina Wexler of ICM went out of their way to be helpful; I thank them both. Another agent, Barney Karpfinger, gave me an early push in the direction of writing this biography; thanks to him for setting the process in motion.

Mark Sendroff, my lawyer, is truly a friend in need. So is Adam Feldman, *Time Out New York*'s theater and cabaret writer. Adam, this book owes so much to your superb editorial eye. Big thanks to Peter Keepnews for his eleventh-hour fact checking and proofing. Photographer William Claxton was an angel on my shoulder from 1994 until his death in 2008. I'm grateful that his work appears in this book thanks to the kindness of his wife, Peggy Moffitt, and son, Christopher Claxton. To my dearest friend, Cindy Bitterman: Thank you for making some of the best things in my life possible. My ultimate thanks go to my parents, Viola and Jack, who are there for me always and never ask, "Why don't you get a real job?"

NOTES

INTRODUCTION

2 "too little": See Bernard Drew, "Lena Horne: The Rage Now Is Gone, and She's 'Free to Be Me.'"

2 "Negro Cinderella": from Richard Durham's radio play *Negro Cinderella*, broadcast on *Destination Freedom*, WMAQ, Chicago, Jun 12, 1949.

2 "I'm sorry": Lena Horne to JG, Mar 14, 1994.

3 "couldn't sing" and was a "*bad* dancer": *The Rosie O'Donnell Show*, ABC-TV, May 22, 1998.

3 "Her command": Abbey Lincoln to JG, Dec 22, 1992.

3 "weren't anything": LH to JG, Mar 14, 1994.

3 "She looks good": Ibid.

3 "I thought": Peggy Moffitt to JG, Jul 24, 2004.

3 "Lena is": Anonymous source to JG.

3 "Why am": LH to JG, Mar 14, 1994.

4 "I was never": LH to John Gruen, New School for Social Research, New York, Nov 27, 1972.

4 "evil": LH to JG, Mar 14, 1994.

4 "I never": Ibid.

5 "Lena is": Louis Johnson to JG, Feb 12, 2006.

5 "In a way": Arthur Laurents to JG, Nov 18, 2004.

5 "What was it": LH to JG, Mar 14, 1994.

CHAPTER 1

Author's note: Gail Lumet Buckley's book *The Hornes: An American Family* was invaluable in the research of this chapter.

7 "Every Saturday": Lorraine Gerard to JG, Sep 5, 2004.

8   "danced for pennies": See Robert Rice, "The Real Story of Lena Horne."

8   "I came": See Lena Horne, "I Just Want to Be Myself."

9   "You didn't": Jane White to JG, Feb 24, 2004.

9   "There would": Ibid.

10   "Lighter": Gene Davis to JG, Jan 21, 2006.

10   "cultural roots": See John Munro, "Black Bourgeoisie at 50: Class, Civil Rights, and the Cold War in America."

11   "As a family": See Kathy Larkin, "Lena Horne: A Stage Presence with a TV Future."

12   "violent": *The Mike Douglas Show,* Dec 1965.

12   "beautiful, sad": *Lena,* p. 14.

12   "sucker": Ibid., p. 6.

13   "pursuing": Ibid., p. 1.

13   "youngest members": See NAACP *Branch Bulletin.*

13   "was too young": *In Person: Lena Horne,* p. 5.

13   "a pimp": LH to John Gruen, Nov 27, 1972.

13   "You worked": LH to Gene Delassi, Pacifica Radio, KPFA, San Francisco, Apr 12, 1966.

14   "Think for yourself": LH to JG, Mar 14, 1994.

14   "You will never": See Michiko Kakutani, "Aloofness Hid the Pain, Until Time Cooled Her Anger."

14   "She never": LH to Jim Hartz, *Over Easy,* PBS, Apr 25, 1982.

14   "a very": See Leonard Feather, "Hornes of Plenty."

14   "At that time": Carmen de Lavallade to JG, Jan 17, 2008.

14   "been raised": See Sidney Fields, "Success in Mixed Marriage."

15   "I was certain": Lena Horne, *In Person: Lena Horne,* p. 9.

16   "I can": Ibid., p. 6.

16   "The show was": Frank C. Taylor (with Gerald Cook), *Alberta Hunter: A Celebration in Blues,* p. 80.

17   "hellish": Bill Reed, *Hot from Harlem,* p. 5.

17   "tumble-down": *In Person: Lena Horne,* p. 13.

17   "a foul": Ibid., p. 14.

18   "dumb": See Cheryl Lavin, *California Living.*

18   "stranded": *Broadway—The Great White Way,* Arts & Entertainment Channel, 1989.

18   *"The crackers"*: *In Person: Lena Horne,* p. 19.

18   "They're mean": Ibid., p. 16.

18   "only sense": LH to JG, Mar 14, 1994.

19   "Come on": Claude Thompson to JG, Jan 20, 2006.

19   *"afraid"*: LH to JG, Mar 14, 1994.

19   "I made my": See Nancy Collins, *W.*

19   "a very elderly": LH to JG, Mar 14, 1994.

20   "She tried": See Robert Ruark, "Lady in a High Key."

20   "apt to be": LH to Gene Delassi, Pacifica Radio, KPFA, Apr 12, 1966.

20   "We've had a great loss": See Herbert Feinstein, "Lena Horne Speaks Freely on Race, Marriage, Stage."

20   "Yaller! Yaller!": *In Person: Lena Horne*, p. 11.

21   "two or three people": *Lena*, p. 32.

22   "Ask for": LH to JG, Mar 14, 1994.

22   "Don't trust": Ibid.

22   "Because he": Brian Lanker, *I Dream a World*.

22   "a willingness": See Leonard Feather, "The Three Faces of Lena."

23   "Back in Macon": *Lena*, p. 36.

23   "So much": Marcia Ann Gillespie to JG, Aug 10, 2004.

23   "I became": "Lena Horne: In Her Own Words," *American Masters*, PBS, Nov 25, 1996.

23   "What a cute": LH to John Gruen, Nov 27, 1972.

24   "Lena felt": Gail Lumet Buckley, *The Hornes*, p. 106.

24   "silly, foolish": LH to JG, Mar 14, 1994.

24   "You must": LH to Jim Hartz, *Over Easy*, PBS, Apr 25, 1982.

24   "battling": LH to JG, Mar 14, 1994.

25   "We were the": *In Person: Lena Horne*, p. 23.

25   "'tops'": See "Lena Horne Weds, Quitting Footlights."

25   "fierce": *Lena*, p. 45.

25   "a nuisance": See Clive Hirschhorn, "The Man Lena Married Even Though She Wasn't in Love."

26   "dear little girl": Gail Lumet Buckley, *The Hornes*, p. 109.

26   "a group": See "Ann Jones' Dancers to Be at Lafayette."

27   "the most": See Alfred Duckett, "A Warm Embrace."

27   "She had a few": See Alfred Duckett, "Fabulous Lena Horne Rivals That 'Tree Growing in Brooklyn.'"

27   "She carried": See Alfred Duckett, "A Warm Embrace."

27   "I remember": See Alfred Duckett, "Fabulous Lena Horne."

27   "The regal": See Alfred Duckett, "A Warm Embrace."

27   "Miss": Ibid.

CHAPTER 2

29   "If you were": Bobby Short to JG, Dec 5, 2004.

29   "You couldn't": Cleo Hayes to JG, Apr 20, 2005.

30   "Everyone tried": *The Cotton Club Remembered* (Great Performances, PBS), Nigel Finch, dir., 1985.

30   "that we had": See Ossie Davis, *Life Lit By Some Large Vision*.

30   "At five": Cleo Hayes to JG, Apr 20, 2005.

31   "All our clientele": Doris Bye Nazaire to JG, Jul 25, 2005.

31   "Racist images": See Steven Watson, *The Harlem Renaissance*.

32   "the greatest": From Duke Ellington's RCA Victor recording "Cotton Club Stomp," Apr 12, 1929.

33   "We'd have twenty-four": See David Hinckley, "Cotton Tales."

33   "take a strong": See George Ross, New York *World–Telegram*.

33   "You know better": LH, *The Dick Cavett Show*, PBS, 1981.

33   "You don't have": Fayard Nicholas to JG, Dec 9, 2004.

34   "The Cotton Club": See "Billy Rowe's Notebook," Aug 19, 1950.

34   "fantastic": LH to Rex Reed, *Tomorrow* (NBC-TV), Nov 17, 1981.

35   "When I got": Ethel Waters, *His Eye Is on the Sparrow*, p. 220.

35   "scared": See Rex Reed, "A Life on Stage."

35   "Instead of": *In Person: Lena Horne*, p. 39.

35   "Black women": *Lyrically Speaking*, Black Entertainment Television, 1994.

36   "Many were": "Cotton Club Girls," *Ebony*, Apr 1949.

36   "1. Beauty": Ibid.

36   "stumbled": *In Person: Lena Horne*, p. 40.

36   "I had no": See Ponchitta Pierce, "Lena Horne at 51."

36   "A likely": *The Complete Life of Lena Horne: A Pocket Celebrity Scrapbook*, p. 6.

36   "very shy": LH profile, BBC-4 radio (U.K.), Aug 24, 1984.

37   "very sweet": Avon Long to James V. Hatch, recorded lecture, City College, New York, Sep 25, 1969.

37   "She was very": Isobel Washington Powell to JG, Jun 20, 2005.

37   "You should": Alan Ebert, *Intimacies*, p. 160.

37   "I saw": Fayard Nicholas to JG, Dec 9, 2004.

37   "Jail bait": Delilah Jackson to JG, Dec 21, 2005.

38   "most undressed": See "Lena Horne Weds, Quitting Footlights."

38   "objected violently": Ibid.

38   "She was always": Ruby Dallas Young to JG, Mar 29, 2005.

38   "Call me": Delilah Jackson to JG, Dec 21, 2005.

38   "accidentally": Ruby Dallas Young to JG, Mar 29, 2005.

38   There was no": See Robert Wahls, "Stormy Weather Is All Behind Her."

39   "get to": Fayard Nicholas to JG, Dec 9, 2004.

39   "the most frustrated": LH to John Gruen, Nov 27, 1972.

39   "My daughter": LH to Jim Harlan, "Legends," WNEW-AM, Jun 23, 1991.

39   "I couldn't": LH to JG, Mar 14, 1994.

39   "sing in the": See Rosemary Layng, "Dark Angel."

39   "Lena was *never*": Cleo Hayes to JG, Apr 20, 2005.

40   "is a lady": See Cab Calloway, *Of Minnie the Moocher and Me,* p. 113.

40   "I promptly": See John Corry, "An Anatomy of Lena Horne's Triumph."

40   "had to go": Fayard Nicholas to JG, Dec 9, 2004.

40   "Whenever I": LH to John Gruen, Nov 27, 1972.

41   "black nigger": Avon Long to James V. Hatch, recorded lecture, City College, New York, Sep 25, 1969.

42   "Now it seems": Ruby Dallas Young to JG, Jan 2, 2007.

42   "It was a real": See "Cotton Club Girls."

42   "That's the way": Doris Bye Nazaire to JG, Jul 25, 2005.

42   "a snobbish": See David Hinckley, "Cotton Tales."

43   "That was about": Cleo Hayes to JG, Apr 20, 2005.

43   "A couple": Ibid.

43   "an ability": See Glenn Plaskin, "The Ageless Appeal of Lena."

43   "I *hated*": LH to Gene Delassi, Pacifica Radio, KPFA, San Francisco, Apr 12, 1966.

44   "pigsty": Ibid.

44   "Harlem Negroes": Langston Hughes, *The Collected Works of Langston Hughes,* p. 176.

44   "The money": Cab Calloway, *Of Minnie the Moocher and Me,* p. 90.

44   "didn't want to be onstage": LH to Jim Hartz, *Over Easy,* PBS, Apr 25, 1982.

45   "Someday I'm": Delilah Jackson to JG, Dec 21, 2005.

45   "But it was": Alan Ebert, *Intimacies,* p. 160.

45   "He couldn't": LH to John Gruen, Nov 27, 1972.

45   "a misty": See Alfred Duckett, "A Warm Embrace."

46   "All she needed": Avon Long to James V. Hatch, recorded lecture, New York University, Mar 9, 1981.

46   "might be more": M-G-M Publicity Department Questionnaire, Jan 1942.

46   "You sure": See Max Jones, "The Singer They Went to See."

46   "You're telling": *In Person: Lena Horne,* p. 57.

46   "I would sing": LH, ASCAP video interview, 1989.

46   "If I had": See Lisa Schwarzbaum, "Horne Again."

46   "a very unhappy": Ruby Dallas Young to JG, Mar 29, 2005.

47   "Swaggering": See John Chapman, New York *Daily News.*

48   "In a wild": Ibid.

48   "very silly": *Broadway: The Great White Way,* Arts & Entertainment Channel, 1988.

48   "I liked getting": See Steve Warren, "At Her Mellow Age, Lena Horne Still as Tough as Nails."

48   "animated": See Arthur Ruhl, *New York Herald Tribune*.

48   "had worked": See "As Long as I Live."

48   "too sophisticated": See Lena Horne, "'An Actress Mother Inspired My
       Stage Career,' Says Lena Horne."

48   "The champ": *Variety*, Sep 18, 1935.

49   "Lena Horne, the Cotton": See Roi Ottley, "Hectic Harlem."

49   "escaped": LH to John Gruen, Nov 27, 1972.

49   "lifetime contract": Ibid.

49   "That was": See Lena Horne, "I Just Want to Be Myself."

49   "they did terrible": LH to John Gruen, Nov 27, 1972.

49   "Actually": Ibid.

49   "I don't think": Ernest Brown to JG, Sep 9, 2008.

49   "If *Lena* thought": Cleo Hayes to JG, Apr 20, 2005.

49   "We didn't have": Ruby Dallas Young to JG, Jan 2, 2007.

50   "What would": See Rosemary Layng, "Dark Angel."

50   "dark Harlem": See Alain Locke, "Harlem: Dark Weather-Vane."

51   "the better class": See "Cotton Club Girls."

51   "She was not": Isobel Washington Powell to JG, Jun 20, 2005.

CHAPTER 3

52   "lean": *In Person—Lena Horne*, p. 66.

52   "exemplary": Ibid.

52   "very opinionated": Cleo Hayes to JG, Apr 20, 2005.

53   "Noble had": Ibid.

53   "You must be": LH to Gene Delassi, Pacifica Radio, KPFA, San Fran-
       cisco, Apr 12, 1966.

53   "You are not": LH to John Gruen, Nov 27, 1972.

54   "Sissle's new": See Jesse Mann, "Washington's Social Whirl."

54   "Lena was just": Cleo Hayes to JG, Apr 20, 2005.

55   "How could": See Bernard Drew, "Lena Horne: The Rage Now Is Gone,
       and She's 'Free to Be Me.'"

56   "In one voice": From Mary Lou Williams's 1936 diary, courtesy of Linda
       Dahl, June 28, 2006.

56   "Girls!" it said: *Pittsburgh Courier*, May 16, 1936.

57   "nothing": Vernon Jordan to JG, Sep 4, 2008.

57   "the impression": Ruby Dee to JG, Jan 10, 2008.

57   "No!": *Lena*, p. 74.

57   "a cute little": LH to Gene Delassi, Pacifica Radio, KPFA, San Francisco,
       Apr 12, 1966.

58   "After the first": See Rosemary Layng, "Dark Angel."

58   "She was supposed": "Gene Mikell Talks to Peter Carr and Al Vollmer," *Storyville 1989–1999*, p. 94.

58   "took the patrons": See "Lena Horne's Fame Grows as Sensational Dance Director."

58   "She is widely": See "Lena Horne Is Sensation in Absence of Noble Sissle."

58   "intensely interested": See "Lena Horne's Fame Grows as Sensational Dance Director."

59   Louis "would always": David Margolick, *Beyond Glory*.

59   "If I ever": "Life Story by Joe Louis," *Our World*, Jun 1948.

59   "But I do": LH to Gene Delassi, Pacifica Radio, KPFA, San Francisco, Apr 12, 1966.

59   "For one night": Larry Schwartz, "'Brown Bomber' Was a Hero to All," www.espn.com.

60   "blacks throughout": Leonard Reed (as told to Bill Reed), *A Hell of a Life* (unpublished memoir), c. 1990.

60   "I was identifying": LH to Gene Delassi, Pacifica Radio, KPFA, San Francisco, Apr 12, 1966.

60   "This was a": Esther Cooper Jackson to JG, May 11, 2005.

60   "cooled": See "Lena Horne Weds, Quitting Footlights."

60   "shifted Lena": Ibid.

60   "was as rigid": See Hans J. Massaquoi, "Lena Horne on Her Loveless Childhood."

60   "if I didn't" . . . "hot-blooded": LH to John Gruen, Nov 27, 1972.

61   "snob": Avanelle Harris to JG, Mar 20, 2006.

61   "very handsome": Alan Ebert, *Intimacies*, p. 161.

61   "He was peculiar-looking": Doris Bye Nazaire to JG, Jul 25, 2005.

61   "He charmed" . . . "you *do?*": Cleo Hayes to JG, Apr 20, 2005.

61   "I don't know": *Lena*, p. 78.

62   "Why wait?": See "'Love at First Sight' Romance Ends at Altar."

62   "It's the end": *Lena*, p. 81.

62   "But love": See "'Love at First Sight' Romance Ends at Altar."

62   "Mother sends": Ibid.

62   "Lena said he": Elle Elliott to JG, May 23, 2006.

62   "that sex": See Glenn Plaskin, "The Ageless Appeal of Lena."

62   "My grandfather": Samadhi Jones to JG, Oct 28, 2007.

62   "Here I was": LH to John Gruen, Nov 27, 1972.

63   "I thought that": Ibid.

63   "You dumb": See Maurice Zolotow, "Lena: The Lady Who Just Wasn't Black Enough."

63   "You're in": Brett Howard, *Lena Horne—Singer and Actress*, p. 19.

64   the "Prettiest": See "Lena Horne Accepts Hollywood Film Offer."
65   "Just seeing": Esther Cooper Jackson to JG, May 11, 2005.
66   "They wanted": Avanelle Harris to JG, Mar 20, 2006.
66   "we welcomed" . . . "going on": Ibid.
66   "Oh, fine": See Harry Levette, "Miss Lena Horne, Million Dollar Star, Devoted to Retiring Home Life."
66   "*very* ambitious": Avanelle Harris to JG, Mar 20, 2006.
67   "REFUSES" . . . "talk of Pittsburgh": See "Refuses to Appear at Premiere of Own Film."
68   "Lena Horne, gifted": See Harry Levette, "L. Horne Screens Well."
68   "discovered" . . . "Lena and me": Leonard Reed (as told to Bill Reed), *A Hell of a Life.*
69   "It was clear": Anonymous source to JG.
69   "Lena *loved*": Delilah Jackson to JG, Nov 9, 2008.
69   "flighty": *Lena,* p. 82.
69   "Black men": Gene Davis to JG, Jan 21, 2006.
69   "The lure": See Avery Williams, "The Lena Horne Love Story."
70   "She can sing": *New York World-Telegram,* Dec 1938.
70   "Louder": Ibid., p. 123.
71   "*I'm doing*": Ibid.
71   "large number": See Kelcey Allen, "Blackbirds of 1939."
71   "Lena should never": Cleo Hayes to JG, Apr 20, 2005.
71   "woefully" . . . "punch and drive": See "'Blackbirds' Gets So-So Reception."
71   "extraordinary beauty": Ibid.
71   "lack of": Ibid.
72   "All the performers": See Brooks Atkinson, "Lew Leslie Gets His 'Blackbirds of 1939' onto the Stage of the Hudson Theatre."
72   "What kind": *In Person: Lena Horne,* p. 131.
73   "It was a pretty": See Marilyn Beck, "I'm Making Up for the Time I Sat Back."
73   "That was a": *In Person: Lena Horne,* p. 131.
73   "My husband wanted": See Avery Williams, "The Lena Horne Love Story."
73   "His personality": *In Person: Lena Horne,* p. 132.
73   "You'll come back": *Lena,* p. 102.

CHAPTER 4

74   "I was just": Ralph J. Gleason, *San Francisco Chronicle,* Apr 29, 1951.
75   "They said": *The Dick Cavett Show,* PBS, 1981.
75   "What difference": *In Person: Lena Horne,* p. 149.

75   "sensational Broadway": See "Dave's Café Opening Is Terrific."

75   "Lena Horne . . . has her": See Billy Rowe, "Rowe's Notebook."

75   "I remember": *In Person: Lena Horne,* p. 150.

75   "the blackest": *Metronome,* 1941.

76   "I've found": *In Person: Lena Horne,* p. 150.

76   "I remember": Brett Howard, *Lena Horne—Singer and Actress,* p. 105.

76   "Somehow, they": See Robert Rice, "The Real Story of Lena Horne."

77   "tore up": *Those Swinging Years: The Autobiography of Charlie Barnet,* p. 95.

77   "How do you suppose": *In Person: Lena Horne,* p. 166.

77   "We can't have": Ibid., p. 168.

78   "She eats": Ibid., p. 160.

78   "Then I'd": Ibid., p. 162.

78   "Give me": Ibid., p. 167.

78   "I thought she": Doris Bye Nazaire to JG, Jul 25, 2005.

79   "She was a": Artie Shaw to JG, Aug 27, 2004.

79   "hot-blooded": LH to John Gruen, Nov 27, 1972.

79   "traumatic": Gail Lumet Buckley, *The Hornes,* p. 139.

79   "Lena C. Jones": Divorce petition no. 1386, Louis J. Jones vs. Lena C. Jones, Allegheny County, Pa., Apr 1941.

79   "DESERTION": *Pittsburgh Courier,* Feb 15, 1941.

79   "This marital": See "Lena Horne Sues Mate for Divorce."

80   "I remember": Gail Lumet Buckley, *The Hornes,* p. 139.

80   "cruel" . . . "such indignities": Divorce petition no. 3661, Lena C. Jones vs. Louis J. Jones, Allegheny County, Pa., Apr 1941.

80   "I didn't want": Clint Rosemond to JG, May 25, 2006.

80   "many rumors": See Maurice Dancer, "Lena Horne and Charlie Barnet to Exchange Guest Appearances."

80   "practically": Jack Schiffman, *Uptown: The Story of Harlem's Apollo Theatre,* pp. 76–77.

81   "I was impressed": Barney Josephson to JG, Apr 4, 1988.

81   "Now, people": Ibid.

81   "Fine," said Horne.: Ibid.

81   "the sweetest": LH to John Gruen, Nov 27, 1972.

82   "I was sick": *New York Post,* Nov 4, 1946.

82   "All these white": Josephson to JG, Apr 4, 1988.

83   "It drew": Madeline Lee Gilford to JG, Sep 14, 2007.

83   "I'd like": Josephson to JG, Apr 4, 1988.

83   "What are you" . . . "Café Society": Josephson to JG, Apr 4, 1988.

83   "Hoodlums": Madeline Lee Gilford to JG, Sep 14, 2007.

84   "I noticed" . . . "Negro talent": See "Barney Josephson: How He Changed America for Good."

84   "hell" she later said: LH to JG, Mar 14, 1994.

84   "When she looked": See Whitney Balliett, "The Happiest Days of My Life."

84   "Barney said": LH to Jonathan Schwartz, WNEW-AM, Aug 1981.

84   "There were so": LH to JG, Mar 14, 1994.

85   "The first time": Paul Robeson, Jr., to JG, Feb 23, 2006.

85   "I had a lot": LH to JG, Mar 14, 1994.

85   "Oh, God": Betty Comden to JG, Aug 6, 2004.

85   "sing some Billie": *The Rosie O'Donnell Show*, May 22, 1998.

85   "Blues Singer": Source unknown.

85   "I got her": Jim Piazza to JG, Aug 12, 2008.

86   "That is *horrible*": LH to Jonathan Schwartz, WNEW-AM, Aug 1981.

86   "I had this terrible": LH to JG, Mar 14, 1994.

86   "cabaret was": LH to Johnny Carson, *Tonight*, NBC-TV, Dec 1965.

87   "He had a": Esther Cooper Jackson to JG, May 11, 2005.

87   "Paul came": LH to Gene Delassi, Pacifica Radio, KPFA, San Francisco, Apr 12, 1966.

87   "He was a": Doris Bye Nazaire to JG, Jul 25, 2005.

88   "She lived": Madeline Lee Gilford to JG, Sep 14, 2007.

88   "I'd had": LH to JG, Mar 14, 1994.

88   "She was a": Artie Shaw to JG, Aug 27, 2004.

88   "only weakness": *Variety*, Jul 30, 1941.

89   "terrified" . . . "complex man": LH to Ray Otis, "The Great Sounds," USP Programming Network, Sep 1989.

89   "That's not" . . . "black guy": Artie Shaw to JG, Aug 27, 2004.

89   "and his mental domination": Lena Horne (Introduction), *Ava Gardner: My Story*, p. 146.

89   "She knew": Artie Shaw to JG, Aug 27, 2004.

89   "the reigning": See "Late and Later at the Night Clubs."

89   "very ambitious": Madeline Lee Gilford to JG, Sep 14, 2004.

89   "Patrons jammed": *Lion's Roar*, Sep 1943.

89   "Hazel Scott *hated*": Delilah Jackson to JG, Dec 21, 2005.

89   "In the beginning": See Kay Gardella, "Lena Tells It Like It Is."

90   "to join": *Chicago Defender*, Aug 30, 1941.

90   "She says her": See "Swingin' the News."

92   "It was very hard": Cleo Hayes to JG, Apr 20, 2005.

92   "I was struck": Katherine Dunham to JG, Dec 20, 2004.

92   "got talked": LH to Ray Otis, "The Great Sounds."

93   "I told him": See Shonte Penland.

CHAPTER 5

94   "rather Oriental-looking": *Lena,* p. 122.

94   "The questioning": Ibid.

94   "When I got": LH to Ray Otis, "The Great Sounds."

95   "Give it time": See Rosemary Layng, "Dark Angel."

95   "I used to": Cleo Hayes to JG, Apr 20, 2005.

95   "She was very": Alice Key to JG, Mar 10, 2006.

95   "You could never": Bruce Lundvall to JG, Nov 7, 2007.

95   *Jump for Joy:* Alice Key to JG, Mar 10, 2006.

95   "It was such": LH to JG, Mar 14, 1994.

96   "Miss Horne . . . you know?": Ibid.

97   "I was very": LH to JG, Mar 14, 1994.

97   "sense of being": See "Proust Questionnaire: Lena Horne."

97   "I was just": LH to JG, Mar 14, 1994.

97   "By the next": Katherine Dunham to JG, Dec 20, 2005.

98   "I *hate* hearing": LH to Jonathan Schwartz, WQEW-AM, May 15, 1994.

98   "She blew": Skitch Henderson to JG, Oct 12, 2004.

98   "She's the best": See Sidney Skolsky, "Close-up of Lena Horne."

99   "ladylike bitchiness": Nicolet V. Elert et al., eds., *International Dictionary of Film and Filmmakers: Actors and Actresses.*

99   "so gracious": *Lena,* p. 128.

99   "In one of": Memo, Steve Trillin to Hal Willis, Feb 5, 1942.

100 "It was Roger": Lorna Luft, *Me and My Shadows,* p. 31

100 "a normal human": Kenneth Robert Janken, *White: The Biography of Walter White,* p. 268.

100 "The director said": Leonard Bluett to JG, Feb 8, 2006.

100 "If the part": Ibid.

100 "jail fiend": Ibid.

101 "I sincerely hope": Carlton Jackson, *Hattie: The Life of Hattie McDaniel,* p. 52.

101 "He made Hollywood" . . . "anybody": Ossie Davis, *Life Lit by Some Large Vision,* p. 163.

102 "I am through": See Herman Hill, "Toddy Offers Robeson Part in New Picture."

102 "I remember": Alice Key to JG, Mar 10, 2006.

103 "perpetuating": *A Man Called White: The Autobiography of Walter White,* p. 199.

103 "interesting weapon": See Paul Rosenfield, "Lena on Lena, Late at Night."

104 "I was so": Video interview, *That's Entertainment! III,* spring 1994.

104 "He said, 'Mr. Mayer'": *The Dick Cavett Show,* PBS, 1981.

105 "would sing": See Sidney Skolsky, "Close-up of Lena Horne."

105   "The NAACP": See Kathy Larkin, "Lena Horne: A Stage Presence with a TV Future."

106   "It was a good": Sharon Rich, *Sweethearts*, p. 290.

106   "And then": Ibid.

106   "poor Rochester": LH to Johnny Carson, *Tonight*, NBC-TV, Nov 22, 1982.

107   "wasn't very good": Jeni LeGon to JG, Jun 29, 2005.

107   "This woman": Helen Rose, *Just Make Them Beautiful*, p. 54.

108   "*I* will do . . . accept her": Video interview, *That's Entertainment! III*, spring 1994.

108   "tired": Source unknown.

108   "spectacular": See Edwin Schallert, "Fun, Music Blend in *Panama Hattie*."

108   "the high point": See "Chocolate Cream Chanteuse."

108   "She demonstrates": Archer Winstein, *New York Post*, Sep 1942.

108   "like an angel": Leonard Bluett to JG, Feb 8, 2006.

109   "When Lena": Delilah Jackson to JG, Dec 21, 2005.

109   "Everybody said": LH to Rex Reed, *Tomorrow*, NBC-TV, Nov 17, 1981.

109   "Some Negroes": *Lena*, p. 140.

CHAPTER 6

110   "There was a": Betsy Blair, *The Memory of All That*, p. 107.

110   "strode": Helen Rose, *Just Make Them Beautiful*, p. 50.

111   "His favorite": Betsy Blair, *The Memory of All That*, p. 206.

112   "looking into": Gloria DeHaven to JG, Nov 24, 2004.

112   "Harmless": Betsy Blair, *The Memory of All That*, p. 108.

112   "from the": See Almena Davis, "How 'bout This?"

112   "Assembly-line": LH to Johnny Carson, *Tonight*, NBC-TV, Dec 1965.

112   "exactly like": LH to Gil Noble, "Like It Is," ABC-TV, 1982.

112   "M-G-M had": Betty Garrett, *Betty Garrett and Other Songs*, p. 116.

112   "it more or": William Tuttle to JG, Feb 25, 2005.

113   "I'd known him": LH to JG, Mar 14, 1994.

113   "Lena has remained": See Philip Carter, "Lena Horne Is the Gal."

113   "remember your": LH to Rex Reed, *Tomorrow*, NBC-TV, Nov 17, 1981.

113   "If it is": See Philip Carter, "Lena Horne Is the Gal."

113   "sepian songstress": Irving Hoffman, "'Panama Hattie' Is Nixed by Critics," *Hollywood Reporter*, Oct 5, 1942.

113   "beauteous bronze": *Chicago Defender*, c. 1942.

113   "Chocolate": See "Chocolate Cream Chanteuse."

113   "My dear": See "Meet the Real Lena Horne."

114   "took my": Lena Horne, *The Lady and Her Music*, Quest Warner Bros. CD 3597-2.

114   "no friends": See Kay Gardella, "Lena Tells It like It Was."

114   "displaced": *Lena,* p. 150.

114   "He is so wise": See Irene Thirer, "Lena Horne's Double Career."

114   "those lips": Mart Crowley to JG, Mar 17, 2007.

115   "Honey": John Fricke to JG, Feb 11, 2008.

115   "I believe": Richard Schickel to JG, Oct 8, 2004.

115   "frustrated": Butterfly McQueen to Richard Lamparski, *Whatever Became of . . . ,* WBAI-FM, 1968.

115   "very friendly . . . embarrassment": Vincente Minnelli, notes for *I Remember It Well.*

116   "Upon its success": See Billy Rowe, "'Cabin in the Sky': Liberal Producer Says Picture Will Make Movie History."

116   "If I was going . . . possible": Vincente Minnelli, *I Remember It Well,* p. 125.

117   "produced on a par": See Billy Rowe, "'Cabin in the Sky.'"

118   "a weird but": Letter, Hall Johnson to Albert Lewis, July 24, 1942.

118   "When is Hollywood": Letter, Charlie Sands to Arthur Freed, Feb 12, 1942.

118   "the greatest": Bobby Short to JG, Dec 5, 2004.

118   "matchless": Bobby Short, *Black and White Baby,* p. 162.

118   "Everything about her": Bobby Short to JG, Dec 5, 2004.

118   "Ethel was": Gene Davis to JG, Apr 7, 2005.

118   "the sexual": See Susannah McCorkle, "The Mother of Us All."

118   "Ethel survived": Bobby Short to JG, Dec 5, 2004.

119   "I never was": Ethel Waters, *His Eye Is on the Sparrow,* p. 1.

119   "the way I like": Bobby Short to JG, Dec 5, 2004.

119   "I was scared": Cleo Hayes to JG, Apr 20, 2005.

120   "It's a joy": Ethel Waters, *The Tex & Jinx Show,* Aug 4, 1947.

120   "If I can do": See "Better than a Rabbit's Foot."

120   "She always": Avanelle Harris to JG, Mar 20, 2006.

120   "I'm the kind": Earl Wilson, source unknown, 1940.

121   "*God* is": Donald Spoto, *Stanley Kramer: Film Maker,* p. 48.

121   "Ethel was on": Vincente Minnelli, notes for *I Remember It Well.*

121   "Before the camera": LH profile, source unknown, c. 1942.

121   "I don't mind": Ibid.

121   "You could sit": Avanelle Harris to JG, Mar 20, 2006.

122   "My God": Leonard Bluett to JG, Feb 8, 2006.

122   "All through": Ethel Waters, *His Eye Is on the Sparrow,* p. 258.

122   "down on": Leonard Bluett to JG, Feb 8, 2006.

122   "sex had": *The Dick Cavett Show,* PBS, 1981.

122   "the *beautiful*" Butterfly McQueen to Richard Lamparski, *Whatever Became of . . . ,* WBAI-FM, 1968.

122   "When I read": Ibid.

123   "as if she": Leonard Bluett to JG, Feb 8, 2006.

123   "The Lord": Alice Key to JG, Mar 10, 2006.

123   "Miss Waters started": *Lena,* p. 154.

123   "a semi-coherent": Gail Lumet Buckley, *The Hornes,* p. 165.

124   "Billy was intrigued": Alice Key to JG, Mar 10, 2006.

124   "the wonderful": Earl Dancer, letter to the editor, *Pittsburgh Courier,* Feb 20, 1943.

124   "that fast-approaching": See Billy Rowe, "'Cabin in the Sky.'"

124   "He had great": Evelyn Cunningham to JG, Mar 13, 2005.

124   "there would be": See Billy Rowe, "'Cabin in the Sky.'"

124   "friendship": Letter, Billy Rowe to Arthur Freed, Nov 17, 1942.

125   "You may rest": Letter, Billy Rowe to Howard Strickling, Nov 16, 1942.

125   "the arrogant": See Almena Davis, "How 'bout This?"

125   "Everywhere you": Ibid.

125   "Please avoid": Memo, Joseph I. Breen to Louis B. Mayer, Jun 29, 1942.

125   "Please change": Ibid.

126   "A kiss": Ilona Massey to Richard Lamparski, *Whatever Became of . . . ,* WBAI-FM, 1968.

126   "This young": Esther Williams to JG, Apr 15, 2005.

126   "There must": Memo, Joseph I. Breen to Louis B. Mayer, Jun 1942.

126   "historical debut": See "Lena Horne Clicks at Savoy-Plaza in Historical Debut."

126   "sepia eyeful": *All Around the Town,* Jan 1943.

127   "snooty" . . . "discussion": Ibid.

127   "surrounded" . . . "world": See "Lena Horne Clicks at Savoy-Plaza in Historical Debut."

127   "She came down": Arthur Laurents to JG, Nov 18, 2004.

128   "a looker": *All Around the Town,* Jan 1943.

128   "the café": See "Lena Horne Clicks at Savoy-Plaza in Historical Debut."

128   "What they're really": Diahann Carroll to JG, Nov 10, 2005.

128   "that colored": See Mike Levin, "Lena Horne Now Hears Society's Coveted 'Ah's!'"

128   "In the ultra-" . . . "newspapers": See "Savoy-Plaza Ousts Two Men Following Lena Horne Booking."

129   "over something else": See Bill Chase, "All Ears."

129   "She claims": See Robert Rice, "The Real Story of Lena Horne."

129   "I haven't got": See "Chocolate Cream Chanteuse."

129   "never had heard": *PM,* Dec 15, 1942.

129   "I knew I was": *Lena,* p. 145.

CHAPTER 7

130   "sensational colored chanteuse": *Lion's Roar,* Sep-Oct 1942.

131   "He broke": Delilah Jackson to JG, Dec 21, 2005.

131   "he jumped": Ibid.

131   "He was a pro": Gene Davis to JG, Jan 21, 2006.

131   "provocative": *Jet,* 1951.

131   "Some studios": Avanelle Harris to JG, Mar 20, 2006.

132   "He had never": Cleo Hayes to JG, Apr 20, 2005.

132   "terrified": See Charles Michener, "The Awesome Lena Horne."

132   "He was the": Alice Key to JG, Mar 10, 2006.

132   "feel it": LH to Rex Reed, *Tomorrow,* NBC-TV, Nov 17, 1981.

132   "thought that": LH, M-G-M archival interview, Jan 1996.

132   "I'd always": LH to Rex Reed, *Tomorrow,* NBC-TV, Nov 17, 1981.

132   "Lena sang it": See Frank Nugent, "She's Nobody's Mammy."

132   "Girl, what are": LH to Ray Otis, "The Great Sounds."

133   "Think about": *Lyrically Speaking,* BET, 1994.

133   "whispered" . . . "that's all": See Frank Nugent, "She's Nobody's Mammy."

133   "Ethel Waters": Ruby Dallas Young to JG, Mar 29, 2005.

133   "very unhappy": Avanelle Harris to JG, Mar 20, 2006.

133   "Everybody was": Cleo Hayes to JG, Apr 20, 2005.

133   "paid it": See "Movie Star Lena Horne."

133   "At that time": Helen Rose, *Just Make Them Beautiful,* p. 54.

133   "only romantic leads" . . . "pictures": See "Romantic Lena Horne."

134   "I never had": St. Clair Pugh to JG, Oct 27, 2004.

135   "tolerance": Orson Welles, *It's All True* (1993 documentary).

135   "suntan": See Max Jones, "The Singer They Went to See."

135   "not at all": LH profile, BBC-4 radio, U.K., Aug 18, 1984.

135   "Race hate": See Orson Welles, "Why I Am Interested in the Woodard Case."

136   "They see": *It's All True.*

136   "She was crazy": Marcia Ann Gillespie to JG, Aug 10, 2004.

136   "only real friend": See Clive Hirschhorn, "The Man Lena Married Even Though She Wasn't in Love."

136   "not easy": LH profile, BBC-4 radio, U.K., Aug 18, 1984.

136   "undisciplined" . . . "the set": Joan Fontaine, *No Bed of Roses,* p. 154.

137   "I said, 'What'": LH profile, BBC-4 radio (U.K.), Aug 18, 1984.

137   "I think that": See Billy Rowe, "Hollywood Star and Heavy Champ Scoff at Claims."

137   "Sergeant Louis": Ibid.

138   "he was my": Cleo Hayes to JG, Apr 20, 2005.

138   "his member": Leonard Bluett to JG, Feb 8, 2006.

138 "No, she didn't!": Alice Key to JG, Mar 10, 2006.

138 "cheating" . . . "choking her": Joe Louis, *Joe Louis: My Life*.

138 "Lena can cuss": *Joe Louis: My Life*.

139 "That breakup": Cleo Hayes to JG, Apr 20, 2005.

139 "I said, 'Champ'": Alice Key to JG, Mar 10, 2006.

139 "It was the": Cleo Hayes to JG, Apr 20, 2005.

139 "the sidewalks": See John Rosenfield, "First Audience Loves M-G-M's Cabin in the Sky."

140 "We experimented": Vincente Minnelli, notes for *I Remember It Well*.

141 "At one point": See J.T.M., "It's a Sure 'Nuff Cabin in the Sky."

141 "I think that": Gene Davis to JG, Apr 7, 2005.

141 "eliminate" . . . "view": Memo, Joseph I. Breen to Louis B. Mayer, 1942.

141 "rhythmic-hipped": See Frank Nugent, "She's Nobody's Mammy."

141 "indecent" . . . "distributors": Vincente Minnelli, notes for *I Remember It Well*.

142 "thoroughly enchanting": See Irene Thirer, *New York Evening Post*.

142 "feverish": *Variety*, Feb 10, 1943.

142 "rather forced": *Hollywood Reporter*, Feb 10, 1943.

142 "a magnificent": See "It's a Sure 'Nuff Cabin in the Sky."

142 "gorgeous, but": Ruby Dee to JG, Jan 10, 2008.

142 "For its time": Leonard Bluett to JG, Feb 8, 2006.

142 "could have died": See Wayne Warga, "Lena Horne Stars in Special on NBC."

143 "That's the only": LH, M-G-M archival interview, Jan 1996.

143 "probably": See Jesse Zunser, "'Stormy Weather' Opens at Roxy."

143 "the most of": See "Stormy Weather Certain to Mop Up at Box Office."

143 "not as what": See Charlie Emge, *Down Beat*.

143 "I think": Alice Key to JG, Mar 10, 2006.

143 "I got stuck": See Charles Michener, "The Awesome Lena Horne."

143 "More than a": See "Lena Horne Takes the Duke Over on Broadway."

144 "fantastic": *Chicago Defender*, Oct 23, 1943.

144 "She was stubborn": Gene Davis to JG, Feb. 1, 2006.

144 "In Philadelphia" . . . "thankful": Ibid.

144 "I mean": Carmen de Lavallade to JG, Jan 17, 2008.

144 "despicable": *Chicago Defender*, 1943.

145 "with the tone" . . . "parts": Jill Watts, *Hattie McDaniel: Black Ambition, White Hollywood*, p. 242.

145 "She said to me": *The Dick Cavett Show*, PBS, 1981.

145 "Darling, don't": Alan Ebert, *Intimacies*, p. 160.

145 "ran away": LH to Jim Harlan, "Legends," WNEW-AM, Jun 23, 1991.

146 "The blacks": See Rex Reed, "A Life on Stage."

CHAPTER 8

147 "She is the": See Frank Nugent, "She's Nobody's Mammy."

147 "She is unique": See Sidney Skolsky, "Close-up of Lena Horne."

147 "They told me": See Robert Higgins, "Harry and Lena."

148 "He yelled": Esther Williams to JG, Apr 15, 2005.

148 "a jolly, stout": *Lena,* p. 185.

148 "Lena is not" . . . "at a time": See Robert Rice, "The Real Story of Lena Horne."

148 "She gets loads": See "A Day in Hollywood with Lena Horne."

148 "brilliant display": *Motion Picture,* Jan 1945.

148 "I consider": Ibid.

149 "As a youngster": Ruby Dee to JG, Jan.10, 2008.

149 "The studio": See "Perfection Only Thing Satisfies Movie Star."

149 "White people": LH to JG, Mar 14, 1994.

149 "have an important part": See "Lena Horne with Garland and Rooney in 'Girl Crazy.'"

151 "bouquet" . . . "haunting": See T.M.P., "Thousands Cheer."

151 "I had friends": Louis Johnson to JG, Feb 12, 2006.

151 "They'll raid": LH to JG, Mar 14, 1994.

151 "very laid back": Arthur Laurents to JG, Nov 18, 2004.

152 "I had watched": LH to Jim Harlan, *Legends,* WNEW-AM, Jun 23, 1991.

152 "And he thought": LH, M-G-M archival interview, Jan 1996.

152 "I hated him": Video interview, *That's Entertainment! III,* spring 1994.

153 "If Lennie": LH to JG, Mar 14, 1994.

153 "this little joint": LH, M-G-M archival interview, Jan 1996.

153 "She can't be": LH to Jim Harlan, *Legends,* WNEW-AM, Jun 23, 1991.

153 "I'd thought": LH to Jonathan Schwartz, WNEW-AM, Aug 1981.

153 "civil": LH to JG, Mar 14, 1994.

153 "If somebody": LH to Gil Noble, "Like It Is," ABC-TV, 1982.

153 "He played" . . . "that evening": LH, M-G-M archival interview, Jan 1996.

153 "very glittery": LH to JG, Mar 14, 1994.

154 "When we knew": LH, M-G-M archival interview, Jan 1996.

154 "It was the rumor": Hugh Martin to JG, Oct 1, 2004.

155 "I don't want": John Lewis to JG, Mar 21, 2007.

155 "Hello, girl": See Sidney Fields, "Only Human."

155 "violently prejudiced": LH to Johnny Carson, *Tonight,* NBC-TV, Dec 1965.

155 "seek an accounting": See "Lena Files Counter Suit."

156 "I do think": See "Perfection Only Thing Satisfies Movie Star."

157 "Every time Lena": Gene Davis to JG, Apr 7, 2005.

157 "strong impact": Geoffrey Holder to JG, Apr 28, 2006.

157 "Lena Horne syndrome": Jeanne Noble, *Beautiful, Also, Are the Souls of My Black Sisters*, p. 236.

157 "The one thing": See Karen Grigsby Bates, *Los Angeles Times Magazine*.

158 "look like Lena": Jeanne Noble, *Beautiful, Also, Are the Souls of My Black Sisters*, p. 236.

158 "daydream" . . . "looked": Brian Lanker, *I Dream a World*.

158 "Lena goes anywhere": See "Call Her Tomorrow."

158 "A gal who": *Mail Call*, Armed Forces Radio Service, Jan 3, 1945.

159 "We want Lena!": *Command Performance,* Show no. 142, Armed Forces Radio Service, Oct 14, 1944.

159 "Fellas": *Personal Album* no. 582, AFRS, 1943.

159 "although I was": See Mike Jackson, "She Leads Two Lives and Does Both Nicely."

160 "written in": See Richard Kenyada, "Love, Lena Horne."

160 "They were a group": See Charles Hillinger, "WWII's Black Pilots Salute 'Pinup.'"

160 "What impressed me": Bill Broadwater to JG, Jul 17, 2007.

161 "The men who": LH to Gil Noble. "Like It Is," ABC-TV, 1982.

161 "I'm sorry": See Frank Nugent, "She's Nobody's Mammy."

161 "automatically": Bill Broadwater to JG, Jul 17, 2007.

161 "I've given wings": LH profile, source unknown, c. 1944.

161 "the charm": See Frank Nugent, "She's Nobody's Mammy."

162 "He was prepared": Anonymous source to JG.

162 "and temporary": Divorce order no. 31857, Louis J. Jones vs. Lena C. Jones, Jun 15, 1944.

162 "The court finds": Ibid.

162 "did not contest": *Down Beat*, Jul 1, 1944.

162 "But, then": See Hans J. Massaquoi, "Lena Horne on Her Loveless Childhood."

162 "but when he": See Glenn Plaskin, "The Ageless Appeal of Lena."

163 "great, quiet strength": *Lena*, p. 168.

163 "lived up to": See "Lovely Lena Horne Captivating in Short Stopover Thurs. Nite."

163 "rude" . . . "unforgivable": See "Lena Horne Quits USO Tour in Row Over Army Jim Crow."

163 "The next day": See "Lena Horne Tells Why She Quit Camp Show."

163 "to the annoyance": See "Lena Horne Quits USO Tour in Row over Army Jim Crow."

164 "on a sort of": *Lyrically Speaking,* Black Entertainment Television, 1994.

164   "So much fun": See "Horne—of Plenty."

164   "Lena Horne is a one-gal": See Howard Heyn, "Leapin' Lena Just Can't Stay Still."

164   "It's titled": *Colgate Sports Newsreel,* Apr 1945.

165   "More stars": *Lion's Roar,* Nov 1945.

165   "There are many": LH to JG, Mar 14, 1994.

165   "Let's try": Hugh Martin to JG, Oct 1, 2004.

165   "I'd had the" . . . "about her": Ibid.

166   "He played music": LH to Gil Noble, "Like It Is," ABC-TV, 1982.

166   "the best vocal": See Marie Brenner, "Kay and Eloise."

166   "It's there": LH to JG, Mar 14, 1994.

166   "The girl with": *Your Hit Parade,* 1935 broadcast.

166   "a living tornado": Buster Davis, *Ask Her If She's Got a Kid Brother: A Somewhat Tattered Life.*

166   "always on" . . . "ride-out": Ibid.

167   "I liked being": LH to JG, Mar 14, 1994.

167   "filled with" . . . "like this": Hilary Knight to JG, May 14, 2005.

167   "sweet, generous": *Movieland,* 1945.

167   "Kay was a": Hilary Knight to JG, May 14, 2005.

167   "no tits": James Melody to JG, Oct 22, 2005.

168   "pure Minnelli": Gene Davis to JG, Apr 7, 2005.

168   "Hundreds of" . . . "much out": See Avanelle Harris, "I Tried to Crash the Movies."

169   "I never thought": See Frank Nugent, "She's Nobody's Mammy."

169   "In my little": Vernon Jordan to JG, Sep 4, 2008.

169   "I saw what": Hilary Knight to JG, May 14, 2005.

170   "I worked out": *Lena,* p. 171.

170   "I understood": See Marcia Ann Gillespie, "Lena Horne Finds Her Music."

170   "Metro in the past": See Frank Nugent, "She's Nobody's Mammy."

171   "Of course Miss Mills": LH profile, source unknown, 1945.

171   "We tire": See Leon H. Hardwick, "Lena Horne Turns Down Lead in Filming of 'Uncle Tom's Cabin.'"

171   "We just presumed": Ibid.

171   "one could note": See David Hanna, "Lena Horne Makes Plea for Better Roles for Negroes."

172   "The same thing": John Fricke to JG, Oct 21, 2008.

172   "I suspect": Richard Schickel to JG, Oct 8, 2004.

172   "victim": See "Screen Guild Elects Lena to Its Exec Board."

172   "the songstress" . . . "the effort": See "Lena Horne's Contract Cuts Wages in Half."

173   "Her performance": See "Lena Horne Heard in New Kind of Role on Network."

174   "sordid" . . . "characteristics": *A Man Called White: The Autobiography of Walter White,* p. 338.

174   "atrocious dialect": See "Guild Seeks to Eliminate Lena Horne or 'Dis and Dat' from 'St. Louis Woman.'"

174   "has nothing to do": See Arna Bontemps, "'St. Louis Woman' Basically a Folk Play."

175   "She actually": See Harry Levette, "Says Lena Nixed Role in 'St. Louis Woman.'"

175   "I'm loath": See "Mayer Differs with Winchell in Disciplining Lena Horne."

176   "I don't really": Betty Garrett to JG, Sep 6, 2004.

176   "glorious": LH, M-G-M archival interview, Jan 1996.

176   "come down hard": See Rex Reed, "A Life on Stage."

176   "pawn": *The Dick Cavett Show,* PBS, 1981.

177   "a bit undemocratic": See Rosa R. Riley, "Lena Denies Marriage in Exclusive Sentinel Interview."

CHAPTER 9

178   "I'm very gratified": See "A Day in Hollywood with Lena Horne."

179   "When Lena Horne": LH profile, source unknown, 1945.

179   "In fact": LH, M-G-M archival interview, Jan 1996.

180   "hackneyed": See Bosley Crowther, "'Till Clouds Roll By.'"

180   "comes off": See Edwin Schallert, "Till the Clouds Roll By."

180   "Lena Horne in a": *Variety,* Apr 1945.

180   "And the number": Hugh Martin to JG, Oct 1, 2004.

181   "might prove": *Down Beat,* 1946.

181   "No film": See "Binford, Dixie Censor."

181   "the morals" . . . "old niggers": See Michael Finger, "Banned in Memphis."

182   "you can see": Hugh Martin to JG, Oct 1, 2004.

183   "nigger": *Lena,* p. 169.

183   "knew they": See "Lena Horne Discussed Problems Youth Meets, Hers and Neighbors."

184   "Don't worry": *Lena,* p. 170.

184   "She was very": Evelyn Cunningham to JG, Mar 13, 2005.

184   "just the grandest": See "Lena Horne Joins Notables Backing FDR's Reelection."

185   "Besides beauty": See "Lena Brings Colored, White Newspapermen Together in Dee Cee."

185   "With deep": See Harry Levette, "Lena Horne Says No Mother's Children Safe in Calif. Rally."

185   "Shoo shoo": Liner notes, *Remembering the '40s* (Reader's Digest LP set).

186   "offers much": *Metronome*, Sep 1947.

187   "where the guys": See Robert Ruark, "Lady in a High Key."

187   "Having started": LH to JG, Mar 14, 1994.

187   "a temple" . . . "unreality": Bosley Crowther, WQXR-FM report on closing of Capitol Theatre, Sep 11, 1968.

188   "Miss Horne's": See Bert McCord, "The Horne of Plenty."

188   "I've watched": Skitch Henderson to JG, Oct 12, 2004.

188   "had the ability": Ibid.

189   "where your people" . . . "could happen": See Ted Poston, "Prejudice and Progress."

189   "I admire": See Jerry Chester, "Why Lena Horne Refuses to Blow Her Own Horne."

190   "and no star": *The Big Break,* NBC radio, Aug 3, 1947.

190   "She wasn't": See Alfred Duckett, "Fabulous Lena Horne Rivals That 'Tree Growing in Brooklyn.'"

190   "There will always": See "Lena Horne Comes Back to Brooklyn."

190   "Displaying": See "200,000 Brooklynites Cheer Lena Horne; Tributes Made."

190   "You can't let" . . . "anything": See Earl Wilson, Los Angeles *Daily News.*

191   "Almost every": Nate Gross, quoted in "Lena Horne Swats Radio's Jim Crow."

191   "silly, simple": See "Lena Horne on the Entertainment Profession."

191   "We made it": From the documentary *Scandalize My Name: Stories from the Blacklist* (1998), dir. by Alexandra Isles.

191   "The Communist": Gene Davis to JG, Feb. 1, 2006.

192   "The more involved": Betty Garrett, *Betty Garrett and Other Songs,* p. 57.

192   "we didn't know": *Scandalize My Name.*

192   "I like any" . . . "work here": See "Lena Horne Tells All to Scribes—She Likes Men."

193   "very young" . . . "don't understand": Annie Ross to JG, Mar 12, 2005.

193   "I always had": LH to Gil Noble, "Like It Is." ABC-TV, 1982.

193   "didn't have": LH profile, source unknown, c. 1955.

193   "an ax": See Lena Horne, "I Just Want to Be Myself."

193   "It was good": LH, M-G-M archival interview, Jan 1996.

193   "He couldn't": Arthur Laurents to JG, Nov 18, 2004.

193   "They stayed": See Avery Williams, "The Lena Horne Love Story."

193   "We all knew": Kathryn Grayson to JG, Mar 4, 2005.

194   "Is Lena" . . . "daily": See Albert Anderson, "Is Lena Horne Married?"

194 "romance" . . . "Hollywood": See Earl Wilson, *Los Angeles Daily News.*

194 "Her husband": See Dale Harrison, "All About the Town."

194 "ugly things": See Rosa R. Riley, "Lena Denies Marriage in Exclusive Sentinel Interview."

194 "I was in": See Sidney Fields, "Success in Mixed Marriage."

194 "To L.H.": "Is Lena Horne Married?," *Our World,* Apr 1948.

194 "Something away": See Earl Wilson, *Los Angeles Daily News.*

195 "to return home": See Lena Horne, "My Story."

195 "I kept it": Sidney Fields, "Only Human."

195 "Every Sunday": LH to Jonathan Schwartz, WNEW-AM, Aug 1981.

195 "I was either": Betty Garrett, *Betty Garrett and Other Songs,* p. 99.

196 "The road" . . . "cents": Betty Garrett to JG, Sep 6, 2004.

197 "a great refuge" . . . "freak": See Joan Barthel, "Lena Horne: 'Now I Feel Good About Being Me.'"

197 "to see how": See Max Jones, "The Singer They Went to See."

197 "was not reluctant": See Rudolph Dunbar, "Lena Horne Charms London Audiences."

197 "to see": *Variety,* Nov 19, 1947.

197 "Listen, Charlie" . . . "Drinks, Lennie?": Jack Parnell to JG, May 20, 2008.

198 "an old cab" . . . "the roof:" See Tex McCrary and Jinx Falkenburg, "New York Close-Up: Lena Horne Didn't Want to Sing."

198 "Just go straight": LH to Johnny Carson, *Tonight* show, NBC-TV, Dec 1965.

198 "were hysterical": "New York Close-up."

198 what took: LH to Johnny Carson, *Tonight* show, NBC-TV, Dec 1965.

198 "obviously": "Lena in Paris," *Time,* Dec 8, 1947.

CHAPTER 10

200 "wonderful": See Lena Horne, "I Just Want to Be Myself."

200 "Lennie was Jewish": Judy Davis Francis to JG, Feb 28, 2005.

200 "very much": Gloria DeHaven to JG, Nov 24, 2004.

200 "She always had": Skitch Henderson to JG, Oct 12, 2004.

201 "Luther really": Billie Allen Henderson to JG, Mar 10, 2005.

201 "I kept": Chico Hamilton to JG, Sep 2, 2004.

201 "nowhere, no way": *Lena,* ATV special (U.K.), Nov 1, 1964.

201 "She was one" . . . "silk": Chico Hamilton to JG, Sep 2, 2004.

202 "a famous": See Brenda Cross, "Honeysuckle Rose."

202 "Why is it": See Carlton Moss, "Your Future in Hollywood."

203 "She scared me": Charles Cochran to JG, Jun 20, 2005.

203 "There's just": See Archer Winstein, *New York Post.*

203   "superb work": *Variety,* Dec 7, 1948.

203   "I began to": See Seymour Peck, "Calling on Lena Horne."

203   "The moment she": Arthur Laurents to JG, Nov 18, 2004.

204   "Regardless": See Lawrence LaMar, "Lena Horne Captivates Fans in Night Club Debut."

204   "We were royally": See Eddie Burbridge, "No Fooling."

204   "One can almost": LH review, source unknown, May 1949.

204   "astute": LH profile, source unknown, 1949.

204   "Most of the time": See "Song for Horne."

204   "was not a": Artie Shaw to JG, Aug 27, 2004.

204   "I never sensed": Betty Comden to JG, Aug 6, 2004.

204   "In our circles": Betsy Blair to JG, Sep 22, 2004.

205   "fun and raucous": André Previn to JG, Oct 9, 2006.

205   "Democrats": LH to JG, Mar 14, 1994.

205   "she could be": Gloria DeHaven to JG, Nov 24, 2004.

205   "very vital" . . . "beautiful have": Betsy Blair to JG, Sep 22, 2004.

205   "He has almost": LH interview, source unknown, c. 1965.

205   "Lena was very": Arthur Laurents to JG, Nov 18, 2004.

205   "Why doesn't" . . . "forgot": Betsy Blair, *The Memory of All That,* p. 151.

206   "Hollywood Digs": See A. S. "Doc" Young, "Hollywood Digs 'Black Gold.'"

206   "extraordinary courage": See Bosley Crowther, "Lost Boundaries."

206   "masturbation": J. Fred MacDonald, ed., *Richard Durham's Destination Freedom,* p. 3.

206   "a long way": See "La Horne Proud of Films About Negroes."

207   "Everybody": Jane White to JG, Feb 24, 2004.

207   "I'm only concerned": Original source unknown; quoted in Susannah McCorkle, "The Mother of Us All," *American Heritage,* Feb–Mar 1994.

208   "Lena, *you*": *Lena Horne: The Lady and Her Music,* Qwest/Warner Bros. CD 3597-2.

208   "the last straw": See Lem Graves, Jr., "Lena Grants Courier Exclusive Interview."

208   "given up": Ibid.

208   "Over and over": Marie Brenner, *Intimate Distance,* p. 137.

208   "I've just": See Darr Smith, *Los Angeles Daily News,* 1949.

208   "She is a little": Ibid.

208   "the type": See Frank Eng, *Los Angeles Daily News.*

208   "The Girl": See "The Girl Whom the Movies Buried."

209   "I was the": St. Clair Pugh to JG, Oct 27, 2004.

209   "After a while": Video interview for *That's Entertainment! III,* spring 1994.

209   "Being a": See Ira Peck, "Meet Miss Lena Horne."

209   "the camouflage": J. Fred MacDonald, editor, *Richard Durham's Destination Freedom,* p. 3.

210   "membership" . . . "*Negroes?*": See "Lena Horne Sues Chicago Café."

210   "She wasn't": Gloria DeHaven to JG, Nov 24, 2004.

210   "I'd like to": See Earl Wilson, *Los Angeles Daily News.*

210   "one nasty": LH profile, source unknown, c. 1952.

211   "Wherever": Chico Hamilton to JG, Sep 2, 2004.

211   "The Horne songs": See Ole Nosey, "Everybody Goes When the Wagon Comes."

211   "Are you" . . . "signature": See Darr Smith, *Los Angeles Daily News,* 1950.

212   "The people": See "I'd Love My Own Show."

213   "They didn't sound": See William Peper, *New York World-Telegram & Sun.*

213   "I try not": See "Meet the Real Lena Horne."

213   "only for one": See "The Duke and Duchess of the Music World."

214   "I thought I": LH to Johnny Carson, *Tonight* show, NBC-TV, Nov 23, 1982.

214   "There's no question" . . . "possibility": John Fricke to JG, Sep 9, 2008.

214   "She was never": George Sidney, *Los Angeles Times,* Dec 9, 1982.

214   "Lena wanted": Gene Davis to JG, Feb 1, 2006.

215   "Lena Horne and M-G-M": *Hollywood Reporter,* Mar 17, 1950.

215   "I learned": See "La Horne Proud of Films About Negroes."

215   "I was a sheep": Francis Marion, *Off with Their Heads,* p. 321.

215   "When Dore": Kathryn Grayson to JG, Mar 4, 2005.

216   "She dilated": See Rudolph Dunbar, "Lena Horne Sets Londoners on Their 'Royal' Ears."

216   "great tragedy queen": Ibid.

216   "I started": See Jerry Chester, "Why Lena Horne Refuses to Blow Her Own Horne."

216   "Here, for": See John Patrick Diggins, "I Walk in Dignity."

216   "refused flatly": Jerry Chester, "Why Lena Horne Refuses to Blow Her Own Horne."

216   "I don't know": See Robert Higgins, "Harry and Lena."

217   "pro-Communist": See "Lee and Lena Deny Red Charge."

217   "indignation": Ibid.

217   "Suitcases": Betsy Blair, *The Memory of All That,* p. 197.

218   "Anything": Esther Cooper Jackson to JG, Apr 5, 2005.

218   "And there is": See Marvin Jones, "Barney Josephson . . . How He Changed America for Good."

218   "My head": Ibid.

219   "Is Lena": See S. W. Garlington, "Pointed Points: Is Lena Wrecking Her Future?"

219 "has publicly": See "Harlem Says Lena Horne Is Married."

219 "hubby": See "Lena Horne, Hubby Share Chicago Stage, Set for Europe."

219 "husband": See "Harlem Says Lena Horne Is Married."

219 "We sat": LH to JG, Mar 14, 1994.

219 "for professional": See "Lena Horne's 1947 Wedding Disclosed."

220 "And then": LH to JG, Mar 14, 1994.

220 "Lena Horne's 1947": See "Lena Horne's 1947 Wedding Disclosed."

220 "Red Fascists": *Red Channels,* p. 6.

220 "The beige lovely": See "Billy Rowe's Notebook," Sep 30, 1950.

221 "She signed": Madeline Lee Gilford to JG, Sep 14, 2007.

221 "So inspiring": *Scandalize My Name.*

221 "The letter said": See Arthur Bell, "Lena Horne: All Storms Weathered."

222 "A lot of": Carmen de Lavallade to JG, Jan 17, 2008.

222 "10 Most": See "10 Most Beautiful Negro Women."

222 "Miss Horne": See "Critics Rave over Lena Horne Protégé."

222 "this uneducated": Betsy Blair to JG, Sep 22, 2004.

223 "Girl, I'm": See Rex Reed, "A Life on Stage."

223 "I know that": Marge Champion to JG, Nov 9, 2004.

223 "the good-bad": See Peter Bogdanovich, "Ava's Allure."

223 "was *down*": Lena Horne (Introduction), *Ava Gardner: My Story,* p. 147.

223 "she had": LH to Johnny Carson, *Tonight* show, NBC-TV, Nov 3, 1982.

223 "I'm just poor": Esther Williams to JG, Apr 15, 2005.

223 "loaded": LH to Johnny Carson, *Tonight,* NBC-TV, Nov 3, 1982.

223 "screwed" . . . "acceptable": See Hans J. Massaquoi, "Lena Horne on Her Loveless Childhood."

224 "We don't like": See R. Couri Hay, "Lena!"

224 "Ava was one": Ray Ellis to JG, Nov 30, 2004.

224 *"Lesbians!":* Lee Server, *Ava Gardner: Love Is Nothing,* p. 246.

225 "The role of": See Miles Krueger, *Show Boat: The Story of a Classic American Musical,* p. 182.

225 "But she did": Geoffrey Holder to JG, Apr 28, 2006.

225 "I really didn't": See Liz Smith, *New York Newsday.*

225 "Lena Horne was never": George Sidney, voice-over commentary, *Show Boat* laser disc edition, M-G-M/UA Home Entertainment, 1991.

226 "monumental": See Samuel Marx, "Lena at M-G-M—Take Two."

226 "somebody white": LH to Jonathan Schwartz, WNEW-AM, Aug 1981.

226 "When the first": See R. Couri Hay, "Lena!"

226 "all a lie": See Joan Barthel, "Lena Horne: 'Now I Feel Good About Being Me.'"

226 "I begged": See Erskine Johnson, *Los Angeles Daily News.*

227 "None of them": See R. Couri Hay, "Lena!"

227   "Well, they": See Liz Smith, *New York Newsday*.

227   "The feelings": John Fricke to JG, Jun 12, 2006.

227   "There wasn't": André Previn to JG, Oct 9, 2006.

227   "Everybody adored": Gloria DeHaven to JG, Nov 24, 2004.

227   "Lena couldn't": Esther Williams to JG, Apr 15, 2005.

228   "Let's face it": Rex Reed to JG, Aug 28, 2004.

228   "Forget this": *Lena Horne: In Her Own Words, American Masters*, PBS, Nov 25, 1996.

228   "All the gaiety": Betsy Blair, *The Memory of All That*, p. 199.

228   "booted": LH to Gil Noble, "Like It Is." ABC-TV, 1982.

228   "Why would": Artie Shaw to JG, Aug 27, 2004.

228   "There were times": Alan Ebert, *Intimacies*, p. 160.

CHAPTER 11

229   "It is very": *In Person: Lena Horne*, p. 237.

229   "Color!": Ibid., p. 163.

230   "Would it": See P. L. Prattis, "The Horizon."

230   "It is natural": See George Freedley, *New York Morning Telegraph*.

230   "I didn't really": See R. D. Heldenfels, "Times Are Pretty Good for Lena Horne."

230   "Lena wanted": Arthur Laurents to JG, Nov 18, 2004.

230   "stomping": *Lena*, p. 242.

230   "She sings": See "Lena Horne's New Singing Style."

230   "She sings to": See J. V. Cottom, "Vénus et Carmens Noires."

231   "which they hate": Chico Hamilton to JG, Sep 2, 2004.

231   "the manager": Arthur Laurents to JG, Nov 18, 2004.

231   "queen of": See "This Is Show Business."

231   "finding places": *Lena*, p. 241.

231   "Oh, darling": LH to Ray Otis, "The Great Sounds."

232   "seemed self-conscious": *Variety*, Jan 22, 1951.

232   "Lena could kill": Arthur Laurents to JG, Nov 18, 2004.

232   "With a gown": Source unknown, Feb 27, 1951.

233   "She wanted": Arthur Laurents to JG, Nov 18, 2004.

233   "Over 500": See Radie Harris, "Lena Horne Turns 'Em Away; Other Nitery Acts Score."

234   "rude": See "Counterattack."

234   "this latest": See John Roddy, "Attempt to Bar Lena Horne from TV Show Rebuffed."

234   "I'm not going": See "Hearst Press Off Again; This Time vs. Lena Horne."

234   "fracture": Ibid.

235   "many complaints": See Jack O'Brian, *New York Journal-American*.

235   "dream-like quality": *Lena,* p. 255.

235   "very little": Ibid., p. 256.

235   "He said he": See Arthur Bell, "Lena Horne: All Storms Weathered."

236   "necessarily vague": *Lena,* p. 255.

236   "made her peace": See Marvel Cooke, "Lena Horne's Manager Says She'll Refuse to 'Name Names.'"

236   "do exactly": See John Roddy, "Lena Horne's Manager Says 'Counterattack' Clears Her."

237   "First there": *Lena,* p. 252.

237   "whitest": See Fred Rayfield, "What's the Stork Club Got?"

238   "Josephine is": Jean-Claude Baker to JG, Aug 4, 2005.

238   "Bessie plotted": Ralph Blumenthal, *Stork Club,* p. 163.

238   "Josephine didn't" . . . "years": Jean-Claude Baker to JG, Aug 4, 2005.

238   "FAMOUS NITE": See Dick Armstrong and Max Sien, "Stork Picketed over Jo Baker."

239   "and in a style": Arthur Laurents to JG, Nov 18, 2004.

239   "NIGGER LOVER": See Luke Roberts, "Untold Story of Lena Horne's Love Affair!"

239   "selfish" . . . "ladder": Skitch Henderson to JG, Oct 12, 2004.

239   "We just couldn't": See Nancy Collins, *W.*

239   "When I saw": Arthur Laurents to JG, Nov 18, 2004.

239   "Lena performed": Bobby Short to JG, Dec 5, 2004.

240   "Lena *demanded*": Billie Allen-Henderson to JG, Dec 10, 2004.

240   "sticks": See Robert Ruark, "Lady in a High Key."

240   "You could tell": Trygve Harris to JG, Aug 23, 2004.

240   "a sort of": Arthur Laurents to JG, Nov 18, 2004.

241   "She called him": Ibid.

241   "nothing until": Alan Ebert, *Intimacies,* p. 163.

241   "I began to": See Seymour Peck, "Calling on Lena Horne."

241   "torture": *Lena,* p. 266.

241   "The trouble": *The Complete Life of Lena Horne,* p. 53.

241   "was a *consummate*": Skitch Henderson to JG, Oct 12, 2004.

241   "They opened": Edward Berger and David Chevan, *Bassically Speaking,* p. 96.

241   "the world's best bass player": LH to JG, Mar 14, 1994.

241   "Like most": Edward Berger and David Chevan, *Bassically Speaking,* pp. 99–100.

242   "Listen. Playing": Jack Parnell to JG, May 20, 2008.

242   "if I ran": LH to JG, Mar 14, 1994.

242   "got tired": Chico Hamilton to JG, Sep 2, 2004.

242   "She was more": Gene DiNovi to JG, Dec 11, 2004.

242   "Ralph Harris told": Richard Schickel to JG, Oct 8, 2004.

243   "When I first": Alice Key to JG, Mar 10, 2006.

243   "She could not": Grange Rutan to JG, Feb 12, 2005.

243   "The Queen": Sands flyer, c. 1954.

244   "poured herself": Gail Lumet Buckley, *The Hornes,* p. 214.

244   "When I settle": See "Lena Horne Enjoys Her Longest Vacation."

244   "a man almost" . . . "Doris Night": Arthur Laurents to JG, Nov 18, 2004.

244   "You know": Bobby Short to JG, Dec 5, 2004.

244   "changed my life": See "I'm Proud to Be a Mother."

245   "Oh, pickaninnies": Jack Larson to JG, Feb 23, 2008.

245   "beach hotel": See "Lena Horne Says Hotel Barred Her."

245   "This hotel": *New York World-Telegram,* Feb 18, 1955.

246   "because the problem": See "Lena Horne Says Hotel Barred Her."

246   "first-class": Ibid.

246   "With her popularity": See Jack Mitchell, "Lena Horne: Why Did She Run Out on Her Miami Date?"

246   "disgraceful": See "Lena Horne Says Hotel Barred Her."

246   "What the hell": Ibid.

246   "God's country": Ibid.

247   "obliged" . . . "selfish": See Mike Wallace, "Mike Wallace Asks Lena Horne."

247   "it would be": See James Green, "My Men, My Sex, My Work and Me—by Lena."

247   "dried-up": See Robert Ruark, "Lady in a High Key."

247   "I don't think": See Aline Mosby, "Lena Horne to Quit Clubs, Enter Theater."

247   "sexy look" . . . "near-sighted": See Arch Ayres, "How Long Can a Glamour Girl Last?"

247   "that beneath": Dorothy Dandridge, *Everything and Nothing.*

248   "There was nothing": Diahann Carroll to JG, Nov 10, 2005.

248   "the most beautiful": *Life,* Nov 1, 1954.

248   "Is Lena": See "Is Lena Still the Queen?"

248   "Can Dandridge" . . . "first place": See "Can Dandridge Outshine Lena Horne?"

248   "She has the voice": *Our World,* Dec 1951.

248   "Lena in a way": Bobby Short to JG, Dec 5, 2004.

248   "I'm easy": See "Song for Horne."

249   "She was mad": Claude Thompson to JG, Jan 20, 2006.

249   "She has shown": See "Is Lena Still the Queen?"

249 "Whenever I": Diahann Carroll to JG, Nov 10, 2005.

250 "It was a damn": Brian Lanker, *I Dream a World.*

250 "I think": *Disc Derby,* CBS radio, Apr 26, 1955.

250 "just kidding around": Edward Berger and David Chevan, *Bassically Speaking,* p. 99.

251 "Lena at her": See Bill Coss, review, "I Love to Love."

251 "offensive": See "CBS Bans Recording by Lena Horne."

251 "unsuitable": Laurie Henshaw, See "The Records Are Playing That Banned Song."

251 "Lena can be": See Arch Ayres, "How Long Can a Glamour Girl Last?"

251 "poisonous and fun": LH to JG, Mar 14, 1994.

252 "smart and funny" . . . "laughing": Arthur Laurents to JG, Nov 18, 2004.

252 "Oh, Daddy": Charles Busch to JG, Mar 10, 2008.

252 "tremendous": See "Is Lena Still the Queen?"

253 *"Kiss my ass!"*: Chico Hamilton to JG, Sep 2, 2004.

253 "She had more": Ibid.

253 "Chico had strep": Billie Allen-Henderson to JG, Mar 10, 2005.

254 "That was the": See Shirley Norman, "Lena Horne at 60."

254 "It was always": Bob Freedman to JG, Sep 28, 2004.

254 "It's the first": See Gael Greene, "Happiness Comes Last."

254 "Come up": See Leonard Feather, "The Horne of Plenty."

255 "Lena was not": Arthur Laurents to JG, Nov 18, 2004.

255 "at odd moments": Anonymous source to JG.

255 "hotel baby": LH to Ray Otis, "The Great Sounds."

255 "more frightened": See John Sansoni, "Untold Story of Lena Horne's Children."

255 "Gail was": *Lena,* p. 245.

255 "had a lot": Judy Davis Francis to JG, Feb 28, 2005.

255 "Gail was brought": Arthur Laurents to JG, Nov 18, 2004.

255 "My son used": LH to JG, Mar 14, 1994.

256 "a very confused guy": Chico Hamilton to JG, Sep 2, 2004.

256 "A kid": Francine Kahan Weiss to JG, Nov 21, 2004.

256 "She took": Clint Rosemond to JG, May 25, 2006.

256 "mysterious" . . . "shirts": Ibid.

256 "Yes, Ted": Francine Kahan Weiss to JG, Nov 21, 2004.

257 "the smartest": Clint Rosemond to JG, May 25, 2006.

257 "He was a": Francine Kahan Weiss to JG, Nov 21, 2004.

257 "by an overwhelming": Roland Jefferson to JG, Nov 17, 2004.

257 "I'm sure": Francine Kahan Weiss to JG, Nov 21, 2004.

257 "take a car": See John Sansoni, "Untold Story of Lena Horne's Children."

257   "*the* modern": See Leonard Feather, "The Horne of Plenty."

257   "He would love": See John Sansoni, "Untold Story of Lena Horne's Children."

257   "Lou was a": Clint Rosemond to JG, May 25, 2006.

CHAPTER 12

258   "I went to": Bobby Short to JG, Dec 5, 2004.

258   "When performing": Alan Ebert, *Intimacies,* pp. 161–2.

259   "When Hilton placed" . . . "walked out": See Max Maxwell, "Negro Stars Wow High Society."

259   "I can't remember": See Robert Dana, "Lena Packs 'Em In at Waldorf."

259   "toilets": Ray Ellis to JG, Nov 30, 2004.

260   "the ultimate": Bobby Short to JG, Dec 5, 2004.

260   "geisha walk": Arthur Laurents to JG, Nov 18, 2004.

260   "You can have": Gene Davis to JG, Apr 7, 2005.

260   "It made people": Polly Bergen to JG, Jul 13, 2004.

260   "Thank you" . . . "tunes": From the RCA album *Lena Horne at the Waldorf-Astoria,* RCA LSO-1028.

261   "It would" . . . "nightclubs": LH to JG, Mar 14, 1994.

261   "There is not": John Wallowitch to JG, Dec 6, 2004.

261   "But I could": Polly Bergen to JG, Jul 13, 2004.

262   "He had this": LH to Ray Otis, "The Great Sounds."

262   "not to be": Stephen Citron, *Noel & Cole: The Sophisticates.*

262   "hated": George Eells, *The Life That Late He Led,* p. 283.

262   "I learned": LH to JG, Mar 14, 1994.

262   "It's like, 'Now'": Billie Allen-Henderson to JG, Dec 10, 2004.

263   "acted up a storm": Arthur Laurents to JG, Nov 18, 2004.

263   "Any minute": Claude Thompson to JG, Jan 20, 2006.

263   "I wanted": Johnny Mathis to JG, Nov 1993.

263   "Lena Horne can't": See William C. Payette, "'Can't Girl' Hits High Spot in Films."

264   "My blood" . . . "loved it!": Charles Cochran to JG, Jun 20, 2005.

264   "spoiled" . . . "children's lives": Judy Davis Francis to JG, Feb 28, 2005.

265   "I think": Gail Lumet Buckley to JG, Jul 16, 1998.

265   "the naked": *Lena,* p. 260.

265   "Nothing": See Aline Mosby, "Lena Horne to Quit Clubs, Enter Theater."

266   "I'm too old": LH profile, source unknown, c. 1954.

267   "a stupid broad": *Lena,* pp. 258–9.

267   "glorified": Arthur Laurents to JG, Nov 18, 2004.

267   "I had such": LH to JG, Mar 14, 1994.

267   "I have a": See William Peper, *New York World-Telegram & Sun.*

268   "Adelaide was far": Iain Cameron Williams to JG, 2008.

268   "it became": Stephen Bourne to JG, Mar 20, 2008.

269   "my Auntie": Ibid.

269   "Isn't it sad": See "An Interview: Lena Horne."

269   "some of the most": Alvin Ailey, *Revelations*, p. 1.

269   "What a gorgeous": Ibid., p. 39.

269   "When Alvin": Cristyne Lawson to JG, May 25, 2006.

270   "I think I": Nat Horne to JG, May 10, 2006.

270   "My feet": Alvin Ailey, *Revelations*, p. 81.

270   "those young people": Ibid., p. 2.

271   "Horne, in her": Howard Kissel, *David Merrick: The Abominable Showman*, p. 133.

271   "Lena's face": Alan Eichler to JG, Aug 4, 2008.

271   "dreadful": See Elinor Hughes, *Boston Globe.*

271   "*I hate*" . . . "before": See Seymour Peck, "Calling on Lena Horne."

271   "I thought this": See Earl Wilson, *New York Post,* Nov 1, 1957.

271   "Yip said" . . . "in the way": Joseph Stein to JG, Jan 29, 2008.

272   "You find" . . . "ingénue": *Lena,* p. 262.

272   "To hell": St. Clair Pugh to JG, Nov 19, 2004.

273   "inspired her": *David Merrick: The Abominable Showman,* p. 133.

273   "walked around": Claude Thompson to JG, Jan 20, 2006.

274   "better than sex": Ibid.

274   "sick again": *The Steve Allen Show,* NBC-TV, Mar 16, 1958.

274   "Let's get": *Lena,* p. 263.

274   "completely overhauled": Liner notes by Steven Suskin, *Jamaica,* CD reissue: RCA Victor 09026-68041-2.

274   "I felt like": Joseph Stein to JG, Jan 29, 2008.

274   "*Jamaica* was": Arthur Laurents to JG, Nov 18, 2004.

274   "She has nothing": Robert Sylvester, New York *Daily News,* Nov 24, 1957.

275   "On Monday": Graham Payn and Sheridan Morley, eds., *The Noël Coward Diaries,* p. 366.

275   "No one": See Brooks Atkinson, "One Yes: One No."

275   "I was knocked": Mart Crowley to JG, Mar 17, 2007.

275   "I am flabbergasted": See Tina Morris, "Lena Horne and That 'Jamaica' Kiss."

275   "I don't feel": See Gael Greene, "Happiness Came Last."

275   "heaven": *Lena,* p. 265.

275   "we had an": *The Rosie O'Donnell Show,* ABC-TV, Jun 16, 1997.

275   "I was very": LH to JG, Mar 14, 1994.

276 "haze of goodwill": *Original Story by Arthur Laurents,* p. 291.

276 "Lennie was devoted": Gail Lumet Buckley, *The Hornes,* p. 186.

276 "Lena was drinking": Cristyne Lawson to JG, May 25, 2006.

276 "Daddy gives" . . . "at all": See Robert Wahls, "Cocktails with Lena; What Could Be Keener."

277 "very sweet": Claude Thompson to JG, Jan 20, 2006.

277 "Every time": *The Dick Cavett Show,* PBS, 1981.

277 "Her mother": Arthur Laurents to JG, Nov 18, 2004.

277 "terrible frustration": Carmen de Lavallade to JG, Jan 17, 2008.

277 "not pretty" . . . "ever seen": Susan Fales-Hill, *Always Wear Joy,* pp. 34–5.

278 "real sense" . . . "would say": Alvin Ailey, *Revelations,* p. 82.

278 "But from": Geoffrey Holder to JG, Apr 28, 2006.

278 "We never saw": Nat Horne to JG, May 10, 2006.

279 "I'd never": Claude Thompson to JG, Jan 20, 2006.

279 "The world": Cristyne Lawson to JG, May 25, 2006.

279 "Lena needed": Nat Horne to JG, May 10, 2006.

279 "I didn't": Claude Thompson to JG, Jan 20, 2006.

280 "I sat": Alan Ebert, *Intimacies,* p. 160.

280 "that surreal": André Previn to JG, Oct 9, 2006.

280 "Oh, it's: Charles Cochran to JG, Jun 20, 2005.

280 "She would never": Gene DiNovi to JG, Dec 11, 2004.

281 "Frank Sinatra": Alice Key to JG, Mar 10, 2006.

281 You have: Robert B. Weide, dir., *Swear to Tell the Truth* (documentary), 1998.

281 "were this" . . . "tower": LH to JG, Mar 14, 1994.

282 "a finger-snapping": Charles Cochran to JG, Jun 20, 2005.

282 "Lena said": St. Clair Pugh to JG, Nov 19, 2004.

282 "Lena would use": Liz Smith, *Natural Blonde,* p. 116.

282 "glamorous" . . . "before": Kitty D'Alessio to JG, Nov 26, 2004.

282 "But Ginette": Geoffrey Holder to JG, Apr 28, 2006.

282 "there was a": *The Noël Coward Diaries,* p. 419.

283 "Now Lena's: See Jerry Chester, "Why Lena Horne Refuses to Blow Her Own Horne."

283 "She had that": Anonymous source to JG.

283 "knew all": Claude Thompson to JG, Jan 20, 2006.

283 "My mother": Whitney Bolton, "Lena's Daughter Is Set for Debut."

283 "were at odds": Arthur Laurents to JG, Nov 18, 2004.

283 "serious love-hate": Rex Reed to JG, Aug 1, 2004.

283 "I had always": Sidney Myer to JG, Nov 10, 2005.

284 "was very rare": Nelson Atkins to JG, Dec 7, 2004.

284 "I was one": Terrie Burton-Charles to JG, Apr 25, 2006.

284   "sweet, vivacious": Los Angeles High yearbook, 1957.

284   "I always": Terrie Burton-Charles to JG, Apr 25, 2006.

285   "he just" . . . "apartments": Ibid.

285   "newly": Article, source unknown, Mar 4, 1958.

285   "It kills me": See Mike Wallace, "Mike Wallace Asks Lena Horne."

286   "who had bitterly": See "Lena's 'Ex' Named in Vote Fraud."

286   "He loved my": *Lyrically Speaking*, BET, 1994.

286   "Teddy did": Judy Davis Francis to JG, Mar 1, 2005.

287   "I really think": Samadhi Jones to JG, Oct 28, 2007.

288   "It was very": LH to JG, Mar 14, 1994.

288   "get it right": Ibid.

288   "knew what": Gene DiNovi to JG, Dec 11, 2004.

288   "lyricist's dream": André Previn to JG, Oct 9, 2006.

288   "I detest": See Peter Reilly, "Interview: Lena Horne."

288   "one of the": See Murray Schumach, Review of *Stormy Weather*.

289   "Harry was like": Claude Thompson to JG, Jan 20, 2006.

289   "Harry was not": Polly Bergen to JG, Jul 13, 2004.

290   "irreparable damage": See "Lena Horne Sues to Halt Sale of Album."

290   "I didn't speak": See Eliot Tiegel, "The Art of Survival: Lena."

290   "No network would": Ralph Harris to Stephen Bourne, May 24, 1990.

290   "I feel I've": See "I'd Love My Own Show."

290   "Although the": *Variety*, 1959.

291   "She was not": Gene Davis to JG, Jan 21, 2006.

291   "I like money": LH to Herbert Feinstein, Pacifica Radio, KPFA, San Francisco, 1963.

291   "It's pretty clear": See "I'd Love My Own Show."

291   "someone they": LH interview, source unknown, c. 1965.

291   "*Fuck 'em*" . . . "armor": Claude Thompson to JG, Jan 20, 2006.

291   "I remember": Arthur Laurents to JG, Nov 18, 2004.

291   "I'm an excellent": *Lena*, p. 273.

292   "I felt he": Alan Ebert, *Intimacies*, p. 160.

292   He reads": See Bernard H. Gould, "The Smile That Hides a Singer's Sorrow."

292   "They had": Samadhi Jones to JG, Oct 28, 2007.

292   "I thought" . . . "and feel": Terrie Burton-Charles to JG, Apr 25, 2006.

292   "Mother, you": See Leonard Feather, "The Horne of Plenty."

292   "I think" . . . "*Hello*, dear": Terrie Burton-Charles to JG, Apr 25, 2006.

293   "for publicity": Samadhi Jones to JG, Oct 28, 2007.

293   "a better life": See Peter Reilly, "Lena Horne: Interview."

293   "didn't like" . . . "fortune": Clint Rosemond to JG, May 25, 2006.

293   "feel the": Francine Kahan Weiss to JG, Nov 21, 2004.

CHAPTER 13

294   "Ted left": Clint Rosemond to JG, May 25, 2006.

294   "She was": Elle Elliott to JG, May 23, 2006.

294   "My grandfather": Samadhi Jones to JG, Oct 28, 2007.

295   "a beautiful lady": See Frank Sinatra, "Me and My Music."

295   "kitsch": Mart Crowley to JG, Mar 17, 2007.

296   "Miss Horne's table": *Lena*, p. 273.

296   "There's Lena": See "Lena Horne Clobbers Race Baiter."

296   "So that's": See "Swingin' Lena Horne Backed by Fans."

296   "I can hear": See "Lena Horne Pelts 'Insulter' in Café."

296   "Well," he barked: "Swingin' Lena Horne Backed by Fans."

296   "nigger bitch": See "I Don't Like Being Insulted!"

296   "all red": LH to Jim Harlan, "Legends," WNEW-AM, Jun 23, 1991.

296   "For God's sake": See Lena Horne, "I Just Want to Want to Be Myself."

296   *"He called"*: Claude Thompson to JG, Jan 20, 2006.

296   "Why'd she": LH to Jim Harlan, "Legends."

296   "Did you": *Lena*, p. 273.

296   *"Yes, I did!"*: Claude Thompson to JG, Jan 20, 2006.

296   "We're taking": See "Swingin' Lena Horne Backed by Fans."

296   "He's bleeding!": See "What the Man Said to Lena Horne."

297   "What do you": See "Lena's a Bit Uneasy, but She's Not Apologizing."

297   "He called me": Claude Thompson to JG, Jan 20, 2006.

297   "I am not" . . . "stuff": See "Lena's a Bit Uneasy, but She's Not Apologizing."

297   "few Negroes": *Time*, Feb 29, 1960.

297   "thought because": Brian Lanker, *I Dream a World*.

297   "My anger": See Rex Reed, "A Life on Stage."

297   "I had never": LH to Rex Reed, *Tomorrow*, NBC-TV, Nov 17, 1981.

297   "We submit": See "The Right to Be Wrong."

298   "an apparent bid": See "Not Sorry for Brawl, Says Lena Horne."

298   "New York": See "Swingin' Lena Horne Backed by Fans."

298   "When she did": said Arthur Laurents to JG, Nov 18, 2004.

299   "used a minimum": Edward Berger and David Chevan, *Bassically Speaking*, p. 99.

299   "He likes": See "Lena Picks an Easter Hat," *Ebony*.

299   "If they'd both": Ray Ellis to JG, Nov 30, 2004.

299   "Lennie was": Geoffrey Holder to JG, Apr 29, 2006.

299   "strange, mystic": See Ponchitta Pierce, "Lena Horne at 51."

299   "Lena was more": Arthur Laurents to JG, Nov 18, 2004.

300   "color-blind": LH to JG, Mar 14, 1994.

300   "I would come": *Lyrically Speaking*, BET, 1994.

300   "Luther told me": Billie Allen Henderson to JG, Dec 10, 2004.

300   "part of a": See "Lena Horne to Headline Benefit at Ahmanson."

300   "He asked me": See Gene Wright, "Have You Met Miss Jones?"

301   "I really didn't": LH to John Gruen, Nov 27, 2972.

301   "I'm terrified" . . . "opening night": See Gene Wright, "Have You Met Miss Jones."

301   "I want Gail": See "Lena's Daughter Makes Stage Debut."

301   "Tired Musical": See Howard Taubman, "Tired Musical."

301   "intellectualism": See Whitney Bolton, "Lena's Daughter Is Set for Debut."

301   "I wouldn't": See Leonard Feather, "Hornes of Plenty."

301   "now engrossed": See Helen McNamara, "Lena's Plan for Her Tour."

302   "I'm going": See Vinícius de Moraes, *A Manhã*.

302   "went crazy": See Ary Vasconcelos, "Lena Horne 'Desafina' com João Gilberto."

302   "I'm getting": See Helen McNamara, "Lena's Plan for Her Tour."

303   "I'm not a": LH to JG, Mar 14, 1994.

304   "Her voice": Private tape, *A Celebration of the Music of Ella Fitzgerald*, Carnegie Hall, New York, Jul 9, 1996.

304   "Repudiating": See S.G., review of *Lena . . . Lovely and Alive.*

305   "terrible" . . . "couldn't sing": Paul Robeson, Jr., to JG, Feb 23, 2006.

306   "I know he": Bob Florence to JG, Feb 8, 2008.

306   "an absolutely": J.F.I., review: *Lena Horne Sings Your Requests, High Fidelity*, 1962.

306   "I'm always": LH interview, source unknown, c. 1965.

306   "I was never": *The Dick Cavett Show*, PBS, 1981.

307   "I didn't realize": Diahann Carroll to JG, Nov 10, 2005.

307   "She had this": Ray Ellis to JG, Nov 30, 2004.

307   "I examined": *The Dick Cavett Show*, PBS, 1981.

308   "heroic": LH to JG, Mar 14, 1994.

308   "lie": See Joan Barthel, "Lena Horne: Now I Feel Good About Being Me."

308   "buy-offs": LH interview, source unknown, c. 1972.

308   "good little symbol": LH to JG, Mar 14, 1994.

308   "very imposing-looking": St. Clair Pugh to JG, Nov 19, 2004.

309   "*big* controlling force": Arthur Laurents to JG, Nov 18, 2004.

309   "She was the": Marcia Ann Gillespie to JG, Aug 10, 2004.

309   "To know Jeanne": Novella Nelson to JG, Aug 28, 2005.

309   "She hated": Arthur Laurents to JG, Nov 18, 2004.

310   "I may be": See Joanne Stang, "Lena, No Identification Necessary."

310   "to devote": See Herbert Feinstein, "Lena Horne Speaks Freely on Race, Marriage, Stage."

310   "was in a mess": See Rex Reed, "A Life on Stage."

311   "Suppose from": Roy Wilkins, *Today* (NBC-TV), Jun 13, 1963.

311   "I want 'em": See "Dogs, Kids & Clubs."

311   "The extraordinary": James Baldwin, *The Mike Wallace Interview*, 1959.

312   "see color": LH to JG, Mar 14, 1994.

312   "I suddenly": Alan Ebert, *Intimacies*, p. 162.

312   "chic": See Peter Reilly, "Lena Horne: Interview."

313   "not used": See "War in the North."

313   "the day" . . . "for broke": James Baldwin, *The Mike Wallace Interview*.

313   "There is": James Baldwin, *Notes of a Native Son*, p. 38.

315   "very tall": LH interview, source unknown, c. 1982.

315   "I had never": LH to Jim Hartz, *Over Easy*, PBS, Apr 25, 1982.

316   "in inhumanity": *Today*, NBC-TV, Jun 13, 1963.

316   "Their names": See Karen Grigsby Bates, *Emerge*.

316   "The hatred": See Hodding Carter, "Mississippi Now—Hate and Fear."

316   "Medgar is our": *Today*, NBC-TV, Jun 13, 1963.

316   "He's the one": See Karen Grigsby Bates, *Emerge*.

316   "I am a woman": LH interview, source unknown, c. 1965.

317   "Hold your flags": See Sara Slack, "Lena Horne Going to Jackson, Miss."

317   "How do we": *Today*, NBC-TV, Jun 13, 1963.

317   "Nobody black": Jackson, Mississippi, news footage, Jun 8, 1963.

317   "He always had": LH to JG, Mar 14, 1994.

318   "I never will": "Lena Horne: In Her Own Words," *American Masters*, PBS Nov 25, 1996.

318   "It was the": Brian Lanker, *I Dream a World*.

318   "Segregation now": Paul Stekler and Daniel McCabe, prods./dirs., *George Wallace: Settin' the Woods on Fire* (documentary), *The American Experience* (PBS), 2000.

318   "If an American": John F. Kennedy, Civil Rights Address, Jun 11, 1963.

319   "considering": *Lena*, p. 285.

320   "a casualty" . . . "like this!": *Today*, NBC-TV, Jun 13, 1963.

321   "crazy" . . . "used my tears": See Arthur Unger, "The Lady and Her Life."

321   "Miss Lena Horne": LH, filmed public-service announcement, 1963.

321   "the worst" . . . "unloving": Alan Ebert, *Intimacies*, p. 160.

CHAPTER 14

323   "the height": Mel Tormé, *The Other Side of the Rainbow*, p. 76.

324   "fiery temper": Ibid.

324   "Aw, screw": Ibid., p. 77.

324 "Dress rehearsal": Ibid., p. 81.

325 "Everybody said": Diahann Carroll to JG, Nov 10, 2005.

325 "People have": LH to Herbert Feinstein, Pacifica Radio, KPFA, San Francisco, 1963.

326 "It was wonderful": Diahann Carroll to JG, Nov 10, 2005.

327 "I got": Esther Cooper Jackson to JG, Apr 5, 2005.

327 "I found her": Richard Schickel to JG, Oct 8, 2004.

328 "exploited": Lena Horne, "I Just Want to Be Myself."

328 "a sophisticated": Ibid.

328 "We were divorced": Ibid.

328 "that when": Ibid.

329 "didn't like": Ray Ellis to JG, Nov 30, 2004.

329 "Bible": LH to Jim Harlan, "Legends," WNEW-AM, Jun 23, 1991.

329 "Now how": "Louis Lomax, "Louis Lomax Interviews Malcolm X."

330 "under": Arthur Laurents to JG, Nov 18, 2004.

330 "desperate chance": See Ponchitta Pierce, "Lena Horne at 51."

330 "I said, 'Lennie'" . . . "didn't fuss": LH to John Gruen, Nov 27, 1972.

330 "Maybe it": Geoffrey Holder to JG, Apr 28, 2006.

330 "When they": Ray Ellis to JG, Nov 30, 2004.

332 "tough": Ibid.

332 "new worlds": See "2 Sinatra-Horne Carnegie Hall Benefits Garner 100G for Civil Rights & Kids."

332 "a truly memorable": See Robert Salmaggi, "Frankie and Lena: Wow!"

332 "infuriated" . . . "Martin Luther King": See "Lena Horne's Daughter Hits Sinatra Hypocrisy."

332 "she usually": Ray Ellis to JG, Nov 30, 2004.

332 "lit up": Ibid.

332 "big hassle": LH to John Gruen, Nov 27, 1972.

333 "It doesn't": See "Lena Horne Integration Record Stirs Radio Ban."

333 "KMPC": Source unknown, quoted in above.

333 "Seven out": See "Lena Horne Integration Record Stirs Radio Ban."

333 "puzzled": See Bernard Lefkowitz, "Lena Horne Is Puzzled by CBS 'Ban' on a Song."

333 "I'm airing": See Mort Young, "WCBS Bars Lena's Civil Rights Disc."

333 "It never": Betty Comden to JG, Aug 6, 2004.

334 "How can I": See Michiko Kakutani, "Aloofness Hid the Pain, Until Time Cooled Her Anger."

334 "I can't get": See Art Buchwald, "Lena Horne Isn't the Memoir Type."

334 "I never had": See Arthur Unger, "The Lady and Her Life."

334 "she walked": Ray Ellis to JG, Nov 30, 2004.

335 "was *very*" . . . "pretty good": Ibid.

336   "horrified"... "marry him": Arthur Laurents to JG, Nov 18, 2004.

336   "Lennie felt": See Margaret McManus, "How to Look as Graceful as Lena Horne Under Pressure."

337   "I've always": Marie Brenner, *Intimate Distance*, p. 138.

337   "What's the matter"... "pills": *New York Mirror*, Aug 27, 1963.

337   "a rather": Source unknown, Aug 27, 1963.

337   "And I would": *New York Mirror*, Aug 27, 1963.

337   "stark black"... "match": *New York Journal-American*, Nov 29, 1963.

338   "My father": Samadhi Jones to JG, Oct 28, 2007.

338   "I asked him": Terrie Burton-Charles to JG, Apr 25, 2006.

338   "Lena Horne": Samadhi Jones to JG, Oct 28, 2007.

338   "He wants": LH to Herbert Feinstein, Pacifica Radio, KPFA, San Francisco, 1963.

339   "this thing"... "berserk": LH to Ray Otis, "The Great Sounds."

340   "Why should I": See Shirley Norman, "Lena Horne at 60."

340   "I must have": *Lena*, ATV (U.K.), Nov 1, 1964.

341   "The advertising": Ralph Harris to Stephen Bourne, May 24, 1990.

341   "someone TV": *New York Herald Tribune*, Dec 27, 1964.

341   "spellbinding": Toronto *Daily Star*, Jan 5, 1965.

341   "splendid": *Los Angeles Herald*, Mar 21, 1965.

341   "magnificent": *Pittsburgh Post-Gazette*, Apr 22, 1965.

341   "It was a": *Lena*, p. 296.

341   "It's part": *Variety*, Jun 2, 1964.

341   "because she": See Art Buchwald, "Lena Horne Isn't the Memoir Type."

341   "We got very"... "electrifying": Richard Schickel to JG, Oct 8, 2004.

343   "I suddenly": LH to Jonathan Schwartz, WNEW-AM, Aug 1981.

CHAPTER 15

344   "One was": Claude Thompson to JG, Jan 20, 2006.

344   "Grandfather": Samadhi Jones to JG, Oct 28, 2007.

344   "That sort of": Daniel L. Johnson to JG, Apr 18, 2008.

345   "Gail is very": Alan Ebert, *Intimacies*, p. 160.

345   "idol": LH to Gil Noble, "Like It Is," ABC-TV, 1982.

345   a "saint": See Ponchitta Pierce, "Lena Horne at 51."

345   "saw white": Malcolm X, *The Autobiography of Malcolm X*, p. 429.

346   "Those radicals": See Michiko Kakutani, "Aloofness Hid the Pain, Until Time Cooled Her Anger."

346   "Yes, but": See Kay Gardella, "Lena Tells It like It Was."

346   "revulsion": See Peter Reilly, "Lena Horne: Interview."

346   "I tell you": See Rex Reed, "A Life on Stage."

346   "I used to": Ray Ellis to JG, Nov 30, 2004.

347   "a ball": Ibid.

347   "Then she started": Ibid.

347   "I don't think": *The Mike Douglas Show,* Dec 1965.

347   "more militant": See Ponchitta Pierce, "Lena Horne at 51."

347   "her slavies": Arthur Laurents to JG, Nov 18, 2004.

348   "All of a": Geoffrey Holder to JG, Apr 28, 2006.

348   "I had no": See Joan Barthel, "Lena Horne: 'Now I Feel Good About Being Me.'"

348   "I realized": Liz Smith, *Natural Blonde,* p. 117.

348   "you'd feel" . . . "gangbusters": Geoffrey Holder to JG, Apr 28, 2006.

348   "We had extolled": Liz Smith, *Natural Blonde,* p. 117.

348   "I didn't like": St. Clair Pugh to JG, Oct 27, 2004.

349   "reaching into": See Lena Horne, "Three-Horned Dilemma Facing Negro Women."

349   "She and Lena": Anonymous source to JG.

349   "the woman she had": Tom Hatcher to JG, Nov 18, 2004.

350   "The public profile": Marcia Ann Gillespie to JG, Aug 10, 2004.

350   "There was a": Billie Allen Henderson to JG, Dec 10, 2004.

350   "a clandestine": Gene Davis to JG, Jan 21, 2006.

350   "rough racket": See Herbert Feinstein, "Lena Horne Speaks Freely on Race, Marriage, Stage."

350   "That's tragic": LH to Herbert Feinstein, Pacifica Radio, KPFA, San Francisco, 1963.

351   "Somewhere people": Gail Lumet Buckley, *The Hornes,* p. 249.

351   "a very angry" . . . "windows": Ibid., p. 254.

352   "He was not a" . . . "have had": Samadhi Jones to JG, Oct 27, 2007.

352   "crushed": Claude Thompson to JG, Jan 20, 2006.

352   "Lena was buying": Terrie Burton-Charles to JG, Apr 25, 2006.

352   "potentially": See Wayne Warga, "Lena Horne Returns to Hollywood."

352   "She did all": Terrie Burton-Charles to JG, Apr 25, 2006.

353   "She was sitting": Ray Ellis to JG, Nov 30, 2004.

353   "She had full": Richard Schickel to JG, Oct 8, 2004.

353   "The first time": See Mary Wilson, "Lena Horne—We Don't Need a Superblack!"

353   "my brother": See Shirley Norman, "Lena Horne at 60."

354   "No": LH to Johnny Carson, *Tonight,* NBC-TV, Dec 1965.

345   "I thought": Arthur Laurents to JG, Nov 18, 2004.

354   "simply got" . . . "Christmas card": Richard Schickel to JG, Oct 8, 2004.

354   "Now I": *Lena,* p. 296.

355   "That is not": Gene Davis to JG, Apr 7, 2005.

355 "much more": See R. Couri Hay, "Lena!"

355 "to find" . . . "flashback": LH to Rex Reed, *Tomorrow*, NBC-TV, Nov 17, 1981.

355 "I said, 'Thelma'": *60 Minutes* (CBS-TV), 1981.

355 "terrible coldness" . . . "inside me": See Peter Reilly, "Lena Horne: Interview."

355 "It was not": Ray Ellis to JG, Nov 30, 2004.

356 "I have to": Ibid.

356 "would be kind": Jackson R. Bryer, *The Art of the American Musical*, p. 133.

357 "Arthur wrote": Buster Davis, *Ask Her If She's Got a Kid Brother*.

357 "Arthur kept": St. Clair Pugh to JG, Oct 27, 2004.

358 "She hated it" . . . "got out": Ray Ellis to JG, Nov 30, 2004.

358 "There were": Arthur Laurents to JG, Nov 18, 2004.

358 "*Hallelujah, Baby!* was": Jeanne Noble, *Beautiful, Also, Are the Souls of My Black Sisters*, p. 258.

358 "*enormous*": See Jane Horwitz, "For Laurents, Time to Revise and Shine."

358 "about as unprejudiced": Ibid.

359 "She gave": Arthur Laurents to JG, Nov 18, 2004.

359 "Then why": Margaret Styne to JG, Sep 22, 2004.

359 "never read" . . . "meant it": Arthur Laurents to JG, Nov 18, 2004.

359 "old-fashioned": See Joan Barthel, "Lena Horne: 'Now I Feel Good About Being Me.'"

359 "was too radical": Margaret Styne to JG, Sep 22, 2004.

359 "ran like thieves": Arthur Laurents to JG, Nov 18, 2004.

359 "Fortunately": Buster Davis, *Ask Her If She's Got a Kid Brother*.

359 "charming comic" . . . "she sing!": *The Lee Jordan Show*, WCBS, Feb 19, 1967.

360 "one of the loveliest" . . . "in it": Arthur Laurents to JG, Nov 18, 2004.

360 "There was no": Betty Comden to JG, Aug 6, 2004.

360 "were a little": Buster Davis, *Ask Her If She's Got a Kid Brother*.

360 "atmosphere": Theodore Taylor, *Jule: The Story of Composer Jule Styne*, p. 256.

360 "a course": See Trey Graham, "Playwright Returns to His 1960's Musical with a New Vision and Voice."

360 "The show was": Ibid.

360 "There comes": Theodore Taylor, *Jule: The Story of Composer Jule Styne*, p. 257.

360 "be in some": See Marcia Ann Gillespie, "Lena Horne Finds Her Music, Her Daughter, and Her Self."

361 "I think I'd" . . . "and died": LH to JG, Mar 14, 1994.

362 "They were gonna" . . . "after that": Ray Ellis to JG, Nov 30, 2004.

362 "would soften": See Ponchitta Pierce, "Lena Horne at 51."

363 "I'd like someone": "The Life and Words of Martin Luther King, Jr.," www.scholastic.com.

363 "arrogance": See Ponchitta Pierce, "Lena Horne at 51."

363 "the remarkable": *Freedomways Salute to Paul Robeson* (WBAI-FM, Jun 18, 1965).

364 "I said, 'What" . . . "capable of it": Ray Ellis to JG, Nov 30, 2004.

CHAPTER 16

366 "She told me": Elle Elliott to JG, May 23, 2006.

366 "When I found": Claude Thompson to JG, Jan 20, 2006.

367 "with twenty years": See "A Deadly Iteration."

367 "I got hysterical": LH to JG, Mar 14, 1994.

367 "God, please": LH interview, source unknown, c. 1972.

368 "Oh, I cried!": LH to JG, Mar 14, 1994.

368 "I say": LH to Nikki Giovanni, *WNET Black Journal,* Dec 29, 1970.

368 "this girl" . . . "dragged me out": LH to JG, Mar 14, 1994.

368 "He wasn't": Daniel L. Johnson to JG, Apr 18, 2008.

369 "No one could": Francine Kahan Weiss to JG, Nov 21, 2004.

369 "He wasn't": Nelson Atkins to JG, Dec 7, 2004.

369 "He was absolutely": Francine Kahan Weiss to JG, Nov 21, 2004.

369 "always accepted": Judy Davis Francis to JG, Mar 1, 2005.

371 "Richard was": LH, M-G-M archival interview, Jan 1996.

371 "I'm gonna learn": Sidney Skolsky, *Citizen News.* Jul 20, 1968.

371 "scared to death" . . . "stand it": See Wayna Warga, "Lena Horne, Working Tourist."

371 "terrified" her: See Sidney Skolsky, *Citizen News.*

371 "He is turning": LH interview, source unknown, summer 1968.

371 "It was distinctly": Richard Schickel to JG, Oct 8, 2004.

372 "I wasn't that": LH, M-G-M archival interview, Jan 1996.

372 "blue-eyed": See Wayne Warga, "Lena Horne, Working Tourist."

372 "half-well" . . . "I guess": See Ponchitta Pierce, "Lena Horne at 51."

373 "She said to me": Ray Ellis, Nov 30, 2004.

373 "I'm like that": *The Mike Douglas Show,* May 23, 1968.

374 "I had fun": LH to JG, Mar 14, 1994.

375 "conquered": See Jack Gould, "Lena Horne, Young in Spirit, on N.B.C. Special."

375 "I'm a better": See Kay Gardella, New York *Daily News.*

375   *"Now,* I": See Robert Higgins, "Harry and Lena."

375   "exquisiteness"... "brothers": *Tonight,* NBC-TV, 1967.

375   "They weren't": Claude Thompson to JG, Jan 20, 2006.

376   "both Harry": See Robert Higgins, "Harry and Lena."

376   a "triumph": See Jack Gould, "Lena Horne, Belafonte Offer Poignant Hour."

377   "Against doctor's orders": Gail Lumet Buckley, *The Hornes,* p. 254.

377   "She was going": Daniel L. Johnson to JG, Apr 18, 2008.

377   "I said to her": Anonymous source to JG.

377   "Lena really": Judy Davis Francis to JG, Feb 28, 2005.

377   "He was in": Clint Rosemond to JG, May 25, 2006.

378   "We went to": Kitty D'Alessio to JG, Nov 26, 2004.

378   "Ted was": Daniel L. Johnson to JG, Apr 18, 2008.

378   "We had": *Lena,* p. 297

378   "circumstances": LH to Jonathan Schwartz, WQEW-AM, May 15, 1994.

379   "I thought": See Jan Hodenfield, "Lena Horne: Back on Broadway."

379   "That was the": Claude Thompson to JG, Jan 20, 2006.

380   "The morning": LH to Jonathan Schwartz, WNEW-AM, Aug 1981.

380   "We walked": Claude Thompson to JG, Jan 20, 2006.

380   "He looked": Roland Jefferson to JG, Nov 17, 2004.

380   "His attitude"... "state": Daniel L. Johnson to JG, Apr 18, 2008.

381   "It didn't dawn": Clint Rosemond to JG, May 25, 2006.

381   "an intelligent": Tom Reed to JG, 2005.

381   "crushed": Kitty D'Alessio to JG, Nov 26, 2004.

381   "devastated": Judy Davis Francis to JG, Mar 1, 2005.

381   "I cried": Terrie Burton-Charles to JG, Apr 25, 2006.

382   "very positive": Judy Davis Francis to JG, Feb 28, 2005.

382   "or even advised": Samadhi Jones to JG, Oct 28, 2007.

382   "He wanted": Clint Rosemond to JG, May 25, 2006.

382   "forcibly": See Stephen Wilding and J. M. Weyburn, Jr., "Lena Horne: The Beautiful Survivor."

382   "I think": Clint Rosemond to JG, May 25, 2006.

383   "None of": Skitch Henderson to JG, Oct 12, 2004.

383   "All he talked": Eileen Barton to JG, Jun 24, 2006.

383   "I never heard": Bob Freedman to JG, Sep 28, 2004.

383   "Sinatra said": Fred Walker to JG, Aug 17, 2004.

384   "kind of calm": Claude Thompson to JG, Jan 20, 2006.

384   "All the men": LH to JG, Mar 14, 1994.

384   "I'm very fatalistic": LH interview, source unknown, c. 1972.

384   "I was furious": See Rex Reed, "A Life on Stage."

CHAPTER 17

385   "Alan, we've": Alan King, *Name-Dropping*, p. 89.

385   "I couldn't": See Glenn Plaskin, "The Ageless Appeal of Lena."

385   "Why am": LH to Jonathan Schwartz, WNEW-AM, Aug 1981.

385   "You're too young": Alan King, *Name-Dropping*, p. 89.

385   "Are you crazy?": See "Ask."

385   "I can't work!": Alan King, *Name-Dropping*, p. 89.

385   "Don't give" . . . "anymore?" LH to John Gruen, Nov 17, 1972.

385   "I don't know": Alan King, *Name-Dropping*, p. 89.

386   "letting people in": LH to JG, Mar 14, 1994.

386   "I never really": See Mary Campbell, "She Just Loves It, Laughs Lena Horne."

386   "I guess I": See Shirley Norman, "Lena Horne at 60."

386   "I owe Lennie" . . . "till Lennie": Alan Ebert, *Intimacies*, p. 160.

387   "a real Cancer": Ibid.

387   "She said once" . . . "the kids": Sherri Sneed to JG, Jun 25, 2008.

388   "They don't": Bob Williams, *New York Post,* Apr 2, 1974.

388   "My Jenny": *Lyrically Speaking,* BET, 1994.

388   "I respect": See Margaret McManus, "How to Look as Graceful as Lena Horne Under Pressure."

388   "I have never": See Judy Klemesrud, "On Reverse Sides of Generation Gap?"

389   "Black symbols": See Mary Wilson, "Lena Horne—We Don't Need a Superblack!"

389   "I'm sort of": See R. Couri Hay, "Lena!"

389   "an old lady": Ibid.

390   "been waiting": See Cecil Smith, "Redd Foxx's Date with Lena Horne."

390   "What do you" . . . "Hermès": Elle Elliott to JG, May 23, 2006.

391   "a supernova": See David Colman, "Giorgio Sant'Angelo: Wild Child," *New York,* Feb 18, 2002.

391   "Giorgio had": Kitty D'Alessio to JG, Nov 26, 2004.

391   "her highly": See S.G., review of *Lena . . . Lovely and Alive.*

391   "uptight" . . . "unreal": See Ponchitta Pierce, "Lena Horne at 51."

391   "He plays": LH to John Gruen, Nov 27, 1972.

392   "She was kind": Ann Ruckert to JG, Sep 12, 2008.

392   "That's the way": LH to John Gruen, Nov 27, 1972.

392   "I was completely": LH to JG, Mar 14, 1994.

393   "Once in a": LH to JG, Mar 14, 1994.

393   "Miss Horne": See Morgan Ames, review of *Nature's Baby.*

393   "excited for": LH to JG, Mar 14, 1994.

393   "She did *not*": Bob Freedman to JG, Sep 28, 2004.

393 "indulges herself": See James Green, "So Bewitching, Lena, but Stick to the Old Hits."

393 "That was a": Tony Bennett to JG, Jun 2, 2005.

394 "Gone was": See Jan Hodenfield, "Lena Horne: Back on Broadway."

394 "I found myself" . . . "like that": Tony Bennett to JG, Jun 2, 2005.

394 "Tony looks": See Earl Wilson, *New York Post,* Oct 31, 1974.

394 "I put the show": Tony Bennett to JG, Jun 2, 2005.

395 "Tony Bennett, 48": *Newsweek,* 1973.

395 "Tony Bennett found": Ibid.

395 "a genuine": Ibid.

395 "I've seldom": See Nat Hentoff, "Who Loves Performing, Tony or Lena?"

395 "Honey" . . . "whore": See Nancy Collins, "Alone with Lena."

395 "this feeling": LH to Jonathan Schwartz, WNEW-AM, Aug 1981.

396 "If you're doing": Tony Bennett to JG, Jun 2, 2005.

396 "I don't think": See Mary Campbell, "She Just Loves It, Laughs Lena Horne."

396 "Look, he's" . . . "umbrella!": Elle Elliott to JG, May 23, 2006.

396 "The worst part": See Cheryl Lavin, *California Living.*

396 "Did you hear": Elle Elliott to JG, May 23, 2006.

396 "TV is": See Gene Arceri, "Lena Horne: The Girl Who Wore the Glass Slipper."

397 "had it": See Maurice Zolotow, "Lena: The Lady Who Just Wasn't Black Enough."

397 "I think now I'm": See Nancy Collins, *W.*

397 "I don't do": See Jan Hodenfield, "Lena Horne: Back on Broadway."

397 a "real storybook": See Leonard Feather, "Lena at 60 Still a Horne of Plenty."

397 "weak moment": *The Lady and Her Music* (Showtime), 1982.

397 "I was making": See "A Glamorous Grandmother Wants Audiences to Wonder: How Does the Old Broad Do It?"

397 "soft voices": See Maurice Zolotow, "Lena Horne: The Lady Who Just Wasn't Black Enough."

398 "silly" . . . "myself": See Stephen Wilding and J. M. Weyburn, Jr., "Lena Horne: The Beautiful Survivor."

CHAPTER 18

399 "She said, 'I'": Michel Legrand to JG, Apr 12, 2003.

400 "hell to sing" . . . "giants": See Leonard Feather, "The Three Faces of Lena."

400 "Another has it": See Peter Reilly, "The Art of *La Belle* Lena."

400 "It was beautiful": Michel Legrand to JG, Apr 12, 2003.

401   "packed in ice" . . . "comes out": LH to JG, Mar 14, 1994.

401   "Norman didn't": Phil Woods to JG, May 4, 2005.

401   "It's a scene" . . . "freer": LH to JG, Mar 14, 1994.

402   "The musicians" . . . "this day": Phil Woods to JG, May 4, 2005.

402   "I guess": LH to JG, Mar 14, 1994.

402   "I sang that": *Lyrically Speaking,* BET, 1994.

403   "Lena never": Claude Thompson to JG, Jan 20, 2006.

403   "bad": Ibid.

403   "I did as": See Kathy Larkin, "Lena Horne: A Stage Presence with a TV Future."

403   "I always": Alan Ebert, *Intimacies,* p. 160.

403   "I had to" . . . "after all": Marie Brenner, *Intimate Distance.*

404   "The agony": See Shirley Norman, "Lena Horne at 60."

404   "I had a *brief*": *Evening at Pops,* PBS, 1976.

404   "stickin' it to 'the Man'": S. Torriano Berry, *The 50 Most Influential Black Films,* p. 116.

405   "Law-abiding": See Ellen Holly, "Where Are the Films About Real Black Men and Women?"

405   "some lady": LH to John Gruen, Nov 27, 1972.

406   "Dorothy's trip": See Tom Burke, "Suddenly, I Knew How to Film the Play."

406   "little bitty scene": See Hans J. Massaquoi, "Lena Horne on Her Loveless Childhood."

407   "perfect": See Leonard Feather, "Lena at 60 Is Still a Horne of Plenty."

407   "frivolous, bored" . . . "*I* have": See Leonard Gross, "On Stage."

407   "Vera used": See "Two Revivals: One Live and One Dead."

408   "Gower said": Marge Champion to JG, Nov 9, 2004.

408   "When Jo" . . . "cut, cut, cut": Claude Thompson to JG, Jan 20, 2006.

409   "That was just": Carmen de Lavallade to JG, Jan 17, 2008.

409   "a bit arrogant": See Joan Pikula, "Clifton Davis: Flying over the Mountain."

409   "fucked up" . . . "It's ugly": Claude Thompson to JG, Jan 20, 2006.

410   "know how": See Sylvie Drake, "'Pal' Factions in a Deadlock."

410   "We're happy": Ibid.

411   "very real" . . . "my role": *Los Angeles Times,* Apr 16, 1978.

411   "looks and sounds": See Ron Pennington, "Pal Joey '78."

411   "Onstage I don't think she": Gene Davis to JG, Apr 7, 2005.

411   "a sort of": See Dan Sullivan, "'Joey' Caught in a Time Warp."

411   "jive talk": See Jim Johnson, "Poor Pal Joey."

411   "Thanks a lot": Marge Champion to JG, Nov 9, 2004.

411   "suspended": See "Lena Horne Ailing; Performances of 'Pal Joey,' Are Suspended."

412   "adverse": See Stanley Eichelbaum, "Lena on How 'Joey' Moved to '78."

412 "who said": Ibid.

412 "innuendoes" . . . "influence": Ibid.

412 "like an" . . . "fairy tale": See Vincent Canby, "When Budgets Soar over the Rainbow."

413 "If Diana Ross": Geoffrey Holder to JG, Apr 28, 2006.

413 "I went to": Anonymous source to JG.

413 "Sidney and I": See Leonard Feather, "Hornes of Plenty."

414 "in shock" . . . "fairy tale": *Los Angeles Times*, c. 1979.

414 "the bastard": See Arthur Bell, "Bell Tells."

414 "My two grandchildren": LH, M-G-M archival interview, Jan 1996.

414 "he started" . . . "sister": Judy Davis Francis to JG, Mar 1, 2005.

414 "the sort of": Samadhi Jones to JG, Oct 28, 2007.

415 "a professional": Clint Rosemond to JG, May 25, 2006.

415 "I think she was": Samadhi Jones to JG, Oct 28, 2007.

415 "Lou was": Clint Rosemond to JG, May 25, 2006.

415 "She would come": Samadhi Jones to JG, Oct 28, 2007.

415 "He and my": Ibid.

415 "saw where" . . . "pocket": Clint Rosemond to JG, May 25, 2006.

415 "She got": Samadhi Jones to JG, Oct 28, 2007.

416 "With a boost": Clint Rosemond to JG, May 25, 2006.

416 "She said, 'Mummy'": Arthur Laurents to JG, Nov 18, 2004.

417 "Now *this* is Lena": *Live at Caesar's Palace*, Neon Tonic Records NTD-6502-2.

417 "One of the": Private tape, LH and Vic Damone, South Shore Music Circus, Cohasset, Mass., Aug 17, 1978.

417 "bumping": Billie Allen-Henderson to JG, Mar 10, 2005.

417 "He said, it's'": LH to JG, Mar 14, 1994.

417 "a really big" . . . "*part out!*": Private tape, LH and Vic Damone.

418 "sour grapes": See Paul Mooney, *The Plain Dealer*.

418 "I would like": See Francesca Hare, "The Star Who Wants Her Career to Fade."

418 "The theater": Stephen Bourne to JG, Apr 10, 2008.

419 "I tell you": See "For the Late Bloomer, Life Begins at 50."

419 "I don't want": See Steve Warren, "At Her Mellow Age, Lena Horne Still as Tough as Nails."

419 "stunned crowd": See "Lena Horne to Retire."

419 "just cutting": *Variety*, Jun 17, 1980.

419 "offered a": David Weiss, "Going on 63 and Still Sizzling," *Los Angeles Herald-Examiner*, Jun 18, 1980.

419 "good pal" . . . "too much": See "Thalians 25th-Anniversary Party at Beverly Wilshire."

420 "I felt I": See Charles Michener, "The Awesome Lena Horne."

CHAPTER 19

421   "I don't want": LH to Jim Harlan, "Legends," WNEW-AM, Jun 23, 1991.

421   "I just had": See John Corry, "An Anatomy of Lena Horne's Triumph."

421   "I can work": LH to Jim Harlan, "Legends," WNEW-AM, Jun 23, 1991.

421   "She was totally": Michael Frazier to JG, Aug 4, 2004.

422   "No messages!": Fred Walker to JG, Aug 17, 2004.

422   "I can tell": Michael Frazier to JG, Aug 4, 2004.

422   "Luther loved": Billie Allen Henderson to JG, Dec 10, 2004.

423   "We'll be here": *Lyrically Speaking,* BET, 1994.

423   "Ralph said": Fred Walker to JG, Aug 17, 2004.

423   "We were just": Michael Frazier to JG, Aug 4, 2004.

423   "and she let": Ibid.

424   "Possibly this": *Good Morning America,* ABC-TV, Apr 20, 1981.

424   "They named": Josh Ellis to JG, Mar 8, 2005.

425   "good, not": Ibid.

425   "Yes, I'm out": See Marcia Ann Gillespie, "Lena Horne Finds Her Music, Her Daughter, and Her Self."

425   "She hit": Josh Ellis to JG, Mar 8, 2005.

425   "The way she": Linda Dahl to JG, Aug 3, 2004.

426   "It's very difficult": See Mary Campbell, "Lena Horne—In Her Own Voice."

427   "I felt something": LH to Sherry Carter, *Jazz Scene,* BET, Sep 22, 1998.

427   "They're the best": Josh Ellis to JG, Mar 8, 2005.

427   "I'm numb": See Charles Michener, "The Awesome Lena Horne."

427   "an evening": See Frank Rich, "Theater: Lena Horne: The Lady and Her Music."

427   "Perfection!": Jeffrey Lyons, WPIX-TV, Jun 30, 1982.

427   "The most": See Howard Kissel, review of *Lena Horne: The Lady and Her Music.*

427   "The season's": See Douglas Watt, review of *Lena Horne: The Lady and Her Music.*

428   "All the black": Delilah Jackson to JG, Dec 21, 2005.

428   "the buses": *Lyrically Speaking,* BET, 1994.

428   "I can make": See John Corry, "An Anatomy of Lena Horne's Triumph."

428   "I thought": Marcia Ann Gillespie to JG, Aug 10, 2004.

428   "Honey" . . . "broad": See Rex Reed, "A Life on Stage."

428   "It was cold-blooded": See Gerald Clarke, "Stormy Weather on Broadway."

429   "I learned": *60 Minutes,* 1981.

429   "I had a": See Francesca Hare, "The Star Who Wants Her Career to Fade."

429   "just a minute": See Arthur Unger, "Lena, the Lady and Her Life."

429   "I couldn't": LH to Jonathan Schwartz, WNEW-AM, Aug 1981.

429   "I wasn't gonna": See George Hadley-Garcia, "Lena Horne Is Still Misbehavin' After All These Years!"

429   "refused to play": See Darr Smith, *Los Angeles Daily News*, Aug 15, 1949.

429   "stopped singing": LH to Rex Reed, *Tomorrow,* NBC-TV, Nov 17, 1981.

429   "I think any": Alan Ebert to JG, Mar 14, 2004.

429   "a butterfly pinned": See Oorde Coombs, "Lena Horne Is 60."

430   "the dead years": *60 Minutes,* 1981.

430   "I almost": Trygve Harris to JG, Aug 23, 2004.

430   "angry as hell": Mart Crowley to JG, Mar 17, 2007.

430   "It has been": Geoffrey Holder to JG, Apr 28, 2006.

430   "Grandma": LH to JG, Mar 14, 1994.

430   "This was no": Arthur Laurents to JG, Nov 18, 2004.

430   "In Harlem": Nat Horne to JG, May 10, 2006.

431   "Henry Kissinger": Michael Frazier to JG, Aug 4, 2004.

431   "Later on": Ibid.

432   "And waited" . . ."*again!*": Diahann Carroll to JG, Nov 10, 2005.

432   "I don't think": See Arthur Bell, "Lena Horne: All Storms Weathered."

432   "Mrs. Reagan" . . . "for Reagan": Michael Frazier to JG, Aug 4, 2004.

432   "This Broadway": See Rex Reed, "A Life on Stage."

432   "She'd come into": Fred Walker to JG, Aug 17, 2004.

433   "Sherman and" . . . "the lady": Ibid.

433   "Sherman always": Mike Renzi to JG, Aug 15, 2008.

433   "I would call": Chico Hamilton to JG,

433   "Lena Is My Mom": See Mel Tapley, "Lena Is My Mom."

433   "was like": Josh Ellis to JG, Mar 8, 2005.

434   "Lady," he announced: Ibid.

434   "She always used": See Clive Hirschhorn, "The Man Lena Married Even Though She Wasn't in Love."

434   "She said to me": LH profile, BBC-4 radio (U.K.), Aug 24, 1984.

435   "The gift": Letter, Kitty D'Alessio to LH, Jan 3, 1982.

435   "From two guys": Card, William and Thomas Jones to LH, Dec 1981.

435   "I love you": Letter, Lena Mary Jones to LH, 1981.

435   "I can't imagine": Samadhi Jones to JG, Oct 28, 2007.

436   "My grandkids": See George Hadley-Garcia, "Lena Horne Is Still Misbehavin' After All These Years!"

436   "crazy old": LH to JG, Mar 14, 1994.

436   "lets me" . . . "a minute": LH to Jim Hartz, *Over Easy,* PBS, Apr 25, 1982.

436   "Why don't": Claude Thompson to JG, Jan 20, 2006.

436   "I find with": LH to Jim Hartz, *Over Easy*, PBS, Apr 25, 1982.

436   "If I'd been": See Bernard Drew, "The Rage Now Is Gone, and She's 'Free to Be Me.'"

436   "If I were": Mike Renzi to JG, Aug 15, 2008.

436   "This place" . . . "looking at": See Rex Reed, "A Life on Stage."

437   "Nobody I": See David Colker, "Lena Horne: The Making of a Superstar."

437   "oozin' around" . . . "crazy": *The Lady and Her Music* (Showtime), 1982.

437   "tired" . . . "always": LH to JG, Mar 14, 1994.

437   "surprise that": See Ruthe Stein, "Stormy Weather Doesn't Stop Lena Horne."

438   "I looked down" . . . "is mine": *The Lady and Her Music* (Showtime), 1982.

438   "By the time": See Arthur Bell, "Bell Tells."

438   "But if I": LH, M-G-M archival interview, Jan 1996.

438   "orgy of food" . . . "Nederlander": See Liz Smith, New York *Daily News* Jun 1982.

439   "It's not a": See "Horne of Plenty," *People*.

439   "I think I'm": CBS News, Jun 30, 1982.

CHAPTER 20

440   "I can't believe": *The Lady and Her Music* (Showtime), 1982.

440   "I'll take the": See Gerald Nachman, "Horne-Swoggled."

441   "slapdash": See Michael Mascioli, "Sweatin', Spittin', Makin' a Damn Fool of Myself."

441   "I don't make": See Ruthe Stein, "Stormy Weather Doesn't Stop Lena Horne."

441   "bananas": See Gerald Nachman, "Horne-Swoggled."

441   "fantastic" . . . "outskirts": See David Colker, "Lena Horne: The Making of a Superstar."

441   "She has helped": See "Lena Horne Draws Crowd to Benefit."

442   "outraged": See Samuel Marx, "Lena at M-G-M—Take Two."

442   "Charity is": *Sacramento Bee*, Oct 20, 1982.

442   "she was fit": Michael Frazier to JG, Aug 4, 2004.

442   "I've noticed": See "The Star-Spangled Manner of Zev Bufman."

443   "Lena was very": Elle Elliott to JG, May 23, 2006.

444   "We were really": Quincy Jones to Will Friedwald, c. 1992.

444   "All I know": *Los Angeles Times*, Feb 25, 1983.

444   "It's no more": See Marilyn Beck, New York *Daily News*.

444   "all that was" . . . "Vegas": Charles Pignone, *Sinatra Treasures: Intimate Photos, Mementos, and Music from the Sinatra Family Collection*, p. 161.

444   "would have been": Quincy Jones to Will Friedwald, c. 1992.

445   "The road show": Marcia Ann Gillespie to JG, Aug 10, 2004.

445   "He used to": Mike Renzi to JG, Aug 15, 2008.

445   "Sherman tried": Fred Walker to JG, Aug 17, 2004.

445   "laying rumors": See Irving Wardle, "Lena Horne: The Lady and Her Music."

446   "Enough is enough": See Clive Hirschhorn, "The Man Lena Married Even Though She Wasn't in Love."

446   "It wasn't": See Paul Rosenfield, "Lena on Lena, Late at Night."

446   "spoke of" . . . "can get": See Clarke Taylor, "Lena Horne in London: Thriving on Surviving."

447   "just a": Letter, Joyce Eskridge to Wendy Munson, 2005.

447   "instant rapport": Letter, Sherman Sneed to Joyce Eskridge, Sep 7, 1984.

447   "grabbed me" . . . "Waxahachie": Letter, Joyce Eskridge to Wendy Munson, 2005.

447   "Rested in room": Diary, Joyce Eskridge, Aug 30, 1984.

447   "Back to hotel": Diary, Joyce Eskridge, Sep 2, 1984.

447   "Your visit": Letter, Sherman Sneed to Joyce Eskridge, Sep 7, 1984.

448   "personal and": Letter, Joyce Eskridge to Wendy Munson, 2005.

448   "Not having": See Cheryl Lavin, *California Living.*

448   "I call Lena" . . . "she was black": *Kennedy Center Honors,* CBS-TV, Dec 25, 1984.

449   "I'm too": See Arthur Unger, "The Lady and Her Life."

449   "fucking recluse": See Cindy Adams, *New York Post.*

449   "He is true": See Arthur Unger, "The Lady and Her Life."

450   "Not just me": See Kathy Larkin, "Lena Horne: A Stage Presence with a TV Future."

450   "The fact is": See Cindy Adams, "The Lady & Her Life."

450   "There were so": Marcia Ann Gillespie to JG, Aug 10, 2004.

450   "I knew she": Ibid.

451   "I wasn't what": See Marcia Ann Gillespie, "Lena Horne Finds Her Music, Her Daughter, and Her Self."

450   "exactly the same" . . . "Lourdes": See Leonard Feather, "Hornes of Plenty."

451   "hadn't done": *Coming Together with Tanya Hart,* WGBH-TV, Boston, Jul 19, 1987.

451   "lived the lazy": Gail Lumet Buckley, *The Hornes,* p. 243.

451   "Personally": Ibid., p. 231.

451   "Buckley chooses": See Melvin Maddocks, "Dancing Partners of Chic."

452   "I do feel": *Coming Together with Tanya Hart.*

452   "The price" . . . "a lot": See Susan Mulcahy, "The Lady Loves N.Y.—She Just Can't Stand It."

452   "ultimate": See Howard Fineman, "The Bespoke Broker."

453   "To Hollywood's": Vernon Jordan, Spingarn Medal Address, New Or-
       leans, Jul 15, 1982.

453   "To this day"... "after that": Vernon Jordan to JG, Sep 4, 2008.

454   "I can't believe"... "that bitch": Trygve Harris to JG, Aug 23, 2004.

455   "She was like": Sandy Stewart to JG, Oct 15, 2004.

455   "Shirley had": Rex Reed to JG, Feb 3, 2006.

455   "Gigi was": Gloria DeHaven to JG, Nov 24, 2004.

455   "Actually a lot": *CBS This Morning,* Oct 17, 1988.

455   "I like to": See Barbara Gordon, "Day by Day."

456   "It's boring": See Eliot Tiegel, "The Art of Survival: Lena."

456   "She loved": Mike Renzi to JG, Aug 15, 2008.

456   "It's very": LH interview, source unknown, 1994.

457   "She didn't really": Mike Renzi to JG, Aug 15, 2008.

457   "I fought it" LH to JG, Mar 14, 1994.

457   "angry"... "tell me": *Lifestyles of the Rich and Famous,* May 12, 1995.

457   "I never thought": Brian Lanker, *I Dream a World.*

457   "Lena completely": Samadhi Jones to JG, Oct 28, 2007.

457   "I went into": LH to JG, Mar 14, 1994.

CHAPTER 21

458   "very well appointed": Mike Renzi to JG, Aug 15, 2008.

458   "I'm looking": LH to JG, Mar 14, 1994.

458   "I had some": See Ponchitta Pierce, "Lady Attitude."

459   "She wanted": Sherri Sneed to JG, Jun 25, 2008.

459   "Ask her"... "that day": George Feltenstein to JG, Nov 8, 2004.

460   "I have many"... "wonderful in it": *That's Entertainment! III,* 1994.

460   "Oh, please!": *Live with Regis & Kathie Lee,* ABC-TV, Sep 6, 1994.

460   "I'd love": LH, M-G-M archival interview, Jan 1996.

460   "It's hard": See Liz Smith, *New York Newsday.*

461   "for your artistry"... "this long": *Essence Awards,* Jun 1993.

461   "I'm too old": See "Memories of Harlem."

461   "I'm not a"... "pushed me": LH to JG, Mar 14, 1994.

462   "she was"... "nerves": Mike Renzi to JG, Aug 15, 2008.

462   "rivetingly"... "legend": See Stephen Holden, "Lena Horne and the
       Stuff of Legends."

462   "The audience": LH to Jonathan Schwartz, WQEW-AM, May 15, 1994.

462   "walking": See Lisa Schwarzbaum, "Horne Again."

462   "Are you ready": See Gene Seymour, "Horne Still Has It 'Together.'"

462   "I don't just": LH to JG, Mar 14, 1994.

462   "I'm just": LH to JG, Mar 14, 1994.

462   "In my dealings": Helene Greece to JG, Aug 24, 2008.

463   "They keep": LH to JG, Mar 14, 1994.

463   "It's not easy": Ibid.

463   "Hi, Miss Horne" . . . "Easy": Jim Czak to JG, Aug 26, 2008.

464   "I love it": LH to JG, Mar 14, 1994.

464   "Many times": LH to Jonathan Schwartz, WQEW-AM, May 15, 1994.

464   "talking" . . . "like that": LH to JG, Mar 14, 1994.

464   "To have": Johnny Mathis to JG, Nov 1993.

464   "It's difficult": LH to JG, Mar 14, 1994.

464   "I can remember": *Lyrically Speaking*, BET, 1994.

464   "I thought": LH to JG, Mar 14, 1994.

464   "She won't: See Gene Seymour, "Horne Still Has It 'Together.'"

465   "To me, Lena": Bruce Lundvall to JG, Nov 7, 2007.

465   "I feel like" . . . "trouble!": LH to JG, Mar 14, 1994.

465   "I'm in love": Ibid.

466   "and the audience": Bruce Lundvall to JG, Nov 7, 2007.

466   "I did it" . . . "happening": LH to JG, Mar 14, 1994.

466   "one of the": See Stephen Holden, review of *We'll Be Together Again*.

466   "The ego": Mike Renzi to JG, Aug 15, 2008.

466   "Too little": LH to Jonathan Schwartz, May 15, 1994.

467   "It was a" . . . "I thank you": Ibid.

467   "Everybody's got": See Carol Rosen, "Lena Horne—A Lovesome Thing."

467   "The minute": Helene Greece to JG, Aug 24, 2008.

467   "I'm terrified": See David Patrick Stearns, "Elegant Lena Horne Is Singing Up a Storm Again."

467   "They're waiting": See Carol Rosen, "Lena Horne—A Lovesome Thing."

468   "pandemonium": Jim Czak to JG, Aug 26, 2008.

469   "That's probably": Bruce Lundvall to JG, Nov 7, 2007.

469   "From what": Helene Greece to JG, Aug 24, 2008.

469   "Her smile": See Mary Campbell, "Lena Horne—In Her Own Voice."

470   "Hey, get" . . . "handsome man": Jim Czak to JG, Aug 26, 2008.

470   "Yes, that's": *Jazz Scene*, BET, Sep 22, 1998.

471   "It will": See Marilyn Beck and Stacy Jenel Smith, "Horne Sings the Blues over Attending Premiere."

471   "I guess": See Liz Smith, "Lady Lena Sizzles Again."

471   "rehearsing": See Marilyn Beck and Stacy Jenel Smith, "Horne Sings the Blues over Attending Premiere."

471   "heart": *The Rosie O'Donnell Show*, ABC-TV, May 22, 1998.

471   "chaotic": Mike Renzi to JG, Aug 15, 2008.

471 "He treated" . . . "one more": Jim Czak to JG, Aug 26, 2008.

473 "She looked": Michael Frazier to JG, Aug 4, 2004.

473 "Let's see": See Frank Scheck, "Lena: 80th Birthday."

473 "She took": Michael Frazier to JG, Aug 4, 2004.

474 "No," said Horne: Carmen de Lavallade to JG, Jan 17, 2008.

474 "It went OK": Mike Renzi to JG, Aug 15, 2008.

474 "one-hundred-percent": See Clarence Waldron, "Lena Horne, Officially Retired from Showbiz, Turns 90 in June."

474 "There are people": Gene Davis to JG, Apr 7, 2005.

475 "How dare": LH to Jonathan Schwartz, WQEW-AM, May 15, 1994.

475 "I'm winding": LH to JG, Mar 14, 1994.

475 "Was it" . . . "anything back": Claude Thompson to JG, Jan 20, 2006.

475 "Isabel would": Delilah Jackson to JG, Dec 21, 2005.

476 "We were": LH to JG, Mar 14, 1994.

476 "That was it" . . . "going out?": Sherri Sneed to JG, Jun 25, 2008.

477 "Rodney said": Bruce Lundvall to JG, Nov 7, 2007.

477 "Oh, you": Jim Czak to JG, Aug 26, 2008.

477 "That's my": Pledge-break appearance during *American Masters,* PBS, Nov 25, 1996.

477 "I don't": LH to JG, Mar 14, 1994.

477 "She always": Anonymous source to JG.

478 "she went": Judy Davis Francis to JG, Mar 1, 2005.

478 "Tom was": Jim Piazza to JG, Aug 12, 2008.

478 "William was" . . . "with grief": Samadhi Jones to JG, Oct 28, 2007.

478 "She didn't" . . . "be interested": Sherri Sneed to JG, Jun 25, 2008.

479 "as a victor": Roy Campanella, Jr., to JG, Aug 20, 2008.

480 "She is someone": See "Jackson Pulls Out of 'Horne' Film."

480 "I can't think" . . . "sandwich plans": See Gary Susman, "'Weather' Report."

480 "I said, 'This deal'": Richard Schickel to JG, Oct 8, 2004.

480 "Before they" . . . "better deal": Roy Campanella, Jr., to JG, Aug 20, 2008.

481 "I believe": Richard Schickel to JG, Oct 8, 2004.

482 "In my deepest": See Liz Smith, "Janet Should Be Making Films."

482 "I feel Sony": Roy Campanella, Jr. to JG, Aug 20, 2008.

482 "I used to" . . . "bandstand": LH to JG, Mar 14, 1994.

482 "The key": Geoffrey Holder to JG, Apr 28, 2006.

482 "I had to read . . . "goes on": Arthur Laurents to JG, Nov 18, 2004.

483 "mentally great": See Clarence Waldron, "Lena Horne, Officially Retired from Showbiz."

483 "I was always": Arthur Laurents to JG, Nov 18, 2004.

483 "She liked": Jim Czak to JG, Aug 26, 2008.

483   "gray": Mike Renzi to JG, Aug 15, 2008.

484   "Someone once": LH to JG, Mar 14, 1994.

484   "I got a": Hilary Knight to JG, May 14, 2005.

484   "The men" . . . "Come on'": LH to JG, Mar 14, 1994.

484   "I don't care": LH to Jonathan Schwartz, WQEW-AM, May 15, 1994.

485   "Lena Horne knows": See Cindy Adams, *New York Post,* May 2, 2008.

485   "I had a": LH to JG, Mar 14, 1994.

486   "You look" . . . "I know": Jim Czak to JG, Aug 26, 2008.

486   "I should have": LH to JG, Mar 14, 1994.

486   "Pain is": See Rex Reed, "A Life on Stage."

486   "Don't be": Brian Lanker, *I Dream a World.*

BIBLIOGRAPHY

BOOKS

AILEY, ALVIN (WITH A. PETER BAILEY). *Revelations: The Autobiography of Alvin Ailey*. New York: Birch Lane Press, 1995.

BALDWIN, JAMES. *Notes of a Native Son*. Boston: Beacon Press, 1984.

BARNET, CHARLIE (WITH STANLEY DANCE). *Those Swinging Years: The Autobiography of Charlie Barnet*. Baton Rouge: Louisiana State University Press, 1984.

BERGER, EDWARD, AND DAVID CHEVAN. *Bassically Speaking: An Oral History of George Duvivier*. Lanham, MD: Scarecrow Press, 1993.

BERRY, S. TORRIANO (WITH VENISE T. BERRY). *The 50 Most Influential Black Films*. New York: Citadel Press.

BLAIR, BETSY. *The Memory of All That: Love and Politics in New York, Hollywood, and Paris*. New York: Alfred A. Knopf, 2003.

BLUMENTHAL, RALPH. *Stork Club*. New York: Back Bay Books, 2000.

BOURNE, STEPHEN. *Sophisticated Lady: A Celebration of Adelaide Hall*. London: Ethnic Communities Oral History Project, 2001.

BRENNER, MARIE. *Intimate Distance*. New York: William Morrow & Co., 1983.

BRYER, JACKSON R. *The Art of the American Musical: Conversations with the Creators*. Newark, NJ: Rutgers University Press, 2005.

CALLOWAY, CAB (AND BRYANT ROLLINS). *Of Minnie the Moocher and Me*. New York: Thomas Y. Crowell Co., 1976.

CITRON, STEPHEN. *Noel & Cole: The Sophisticates*. New York: Oxford University Press, 1993.

THE COMPLETE LIFE OF LENA HORNE: A POCKET CELEBRITY SCRAPBOOK. New York: Pocket Magazines, 1955.

DANDRIDGE, DOROTHY (WITH EARL CONRAD). *Everything and Nothing: The Dorothy Dandridge Tragedy*. New York: HarperCollins, 2000.

DAVIS, BUSTER. "Ask Her If She's Got a Kid Brother: A Somewhat Tattered Life." Unpublished memoir, c. 1986.

DAVIS, OSSIE. *Life Lit By Some Large Vision*. New York: Atria Books, 2007.

EBERT, ALAN. *Intimacies: Private Conversations with Very Public Women*. Raleigh, NC: Lightning Bug Press, 2001.

EELLS, GEORGE. *The Life That Late He Led*. New York: Putnam, 1967, 283.

ELERT, NICOLET V., et al., eds. *International Dictionary of Film and Filmmakers: Actors and Actresses*. Farmington Hills, MI: Gale Group, 1996.

FALES-HILL, SUSAN. *Always Wear Joy*. New York: HarperCollins, 2003.

FONTAINE, JOAN. *No Bed of Roses*. New York: William Morrow & Co., 1978.

GARDNER, AVA. *Ava Gardner: My Story*. New York: Bantam Books, 1990.

GARRETT, BETTY (WITH RON RAPOPORT). *Betty Garrett and Other Songs*. Lanham, MD: Madison Books, 1998.

HORNE, LENA (AS TOLD TO HELEN ARSTEIN AND CARLTON MOSS). *In Person: Lena Horne*. New York: Greenberg, 1950.

HORNE, LENA (WITH RICHARD SCHICKEL). *Lena*. New York: Doubleday, 1965.

HOWARD, BRETT. *Lena Horne—Singer and Actress*. Los Angeles: Melrose Square Publishing Company, 1981.

HUGHES, LANGSTON. *The Collected Works of Langston Hughes*. Vol. 13. Columbia: University of Missouri Press.

JACKSON, CARLTON. *Hattie: The Life of Hattie McDaniel*. Lanham, MD: Madison Books, 1993.

JANKEN, KENNETH ROBERT. *White: The Biography of Walter White, Mr. NAACP*. New York: New Press, 2003.

KING, ALAN. *Name-Dropping: The Life and Lies of Alan King*. New York: Scribner's, 1996.

KISSEL, HOWARD. *David Merrick: The Abominable Showman*. New York: Applause Books, 2000.

KRUEGER, MILES. *Show Boat: The Story of a Classic American Musical*. New York: Oxford University Press, 1977.

LANKER, BRIAN. *I Dream a World: Portraits of Black Women Who Changed America*. New York: Stewart, Tabori & Chang, 1989.

LAURENTS, ARTHUR. *Original Story by Arthur Laurents*. New York: Alfred A. Knopf, 2000.

LOUIS, JOE (WITH EDNA AND ART RUST JR.). *Joe Louis: My Life*. New York: Harcourt, Brace & Jovanovich, 1978.

LUFT, LORNA. *Me and My Shadows*. New York: Pocket Books, 1998.

LUMET BUCKLEY, GAIL. *The Hornes: An American Family*. New York: Alfred A. Knopf, 1986.

MACDONALD, J. FRED, ED. *Richard Durham's Destination Freedom*. New York: Praeger, 1989

MARGOLICK, DAVID. *Beyond Glory: Joe Louis vs. Max Schmeling, and a World on the Brink*. New York: Alfred A. Knopf, 2005.

MARION, FRANCIS. *Off with Their Heads: A Serio-Comic Tale of Hollywood*. New York: Macmillan, 1972.

MINNELLI, VINCENTE (WITH HECTOR ARCE). *I Remember It Well*. New York: Berkeley Medallion Books, 1974.

NOBLE, JEANNE. *Beautiful, Also, Are the Souls of My Black Sisters*. Englewood Cliffs, NJ: Prentice Hall, 1978.

PAYN, GRAHAM, AND SHERIDAN MORLEY, EDS., *The Noël Coward Diaries*. Boston: Little, Brown & Co., 1982.

PIGNONE, CHARLES. *Sinatra Treasures: Intimate Photos, Mementos, and Music from the Sinatra Family Collection*. New York: Bulfinch Press, 2004.

Red Channels, New York: Counterattack, 1950.

REED, BILL. *Hot from Harlem*. Los Angeles: Cellar Door Books, 1998.

REED, LEONARD (AS TOLD TO BILL REED). "A Hell of a Life." Unpublished manuscript, c. 1986.

RICH, SHARON. *Sweethearts*. New York: Donald I. Fine, 1994.

ROSE, HELEN. *Just Make Them Beautiful: The Many Worlds of a Designing Woman*. Santa Monica, CA: Dennis Landman Publishers, 1976.

SCHIFFMAN, JACK. *Uptown: The Story of Harlem's Apollo Theatre*. New York: Cowles Book Company, 1971.

SERVER, LEE. *Ava Gardner: Love Is Nothing*. New York: Macmillan, 2006.

SHORT, BOBBY. *Black and White Baby*. New York: Dodd, Mead & Company, 1974.

SMITH, LIZ. *Natural Blonde*. New York: Hyperion Books, 2000.

SPOTO, DONALD. *Stanley Kramer: Film Maker*. New York: G. P. Putnam's Sons, 1978.

TAYLOR, FRANK C. (WITH GERALD COOK). *Alberta Hunter: A Celebration in Blues*. New York: McGraw-Hill, 1987.

TAYLOR, THEODORE. *Jule: The Story of Composer Jule Styne*. New York: Random House, 1979.

TORMÉ, MEL. *The Other Side of the Rainbow*. New York: Bantam Books, 1971.

WATERS, ETHEL. *His Eye Is on the Sparrow*. New York: Doubleday, 1951.

WATSON, STEVEN. *The Harlem Renaissance*. New York: Pantheon, 1995.

WATTS, JILL. *Hattie McDaniel: Black Ambition, White Hollywood*. New York: HarperCollins, 2005.

WHITE, WALTER. *A Man Called White: The Autobiography of Walter White*. Athens: University of Georgia Press, 1948.

WILLIAMS, IAIN CAMERON. *Underneath a Harlem Moon: The Harlem to Paris Years of Adelaide Hall*. London: Continuum, 2002.

X, MALCOLM (WITH ALEX HALEY). *The Autobiography of Malcolm X*. New York: Grove Press, 1965.

PERIODICALS

ADAMS, CINDY. "The Lady & Her Life." *New York Post,* May 24, 1985.

———. *New York Post,* Apr 23, 1985.

———. *New York Post,* May 2, 2008.

ALLEN, KELCEY. "Blackbirds of 1939." *Women's Wear Daily,* Feb 13, 1939.

AMES, MORGAN. Review of *Nature's Baby. High Fidelity,* 1973.

ANDERSON, ALBERT. "Is Lena Horne Married—Rumor Lena Horne Wed to M-G-M Conductor." *Chicago Defender,* Sep 7, 1946.

"ANN JONES' DANCERS TO BE AT LAFAYETTE." *New York Amsterdam News,* Aug 2, 1933.

ARCERI, GENE. "Lena Horne: The Girl Who Wore the Glass Slipper." *David,* Jul 1973.

ARMSTRONG, DICK, AND MAX SIEN, "Stork Picketed over Jo Baker." *Daily Compass,* Oct 23, 1951.

"AS LONG AS I LIVE." *Pittsburgh Courier,* Oct 20, 1934.

"ASK." *Family Circle,* Aug 14, 1982.

ATKINSON, BROOKS. "Lew Leslie Gets His 'Blackbirds of 1939' onto the Stage of the Hudson Theatre." *New York Times,* Feb 13, 1939.

———. "One Yes: One No." *New York Times,* Nov 10, 1957.

AYRES, ARCH. "How Long Can a Glamour Girl Last?" *Cabaret (The Adult Entertainment Magazine),* Mar 1957.

BALLIETT, WHITNEY. "The Happiest Days of My Life." *The New Yorker,* Oct 9, 1971.

BARTHEL, JOAN. "Lena Horne: 'Now I Feel Good About Being Me.'" *New York Times,* Jul 28, 1968.

BATES, KAREN GRIGSBY. [Title unknown]. *Los Angeles Times Magazine,* Jan 26, 1992.

———. *Emerge,* [date unknown].

BECK, MARILYN. "I'm Making Up for the Time I Sat Back." *Movie Mirror,* Nov 1968.

———. *Daily News* (New York), Jan 24, 1983.

BECK, MARILYN, AND STACY JENEL SMITH. "Horne Sings the Blues over Attending Premiere." *Daily News* (New York), Nov 12, 1996.

BELL, ARTHUR. "Lena Horne: All Storms Weathered." *Village Voice,* May 6–12, 1981.

BELL, ARTHUR. *Village Voice,* Aug 12, 1981.

"BETTER THAN A RABBIT'S FOOT." *Lion's Roar,* Apr 1943.

"BINFORD, DIXIE CENSOR, SHOULD BE PITIED SAYS SCRIBE REVIEWING ACTS." *Chicago Defender,* Dec 31, 1955.

"'BLACKBIRDS' GETS SO-SO RECEPTION." *New York Amsterdam News,* Nov 26, 1938.

BOGDANOVICH, PETER. "Ava's Allure." *New York Times Book Review,* Apr 23, 2006.

BOLTON, WHITNEY. "Lena's Daughter Is Set for Debut." *New York Morning Telegraph,* Sep 6, 1960.

BONTEMPS, ARNA. "'St. Louis Woman' Basically a Folk Play." [Unknown Boston newspaper], Feb 17, 1946.

BRENNER, MARIE. "Kay and Eloise." *Vanity Fair,* Dec 1996.

BUCHWALD, ART. "Lena Horne Isn't the Memoir Type." *New York Herald Tribune,* Jan 10, 1960.

BURBRIDGE, EDDIE. "No Fooling." *Los Angeles Sentinel,* Jun 3, 1948.

BURKE, TOM. "Suddenly, I Knew How to Film the Play." *New York Times,* Jul 24, 1977.

"CALL HER TOMORROW." *Lion's Roar,* Jan 1944.

CAMPBELL, MARY. "Lena Horne—In Her Own Voice." Associated Press, Nov 25, 1996.

———. "She Just Loves It, Laughs Lena Horne." *Philadelphia Inquirer,* Dec 29, 1974.

"CAN DANDRIDGE OUTSHINE LENA HORNE?" *Our World,* Jun 1952.

CANBY, VINCENT. "When Budgets Soar over the Rainbow." *New York Times,* Nov 26, 1978.

CARTER, HODDING. "Mississippi Now—Hate and Fear." *New York Times,* Jun 23, 1963.

CARTER, PHILIP. "Lena Horne Is the Gal; Her Talent the Stuff for Films." *Chicago Defender,* Nov 21, 1942.

"CBS BANS RECORDING BY LENA HORNE." *Los Angeles Sentinel,* Apr 14, 1955.

CHAPMAN, JOHN. *Daily News* (New York), Oct 7, 1934.

CHASE, BILL. "All Ears." *New York Amsterdam Star-News,* Feb 6, 1943.

CHESTER, JERRY. "Why Lena Horne Refuses to Blow Her Own Horne." *Top Secret,* Apr 1958.

"CHOCOLATE CREAM CHANTEUSE." *Time,* Jan 4, 1943.

CLARKE, GERALD. "Stormy Weather on Broadway." *Time,* May 25, 1981.

COLKER, DAVID. "Lena Horne: The Making of a Superstar." *Los Angeles Herald Examiner,* Nov 12, 1982.

COLLINS, NANCY. "Alone with Lena." *Women's Wear Daily,* Oct 24, 1974.

———. *W,* Nov 1, 1974.

COLMAN, DAVID. "Giorgio Sant'Angelo: Wild Child." *New York,* Feb 18, 2002.

COOKE, MARVEL. "Lena Horne's Manager Says She'll Refuse to 'Name Names.'" *Daily Compass,* Oct 11, 1951.

COOMBS, OORDE. "Lena Horne Is 60." *Esquire,* Aug 1977.

CORRY, JOHN. "An Anatomy of Lena Horne's Triumph." *New York Times,* May 15, 1981.

Coss, Bill. Review of "I Love to Love." *Metronome*, Jun 1955.

Cottom, J. V. "Vénus et Carmens Noires." *Ciné Revue* (France), Jun 1956.

"Cotton Club Girls." *Ebony*, Apr 1949.

"Counterattack." *Time*, March 31, 1958.

"Critics Rave over Lena Horne Protégé." *Los Angeles Sentinel*, May 11, 1950.

Cross, Brenda. "Honeysuckle Rose." *Picturegoer*, Jan 17, 1948.

Crowther, Bosley. "'Till Clouds Roll By,' Musical Biography of Life of Jerome Kern." *New York Times*, Dec 6, 1946.

———. "'Lost Boundaries,' Racial Study with Ferrer in Lead, New Feature at Astor." *New York Times*, Jul 1, 1949.

Dana, Robert. "Lena Packs 'Em In at Waldorf." *New York World-Telegram & Sun*, Jan 14, 1957.

Dancer, Maurice. "Lena Horne and Charlie Barnet to Exchange Guest Appearances." *Chicago Defender*, Apr 26, 1941.

"Dave's Café Opening Is Terrific." *Chicago Defender*, Sep 14, 1940.

Davis, Almena. "How 'Bout This?" *Los Angeles Tribune*, Oct 19, 1942.

"A Day in Hollywood with Lena Horne." *Ebony*, Mar 1946.

"A Deadly Iteration." *Time*, Mar 7, 1969.

Diggins, John Patrick. "I Walk in Dignity." *New York Times*, Feb 12, 1989.

"Dogs, Kids & Clubs." *Time*, May 10, 1963.

Drake, Sylvie. "'Pal' Factions in a Deadlock." *Los Angeles Times*, May 4, 1978.

Drew, Bernard. "Lena Horne: The Rage Now Is Gone, and She's 'Free to Be Me.'" Gannett Westchester Newspapers, May 10, 1981.

Duckett, Alfred. "Fabulous Lena Horne Rivals That 'Tree Growing in Brooklyn.'" *Chicago Defender*, Aug 28, 1954.

———. "A Warm Embrace." *élan*, Feb 1982.

"The Duke and Duchess of the Music World." *Ebony*, Oct 1949.

Dunbar, Rudolph. "Lena Horne Charms London Audiences." *Atlanta Daily World*, Dec 20, 1947.

Eichelbaum, Stanley. "Lena on How 'Joey' Moved to '78." *San Francisco Chronicle*, Sep 28, 1978.

Emge, Charlie. *Down Beat*, Apr 27, 1943.

Eng, Frank. *Los Angeles Daily News*, Jun 3, 1948.

Feather, Leonard. "The Horne of Plenty." *Down Beat*, Jan 9, 1958.

———. "The Three Faces of Lena." *Los Angeles Times*, Mar 23, 1975.

———. "Hornes of Plenty." *Los Angeles Times*, Jul 20, 1986.

———. "Lena at 60 Still a Horne of Plenty." *Los Angeles Times*, Apr 16, 1978.

Feinstein, Herbert. "Lena Horne Speaks Freely on Race, Marriage, Stage." *Ebony*, May 1963.

Fields, Sidney. "Only Human." *New York Daily Mirror*, May 18, 1953.

———. "Success in Mixed Marriage." *New York Daily Mirror,* Dec 8, 1957.

FINEMAN, HOWARD. "The Bespoke Broker." *Newsweek,* Apr 14, 2008.

FINGER, MICHAEL. "Banned in Memphis." *Memphis Flyer,* May 8, 2008.

"FOR THE LATE BLOOMER, LIFE BEGINS AT 50." *TV Times* (U.K.), Jun 1979.

FREEDLEY, GEORGE. *New York Morning Telegraph,* Oct 18, 1950.

S.G. Review of *Lena . . . Lovely and Alive. Stereo Review,* Mar 1963.

GARDELLA, KAY. *Daily News* (New York). Sep 8, 1969.

———. "Lena Tells It like It Is." *A&E Monthly,* Dec 1994.

GARLINGTON, S. W. "Pointed Points: Is Lena Wrecking Her Future?" *New York Amsterdam News,* Nov 12, 1949.

GILLESPIE, MARCIA ANN. "Lena Horne Finds Her Music, Her Daughter, and Her Self." *Ms.,* Aug 1981.

"THE GIRL WHOM THE MOVIES BURIED IS SEASON'S TOP NIGHTCLUB STAR." *Life,* Oct 18, 1948.

"A GLAMOROUS GRANDMOTHER WANTS AUDIENCES TO WONDER: HOW DOES THE OLD BROAD DO IT?" *People,* 1981.

GORDON, BARBARA. "Day by Day." *Parade,* Apr 30, 1989.

GOULD, BERNARD H. "The Smile That Hides a Singer's Sorrow." *National Enquirer,* Aug 12, 1973.

GOULD, JACK. "Lena Horne, Belafonte Offer Poignant Hour." *New York Times,* Mar 23, 1970.

———. "Lena Horne, Young in Spirit, on N.B.C. Special." *New York Times,* Sep 11, 1969.

GRAHAM, TREY. "Playwright Returns to His 1960's Musical with a New Vision and Voice." *New York Times,* Dec 25, 2004.

GRAVES, LEM JR. "Lena Grants Courier Exclusive Interview." *Pittsburgh Courier,* Jul 1, 1950.

GREEN, JAMES. "My Men, My Sex, My Work and Me—by Lena." *Evening News* (U.K.), Apr 12, 1973.

———. "So Bewitching, Lena, but Stick to the Old Hits." *Evening News* (U.K.), Jul 18, 1979.

GREENE, GAEL. "Happiness Comes Last." *New York Post,* Feb 2, 1958.

GROSS, LEONARD. "On Stage." *Westways,* Jun 1978.

"GUILD SEEKS TO ELIMINATE LENA HORNE OR 'DIS AND DAT' FROM 'ST. Louis Woman.'" *Chicago Defender,* Sep 8, 1945.

HADLEY-GARCIA, GEORGE. "Lena Horne Is Still Misbehavin' After All These Years!" *Class,* Apr 1983.

HANNA, DAVID. "Lena Horne Makes Plea for Better Roles for Negroes." *Atlanta Daily World,* Jun 11, 1944.

HARDWICK, LEON H. "Lena Horne Turns Down Lead in Filming of 'Uncle Tom's Cabin.'" *Atlanta Daily World,* Feb 15, 1944.

HARE, FRANCESCA. "The Star Who Wants Her Career to Fade." [Source unknown, U.K.], 1979.

"HARLEM SAYS LENA HORNE IS MARRIED." *Atlanta Daily World*, Nov 8, 1949.

HARRIS, AVANELLE. "I Tried to Crash the Movies." *Ebony*, 1946.

HARRIS, RADIE. "Lena Horne Turns 'Em Away; Other Nitery Acts Score." *Los Angeles Times*, Sep 23, 1951.

HARRISON, DALE. "All About the Town." *Chicago Sun*, May 22, 1947.

HAY, R. COURI. "Lena!" *Interview*, Jan 1973.

"HEARST PRESS OFF AGAIN; THIS TIME VS. Lena Horne." *Down Beat*, Oct 19, 1951.

HELDENFELS, R. D. "Times Are Pretty Good for Lena Horne." *Saratoga Gazette* (Schenectady, NY), Jul 22, 1983.

HENSHAW, LAURIE. "The Records Are Playing That Banned Song." *Picturegoer*, Jun 11, 1955.

HENTOFF, NAT. "Who Loves Performing, Tony or Lena?" *Village Voice*, Nov 7, 1974.

HEYN, HOWARD. "Leapin' Lena Just Can't Stay Still." *Milwaukee Journal–Screen and Radio Sun*, Nov 14, 1943.

HIGGINS, ROBERT. "Harry and Lena." *TV Guide*, Mar 21, 1970.

HILL, HERMAN. "Toddy Offers Robeson Part in New Picture." *Pittsburgh Courier*, Oct 3, 1942.

HILLINGER, CHARLES. "WWII's Black Pilots Salute 'Pinup.'" *Los Angeles Times*, Dec 7, 1982.

HINCKLEY, DAVID. "Cotton Tales." *Daily News* (New York), Dec 9, 1984.

HIRSCHHORN, CLIVE. "The Man Lena Married Even Though She Wasn't in Love." *London Sunday Express*, Aug 12, 1984.

HODENFIELD, JAN. "Lena Horne: Back on Broadway." *New York Post*, Oct 26, 1974.

HOFFMAN, IRVING. "'Panama Hattie' Is Nixed by Critics." *Hollywood Reporter*, Oct 5, 1942.

HOLDEN, STEPHEN. "Lena Horne and the Stuff of Legends." *New York Times*, Jun 22, 1993.

———. Review of *We'll Be Together Again*. *New York Times*, Jun 5, 1994.

HOLLY, ELLEN. "Where Are the Films About Real Black Men and Women?" *New York Times*, Jun 2, 1974.

HORNE, LENA (AS TOLD TO AL MONROE). "'An Actress Mother Inspired My Stage Career,' Says Lena Horne." *Chicago Defender*, May 17, 1947.

——— (AS TOLD TO AL MONROE). "My Story." *Chicago Defender*, May 31, 1947.

HORNE, LENA (WITH JEANNE NOBLE). "Three-Horned Dilemma Facing Negro Women." *Ebony*, Aug 1966.

HORNE, LENA (WITH RICHARD SCHICKEL). "I Just Want to Be Myself." *Show,* Sep 1963.

"HORNE—OF PLENTY." *Lion's Roar,* Nov 1945.

"HORNE OF PLENTY." *People,* Jul 19, 1982.

HORWITZ, JANE. "For Laurents, Time to Revise and Shine." *Washington Post,* Dec 14, 2004.

HUGHES, ELINOR. Review of *Jamaica. Boston Globe,* Sep 1957.

"I DON'T LIKE BEING INSULTED!" *New York Journal-American,* Feb 17, 1960.

"I'D LOVE MY OWN SHOW." *New York Herald Tribune,* Feb 14, 1960.

"I'M PROUD TO BE A MOTHER." *Ebony,* Apr 1959.

"AN INTERVIEW: LENA HORNE." *Equity,* Apr 1958.

"IS LENA HORNE MARRIED?" *Our World,* Apr 1948.

"IS LENA STILL THE QUEEN?" *Ebony,* Feb 1956.

JACKSON, MIKE. "She Leads Two Lives and Does Both Nicely." *Los Angeles Herald-Examiner,* Feb 16, 1962.

"JACKSON PULLS OUT OF 'HORNE' FILM." BBC News, Feb 24, 2004.

JOHNSON, ERSKINE. "South Seas Are Tiring Lena Horne." *New York World-Telegram & Sun* (reprinted from *Los Angles Daily News*), Jun 14, 1951.

JOHNSON, JIM. "Poor Pal Joey." [Source unknown], Apr 1978.

JONES, MARVIN. "Barney Josephson: How He Changed America for Good." *The New Common Good,* Nov 1984.

JONES, MAX. "The Singer They Went to See." *Melody Maker* (U.K.), Oct 30, 1954.

KAKUTANI, MICHIKO. "Aloofness Hid the Pain, Until Time Cooled Her Anger." *New York Times,* May 3, 1981.

KENYADA, RICHARD. "Love, Lena Horne." "Mr. Kenyada's Neighborhood," www.kenyada.com/lena.htm.

KISSEL, HOWARD. Review of *The Lady and Her Music. Women's Wear Daily,* May 13, 1981.

KLEMESRUD, JUDY. "On Reverse Sides of Generation Gap?" *New York Times,* Apr 23, 1971.

"LA HORNE PROUD OF FILMS ABOUT NEGROES." *New York Amsterdam News,* Apr 16, 1949.

LAMAR, LAWRENCE. "Lena Horne Captivates Fans in Night Club Debut." *Atlanta Daily World,* Jun 2, 1948.

LARKIN, KATHY. "Lena Horne: A Stage Presence with a TV Future." *Daily News* (New York), May 26, 1985.

"LATE AND LATER AT THE NIGHT CLUBS." *Harper's Bazaar,* Nov 1941.

LAVIN, CHERYL. *California Living,* Aug 5, 1984.

LAYNG, ROSEMARY, "Dark Angel." [Source unknown], 1944.

"LEE AND LENA DENY RED CHARGE." *Chicago Defender,* Jun 18, 1949.

LEFKOWITZ, BERNARD. "Lena Horne Is Puzzled by CBS 'Ban' on a Song."
    New York Post, Oct 28, 1963.
"LENA BRINGS COLORED, WHITE NEWSPAPERMEN TOGETHER IN DEE CEE."
    Los Angeles Sentinel, c. 1944.
"LENA FILES COUNTER SUIT." *Pittsburgh Courier,* Nov 13, 1943.
"LENA HORNE ACCEPTS HOLLYWOOD FILM OFFER." *Pittsburgh Courier,* Feb 5,
    1938.
"LENA HORNE AILING; PERFORMANCES OF 'PAL JOEY,' ARE SUSPENDED."
    [Source unknown], 1978.
"LENA HORNE CLICKS AT SAVOY-PLAZA IN HISTORICAL DEBUT." *Pittsburgh
    Courier,* Dec 5, 1942.
"LENA HORNE CLOBBERS RACE BAITER." [Source unknown], Feb 1960.
"LENA HORNE COMES BACK TO BROOKLYN." [Source unknown], Aug 1947.
"LENA HORNE DISCUSSED PROBLEMS YOUTH MEETS, HERS AND NEIGH-
    BORS." *Chicago Defender* (reprinted from *Datebook*), Nov 8, 1958.
"LENA HORNE DRAWS CROWD TO BENEFIT." *Los Angeles Times,* Nov 25, 1982.
"LENA HORNE ENJOYS HER LONGEST VACATION." *Ebony,* Dec 1954.
"LENA HORNE HEARD IN NEW KIND OF ROLE ON NETWORK." *Atlanta Daily
    World,* Nov 19, 1944.
"LENA HORNE, HUBBY SHARE CHICAGO STAGE, SET FOR EUROPE." *Los Angeles
    Sentinel,* Apr 27, 1950.
"LENA HORNE INTEGRATION RECORD STIRS RADIO BAN." *Los Angeles Times,*
    Nov 1, 1963.
"LENA HORNE IS SENSATION IN ABSENCE OF NOBLE SISSLE." *Pittsburgh Cou-
    rier,* Jun 20, 1936.
"LENA HORNE JOINS NOTABLES BACKING FDR'S REELECTION." *Chicago De-
    fender,* Oct 21, 1944.
"LENA HORNE ON THE ENTERTAINMENT PROFESSION." *People's Voice,* Summer
    1947.
"LENA HORNE PELTS 'INSULTER' IN CAFÉ." *New York Journal-American,* Feb 1960.
"LENA HORNE QUITS USO TOUR IN ROW OVER ARMY JIM CROW." *Chicago
    Defender,* Jan 6, 1945.
"LENA HORNE REFUSES LEAD ROLE IN M-G-M's 'ST. Louis Woman.'" *Chi-
    cago Defender,* Sep 29, 1945.
"LENA HORNE SAYS HOTEL BARRED HER—CANCELS MIAMI BEACH CLUB
    DATE." *New York Post,* Feb 13, 1955.
"LENA HORNE SUES CHICAGO CAFÉ FOR $500 DAMAGES UPON REFUSAL TO
    SERVE HER PARTY." *Los Angeles Sentinel,* Sep 22, 1949.
"LENA HORNE SUES MATE FOR DIVORCE." *Chicago Defender,* Aug 21, 1943.
"LENA HORNE SUES TO HALT SALE OF ALBUM." *New York Post,* May 4, 1959.
"LENA HORNE SWATS RADIO'S JIM CROW." *Chicago Defender,* Sep 20, 1947.

"Lena Horne Takes the Duke Over on Broadway." *Chicago Defender*, Oct 23, 1943.

"Lena Horne Tells All to Scribes—She Likes Men." *Chicago Defender*, Nov 4, 1944.

"Lena Horne Tells Why She Quit Camp Show." *Pittsburgh Courier*, Jan 20, 1945.

"Lena Horne to Headline Benefit at Ahmanson." *Los Angeles Times*, Jun 3, 1980.

"Lena Horne to Retire." United Press International, Mar 24, 1980.

"Lena Horne Weds, Quitting Footlights." *New York Amsterdam News*, Jan 16, 1937.

"Lena Horne with Garland and Rooney in 'Girl Crazy.'" *Chicago Defender*, Jan 23, 1943.

"Lena Horne's Contract Cuts Wages in Half." *New York Amsterdam News*, Jul 1, 1944.

"Lena Horne's Daughter Hits Sinatra Hypocrisy." *Chicago Daily Defender*, Nov 4, 1963.

"Lena Horne's Fame Grows as Sensational Dance Director." *Pittsburgh Courier*, Jun 20, 1936.

"Lena Horne's New Singing Style." [Source unknown], Fall 1950.

"Lena Horne's 1947 Wedding Disclosed." *Los Angeles Times*, Jun 22, 1950.

"Lena Picks an Easter Hat." *Ebony*, Apr 1962.

"Lena's a Bit Uneasy, but She's Not Apologizing." *New York Journal-American*, Feb 17, 1960.

"Lena's Daughter Makes Stage Debut." *Ebony*, Nov 1960.

"Lena's 'Ex' Named in Vote Fraud." *Pittsburgh Courier*, Jul 26, 1958.

Levette, Harry. "L. Horne Screens Well." *Chicago Defender*, May 7, 1938.

———. "Lena Horne Says No Mother's Children Safe in Calif. Rally." *Atlanta Daily World*, Aug 16, 1946.

———. "Miss Lena Horne, Million Dollar Star, Devoted to Retiring Home Life." *Atlanta Daily World*, Feb 28, 1938.

———. "Says Lena Nixed Role in 'St. Louis Woman.'" *New York Amsterdam News*, Sep 19, 1953.

Levin, Mike. "Lena Horne Now Hears Society's Coveted 'Ah's!'" *Down Beat* (reprinted in *Pittsburgh Courier*, Dec 19, 1942).

"Life Story by Joe Louis." *Our World*, Jun 1948.

Locke, Alain. "Harlem: Dark Weather-Vane." *Survey Graphic*, Aug 1936.

Lomax, Louis. "Louis Lomax Interviews Malcolm X." 1963, TeachingAmerican History.org.

"'Love at First Sight' Romance Ends at Altar." *Pittsburgh Courier*, Jan 23, 1937.

"Lovely Lena Horne Captivating in Short Stopover Thurs. Nite." *Atlanta Daily World,* Dec 22, 1944.

J.T.M. "It's a Sure 'Nuff Cabin in the Sky." *PM,* May 28, 1943.

MacNamara, Helen. "Lena's Plan for Her Tour: Showbiz and Civic Duties." *The Telegram* (Toronto), Oct 7, 1961.

Maddocks, Melvin. "Dancing Partners of Chic." *Time,* Jun 23, 1986.

Mann, Jesse. "Washington's Social Whirl." *Chicago Defender,* Feb 22, 1936.

Marx, Samuel. "Lena at M-G-M—Take Two." *Los Angeles Times,* Dec. 5, 1982.

Mascioli, Michael. "Sweatin', Spittin', Makin' a Damn Fool of Myself." *The Sentinel* (San Francisco), Sep 30, 1982.

Massaquoi, Hans J. "Lena Horne on Her Loveless Childhood, Her Durable Beauty, Sex and the Older Woman, Her Life's Triple Tragedy." *Ebony,* May 1980.

Maxwell, Max. "Negro Stars Wow High Society." *Whisper,* May 1958.

"Mayer Differs with Winchell in Disciplining Lena Horne." *Atlanta Daily World,* Oct 13, 1945.

McCord, Bert. "The Horne of Plenty." *New York Herald Tribune,* c. 1946.

McCorkle, Susannah. "The Mother of Us All." *American Heritage,* Feb–Mar 1994.

McCrary, Tex, and Jinx Falkenburg. "New York Close-Up: Lena Horne Didn't Want to Sing." *New York Herald Tribune,* 1950.

McManus, Margaret. "How to Look as Graceful as Lena Horne Under Pressure." [Source unknown], Mar 22, 1970.

"Meet the Real Lena Horne." *Ebony,* Nov 1947.

"Memories of Harlem." *New York Times,* May 23, 1993.

Michener, Charles. "The Awesome Lena Horne." *Newsweek,* May 25, 1981.

Mitchell, Jack. "Lena Horne: Why Did She Run Out on Her Miami Date?" *Hush-Hush,* Jul 1955.

Monroe, Al. "Swingin' the News." *Chicago Defender,* Sep 6, 1941.

Mooney, Paul. *Plain Dealer* (Cleveland), 1979.

Moraes, Vinícius de. *A Manhã* (Rio de Janeiro, Brazil), 1943.

Morris, Tina. "Lena Horne and That 'Jamaica' Kiss." *Whisper,* Feb 1958.

Mosby, Aline. "Lena Horne to Quit Clubs, Enter Theater." *Hollywood Citizen-News,* Jul 2, 1957.

Moss, Carlton. "Your Future in Hollywood." *Our World,* May 1946.

"Movie Star Lena Horne." *Pittsburgh Courier,* c. 1942.

Mulcahy, Susan. "The Lady Loves N.Y.—She Just Can't Stand It." *New York Post,* Jun 24, 1985.

Munro, John. "Black Bourgeoisie at 50: Class, Civil Rights, and the Cold War in America." *Seven Oaks,* Mar 1, 2005.

NAACP *Branch Bulletin,* Oct 1919.

Nachman, Gerald. "Horne-Swoggled." *San Francisco Chronicle,* Sep 15, 1982.

Norman, Shirley. "Lena Horne at 60." *Sepia,* Jun 1977.

Nosey, Ole. "Everybody Goes When the Wagon Comes." *Chicago Defender,* Mar 5, 1949.

"Not Sorry for Brawl, Says Lena Horne." *Los Angeles Times,* Feb 17, 1960.

Nugent, Frank. "She's Nobody's Mammy." *Daily News Sunday Magazine* (New York), Apr 7, 1945.

O'Brian, Jack. *New York Journal-American,* Sep 10, 1951.

Ottley, Roi. "Hectic Harlem." *New York Amsterdam News,* May 18, 1935.

Payette, William C. "'Can't Girl' Hits High Spot in Films." [Source unknown], Aug 3, 1943.

Peck, Ira. "Meet Miss Lena Horne." *PM Picture News,* c. 1948.

Peck, Seymour. "Calling on Lena Horne." *New York Times,* Oct 27, 1957.

Penland, Shonte. [Title unknown]. *Los Angeles Sentinel,* Nov 25, 1982.

Pennington, Ron. "Pal Joey '78." *Hollywood Reporter,* Apr 24, 1978.

Peper, William. *New York World-Telegram & Sun,* Feb 12, 1957.

"Perfection Only Thing Satisfies Movie Star; Tells of Her Ambitions." *New York Amsterdam News,* Oct 30, 1943.

Pierce, Ponchitta. "Lady Attitude." *Modern Maturity,* Jan–Feb 2000.

———. "Lena Horne at 51." *Ebony,* Jul 1968.

Pikula, Joan. "Clifton Davis: Flying over the Mountain." *After Dark,* Jan 1976.

Plaskin, Glenn. "The Ageless Appeal of Lena." *Family Circle,* Apr 15, 1986.

Poston, Ted. "Prejudice and Progress: Jim Crow in New York." *New York Post,* Apr 19, 1956.

Prattis, P. L. "The Horizon." *Pittsburgh Courier,* Nov 18, 1950.

"Proust Questionnaire: Lena Horne." *Vanity Fair,* May 1997.

Rayfield, Fred. "What's the Stork Club Got That Duffy's Hasn't, Except Jim Crow?" *Daily Compass,* Oct 23, 1951.

Reed, Rex. "A Life on Stage." *Daily News* (New York), May 10, 1981.

Reilly, Peter. "The Art of *La Belle* Lena: Far Too Special to Categorize." *Stereo Review,* Oct 1975.

———. "Interview: Lena Horne." *Stereo Review,* Feb 1982.

"Refuses to Appear at Premiere of Own Film." *Pittsburgh Courier,* Jun 18, 1938.

Rice, Robert. "The Real Story of Lena Horne." *PM Sunday Picture News,* Jan 10, 1943.

Rich, Frank. "Theater: Lena Horne: The Lady and Her Music." *New York Times,* May 13, 1981.

"The Right to Be Wrong." *New York Amsterdam News,* Feb 20, 1960.

RILEY, ROSA R. "Lena Denies Marriage in Exclusive Sentinel Interview." *Los Angeles Sentinel,* Jan 31, 1946.

ROBERTS, LUKE. "Untold Story Of Lena Horne's Love Affair!" [Source unknown], Sep 1956.

RODDY, JOHN. "Attempt to Bar Lena Horne from TV Show Rebuffed." *Daily Compass,* Sep 10, 1951.

———. "Lena Horne's Manager Says 'Counterattack' Clears Her." *Daily Compass,* Oct 9, 1951.

"ROMANTIC LENA HORNE." *Chicago Defender,* Feb 27, 1943.

ROSEN, CAROL. "Lena Horne—A Lovesome Thing." *TheatreWeek,* Sep 19–25, 1994.

ROSENFIELD, JOHN. "First Audience Loves M-G-M's Cabin in the Sky." *Dallas Morning News,* Mar 11, 1943.

ROSENFIELD, PAUL. "Lena on Lena, Late at Night." *Los Angeles Times,* Nov 14, 1982.

ROSS, GEORGE. *New York World-Telegram & Sun,* 1934.

ROWE, BILLY. "Billy Rowe's Notebook." *Pittsburgh Courier,* Aug 19, 1950.

———. "Billy Rowe's Notebook." *Pittsburgh Courier,* Sep 30, 1950.

———. "'Cabin in the Sky': Liberal Producer Says Picture Will Make Movie History." *Pittsburgh Courier,* Oct 3, 1942.

———. "Hollywood Star and Heavy Champ Scoff at Claims." *Pittsburgh Courier,* Nov 1942.

———. "Rowe's Notebook." *Pittsburgh Courier,* Nov 9, 1940.

RUARK, ROBERT. "Lady in a High Key." *Esquire,* Sep 1952.

RUHL, ARTHUR. *New York Herald Tribune,* Oct 7, 1934.

SALMAGGI, ROBERT. "Frankie and Lena: Wow!" *New York Herald Tribune,* Oct 7, 1963.

SANSONI, JOHN. "Untold Story of Lena Horne's Children." *Inside Story,* Mar 1956.

"SAVOY-PLAZA OUSTS TWO MEN FOLLOWING LENA HORNE BOOKING." *Pittsburgh Courier,* Jan 23, 1943.

SCHALLERT, EDWIN. "Fun, Music Blend in *Panama Hattie*." *Los Angeles Times,* Sep 18, 1942.

———. "Till the Clouds Roll By." *Los Angeles Times,* Apr 9, 1946.

SCHECK, FRANK. "Lena: 80th Birthday." *Hollywood Reporter,* Jun 25, 1997.

SCHUMACH, MURRAY. "The Music Between." *High Fidelity,* Aug 1957.

———. Review of *Stormy Weather. High Fidelity,* Nov 1957.

SCHWARZBAUM, LISA. "Horne Again." *Entertainment Weekly,* May 13, 1994.

"SCREEN GUILD ELECTS LENA TO ITS EXEC BOARD." *New York Amsterdam News,* Sep 30, 1944.

SEYMOUR, GENE. "Horne Still Has It 'Together.'" *New York Newsday,* May 31, 1994.

SINATRA, FRANK. "Me and My Music." *Life,* Apr 23, 1965.

SKOLSKY, SIDNEY. "Close-up of Lena Horne." *Motion Picture,* Oct 1944.

———. *Citizen News* (Connecticut), Jul 20, 1968.

SLACK, SARA. "Lena Horne Going to Jackson, Miss." *New York Amsterdam News,* Jun 8, 1963.

SMITH, CECIL. "Redd Foxx's Date with Lena Horne." *Los Angeles Times,* Jan 12, 1973.

SMITH, DARR. *Los Angeles Daily News,* Aug 15, 1949.

———. *Los Angeles Daily News,* 1950.

SMITH, LIZ. *Daily News* (New York), Jun 1982.

———. "Janet Should Be Making Films." *New York Post,* Nov 8, 2006.

———. "Lady Lena Sizzles Again." *Los Angeles Times,* Nov 15, 1996.

———. *New York Newsday,* Mar 17, 1993.

"SONG FOR HORNE." *Look,* May 8, 1951.

STANG, JOANNE. "Lena, No Identification Necessary." *New York Times,* Dec 27, 1964.

"THE STAR-SPANGLED MANNER OF ZEV BUFMAN." *W,* Mar 25, 1983.

STEARNS, DAVID PATRICK. "Elegant Lena Horne Is Singing Up a Storm Again." *USA Today,* May 20–22, 1994.

STEIN, RUTHE. "Stormy Weather Doesn't Stop Lena Horne." *San Francisco Examiner & Chronicle,* Sep 5, 1982.

"STORMY WEATHER CERTAIN TO MOP UP AT BOX OFFICE." *Hollywood Reporter,* May 27, 1943.

SULLIVAN, DAN. "'Joey' Caught in a Time Warp." *Los Angeles Times,* Apr 22, 1978.

SULLIVAN, ED. "Little Old New York." *Daily News* (New York), Oct 10, 1951.

SUSMAN, GARY. "'Weather' Report." EW.com, Sep 3, 2003.

"SWINGIN' LENA HORNE BACKED BY FANS." *New York Post,* Feb 17, 1960.

TAPLEY, MEL. "Lena Is My Mom." *New York Amsterdam News,* May 22, 1982.

TAUBMAN, HOWARD. "Tired Musical." *New York Times,* Oct 7, 1960.

TAYLOR, CLARKE. "Lena Horne in London: Thriving on Surviving." *Los Angeles Times,* Aug 27, 1984.

"10 MOST BEAUTIFUL NEGRO WOMEN." *Our World,* Nov 1950.

"THALIANS 25TH-ANNIVERSARY PARTY AT BEVERLY WILSHIRE." [Source unknown], Oct 19, 1980.

THIRER, IRENE. *New York Evening Post,* May 28, 1943.

———. "Lena Horne's Double Career." *New York Post,* Oct 27, 1943.

"THIS IS SHOW BUSINESS." *Our World,* Sep 1953.

TIEGEL, ELIOT. "The Art of Survival: Lena." *Pulse,* Mar 1989.

T.M.P. "'Thousands Cheer,' Lavish Metro Musical with an All-Star Cast, Makes Its Appearance at War Bond Rally at Astor." *New York Times,* Sep 14, 1943.

"200,000 BROOKLYNITES CHEER LENA HORNE; TRIBUTES MADE." *New York Amsterdam News,* Aug 23, 1947.

"TWO REVIVALS: ONE LIVE AND ONE DEAD." [Source unknown], Jun 11, 1978.

"2 SINATRA-HORNE CARNEGIE HALL BENEFITS GARNER 100G FOR CIVIL RIGHTS & KIDS." *Variety,* Oct 9, 1963.

UNGER, ARTHUR. "The Lady and Her Life: Breaking Down Walls of Prejudice." *Christian Science Monitor,* Nov 30, 1984.

VASCONCELOS, ARY. "Lena Horne 'Desafina' com João Gilberto." *O Cruzeiro,* Jun 11, 1960.

WAHLS, ROBERT. "Cocktails with Lena; What Could Be Keener." *Daily News* (New York), May 11, 1958.

———. "Stormy Weather Is All Behind Her." *New York Sunday News,* Oct 27, 1974.

WALDRON, CLARENCE. "Lena Horne, Officially Retired from Showbiz, Turns 90 in June." *Jet,* Apr 23, 2007.

WALLACE, MIKE. "Mike Wallace Asks Lena Horne." *New York Post,* Mar 6, 1958.

"WAR IN THE NORTH." *Time,* May 31, 1963.

WARDLE, IRVING. "Lena Horne: The Lady and Her Music." *Times* (London), Aug 8, 1984.

WARGA, WAYNE. "Lena Horne Returns to Hollywood." *Los Angeles Times,* Jun 13, 1968.

———. "Lena Horne Stars in Special on NBC." *Los Angeles Times,* Aug 27, 1969.

———. "Lena Horne, Working Tourist." *New York Post,* Jun 17, 1968.

WARREN, STEVE. "At Her Mellow Age, Lena Horne Still as Tough as Nails." *Atlanta Constitution,* Jun 28, 1979.

WATT, DOUGLAS. Review of *Lena Horne: The Lady and Her Music. Daily News* (New York), May 13, 1981.

WEISS, DAVID. "Going on 63 and Still Sizzling." *Los Angeles Herald-Examiner,* Jun 18, 1980.

WELLES, ORSON. "Why I Am Interested in the Woodard Case." *Our World,* Dec 1946.

"WHAT THE MAN SAID TO LENA HORNE." [Source unknown], Feb 1960.

WILDING, STEPHEN, AND J. M. Weyburn Jr. "Lena Horne: The Beautiful Survivor." *Black Stars,* Apr 1977.

WILLIAMS, AVERY. "The Lena Horne Love Story." *Tan,* Dec 1954.

WILLIAMS, BOB. *New York Post,* Apr 2, 1974.

WILSON, EARL. *Los Angeles Daily News,* Jul 2, 1947.

———. *New York Post,* Nov 1, 1957.

———. *New York Post,* Oct 31, 1974.

WILSON, MARY. "Lena Horne—We Don't Need a Superblack!" *National Tattler,* May 10, 1970.

WINSTEIN, ARCHER. *New York Post,* Dec 10, 1948.

WRIGHT, GENE. "Have You Met Miss Jones?" *The Theatre,* Oct 1960.

YOUNG, A. S. "Doc." "Hollywood Digs 'Black Gold.'" *Chicago Defender,* Dec 17, 1949.

YOUNG, MORT. "WCBS Bars Lena's Civil Rights Disc." *New York Journal-American,* Oct 26, 1963.

ZOLOTOW, MAURICE. "Lena: The Lady Who Just Wasn't Black Enough." *Los Angeles Times,* Nov 1982.

ZUNSER, JESSE. "'Stormy Weather' Opens at Roxy." *Cue,* Jul 24, 1943.

DISCOGRAPHY

The Birth of the Blues: An Album of W. C. Handy Music (1941)
NBC's Chamber Music Society of Lower Basin Street; four vocals by Lena Horne.
78-rpm album: Victor P82

Moanin' Low: Torch Songs by Lena Horne (1941)
78-rpm album: Victor 118
LP: *This Is Lena Horne*, RCA Victor LPT 3061

La Sélection 1936–1941 (French compilation of every commercial, pre-M-G-M Horne recording)
CD: *L'Art Vocal*, Volume 11

Ain't It the Truth: Lena Horne at Metro-Goldwyn-Mayer (1942–1955)
CD: Rhino R2 72246

Little Girl Blue (1947)
78-rpm album: Black and White 70

Classics in Blue (1947)
78-rpm album: Black and White 75
CD of above two albums: *The Complete Black and White Recordings*, Simitar 567820

Lena Horne: V-Disc (World War II–era recordings)
CD: Collector's Choice Music; no catalogue number

Lena Horne: The Young Star (RCA recordings, 1941–1944)
CD: Bluebird 09026-63964-2

Lena Horne Sings (M-G-M singles, 1947–1949)
LP: M-G-M E545

The One & Only (M-G-M singles, 1947–1949)
LP: M-G-M MGB-1-5409

It's Love (1955)
LP: RCA Victor LPM-1148
CD: BMG (U.K.) 625972

Lena Horne at the Waldorf-Astoria (1956)
LP: RCA Victor LSO-1028
CD: Collectables COL-CD-2841

Stormy Weather (1956–1957)
LP: RCA Victor LPM-1375
CD: Bluebird 09026-63911-2

Lena Horne at the Cocoanut Grove (1957)
Vinyl EP: RCA Victor EPA-4098

Jamaica (four tracks recorded in 1957, prior to Broadway opening)
Vinyl EP: RCA Victor EPA-4038

Jamaica (Original Broadway cast, 1957)
LP: RCA LSO-1036
CD: Collectables COL-CD-2845

Give the Lady What She Wants (1958)
LP: RCA LSP-1879
CD: BMG (Japan) BVCJ-1011

Songs by Burke and Van Heusen (1959)
LP: RCA Victor LSP-1895
CD: BMG (U.K.) 625972

Porgy and Bess (with Harry Belafonte) (1959)
LP: RCA Victor LSO-1507
CD: Collectables COL-CD-2845

Lena at the Sands (1960)
LP: RCA Victor LSP-2364
CD: Collectables COL-CD-2841

Lena on the Blue Side (1961)
LP: RCA Victor LSP-2465
CD: BMG (Japan) BVCJ 2023

Lena . . . Lovely and Alive (1962)
LP: RCA Victor LSP-2567
CD: BMG (Spain) 74321421252

Lena Horne Sings Your Requests (1962)
LP: Charter CLS 101

Lena Like Latin (1963)
LP: Charter CLS 106
CD of above two albums: Fresh Sound (Spain) FSRCD525

Here's Lena Now! (1962)
LP: 20th Century-Fox TFS-4115

Feelin' Good (1964)
LP: United Artists UAS 6433

Lena in Hollywood (1964)
LP: United Artists UAS 6470
CD of above two albums: DRG 91503

Soul (1966)
LP: United Artists UAS 6496
CD: DRG 91504

Merry from Lena (1966)
LP: United Artists UAS 6546
CD: DRG 77503

Lena & Gabor (1969)
LP: Skye SK15
CD: *My Mood Is You*, Music of Your Life 40979-2

Harry & Lena (with Harry Belafonte) (1970)
LP: RCA PRS-295

Nature's Baby (1971)
LP: Buddah BDS5084
CD: All That Jazz ATJCD 5962

Lena and Michel (1975)
LP: RCA BGL1-1026
CD: BMG (Japan) BVCJ37565

Lena, a New Album (1976)
LP: RCA BXL1-1799
CD: Vocalion (Japan) CDLK4342

Lena Horne: The Lady and Her Music (1981)
LP: Qwest/Warner Brothers 2QW 3597
CD: Qwest/Warner Brothers 3597-2

The Men in My Life (1988)
CD: Three Cherries TC 64411

We'll Be Together Again (1993)
CD: Blue Note CDP 7243 8 28974 2 2

An Evening with Lena Horne Live at the Supper Club (1994)
CD: Blue Note CDP 7243 8 31877 2 0

Being Myself (mid-'90s sessions)
CD: Blue Note CDP 7243 8 34286 2 5

Seasons of a Life (mid-'90s sessions)
CD: Blue Note 7243 4 94265 2 8

Classic Ellington (Birmingham Symphony Orchestra; Simon Rattle, cond.;
  Luther Henderson, arr.; with three Horne vocals; recorded 1996)
CD: EMI 7243 5 57014 2 8

COMPILATIONS

The Best of the RCA Years
CD: Koch Jazz KOC-CD-7993

The Best of Lena Horne: The United Artists and Blue Note Recordings
CD: EMI W3973882

FILMOGRAPHY

Cab Calloway's Jitterbug Party (Paramount, 1935)
    Lena Horne appears in the ensemble of "Call of the Jitterbug."
The Duke Is Tops (Million Dollar Productions, 1938)
Panama Hattie (M-G-M, 1942)
Cabin in the Sky (M-G-M, 1943)
Stormy Weather (20th Century Fox, 1943)
Thousands Cheer (M-G-M, 1943)
I Dood It (M-G-M, 1943)
Swing Fever (M-G-M, 1943)
Boogie Woogie Dream (B. W. Film Shorts, Inc., 1944)
Broadway Rhythm (M-G-M, 1944)
Two Girls and a Sailor (M-G-M, 1944)
Ziegfeld Follies (M-G-M, 1946)
Studio Visit (Pete Smith short, M-G-M, 1946)
'Till the Clouds Roll By (M-G-M, 1946)
Words and Music (M-G-M, 1948)
Duchess of Idaho (M-G-M, 1950)
Meet Me in Las Vegas (M-G-M, 1956)
Death of a Gunfighter (Universal Pictures, 1969)
The Wiz (Universal Pictures, 1978)
That's Entertainment! III (M-G-M, 1994)

INDEX